# THE COLLECTED WORKS OF MAX HAINES, VOLUME 5: 1996–1999

MAX HAINES's "Crime Flashback" column made its debut in the *Toronto Sun* in 1972. Since that time, Haines has researched more than two thousand murder cases from around the world. Today, "Crime Flashback" appears weekly in the *Toronto Sun* and is syndicated around the world and in more than forty newspapers across Canada. The column has a weekly readership of more than three million and has been translated into Spanish, French, and Chinese. Haines is also the author of twenty-five bestselling anthologies of crime vignettes, including *Unnatural Causes*, *Canadian Crimes*, *Murder Most Foul*, and *The Collected Works of Max Haines*. He lives in Toronto with his wife, Marilyn.

## ALSO BY MAX HAINES

*Bothersome Bodies*

*Calendar of Criminal Capers*

*Crime Flashback #1*

*Crime Flashback #2*

*Crime Flashback #3*

*The Murderous Kind*

*Murder & Mayhem*

*The Collected Works of Max Haines, Volume 1*

*That's Life*

*True Crime Stories*

*True Crime Stories, Book II*

*True Crime Stories, Book III*

*True Crime Stories, Book IV*

*The Collected Works of Max Haines, Volume 2*

*True Crime Stories, Book V*

*Doctors Who Kill*

*Multiple Murderers*

*Multiple Murderers II*

*Celebrity Murders*

*The Collected Works of Max Haines, Volume 3*

*Murders Strange But True*

*Canadian Crimes*

*Murder Most Foul*

*The Collected Works of Max Haines, Volume 4*

*Unnatural Causes*

*Instruments of Murder*

# THE COLLECTED WORKS OF MAX HAINES

VOLUME 5
1996–1999

MAX HAINES

PENGUIN
CANADA

PENGUIN CANADA

Published by the Penguin Group

Penguin Group (Canada), 90 Eglinton Avenue East, Suite 700, Toronto, Ontario, Canada M4P 2Y3 (a division of Pearson Penguin Canada Inc.)

Penguin Group (USA) Inc., 375 Hudson Street, New York, New York 10014, U.S.A.
Penguin Books Ltd, 80 Strand, London WC2R 0RL, England
Penguin Ireland, 25 St Stephen's Green, Dublin 2, Ireland (a division of Penguin Books Ltd)
Penguin Group (Australia), 250 Camberwell Road, Camberwell, Victoria 3124, Australia (a division of Pearson Australia Group Pty Ltd)
Penguin Books India Pvt Ltd, 11 Community Centre, Panchsheel Park, New Delhi – 110 017, India
Penguin Group (NZ), cnr Airborne and Rosedale Roads, Albany, Auckland 1310, New Zealand (a division of Pearson New Zealand Ltd)
Penguin Books (South Africa) (Pty) Ltd, 24 Sturdee Avenue, Rosebank, Johannesburg 2196, South Africa

Penguin Books Ltd, Registered Offices: 80 Strand, London WC2R 0RL, England

First published 2005

1 2 3 4 5 6 7 8 9 10 (WEB)



Manufactured in Canada.

---

LIBRARY AND ARCHIVES CANADA CATALOGUING IN PUBLICATION

Haines, Max
The collected works of Max Haines.

Vols. 3-5 published by Penguin Books.
ISBN 0-919233-18-X (v. 1).—ISBN 0-919233-37-6 (v. 2 : bound).—
ISBN 0-919233-38-4 (v. 2 : pbk.).—ISBN 0-14-026109-5 (v. 3).—
ISBN 0-14-029515-1 (v. 4).—ISBN 0-14-305063-X (v. 5)

1. Murder. I. Title.

HV6515.H355 1985 364.1'523 C86-008656-9 rev

---

Visit the Penguin Group (Canada) website at **www.penguin.ca**

*To the memory of Douglas Creighton*

# CONTENTS

# PART 1

## CELEBRITY MURDERS AND OTHER NEFARIOUS DEEDS

# ROSCOE "FATTY" ARBUCKLE

WITH the exception of Charlie Chaplin, Roscoe "Fatty" Arbuckle was the world's leading funny man. He weighed 280 pounds and had a way of manipulating his enormous bulk and expressive face that was truly humorous and that won him the hearts of the movie-going public all over the world.

Fatty Arbuckle started out in silent movies earning three dollars a day as a Keystone Cop. He ended up signing a three-million-dollar contract covering his services for three years. That kind of money is a fortune today, but in 1920 it was a king's ransom.

To depict Fatty and the times in their proper light, it must be pointed out that the morals of early Hollywood were not the highest. The stars were bigger than life. They could do no wrong. Sometimes, however, they went too far. Big cars, wild parties and loose women were the order of the day; Fatty Arbuckle was in no way an exception. The players lived it up and their fans ate it up.

On Sunday, September 4, 1921, Fatty Arbuckle drove into San Francisco in his Rolls-Royce and parked in front of the St. Francis Hotel. He took the manager aside and told him to take care of the car and the booze. Fatty said he would take care of the girls personally. He was going to have a party to end all parties. A continuous parade of chorus girls, bit players, champagne and gin by the case were delivered to Fatty's room. Laughter and music blared from the party. Fatty's female companions knew that to be friendly to a star could lead to small parts in the movies, and small parts exposed them to a chance at stardom. They would do anything for a grab at the golden ring. The party raged on.

Unknown to the rest of the merrymakers, a bit player named Virginia Rappe was staying at the Palace Hotel with her agent and a personal friend, Mrs Delamont. The funny man had been making advances to Virginia for years and for years she had been repulsed by his appearance. For some reason that was never definitely established, Virginia knew that Fatty would be in San Francisco that Sunday and had given him her telephone number. She waited for his call. No doubt she expected some sort of break in the film industry in exchange for certain favours. In the meantime, Fatty started to tire of his guests. He picked up the phone and called the Palace. Virginia didn't waste any time getting over to the St. Francis. She brought along Mrs Delamont and her agent. They had a few drinks with the comedian until the conversation centred around what Fatty would do to help Virginia's career. Then, without a word, Fatty got up, took Virginia by the arm and led her into a private bedroom. Some who witnessed the scene said Fatty pushed Virginia into the room. Others said she entered not only voluntarily, but eagerly.

Suddenly the party atmosphere was shattered by screams from the bedroom, the kind that indicated something was drastically wrong. Mrs Delamont rushed to the door, but it was locked from the inside. The frantic screams continued. Virginia's friend picked up the phone and called the reception desk, asking for help. Just as the assistant manager entered the room, Fatty opened the bedroom door. Everyone agreed that he said, "Go in and get her dressed. Take her back to where she came from. She makes too much noise." Lying on the floor was the pale nude form of Virginia Rappe. She was moaning heavily and sobbed to Mrs Delamont, "I'm dying, I'm dying. Roscoe did it." Fatty shouted, "Shut up, you phoney, shut your mouth or I'll throw you outta the window." A doctor was called and Virginia was rushed to hospital. She lingered between life and death until Thursday, when she died. An autopsy revealed that she had not died of natural causes. The coroner attributed her death to a ruptured bladder.

A preliminary hearing was held which caused a sensation. There was much speculation as to whether or not Virginia had been raped. The details of the hearing were considered to be so appalling that the witnesses' statements of what went on in the hotel room that afternoon were written out on bits of paper and passed around the court. In this way, descriptions of the events were not audible to spectators.

In many well-publicized murder cases, an individual's statements or a single piece of evidence have affected the outcome of a case one way or the other. When death does not occur immediately, people sometimes say and do things that return to haunt them. In this case, Fatty never felt for a minute that Virginia would actually die. During the days in which she remained in hospital, he joked about her. One witness later testified that Fatty told him he didn't rape Virginia at all. In his own words, the witness said, "He simply took a piece of ice from an ice bucket and thrust it into her genitals." This one revolting statement turned the public against Fatty. They would forgive the beloved comedian almost anything, but not this. The truth of the statement was never proven, but it didn't matter. The damage was done.

Fatty was tried three times for murder. The first two trials ended in hung juries. The third jury to hear the case returned a verdict of not guilty. In the years during which his case dragged through the courts, Fatty spent his entire fortune in his successful efforts to stay out of jail. Hollywood would have nothing more to do with him. He attempted to tour small towns, but even there he was sometimes booed off the stage. Later he tried directing under an assumed name. Nothing worked for him. His career was over.

One hot day in 1933, Roscoe "Fatty" Arbuckle returned to his hotel room in New York after attending a party. He suffered a heart attack and died alone in the middle of the night.

# ALAN BERG

ALAN Berg was many things to many people.

In 1969, the successful but bored trial lawyer gave up his practice and moved from Chicago to Denver, where he obtained employment as a $65-a-week shoe salesman. The six-foot-two-inch, 150-pound string bean had had a topsy-turvy career before arriving in Denver. Scars received from a successful brain tumour operation were hidden by a full head of coarse gray hair. His shaggy appearance was enhanced by a full beard. There was no mistaking Alan Berg.

By 1984, his love affairs, broken marriage, brain operation and sales jobs were all behind Alan Berg. His life had abruptly changed years earlier when a talk-show host asked him to take over for one day. On the air, Berg was witty, obstreperous, bold and downright honest. He was an immediate hit and soon moved up to KOA, the most powerful radio station in Colorado. Those who listened to Alan Berg's enormously popular radio show have difficulty explaining the man's charisma. Berg could be kind and gentle, but this was not his forte. He was totally outspoken and often cursed on air. He would go into tirades on sensitive subjects such as homosexuality, white supremacy, communism, race relations in America, anti-Semitism and many other topics not often aired openly on talk-show radio at the time. Berg argued with his audience, insulted them and often hung up when he didn't agree with them. At other times, he would discuss his Airedale's latest illness in detail. There was no middle ground with Alan Berg. You either loved the man or hated him. Everyone listened to the Alan Berg Show, which had the highest ratings in the history of Denver radio. A contest in Denver once invited the public to vote for the most hated personality in radio and the most loved: Berg placed first in both categories.

Berg saved his classic harangues for white supremacists. He labelled them Nazis and could ramble on for most of his show on the one topic. The Ku Klux Klan was often the subject of Berg's caustic tongue. Indeed, Alan Berg became a thorn in the side of organized racist groups. The Aryan Nations, headquartered about five miles east of Hayden Lake, Idaho, is such a group. Founded by Gerald Smith, who purchased twenty acres of virgin woodland, the Hayden Lake area is relatively untouched, except for the structures built there by the Aryans. The first building erected in the compound was Aryan Hall, where Rev. Richard Butler, a former air force flight engineer instructor, gave sermons denouncing blacks, Jews, homosexuals, Communists and almost everything else that wasn't white Christian. At night, the Aryans burned crosses just for fun. During the day, instructors gave courses on weapons handling. New recruits were solicited from prisons, which were inundated with Aryan literature. By the early 1980s, the Aryan Nations was a force to reckon with.

William Pierce was a hate-monger. Using the alias Earl Turner, he wrote a book in 1968, which railed against big business, big institutions, liberals, the system, the FBI and just about anything larger than a Saturday-night town hall meeting. Pierce developed his hate on a personal level: How would you feel if a black person was hired for a job you wanted? Do you want your children taught by homosexuals? He advocated killing the imagined interlopers. By the early 1980s, his book was in great demand by militant white supremacist groups.

David Lane didn't have an organization capable of dispensing his very special variety of hate. In 1980, he joined the United Klans of America, a hate organization headed by Charles Howarth. The association didn't last long. Howarth was arrested when he was caught with a truckload of TNT, which was about to be used to blow up a federal Courthouse in Denver. Dave Lane looked around for another "family." He joined Butler's Aryan Nations.

Robert Jay Mathews was a racist from the time of his high school days. Born in Texas, raised in Arizona, he settled in the village of Mataline Falls, Washington, where he worked in a lead and zinc mine, later gravitating to farming. But Mathews was like a fish out of water. There were no minorities to hate in Mataline Falls. It didn't take long for him to hear of the Aryan Nations organization. He met Tom Martinez and William Soderquist. Both men urged Mathews to visit the Idaho compound and take in the lectures of Rev. Richard Butler. Bob Mathews went to Hayden Lake and liked what he heard, with one exception. The Aryan Nations preached that killings would take place at an opportune year in the future. Mathews believed the purification of the white race should take place immediately. In preparation for his warlike campaign, Mathews built a barracks on his property. He had no trouble recruiting racists to his group, which he called the Order. Mathews, Lane, Martinez and Soderquist were joined by five others, including Bruce Pierce. Bruce had been an avid follower of the Aryan Nations, but had grown impatient with their lack of action.

After all, there had to be more to their revolution than shooting at cardboard images of Menachem Begin mounted on trees for target practice. He threw in his lot with Mathews and the Order.

One of the main aims of the Order was the assassination of Jews, as well as gentile traitors. High on their hit list were former secretary of state Henry Kissinger, Chase Manhattan Bank president David Rockefeller and Fred Silverman, president of NBC Television. To finance their activities, the Order printed counterfeit fifty-dollar bills. When this venture proved to be somewhat less than successful, they robbed stores and banks.

Alan Berg became a target of the Order when he had Rev. Pete Peters of the Laporte Church of Christ, located just north of Fort Collins, Colorado, and Col. Gordon Jack Mohr of Mississippi on a telephone hookup with his program. An on-air argument ensued, during which Berg shouted, "Both of you are cowards. Bail out right now." Mohr hung up. Alan Berg was placed on the Order's hit list. The gang met in Denver to eliminate the Berg problem. Mathews enlisted the aid of Jean Craig to learn all she could about Berg's appearance and habits. Jean knew Bob Mathews well. He was responsible for the pregnancy of her thirty-year-old daughter, Zillah, several months earlier.

Alan Berg finished his show for the evening of June 18, 1984, and left the station. He brought his Volkswagen to a stop in front of 1445 Adams St. As he swung his thin body from the vehicle, a burst of gunfire hit his chest, neck and head, sending him sprawling to the pavement. The Order had perpetrated their first assassination. Big-mouth Alan Berg would no longer insult the Order's racist friends. Police investigated the widely publicized killing. Berg had many enemies. The murderer could have been anyone who had been the target of his insults, and that number was legion. Months passed, but no arrests were made.

The gang boldly continued to operate. Twelve members, headed by Mathews, held up a Brinks armoured truck in Northern California. The take was 3.6 million dollars. This newfound wealth provided them with cars and trucks, as well as more acreage in Priest River, Idaho. The gang might have gone on robbing and killing but for Tom Martinez. Martinez was picked up passing the gang's counterfeit money. In exchange for a suspended sentence, he told investigating officers the amazing tale of the Order. In so doing, he brought the FBI into the case, as well as the Bureau of Alcohol, Tobacco and Firearms, the Internal Revenue Service and various police forces throughout the West.

Working with the police, Martinez set up a meeting with Mathews. He flew to Portland and was met at the airport by Mathews and another gang member,

Gary Yarbrough. An FBI SWAT team surrounded the bandits' hotel. Mathews made a dash across the hotel's parking lot. He spotted FBI agent Arthur Hansel, and fired twice. Hansel was wounded in the left shin and the toes of his left foot, while Mathews escaped. Yarbrough was taken into custody without incident. Mathews made his way to Whidbey Island, Washington, where many gang members had homes. The FBI swooped down on the gang. Several were taken into custody, but not Bob Mathews. He opened fire on the agents with an automatic weapon and, after a thirty-six-hour siege, was killed when the house in which he was barricaded burned to the ground.

Most members of the Order were rounded up. On June 18, 1985, exactly one year after Alan Berg was gunned down, they stood trial in Seattle on a variety of criminal charges. Some were granted immunity from prosecution in exchange for their evidence. After a three and a half month trial, ten defendants were found guilty of racketeering and conspiring to racketeer. All received sentences of from forty to one hundred years' imprisonment for their crimes.

In November 1987, four members of the Order stood trial on the charge of "depriving Alan Berg of his civil liberties by killing him." The main prosecution witness was Zillah Craig. The results of that trial are as follows: gang member Richard Scutari was acquitted; Jean Craig, the fifty-four-year-old mother of the chief prosecution witness, was acquitted; and Bruce Pierce and David Lane were both found guilty and sentenced to 150 years' imprisonment each. The judge stipulated that these sentences were to run consecutively to the forty years already being served by both men.

# CHARLIE CHAPLIN

CHARLIE Chaplin—the Little Tramp. The name may mean little to the Michael Jackson generation, but to the millions throughout the world whose memories go back more than thirty years, Charlie Chaplin is synonymous with comedic genius. Charlie's movies, both silent and talkies, which he wrote, produced and starred in, stand as classics of the film art.

The Little Tramp was born to poverty in the Kensington district of London, England, in 1889. His parents, unsuccessful vaudeville entertainers, lived from hand to mouth. When Charlie was three and his older brother, Sydney, was seven, his father died of alcoholism. Mrs Chaplin left the theatre in an attempt to support herself and her sons, but found that the periodic sewing jobs which came her way were not enough. Desperate and alone, Hannah Chaplin suffered a nervous breakdown and was institutionalized. Sydney and Charlie were placed in an orphanage. Fortunately, Hannah recovered and her two sons were returned to her. Their life of poverty continued. Charlie sold newspapers and worked at odd jobs around pubs. Often he wore nothing more than rags and roamed the streets barefoot. In desperation, Charlie sometimes made faces, sang ditties and danced for impromptu audiences. He soon discovered that he had the ability to make people laugh or cry as he chose. Charlie developed his talent and was successful in obtaining a few small parts in English music halls.

Charlie's big break came when he joined Karno's Comedians, a well-known act that had several bookings in the United States. While performing in New York, he was noticed by Mack Sennet of Keystone Cop fame and was lured away from the Karno troupe to make a movie. Charlie was paid $150 a week to act in the film. He was a hit from the very beginning, and went from $150 to $1,250 a week with one raise in pay. Of course, with stardom came the spotlight. Some resented the fact that Charlie never became a U.S. citizen. Others never cared for the Little Tramp because of his well-known sympathy toward the Communist party. But it was not politics that catapulted Charlie into hot water. It was, in a word, women. In 1918, when Charlie was approaching age thirty, he was seen regularly with cute little blonde Mildred Harris. No one would have blinked an eye were it not for one thing: Mildred was an overdeveloped sixteen. The romance evoked a mild scandal. But Charlie had an answer for the rumour-mongers. He married Mildred. Unfortunately, the fun didn't last. The odd couple divorced in 1920.

Sixteen seems to have been Charlie's favourite number. In 1924, at the mature age of thirty-five, he took up with Lita Gray. You guessed it: Lita was sixteen. After Charlie and Lita became an item, as they used to say in Hollywood, Charlie was visited by Lita's uncle who (surprise) happened to be a lawyer. Unc pointed out rather forcefully that intimacy with an under-age girl was, in legalese, statutory rape. On November 24, 1924, in dreary downtown Empalme, Mexico, Lita and Charlie became husband and wife. That same afternoon, Charlie went fishing. Charlie's indifference was a sign of things to come. The newlyweds simply didn't hit it off. They tolerated each other for three years, until January 10, 1927, the day Lita filed a forty-two-page complaint against Charlie. Let's see now, there was the little matter of intimacy before they were married, when she was under-age. Then there was Charlie's abnormal sexual demands. Throw in mental cruelty and running around with other women and you get the general idea. The comedian caught everyone by surprise when he announced to the press that he loved his wife and was deeply hurt that she didn't care for him anymore. Eventually, the charges concerning events which had occurred before the marriage were dropped. Charlie settled out of court on the other charges and somehow managed to weather the storm.

Charlie's star continued to shine brightly, his marital problems notwithstanding. Unlike some silent-movie actors, he made the transition to talkies without any difficulty. Soon he owned a large estate and was considered one of the wealthiest men in Hollywood. At the height of his fame, Charlie never wavered in his leanings toward the Soviet Union. Perhaps it was his impoverished youth that influenced his pro-Communist tendencies. Whatever the reason, he raised the ire of anti-Communist groups in the film industry.

In 1936, Charlie married movie star Paulette Goddard on a ship off Canton, China. They stayed together for five years before Paulette obtained a Mexican divorce. Shortly after his divorce from Goddard, Charlie was introduced to twenty-year-old Joan Barry. Within a year, Joan contacted powerful Hollywood gossip columnist Hedda Hopper with the rather startling news that she was pregnant. Hedda, who didn't trust her own mother, took Joan to a doctor, who confirmed that the young woman was indeed expecting a child. Joan claimed that Charlie Chaplin was the father and what's more, he would not even allow her into his mansion where she had once been so very welcome.

It was all too much for Joan. She took an overdose of sleeping pills and was only saved by an alert police officer who rushed her to hospital, where doctors pumped out her stomach. Joan was booked as a vagrant. The charges were dropped in exchange for a promise to leave town. She hopped a train for New York, but got off in Omaha and headed back to Hollywood, where she broke into Charlie's home. Police were summoned and Joan was sentenced to ninety days in jail. Charlie interceded. He had Joan transferred from the jail to a hospital in Santa Monica. In return for the favour, Joan slapped Charlie with a paternity suit. He was also charged with violation of the Mann Act (the act prohibiting interstate transportation of women for immoral purposes) and with having denied Joan her civil rights. Joan claimed that earlier that year Charlie had travelled to New York, where she was staying at the time. He booked into the Waldorf Towers. Joan roomed elsewhere. One night she joined Charlie at the Waldorf, where sexual intercourse had taken place. In regard to the civil rights action, Joan claimed that her rights were denied her when she was forced to leave Hollywood. She also brought the same action against the judge, lawyer and police officers involved in the incident. The civil rights indictment was eventually dropped, but Charlie stood trial on the Mann Act violation.

Charlie hired famed Hollywood lawyer Jerry Giesler, who proved without a doubt that there was little need for Charlie to follow Joan to New York. She was constantly throwing herself at him, to the point of breaking into his home in Hollywood. On the night Joan claimed they were intimate, Charlie admitted that he had escorted her to the Waldorf, but vehemently denied that intercourse had taken place. Joan took the witness stand. Giesler had her admit that, on one occasion when she broke into Charlie's home, she had held a pistol on the comedian for an hour and a half, after which she'd jumped into bed and had intercourse with Charlie.

Joan also admitted that many of her travels were financed by the richest man in the world at that time, Jean Paul Getty. She usually stayed at the fashionable Hotel Pierre while in New York. This was particularly convenient since Getty owned the Pierre. Charlie beat the rap. He was acquitted of the Mann Act charge, which could have brought him a twenty-five-year prison sentence.

Joan gave birth to her baby, Carol Ann. Blood tests performed on Joan, Charlie and Carol Ann proved conclusively that Charlie could not have been the father of the child. Despite this scientific proof, Charlie was brought to trial. Strangely, the jury could not reach a verdict. Even stranger, at a second trial, Charlie was judged to be the father of little Carol Ann. The baby was awarded

$75 a week and was entitled to use the Chaplin name. The sentimental verdict passed down by the Chaplin jury can never happen again. In 1955, California passed a law prohibiting paternity trials after blood tests have proven the impossibility of the defendant's being the father.

While still on trial, Charlie, now fifty-four, married eighteen-year-old Oona O'Neill, daughter of playwright Eugene O'Neill. Charlie's fourth marriage proved to be his most successful. Over the years, he and Oona had seven children. But Charlie Chaplin was to have still more problems from another direction. At the conclusion of the Second World War, the United States became enmeshed in the Cold War. Everything Communist was seen as pernicious. Charlie openly supported Communist causes. In 1952, he and Oona sailed for Europe on vacation. While at sea, they were informed that U.S. Attorney General James F. McGranery had announced that he was rescinding Chaplin's re-entry permit. Charlie decided not to fight, and moved himself and his family to Vevey, Switzerland.

Charlie would not return to the United States until twenty years later. In 1972, in one of the most emotional ceremonies ever witnessed on television, Hollywood presented Charlie with an honorary Oscar "in recognition of the incalculable effect he has had in making motion pictures the art form of this century." Three years later, confined to a wheechair, Charlie was knighted by the Queen of England.

In 1977, Sir Charles Chaplin, the Little Tramp, father of ten children, married four times, innovative genius who had made millions laugh and cry, died peacefully at his home in Switzerland with his wife and seven of his children by his side. He was eighty-eight.

The Little Tramp from Kensington had lived a very full life.

# RICHARD DADD

ROBERT Dadd was a retired apothecary, the father of gifted painter Richard Dadd. On Monday, August 28, 1843, Robert drove into the tiny village of Cobham with his son Richard in tow. Robert Dadd knew that his son was extremely unstable. The young man had just returned from the Mediterranean. From all reports, Richard had behaved irrationally and had caused several disturbances. Concerned, Robert had his son examined by doctors who agreed that Richard was dangerously unstable. Richard Dadd was also an artist of some renown and promise. His paintings featured fantastic images drawn from his fertile imagination. They were a commercial success and had been the subject of several exclusive shows.

On this day in late August 1843, Robert Dadd was accompanying Richard on the short trip to Cobham as a sort of vacation, which he felt his son needed. The elder Dadd had no way of knowing that his son was hallucinating. Richard was receiving messages from the ancient Egyptian god Osiris. In his hallucinatory state, he had come to regard his father as "the man who calls himself my father." Unknown to Robert, his son was stalking him under the direction of Osiris.

The Dadds pulled up to The Ship, a well-known watering hole in the village. Robert asked if they could provide beds for the night. John Adams, who knew Robert slightly, explained that they didn't have rooms, but because they received so many requests for accommodations, they had a working arrangement with locals who lived in cottages close to the pub, who could provide one double bed. Before Adams could continue, Robert Dadd said that one double bed would do just fine. He introduced Adams to his son. Surlily, Richard stated that he wanted his own bed. Adams explained that there would be no trouble providing single beds, but the two would have to sleep in separate cottages. Richard agreed to these arrangements.

Father and son had a beer and then went out for a walk to take in the pleasant summer evening. An hour later, they returned and ordered supper, during which Richard Dadd behaved somewhat erratically. At one point during the meal, he dashed to another area of the pub and gulped down two glasses of water when all the while there was a tumbler of water within arm's reach at his table. At about 8:45 p.m., Robert and Richard went for another walk in the fading light. Near a gravel pit beside a large tree whose branches almost touched the ground, Richard suddenly hit his father from behind. The blow to the head stunned the older man, who fell to the ground. Richard was on his father like a crazed animal, raining blows on the man's head and body. He pulled his half-conscious father under the branches of the tree, took a straight razor out of his pocket and relentlessly slashed at his helpless victim. Because Robert's clothing was bunched up as a result of his being dragged under the tree, the razor didn't inflict any real damage. Frustrated, Richard extracted a large new seaman's spring-bladed knife from his pocket. Well-directed blows with this formidable weapon ended his father's life. In Richard's warped mind, he had killed Satan, who had been posing as his father.

That evening, some villagers passed near the body of Robert Dadd. They paid scant attention, figuring that someone had had too much grog and was sleeping it off. The following morning, one of the villagers who had seen the still form the night before decided to investigate. It was he who raised the cry of bloody murder. Richard had had a night's head start. He made his way to Dover, where he hired a small private boat to take him to France. From Calais, he travelled to Paris. Fellow passengers on the coach remembered the wild-eyed Englishman who had been their travelling companion. After a shopping spree for a new wardrobe in Paris, Richard booked passage on a stagecoach bound for Vienna, Austria.

Before Richard left French soil, the god Osiris spoke to him once more. Osiris told him that Satan was the lone fellow traveller sitting right beside him. Satan had to be annihilated. Richard slashed viciously at the man's throat, but the attack was far different from the one that had taken place on the deserted country road in England. The intended victim screamed and the coachman quickly came to his rescue, pulling Richard away. Once overpowered, Richard settled down and was turned over to the authorities. He was sent to an asylum at Melun and later to Clermont-Ferrand, where he stayed ten months. Initially, the French were reluctant to allow Richard to be extradited, fearing that an English court would execute an insane man. However, once they received assurances from English authorities that he would be certified insane, they agreed to send him back.

It is interesting to note that, despite the murderous attack on his father, Richard's family considered the gifted painter to be a sick person rather than a criminal—certainly an enlightened view for those times. Richard was sent to Bethlehem Royal Hospital, the insane asylum credited with giving us the word *bedlam*. Many believed that a masterful artist would be lost to the world, but such was not the case. Richard was transferred to Broadmoor when that infamous institution was opened. Here he painted diligently and produced some of his finest works, featuring fairies and fantasy scenes from his imagination. He died of natural causes in the institution in 1887, at the age of seventy.

In 1960, much of Richard's work was discovered by an archivist who had been left the old Bethlehem Royal Hospital's records and files. Scholars have studied the paintings and believe them to be the work of a genius. In 1974, the prestigious Tate Gallery in London, England, held an exhibition of his works. Today, one of Richard's finest works, *The Fairy Feller's Master Stroke,* is on permanent display in the Tate Gallery. If you look closely enough at the obsessively detailed studies of gnomes and elves, you will see the likeness of Robert Dadd. Somewhere along the line, apparently, Osiris had decreed that the image of Richard's murdered father would live forever in the work of his brilliant, tormented son.

# CULLEN DAVIS

JUST how rich were the Davises of Fort Worth, Texas? Well, to give you an idea, the family's holding company, Kendavis Industries International Inc., had a net profit in 1975 of $57 million. Sales of the wholly family-owned conglomerate exceeded one billion dollars annually and involved eighty-three individual companies.

In 1968, old man Davis died, leaving his vast business empire to his three sons, Ken Jr., Cullen and Bill. Cullen, the most flamboyant of the three, shocked Fort Worth society when he married Priscilla Lee Wilborn, a tiny sexy blond bombshell from the other side of the tracks who had been married twice before. Priscilla brought to the marriage her eldest daughter, Dee, whom Cullen adopted. Two other children, Jack and Andrea Wilborn, lived with their father, although they visited Priscilla frequently. Cullen brought three hundred million dollars to the union.

Priscilla was a fun-loving morsel who preferred life in the fast lane. Although she didn't fit in with the country-club-cum-jet-set crowd, it didn't take her long to acquire expensive habits, such as blowing $20,000 a month on clothing. Shortly after their marriage, Cullen built a new home for his ever-loving bride on a piece of property in Fort Worth's most prestigious residential area. The Mansion, as it came to be known, covered 19,000 square feet and cost an estimated six million dollars to build. The estate, at 4200 Mockingbird Lane, encompassed 181 acres. Cullen and Priscilla travelled extensively throughout Europe and South America purchasing furniture for their ultraluxurious showplace. Superficially, everything looked fine.

The first rumblings of trouble in paradise developed when Cullen insisted on disciplining Priscilla's daughter Andrea when she visited the Mansion. Soon Andrea would only visit with her mother when Cullen was not home. With the bloom gradually fading off the rose, Cullen took more business trips without Priscilla. This brought out the worst in Priscilla's restless nature. She craved company, but she didn't crave company bedecked in white shirts and thousand-dollar suits. She carried on a series of affairs with unemployed rock singers, dope addicts, motorcycle gang members and just plain drifters. There was usually a roaring party taking place at 4200 Mockingbird Lane. Six years after their marriage, Priscilla filed for divorce. Cullen moved out of the Mansion and into a motel. This arrangement didn't last long. Cullen met Karen Master, the mother of two handicapped children, and moved into her home. Meanwhile, Priscilla settled down with six-foot-nine-inch former Texas Christian University basketball player, Stan Farr.

On August 2, 1976, an event took place which is believed to have been the catalyst for the tragedy that followed. While attending a business meeting, Cullen was informed that Priscilla had received a delay in her divorce proceedings against him. Judge Joseph Eidson, who was hearing the divorce case, ordered Cullen to pay Priscilla the sum of $52,000 immediately and raise her monthly support from $3,500 to $5,000. Cullen was also ordered not to visit the Mansion or bother his wife in any way. Above all, ever since Priscilla had instituted proceedings, Judge Eidson reserved the right to approve all business deals of the vast Davis empire, presumably to protect Priscilla's interests. The entire package was a bitter pill for Cullen to swallow. That night, events in the lives of Mr and Mrs Davis took a turn which shocked the nation and gave rise to the longest, most expensive murder trial ever to take place in Texas.

Priscilla and Stan Farr went out for dinner with some friends. After dinner they visited the Rangoon Racquet Club, where they bumped into Bev Bass, a friend of Priscilla's daughter Dee, and Bev's boyfriend, Bubba Gavrel. Bev mentioned that she planned on sleeping over at Dee's that night and would see Priscilla later. It was approximately 11 p.m. Back at the Mansion, twelve-year-old Andrea had just finished chatting on the phone with Stan Farr's sister. It was 10:30 p.m. Sometime after that, Andrea had a visitor. She probably opened the door to her killer, because the Mansion's alarm system was later found to be deactivated. Her murderer led her down to the basement and shot her below the left breast with a .38 Smith and Wesson. She died instantly.

Priscilla and Stan arrived home. Priscilla was annoyed at her two daughters when she found that the alarm system was deactivated. She was unaware that Dee was spending the night at a friend's home and so had escaped the tragedy of that evening. Stan headed up the stairs to the master bedroom. Suddenly, according to Priscilla, Cullen stepped out of the laundry room. He was wearing a shoulder-length black wig and was dressed in black. Again according to Priscilla's testimony, Cullen said, "Hi," and shot her. Priscilla screamed, "I've been shot! Cullen shot me! Stan, go back." At this time, Priscilla later stated, Stan, a huge man, came running down the stairs. Cullen fired through a door, wounding Stan. Then he pushed the door open. The two men struggled before Cullen wrenched free and shot Stan again. Stan went down and his assailant fired two more shots into his body. The killer turned to the badly wounded Priscilla, who managed to run outside, believing that a second bullet would end her life at any moment. She stumbled and fell. Her antagonist was once more at her side. He pulled at her arm, half dragging her toward the house. Suddenly he let go and returned to Stan's body, attempting to drag the large corpse to the cellar.

Outside, Priscilla ran to a neighbour's home. Just then, Bubba Gavrel and Bev Bass pulled up in the driveway. Later, Gavrel corroborated Priscilla's story by recalling how he had come upon the scene. Not comprehending the seriousness of the situation, he and Bev approached the house. The man in black greeted them and said, "They are right this way. Follow me." The two followed the man as he led the way in the darkness. When they approached the breakfast-room door, light from the interior of the house fell upon the man in black. Bev recognized him immediately. "Bubba, that's Cullen," she blurted out. Without hesitation, the gunman turned and shot Bubba in the stomach. In terror, Bev Bass ran outside and managed to flag down a passing motorist. Back at the Mansion, Bubba Gavrel, paralysed from the waist down, played dead. All was quiet. The massacre was over.

At 4:30 a.m., police surrounded Karen Master's home. Cullen Davis surrendered to the authorities. In the summer of 1977, in Amarillo, Texas, Cullen Davis, probably the richest man ever tried for murder in the United States, stood trial for the murder of Andrea Wilborn. Davis hired the best legal team available in the country. He even spent $30,000 to finance a research project to determine what type of individual would make the most favourable jurors for the defence. In all, more than fourteen top-drawer lawyers worked on his behalf.

Despite three eyewitnesses positively identifying Cullen as the killer, the jury brought in a verdict of not guilty. Davis and his girlfriend, Karen Master, celebrated the decision by taking a ski vacation in Aspen, Colorado. The verdict, so at odds with the evidence, probably was swayed by one conjecture: If a man of Cullen's means really wanted someone killed, would he not hire a professional to do it? Several jurors later stated that they couldn't dismiss that thought from their minds.

Of course, Cullen still had minor problems. He claimed that the long murder trial had cost him three million dollars. Priscilla was still pressing her divorce case, which could add up to several million more, and Bubba Gavrel was suing for thirteen million dollars. That's when Cullen hit the headlines again. David McCrory was a good friend of Cullen's who worked for one of his companies. He informed the FBI that Davis had approached him to hire a hit man to kill Judge Joe Eidson. In all, McCrory alleged that Cullen's hit list contained fifteen names, including all those who had testified against him at his murder trial. The FBI outfitted McCrory with a tape recorder and had him go along with the scheme. He recorded Cullen discussing the murders and the cost of each killing. The FBI even photographed several meetings between the two men.

Judge Eidson was to be the first victim. The judge cooperated with police by having his picture taken in a death pose. Cigarette burns in the judge's shirt simulated bullet wounds. McCrory triumphantly showed Cullen the picture of the supposedly dead judge while Cullen's reactions were taped. Cullen was picked up and charged with solicitation of murder. Again he faced an apparently overwhelming array of irrefutable evidence. Once more, his high-priced legal team went into action.

After debating forty-four hours and taking fourteen ballots, the jury stood eight for conviction and four for acquittal. They couldn't agree. A mistrial was declared and Cullen Davis was set free. Late in 1979, Cullen again stood trial for soliciting the murder of Judge Joseph Eidson. This time, the jury deliberated only fourteen hours before finding Cullen not guilty. When this decision was handed down, the remaining charges of murdering Stan Farr and wounding Priscilla and Bubba Gavrel were dropped.

Priscilla finally obtained her divorce and received a settlement of $3.4 million in cash and property. Cullen Davis married Karen Master. As part of his divorce settlement from Priscilla, Cullen was awarded the six-million-dollar home on 4200 Mockingbird Lane.

# ALFRED DREYFUS

PERHAPS no other criminal case in history dominated the news of the world as France's infamous Dreyfus affair. For twelve years, details regarding the status of the case spilled out of its country of origin to capture the attention of the entire world.

Alfred Dreyfus was a career army man, the only Jewish member of the general staff of the French army. The son of a wealthy textile manufacturer, Dreyfus entered the École Polytechnique at age nineteen with one aim in mind—to become an army officer. Dreyfus was an excellent horseman and fencer, as well as a brilliant student. However, he was an aloof, formal loner who was not well liked by his colleagues.

In 1889, at age thirty, Dreyfus had attained a captaincy in the Central School of Explosives at Bourges. The day he was accepted to the École de Guerre, he married Lucie Hadamard, the daughter of an influential French family. In the next three years, the Dreyfuses had two children, a boy and a girl. Dreyfus graduated from the École de Guerre in ninth place in a class of eighty-one. In 1893, with anti-semitism raging throughout France, he was appointed to the general staff. Thus Dreyfus became the only Jew ever to enter the higher echelon of the French army.

On July 20, 1894, an event took place that changed Dreyfus's life forever. Col. Max von Schwartzhoppen, military attaché to the German Embassy in Paris, was approached by Maj. Count Ferdinand Walsin-Esterhazy of the French army. Esterhazy offered to act as a spy for Germany. Two days after their meeting, he was turning over top-secret documents to Schwartzhoppen in exchange for money. In the ensuing weeks, several documents changed hands. Often, the Germans shared their French secrets with the Italian army. On one such occasion, Schwartzhoppen sent his Italian counterpart a letter which was intercepted by French counter-intelligence. It read, "Enclosed are 12 detailed maps of Nice that the scoundrel D left with me for you. I told him you had no intention of taking up relations with him again. He said there was a misunderstanding and that he will do his best to satisfy you."

The letter was passed on to the head of counter-espionage, Col. Jean Conrad Sandherr, who wanted desperately to know the identity of "D." Another group of documents was intercepted. A summary attached to these documents read, "I am sending you some interesting information. 1. A note on the hydraulic brake of the 120 mm gun. 2. A note on the new plan for the supporting troops. 3. A note on the modification of artillery formations. 4. A note concerning Madagascar. 5. The provisional Firing Manual for Field Artillery. The last document is extraordinarily difficult to procure and I have it in my possession only for a few days. If therefore you will take notes of whatever is of interest to you and hold it at my disposal, I shall take it back. I am off to the manoeuvres."

Colonel Sandherr now knew for certain that the spy was a member of the general staff. He scanned the list of staff members whose names began with the letter D. When he came to Alfred Dreyfus, he went no further. Copies of Dreyfus's handwriting were compared to the handwriting on the summary. It was decided that the two were similar. Gen. Auguste Mercier, the minister of war, met with the premier of France, Charles Dupuy. As a result of their meeting, Alfred Dreyfus was arrested. In true French fashion, Dreyfus was presented with a revolver and invited to kill himself. He was astonished to be accused of treason: his whole life had been devoted to the army and the honour of his country.

The news of the arrest of a general staff member as a traitor caused a tremendous uproar throughout France. Dreyfus was held incommunicado. Army lawyers scanned his past from the day he was born, in an attempt to paint him as a criminal who had managed to rise to a lofty position in the French army, this in spite of the fact that Dreyfus's past was filled with academic and military achievements. These honours notwithstanding, Dreyfus was court-martialled, the main piece of evidence against him being the summary, which some experts claimed might have been written by him. Other experts disagreed.

On December 19, 1894, Dreyfus was tried for treason. Throughout the trial, he maintained his aloof aristocratic bearing, which did nothing to win sympathy for him. He was ably defended by criminal lawyer Edgar Demange, who was firmly convinced that Dreyfus was innocent. The proceedings were held in camera. Demange brought out that Dreyfus would never write, "I'm off to the manoeuvres" because, in fact, records verified that he had not gone on manoeuvres at or around the time the note was written.

Despite the best efforts of the defence, Dreyfus was doomed. High-ranking French army personnel swore that they had been informed he was a spy. They were able to give this type of testimony without revealing their sources. Captain Dreyfus was uncermoniously found guilty of treason and sentenced to deportation for life to the dreaded penal colony on Devil's Island. On January 5, 1895, Dreyfus was officially drummed out of the army at the parade grounds of the École Militaire. As epaulettes and red stripes were torn from his uniform, Dreyfus stood at attention and shouted, "An innocent is discharged. Long live France!" On his way to exile, Dreyfus came close to being lynched on several occasions as mobs attempted to pull him from his train. He arrived in chains at Devil's Island and was placed in a small stone hut with barred doors and windows. A wall was built around the hut. Five guards who never spoke stood watch over him night and day. He was allowed no mail and no visitors.

Fifteen months later, French counter-intelligence came into possession of a postcard written by German Colonel von Schwartzhoppen to Major Esterhazy. Esterhazy was put under surveillance. His handwriting was studied. It was compared to the summary purportedly written by Dreyfus. There was no doubt about it: the two documents had been written by Esterhazy. Lt.-Col. Georges Picquant, the man who discovered Dreyfus's innocence, could get no one interested in reopening the Dreyfus affair. In the months and years that followed, Picquant's military career was ruined because of his insistence on Dreyfus's innocence. It was only when he finally consulted a lawyer that the first rumblings that Dreyfus had been made a scapegoat reached the public. Pamphlets were distributed. Dreyfus's brother Mathieu kept the case alive and even brought a court action against Esterhazy. Behind closed doors, Esterhazy was vindicated.

Five thousand miles away, Dreyfus was unaware that year after year his case was being argued in the press. It wasn't until January 13, 1898 that the public became fully aware of the new status of the Dreyfus case. Famed author Emile Zola published his piece "J'accuse" in the tiny French newspaper *L'Aurore,* in which he clearly accused the French army of convicting an innocent man and now knowing the identity of the guilty party. The piece caused a sensation. The paper sold 300,000 copies and received 30,000 letters concerning the case. Zola was charged with libel. The world watched as France shamelessly convicted its renowned journalist. Zola was sentenced to a year in prison, but the excitement he had ignited would not die. Eventually, several documents which had been instrumental in convicting Dreyfus were exposed as forgeries. A retrial of the case became inevitable. Dreyfus was brought back to France. He was only thirty-nine, but looked years older. Unbelievably, Dreyfus once more was found guilty of treason.

The world was horrified at this travesty of justice. In 1899, the premier of France hurriedly issued a full pardon to Dreyfus. At last he was a free man. Not content with a pardon for his brother, Mathieu Dreyfus successfully pressed for a new trial. On July 12, 1906, the High Court of Appeal set aside the former sentence and declared its guilty verdict to be an error. The court agreed that at no time did any incriminating evidence exist against Dreyfus. After capturing the headlines for twelve years, the case was closed.

At a ceremony at the École Militaire, on the exact spot where years before he had been disgraced, Dreyfus was decorated with the Legion of Honor. Later, in 1914, he fought with distinction side by side with Canadian troops at Chemin des Dames and Verdun, two of the bloodiest battles of the First World War. He died in 1935.

Major Esterhazy, who had been discharged from the army, died destitute in 1923 in the slums of London, where he had lived under an assumed name.

# ADOLF EICHMANN

THE name Adolf Eichmann conjures up images of a man who, with one telephone call, could send thousands of innocent people to their deaths. Men, women and children were stripped of their possessions, shoved into cattle cars and transported to Nazi Germany's extermination camps, where they were gassed to death. This man could bark out an order and have the entire Jewish populations of Europe's major cities herded into ghettos.

The "Final Solution" of the so-called Jewish problem, which in reality translated into the annihilation of an entire segment of Europe's population, was already taking place. A high-priority meeting was called by the German High Command on January 20, 1942, in the Berlin suburb of Wannsee. Reinhard Heydrich addressed the group from material compiled by Adolf Eichmann. The fate of the Jewish people was sealed. In the future, moving Jews out of areas occupied by Germans was not sufficient. The order had come down from none other than the fuehrer himself, Adolf Hitler. He wanted the Final Solution implemented, with all its horrendous ramifications.

Everything was now in place. Camps were built or were being built. The names would became infamous—Auschwitz, Belzec, Buchenwald, Chelmno, Dachau, Maidanek, Sobibor, Treblinka. Moreover, experiments had been carried out with poison gas until deadly Zyklon B., supplied in quantity by the firm of Tesch and Stabenow, was chosen to be used to kill Jews. Heydrich estimated that the Jews of countries occupied by Germany, in addition to those of Spain, Turkey, Switzerland, Sweden, Britain, Russia and Ireland, would approximate eleven million. The man in charge of the entire extermination operation was SS Sturmbannfuehrer Adolf Eichmann. In the years that followed, he would go about his task with unusual zeal and demonic imagination. In all, six million Jews would perish in the Holocaust.

At the conclusion of the Second World War, many war criminals were executed or imprisoned. Others, like Hitler himself, took their own lives. Still others melted into the chaos of war-torn Europe, emigrated to North America or made their way to South America. Adolf Eichmann disappeared from view. His notoriety never suspected, Eichmann was interned in a prisoner-of-war camp in

Austria. He escaped and made his way to the German town of Celle, where he spent the next three years staying out of the limelight. With the aid of a well-established Nazi underground, he went to Italy, where he was outfitted with a passport in the name of Ricardo Klement. Together with his wife, Vera, and their three sons, Ricardo Klement sailed for Argentina, where he settled down near Buenos Aires. There, the Klements had a fourth son. Meanwhile, Eichmann worked quietly for a water-supply company.

One of the most prolific mass murderers of all time wanted the world to forget Adolf Eichmann. But those who remembered the gas chambers of the camps, the human experiments at Dachau and the eighty-one children of Lidice, murdered in reprisal for the assassination of Heydrich, could not forget. Men and women who survived the Holocaust took an active interest in hunting down war criminals: Adolf Eichmann was at the top of their list. Rumours persisted that Eichmann was alive in Kuwait, Switzerland and Austria. The hunt was on.

Probably the first concrete evidence of Eichmann's participation in the Final Solution came when Tuvia Friedman, a man involved in hunting Nazi war criminals, received a document from the Austrian police. The document, signed by Eichmann, authorized the deportation of 50,000 Hungarian Jews to a death camp in Poland. Friedman interviewed Eichmann's former chauffeur, Joseph Wiesel. He was told that a former mistress of Eichmann's, Frau Missenbach, lived near Linz. Friedman believed the ex-girlfriend might have a photo of her dashing wartime companion. He enlisted the aid of a handsome German-born Israeli agent to ingratiate himself with the still-attractive Frau Missenbach.

Friedman and Missenbach met by a prearranged accident. Soon the agent gained Frau Missenbach's confidence and was invited to her home on several occasions. On one such visit, the conversation turned to talk of the old war days. Photo albums were taken out of drawers and shown to the Israeli agent. One of the photos was of an SS officer who could be Adolf Eichmann. Later, Israeli agents entered the house and stole the photo. It was never missed. Friedman showed the photo to Eichmann's former chauffeur, who confirmed that it was a photograph of his former superior officer. It was exciting news, but it was still only an old photo. It was 1948, and Israeli statehood took precedence over all other activities for a time. In 1950, Friedman established that Eichmann's wife and three children had lived in the Austrian resort town of Bad Ausee before they disappeared. When questioned, friends and relatives claimed that Vera had remarried and moved away with her children; no one heard from her anymore.

Meanwhile, another Nazi hunter, Simon Wiesenthal, had garnered much material indicating that Eichmann was living near Buenos Aires and working for a water-supply company. An old friend who exchanged stamps with Wiesenthal from Argentina was sure Eichmann was living under an alias and leading a pleasant, if quiet, life. Wiesenthal turned over all his information to the Israeli government. Very little was done in the hunt for Eichmann until the prime minister of Israel, David Ben Gurion, offered a $10,000 reward for anyone providing information leading to the capture of the wanted man. Tuvia Friedman, still obsessed with bringing Eichmann to justice, saw to it that the offer was well publicized. He received replies from all over the world. It took him days just to separate the hoaxes from the genuine possibilities.

One letter stood out from all others. It was from Buenos Aires, Argentina, and was signed by Lothar Herman, who explained that he could provide absolute proof as to Eichmann's identity and whereabouts. Lothar, a blind Jewish lawyer, went on to explain that he had this information because his daughter was dating Adolf Eichmann's son. In due course, an Israeli agent contacted Lothar Herman, who did as he had promised. He turned over all the information he had in his possession. On May 23, 1960, Israeli agents swooped down on Adolf Eichmann. They quickly drugged their captive and flew him to Israel to stand trial for crimes against humanity. In a trial publicized around the world, Eichmann was found guilty of crimes against the Jewish people, crimes against humanity and various war crimes. He was hanged on May 31, 1962.

In 1972, Reuters News Agency released a four-inch news bulletin datelined Tel Aviv. The item was relegated to the back pages of the few newspapers that picked it up. The insignificant news story related that Israeli authorities were releasing the $10,000 reward money for the information which had led to the apprehension of Adolf Eichmann. The recipient was Lothar Herman. Fourteen years had passed since the now-seventy-year-old lawyer wrote to Tuvia Friedman to tell him that his daughter was dating Adolf Eichmann's son.

# JOSEPH BONNE ELWELL

AT the turn of the century, Joseph Bonne Elwell was gainfully employed as a hardware-store salesman. He was a terrific cardplayer, but had no idea that he would become one of the best-known bridge authorities of his day. By the time he was twenty-five, Joe had written two books on bridge which came to be accepted as the definitive works on the subject. He also taught the game to wealthy New Yorkers. Soon the bridge expert was associating with the crème de la crème of Big Apple society.

In 1904, Joe married the former wife of a Long Island lawyer. The marriage was to last sixteen years, during which the Elwells had one son, Richard. In the course of their married life, Joe's wife was a great help to him in his writing. His books owed as much to her contribution as they did to his knowledge of bridge.

The years passed. As Joe's fame spread, he became bored with married life. It must have come as somewhat of a shock to his wife when he asked her for a divorce. Arrangements were amicable enough. Joe paid the shot. He gave a monthly allowance to the former Mrs Elwell and took care of all his fifteen-year-old son's expenses.

Looking back over the years, it is not difficult to imagine Joe's fame. He was in demand as a teacher of bridge and as a public speaker on the subject. His wealth grew in proportion to his fame. During the height of his career he maintained summer homes in Saratoga Springs, Palm Beach and Long Island, as well as quarters in New York City. His city home, which he occupied alone, was a three-storey building located at 244 West Seventieth St. Joe was riding high, wide and handsome.

Now that Joe was hobnobbing with the elite of the city, he often received valuable stock-market tips from wealthy, well-informed friends. He invested wisely, which enabled him to maintain a privileged lifestyle, as well as to provide for his former wife and son. In time, Joe invested in a stud farm in Covington, Kentucky. His Beach Racing Stable, unlike many horsy investments, returned a sizeable profit. It seemed that everything Joe touched turned to gold.

So much for Mr Elwell's business ventures. His personal life revolved around wine, women and song. Joe kept a steady stream of Broadway lovelies entering his bachelor digs on West Seventieth. It didn't matter whether they were married, single, separated or whatever. From aspiring matronly bridge mavens, to buxom chorus girls, Joe partied with them all. Expensive booze and catered goodies were always at hand for Joe and his female guest—or female guests. In keeping with his lifestyle and opulent home, Joe maintained a staff of three, none of whom lived on the premises. William Barnes acted as secretary and valet; Edward Rhodes was Joe's chauffeur; and Mrs Marie Larsen was his housekeeper.

Let's pause for a moment and go over the night of Thursday, June 10, 1920, in some detail. It would be Joe Elwell's last night on earth.

At 7:30 p.m., Joe was in the company of Mr and Mrs Walter Lewisohn and Mrs Lewisohn's sister Viola Kraus, having dinner at the Ritz Carlton Hotel. They were observed leaving the hotel by several acquaintances. The dinner companions made their way to the New Amsterdam Theatre roof to take in the *Midnight Follies*. They stayed at the New Amsterdam until 2 a.m. and were seen by many to be enjoying themselves. The party of four took the elevator down to the street. Mr Lewisohn hailed a cab and together with his wife and sister-in-law climbed in. Joe felt the cab was too crowded. Despite the Lewisohns' urgings, he insisted they go on without him. Good nights were exchanged. The Lewisohns last saw Joe walking alone toward Seventh Avenue.

Cab driver Edgar Walters was not having a busy night and was glad to see someone on the street obviously looking for a cab. Edgar pulled up and Joe entered his taxi. At Sixty-sixth Street, Joe asked Edgar to stop at a newsstand. He got out, picked up a *Morning Telegram* and reentered the cab. Delivered to his house, Joe gave Edgar a thirty-five cent tip. Edgar observed him walking up the three steps of his home. It was 2:30 a.m.

Dawn came to little old New York. At 6:15 a.m., Henry Otter was well into his route as a driver for the Sheffield Dairy Co. He left a quart of milk in Joe's porch. Fifty-five minutes later, at 7:10 a.m., postman Charles Torey opened the storm door, dropped Joe's mail on the floor and pressed the buzzer as he did on all his deliveries. At 8:10 a.m., an hour after the mail had been dropped off, housekeeper Marie Larsen, who had the key to the residence, showed up for work. Marie absentmindedly picked up the bottle of milk, used her key to open the door and entered the house.

Marie walked down the hall and glanced into the living room. There was Joe Elwell sitting in a large chair facing a fireplace across the room, a bullet hole squarely between his eyes. Joe was dressed only in pyjamas. Several unopened envelopes lay on the floor around the chair. One letter had been opened and rested on Joe's lap. He had obviously been reading it when he was shot. Blood was spattered on the walls and on the floor. Marie could hear her boss's laboured breathing. She ran from the house and bumped into milkman Henry Otter, who had returned to the street to collect unpaid bills from customers who were now rising. Marie shouted to Otter, "Call an ambulance, quick!" Otter looked confused and told Marie to tell a traffic cop up the street. Marie ran to the police officer, who accompanied her back to Joe's residence. At 8:30 a.m., he attempted to use Joe's phone to summon help, but found it to be out of order. A minute later, he called from a neighbour's phone. An ambulance was dispatched. Attendants rushed Joe to hospital, where he died two hours later.

From the moment Joe died, his murder was a national sensation. Here was a man known and admired by millions. The public was mystified. Who would kill the bridge expert in his own home during the early hours of an otherwise pleasant summer morning? New York's top homicide detectives were assigned to the case. They thoroughly examined Elwell's three-storey home. Two of the three doors leading into the first floor were locked from the inside. The only window open was in Joe's bedroom on the third floor. It would have been impossible for the killer to have entered through this window. And Marie and Joe had the only two keys to the front door.

Detectives quickly ascertained that Joe had been shot sometime between 7:10 a.m. when the mail was delivered and 8:10 a.m. when Marie Larsen showed up for work. They also believed that the killer had been known to Joe, since all the physical evidence pointed to Joe's having opened the door to his assailant. Of course, he could have inadvertently left the door open that morning, but Joe was a creature of habit. Those who knew him swore that he always locked his door before retiring.

Joe's bedroom was examined. It appeared that he had lain down on top of the bedclothes on one side of the bed. It was an extremely hot night. Joe had probably left his window open because of the heat and had situated himself on top of the bedclothes for the same reason. The other side of the bed showed no sign that anyone other than Joe had been in his bedroom that night. From Joe's trouser pockets detectives retrieved $400 in cash. His toupee, false teeth and jewellery were undisturbed on a dresser. His slippers were neatly placed on the bedroom floor.

A spare bedroom on the third floor, decorated in a sensuous motif, which was obviously used for purposes other than sleeping, bore no evidence that it had been occupied that night. The living room, where the murder had taken place, came under close scrutiny. A .45-calibre steel-jacket bullet lay on a table to Joe's right. It had gone directly through his head, ricocheted off a wall and had come to rest on the table. Near his feet was the empty shell that had been ejected automatically when the murder weapon was fired. The ammunition had been manufactured three years earlier by the U.S. Cartridge Co. Powder burns indicated that the .45-calibre weapon had been held between three and four feet from Joe's head.

Examination of the bullet holes in Joe's head revealed that the entry bullet between the eyes was one inch lower than the exit wound. In addition, the mark on the living-room wall was slightly higher than the exit wound. Whoever had shot Joe had either been in a slouching position or had fired upward from the hip. No strange fingerprints were found anywhere in the residence, nor was there any sign of a struggle.

As days turned into weeks, detectives were left with little more than two theories. It was unlikely, but possible, that a robber had somehow gained entrance to the house before Joe came home. He could have lain in wait for his unsuspecting victim and shot Joe dead while he opened his mail. Under examination, this theory doesn't hold water. If a robber was in the house, why wouldn't he have shot Joe in his bed? If he killed Joe as he sat in his chair opening his mail, how did he get within three or four feet of his victim without being seen by him? Nothing was missing from the house, which would make our robber a strange criminal indeed.

Theory number two was by far the more popular: Joe had been murdered by someone he knew well, someone who could come within three or four feet of his chair, pull a gun and shoot him. It had to be an individual who Joe knew and trusted implicitly. With this in mind, police questioned every member of Joe's family, including his ex-wife. None had motive and all had airtight alibis. The letter Joe was reading when he was shot was from his horse trainer, Lloyd Gentry, in Kentucky. It proved to have no connection whatever with the murder. Detectives came to know every idiosyncrasy of the dead man. He was a vain individual who they felt would never let any of his acquaintances see him without teeth or toupee.

The mystery was compounded when detectives found a card index containing the names and pertinent details of fifty-three women, most of whom had at one time or another occupied that sensually decorated room on the third floor. Along with the informative cards were numerous love letters and photographs.

Every single person whose name appeared on cards or letters was located and interviewed. This was quite a task, involving extensive travel around the country.

Without exception, the women were able to prove conclusively that they were somewhere else when Joe was shot to death. Many a married woman begged detectives to be discreet concerning their association with the bridge expert. In the main, their names were kept confidential, but others were not as fortunate. Viola Kraus had to account for her every moment after she said goodnight to Joe from the Lewisohns' cab. The Lewisohns also had to account for their time. All three were exonerated. Joe's racing associates in Kentucky were dragged into the net of the investigation. None were anywhere near New York at the time of the murder. Valet William Barnes, chauffeur Edward Rhodes and housekeeper Marie Larsen were thoroughly investigated. Joe wasn't a monster to work for, nor was he a skinflint, they told police. The hired help liked their boss and spoke highly of him. They were cleared of any complicity in the crime.

The murder case wound down, as most unsolved murder cases do. From time to time, a new suspect would take centre stage, only to be cleared. Unlike fictional plots, no clever detective came up with a convoluted clue leading to the apprehension of the culprit. It has been sixty-seven years since Marie Larsen looked into Joe Elwell's living room and observed that someone had shot him between the eyes. That someone has not been identified to this day.

# ERROL FLYNN

THOSE who remember Errol Flynn readily identify him with his movie portrayals of pirates and cavalry officers. If you are too young to have seen Flynn act on the screen, try to imagine Tom Cruise and Mel Gibson rolled into one and you have some idea of his magnetism.

By 1942, Errol Flynn's stature in Hollywood was equalled only by that of Clark Gable. Flynn was box-office gold and he acted the part on and off the screen. Flynn lived in a mansion in Hollywood. Although he wasn't an art collector, he had a Gauguin and Van Gogh hanging on his walls, just to be fashionable. His estate boasted a swimming pool, cockfighting arena, tennis court and riding ring. When he ventured out for an evening's entertainment, his companions included the most beautiful and desirable women in the world. He had just shed his first wife, glamorous Lily Damita, and was free to womanize to his heart's content. The handsome, sexy Flynn had everything any man could want.

It was a shock to him and the world when one fine day the Los Angeles police arrested him and charged him with statutory rape. Betty Hanson, an attractive seventeen-year-old, said that she met Flynn at a party and that the hard-drinking, good-looking actor had taken her into the bedroom and raped her. She admitted that the sexual activity was really with her consent. Well, actually, with her encouragement, but it didn't matter to Flynn. Statutory rape, by definition, meant having "carnal knowledge" of any member of the opposite sex under eighteen years of age, whether they consented or not. To give you an idea of the life Flynn led, he later revealed that he had a hard time remembering the girl. He vaguely recalled hustling some "blonde floozie" up to a bedroom during some party or other.

When Betty gave her statement to police, she left nothing to the imagination. Arguably the most embarrassing moment for Flynn was when she said he had undressed completely, but had kept his shoes and socks on. The actor had just completed a movie based on General Custer's last stand. It was entitled *They Died With Their Boots On*. Flynn knew he would have a hard time living that one down.

Not to be outdone by Betty, a nightclub dancer, Peggy Satterlee, came forward with the story that Flynn raped her aboard his yacht, *Sirocco*. The actor embarrassed everyone when he couldn't place her. The fifteen-year-old Peggy had no trouble placing Errol. She claimed she was a guest on the yacht one night and bumped into Flynn while strolling on the deck. The suave movie idol had invited her to his cabin. Once inside, he'd thrust her onto the bed and violently raped her. She described every detail, including the view from the bed. It seems she had a clear view of the moon through a porthole of the cabin.

Both girls appeared in court, looking as if they were vying for the position of Shirley Temple's understudy. They looked like children; Flynn stated that they hadn't looked or acted like children on the nights he had spent with them.

The episode made headlines around the world. For a few weeks in 1942, the war news took a back seat to the escapades of Errol Flynn and his partners in sex. To Flynn it was no joke. If convicted, he stood to spend five years in prison. Like many stars who found themselves in trouble in those days, Flynn engaged the famed Hollywood lawyer Jerry Giesler. Now, Giesler could talk a partridge out of a pear tree and it wasn't long before he revealed to the court the inconsistencies in the girls' testimonies. For instance, Peggy couldn't have been lying on her back looking at the moon out of the porthole in Flynn's cabin. The moon was over the yacht that night, but Giesler proved that it was on the other side of the boat. Peggy would have had to look through sheets of steel to have seen the moon that night. Every adult realized that Flynn was being dragged over the coals. The jury thought so too. They took only four hours to find the actor not guilty. Giesler's fee was $50,000. Flynn always thought it was a bargain. Later, Flynn, flamboyant character that he was, revealed that he was dating an eighteen-year-old girl while his trial was in progress. She was a city-employed clerk at the refreshment stand in the lobby of the courthouse where the trial was being held.

The trial branded Errol Flynn as a rascal for the rest of his life. In October, 1959, Flynn suffered a fatal heart attack while living it up in Vancouver. He was only fifty years old, but had the dissipated body of a man of seventy. A young lady, Beverly Aadland, was with Flynn when he died. She had been living with him since she was fifteen years old.

# GREY OWL

THE little boy liked to play cowboys and Indians. Unlike other little boys, he always wanted to be an Indian. Much later, he would tell his story to tens of thousands: how he was born in Hermosillo, Mexico, in 1888; how his mother was an Apache, Katherine Cochise, and his father a Scotsman, George MacNeil, a buddy of Buffalo Bill Cody; how, at the age of fifteen, he left his parents and made his way to Ontario, where he was adopted by Ojibways; how it was they who gave him the name Grey Owl.

It was a great story. Unfortunately, it was a pack of lies. But let's not divest Grey Owl of all his laurels. He did become an accomplished lecturer, successful author and conservationist. One of his books, *Tales of an Empty Cabin,* went into seven printings. Another, *The Adventures of Sajo and Her Beaver People,* ran to fourteen printings.

Grey Owl was born Archie Belaney in Hastings, England, on September 18, 1888. Shortly after his birth, his father deserted the family. Archie was brought up by two maiden aunts, Ada and Carrie. The little boy, always a bit of a loner, loved to read about the life of Indians in the north woods of Canada. He kept small animals in the attic and amused school chums by bringing his little friends to school. Archie spent a lot of time outdoors in Hastings and developed a swarthy complexion. He attempted to emulate Canadian Indians at every opportunity and dreamed of travelling to Canada to live in the woods. In 1906, at the age of eighteen, he persuaded his aunts to pay his fare to Toronto. While other young boys only dreamed of life in the wilds, here was a young man determined to make his dream come true. For a year, Archie worked as a clerk in a dry-goods store. He then made his way to Cobalt, Ontario, where he obtained a job with a tourist-camp operator and learned how to handle a canoe from the Ojibways.

While working at the tourist camp, Archie met a young Ojibway girl, Angel Aquena. Angel was a religious girl who didn't believe in sexual activity outside the sacrament of marriage. The couple went together for two years before Archie asked Angel to marry him. She agreed. Rev. D. A. Schaefer conducted the marriage ceremony on August 23, 1910. Angel was twenty, Archie twenty-two. Initially, the marriage seemed to be made in heaven. Archie and Angel took long canoe trips into the bush. They hunted and fished and made love. Slowly, Archie took on the mannerisms of his wife and her people. The pair settled in Temagami. To support himself and his wife, Archie would often be away hunting for three or four months. Patient Angel would always be there waiting for her man. When she received a message that Archie had joined the army, Angel waited. It wasn't that different from the usual hunting trip.

Archie served overseas and was shot in the foot, a wound which enabled him to receive a $75-a-month pension for the rest of his life. He was sent to England, where he bigamously married a childhood sweetheart. Archie tried to persuade his new bride to accompany him to Canada, but the proper English girl would have none of it. After he returned to Canada, wife number two obtained a divorce. In 1919, Archie returned to his Angel, but stayed with her only a short while. He left to steep himself in the Ojibway culture and way of life. The tall hawk-nosed Englishman mastered the crafts of the Indians and took on the personality of the Indians. The Ojibways adopted him into their tribe. Grey Owl was born. Now an Indian in every practical way, in 1925 he returned to Angel and their three children for the last time. Then he left her for good.

In May 1925, Grey Owl met a beautiful Iroquois woman, Anahareo, and was immediately smitten. Within two years they were married in an Indian ceremony. If you are keeping track, Grey Owl has now taken his third bride. The happy couple settled in Coudet, Quebec. A daughter, Shirley Dawn, blessed the union in 1932.

It was while living in a cabin he had built for his wife and daughter that Grey Owl began submitting articles to newspapers and magazines. His writing emphasized conservation of our natural resources, particularly wildlife. The pieces were touching and sincere. Grey Owl had long since given up hunting. Slowly, the saga of the Indian who could write well and champion the cause of our natural heritage caught the imagination of the public. The federal government, intrigued with Grey Owl, gave him a position in Prince Albert National Park, where he cared for a colony of beavers, as well as other animals, in their natural habitat.

Grey Owl's popularity and fame spread. He was invited to England to go on a lecture tour extolling the virtues of conservation. Accompanied by Anahareo, he was an instant hit. Here was this tall, lean Indian, the epitome of a man who pitted his brawn and brain against the harshness of the Candian North and came away victorious. When summoned to Ottawa in connection with his post at the park, Grey Owl met Yvonne Perrier. She and Grey Owl married in St. James United Church in Montreal, number four if you're still counting.

Once again, Grey Owl was invited to lecture in England. This time, Yvonne accompanied him. Today, Grey Owl's popularity is hard to fathom, but in those days he was a phenomenal hit. He spoke to standing-room-only audiences. Always, he told of his respect for animals. He also had a dry wit, which the English loved. At the conclusion of the tour, Grey Owl was invited to Buckingham Palace to be presented to King George and Queen Elizabeth. Also present were Princesses Elizabeth and Margaret. At the conclusion of his lecture, Grey Owl bade goodbye to his host. He lightly slapped King George on the shoulder and said, "Goodbye, brother, I'll be seeing you." The royal entourage ate it up.

Grey Owl was an international celebrity. Photos of him, erect and proud in his buckskins, adorned the front pages of newspapers all over the world. What wasn't printed was that, to alleviate the pressure of his hectic schedule, Grey Owl had become a heavy drinker. Only his close associates knew of his moods and bad temper; to the public, he was the tall Indian who pleaded for the conservation of wild animals.

Meanwhile, throughout all the glory years, a woman named Angel waited in Temagami for her man. He never returned. Once, Angel heard of Grey Owl's giving a lecture in Toronto's Massey Hall, but that was the only news she had of her husband until she learned that he had died of pneumonia in April 1938. That's when the beavers, so to speak, hit the dam. Grey Owl's false history was exposed by the *North Bay Nugget* the day after his death. The newspaper had learned the truth of Grey Owl's identity some time earlier, but had chosen to suppress the story. Now, newspapers throughout the world carried the story of the Englishman who had posed as an Indian. Why, he had even fooled the King of England.

Grey Owl had drawn up a will over a year before his death. His estate amounted to about $15,000, not a great deal of money now, but a sizeable amount in 1938. He bequeathed one-half of his estate and future royalties from his books to his daughter, Shirley Dawn. The balance was left to his last wife, Yvonne Perrier. He didn't leave a cent to Angel. Angel applied for a share of the estate under the Widows' Relief Act of 1930. The act allowed a widow to apply for a share of her husband's estate if she is left less than she would have received had her husband died without a will. Angel had a good case. Her application stated that she was Archie Belaney's only legal wife. She claimed one-third of the estate and appeared to deserve every penny. There was one catch, however.

Another section of the act stated that the widow would not share in the will if her behaviour was such that she would not have the right to receive alimony payments if her husband were alive. A young lawyer named John Diefenbaker acted for Yvonne Perrier. Diefenbaker attempted to prove that Angel had committed adultery and was therefore not entitled to her claim.

During the hearing it was established that from the time of his last visit to Angel after the First World War, Grey Owl had contributed nothing towards the support of his wife and three children. She had brought up the children herself and had waited for her man to return. It was true that, during Grey Owl's absence, she had given birth to a boy who had died at the age of three months. Angel claimed that the pregnancy was the result of being raped by one Charlie Potts. Charlie stated that Angel had consented to the sexual encounter and had thus committed adultery.

The judge hearing the case chose to believe Angel. After legal fees, she received one-third of Grey Owl's estate. Incidentally, the young lawyer named John Diefenbaker went on to make somewhat of a name for himself in Canadian politics.

# JEAN HARLOW

THERE are many similarities between Marilyn Monroe and Jean Harlow. Both were blond sex symbols who achieved fame and fortune in the movies. Above all, the deaths of both women were surrounded by mystery and intrigue. The details of Miss Monroe's life and untimely death are well documented in some forty books, in itself a tribute to her charismatic personality and lingering popularity. Jean Harlow's life is not as well known.

Jean was born Harlean Carpentier in Kansas City on March 3, 1911. When she was only sixteen, she ran away and married wealthy bond broker Charles McGrew. The young bride returned to her parents and received their blessing. The McGrews settled down in California, where they lived off the income from a fortune inherited by McGrew. Two years later, they were divorced.

Still only eighteen, with an outstanding figure, good looks and long, flowing blond hair, Jean entered the entertainment world by accident. One day she drove a friend to a movie studio. A motion picture executive spotted her and sent her to the Central Casting Office. She immediately received work as an extra and was noticed by famed moviemaker Hal Roach, who signed her to a five-year contract. Jean worked for months in small walk-on parts until 1930, when millionaire Howard Hughes chose her to play the lead in the movie *Hell's Angels*. The ensuing publicity and the movie itself made Jean Harlow a star. Overnight, young girls were copying her sultry walk, and women across the country were dyeing their hair platinum blond.

After a while, Jean met Paul Bern, assistant to the head of production of MGM Studios. Bern was twenty-two years Jean's senior. He had come up the hard way, starting off with $3.50 a week working for the Produce Exchange Co. in New York. Later, he entered the Academy of Dramatic Arts and was bitten by the entertainment bug. Bern travelled to Hollywood, worked as a film cutter, became a script editor, then a director, until finally, at age thirty-seven, he achieved the status of supervisor at MGM. Soon after, he was promoted to assistant of production.

Bern was well liked and respected in Hollywood, an extremely intelligent, introspective man. There were many who thought there never was a more unlikely pair than Jean Harlow and Paul Bern. Indeed, the Hollywood crowd was surprised when the couple married. It was a sudden decision. On July 2, 1932, the day Harlow and Bern were wed, both had supposedly unbreakable schedules. They didn't take a honeymoon right away, but opted to wait a few months until they were free of their respective obligations.

In the weeks following their marriage, Paul and Jean appeared to be extremely happy. Individually they told acquaintances how thrilled they were with their married life. Paul presented Jean with a beautiful new home in Benedict Canyon in Beverly Hills. Towards the end of August there was an abrupt change in Paul's behaviour. He no longer appeared to be happy. Instead, he went into long periods of depression during which he hardly spoke. Acquaintances and colleagues noticed the marked difference in his personality.

On September 5, 1932, two months after his marriage, Paul Bern put a .38-calibre pistol to his head and killed himself. The bullet entered his right temple, ploughed through his brain and ended up imbedded in a wall. Paul left a note which read, "Dearest Dear; Unfortunately this is the only way to make good the frightening wrong I have done you and wipe out my abject humility. I love you, Paul. P.S. You understand that last night was only a comedy." Hollywood was aghast at the sudden death. What had caused such a successful man, married to one of the most glamorous women in the world, to kill himself? Rumours flew throughout the movie capital.

An inquest into the suicide was held. The only point of contention was motive. The most widely accepted reason for Bern taking his own life proved to be an embarrassment for all concerned. Evidently, Bern had suffered from a physical deficiency that made the consummation of his marriage impossible. His reference to "last night being a comedy" was held to mean that a desperate Bern had attempted to consummate the marriage by artificial means. If this was true, one wonders why Bern ever married Jean Harlow.

Shortly after Bern's suicide, it was revealed that he had previously lived with movie actress Dorothy Millette. Miss Millette became mentally ill and was confined to an institution. Paul Bern paid all expenses during her illness and provided her with a living allowance after her release. At the time of Bern's death, Miss Millette resided in the Algonquin Hotel in New York. The day after Bern's suicide, Dorothy was staying at the Plaza Hotel in San Francisco. She boarded the *Delta King,* a Sacramento River steamer sailing from San Francisco to Sacramento. A pair of shoes and a ladies' coat were found beside the steamer's railing. Two weeks later, fishermen found Dorothy Millette's body. The official verdict was suicide, possibly over the loss of a great love or possibly over the loss of her only means of support.

Meanwhile, back in Hollywood, Jean Harlow was so distraught she had to be placed under a doctor's care. She recovered rapidly and remained one of Hollywood's leading actresses. In 1933, she married cameraman Harold Rosson. A little over a year later, she divorced Rosson, charging cruelty. Seems Harold kept the light on late at night reading. Harlow couldn't get the sleep required to enable her to go before the cameras the next day.

Jean Harlow continued to star in the movies. Beloved by all, the dynamic blond actress had the world by the tail. Her public was shocked when, in June, 1937, her mother announced that Jean was seriously ill. Four days later Jean Harlow was dead. Apparently she had suffered from influenza, which had caused inflammation of the gall bladder. The cause of death was stated to be uremic poisoning. Many didn't believe the official explanation and rumours spread throughout the entertainment community that Jean had met with foul play. Nothing of a concrete nature was ever uncovered to give credence to the rumours.

Jean Harlow was only twenty-six years old at the time of her death.

# JIMMY HOFFA

ON July 30, 1975, Jimmy Hoffa told his wife, Josephine, that he had an appointment to meet friends for lunch. He left his summer home north of Detroit for the twenty-five-mile trip to the suburb of Birmingham. The sixty-two-year-old Hoffa arrived at the Red Fox Restaurant and was observed parking his green 1974 Pontiac sometime after 11:30 a.m. When his friends didn't show up, he called Josephine and told her that Anthony "Tony Jack" Giacalone had stood him up. He asked her if his friend had called to cancel the appointment. Josephine assured him that she had received no such call. Hoffa made another phone call to a friend. This time he mentioned that Anthony "Tony Pro" Provenzano had not arrived, either. Jimmy Hoffa never had lunch that day or any other day. He disappeared off the face of the earth.

Jimmy kept dubious company. Tony Jack, a reported Mafia enforcer, was awaiting trial on income tax evasion. Tony Pro had at one time been a Teamsters union vice-president and had been a friend of Jimmy's while both were serving time in Lewisburg Federal Prison. The boys had a falling-out in prison and were no longer on good terms. Both Giacalone and Provenzano would later deny any involvement in the greatest disappearance since Ambrose Small walked into a snowstorm in Toronto and vanished forever.

Over a period of fourteen years, Hoffa built the Teamsters union into the strongest and wealthiest union in North America. Jimmy Hoffa was a short stocky outspoken man who must have made hundreds of enemies during his climb to the top of the most powerful union in the land. At its zenith, the union boasted two million members and held sway over thousands of companies, truly a potent economic and political force. Defrocked and tossed into prison for jury tampering and mail fraud, Jimmy had recently been released. The current president of the union, Frank Fitzsimmons, heard the rumours. He couldn't help it. Jimmy Hoffa was making noise. He wanted the presidency back and meant to do everything in his power to wrest control from Fitzsimmons. These men played hardball. Fitzsimmons's son Richard had narrowly escaped death a month earlier when his car had been blown up. President Fitzsimmons claimed he had no idea who had abducted Jimmy Hoffa.

For several days after Hoffa's disappearance, police, most notably the FBI, held out hope that Hoffa had been abducted in some sort of labour power play and would soon turn up. As time passed, it became obvious that he had been murdered.

It was also theorized that Hoffa, fearing for his life, had fled the country, but few believed that Jimmy, a devoted family man, would leave his wife, daughter and son. Some think that Hoffa was planning to testify against top union officials suspected of receiving huge kickbacks paid out of the union's pension fund. Eliminating a witness ready to spill his guts is a time-honoured mob practice. The most probable theory of all alludes to Jimmy as a major threat to once again become president of the Teamsters union. It must be remembered that hundreds of thousands of truckers owed their increased paycheques to Hoffa, who almost single-handedly had been instrumental in gaining those increases. Many revered the man.

When Jimmy was paroled from prison, one of the conditions of his parole forbade his participation in union activities. Jimmy was legally fighting to have this condition set aside. It was an open secret that he planned to run for the presidency in 1976. This was considered a direct threat to many people. The current president, Fitzsimmons, had delegated power to fifteen vice-presidents. This was in direct contrast to Hoffa's style. Jimmy had always insisted on total control. Then there was the Mafia itself. They had formulated gentlemen's agreements with the union during Jimmy's tenure in prison. Would all this change if Jimmy regained the presidency?

Jimmy Hoffa's adopted son, Chuckie O'Brien, came under close examination. It was rumoured that O'Brien joined the Fitzsimmons camp while Hoffa was in jail and stood to lose should Jimmy once again become Teamster president. O'Brien, who dropped out of sight for a short while after his father's disappearance, had an alibi for the afternoon of Jimmy's abduction. He claims that he borrowed Joseph Giacalone's car to deliver a salmon to a union official at the time in question. The FBI have not been able to disprove his alibi.

What happened to Hoffa's body? The FBI tells me they still receive tips pinpointing Jimmy's last resting place. Some say he was dumped in a Florida swamp. Others claim to have watched him being buried beside the end zone in Giant Stadium after his body was transported from Michigan. Still others believe that Jimmy's body was ground up and incinerated in a Mafia-owned operation in New Jersey.

Jimmy Hoffa left a loving family who saw him in a far different light than the public or the Teamsters. James Jr., a labour lawyer in Detroit, always believed that his father had been maligned by the press. Jimmy's only daughter, Barbara Ann Hoffa Crancer, a practising judge, believes the same thing.

The disappearance of Jimmy Hoffa leaves many questions unanswered. We may never know the details surrounding his death.

# CLIFFORD IRVING

THERE was nothing in Clifford Irving's past to hint that he would attempt to pull off the literary hoax of the century.

Born in New York in 1930, Clifford graduated from high school in 1947 and went on to study the arts at Cornell University. By 1956, he was a relatively successful author, having written his first novel, *On a Darkling Plain*. Another novel entitled *The Losers* quickly followed.

Clifford married twice. He divorced his first wife and lost his second wife in a tragic car accident in California. Along the way, he discovered the pleasures of Ibiza, one of the Balearic Islands off the coast of Spain, which was a well-known haven for writers and artists. This was the life, lapping up the wine and the sun, surrounded by tanned beauties in bikinis.

But Clifford Irving was not a contented man. While moderately successful, he longed for recognition as a great writer whose works would be remembered long after he was gone. The recognition afforded Hemingway or Steinbeck would do nicely. Meanwhile, Clifford kept writing. A western, *The Valley,* was followed by a fourth novel, *The Thirty-Eighth Floor*. He married for the third time, but in 1965 this marriage, too, ended in divorce.

Clifford had become a brooding, sullen man. From his retreat in Ibiza it was obvious to him that his novels would never bring him the international acclaim he craved. No, he had to do something different, something big that would make the literary world sit up and take notice. The idea became an obsession. In the meantime, Clifford met Edith Sommer, a pretty young artist living on Ibiza. Edith had just come through a bad marriage and jumped at the opportunity to share her life with Clifford. They soon wed.

Clifford produced his last book, *Fake,* before he met another writer, Richard Suskind, who also lived on Ibiza. The two men became friends and decided to work on Clifford's next book together. While visiting Las Vegas, the pair heard of multimillionaire Howard Hughes, who at that time controlled a big hunk of the gambling action in that city. Hughes and his unorthodox lifestyle fascinated the two writers. Here was a man who had made his money through a variety of industries, including tool manufacturing, aircraft production, movies, hotels and gambling casinos, to name just a few. Yet for approximately fifteen years Hughes had lived as a recluse, dodging all attempts by the press to interview him. Hughes had even ducked court appearances.

True, there had been many books written about Hughes and his strange life, but this enigmatic man had never written an autobiography. However, Clifford and Suskind considered there were reams of newspaper clippings available to the researcher, as well as magazine articles, which outlined in detail all of Hughes's unpredictable exploits. Could a conscientious researcher dig out those personal idiosyncrasies and inject them into the available facts, thus giving the stamp of authenticity to an autobiography? The two friends agreed it could be done. Suskind would do the research and feed it to Clifford, who would falsely claim that he had exclusively interviewed Hughes over a period of months. This would be a first—an authorized biography of Howard Hughes. It was bound to be a runaway best-seller.

Clifford's first illegal act was to forge a letter from Hughes to himself indicating that the two men had met and that Hughes had agreed to reveal the details of his life to Clifford Irving. Clifford's publishers, McGraw-Hill, took one look at the letter signed H. R. Hughes and jumped at the opportunity. A deal was struck. They agreed to pay Hughes $100,000 upon signing of the contract, a further $100,000 upon completion of the research and $300,000 upon delivery of the manuscript—a cool half-million dollars in all.

As only Clifford had access to Hughes, all cheques were to be made out to H. R. Hughes and delivered by Clifford. The giant publishing company suggested that a representative of the firm be present at the signing of the contract, but Clifford assured them that this would not sit well with Hughes. After all, his own lawyers were denied private meetings with the great man. McGraw-Hill executives understood. Clifford later returned with the contract duly signed by H. R. Hughes. Clifford made it known to McGraw-Hill that despite the signed contract, Hughes felt that the price just wasn't high enough. Knowing they were dealing with an eccentric, and believing they had a blockbuster on their hands, the publisher upped the ante. One cheque for $25,000, made out to Clifford Irving, and another made out to H. R. Hughes in the amount of $275,000, were handed over to Clifford.

McGraw-Hill staff read over the roughly edited partial manuscript provided by Clifford and agreed that it was good. Hughes had given his personal viewpoint on a variety of subjects and explained many of his own idiosyncrasies. The book made interesting, exciting reading. A further $25,000 was turned over to Clifford, accompanied by another cheque of $325,000 made out to H. R. Hughes. Little did McGraw-Hill know that Clifford's wife, Edith, had opened an account with the Swiss Credit Bank in Zurich under the name Helga R. Hughes. She was endorsing and cashing McGraw-Hill's cheques by signing them H. R. Hughes.

From time to time, the entire project came under close scrutiny by the publisher, but their suspicions were laid to rest each time. They attempted to have Hughes's signature verified on the original letter given to them by Clifford. It was turned over to a handwriting expert. The man compared it with an authentic Hughes signature, and attested that the signature was genuine. McGraw-Hill inquired as to who had endorsed the first cheque given to Clifford. They were relieved to learn that it had been endorsed by H. R. Hughes, never suspecting that H. R. Hughes was in reality Mrs. Clifford Irving.

In 1971, the famed confidential biography of Howard Hughes was completed. It was an excellent book, containing all the little personal touches that could only be known by the man who had lived them. Or so it appeared. Richard Suskind had done an amazingly thorough job of researching his subject. Then the unexpected occurred. Frank McCulloch, a journalist with *Life* magazine who had interviewed Hughes back in 1957, read the manuscript. He thought it was authentic and was surprised when he received a phone call from the reclusive Howard Hughes himself. The eccentric Hughes had read the book, and in a voice loud and clear, told McCulloch that the book was a fake. He didn't know any Clifford Irving. He had never even met the man. *Life* magazine, which was interested in the serial rights to the book, became suspicious. A team of experts were put to work going over the book word by word. Gradually, small errors were uncovered. Suskind's educated guesses had come close to the truth, but upon further examination, they didn't hold up. A gigantic hoax had been perpetrated.

Initially, Clifford claimed that the book was as he had represented it. Later, he told the true story. One question puzzled investigators. Surely Clifford realized the hoax would be discovered when Hughes read the book. Not so, explained Clifford. Hughes had remained in hiding, even when being sued. His own top executives didn't speak directly to him. Other books containing slanderous material had been written about Hughes without a peep out of the erratic recluse. Clifford thought it worth the chance. He figured Hughes would remain in seclusion and not say a word.

Clifford had gambled and lost. He, his wife, Edith, and Richard Suskind were arrested. In all, fourteen charges pertaining to forgery and conspiracy with intent to defraud were brought against them. The three pleaded guilty. The conspirators returned an undisclosed amount of money to McGraw-Hill. Each received a sentence of from three to five years' imprisonment. Clifford, who was ordered to begin serving his sentence earlier than his wife, was paroled in 1974. Edith was released in 1975. Both planned on continuing their careers as writer and artist. On April 5, 1976, Howard Hughes died of natural causes, at age seventy.

For Clifford Irving, the entire exercise had not been a complete failure. He did achieve the notoriety he so desperately craved.

# REVEREND JIM JONES

THE more than 900 corpses decomposed rapidly in the intense heat of the Guyanese jungle. Eighteen years have passed since that day of November 18, 1978, when vague news dispatches hinted at the mass suicide of some obscure religious cult in a jungle commune in South America. The dispatches also alluded to the possible murder of a United States congressman. The individual behind the horror story, which was soon to make headlines around the world, was the Reverend Jim Jones.

Jones was born in Lynn, Indiana, in 1931. He was the son of an army veteran who was gassed in the First World War. Jones's father was an enthusiastic member of the Ku Klux Klan. In 1951, the twenty-year-old Jones attended Butler University, a school operated by the Disciples of Christ. He took courses at Butler off and on for the next ten years, receiving his B.A. degree in education in 1961. However, in 1958, Jones founded his own interdenominational church, the Christian Assembly of God. By 1960, his Peoples' Temple, located in Los Angeles, was a bona fide congregation of the Disciples of Christ, which had a membership of almost a million and a half people, mostly living in the midwest states.

From 1961 to 1963, Jones performed missionary work in Brazil, organizing orphanages. There is evidence that he visited Guyana while in South America and, quite possibly, it was during this period that the seeds of starting his own colony in the jungle took root in his mind. Upon his return from Brazil, Jones displayed a degree of entrepreneurial acumen by forming two non-profit organizations with headquarters in Indianapolis. The Wings of Deliverance was organized to spread the word of God, while the Jim-Lu-Mar Corp. was formed to purchase every successful venture that was available. The latter company's elongated name was made up of his own first name as well as those of his mother, Lynette, and his wife, Marceline.

During the sixties, Jones operated out of Ukiah, a small town located about a hundred miles north of San Francisco. His headquarters, known simply as the Peoples' Church, became a moneymaking machine. The strategically located church afforded Jones and his followers the opportunity to swoop down to San

Francisco and Los Angeles on weekends to spread the word, win followers and raise hard cash.

The group would sometimes return to headquarters richer by as much as $40,000. Members of the congregation turned over their social security cheques to Jones. As the flock grew, so did the routine amount of cash flowing into the church's coffers. Many members, completely enraptured with the charismatic Jones, turned over their entire life savings. Some cashed in their life insurance policies. Others moved into the church's dormitories to live. Jones wasn't above slick hucksterism. Photographs of "The Father," as he was now called by his followers, were considered to have healing powers. These bogus medical aids fetched a pretty penny, as did other religious artifacts.

In 1971, Jones purchased a former synagogue and moved the centre of his operations to San Francisco. The Peoples' Temple held its opening service with much fanfare. Scores of gospel singers raised their voices in praise of the Lord. Well-known activist Angela Davis spoke. The Peoples' Temple appeared to be a model of what God-fearing folks could achieve. It boasted a day care centre, infirmary, printing press, carpentry shop and facilities to feed hundreds of the poor each day. Soon the devoted congregation and its dynamic leader were being lauded by the media as a fine example of an efficiently operated pure charity. Jones's photograph, depicting him handing over sizeable cheques to worthwhile causes, often appeared in the press. His now eight-thousand-member church also became politically powerful. At the snap of a finger, Jones could muster hundreds of followers to work on a political campaign. Many dignitaries wooed the religious leader, sometimes for manpower, sometimes for substantial donations.

In 1973, Jones dispatched twenty members of the Peoples' Church to Guyana with the express purpose of finding a site for an agricultural mission. A year later, Father Jones leased 27,000 acres in the jungle near the town of Port Kaituma from the government of Guyana. The commune was called Jonestown after its founder. As the colony was populated, glowing reports were received by relatives back in the States: crops were flourishing, housing was more than adequate and, above all, the individual freedom that the disciples enjoyed was lauded by all. The minister of foreign affairs for Guyana reported that Jonestown was "peace and love in action."

In 1975, Rev. Jim Jones was named one of the most outstanding clergymen in the United States by an interfaith organization, Religion in American Life. The following year, he was named Humanitarian of the Year by the *Los Angeles*

*Herald*. That same year, he was appointed to the San Francisco Housing Authority by his good friend Mayor George Moscone. In January 1977, Jones received the annual Martin Luther King Jr. Humanitarian Award. But in the midst of all this praise were some ominous rumblings. A few members dropped out of the congregation. Others sued, claiming they'd been brainwashed, beaten and stripped of their wealth. Interested in investigating the story, a handful of journalists made their way to Jonestown. Their reports were far from complimentary. They described poor living conditions and disillusioned members. After their reports appeared in California papers, many of these journalists were threatened. The adverse publicity initiated an investigation of the commune by the government of Guyana. They reported "not one confirmation of an allegation of mistreatment."

California congressman Leo Ryan, fifty-three, was serving his fourth term when he became interested in the Jonestown commune and the reports that its members were being abused and were being denied their civil rights. He decided to look into the matter. This was not Ryan's first excursion into a high-profile, well-publicized investigation. It was Ryan who had strongly and successfully petitioned for the release from prison of his constituent Patty Hearst. In 1965, he made a trip to Newfoundland and came away denouncing the hunting of seal pups. The International Wildlife Fund named him Man of the Year for that effort.

Ryan's entourage, including aides, lawyers, a Guyanese government official, newspaper reporters and a TV crew from NBC, landed at the closest airstrip to Jonestown, Port Kaituma. Only Ryan and four members of his party were allowed to proceed immediately to the commune. The remainder of the entourage were made to wait four hours before they too were transported over the muddy single-lane road to Jonestown. Initial impressions of the commune were favourable. Food appeared to be plentiful. The visitors clapped to gospel music as they finished a pleasant meal. Members of the congregation conversed with Congressman Ryan. They told him they were experiencing the happiest years of their lives. Throughout the informal introduction to Jonestown, benevolent Father Jim Jones presided, volunteering his views when asked.

Later, only Ryan and his four original party members were allowed to spend the night at the commune. The balance were transported back to Port Kaituma in a dump truck. Next morning, they returned to Jonestown and were escorted around the compound by Marceline Jones. Impressive nurseries and classrooms were shown to the journalists. Curiously, some buildings were shut tight. The visitors were told the inhabitants were sleeping and were not to be disturbed.

Questioned by the reporters, Jones denied the veracity of the bad press he had lately received in the United States. He vehemently denied the allegations of poor treatment by former members of his flock. During the questioning, word drifted to Jones and his interrogators that several members of the commune wanted to leave with Congressman Ryan and his group. Jones flew into a rage. Tension mounted. But no one prevented the dissident members from leaving. As Ryan talked to the disturbed Jones, a member of the commune pulled a knife and attempted to stab the congressman. While he was being disarmed, the attacker was wounded. Ryan was noticeably shaken by the experience.

Finally, Ryan, his entourage and the defectors boarded the dump truck for the return trip to the airstrip at Port Kaituma. The journalists in the group would later state that at this point they believed Jones was an unstable character, but that he was sincere in his desire to do good for his fellow man. True, there were some flaws to Jonestown, they said, but such things were to be expected. Sixteen homesick dissidents out of nine hundred members was not unusual. No one seemed to be there against their will. No one appeared to be mistreated.

We can only speculate about Jim Jones's state of mind as the visitors left the commune. Unstable, paranoid Jones believed the adverse publicity generated by the stories the reporters would file spelled ruination for his colony in the jungle. He also believed that the dissidents who joined Ryan and his group were only the beginning of a wave of dissension that would sweep Jonestown. He decided to force the world to sit up and take notice.

As small planes landed at the Port Kaituma airstrip to take the visitors home, the dump truck which had originally carried the Ryan group to the landing strip pulled up with a tractor and flatbed. The truck parked, but the tractor towing the flatbed drove up between the two aircraft. Suddenly, the men on the tractor and flatbed opened fire. Airplane tires were punctured. Jonestown defector Patricia Parks lay dead. Also killed in the rain of bullets were *San Francisco Examiner* photographer Greg Robinson, NBC cameraman Bob Brown, NBC correspondent Don Harris and Congressman Leo Ryan. Others were wounded, some severely.

While the Guyanese police looked on from a distance, one of the defectors pointed out that Larry Layton, posing as a defector, had opened fire on his fellow commune brothers. When uninjured Dick Dwyer, head of the U.S. Embassy in Georgetown, Guyana, and himself a member of the ill-fated mission, was told this, he insisted that the police arrest Layton on the spot. The slow-to-react Guyanese police, together with soldiers, assisted the wounded. After a night of horror, what remained of the Ryan party was flown to safety in Georgetown.

Back in Jonestown, an unbelievable scene was taking place. Cyanide was mixed with Kool-Aid and quickly distributed to members of the commune. Mothers forced the liquid down small children's throats. No one else refused to take the poison. Black and white, young and old, people who had fled the ghettos and streets of America for the jungles of Guyana were committing mass suicide. They had followed the charismatic leader who had promised them a better life. Instead, he had led them to death. All 913 died.

On December 2, 1986, forty-one-year-old Larry Layton was convicted of conspiring to murder a U.S. congressman. He was sentenced to life imprisonment. Layton was the only person ever tried for the incident that took a total of 918 lives.

# TED KENNEDY

HOW does a married U.S. senator find himself trying to get a beautiful young girl out of a sunken car in the middle of the night? Twenty-seven years ago, that question was on everyone's lips. The man on the lonely road that summer night in 1969 was Senator Ted Kennedy, a prime prospect for the presidency of the United States.

Joe Kennedy and his wife, Rose, had a remarkable family. Money and politics were topics dear to all the Kennedy children. Rose's father, John (Honey Fitz) Fitzgerald, had been mayor of Boston. The Kennedys' eldest son, Joe Jr., was killed in action as a bomber pilot during the Second World War. Son John became president of the United States while still a young man. The tragedy of JFK's assassination is still a vivid memory. Youthful-looking Bobby became the U.S. attorney-general and was a serious challenger for the presidency when he, too, was killed by an assassin's bullet in Los Angeles.

The saga of the youngest brother, Edward Moore Kennedy, began back in 1960. His brother John had just given up his Senate seat to successfully run for the presidency. Ted, then twenty-eight years old, was newly graduated from Harvard Law School. Earlier, he had been expelled from Harvard for getting another student to write an exam for him. After his expulsion, he joined the army. When Joe Kennedy, then U.S. ambassador to England, heard that his son had signed up for four years, he was furious. A few discreet telephone calls set the matter straight. Ted's term of enlistment was halved. Conveniently, Ted missed the entire Korean War, spending most of his two years serving in England. He was discharged in 1953 as a private first-class.

In 1960, with Ted out of law school, the Kennedy family had a problem. Joe Sr. made no bones about it: he wanted son John's senatorial seat for the youngest boy, Ted. The Constitution of the United States was clear. It was necessary to be thirty years of age in order to become a senator. Ted was twenty-eight. Brother John, president of the United States, solved the problem. He appointed unknown Ben Smith, mayor of the fishing town of Gloucester, Massachusetts, to serve the remaining two years in his old Senate seat. Ben was highly qualified; he had been John Kennedy's roommate in college. Ben Smith kept the seat warm for Ted.

In 1962, Ted Kennedy, aided by his father's money and his brother's influence, easily won his first primary election against the highly qualified state attorney-general Edward McCormack Jr. Later, Ted demolished Republican George Lodge by close to 300,000 votes to capture the Senate seat for the Democrats. As Joe Sr. once remarked, "I paid plenty for that seat for John. It belongs in the family." And that's how Ted Kennedy became a senator.

After John's assassination in 1963, Ted was flying to Springfield, Massachusetts, to attend the Democratic convention, when his twin-engine Aero Commander lost control and crashed at Southampton. Senator Kennedy suffered a broken back, a collapsed lung and three broken ribs. Without ever appearing at the convention, Ted won the Senate nomination by acclamation. Such was his popularity that he was re-elected to his Senate seat by over a million votes.

In the summer of 1969, Ted Kennedy, one of the most recognizable men in the United States was planning to join friends for a few days of fun at Cape Cod. To fully comprehend the events that took place, one must first understand the popularity and charisma of the Kennedy name in Massachusetts. In Hyannisport, where for years the Kennedy family have spent their summers, the mere mention of the Kennedy name brings inquisitive stares. The natives wonder if you really know a Kennedy or are just another nosy tourist. When I was there, the street leading to their compound in Hyannisport was roped off and guarded. On Sunday morning, a crowd gathered outside the church to see if they could catch a glimpse of a Kennedy.

Leaving his wife, Joan, behind, Senator Kennedy flew to Martha's Vineyard, an island off the coast of Massachusetts. He was scheduled to take part in the Edgartown Regatta. Traditionally, members of the Kennedy clan had taken part in this regatta. This July 18, Ted was met by his chauffeur, Jack Crimmins. They made their way to Chappaquiddick Island. About 120 yards of open water separate Chappaquiddick from Martha's Vineyard. The trip on the two-car ferry, the *On Time,* took only a few minutes. Kennedy had time to spare before the regatta began. He changed into a pair of swimming trunks at a cottage that had been rented for a cookout to be held later that evening. Crimmins drove his boss down to the beach and back to the cottage. The 1967 Oldsmobile crossed the narrow, ten-foot-six-inch Dike Bridge twice, once on the way for the swim and then back. If you drive from the cottage to the beach, you come to a fork in the road. A left turn brings you directly back to the site of the two-car ferry landing. If you turn right, you cross the Dike

Bridge to the beach. Beyond the beach there is nothing other than the Atlantic Ocean.

At 2:50 p.m., Senator Kennedy took part in the Wianno Senior heat of the regatta. His yacht, the *Victura,* finished ninth. Ted boarded the *Bettawan,* the winning yacht, congratulated the winner and left. He returned to the Shiretown Inn in Edgartown, where he was registered, and drank some beer with friends before leaving for the barbecue on Chappaquiddick. Jared Grant, owner of the *On Time,* ferried Senator Kennedy over to Chappaquiddick around 6:30 p.m. Grant thought it a bit strange that the senator didn't return. At 12:30 a.m., Grant closed down the ferry and, at 1:20 a.m., went home.

The barbecue held that evening was a sort of reunion of the young women who had worked for Robert Kennedy in Washington before his assassination. They had often held reunions prior to this gathering on Chappaquiddick. Sometimes, Kennedy aides attended these parties. Some of the Kennedy wives had also attended in the past. On this July 18, Mary Jo Kopechne, Esther Newberg, Rosemary Keogh, Susan Tannenbaum, Maryellen Lyons and her sister Nance had come to the remote cottage to enjoy the barbecue. All had been associated with the Kennedys as political workers in one way or another. All were well-educated, level-headed career sorts, away for a few days' fun. Also at the cookout were Paul Markham, thirty-eight, former U.S. attorney for Massachusetts; Joseph Gargan, thirty-nine, lawyer and bank president; Raymond La Rosa, forty-one, an employee of Massachusetts civil defence; Charles Tretter, thirty, a lawyer with the New England regional commission in Boston; and, of course, chauffeur Crimmins and Senator Kennedy.

The thick steaks sizzled on the small barbecue. Everyone ate heartily, and by about 10:30 p.m. the party turned to joke telling and sing-songs. Almost everyone had a few drinks, but no one drank heavily. Sometime between 11 p.m. and midnight (the time varies according to individual recollection), Mary Jo Kopechne and Ted Kennedy disappeared. Both had earlier complained of being tired, and if anyone gave this any thought, they figured Ted had given Mary Jo a lift back to her hotel. The chauffeur remembers the senator asking for the keys to the car before leaving. Later, the remaining guests realized they had missed the ferry back to Martha's Vineyard and went to sleep wherever they could find a comfortable spot.

Next morning, July 19, some youngsters out on an early-morning fishing expedition spotted the Oldsmobile upside down in the channel running under Dike Bridge. They went to the nearest house and informed the occupant,

Mrs Malm, of their discovery. She called the police. Edgartown police chief Dominick Arena was the first law officer on the scene. He borrowed swimming trunks and dived into the cold water to discover Mary Jo Kopechne's body in the overturned Olds. While still at the scene, Arena was advised that Senator Ted Kennedy had walked into the local police station to make a statement. Kennedy said that he had been the driver of the ill-fated car.

Arena rushed back to Edgartown, where he met with Ted Kennedy and Paul Markham. It was decided that the best thing would be for Kennedy to write out a statement relating just what had taken place the night before. It was written out in longhand, then typed by Arena. Here is that statement:

> On July 18, 1969, at approximately 11:15 p.m., on Chappaquiddick Island, Martha's Vineyard, I was driving my car on Main Street on my way to get the ferry back to Edgartown. I was unfamiliar with the road and turned onto Dike Road instead of bearing left on Main Street. After proceeding for approximately a half mile on Dike Road I descended a hill and came upon a narrow bridge. The car went off the side of the bridge. There was one passenger in the car with me, Miss Kopechne, a former secretary of my brother Robert Kennedy. The car turned over and sank into the water and landed with the roof resting on the bottom. I attempted to open the door and window of the car but have no recollection of how I got out of the car. I came to the surface and then repeatedly dove down to the car in an attempt to see if the passenger was still in the car. I was unsuccessful in the attempt.
>
> I was exhausted and in a state of shock. I recall walking back to where my friends were eating. There was a car parked in front of the cottage and I climbed into the back seat. I then asked for someone to bring me back to Edgartown. I remember walking around for a period of time and then going back to my hotel room. When I fully realized what happened this morning, I immediately contacted the police.

Ted Kennedy retreated to the family compound at Hyannisport for the next three days. On the following Tuesday, a twin-engine aircraft landed at Wilkes-Barre, Pennsylvania. Senator Kennedy had arrived to attend Mary Jo Kopechne's funeral in nearby Plymouth.

Police Chief Arena realized he had a hot potato on his hands. How could the senator try to open the windows of the car when they had blown out on impact with the water? How had the senator, a six-foot-two-inch, 220-pounder, managed to get out of the car, when Mary Jo, half his weight and about a foot shorter, was trapped inside? How did the senator get back to Edgartown, when the little ferry had already stopped running? Why didn't the senator report the accident right after it happened, instead of waiting for over nine hours?

Rumours of immoral conduct spread like wildfire. Kennedy's friends poured into the compound at Hyannisport from all over the country to offer their advice. Some even flew in from abroad. Ted Kennedy was charged with leaving the scene of an accident. He pleaded guilty and was sentenced to two months' incarceration in the House of Correction at Barnstable. The sentence was suspended. Despite his walking out of court a free man, speculation concerning misconduct by the senator was so great that his political advisers strongly suggested he appear on television and address the nation. On Friday, July 25, one week after the accident, Kennedy made his TV appearance. He cleared up some matters and left others unanswered.

According to Kennedy, his wife was ill, which was the reason she couldn't attend the cookout. When the car plunged over the bridge, "the cold water rushed in around my head and I was sure I was drowning. But, somehow, I struggled to the surface alive. I made immediate and repeated efforts to save Mary Jo by diving in the strong and murky current, but succeeded only in increasing my state of utter exhaustion and alarm." The senator went on to say that he returned to the cottage and drove back to the scene with Gargan and Markham, who immediately stripped and, at great risk to their own lives, made repeated attempts to get down to Mary Jo. Kennedy explained away his return to Edgartown after the ferry had closed down by saying that he had jumped in the water and swum across to Martha's Vineyard.

Kennedy's address to the nation received initial acceptance and sympathy. Later, doubts were expressed. He had been a busy boy that night. The senator stated that he had left the party at 11:15 p.m. and had taken a wrong turn on a road he had traversed and a bridge he had crossed twice before that same day. He drove the car over the bridge, managed to save his own life and made several dives to try to save his companion. Then he half walked or ran back to the cottage, summoned two friends and together the threesome drove back to the bridge. He claimed his friends made repeated dives to the submerged car. Finally giving up, he swam from Chappaquiddick to Martha's Vineyard and made his way to the Shropshire Inn by 1:30 a.m. He had spent a very busy two hours and fifteen minutes.

Kennedy may have been out of the woods as far as the public was concerned, but he still had a few technicalities to overcome for the state of Massachusetts. Massachusetts law decrees that a manslaughter charge is mandatory if someone leaves the scene of an accident, if that accident produces a fatality, and that fatality is caused by negligence. During January 1970, a secret inquest was conducted in Edgartown. In April of the same year, the Dukes County grand jury convened to hear the details of the Kopechne accident. The entire procedure lasted two days, during which only twenty-two minutes of evidence was heard. The jurors were told it was not legal for them to see the inquest information. The grand jury was disbanded without coming to any conclusion.

Why was Kennedy never charged with any kind of criminal conduct? He testified that he was travelling at twenty miles per hour when he approached the bridge. In his report, the judge who presided at the inquest agreed that 20 m.p.h. could be construed as reckless driving on that particular bridge. The judge, who failed to act on his inquest findings, retired one week before his report was released. What about the women who had attended the ill-fated cookout? Within twenty-four hours of the discovery of Mary Jo's body, all of them had left Chappaquiddick. Not one was ever questioned by police Chief Arena. Not one has ever testified at any of the hearings or at the inquest. Despite offers of large sums of money, not one has ever volunteered any statement to anyone about what went on at the cookout on July 18, 1969.

Ted Kennedy, once touted as a sure-fire candidate for the presidency of the United States, never completely lived down the scandal which arose from the Chappaquiddick affair. The tragic incident effectively prevented him from ever running for that high office.

# MARTIN LUTHER KING

JAMES Earl Ray was born in Quincy, Illinois, on March 10, 1928, to James and Lucille Ray. He was one of four children born to the dirt-poor couple in the first seven years of their marriage. James Sr. had been to prison for theft before his marriage, and with four children to feed during the worst Depression the world had ever known, he took to drinking heavily. The family moved to Ewing, Missouri. Things were no better there, but like everyone in the tiny hamlet of 350 souls, they did survive. Young James started school at the Ewing Consolidated School and is remembered as a shy, retiring youngster.

By 1943, the head of the family abandoned the farm and moved his household to Galesburg, Illinois, where he obtained employment on the railroad. Just before they pulled up stakes, young Jimmy graduated from the eighth grade. Jimmy didn't accompany the rest of the family to their new destination. Instead, he struck out on his own, getting a job with a shoe manufacturing firm in Alton, Illinois. In 1945, Jimmy joined the army. After serving a stint overseas, he was discharged in 1948. Upon returning home, he found that his mother had given birth to two more children. Lucille was now a confirmed alcoholic who hung around bars with strange men.

James Earl Ray left home and, from the age of twenty-one, became a small-time thief, not a very smart one, at that. In 1949, he was caught stealing a typewriter in Chicago and was sent to jail for ninety days. A few years later, Ray was apprehended by a passing citizen as he held up a cab driver for $11.90. He received a sentence of from one to two years in the state penitentiary at Joliet and was released after serving twenty-two months. When he got out of prison, Ray went home to Alton and found work in a gas station. A short time later, a cop making nightly routine calls along the main street of the tiny town saw a window open. When he went to investigate, a burglar rushed out the door and outdistanced the policeman. Returning to the scene, the policeman found a pair of shoes stuck in the mud beside the sidewalk. Next day, James Earl Ray was picked up walking along the railroad tracks on the outskirts of town. His feet were swollen and bleeding. The total take from the robbery was $23. A relative posted bond for Ray, who promptly skipped.

Ray, who couldn't stay out of trouble, was soon picked up passing forged postal orders. This time, he was sentenced to three years in Leavenworth, gaining his release on April 15, 1958. A little over a year later, Ray received his most severe prison term. A four-time loser, he was sentenced to twenty years for armed robbery of a grocery store in St Louis. After serving approximately eight years in prison, Ray escaped. On April 23, 1967, he secreted himself in a truck-load of bread that was being sent from the prison proper to a prison farm close by. The truck was routinely searched, but Ray had concealed himself in the middle of the load of bread boxes and cleanly escaped.

This, then, was James Earl Ray. To this point in his life, he was one of those grey, faceless thousands who start as juvenile delinquents and progress through correctional institutions for the rest of their lives. Ray's criminal activities were planned and executed ineptly. In everything he did he was totally incompetent. And this man, with this background, was to fire the shot which, in one split second, changed the course of history. In so doing, he also triggered the greatest manhunt in the history of crime.

After his successful escape from prison, Ray called himself John Larry Rayns. He made his way to Chicago, where he washed dishes at the Indian Trail Restaurant. He stayed eight weeks, got along well with the rest of the kitchen staff and earned a total of $700. On July 16, 1967, he crossed the border at Windsor, Ontario and kept going to Montreal. Two days later, he took a six-month lease on a room at the Har-K Apartments at 2589 Notre Dame St. E. He signed the lease as Eric S. Galt. It is believed that at the time of the signing of this lease, Ray was actively involved, in conjunction with others, in a master conspiracy to assassinate Dr Martin Luther King. Eric S. Galt's activities in Montreal are well documented. He paid $150 in advance for his room at the Har-K Apartments. On July 18, he bought a suit, pyjamas, gray slacks, two T-shirts, swimming trunks, underwear and ties at Tip Top Tailors. Two days later, he had his nails manicured at the Queen Elizabeth Hotel.

On July 31, he went to the Laurentian Mountains, where he checked into a luxury resort, remaining there for a week. Where did the money come from? Throughout Ray's travels, this question arises again and again. For a man with no income, money seemed to be no object in Ray's date with destiny. Another mystery is that there appears to be a marked change in Ray's personality at this time. The man who bought drinks at the bar in the Laurentian resort was not a shy hillbilly hood on the lam. Ray was now a confident, smooth-talking free spender. He even managed to bed a cultivated employee of the federal government. This poor lady would be questioned extensively by the federal police of the two countries because of her connection with the dapper Eric Galt.

Later, Ray claimed that he met with a man in Montreal he was to know only as Raoul. Ray says he entered into an agreement with Raoul that he would do anything Raoul asked, but in turn would ask no questions himself. Ray claims that if he was part of a conspiracy, he knew nothing about it. Under the auspices of the mysterious Raoul, who, incidentally, has never been identified, Ray travelled from Montreal to Birmingham, Mexico, New Orleans and Los Angeles. Contact was always made with him and money was provided to finance his travels.

In Birmingham, Alabama, Ray bought a white 1966 Mustang. He answered an ad in the *Birmingham News,* met William D. Paisley and paid cash for the car. This was certainly strange behaviour for an escaped convict who was on a mission to murder a Nobel Peace Prize winner. Dr Martin Luther King was a living legend to both whites and blacks. Those who disagreed with his views still admired his courage. Those who agreed with the black leader considered him a god. All agreed that he was the one man who had any chance of unifying the various black groups in the United States. They also agreed that Dr King had no ulterior motives. He was willing to give his life for his people. In 1968, Dr King had already made public his plan for a camp in Washington, D.C., the whole operation to be called Resurrection City.

On February 19, in Los Angeles, Ray had some plastic surgery performed on the tip of his nose and on his left earlobe in which minor but identifiable marks were successfully removed.

Again receiving instructions from the mysterious Raoul, Ray moved from Los Angeles to Atlanta and on to Birmingham. In Birmingham, using the name Harvey Lowmeyer, Ray bought a 30.06-calibre Remington rifle with a telescopic lens. Ray drove the white Mustang back to Atlanta, then went on to Memphis. Meanwhile, after a bomb scare on his plane, Dr King arrived in Memphis. He was met at the airport and accompanied to the Lorraine Motel where he was assigned Room 306.

Using the name John Willard, Ray checked into a dilapidated boarding house at 422 1/2 South Main St. The manager of the boarding house, Mrs Bessie Brewer, thought her new customer was too well dressed for her establishment. She showed him the best rooms in the house, but Mr Willard didn't like the view. He thought Room 58 was perfect. It was filthy, had a lumpy mattress and a nondescript green spread on the bed. The dirty window afforded Ray an unobstructed view of the Lorraine Motel. In his direct line of vision was Room 306.

Down the hall from his room, Mr Willard noticed that the common bathroom gave a still better view of Room 306. He entered the bathroom and locked the door. At six o'clock that evening, Dr King came onto the balcony of his room for a breath of air. John Willard stepped into the bathtub, rested his Remington on the windowsill and squeezed the trigger. Exactly 205 feet, 3 inches away (the distance was later measured), Dr King was slammed against the wall of the Lorraine Motel. The bullet tore into his lower right jaw and hit his spinal cord. At five minutes past seven, Dr Martin Luther King was officially pronounced dead.

James Earl Ray, alias John Willard, rushed from the boarding house and for some reason dropped his rifle in front of a store close by. He jumped into his white Mustang and, in the confusion, got clean away. He travelled as far as Atlanta in the Mustang before abandoning it. Somehow—no one to this day knows what means he used—Ray headed for Toronto. In his wake, Ray left a nation in a state of hatred. The advocate of non-violence, Dr Martin Luther King lay slain by an assassin's bullet. If a white man would kill the leader of the non-violent movement, could non-violence ever achieve the black man's dream of full equality? The answer came in the form of riots and fires. From Memphis to Washington, Chicago, Albany, Youngstown, Baltimore, Kansas City, Newark and Pittsburgh, the hatred, fires and rioting spread. It is estimated that damage amounted to fifty million dollars in the one week following the murder.

The hunt for Dr King's assassin was on. The FBI recovered a note left by Galt in Atlanta. On the note they discovered a fingerprint. The authorities started matching it with prints of known fugitives of the same description as Galt. On the 702nd card pulled, the print was matched. The name on the card—James Earl Ray.

On April 8, James Earl Ray walked up the steps at 102 Ossington Ave. in Toronto and rang the bell. There was a room-for-rent sign in the window. The red brick has been painted many times since the evening Ray introduced himself to Mrs Szpakowski as Paul Bridgman. Surprisingly, the neighbourhood is the same now as it was then. A potpourri of Italians, Portuguese, Spanish and Chinese live in the area. Typical of Toronto and different from other large cities, these ethnic groups seem to be able to retain their culture and yet mix with the community at large. In this mixture of nationalities, no one noticed Paul Bridgman. Well, almost no one. One day his landlady, Mrs Szpakowski, mentioned to her husband that there was a striking resemblance between their quiet boarder and the fellow the whole world was hunting. Her husband told her not to make a fool of herself—what would such a man be doing in their rooming house? Two days later, the ever-increasing reward offered for James Earl Ray hit $155,000.

On April 11, Ray had a passport photo taken at the Arcade Photo Studio on Yonge Street. Five days later, he entered the Kennedy Travel Agency. He said he wanted a twenty-one-day excursion ticket to London, England, leaving on May 6 and returning on May 27. The agent, Mrs Spencer, explained that he needed a passport. When the stranger said that he had no birth certificate, she suggested that he come up with someone who had known him for the past two years. He replied that he had just returned to Toronto after a long absence and didn't know anyone. Mrs Spencer had faced this problem before. There was one further thing he could do to get a passport. Her customer had to swear before a notary that he was a Canadian citizen. Henry Moos, the president of the travel agency, was a notary and would do the necessary. The agency would send the application to Ottawa. Ray answered some further questions and gave his name as Ramon George Sneyd. It was under this name that the application for a passport was sent to Ottawa.

Eric S. Galt, John Willard, Paul Bridgman, Ramon George Sneyd—where did Ray get this assortment of names? How could he feel so safe using them for passports and freely establishing new identities? He was relatively safe because all four men existed and had the same general physical characteristics as Ray. They were all respected citizens of Scarborough, Ontario. They never knew one another and certainly had never met Ray. Somehow their names had been placed on an underworld list of safe names to use and had been purchased by Ray or someone else on behalf of Ray.

On April 19, with the newspapers full of the latest news of the most wanted man in the world, James Earl Ray changed rooming houses. He moved eight blocks away to 962 Dundas St. W. His new address was in the same ethnic neighbourhood. Ray could still remain a faceless nonentity among thousands. Mrs Sun Fung Loo didn't speak any English. Her new roomer paid his nine dollars for the week in advance with a crisp twenty-dollar bill. On May 2, Ray picked up his ticket from Mrs. Spencer. He had applied for and received a birth certificate in the name of Ramon George Sneyd. He paid $345 in cash for the ticket. Four days later, he left his rooming house on Dundas Street West and hailed a cab. The most wanted man in the world drove up Highway 27 (now 427) to Toronto International Airport. By 6 p.m. that evening he was on his way to London, England. The FBI, realizing the ease with which a Canadian passport could be obtained, reasoned that Ray might try to leave the continent via

Canada. The RCMP were asked to check passports issued since Ray's escape from prison. Over 218,000 had been issued. The Mounties set to work checking passports.

On May 7, Ray left London for Lisbon, Portugal. Still travelling under the name Sneyd, he stayed in Lisbon eight days. It is speculated that a prearranged rendezvous was not kept by someone who was supposed to meet Ray. He was forced to return to London. Once back in London, he checked into the Ekfield House hotel and stayed there until May 28, when he moved to the New Earl's Court Motel in Penywern Road. Meanwhile, the Mounties in Ottawa had been checking passports for ten days. They finally came up with one in the name of Ramon George Sneyd with a general description that could have fit Ray. A phone call to Toronto verified that Ramon George Sneyd did indeed exist, but he had never applied for a passport. The police now had the information supplied by Ray in order to purchase his ticket and passport. They traced his actions and learned of his flight to London.

In London, Ray was starting to panic. Moving to another hotel did nothing to calm his nerves. He made inquiries about becoming a mercenary soldier in Africa. Had the elaborate plot commenced to deteriorate? Was Ray now alone, the same loser who years before had left his shoes at the scene of a robbery? On June 8, he checked out of his hotel and booked a flight to Brussels. By this time, Scotland Yard had been alerted to be on the lookout for Ray travelling in Europe under the name of Sneyd. At 11:30 a.m. on the morning of June 8, when Ray rushed to the airport to catch his Brussels flight, Det. Sgt. Phillip F. Birch was checking passports and keeping an eye open for the name Sneyd. Dapper James Earl Ray dashed up to the booth and flashed his passport. Birch saw the wanted name. He said to the most wanted man in the world, "Would you please step into our office, Mr. Sneyd?"

On Monday, March 10, 1969, in Memphis, Percy Foreman, Ray's defence counsel, informed the court that his client had signed a Petition for Waiver of Trial and a request for Acceptance of Plea of Guilty. This document was signed with the firm understanding that Ray's life was to be spared. He received a sentence of ninety-nine years in prison. No one was ever given the opportunity to inquire about a conspiracy, leaving many unanswered questions.

Some time ago, James Earl Ray's petition for leave to appeal was turned down. Despite several attempts on his life, he remains confined in prison to this day.

# JOHN LABATT

THE most notorious kidnapping to take place in Canada, with the possible exception of the abduction of British trade commissioner James Cross in 1970, was that of millionaire John Labatt. The president of John Labatt Ltd., one of Canada's largest breweries, was a likely kidnap victim. His case evolved into one of the most bizarre crimes ever perpetrated in the country.

The Labatt family owned a summer home at Bright's Cove on Lake Huron. On the morning of August 14, 1934, John Labatt left his summer hideaway for the drive to the Labatt Co. headquarters in London, Ontario. Labatt knew the route intimately. On this particular morning, as was his custom, he took a short cut. He always saved miles by driving through Camlachie Village toward the Warwick Bridge, leading eventually to the provincial highway into London. Labatt had just passed Camlachie when another car, travelling much faster in the same direction, overtook him. The car was soon beyond his range of vision. Suddenly, the same automobile came into sight. This time it was blocking the road. Labatt brought his car to a stop. Three men dashed toward his vehicle, two brandishing revolvers. Then John Labatt heard the dreaded words, "Stick them up, quick, this is a kidnapping."

The men acted swiftly. They inquired if Labatt had any cash. He turned over around a hundred dollars. Two of the men hurriedly placed adhesive tape over Labatt's eyes and hustled him into their car, while the third man drove away in Labatt's car. One of the men sat in the back seat with Labatt while his accomplice drove. Interestingly, Labatt's companion was extremely friendly. He called his victim John, and even inquired if there were any good robbery opportunities around the London area. Labatt later claimed that the adhesive tape covering his eyes left a crack through which he could see his captors. During the long ride, the kidnap car stopped for gas and other supplies. At no time did Labatt seek help. Had he screamed or raised an alarm, there was no way the kidnappers could have avoided apprehension. No one knows why Labatt didn't raise a ruckus.

Toward nightfall, the car pulled up to a cottage. The kidnappers and their hostage were to remain there for three nights and four days. A long dog chain was fastened to Labatt's wrist, the other end attached to a bed. The kidnappers seemed very concerned about their hostage's comfort. A substantial meal was provided, which Labatt ate heartily. These were not desperate threatening bullies, Labatt had decided. Obviously, they actually cared about the welfare of their victim. The lone guard excused himself, went into the other bedroom and went to sleep. The thought of escape never entered Labatt's head. He too went to sleep.

Meanwhile, the Labatt car had been driven to City Hospital in London. Hugh Labatt was anonymously phoned and informed of his brother's kidnapping. He was told to proceed to the car for further instructions. Hugh found this note from the kidnappers on the car seat:

> Mr. Hugh Labatt we are holding your brother John for $150,000 ransom. Go to Toronto immediately and register in the Royal York Hotel. We will negotiate with you from that point, be prepared when I get in touch with you there to furnish me the names of two or three reliable parties who you can trust to deliver this money to us. We advise you to keep this matter away from the police and newspapers so as we can return your brother safely. You will know me as Three Fingered Abe.

Hugh and John were very close and Hugh was understandably distraught at the thought of his brother's life being in danger. With the blessing of the Toronto Police Force, Hugh Labatt was installed in a suite in the Royal York Hotel. He managed to have $150,000 with him in the suite as he waited for his instructions. The Toronto police were now being assisted by the Ontario Provincial Police, the RCMP and the FBI. By Wednesday, all four police forces were scurrying about, running down clues. The Labatt kidnapping was the biggest news in the country.

Meanwhile, in their cosy cottage in the Muskokas, John Labatt and his captors ate well, slept at intervals, and above all else were extremely polite and considerate to one another. On Tuesday morning, John Labatt, sitting on the edge of his bed, chatted amicably with his companions while he received a first-rate shave. This ritual was to be repeated each morning of his captivity. Meals, cigarettes and good conversation made the time pass pleasantly enough. On Wednesday, as far as Labatt could tell, the two men received word (probably from the third kidnapper, who had driven Labatt's car back to London) that the Royal York was teeming with journalists and cops. It would be impossible to pick up the ransom money under those circumstances. Rather than simply calling Hugh Labatt with a change of plans, the kidnappers decided to call the whole thing off. On Thursday, the polite, considerate kidnappers took the unreasonable risk of driving their victim into the heart of Toronto. They let Labatt out at the corner of Bathurst Street and St. Clair Avenue. Considerate to the end, they gave the millionaire a dollar for cab fare to the Royal York. The kidnappers expressed concern about having Hugh worry about his brother even a half hour longer than necessary.

Once at the hotel, Labatt had a hard time proving he was the missing John Labatt. After a few embarrassing moments for everyone, he was reunited with his brother Hugh. The John Labatt kidnapping was over. The victim was safe. Now the hunt was on for his abductors. Labatt was shown hundreds of photographs. Finally, he pointed a finger at one picture and declared that it was his travelling companion and guard. The picture was that of David Meisner. The photograph was distributed throughout the United States and Canada. A couple of days later, David Meisner walked into a Detroit police station and advised a clerk that he had heard the police were looking for him. Meisner had wandered from the Goderich, Ontario area to the United States, where he had drifted from one clerical job to another. At the time of the kidnapping, he was living in Covington, Kentucky, making a precarious living as a racetrack follower and gambler. He was fifty-five years old, and he had never been convicted of a serious crime.

Meisner was a shy, lean man, his most outstanding feature a serious growth in his left eye, which gave his eye the appearance of a white lump. He was extradited to London, where John Labatt took one look at him and stated, "That's the man! Marvellous!"

On January 27, 1935, at the London Assizes, Meisner stood trial for kidnapping. John Labatt took the witness stand and told of his ordeal. He positively identified David Meisner as his kidnapper. Labatt had a few awkward moments. He had previously estimated the kidnapper's weight at around 175 pounds. Meisner weighed in at 118 pounds. Labatt's only explanation for the discrepancy was that he was simply a poor judge of weight. He swore that he had never noticed the white growth over Meisner's eye, which everyone agreed was pretty hard to miss. Several other witnesses also positively identified Meisner as the kidnapper. The man who had sold the dog chain and the lady who had rented the Muskoka cottage to the kidnappers were devastating in their effect on the jury. As a result of the many eye witnesses, Meisner was convicted and received a sentence of fifteen years' imprisonment.

While Meisner languished in Kingston Penitentiary, one John Basil Bannon of Detroit, a sometime criminal turned stool-pigeon, contacted the Toronto police. He was after the reward money for the apprehension of the remaining Labatt kidnappers. Bannon led the police to Crown Point, Indiana, where a small-time hood was incarcerated, having just concluded a gunfight with the local cops. The man's name was Michael McCardell. After being confronted with the facts, he admitted to being "Three Fingered Abe." John Labatt was summoned. He stood face-to-face with McCardell, who greeted Labatt like a long lost friend. McCardell reeled off all the subject matter of their four days of conversation. There was no doubt about it. Labatt had made a terrible mistake. McCardell was the kidnapper. David Meisner was an innocent man.

Upon being brought back to London, McCardell told all. He turned on Bannon and informed the police that while Bannon hadn't taken part in the actual kidnapping, he had planned the whole thing and had rented the cottage in the Muskokas. McCardell named the other kidnappers—Albert Pegram and Russell Knowles. He gave a detailed account of the whole incident from beginning to end. David Meisner had taken no part in the crime.

The four guilty men were bought to trial and received long prison sentences. David Meisner was granted a second trial. In March 1936, after deliberating for over seven hours, a jury found him not guilty of kidnapping John Labatt. He had spent a year and a half in Kingston Penitentiary for a crime he did not commit.

John Labatt died of natural causes on July 8, 1952.

# JOHN LENNON

FAMED ex-Beatle John Lennon lived in the luxurious Dakota apartment building at 72nd Street and Central Park West in New York City. On December 8, 1980, he drove up to the Dakota in a sleek limo with his wife, Yoko Ono. It had been a full and tiring day for the illustrious pair. They had been at the Hit Factory, where Yoko had completed recording "Walking On Thin Ice." Waiting for them in front of their home was thirty-one-year-old Mark David Chapman. Inside his pocket he carried a Charter Arms .38 revolver. In his hands he held a copy of J. D. Salinger's book *The Catcher in the Rye*.

Mark had been many things during his somewhat checkered past. Raised by loving parents in Decatur, Georgia, blessed with above-average intelligence, he did nothing to distinguish himself from other children during his formative years. In high school he experimented with drugs, but after a bad LSD trip, he gave up drugs for good. As a teenager, Mark was a counsellor at a YMCA camp in Decatur and is remembered as being excellent at handling young children. After high school, he accepted a position at a YMCA camp in Fort Chaffee, Arkansas, which specialized in housing Vietnamese refugees. When that job dried up, he became a security guard at the Atlanta airport. In an effort to better himself, he took a shooting-range test. After passing the test, he was hired as an armed guard at De Kalb General Hospital on the outskirts of Atlanta.

In the summer of 1977, Mark treated himself to a Hawaiian vacation. He was totally smitten by the beauty of the place and, after a short visit home, returned to Hawaii convinced that he could start a new, more productive life. But things didn't work out. Instead of a new life full of promise, he sank into a deep depression. Mark was so depressed that he decided to commit suicide. He attached a vacuum cleaner hose to the exhaust pipe of a rented car and led the hose into the car through the window. Mark sat in the vehicle to await death. A Japanese fisherman discovered him before the carbon monoxide could take effect. Recovering in hospital, Mark gave up the idea of killing himself.

In 1978, after being released from hospital, Mark caught on as a maintenance employee at the Castle Medical Center, the same institution where he had been a patient. After saving his money for some months, he decided to take a vacation. When he walked into Waters World Travel, twenty-two-year-old Mark met Gloria, twenty-six, who worked for the travel agency. That June, she would become his wife. Throughout his job changes and marriage, Mark remained an admirer of the Beatles, but had become somewhat disenchanted with John Lennon when the former Beatle was quoted as saying that the Beatles were more popular than Jesus.

Mark read extensively, but was particularly enamored with J. D. Salinger's *The Catcher in the Rye*. Mark related strongly with the main character in the book, Holden Caulfield, and at one point gave serious thought to changing his name to the name of that character. In the dark recesses of his progressively anguished mind, Mark came to the conclusion that John Lennon, who had preached about love of his fellow man and peace in the world, was a phoney who had become a millionaire. To Mark, that was a betrayal. In Mark's tortured mind, that meant Lennon had to die. He would later state that Satan had directed him to carry out the deed.

At home, Mark behaved irrationally, flying into rages without provocation, directing most of his venom towards Gloria. As the months passed, he became more engrossed in the character of Holden Caulfield. For some reason, probably unknown even to himself, he focused his rage on John Lennon. When he learned that Lennon lived in New York, he decided it was time for another vacation. Mark took the long flight to New York. Once there, he changed his mind and returned home to Gloria. She was glad to see him safe and sound. In the past, he had often raved about killing Lennon, but Gloria hadn't believed him. She was relieved that his obsession with Lennon was over. Her relief was short-lived. Mark informed her that he was returning to New York, not to kill Lennon, but to explore career opportunities. He had lied to his wife.

Mark arrived in the Big Apple and took a room within walking distance of the Dakota. He walked over to Lennon's building carrying the ex-Beatle's latest album "Double Fantasy." To the casual observer he was just another fan looking for an autograph. Mark waited around the Dakota, but Lennon didn't show up, so he abandoned his stalking for that day. Next morning, Mark purchased a copy of *The Catcher in the Rye* and made his way to the front of Lennon's building. Around noon, he watched as Lennon's five-year-old son, Sean, entered the building with his nanny. The doorman told him that John was at home being interviewed by RKO Radio.

And then it happened. The moment Mark Chapman had been dreaming about and thinking about for months. The demons that had driven him to this place at this time would at last be satisfied. John and Yoko appeared. Mark approached the famed entertainer with his album. He blurted out, "John, would you sign my album, please?" Lennon replied, "Sure," signed the album and inquired, "Is that what you wanted? Is that all you wanted?" Mark replied, "Thanks a lot." And then John and Yoko sped away in their limo. Things had not gone well for Mark. His quarry hadn't come across as an arrogant millionaire, but as a warm, friendly man appreciative of his fans. Mark was disappointed at his own indecision. Next time would be different. He would wait. Lennon would return if he waited long enough. In the meantime, he chatted with doorman Jose Perdomo to pass the time.

It was about 11 p.m. when the limo drove up. Yoko was the first passenger out. John followed some distance behind. He walked past Mark. Later, under questioning, Mark would state that he heard voices commanding, "Do it, do it, do it." Over and over they shouted, "Do it, do it, do it!" Out came the Charter Arms .38. A quick aim, and five bullets poured into John Lennon's body. The doorman clutched Mark's wrist and violently twisted it. The weapon fell to the driveway and was kicked across the road. The doorman shouted, "What did you do? What have you done? Get out of here. Go away." Mark replied, "I'm sorry."

Once in custody, Mark admitted that he had considered killing other public figures. The list included Johnny Carson, Jackie Onassis, Paul McCartney, Elizabeth Taylor and George C. Scott. In the end, he settled for John Lennon, mainly because Lennon was more accessible than the others and, of course, those voices told him it had to be Lennon. A host of mental health physicians delved into Mark's mind for a more direct motive. Mark himself seemed at a loss to explain his intense hatred of Lennon, at the same time admitting that he really liked and admired the ex-Beatle. Finally, Mark put forth a most improbable motive—to give *The Catcher in the Rye* publicity which would promote the book he believed in.

The day before Mark's murder trial, he withdrew his insanity plea and pleaded guilty to murder. He was sentenced to twenty years to life imprisonment, a term he is serving at the correctional facility in Attica, New York. After Mark's confinement, his wife, Gloria, moved from Hawaii to Attica, where she lived for several months to be near her husband. However, when in February 1983, Mark refused to see her, Gloria returned to Hawaii. Mark's father has never visited him since John Lennon's murder.

For his own safety, Mark David Chapman lives in a segregated section at Attica. He will be eligible for parole in the year 2000.

# THOMAS JOHN LEY

THOMAS John Ley was not your typical murderer. But then, John McMain Mudie was not your average victim, either. You see, Mr. Ley was the wealthy former minister of justice for New South Wales, Australia; Mudie was an English bartender. The tale of these two men and how one killed the other, without ever exchanging a word of conversation, has been described by the Lord Chief Justice of England as one of the strangest cases ever presented to an English jury.

Ley was born in England but moved to Australia when he was eight years old. While still in his twenties, he became deeply involved in politics. In 1922, at the age of forty-one, after a gradual climb up the political ladder, he became minister of justice. For years the Honourable Thomas John Ley was one of the most influential men in Australia. With power came wealth. Ley was the director of several large companies. He left Australia for England in 1928, hurt because he hadn't been chosen deputy premier when the prime minister visited Europe.

Thomas Ley's wife was unaware that he had been supporting a mistress for over twenty years. Mrs Brooks was a widow, whose daughter was married to an Englishman named Barron. When Ley went to England, he took Mrs Brooks with him, leaving his wife behind in Australia. Strangely, Ley ceased having intercourse with Mrs Brooks after returning to England. In fact, she acted as Ley's housekeeper and companion in the twelve years prior to the Mudie murder. When Mrs Brooks's daughter required an operation, Ley suggested that she move in with her son-in-law while her daughter was convalescing in hospital. The Barrons lived on Homefield Road in London in a house of flats operated by a Mrs Evans.

One of the roomers at Homefield Road was John Mudie, a bartender who, as the saying goes, never did anyone any harm. From all reports, Mudie was a decent, hardworking, quiet man. Mrs Evans spoke highly of Mudie and doted upon the only bachelor residing in her establishment. Sometimes she tidied his rooms. In return, Mudie was most obliging in running errands for his landlady. Occasionally, John Ley dropped over to the Evans' establishment to have tea with Mrs Brooks. In this way he met Mrs Evans.

It is not my function to analyse people's minds, but certainly the obsession which was to overtake, envelop and eventually ruin John Ley defies explanation. Later, psychiatrists would conveniently decide that the successful businessman and politician was suffering from paranoia. Whatever the reason, Ley became obsessed with the idea that John Mudie was carrying on a torrid love affair with the sixty-six-year-old Mrs Brooks. He became insanely jealous of the fictitious relationship. Mrs Evans was to state that Mudie met Mrs Brooks only once, and that was in her own company, on a stairway where the three passed the time of day for a moment or two. The seed of insane jealousy firmly planted, Ley proceeded to hatch a diabolical plot to murder Mudie, who was in all probability the most innocent victim of any premeditated murder ever committed.

Ley approached a hotel porter named Minden at the Royal Hotel in Woburn Place. Minden knew Ley as a solicitor and a former guest of the hotel who in the past had visited with his wife from Australia. Ley asked Minden if he knew of a man with a motor car who could be trusted, letting the porter know that such a man could earn as much for one piece of work as he normally would in an entire year. Minden, assuming that the vehicle was to be used by the solicitor for legitimate purposes, put Ley in contact with an acquaintance, William Buckingham. Minden received ten pounds from Ley for the favour.

Ley and Buckingham met and, for the first time, Ley told somone else of his intentions. He alleged that a young man had seduced a mother and daughter and was now blackmailing the two women. It was Ley's plan to kidnap the young man and give him a good scare. Then he would provide him with a sum of money and force the culprit to leave the country. Ley promised he would pay Buckingham well for his assistance. He told Buckingham that another accomplice in the scheme, Lawrence John Smith, a carpenter, would eventually meet with them to iron out the details.

The following evening, the former minister of justice, the man with the car for hire and the carpenter met at the Royal Hotel to finalize their plans. Buckingham suggested bringing along a friend of his, Mrs. Lillian Bruce, in order to lure the victim into the car. Buckingham was so excited about the promise of easy money that he brought his son into the scheme, as well. In fairness to all Ley's co-conspirators, it is quite possible that at this time they believed his story. When Minden suggested that Buckingham had a car for hire, he asked if it would be used for legal purposes. Mrs Bruce, slightly suspicious, also inquired if anything she was getting involved in was illegal. All received assurances from Ley that as a solicitor he was operating well within the law.

And so, all the characters of the diabolical plot are now in position—Ley, Smith, Buckingham, his son, Mrs Bruce, and of course, the bartender at the Reigate Hill Hotel, the unsuspecting John Mudie. Mrs Bruce, posing as a well-to-do customer, made it a point to become acquainted with the pleasant, unassuming Mudie. It wasn't difficult. Young Buckingham posed as her chauffeur. Mrs Bruce asked Mudie if he would care to earn some extra money working as a bartender at a cocktail party she was giving on the evening of November 28, 1946. Mudie jumped at the opportunity.

On the appointed night, young Buckingham and Mrs Bruce picked up Mudie at the Reigate Hill Hotel for the ride into London. Buckingham Jr. drove his father's Wosley. Unknown to Mudie, another vehicle, a Ford, licence number 101, which had been rented a week earlier by Smith, preceded the Wosley to 5 Beaufort Gdns. Smith and his passenger, Buckingham Sr., entered Ley's residence. Mrs Bruce, young Buckingham and Mudie entered 5 Beaufort Gdns. Young Buckingham merely opened the door and returned to the car. Once the victim was delivered, Mrs Bruce's work was done. She excused herself, saying she had to consult with her chauffeur. As the door closed behind her, the senior Buckingham and Smith threw a carpet over poor Mudie's head. He was gagged and firmly tied with rope.

Exactly what went on behind that closed door will never be known for sure. Young Buckingham and Mrs Bruce drove to the Crown and Sceptre for a few drinks. Buckingham and Smith were supposed to join them. Only the elder Buckingham showed up. Meanwhile, the terrified Mudie sat with a carpet tied firmly over his head with no idea what was happening to him. Smith remained in the room. Ley, his brain racing in ecstasy, had managed to pull it off. After all the scheming and plotting, his supposed antagonist was trussed up and helpless before him.

On November 29, 1946, Walter Coombs of Woldingham, Surrey, was walking home after finishing work. It was he who discovered the body of John Mudie in a chalk pit. Death was the result of strangulation with a rope, which was tied around the dead man's neck. John Mudie's body was identified immediately. His killers had overlooked his personal card in his pocket. Buckingham and Mrs Bruce read about the terrible conclusion to the kidnapping plot in the newspapers. The chalk-pit murder, as it became known, received wide publicity. Buckingham and Mrs Bruce went directly to the police and told the whole story, but insisted that Mudie was definitely alive when they left him. A gag and pickaxe found at the scene of the crime were later traced to 5 Beaufort Gdns.

When the entire plot unfolded, Smith and Ley were charged with murder. All the other participants turned King's evidence and were never tried. There was little doubt as to Ley's guilt as the architect of the murder. Smith claimed that the last time he saw Mudie, the bartender was alive. To two alert citizens, the evidence proved that, unlike his fellow conspirators, Smith knew that Mudie was to be murdered, not merely kidnapped. Clifford Tamplin and Fred Smith, two landscape gardeners, were cycling past the chalk pit on November 27, the day before the murder. They were startled to notice a car parked in the desolate area. As they came upon the scene, a man appeared some distance inside the pit. When the man spotted the cyclists, he dashed wildly to his car and quickly drove away. The two men noted the licence-plate number—101—and the make of the vehicle, a Ford. Later, when they heard a body had been found at that exact spot on November 29, they went to the police with their story. As the killing was definitely committed on the twenty-eighth, using a Ford car with licence-plate number 101, their story proved that Smith, who had rented the car earlier in the week, was reconnoitering the location to dump the body the day before the murder took place.

Both Ley and Smith were found guilty of murder and sentenced to death, although it was never established which one actually strangled John Mudie. Their sentences were later commuted. Smith was given life imprisonment, while Ley was judged insane and sent to Broadmoor, where he was one of the wealthiest men ever to be incarcerated in that institution. Three months later, the Honourable Thomas John Ley, former minister of justice for New South Wales, Australia, suffered a stroke and died.

# CLAUDINE LONGET

ASPEN, Colorado, is a resort town that abounds with beautiful women, handsome men and bars on every corner. It's a good place to have fun. If one is so inclined, one can even ski in Aspen. Occasionally, people get shot in Aspen. Vladimir "Spider" Sabich did.

The son of a California police officer, Spider Sabich first came to public attention when he finished fifth in the slalom at the Olympic Games held in Grenoble, France, in 1968. After turning pro, he won the world professional skiing championship in 1970 and 1971. The prize money, augmented by commercial fees, skyrocketed his annual income to well over a quarter of a million dollars. That's when he met Claudine Longet, a French femme fatale, who was gainfully employed in a Folies-Bergères revue in Las Vegas. Claudine was the estranged wife of famed singer Andy Williams. When she and Andy agreed to disagree after fourteen years of marital bliss, it is reported that Claudine walked away with a cool two-million-dollar settlement and custody of their three children, Noelle, Bobby and Christian.

Beautiful Claudine and handsome Spider met at a celebrity ski race in Bear Valley, California. They took to each other like rum and Coke. In 1974, Spider moved the entire menagerie into his posh new $250,000 chalet where they all lived happily ever after. Well, not exactly ever after. They lived happily for over a year. Then, in a civilized, sensible manner, Spider and Claudine had a chat about their future. Spider gently suggested that the love affair was over and thought it best for all concerned if Claudine and her children found other accommodations. Claudine, who was well known throughout Aspen for her acid tongue, didn't take the rejection well, as we will soon find out. Outwardly she acted like a real lady. As far as anyone was concerned, she was making the best of an embarrassing situation. Claudine rented a house and appeared to be preparing to move out of Sabich's digs. But appearances can be deceiving. That's where matters stood until March 21, 1976. It was a pleasant Sunday, perfect for skiing. Claudine spent the morning on the slopes and most of the afternoon downing a couple or three at a local watering hole. Friends who joined her that afternoon later stated that she behaved normally in every way.

At around 6:30 p.m. Aspen police received an urgent call from the Sabich residence. The first officer at the scene was greeted by Claudine, who stated simply, "I shot Spider." Someone shot Spider, all right. He was lying on the bathroom floor clad only in his blue thermal underwear and had obviously been washing his face when he had been shot in the abdomen. Claudine told officers that she had approached Spider with a .22-calibre pistol. While she was asking him how to use it, the gun went off. Claudine's story sounded so much better than the one told by Detective David Gorms, who testified that Claudine told him, "I raised the gun and playfully went boom-boom and it went off."

Spider was rushed by ambulance to Aspen Valley Hospital. Paramedics worked on him in the ambulance, while Claudine assisted, but their efforts proved futile. Spider was declared dead on arrival at hospital. Claudine's diary was confiscated. So was Claudine, but she was released on bail hours later. Andy Williams arrived in Aspen and moved Claudine and the children into the home of his good friend, folksinger John Denver.

In 1977, Claudine Longet's manslaughter trial made headlines around the world. It is reported that her diary contained evidence that her relationship with Spider had deteriorated to the point where she disliked him intensely, but the diary was not allowed to be entered in evidence at her trial. Moreover, the presiding judge would not admit blood and urine samples taken from Claudine at the time of the tragedy. He claimed that they were taken without Claudine's permission. Due to the exclusion of the diary as evidence, the prosecution's case was hindered by lack of motive, which the diary would have revealed. The exclusion of the blood and urine analysis made it difficult to prove that Claudine had been, at least to some degree, intoxicated at the time of the shooting.

Claudine, of course, insisted that she was guilty of no crime whatever. It had all been a tragic accident. She took the witness stand in her own defence. She claimed that she had found the gun as she was putting Spider's sweater into a closet and had reminded herself to ask him how to use it, since he was leaving next day on a ski trip and she wanted to know how the gun worked. Claudine went on, "I planned to ask him what the safety was about." At this point in her story, Claudine said that Spider went into the bathroom. She followed him and asked how to work the weapon. Spider said, "When the red dot is covered, the safety is on, it won't fire." I then raised the gun and said, "Here it is on the red dot and it won't fire." "You've got it," Spider replied. Then the gun went off.

Many spectators in the packed courtroom were in tears as they listened to Claudine describe Spider Sabich's last moments. "Spider called my name many times and sort of slid down and I told him I would call an ambulance. I begged him to talk to me. I could see he was fainting. I told him to try to make it, to talk to me. I tried to give him mouth-to-mouth resuscitation." Despite Claudine's tearful recital, the prosecution pressed on by directly asking her if she had been asked to move out of Spider's villa. She replied just as directly, "No." Without that diary, the prosecution's hands were tied.

Peter Martin, a weapons expert with the Maryland Firearms Lab, testified for the defence. He stated that an examination of the German-manufactured Erma .22-calibre pistol showed that the firing mechanism was packed with stiff grease. As a result, he said, "I found that it would fire if the safety catch was fully engaged." After examining the weapon, other experts agreed with Martin. The jury deliberated only forty minutes before finding Claudine guilty only of "criminally negligent homicide," a much less serious charge than felonious manslaughter, which had been sought by the prosecution. Under Colorado law, Claudine could have been sentenced to two years in prison. Instead, a lenient judge sentenced her to one month in jail, a sentence the beautiful Claudine served from April 18 to May 18, 1977.

In 1986, Claudine Longet married prosperous Aspen lawyer Ron Austin, one of the lawyers who had so ably defended her during her manslaughter trial.

# LORD LUCAN

ART Whitehouse figured it would be another routine night tending bar at the Plumbers Arms in Merrie England's good old London town. Art was wrong. The night of November 7, 1974, would turn out to be one he would never forget.

At 10 p.m., the door of the pub flew open and a woman entered screaming, "Help me, help me! I have just escaped from a murderer! My children, my children … he's in the house … he's murdered the nanny … help me!" Art and his wife rushed to the woman, whose head was bleeding profusely. They learned they were tending to Lady Lucan.

Lady Lucan was rushed by ambulance to the closest hospital, while police sped to the Lucan residence at 46 Lower Belgrave St. They had to force the door of the darkened dwelling. Inside, they observed bloodstains on the wallpaper in the hall. There was a large pool of blood at the bottom of the stairs leading to a breakfast room. Upstairs, on the fifth floor, in the nursery, police came across the Lucan children, seven-year-old George and four-year-old Camilla, sleeping peacefully in their beds. Standing beside them in a confused state was their elder sister, Frances, ten. Downstairs, another officer discovered broken cups and saucers in a pool of blood. Police found a canvas mailbag in the breakfast room with blood dripping out of it. The bag contained the body of the Lucans' twenty-nine-year-old nanny, Sandra Eleanor Rivett.

Unexpectedly, Lord Lucan's mother appeared on the scene. She said she had received a telephone call from her son, imploring her to come right over. He told her there had been "a terrible catastrophe." The countess, accompanied by a police officer, took her three grandchildren to her home. As soon as they arrived, she received a telephone call from Lord Lucan. She told him that the children were with her and were safe and sound. When she asked if he wanted to speak to the police officer who was in the room with her, she was told that he would call back in the morning. It's been over twenty years and no such call has ever been received.

Next morning, Lady Lucan was interrogated in hospital. She informed Scotland Yard detectives that Sandra Rivett, who had been in her employ for only a few weeks, normally took Thursday nights off. On this particular

Thursday, she changed her mind and remained at home. Shortly after 9 p.m., Lady Lucan was watching TV with her older daughter, Frances. Sandra popped her head into the room and asked if they cared for a spot of tea. She then proceeded downstairs carrying cups and saucers which had been used previously in the TV room. When twenty minutes passed with no sign of Sandra, Lady Lucan decided to investigate. She walked downstairs to the basement, calling Sandra's name as she went. Suddenly, a man appeared and, without saying a word, struck her on the head. Later, a two-foot-long pipe with tape around one end was found at the scene. The attacker proceeded to strangle the startled woman. She struggled desperately, until she broke free and ran to the Plumbers Arms.

The day after the murder, William Shand-Kydd, who was married to Lady Lucan's sister, received a letter from Lord Lucan, in which he claimed he had interrupted a fight between his wife and an intruder. He had managed to fight off the attacker and had then helped to wash the blood from his wife's head. When he went to the bathroom for a towel, she ran out of the house. He went on to say that he felt no one would believe him and so he had fled.

Scotland Yard had quite a different theory as to how Sandra Rivett had met her death. There had been no forced entry into the house. Although the Lucans were estranged, Lord Lucan still had a key and was privy to the erroneous information that Sandra would take her usual Thursday night off. Investigators could find no one who would want Sandra dead. She had not been sexually interfered with in any way, nor had any valuables been removed from the residence. Police felt that, in the dark, Lucan had mistaken the nanny for his wife. It was well known that Lord Lucan wanted custody of his children. With his wife out of the way, he would no doubt solve this problem.

Three days after the murder, police found an abandoned Ford Corsair in Newhaven, Sussex. The seats of the vehicle were bloodstained. A two-foot-long piece of lead pipe with a taped handle was in the trunk. This weapon was similar to the one found at the scene of the Rivett murder. The vehicle was traced to one Michael Stoop, a friend of Lord Lucan. When questioned by police, Stoop revealed that he had loaned the vehicle to Lord Lucan two weeks before the murder. As if Stoop's revelation wasn't enough to make Lord Lucan the prime suspect in the murder, there was more to come. At an official inquest into the tragedy, Lady Lucan positively identified her husband as her attacker.

And now let's examine the checkered past of Richard John Bingham, better known as Lord Lucan. He was born with all the creature comforts of

British nobility. At thirteen years of age, the handsome fellow was shipped off to Eton. At eighteen he joined his father's old regiment, the Coldstream Guards. In the Guards he excelled in the decidedly unwarlike pursuits of rowing and bobsledding. Once back on civvy street, the dashing lord devoted his time to being an international playboy. Skiing and golf were his major pursuits, but it was gambling that became an obsession. Because of his heavy losses, he was sarcastically referred to as Lucky Lucan.

On November 28, 1963, the handsome lord married beautiful Veronica Duncan at Holy Trinity Church, Brompton. A few months later, they moved into their prestigious address in Belgravia. By 1970, they were the proud parents of three children. In the meantime, Lucky Lucan had become a big-time habitual gambler and big-time loser. On a bad night, Lucan could drop the equivalent of $25,000. It didn't take long before he had squandered his inheritance and was deeply in debt. At home, Lady Lucan had had her fill of her playboy husband. The pair separated. Lucky was incensed when the courts awarded custody of the three children to their mother. He swore he would do anything to get them back.

The question is—did Lord Lucan kill Sandra Rivett by mistake? Many believe this is the case, but of course we can't know for sure because Lucky Lucan has simply disappeared. The day he abandoned Michael Stoop's Ford Corsair, he was spotted by two trawlermen, who told police they had seen a well-dressed gentleman walking on a pier near the abandoned car. Did Lucky decide to end it all with a plunge into the briny? There are other theories. A retired Scotland Yard detective, Alec Edwards, recently revealed that the Yard had employed detectives to trail Lucan's offspring to South Africa, but that the investigation had been called off due to a lack of funds. George, twenty-eight, now Lord Bingham, has been quoted by British papers as saying that the suggestion that either he or his sisters, Lady Frances, a thirty-one-year-old London lawyer and Lady Camilla, twenty-five, had visited his father in Africa was ludicrous.

Of course, Lucky Lucan could have made his way to Canada. Take that aristocratic sixty-year-old gentleman living next door to you—nah, it couldn't be.

# GENERAL HUMBERTO MARILES

IN 1948, at the Olympic Games in London, England, thirty-four-year-old Gen. Humberto Mariles was a well-respected member of Mexico's equestrian team. He sat upright and proud upon his well-trained horse and went through his jumps flawlessly to win a gold medal in individual jumping. In that memorable Olympics, the Mexican equestrian team won a gold medal in team Grand Prix jumping, a bronze medal in the team three-day event, a silver in individual jumping, as well as Mariles's gold. The Mexican equestrians, led by Mariles, dominated their sport throughout the world for the next ten years.

General Mariles was so popular in Mexico that the anniversary of his gold medal triumph was celebrated for years after the event. Not only was he a great horseman, he was also friendly and good-natured. The son of a cavalry officer, Mariles had naturally gravitated to the army as a career. He rose in the ranks, and as he did so, gained the favour of the politicians in power. The higher-ranked army men in Mexico were considered to be the elite of the country. They could do no wrong and the astute ones made sure that they had all the material comforts of life. It is uncertain how Mariles acquired his wealth, but it is a fact that he was considered to be a wealthy man.

At the height of his fame and popularity, Mariles owned an equestrian ranch and school in Mexico. Equestrians came from all over the world to learn from the master. The jovial but quick-tempered Mariles had a particular affinity for Canadians. He always enjoyed his frequent appearances at the Royal Winter Fair in Toronto and was extremely hospitable to any Canadians who stayed at his ranch. Many Toronton-ians went to Mexico to work and learn under Mariles. They were all impressed with the general's friendliness and charm.

This self-made man, who was known and idolized throughout the world, had his own world changed drastically by what started out as an insignificant event. On the night of August 14, 1964, he was driving through Chapultepec, a beautiful park in the centre of Mexico City, when a car cut Mariles off. Instead of letting the incident pass, he took off after the other vehicle. It is believed that Mariles caught up with the other car, driven by Jésus Valaquez.

A heated argument took place. Mariles pulled out a .45-calibre revolver and shot Valaquez three times. The seriously wounded man was rushed to the hospital.

Four days after the shooting, Mariles failed to show up at the Federal District attorney-general's office, where he was to face charges of firing at and wounding a motorist. The next day, August 19, the wounded man's condition improved and he made the following statement: "Mariles, vociferating loudly, took careful aim and fired, wounding me in the back." Shortly after issuing this statement, Valaquez's conditon worsened and he died. Mariles remained a fugitive for over a year. He had left the country to escape capture, but returned and gave himself up to the authorities.

Adolfo Lopez Mateos was president of Mexico at the time, and Mariles was no longer in favour. He could expect no help from political friends. In fact, he found himself in the unique position of having influential friends throughout the world, but no one to help him in his native land. The question that has bothered many of the general's friends was whether or not Mariles acted in self-defence. Some believe the whole thing was a set-up to provoke Mariles into a fight. They think he was the intended victim. The trial was headline news throughout Mexico. Mariles was charged with manslaughter and was sentenced to ten years in prison.

In 1968, Canadian Sheila Whitaker was a reporter covering the equestrian events at the Olympic Games in Mexico City. She nostalgically remembers visiting Mariles in prison. At that time, Mariles had been in the Cárcel de Tecumberri, Mexico City's penitentiary, for four years. At first, she was kept waiting at the prison gates for over half an hour while her credentials were sent into the prison.

When her papers were returned, Sheila was ushered into a decrepit anteroom. Here, over fifty tarnished silver cups and trays won by Mariles throughout the world, were on display. Her Canadian passport was confiscated. Finally, she was frisked by a two hundred pound matron and made to wait another hour before being ushered into the prison. Sheila expected to find Mariles in chains. She was in for a surprise.

Mariles greeted her in a sunny courtyard, where prisoners and civilians mixed freely. He showed his guest into his living quarters, the equivalent of a well-furnished apartment. Friends and acquaintances popped by to say hello. The phone rang incessantly; even a few young ladies strolled by aimlessly. His meals were brought to him by a chauffeur-driven car. The general was still the

same jovial, heavy-set, handsome man. He had been watching the Olympics on his television set. Ironically, Canada's equestrian team won our country's only gold medal of the entire Olympics that year. Mariles seemed pleased that the Canadians had done so well, but appeared to become despondent as it came time for Sheila to leave. Mariles's last words to her were, "I would like to come to Canada when all this is finished." She was never to see Humberto Mariles again.

Mariles served six years of his ten-year sentence before being released from prison in 1970. On November 25, 1972, he and seven other men were arrested in Paris, France. They had in their possession four suitcases containing heroin, destined for shipment to Mexico.

On December 6, two weeks after his arrest, Mariles died of a heart attack in Santa Prison in Paris. He was fifty-eight years old.

# KID MCCOY

NOT many men have been welterweight and middleweight boxing champion of the world, married nine times and still managed to spend eight years in San Quentin prison for the killing of his prospective tenth bride. Then again, there has never been anyone quite like Kid McCoy.

The Kid's real name was Norman Selby, but for most of his life he was known as Kid McCoy. He fought exactly 200 fights and lost only seven. At the turn of the century, he was one of the most famous athletes in the world. McCoy had that quality sometimes called charisma, sometimes referred to as showmanship. In any case, he definitely had magnetism in the ring *and* in the bedroom. Everybody loved the Kid, especially the ladies. McCoy stood five feet eleven inches, had wavy black hair, and in his prime never weighed over 157 pounds. Let's take a look at his pugilistic career first. We'll get to the bedroom soon enough.

In 1896, McCoy beat Tommy Ryan in fifteen brutal rounds and captured the middleweight championship of the world. A year later, he purchased a saloon in New York, which became a hangout for the sporting fraternity and actors. McCoy was so good at his profession it was difficult for him to find a worthy opponent in his own weight class. Occasionally, a promoter would stage a fight between the Kid and a heavier man. These fights accounted for the Kid's few losses. Gentleman Jim Corbett and Jack Sharkey beat McCoy. Both men outweighed McCoy by over forty pounds and both held the heavyweight championship of the world.

One day a drunk sauntered into McCoy's bar and started to verbally abuse McCoy. Someone told the drunk he'd better watch himself—he was picking on Kid McCoy, welterweight champion of the world. The drunk didn't believe he was in the presence of the champ and continued to berate McCoy. Finally, the Kid lost his patience, and with one punch knocked out the drunk. When the poor man regained consciousness, he rubbed his chin, looked up and said, "That's the real McCoy," and so coined the phrase that is still in use today to denote a genuine article.

In affairs of the heart, the Kid answered the bell nine times. All of his wives were good-looking women. Special mention goes to Julia Woodruff Crosselmire,

who had three return matches with the Kid, each ending in divorce. By 1924, the Kid had run through several fortunes and all nine marriages. The black wavy hair was now sparse and the flat-as-a-pancake midriff had developed an ever-so-slight bulge. Show-business friends from the old days obtained bit parts for him in the movies. In between acting assignments, he was a guard in an airplane factory, where he had been issued a pistol.

At the age of fifty-one, the Kid still had that old charisma when it came to the ladies. Theresa W. Mors, the wife of wealthy art and antique dealer Albert E. Mors, fell under the Kid's spell. Theresa left Albert to live with the Kid. She filed for divorce. Her husband in turn named McCoy co-respondent. On August 12, 1924, Theresa and the Kid were both hitting the bottle pretty hard. Many believe that McCoy had learned that night that Theresa had decided not to become Mrs McCoy number ten. That's when the Kid placed his .32-calibre pistol behind Theresa's left ear and shot her dead. The Kid had a few more blasts of whisky, made out his will and drove to the home of his sister, Jennie Thomas. McCoy told his sister, "I just had to kill that woman."

Next morning, McCoy was still on the prowl. He made his way to the Mors' antique store on Seventh Avenue. He walked inside, where customers William Ross, Sam Stern and V. C. Emden, a clerk, were passing the time of day. The Kid pulled out his .32 and turned on a music box. He then proceeded to wave his pistol, keeping time to the music. Suddenly, he slammed the box shut and robbed the three men of their money. Ross made a sudden motion and the Kid fired, wounding Ross in the leg. The Kid dashed for the street, where he encountered Mr and Mrs Sam Schapp, who owned the store next to the antique shop. Sam knew the Kid. He asked, "Norman, what the hell are you doing?" The Kid answered with two shots. One struck Sam, the other hit his wife. All three individuals shot that morning by McCoy recovered from their wounds. Police soon caught up with McCoy and took him into custody. At the time of his arrest, he admitted to the murder of Theresa Mors, but later changed his story, claiming that she had committed suicide.

Attorney Jerry Giesler, who would subsequently gain fame for defending Hollywood stars during their various trials and tribulations, was in the Kid's corner. Although the lawyer did the best he could, the Kid was convicted of manslaughter in the Mors affair and received from one to ten years in prison. For his early-morning shooting spree, he received two sentences of one to fourteen years and one sentence of six months' to ten years' imprisonment. The Kid was the most popular inmate in San Quentin prison. He received gifts

from all over the world. Friends such as Damon Runyon, Lionel Barrymore and Sophie Tucker stuck by him throughout his years in prison. As a result of the intervention of Henry Ford Sr., McCoy was paroled in 1932 and given employment with the Ford organization.

Kid McCoy lived on for eight years, but suffered bouts of depression from not being in the limelight. In April 1940, he swallowed a bottle of sleeping pills in a Detroit hotel room. The real McCoy was down for the count.

# THOMAS D'ARCY MCGEE

THIS is the story of the first murder in Canadian history.

Thomas D'Arcy McGee was born in 1825 in Carlingford, Ireland. At seventeen he heeded the adventurous call of the New World. He made his way to Boston, where he found work with a Catholic Irish newspaper, the *Boston Pilot*. By the time he was nineteen, he was editor of the paper. The following year, McGee returned to his homeland and became an avid foe of Great Britain's union with Ireland. He was a leading figure in the Fenian Brotherhood, an organization devoted to achieving Irish independence from England.

In 1848, McGee had to flee the country; some say he left disguised as a priest. He went once more to the United States, but moved to Canada in 1857. A year later, he was elected to the Legislative Assembly of Canada, representing Montreal West. Once in Canada, it was assumed by Irish patriots that McGee would continue to expound his Fenian sympathies, but such was not the case. McGee split with the Fenians, believing their policy of violence too extreme. In fact, he became an adversary of the Fenian Brotherhood and was considered a traitor by many sympathizers of that movement.

On the evening of April 6, 1868, exactly nine months and six days after our country officially became the Dominion of Canada, the Honourable D'Arcy McGee, one of the finest orators ever to address the House of Commons, was at his eloquent best. A little after 2 a.m., the House adjourned. McGee, accompanied by Robert MacFarlane, a fellow member of Parliament representing Perth, Ontario, left Parliament Hill. MacFarlane and McGee parted company at the corner of Metcalfe and Sparks. McGee walked towards his boarding house on the south side of Sparks Street, between Metcalfe and O'Connor.

He reached his destination, the Toronto House, at 71 Sparks St., owned and operated by Mary Ann Trotter. As was her custom, Mrs Trotter lay asleep on the cot in the dining room. She thought she heard a noise at the door. Believing it to be her son, thirteen-year-old Willie, a parliamentary page-boy, she rose to open the door. Just as she did so, she witnessed the flash of a discharging revolver and saw the form of a man fall at her doorstep. The Honourable Thomas D'Arcy McGee, one of the thirty-three Fathers of Confederation, was Canada's

first murder victim. As he had bent over to insert his key into the lock of the boarding-house door, his assailant had silently pointed a revolver at the back of his neck. The Smith and Wesson revolver roared as the bullet entered McGee's neck and exited through his mouth. He died instantly.

In the days immediately following the assassination, several men were arrested as co-conspirators in the young country's most infamous single violent act. All would eventually be exonerated and released. All except one—James Whelan.

The bewhiskered Whelan had been employed in Ottawa as a tailor since November. He had previously followed his trade in Quebec City and Montreal. When questioned within twenty-four hours of the assassination, he had a fully loaded revolver in his coat pocket. One chamber appeared to have been recently fired. Whelan was taken into custody. After a lengthy preliminary hearing, he was held over for trial.

On September 7, 1868, Whelan stood trial for the murder of the Honourable D'Arcy McGee. News of the trial dwarfed all other events in the newly formed Dominion. One of the founders of the country lay dead. His suspected killer came under microscopic examination. The prosecution attorney, James O'Reilly, contended that Whelan had attended the House of Commons on the night of the murder, leaving before McGee. He had lain in wait for his victim in a gateway and had shot McGee in front of the door of the MP's rooming house. O'Reilly claimed that the plot to kill McGee had been hatched in Montreal. He asserted that Whelan had once visited McGee's home in Montreal. On that occasion, he was met by John McGee, the victim's brother. He told John of a plot to set fire to the McGee residence. The threat was taken seriously and reported to police, although no attempt was ever made to set McGee's home on fire.

Most damaging of all, O'Reilly stated that one Jean Baptiste Lacroix had actually witnessed the shooting. To back up his contentions, O'Reilly presented strong witnesses. John McGee confirmed Whelan's early-morning visit to the McGee residence in Montreal. Detective Edward O'Neill of Ottawa testified that he had found the .32-calibre revolver in the right-hand side pocket of Whelan's coat. In the opposite pocket he recovered a box of cartridges. Although the revolver was fully loaded when confiscated, O'Neill stated that upon examination it was clear to him that the weapon had been recently fired. "I looked in the cylinder and the six chambers and I found six cartridges. Five of these cartridges looked like they'd been in there for some days. But one seemed to be put in recently." O'Neill went on to explain that one cartridge was bright, while the other five were dark and dull.

Jean Baptiste Lacroix told of walking home at the time of the murder. He saw a man at the door of the Toronto House and saw another man sneak up behind him. A shot rang out. Because the moon was full, Lacroix, from a distance of fifteen yards, saw the whole thing. When he heard the shot he stepped into the shadows. The assassin walked quickly past the witness's place of concealment and Lacroix was able to identify him. It was James Whelan. Other witnesses took the stand, claiming that at various times they had overheard Whelan threaten to kill McGee.

Whelan was defended by the Honourable John Hillyard Cameron, believed by many to be the ablest lawyer in the country. The courtroom was silent. Shy, black-haired Euphemie Lafrance, a servant at Storr's Hotel on Clarence Street, took the stand. Miss Lafrance stated that she knew Whelan. When in Ottawa, Whelan lived at the hotel. One of her duties was making up his bed. One morning she found a revolver under his mattress. She picked up the weapon and it accidentally discharged, wounding her in the area of the left elbow. She displayed her scar to the court. Miss Lafrance claimed the accident had occurred shortly before the McGee murder. This evidence effectively explained the reason for the one shiny bullet in Whelan's revolver.

Prosecution witness Lacroix's reputation was vigorously attacked. An array of tough lumberjacks who had known Lacroix for years took the stand and swore that the Crown's chief witness was a notorious liar. Their testimony had a forceful effect on the court, particularly when it was learned that Lacroix did not reveal his eyewitness account of the crime until he knew that a $20,000 reward had been offered for the apprehension and conviction of the killer.

The trial, attended by Prime Minister John A. Macdonald and his wife, lasted seven days. Whelan was found guilty. When asked if he had anything to say before sentence was passed, Whelan gave a long dissertation covering his history and the events of the night of the murder, all the while professing his innocence. He even absolved the jury for their wrong verdict, stating that based on the erroneous circumstantial evidence placed before them, he too would have reached a guilty verdict.

On Thursday, February 11, 1869, accompanied by Father John O'Connor, James Whelan walked directly to the scaffold built for his public execution. His last words were, "God save Ireland and God save my soul." Father O'Connor pressed a crucifix to the condemned man's lips. The trapdoor sprang open, the crowd gasped, and James Whelan was no more. His was the first and last public execution to take place in Canada.

A plaque commemorating D'Arcy McGee's assassination can still be seen opposite 143 Sparks St. in Ottawa.

# DENNY MCLAIN

RON Taylor toiled for years as a relief pitcher in the major leagues. In four appearances in two World Series, he held his opponents scoreless. Today, Ron Taylor is a medical doctor and is team physician to the Toronto Blue Jays.

Don Getty starred as quarterback for the Edmonton Eskimos in the fifties and sixties. After football, he successfully embarked on a political career. He went on to become premier of Alberta.

Syl Apps starred at centre ice for the Toronto Maple Leafs during their glory days of the thirties and forties. After hockey, the Leafs ex-captain became a member of the Ontario legislature for twelve years and served in the cabinet as minister of correctional services before retiring to his home in Kingston.

These men were achievers in sport and in the game of life. Unfortunately, some athletes step off the playing field and find the game of life off the baseball diamond far different. Maybe the handwriting was on the wall for Denny McLain while he was still basking in the limelight as a true sports hero. One of his old Detroit Tiger teammates, Mickey Lolich, explains, "We used to say he was either going to wind up in concrete shoes or in prison. I guess he got the latter."

Denny was first noticed by the baseball world while still a youngster pitching at Mount Carmet High School in Chicago. No wonder. He had a 38-win, 7-loss record. That same season of 1962, the Chicago White Sox gave Denny a $17,000 signing bonus and assigned him to their Harlan, Kentucky, farm club. In the minors, Denny didn't impress. His record was 5 wins and 8 losses. At the ripe old age of eighteen, Denny was just another gifted kid, one of thousands who played baseball with one dream in mind—to make the big leagues.

In 1963, Denny received what appeared to be a setback. At spring training, the White Sox had three rookie pitchers vying for a place on the team. One of the boys had signed for a larger bonus. The other had a better minor league record than McLain. Denny became expendable. He was exposed to the rookie draft which, in effect, meant that any other major league club could pick him up for $8,000. Denny was drafted by the Detroit Tigers, who shipped him to Duluth.

In Duluth, Denny displayed the magic which was to become his trademark. He chalked up a 13-win, 2-loss record. At the end of the season, he was brought up to the Tigers. Detroit pitching instructors taught fastballer McLain how to throw a change-up curve. Denny became a bona fide major leaguer, compiling records of 16-6 in 1965, 20-14 in 1966 and 17-18 in 1967. Denny's 1967 season ended on a sour note. He didn't win a game after August 29 and the Tigers lost the pennant game to the Boston Red Sox. During that time, Denny was sidelined with an injured foot, which was to raise ugly questions in the not too distant future. But all that was forgotten during the 1968 baseball season. That was Denny McLain's year. Victory after victory was savoured by Denny and the delirious Detroit fans. When it was over, he had compiled the unbelievable record of 31 wins against 6 losses and the Tigers rolled to the American League pennant.

No pitcher had won thirty games in over three decades, not since Dizzy Dean accomplished the feat in 1934. No one has won over thirty games since. Denny's achievement was one of the great sports stories of modern times. That season, baseball heaped honours on Denny. He was voted the American League's Most Valuable Player and won the Cy Young Award as Pitcher of the Year. In 1969, he was almost as invincible. He racked up a 24-9 record with a 2.80 earned run average. Once again, he received the Cy Young Award. Denny McLain had won 108 ball games. He was twenty-five, the toast of baseball and the world of sport.

Denny had become an airplane pilot, a better than average organ player and had married Sharyn Boudreau, daughter of baseball immortal Lou Boudreau. In 1970, Denny's salary was $90,000. His income from other sources, including television appearances, organ concerts and the banquet circuit, added up to another $100,000. Remember, this was back when the average U.S. salary was well under $9,000. The talented all-American hero was riding high.

The rumours began in magazine articles. They were made official by Bowie Kuhn, then commissioner of baseball. Denny McLain's off-field activities, dating back to 1967, were being investigated. It was alleged that Denny had invested in a bookmaking establishment in Flint, Michigan, in 1967. It was further alleged that the celebrated injury to his foot had been incurred by a Mafia enforcer while collecting a $46,000 gambling debt owed by McLain. While the rumours flew, it was revealed that Denny owed $2,450 in back rent on his Lakeland, Florida, home, $799 to Consumer Power Co. in unpaid bills and several months' rent on his $75,000 airplane. After a hearing before Commissioner Kuhn, baseball's brightest star was suspended from the opening day of the 1970 season until July 1, a period of two months and twenty-four days.

On July 1, Denny returned to the Tigers. Over 50,000 fans, the largest crowd to fill the Detroit stadium in nine years, cheered his appearance. The bad boy of baseball was back. He wasn't his old, sharp self, but the Tigers won the game and the multitude paid homage to their talented hero. Unfortunately, Denny couldn't stay out of trouble. In August, he poured a bucket of ice water over the heads of two Detroit sports writers. This time, his own organization suspended him for "conduct unbecoming a professional baseball player." A week later, after apologizing to the two writers, Denny was back in the Tigers' starting rotation. To gain relief from the hordes of creditors hounding him, he declared bankruptcy. It was a rough season for McLain. In September, he was suspended for the balance of the 1970 season by Commissioner Kuhn for carrying a gun.

At the conclusion of the season, Denny was reinstated, but the Detroit organization had had enough of their bad-boy star. The same day he was reinstated, he was traded to the Washington Senators. The end was in sight. That season in Washington, Denny suffered the most losses by a pitcher in the big leagues, with twenty-two defeats. He was later traded to the Oakland A's, and from Oakland to the Atlanta Braves. Then began the lonely trip to the minors.

In May 1974, thirty-year-old Denny McLain was out of shape and vastly overweight. He was signed to pitch a game for the London, Ontario, Majors against Kitchener. In typical McLain fashion, he showed up an hour before game time. Nine hundred and four fans attended the game. The majority were there to see with their own eyes the major league's last thirty-game winner. Denny received thirty dollars for his appearance. He had slid a long way down the ladder. Denny spent the next few years doing sports announcing for minor league teams. He even managed to catch on as manager of an American Association team. Nothing worked. Outside businesses failed. In 1977, Denny filed a personal bankruptcy petition for the second time. He listed debts of over one million dollars and assets of $900.

Throughout Denny's glory days and bad times, his wife, Sharyn, remained at his side. They have four children. She watched her husband deteriorate from a handsome, flamboyant sports hero to a bloated 270-pound failure. During the seventies, the sports world had had enough of Denny McLain. New heroes had taken his place, but McLain's unsuccessful battle to cope with life off the baseball diamond continued.

In 1984, Denny again made the headlines. He was indicted for racketeering, conspiracy, extortion, possession and distribution of cocaine and conspiracy to import cocaine. It was alleged that he had been involved in these activities since June 1978. In 1985, Denny was found guilty of racketeering, conspiracy, extortion and cocaine posssion. He was sentenced to twenty-three years in prison. As the sentence was passed, Sharyn McLain and her two daughters wept openly in court.

For two years, Denny McLain, forty-one, one of baseball's greatest heroes, languished in a cell at the federal penitentiary in Atlanta, Georgia, but the turbulent life of Denny McLain was to take another dramatic turn. In August 1987, the Eleventh Circuit Court of Appeals in Atlanta threw out all of McLain's convictions, citing improper conduct by both judge and prosecutor. He was released from prison.

Today, Denny McLain is a successful radio personality in Detroit, the home of his greatest athletic victories.

# SAL MINEO

LIONEL Ray Williams had been in trouble with the law from the age of fourteen when he was arrested four times within a year. The streetwise youngster probably had broken the law long before that, but had managed to escape detection. A light-complexioned black youth, Lionel had progressed from minor crime to armed robbery, and throughout his teen years was in and out of correctional facilities. At age twenty-two, he was a predator on the seamier streets of New York, rolling drunks, attacking gays and stealing from anyone who crossed his path.

In a perfect world, it is unlikely that Lionel Williams would have ever met actor Sal Mineo. Salvatore Mineo was born on January 10, 1939, in New York City. His father, a coffin maker, had a hard time supporting his large family. The Mineos lived in a rough, tough neighbourhood in the Bronx. At age nine, much to the chagrin of his mother, Josephine, Sal ran with a gang of young hoodlums. To occupy his mind and keep him off the streets, Josephine enrolled her son in dance lessons. It was a move that proved to be the future star's introduction into the entertainment industry.

As sometimes happens in the unpredictable world of show business, Sal was noticed. A Broadway producer who was looking for two Italian-American children to appear in *The Rose Tattoo* hired Sal for a small part. Sal spoke only six words in the production, but his sensitive looks made an impact. His next part was the role of the prince in *The King and I.* While still a teenager, young Sal headed for Hollywood. His first part in the movie *Six Bridges to Cross* didn't receive the acclaim afforded his next role. His outstanding performance as Plato in *Rebel Without A Cause* drew rave reviews. Together with James Dean and Natalie Wood, the boy from the Bronx was on his way. He and Dean symbolized the rebellious youth of the fifties. *Rebel Without A Cause* was followed by *Exodus,* with Paul Newman, in which Sal played terrorist Dov Landau.

During the fifties, Sal Mineo was the heart-throb of millions of young women throughout the world. He purchased a quarter-of-a-million-dollar home for his parents in the exclusive Edgewater Point section of Mamaroneck, New

York, and a luxurious home for himself in Hollywood. He had arrived. His jet-black hair, sensuous lips and sensitive face stared down from movie screens around the world. Then, for no discernible reason, this talented actor fell out of favour. His career gradually went into decline in the sixties. Parts became smaller, until finally they, too, dried up. Money was scarce. His parents sold their home in Mamaroneck. Sal moved into an apartment. Like many a movie star before him, his name was so well known he could still obtain dinner-theatre gigs, but it was a far cry from the star treatment to which he had become accustomed. Eventually, Sal could only afford an apartment off Sunset Strip, an area crawling with the dregs of society.

Early in 1976, Sal landed a job as director of a play, *P.S. Your Cat Is Dead*. The play was in rehearsal and was scheduled to open at the Westwood Playhouse. On the evening of February 13, Sal had driven home from rehearsal, had just parked his Chevelle in the carport of his West Hollywood apartment and was walking away from his vehicle, when he was stopped by a man dressed in dark clothing. A neighbour heard Sal shout, "Oh, God, no, help! Someone help." Ray Evans, a friend of Sal's, ran to the actor's aid. He quickly ascertained that Sal had been stabbed in the chest several times. Evans attempted mouth-to-mouth resuscitation, but his efforts were in vain. Within six or seven minutes, Sal was dead.

Immediately after the murder, police busily canvassed the area for clues. A few witnesses claimed that the attacker was a white man dressed in dark clothing. He had been seen leaving the scene in a small yellow car, but the descriptions were too general to be of any use. The coroner's report added little, other than stating that the stab wounds to the chest had been made by a large knife. The portion of Sal's anatomy afflicted by the wounds was kept in case the murder weapon was ever located. The skimpy information was not much to go on and eventually the investigation wound down. Several of Sal's friends tried to raise money for a reward, but could only collect a few hundred dollars. As the months passed, Sal's murder was dropped from the newspapers.

In May 1977, over a year after the murder, Los Angeles police received a tip from a most unusual source. Mrs Theresa Williams informed them that her husband, Lionel, had told her that he had killed Sal Mineo. He had arrived home on the night of the murder covered with blood and had said, "I just killed this dude in Hollywood." Lionel told his wife that he had committed the murder with a hunting knife. Police knew Lionel rather well. Shortly after Sal's murder, Lionel had been arrested for robbery. At that time, endeavouring to get a shorter jail sentence, he had volunteered that he knew something about the Mineo killing. Lionel told detectives that another man had killed Sal over a drug deal that had turned ugly. Police didn't believe Lionel for two reasons: Sal Mineo was known to have nothing to do with drugs and the killer had been described by witnesses as white. Lionel said the killer was black.

Now that Lionel had entered the web of the investigation, detectives did some sleuthing. Mrs Williams described the hunting knife her husband had had in his possession on the night of the murder. Police purchased an identical knife. The blade fit the wounds inflicted to Sal's chest. Police wanted to have a little chat with Lionel Williams. They had no trouble locating him. Lionel was serving time in a Michigan jail for issuing rubber cheques. Upon communicating with Lionel's keepers in Michigan, detectives learned that he had often bragged to guards that he had murdered Sal Mineo. He told them that he'd had no idea his victim was a famous movie actor, but when he found out, he was rather proud of his actions. Guards, who are quite accustomed to inmates either claiming they are innocent or bragging that they were the perpetrators of high-profile unsolved crimes, figured that Lionel was lying about his exploits. Now they weren't so sure. When questioned by police, Williams denied having anything to do with the murder. Strangely, he had an exact replica of the murder weapon tattooed on his arm.

Three years after Sal's murder, Lionel Williams stood trial for the killing, as well as for a series of eleven robberies in Los Angeles. His lawyer insisted that his client was innocent because Lionel was black and the killer had been described by witnesses as white. However, the prosecuting attorney produced photographs of the light-skinned Lionel taken around the time of the murder. He sported dyed auburn hair at that time. Another incriminating factor was Lionel's car, which at the time of the murder had been a yellow Dodge Colt, the same colour and type of vehicle witnesses swore they had seen leaving the crime scene. Lionel Williams was found guilty of murder in the second degree and guilty of ten of the eleven robberies. The presiding judge sentenced him to a total of fifty-one years' imprisonment.

It had been Sal Mineo's misfortune to cross paths with a human predator.

# MARILYN MONROE

NORMA Jean Mortensen, born in the charity ward of Los Angeles General Hospital on June 1, 1926—Marilyn Monroe, found dead in the bedroom of her Los Angeles home on August 5, 1962.
Family deserted by father.
Mother confined to mental institutions.
Norma Jean placed in the Los Angeles Orphans' Home.
Nine different foster families by the age of fifteen.
Marriage to Jim Dougherty, the boy next door, at age sixteen.
Divorce from Dougherty upon his return from the Merchant Marines in 1944.
Modelling jobs.
Bit parts in the movies.
Posing for a nude calendar.
Stardom in movies, such as *Gentlemen Prefer Blondes, The Seven Year Itch, Bus Stop* and *Some Like It Hot*.
Marriages to former baseball superstar Joe DiMaggio and playwright Arthur Miller.
Rumoured affair with Robert Kennedy, then attorney-general of the United States.
Suddenly, tragically, one of the most publicized women in the world found dead in the summer of 1962. She was thirty-six.

The circumstances surrounding the death of Marilyn Monroe have always been an enigma. There are those who state that there is no mystery at all. They flatly claim that Marilyn Monroe was murdered. Their arguments were so strong, so convincing, that the district attorney's office in Los Angeles reopened the investigation into her death.

Robert F. Slatzer, a Hollywood writer-producer, knew Marilyn intimately during the last sixteen years of her life. In fact, Slatzer contends that one weekend in 1952, he and Marilyn were married in Tijuana, Mexico. Immediately after the marriage, Marilyn had misgivings about the wisdom of their actions. When they returned to Los Angeles after the civil ceremony, Darryl F. Zanuck of Twentieth Century Fox was furious with Marilyn. He ordered her to have the secret marriage annulled immediately. Slatzer says that Zanuck explained that the studio was pouring a fortune into building Marilyn up as a sex goddess. Marriage was out of the question.

As Slatzer explains it, the lawyer who performed the ceremony in one of Tijuana's marriage mills was required by law to register the marriage within forty-eight hours. The cost of the registration to the lawyer was a few dollars. Mexican lawyers often neglected to register marriages, pocketing the money instead. After all, no one ever checked. A quickie trip to Mexico and a payment of fifty dollars to the lawyer was all that was required for the documents to be returned to Slatzer and destroyed. No official documentation of this marriage exists. In order to have the marriage performed, Slatzer had required a witness. Quite by accident, he bumped into Noble "Kid" Chissell in Tijuana that weekend. Chissell, a former U.S. navy boxing champ and part-time actor, knew Marilyn and Slatzer well. He was happy to act as a witness and is the only other person who could verify that the marriage had taken place. Years ago, I was able to track down Chissell, who was seventy-seven years old at the time. He corroborated Slatzer's story of his marriage to Marilyn Monroe so many years before. He said to me, "I have no earthly reason to lie about such a thing."

From the day of Marilyn's death, Slatzer strongly suspected that the official cause of death—"probable suicide"—was incorrect. For years, he independently gathered official documents and professional opinions until the case he developed pointing to murder is stronger than the official suicide theory. Yet no one would listen to Slatzer. No one wanted to listen. After years of frustration, Slatzer took his story to Nick Harris Detectives Inc., where he shared his information with Milo Speriglio, who heads the firm. The Harris organization is no fly-by-night outfit. It is a respected company, in business for over ninety-one years, making it the second oldest private investigative firm in the United States. At any given time the agency has had as many as 200 operatives in the field. Speriglio has been associated with the firm for years.

Initially, Speriglio explained to me, he was dubious about Slatzer's story. "Frankly, I thought he was another kook, until I began confirming his claims. It has taken years, but each and every fact stated by Slatzer that can possibly be authenticated has been proven. It has taken me ten years and is the longest investigation in our company's history, but I'm convinced Marilyn Monroe was murdered."

On the night of the tragedy, Marilyn's housekeeper, Mrs Eunice Murray, called psychiatrist Dr Ralph Greenson. She told Marilyn's psychiatrist that the door to the actress's bedroom was locked. She could see the light shining under the door and was alarmed. The doctor advised her to pound on the door again, look in the bedroom window and call him back. Mrs Murray did so without getting any response. She again called Dr Greenson and told him that Marilyn looked funny. He urged her to call Marilyn's physician, Dr Hyman Engelberg, then departed immediately for Marilyn's home. Upon arriving at 12305 Fifth Helena Dr. in Brentwood, Dr Greenson used a poker to break a window pane and climbed into Marilyn's bedroom. The blond actress was lying nude in her bed, the telephone receiver clutched in her hand. In a few moments, Dr Engelberg arrived. It was he who called the police.

Sgt. Jack Clemmons of the Los Angeles Police Department, the first officer at the scene, was later to provide the information contained in the Coroner's Case Report. He could not fill in the square provided for suicide. Instead, he placed a question mark after the word *suicide*. Clemmons thought something was wrong. Although there were several capsule containers on Marilyn's night table, there was no glass and no sign that the victim had taken capsules orally. Friends of Marilyn's were to state that the actress found it difficult to swallow an aspirin without water. Was it natural for her to take an overdose of several dozen pills without water? More remote still, would she have cleaned a glass and put it away after taking a lethal dose of barbiturates?

There was no sign of anything out of place in the death room. Experienced officers such as Clemmons are accustomed to seeing overdose suicide victims. They die twisted and contorted. Marilyn's body lay peacefully reposed, as if placed in the position where it was found. Inexplicably, there was no vomit in evidence, as is usual in overdose suicide cases. Those who knew Marilyn and had been in touch with her shortly before her death couldn't believe she had killed herself. She had just purchased new clothing and new Mexican-style furniture for her home. She was elated at having been reinstated by her studio.

Then came the autopsy, performed by Dr Thomas Noguchi, at that time deputy medical examiner. Dr Noguchi was later to become chief medical examiner of Los Angeles and would gain fame as the "coroner to the stars," having performed autopsies on William Holden and Natalie Wood. Dr Noguchi was eventually relieved of his position because of irregularities in the conduct of his office. The autopsy seemed to satisfy all doubts. An analysis of Marilyn's blood indicated a high drug level—4.5 mg of barbiturate and 8.0 percent of chloral hydrate. This finding was compatible with the initial police investigation at the scene. It appeared that Marilyn had ingested forty-seven Nembutol capsules.

Dr Greenson informed police that he had prescribed fifty such capsules a few days before her death. The empty Nembutol container was found on Marilyn's night table. Unbelievably, Dr Noguchi's autopsy report, under the heading Digestive System, states, "The stomach is almost completely empty. No residue of the pills is noted." What does this mean? Somehow, Marilyn's bloodstream contained the equivalent of forty-seven Nembutol capsules, yet her stomach contained no evidence of the pills, which certainly would have been the case had she taken the Nembutol capsules orally.

How, then, did she die?

Several experts have been asked to comment on the conflicting aspects of Dr Noguchi's autopsy, the most prominent being Dr Sidney B. Weinberg, chief medical examiner of Suffolk County, New York. Dr. Weinberg is considered a world authority in this field. His report, issued in response to a request by Robert Slatzer, runs to over five pages of single-spaced type. Some excerpts are most revealing: "It would appear from the toxicology reports that specimens of blood, kidney, liver, stomach, urine, and intestines were submitted for analysis. The results of this examination revealed a level 4.5 mg percent barbiturates in the blood and 8.0 percent of chloral hydrate in the blood. Since there are no findings of these drugs in the stomach, and since numerous capsules and tablets of prescription drugs were found at the scene, all of the type which are ingestible, it is difficult to conceive that some trace of these drugs would not be found in the stomach or intestinal tract." In another portion of his report, Dr Weinberg states, "A description of the stomach contents estimated the volume to be no more than 20 cc, which is less than one ounce, and that 'no residue of the pills is noted.' These findings are certainly not characteristic of an oral ingestion of large amounts of barbiturates."

The fact of the matter is Marilyn couldn't have taken the pills orally. How did the drugs get into her bloodstream? The obvious answer is by injection, which leads us to another question. Did Marilyn inject herself, or was the injection administered against her will? Again we turn to Dr Noguchi's autopsy report. A bruised left hip was noted, but not described as the entry site of an injection. Yet, as Dr Weinberg points out, "This bruise is in a positon consistent with the location of an injection site. Injection sites can easily be missed unless one suspects and carefully looks for same."

It is within the realm of possibility, and indeed more compatible with the physical evidence, that Marilyn died as the result of an injection rather than by taking pills orally. She was right-handed. The bruise indicated in the autopsy report is on the left hip, an unnatural and awkward entry site for a right-handed person to inject themselves. (Take a pencil and simulate giving yourself an injection in the back of your left thigh with your right hand. It is a difficult manoeuvre.) We must conclude that it is certainly possible that someone gave Marilyn Monroe a fatal injection, rearranged her body, emptied a Nembutol container simulating suicide and succeeded in leaving her home without being seen by Mrs Murray, her housekeeper. Who would do such a thing? Who had anything to gain by Marilyn's death?

To find the answer, I walked along Hollywood Boulevard, stepping over the brass engraved names of Hollywood stars, until I came to the legendary corner of Hollywood and Vine. Here, Robert Slatzer retains his independent producer's office behind unmarked doors. It was here that he told me of Marilyn's rumoured affair with Robert Kennedy, then attorney-general of the United States. He swears that Marilyn told him many times that Kennedy loved to talk politics with her, although she understood little, and retained less, of what the attorney-general passed along. Slatzer alleges that because Kennedy chided her at her lack of memory, Marilyn made notes of their conversations in a red diary so she would remember the details. Slatzer states that the diary contained details of a plot to assassinate Cuba's Fidel Castro. Fantastic as it may sound, the existence of such a plot was confirmed by Senator Frank Church of Idaho in 1975 during the course of an investigation by the Senate into illegal acts by U.S. intelligence. Marilyn also told Slatzer that Kennedy had promised her that he would leave his wife and family to marry her. Finally, Marilyn told Slatzer that Kennedy had abruptly terminated their affair. She was furious and told several acquaintances that she had a good mind to reveal the contents of her diary. Of course, we have no concrete proof that the conversations between Slatzer and Marilyn actually took place. However, Slatzer has since subjected himself to a lie detector test, the results of which indicate he is telling the truth.

As a second point of verification, I was able to meet and question Lionel Grandison, who, at the time of Marilyn's death, was a deputy coroner's aide in the office of the Los Angeles coroner. He stated that Marilyn's diary and what he believes may have been a suicide note were placed in the coroner's safe, but were missing when the safe was opened the following morning. It is his opinion that the suicide note was a plant. Both the note and diary have never been seen since.

Grandison told me that he didn't read the diary, but did glance through it, looking for the name of Marilyn's next of kin. He distinctly remembered seeing the words *Robert Kennedy, Fidel Castro* and *CIA*. Grandison pointed out that one of his duties in the coroner's office was to see that all documentation was in order. At the time, he was amazed that documents and forms pertaining to Marilyn's death were constantly being altered. Suspicious, he told his superior, then county coroner Theodore Curphey, that he was reluctant to sign the death certificate. Curphey replied in no uncertain terms, "Sign it." It was Grandison's impression that had he not signed the cetificate, he would have lost his job. He explained, "I was twenty-two, had a wife and children and was taking night classes." Grandison signed the death certificate and Marilyn Monroe became an official "probable suicide."

Some of these partially corroborated facts and suppositions are hard to believe. Is it possible that the CIA orchestrated the death of Marilyn Monroe to ensure her silence? Before such an observation is scoffed at as absurd, I must inform you that I have in my possession a photostatic copy of a letter from the U.S. Department of Justice, Office of the Associate Attorney General, in response to a request for information concerning Marilyn Monroe's death. This letter states:

> Certain of the material pertaining to Ms. Monroe is classified and I am affirming the denial of access to it on the basis of 5USC 552(b)(1). The Department Review Committee has determined that this material warrants continued classification under Executive Order 12065. These provisions pertain to materials the release of which would constitute a clearly unwarranted invasion of the personal privacy of a third party and to investigatory records compiled for law enforcement purposes, the release of which would, respectively, constitute an unwarranted invasion of the personal privacy of third parties and disclose the identities of confidential sources. None of the information being withheld is appropriate for discretionary release.

The government of the United States chooses to protect someone's identity. What earthly reason could the Justice Department have for not revealing any and all materials pertaining to a movie actress dead these past thirty-five years?

Obviously, someone has something to hide.

# CANDY MOSSLER

IT has been said that no millionaire has ever been executed in the United States. Candy Mossler almost became the exception to the rule.

Born Candace Weatherby in Buchanan, Georgia, in 1919, she was the sixth of ten children. Her father was a not-too-prosperous rancher. At the age of nine, she was crippled with polio. The dread disease left Candy with one leg completely paralysed. For five years, her brothers carried her to school on their backs. By diligently exercising the leg, she was able to walk again by the time she was fourteen. Everyone agreed that Candy was a bright, beautiful child who was soon to blossom into an extremely attractive young lady.

Candy left school in Grade 11 to marry Norman Johnson, a civil engineer. The young couple had two children, Norman Jr. and Rita. Although they later divorced, they remained good friends. After the split-up, Candy went to New York, where she became a successful model. By 1949, she was in business for herself, profitably running the Candace Finishing School, the Candace Modelling School and the Candace Model Agency.

With success came the resources and ability to take part in charitable causes. It was while soliciting funds for worthy causes that she met Jacques Mossler, who had just lost half of his fortune through a divorce. He had four children and four finance companies. Jacques was down to his last million when he met Candy. He fell hard for the blond beauty. Despite being over twenty years her senior, he married Candy on May 24, 1949, in Fort Lauderdale, Florida.

The Mosslers were devoted to each other, worked hard at the finance business and branched out into banking and insurance. The money poured in, and they became multi-millionaires. In 1957, they made national news when they adopted four children at one time. In Chicago, a psychopathic war veteran had run amok, killing his wife and baby. The remaining four children—Martha, six, Dan, five, Chris, three, and Eddie, two—were adopted by the Mosslers.

The Mosslers and their ten children lived like kings. Their home in Houston was a twenty-eight-room mansion with rolling formal gardens and an Olympic-size swimming pool. Candy received $7,500 a month to run the household, except when there was a birthday or party in the family. Then she usually received an extra $5,000 for incidentals. At this time, the Mossler empire included the American National Bank of South Bend, Indiana; the First National Bank of Coral Gables, Florida; the Mutual Bank of Chicago; and the Central Bank and Trust Co. of Miami. A further thirty-five companies were controlled by a holding company—the Mossler Acceptance Corp. We needn't go into the Mossler's vast real estate and property holdings. Suffice it to say, they were loaded.

In 1961, Mossler gave a job to Candy's nephew, Melvin Powers, the son of one of her older sisters. By 1962, Mel was living with the family in the mansion in Houston. It was around this time that the warm relationship between Candy and her husband began to cool. Candy was the first to hint that she thought her husband had acquired homosexual tendencies. Still, to all appearances, they had an ideal marriage. In June 1963, Mossler fired Mel Powers and had him removed from his home in Houston. Harsh words were exchanged between Mossler and Powers.

Because of the convenience and his mounting business interests, Mossler rented an apartment on Key Biscayne, Florida in May 1964. The family soon joined him. In the early-morning hours of June 30, tragedy descended on the Mossler clan. Candy was suffering from a migraine. She piled her four children into her car and drove to Miami's Jackson Memorial Hospital at about one-thirty in the morning. This may seem like strange behaviour, but the family had taken many such excursions in the middle of the night. They lingered, buying stamps and mailing letters on the way to the hospital. Candy received treatment at the hospital and arrived home at about 4:30 a.m. She and the children found Jacques Mossler lying on the living-room floor with a head wound and thirty-nine stab wounds over his body.

The police ascertained from people who lived in the same apartment building that Mossler's killer had sped away in a white 1960 Chev, which had been parked beside the building. The car was later found in the Miami Airport parking lot and was traced back to Candy. It seems she was accustomed to borrowing a car anytime she wanted from one of her husband's finance companies. Candy had actually taken delivery of the car days before the murder and had delivered it to Mel Powers at Miami Airport. As soon as the police got a line on Powers, other revealing tidbits came to light. Witnesses were found who told of a torrid affair taking place between Candy and her nephew over the past several years. Police also found out that Powers had flown from Houston to Miami the day before the murder.

Because of the wealth and celebrity of those involved, the sensational case was covered extensively by the press. It wasn't until January 17, 1966, that Candy and Mel stood trial for the murder of Jacques Mossler. During the trial, four different criminals testified that Powers and Candy offered them the contract to kill Mossler. All flatly refused, except one, who testified that he had accepted $7,500 in advance. He claimed to have spent the money without ever going through with the scheme.

The prosecution came up with Powers's palm print, lifted from the Formica counter in the Mossler apartment. A handyman testified that he had washed down the counter on the afternoon preceding the murder. Thus Powers was placed in the apartment close to the time of the tragedy. Perhaps the most damaging evidence came from the witness who told of Powers bragging about his sexual prowess with Candy. This evidence was given in detail from the witness stand and caused a hum in the courtroom. The underlying motive of the whole crime was attributed to sex.

Famous defence lawyer Percy Foreman of Texas tried to establish that there were scores of men who, for business reasons, wanted Mossler out of the way. The defence also made light of the affair between Candy and Powers, proving that on many occasions Candy's children accompanied her and Powers on supposedly illicit trips. Foreman pressed home the fact that all the evidence was circumstantial. There were no witnesses to the crime. An all-male jury brought in the surprise verdict of not guilty. Candy and her nephew walked out of court into the Florida sunshine.

Despite her wealth, tragedy continued to stalk the attractive blonde. In 1971, she married again. This time, the groom was Barnett Garrison, an electrical contractor. About a year after the marriage, he fell off the roof of their home in Houston and was seriously injured. Candy divorced him and he remains a semi-invalid to this day.

On October 25, 1976, Candy flew to Florida to attend the monthly meeting of the Central National Bank, which she controlled. The next day, she didn't appear for breakfast. When she failed to respond to phone calls, officials of the Fountainbleu Hotel decided to investigate. They found her dead in her bed. She had apparently passed away peacefully in her sleep.

Melvin Powers became a successful real estate developer in Houston, Texas.

# SIR HARRY OAKES

SIR Harry Oakes was an enigma, beloved by some, despised by others. He was unique in the history of mining, a prospector who ended up owning his own gold mine—not an easy feat.

Harry was born on December 23, 1874, in Sangerville, Maine, and attended Syracuse Medical School for two years. So much for the legend of the uneducated oaf who struck it rich. After leaving school, he prospected for gold all over the world, seeking the elusive metal in the Klondike, Australia, California, the Belgian Congo and back to the Klondike.

In 1896, Dawson City was larger than Winnipeg and Vancouver. Gold was the lure that enticed 30,000 souls to the isolated city. Prostitutes plied their wares in exchange for gold nuggets. Men who couldn't afford a loaf of bread one day were rich the next. Others were bilked out of mines worth a fortune for a few hundred dollars. Harry Oakes was above the frivolous action. He worked long and hard in his quest for gold, but the Klondike never gave up its riches to Harry Oakes.

Harry heard rumours about gold around Swastika, Ontario. He had his doubts. Gold in worthwhile quantities had never been found in Ontario. Nevertheless, he pulled up stakes in the Klondike and tried his luck at yet another location.

In 1911, Harry, with exactly $2.65 in his pocket, was refused credit to purchase the essentials necessary for him to stake out claims in the bush near Kirkland Lake. The claims had been haphazardly worked earlier, but since they hadn't been worked the mandatory forty days a year, they were due to fall open. Harry now felt sure there was gold just waiting to be found, but he couldn't raise the funds he needed to stake the claims. That's when he met Tom and George Tough, two prospectors looking for action. Harry cooked a deal. The brothers Tough would finance the trip in return for half of anything found. The claims were staked and the Tough-Oakes Mine came into existence. Within months, gold was found. Harry, with a singleness of purpose, attempted to obtain financing in order to develop his own mine. He found it more difficult raising funds than it had been to find gold in the first place.

Harry kept on prospecting on his own, employing one man, miner Ernie Martin, to tend his claims when he headed south in his ongoing search for funds.

When Harry returned after one such trip, he found Ernie jumping with joy. They had struck gold. Harry was ecstatic. His strike would prove to be second only to the Homestead Mine in Dakota, the largest in the western hemisphere. Harry incorporated his new find under the name Lakeshore Mines Ltd. and went about issuing shares. Meanwhile, he sold his share of Tough-Oakes for $200,000. Selling shares in his new mine was no easy task. He had two million shares issued at one dollar par value. No one wanted them. It didn't seem possible that a discovery as large as Harry's had been made in Ontario. Harry tried to lure some well-known financial heavyweights to invest. Sir Henry Pellatt turned him down flat. Sir Henry should have reconsidered. Pellatt went on to build Toronto's Casa Loma and went broke in the process. Charlie Chow, who ran a rough tough eaterie in Kirkland Lake, accepted Harry's shares at fifty cents each for food and drink. Each one of Charlie's shares would one day be worth $84.

During the First World War, Harry continued to develop his mine by the seat of his pants. When he hit number-two vein, which yielded $80 of gold per ton, he knew the hard times were over. No one could deny gold had been found in Ontario. A special train left Buffalo full of financiers who wanted to see the mine for themselves. Harry, ill at ease in a store-bought suit, made the trip with them. The financiers purchased half a million shares at thirty-two and a half cents per share. Each one of these shares would also one day be worth $84. By 1921, Harry Oakes had brought in the second largest gold mine in the western hemisphere. He had designed every building on his property and had retained over 50 percent of his discovery. He had won every court battle over ownership of the mine and he had done it all without breaking a promise or reneging on a deal. He was also a multimillionaire, soon to become the richest man in the country.

While on a world cruise, Harry met genteel Eunice MacIntyre. They say opposites attract, and that was never truer than in the case of Harry and Eunice. Rough Harry had spent years in the bush. His manners left something to be desired. By contrast, Eunice was a lady through and through. Harry built a fine chateau in Kirkland Lake and another home in Niagara Falls, complete with his own private airport. He loved to look over the Niagara River, perhaps contemplating the turn of fortune which had seen him rise from a man with $2.65 in his pocket to one who was lord and master of Oak Hall. Those around Niagara Falls who still remember Harry speak fondly of him. He had a large staff and was, from all accounts, pleasant and fair to them. He gave generous gifts of land to the community, and today you can walk in formal gardens donated by Harry.

In 1930, when the Bennett Conservatives came to power in Canada, they taxed Harry $250,000 on gifts he had given the country. Taxes on Lakeshore Mines rose to 85 percent. Harry was fit to be tied. He felt that laws were being enacted specifically to claw away at his wealth. When he learned that there was no income tax in the Bahamas, he moved there with his family. Once in Nassau, Harry didn't waste any time purchasing one of the largest homes on the island. The man who used to work until his hands bled now mixed with high society. Harry's closest friend on the island was Harold Christie, whose main aim was to develop tourism in the Bahamas. By 1939, Harry and Eunice had five children—Nancy, Sidney, Pitt, Harry and Shirley. The war in Europe seemed very far away; it didn't affect the social set in the Bahamas one little bit. Harry gave so generously to British charities that he was knighted, taking on the title of Sir Harry Oakes.

The island was home to one couple every bit as illustrious as the Oakeses. Winston Churchill, prime minister of England, had decided to stash the Duke and Duchess of Windsor in the Bahamas. The Duke, who had well-publicized Nazi leanings, was an embarrassment to the British government. More to get him out of the way than anything else, Churchill appointed him governor of the island. Duchess Wally hated the place from the first day she landed. Still, the former King of England could have found himself in a more disagreeable place than a safe tropical island in which to eat, drink and golf the war away.

In May 1942, Harry's eighteen-year-old daughter Nancy slipped away with thirty-two-year-old playboy Alfred de Marigny to New York, where they were married. Alfred was tall, slim and twice divorced. He was an expert yachtsman and a womanizer of monumental proportions. The couple returned to the Bahamas where Alfred was relatively successful in business. One thing bugged Sir Harry. His new son-in-law didn't seem to want a penny from him. Besides, he and Nancy appeared to be extremely happy. Harry just couldn't cotton to the suave de Marigny.

On the night of July 7, 1943, events were to unfold which would make headlines around the world. That evening, Sir Harry played a game of tennis with his friend Harold Christie. The game was followed by cocktails with friends, who left by 11 p.m. A tropical storm was threatening, so it was decided that Christie would sleep over at Sir Harry's. Both men retired to their respective bedrooms. That same night, de Marigny held a dinner party for eleven guests. Nancy was in the States with her mother. As the night wore on, the storm broke. The last two guests remaining at the de Marigny residence,

Mrs Dorothy Clark and Mrs Jean Ainslie, wives of RCAF officers stationed on the island, were offered a lift home by Alfred. He proceeded to drop them off at their homes on the other side of the Oakes' estate, returning home alone.

The thunder and lightning storm lit up the sky. Sir Harry Oakes parked his Lincoln Continental and prepared to slip under mosquito netting with his newspaper. While he was still out of bed someone gained entrance to his room. The intruder rained four blows to Sir Harry's skull, killing him instantly. He poured gasoline onto the bed, placed Harry on top and set both bed and body on fire. Two bedrooms away, Harold Christie heard nothing. The intruder exited by way of a balcony window, leaving it open. Wind gusting furiously through the open window, extinguished the flames. Feathers from the burning mattress fluttered into the air and came to rest on Sir Harry's body. Early next morning, Harold Christie awoke. Barefoot and dishevelled, he made his way to his host's room and discovered Harry's body.

It fell to the Duke of Windsor to do something about the murder of the Bahamas' most illustrious citizen. He could have called on Scotland Yard. After all, the Bahamas was a British colony. He could even have elicited aid from the RCMP. Sir Harry was a Canadian citizen. Instead, the inept governor called Miami and two very ordinary detectives were sent over to conduct the investigation. They proceeded to contaminate the murder scene, making identification of pertinent fingerprints impossible. The two detectives, Edward Melchen and James Barker of the Miami police, quickly learned of de Marigny's rather turbulent relationship with Sir Harry. They homed in on him as a prime suspect, to the exclusion of anyone else. When they discovered that he had driven by the Oakes' estate at the time when the crime may have taken place, they arrested de Marigny and charged him with the murder of Sir Harry Oakes.

Alfred de Marigny was acquitted of the murder. Later, he took a lie detector test under the strictest of conditions. The test indicated that he had no guilty knowledge of the crime.

Some years ago, I interviewed the then eighty-year-old Alfred de Marigny in Toronto. He told me it was all like a bad dream. Everyone assumed he was guilty; everyone except his wife, Nancy, who stood by him thoughout the trial. He still has a soft spot in his heart for Nancy, even though they were divorced about two years after his trial.

It has been over fifty years since the murder. To this day, the murder of Sir Harry Oakes remains unsolved.

# ALEXANDER PANTAGES

ALEXANDER Pantages had kicked around the world as a sailor before striking out for gold in the Yukon at the turn of the century. Born in Greece, the young man received little education. Although he could neither read nor write, he did not find this to be a drawback in the rough tough Yukon. Here, the twenty-six-year-old found hordes of miners who had nothing to do after freeze-up but spend money on amusing themselves.

Alex was fascinated by the world of entertainment. He shunned pick and shovel for a job as a waiter in the Dawson Opera House. Soon he felt he knew enough to venture forth on his own. Together with two acquaintances, he opened a dance hall. It is believed that Kate Rockwell, better known as the Belle of Dawson, backed Alex in this venture. The dance hall prospered. Alex sold out his interest in 1901 and headed south to Seattle.

For the first time in his life, Alex saw people going into a moving-picture show, and immediately saw dollar signs. He decided to buy the theatre. Later, he explained, "They all thought I was a Klondike millionaire. I didn't argue with them. I just let them think so and bought the moving-picture house."

Alex spent $35,000, a princely sum in those days, to renovate the theatre. He was the first to combine vaudeville with motion pictures. Customers flocked to the spruced-up theatre. Alex purchased more theatres and became a wealthy, powerful entertainment-industry mogul.

Pantages wasn't alone in the industry. Competitors sprung up, including the well-financed Orpheum chain. Joe Kennedy of Boston had invested heavily in FBO Pictures and in Orpheum Theatres. The war between Pantages and Orpheum would last fifteen years. By paying acts the highest possible fees and making showplaces of his theatres, Alex came out of the war on top. Kennedy, who got his start in bootlegging, turned legit in shipbuilding and banking, but never could break through into the number-one position in the entertainment business. He did, however, sire a U.S. senator, an attorney-general and the thirty-fifth president of the United States.

By 1929, Alex Pantages owned sixty theatres in the United States. Vaudeville players realized that the road to stardom lay in being booked to perform on the Pantages circuit.

It is estimated that Alex was worth between fifteen and thirty million dollars. Now, folks, let's go back to the days when hot dogs were a nickel. That kind of money, before taxes and inflation, translates to approximately $600 million today.

In 1929, Alex Pantages was a slim, slight man, who had all the money he could ever spend. Alex's only weakness was a well-turned ankle. In his position, he had the pick of the most beautiful women in the world. Alex may have missed one or two. On August 9, 1929, at precisely four o'clock in the afternoon, seventeen-year-old Eunice Pringle ran out of the Pantages Theatre in Los Angeles screaming to high heaven, "Don't let him get at me." A traffic cop accompanied Eunice back to the theatre in time to see Alex coming out of his mezzanine office, his clothes crumpled and wrinkled. Eunice pointed a finger and yelled, "There he is, the beast!" All Pantages could do was shout, "She's trying to frame me." The shouting was loud enough to disturb the theatre audience, who had been engrossed in a movie aptly entitled *Why Be Good*.

Eunice, an athletic high school dropout, claimed Alex had raped her. Pantages, on the other hand, stated that the teenager had purchased a ticket for the matinée and had entered his office uninvited. She had flung herself at him, pulling off his suspenders, pulling up his shirt and yanking down his pants.

Alex Pantages was charged with forcible rape and so had the dubious distinction of being the richest man ever charged with that crime in the state of California. The trial was a sensation.

Eunice showed up in pigtails, wearing a blue dress with Dutch cuffs. She wore black shoes which matched her little black purse perfectly. Eunice looked like a healthy twelve-year-old who planned on joining the Sisters of Perpetual Innocence at her first opportunity. According to Eunice, the accused told her she was beautiful. He wanted her to be his true love. Eunice explained that she was an aspiring dancer and had been after Pantages to book her act. On August 9, she had been invited to his private office. The leech kissed her hand, then her neck, then her shoulder. There was little doubt in Eunice's mind where Alex was proceeding. Suddenly, he threw her to the floor, pulled her clothes from her body and then... "I don't know what happened," Eunice said from the witness stand. "I fainted." You could hear a pin drop in the courtroom. This was better than anything playing at the Pantages.

Alex took the witness stand in his own defence. He said he had turned down Eunice's dance act because he thought it was too sexy. He went on to say that some of the most desirable women on the planet would give their eye-teeth to bestow their sexual favours upon him. Pantages had hired young Jerry Giesler, later to become famous as the "lawyer to the stars." Giesler established that Eunice could cry on cue. However, he made a tactical error when he requested that Eunice appear in court in exactly the same clothing she had worn on the day the alleged rape took place.

Next day, Eunice was a sensation, decked out in a low-cut red dress which revealed for one and all that she was a well stacked seventeen-year-old who had no notion of joining those nuns down at the Innocence organization. The jury took one look at the new Eunice and could now understand perfectly well how the little Greek millionaire had lost his cool. Alex was found guilty of forcible rape and sentenced to from one to fifty years in San Quentin prison. Giesler appealed and Alex was freed on $100,000 bail. The appeal was successful and a new trial ordered.

At the second trial, Jerry Giesler established precedents that have only recently been partially modified in California. For the first time, an under-age victim was forced to reveal details of her prior sex life. It was established that Eunice, no virginal innocent, and her agent, had for some time been living as husband and wife. Moreover, at the time of the alleged forcible rape, Eunice was an athletic, well-conditioned 115 pounds; Pantages, at fifty-seven years of age, weighed in at 128 pounds. Eunice worked out twice a week; Alex worked out only with starlets—enjoyable exercise, but not designed to keep one in peak physical condition. Giesler asked the jury to consider how this little man could keep his right hand over Eunice's mouth and, with his left hand, undress her as well as himself, keeping in mind that Eunice was allegedly kicking and scratching all the time. Immediately after the incident, Alex didn't have a scratch on him.

Alex Pantages was acquitted. Years later, on her deathbed, Eunice Pringle confessed that the entire scheme had been Joe Kennedy's idea. He had promised to make her his star performer if she went through with the phoney rape charge and destroyed Pantages.

# CHARLES WILLIAM POST

WHEN Charles William Post tired of the healing business, he found solace in puttering around his barn with a batch of liquid cereal. At the time, old C.W. had no way of knowing that the runny liquid swishing and churning in his vat would become his very first commercial product, Postum. In the years to come, his company, at the outset known as the Postum Co. Ltd. of Battle Creek, Michigan, would merge, amalgamate and purchase other organizations until it achieved its present giant status. Today we know the whole kit and kaboodle as General Foods, one of the largest food processing corporations in the world. And to think C.W. started the whole thing back in that little white barn.

Post was born in 1854 in Springfield, Illinois. He gravitated to Battle Creek, Michigan, where by 1893, he was running a sanitorium called the La Vita Inn. C.W. had some strange ideas about treating the afflicted. He felt that all physical ailments stemmed from something he called mental conditions of inharmony. If you thought good thoughts, preached C.W., you could clear up such illnesses as rheumatism, heart disease and cancer. His sanitorium flourished. For two years, Post played around in his barn endeavouring to produce a wholesome, nourishing cereal. On New Year's Day 1895, C.W. managed to manufacture his first commercial batch of Postum. Within a year, Postum Co. Ltd. was profitable and growing. Sales were of a cyclical nature, always peaking in winter and dropping drastically in summer. To balance sales, C.W. came up with another winner—Grape Nuts.

By 1905, colourful, dynamic C. W. Post was at the helm of an expanding multimillion-dollar organization. A great believer in advertising, he spent a million dollars a year extolling the benefits of Postum and Grape Nuts. *Extolling* is too mild a word. C.W. ran contests offering prizes and cash for testimonial letters. These same letters, received by the hundreds of thousands, would be culled for the very best. Sometimes they would even be rewritten then reproduced in ads as bona fide testimonials.

Perhaps because of his background in the healing business, C.W.'s newspaper and magazine advertising leaned heavily on the health angle. Here is an example: "Drop coffee and adopt the food and drink known beyond doubt or question to be the best adopted for the forces to take up and make healthy brain, nerve, and other tissue. Postum and Grape Nuts will prove their solid worth and inestimable value in rebuilding the body if steadily used and the improvement can generally be noticed in a week's time." If this isn't heady enough, take a look at a few more. One ad stated that a loose tooth would tighten right up when Grape Nuts were consumed. Another presented Grape Nuts as "The Stuff That Brains Are Made Of." One dandy ad stated that Grape Nuts was "stronger than meat." And then there was the grandaddy of them all: "It is a practical certainty that when a man has approaching symptoms of appendicitis the attack can be avoided by discontinuing all food except Grape Nuts, and by properly washing out the intestines."

Coincidentally, at the time C.W. was spreading the word, *Collier's* magazine was on something of a crusade exposing false and misleading advertising. The company was running a series of articles attacking misleading advertising, particularly those patent medicines that went much too far in claiming miraculous cures. To add substance to the articles, *Collier's* announced in their own magazine that they would not accept ads making obvious false claims and promises.

Whoever it is up there controlling destiny saw fit to place one of C.W.'s outrageous testimonial-letter ads claiming improvement of nervousness and a heart condition due to the consumption of Grape Nuts right next to *Collier's* high-sounding announcement. It took about five minutes for some busybody to point out the inconsistency to executives at *Collier's*. As a result, their advertising manager, Conde Nast, wrote to the Post advertising agency, Grandin Co., advising them that the testimonial ad claiming improvement of nervousness and a heart condition was not acceptable. He also informed them that since the display ads placed by Post in *Collier's* did not make any medical claims, they would be accepted by the magazine. C.W. hit the roof. He stated that *Collier's* had made up an excuse in order to force him to take out the more expensive display ads. Despite this, a scorching editorial appeared in the July 27, 1907, issue of *Collier's*. Grape Nuts was named as a product which claimed to be responsible for preventing appendicitis. The same editorial branded this claim as a lie.

C. W. Post fought back. In scores of papers throughout New York State, he ran advertisements openly attacking the editors of *Collier's* for downgrading his products through their editorial columns. He publicly stated that the attack was a concerted effort to force him to take out display ads in *Collier's*. In fact, C.W. was screaming blackmail. *Collier's* counter-attacked by suing the Postum Co.

in the amount of $250,000 for libel. The libel trial began on November 22, 1910. It was a dandy. C.W. alternately squirmed and basked in glory as he held forth from the witness stand. Maybe he squirmed more than he basked. During the trial it was established that the testimonial letters in Post ads were solicited. Reputable medical authorities stated that neither Grape Nuts or Postum could prevent appendicitis. The products were analysed. Postum was made of roasted and ground bran, wheat and molasses. Grape Nuts contained wheat, barley, salt and yeast.

After several hours' deliberation, the jury awarded *Collier's* $50,000 damages, at that time the largest award ever given for libel in New York State. Two years later, the judgment was reversed and a new trial ordered. The appellate court denied a motion to reargue. It was judged that *Collier's* attorneys had wandered too far afield procuring their victory. To allow them to do it all again would be prejudicial to the defendant. C.W. didn't turn over a red cent to *Collier's,* but the libel trial served notice to business, advertising agencies and the media that a new element had entered the field of advertising. Gradually, laws were enacted controlling and defining the hazy boundaries of honesty and good taste.

Despite the libel trial, C.W. and his business prospered. He continued to introduce new products, many of which have become household words—Post Toasties, Instant Postum, Post Bran Flakes, Post's Raisin Bran. C. W. Post has long since departed this world. The company he started in the little barn is now known as General Foods. Out of fairness to their founder, no one has ever said that Grape Nuts and Postum are not good nourishing products. But, darn it all, they just don't do a thing for appendicitis.

# PRESIDENTS OF THE UNITED STATES—LINCOLN, GARFIELD, MCKINLEY, KENNEDY

RETIRED general Colin Powell was influenced by his wife Alma's wishes that he not run for the office of president of the United States. Mrs Powell had good reason to be concerned. Four of the forty-two men who have held the most powerful position in the world were assassinated while in office.

The sixteenth president of the United States, Abraham Lincoln, was murdered on the evening of Good Friday, April 14, 1865. Before that ill-fated night, Lincoln had remarked to several colleagues that he was having trouble sleeping due to a recurring dream concerning his death. He felt so strongly about his dreams that he tried to back out of attending a play that evening at Ford's Theatre in Washington. Mrs Lincoln insisted they attend, as the comedy *Our American Cousin,* starring Laura Keene, was playing. Lincoln acquiesced, but not before another sticky detail was overcome. Gen. and Mrs Ulysses S. Grant were scheduled to attend the play with the Lincolns, but Mrs Grant begged off. Mrs Grant didn't get along with Mrs Lincoln and, to everyone's embarrassment, refused to spend an evening in the president's private box with her. As a result, Clara Hale, a senator's daughter, and her fiancé, Maj. Henry Rathbone, accompanied the Lincolns that night.

In contrast to today's elaborate precautions covering every move of the president, only one guard was assigned to the Lincoln entourage that night. As soon as the play began, the lone guard retired to Taltavul's Tavern. And so we have the presidential party relaxed, unguarded and oblivious to the fact that a plot was afoot to kill the president and some members of his cabinet.

John Wilkes Booth was the successful twenty-six-year-old son of a prominent theatrical family. A star in his own right, Booth had toured the South, but had spent the Civil War years in the North as a popular actor. He was sympathetic to the Confederacy and blamed Abe Lincoln for the war and the defeat of the South. Booth gathered around him a gang who had plotted to simultaneously attack the vice-president and various cabinet members while he personally assassinated the president.

Booth passed the time at Taltavul's Tavern until 10 p.m. One wonders if he rubbed shoulders with the guard who was drinking in the same bar at the same time. Booth walked to the theatre and made his way to the presidential box. Opening the door, he quietly walked up behind the president, pointed his one-shot Derringer behind the president's left ear and pulled the trigger. Lincoln slumped in his chair. Booth shouted, "Sic semper tyrannis"—Ever thus to tyrants. President Lincoln would die of his wound the next morning. Major Rathbone jumped towards Booth and received a slash from Booth's dagger for his trouble. Dramatically, the assassin climbed to the rail of the box. Before leaping to the stage, he shouted, "The South is avenged." Then he jumped, catching a spur on the bunting decorating the presidential box. Booth fell awkwardly to the stage, breaking his leg. He managed to limp off and make good his escape.

Slowed down by his injury, Booth reached Maryland, where he met fellow conspirator David Herold. The news Herold related to Booth was most disappointing. He had attempted to assassinate Secretary of State William Seward, but had failed in his mission. The two men sought out Dr Samuel Mudd, who placed Booth's leg in splints. Mudd provided Booth with the names of Southern sympathizers, but none would have anything to do with the fugitives. Hobbling about on crutches, Booth was becoming increasingly desperate. Seven days after the murder, he and Herold managed to cross the Potomac, where they expected to receive assistance from Virginians. They were disappointed. None came to their aid.

Five days later, the two tired, hungry men were holed up in a barn at Garrett's Farm, Bowling Green. When located there by Union soldiers, Herold immediately surrendered. Booth was another matter. He is reported to have shouted, "I'll shoot it out with the whole damn detachment." The barn was set afire. Moments later, a shot rang out and Booth fell. It is still a matter of contention whether he shot himself or was felled by a Union bullet. His body was unceremoniously dragged from the burning barn.

All those involved in the plot to assassinate Lincoln and other government officials were apprehended by authorities. George Atzerodt, a carriage maker who had planned to murder Vice-President Andrew Johnson, Lewis Paine who had attempted to kill Secretary of State Seward, and Mrs Mary Surratt, the proprietor of a boarding house, who had assisted the plotters, were charged with murder. Accused of planning the crimes were Samuel Arnold and Michael O'Laughlin. Dr Mudd was charged with aiding the plotters and Edward Spangler, an employee of Ford's Theater, was charged with helping Booth escape. All eight conspirators were convicted. Atzerodt, Paine, Herold and Mrs Surratt were hanged. Spangler received a sentence of six years' imprisonment. Arnold, Mudd and O'Laughlin were sentenced to life imprisonment. O'Laughlin developed yellow fever and died in prison in 1867. President Andrew Johnson pardoned Arnold, Mudd and Spangler in 1869.

SIXTEEN years after Lincoln's untimely demise, the twentieth president of the United States, James A. Garfield, was felled by an assassin's bullet. The tragedy occurred in the waiting room of the Baltimore and Potomac Railroad station on July 2, 1881, in Washington, D.C. A crowd had gathered to see the president before he embarked on a trip to New York. Instead, they were witness to an assassination. President Garfield had been in office only a matter of months when he was shot. He lingered for two and a half months before dying on September 19. Vice-President Chester A. Arthur succeeded the fallen leader.

The man who fired the fatal shots that day in Washington was Charles Guiteau, who was taken into custody soon after he shot the president. Two months later, he stood trial for murder. So angry was the populace, there was great fear that Guiteau wouldn't live through the trial. In fact, there were two unsuccessful attempts on his life. Guiteau turned out to be a real nut case. He claimed dissatisfaction with his lawyers and continually stated that God had told him to shoot the president. A plea of insanity was entered on his behalf. Although he admitted to the shooting, he claimed he wasn't the killer. Guiteau continually interrupted the court proceedings, insisting that his bullet had not killed the president. He blamed Garfield's doctors for his death. Guiteau shouted, "My bullet was not fatal. Garfield's death was caused by malpractice. I was only inspired to shoot the President. The doctors finished the work. It is the Deity's act, not mine."

Because of Guiteau's constant interruptions, the trial took over four months to complete, but the jury wasn't nearly as patient. They took less than an hour to find him guilty. Asked by the presiding judge if he had anything to say as to why sentence should not be passed upon him, Guiteau replied, "It was God's act, not mine. God will take care of it and won't let the American people forget it." He was then sentenced to death.

Charles Guiteau was hanged in the Washington Jail on June 30, 1882.

ON September 6, 1901, President William McKinley was visiting the Pan-American Exposition in Buffalo, New York. It was a triumphant tour. The previous day McKinley had addressed a cheering crowd of 50,000. On September 6 he visited Niagara Falls before returning to Buffalo, where he was scheduled to shake hands with the crowd at the Temple of Music.

The chief executive was well guarded. Outside the building, twelve exposition guards patrolled the entrances. An additional eighteen guards and eleven soldiers formed a passageway, allowing well-wishers to come forward and shake the president's hand. Four Buffalo detectives stood around McKinley. Three Secret Service agents watched the handshakers. Four soldiers flanked the Buffalo detectives. It was stifling hot. Many spectators used handkerchiefs to wipe perspiration from their brows. One man came forward with a handkerchief wrapped around his hand. As he put his hand forward, he brushed the president's arm away and twice fired his .32-calibre Iver Johnson revolver through the handkerchief. One bullet miraculously bounced off a button. The second bullet entered McKinley's abdomen, penetrating its front and rear walls. For an instant, the two men stared at each other as the handkerchief wrapped around the gunman's hand smouldered and caught fire. Guards pounced on the assassin, who shouted, "I done my duty." The president begged, "Be easy with him, boys." The attacker was identified as Leon Czolgosz, a factory worker, who stated his reason for the shooting: "I thought it would be a good thing for this country to kill the president."

Eight days after the attack, McKinley died of gangrene of the pancreas.

Justice moved quickly at the turn of the century. Nine days after McKinley's death, Czolgosz stood trial for murder. He was convicted and sentenced to death. On October 29, 1901, the sentence was carried out in Auburn Prison's electric chair. As the straps were being adjusted about his body, Leon Czolgosz uttered his last words, "I am not sorry."

ON November 22, 1963, President John F. Kennedy, together with his wife, Jackie, and entourage, flew into Dallas's Love Field on *Air Force 1* at 11.40 a.m. There was some initial apprehension concerning the trip, which was the fourth stop on a tiring three-day tour across Texas. Kennedy had barely carried the state in the 1960 election and had badly lost the vote in Dallas. It was hoped that this swing through the state would go a long way towards ingratiating the president with the electorate.

Once the presidential plane landed, a crowd of over a thousand greeted Kennedy and his charming wife on the tarmac. A few moments later, Texas governor and Mrs John Connally entered the presidential limousine, a 1961 Lincoln Continental four-door convertible. Special Agent William Greer drove, while Special Agent Roy Kellerman sat in the passenger seat. Along with twenty other vehicles, the procession made its way through Dallas towards the Dallas Trade Center, where the president was scheduled to address a gathering of business and civic leaders at a luncheon. Among the dignitaries following in separate vehicles were Vice-President Lyndon Johnson and Senator Ralph Yarborough. The crowd, six deep in places, was enthusiastically greeting the president and the First Lady. The gleaming vehicles swung onto Elm Street, directly below the Texas School Book Depository. They were only five minutes away from the trade center. Mrs Connally was relieved that the president's visit was going so well. She turned to Kennedy and said, "Mr President, you can't say Dallas doesn't love you." Kennedy replied, "That is very obvious."

At 12:30 p.m., shots were fired from a sixth-floor window of the Book Depository building. Kennedy is reported to have said, "My God, I'm hit," as he slumped into Mrs Kennedy's lap. Simultaneously, Governor Connally fell into his wife's lap. Jackie shouted, "What are they doing to you?" The special agents saw to it that the presidential limo sped to nearby Parkland Hospital. At 1 p.m., the president of the United States was officially declared dead. Governor Connally would recover from his wounds.

The man who fired from the sixth floor of the Texas School Book Depository building was Lee Harvey Oswald. Oswald was born on October 18, 1939, in New Orleans. His father died of a heart attack two months before his birth. Oswald spent some time in an orphanage, but was later reclaimed by his mother. The family, which included a brother and half-brother, moved to Dallas to New York and back to New Orleans. Oswald's education ended in Grade 9 when, at the age of seventeen, he joined the U.S. Marines. It was while in the marines that he studied Marxism, learned the Russian language and became extremely interested in anything Russian.

Three years later, Oswald left the marines and defected to the Soviet Union. Once in Russia, he became somewhat of a nuisance to Soviet officials, who ordered him out of the country. Disillusioned and despondent, Oswald slit his wrists, but was discovered by a government official before he bled to death. The Soviet government relented and granted him asylum. In time, Oswald obtained work in a television factory in Minsk. While there he met Marina, whom he married. In 1962, Lee and Marina returned to Dallas. For the next several months, Lee drifted from job to job before landing a position with the

Texas School Book Depository. He purchased an Italian rifle, model 31/98 6.5-millimetre Mannlicher-Carcano, with a telescopic sight, from a mail-order firm. On November 22, 1963, he made his way to the sixth floor where he took up his position waiting for the presidential motorcade. After the shooting, Oswald hid the weapon, which was later found complete with his palm prints. Armed with a revolver, he crossed the path of police officer J.D. Tippit, whom he shot dead. Within hours, Oswald was found hiding in a local theatre.

Despite overwhelming evidence to the contrary, Oswald denied killing Tippit or Kennedy. Two days after the assassination, on November 24, he was being transferred from the Dallas City Jail to the county jail. As he was being led through the building, a Dallas nightclub owner, Jack Ruby, stepped out of a crowd of police officers and journalists and shot Oswald to death with a .38-calibre Colt Cobra before millions of television viewers. Ruby died of cancer on January 3, 1967, while in custody.

From the moment President Kennedy was shot, controversy has centred on whether Oswald acted alone or was involved in a conspiracy. A presidential commission headed by Chief Justice Earl Warren investigated the case in detail. The Warren Commission concluded that Oswald, acting alone, had killed Kennedy and Tippit. Later, a congressional committee came to a diametrically opposite conclusion, stating that Kennedy "was probably assassinated as a result of a conspiracy."

The controversy is as alive today as it was over thirty years ago and will most probably never be resolved.

# WILLIAM MARCH RICE

THIS is the story of William Rice, a self-made man with a vision. Rice dreamed that one day his name would grace an established, respected seat of learning. He accomplished his goal, but at a terrible price—his life.

William March Rice was born in New England in 1816. As a teenager, he moved to Texas because it seemed to him that the Lone Star State was where the money was. The young man showed an amazing flair for anticipating land-value fluctuations and soon became wealthy. He progressed to oil speculation and added a chain of hotels and retail stores to his holdings, making him a bona fide multimillionaire.

Rice married twice. Both wives died without producing an heir. When his second wife, Elizabeth, passed away, she left a will bequeathing half of her husband's estate to her relatives. Rice, now an elderly man, thought, with some justification, that this was grossly unfair. Elizabeth had reasoned correctly that the state of Texas treated husband and wife as equal partners. She felt that she owned half of the Rice holdings, which amounted to several million dollars. The shrewd Rice hadn't accumulated that kind of loot for lack of brainpower. He claimed that he was domiciled in New York State, which had no community property law.

Rice brought a Federal Court suit against the executors of his wife's will. They in turn employed a lawyer, Albert T. Patrick, to defend the conditions of Elizabeth's will. Rice was adamant about the will being squelched, principally because he was involved in the legal negotiations required to set up an entire university. He felt Texas had been good to him and he planned to leave the bulk of his estate to establish the Rice Institute. The financial squabbling raged on for some time and the elderly Rice found it aggravating and tiring. His one solace was that, throughout it all, his close young friend, Charles F. Jones, twenty-seven, was at his side. Charlie had started out as a clerk at the Capitol Hotel, which Rice owned in Houston. One day, Rice had a pleasant chat with Charlie and liked him so much he hired the young man to act as his personal secretary. In 1897, a year after they met, they moved to an apartment on Madison Avenue in New York City. Charlie did everything for Mr Rice and was indispensable to his employer.

During the height of the dispute over Elizabeth's will, lawyer Albert T. Patrick called on Charlie. Patrick came right to the point. He offered Charlie $500 if he could come up with a letter signed by the old man himself stating that Rice was a citizen of Texas. Jones was interested in the proposition, but didn't produce the letter. He was charmed enough by Patrick to allow the lawyer to go through all of Rice's personal records and documents. Patrick then drew up a phoney draft of a will purported to be Rice's. He showed the will to Jones. It left large bequests to each of Elizabeth's relatives who had been mentioned in her will. Patrick figured that this would make them more than happy with the new will. The balance of the estate was equally divided between the Rice Institute and guess who—Albert T. Patrick himself. Jones was to be taken care of out of Patrick's share.

The scheme called for Jones to copy the will on Rice's typewriter. Jones could legitimately sign as a witness and then figure out some way to get the elderly Rice to sign the document. Both men felt the eighty-four-year-old Rice didn't have long to live and that they were a heartbeat away from being millionaires. There were a few catches. Rice had given power of attorney to his lawyers for various financial transactions. The two schemers knew that the power of attorney and other documents had to be countered by more recent documents. All required Rice's signature. They knew the wily Rice wouldn't sign anything with which he wasn't familiar. The two men decided to forge Rice's signature on everything, including the will. Jones had a good supply of legitimate signatures and he meticulously traced the real thing on the bogus documents. The entire plot was unfolding with William Rice still believing that the cunning Charlie Jones was a loyal friend and excellent employee.

There was one rather troublesome obstacle. Rice was a healthy, active man and had no intention of dying. Therefore, Patrick and Jones decided to kill him. They procured a supply of mercury tablets. Jones convinced his employer that they would be good for him. Rice started taking two tablets a day and immedately felt ill. Then Patrick instructed Jones on how to apply chloroform over the old man's mouth and nose. Jones was quick to pick up the technique. On the night of September 23, 1900, he killed his boss. A doctor rushed over to the Madison Avenue apartment and signed the death certificate, attributing Rice's death to old age and a weak heart.

Jones and Patrick had thought of everything. They had even forged Rice's name on a letter authorizing the cremation of his body. The cremation was scheduled to take place three days after Rice's death. The two men seemed to have committed the perfect murder, but greed and impatience proved their undoing. On the morning after Rice's death, they forged his signature on a cheque for $25,000 made out to Albert T. Patrick. When Patrick went to cash it, an old clerk examined the cheque carefully because of its large amount. Old clerks are sent to bother industrious criminals. This one became suspicious and decided to call Mr Rice's secretary. Charlie Jones received the call and told him everything was just fine and to please cash the cheque. Despite this, the clerk smelled a rat and asked to speak to Mr Rice himself. This proved an inconvenience, as at that moment Rice was laid out in an undertaker's parlor. Jones was compelled to tell the clerk that his employer had passed away.

The bank realized that a lawyer such as Patrick knew very well that he couldn't cash a dead man's cheque. They called their own lawyer and things commenced to move rapidly downhill for Patrick and Jones. The cremation was held up and an autopsy performed on Rice's body. It was discovered that he had died by the administration of some unidentified gas. Authorities examined all the forged documents and found the signatures on them were too perfect to be anything but traced copies. Patrick and Jones were taken into custody.

In order to prove murder, the state granted Jones immunity from prosecution in return for his testimony against Patrick. On March 26, 1902, Albert T. Patrick stood trial for murder. Charlie took the witness stand and related in detail how the murder was committed:

> After considerable persuasion I said that I would take the chloroform and do as he instructed me, and I took the chloroform and went home. After looking some time for a sponge, I found one that Mr Rice had used for cleaning his clothes, and I made a cone of a towel, placed the sponge in the small end and took it and saturated it with chloroform and placed it over my own face. I got a very strong effect from it. I then added a little more and went into Mr Rice's room. I found that he was still sleeping, and placed it over his face and ran out of the room.
>
> Mr Patrick had given me these instructions, and I followed them out as near as I could. He told me also to leave the chloroform on his face about thirty minutes. I stayed out of the room thirty minutes, staying in my room part of the time, part of the time in the hall, and part of the time in the dining room. At the expiration of the thirty minutes, someone kept ringing the bell very frequently. Of course, I was very much excited that they should be ringing the bell at this moment, so that I went to the door

and looked through, and I could see someone, but I did not know who they were. My impression was, it was two ladies at the door.

After the thirty minutes expired, I went back to Mr Rice's room and found him in the same position that I had left him, with that cone shape over his face. I removed that and put it in the range in the kitchen and lit a match to it and burned it and returned to Mr Rice's rooms and opened all the windows, straightened everything around to its usual appearance, and telephoned Mr Patrick that Mr Rice was very ill.

The phrase "Mr Rice is very ill" had been agreed upon by the two conspirators to mean that William Rice was dead. After that recitation, Patrick didn't have a chance. He was found guilty and sentenced to death in the electric chair. Every legal ploy was instituted to save his life. Finally, his sentence was commuted to life imprisonment. After spending twelve years in prison, Patrick was granted an unconditional pardon by the outgoing governor of the state, John A. Dix, who claimed that the original trial had been held in a hostile atmosphere.

Today, on the outskirts of Houston, Texas, you can drive through the beautiful grounds of the Rice Institute. The university graduates over 1,600 students each year and not one of them is required to pay tuition. Benevolently gazing down over the rolling lawns is an imposing statue of William March Rice.

# THE SCOPES MONKEY TRIAL

MONKEYS can make big news.

If you happened to wander into Dayton, Tennessee, during the scorching summer of 1925, you would have come face-to-face with every conceivable species of monkey in existence. There were storefront signs of monkeys, monkey dolls, monkey badges, live monkeys. Why all the monkey business? Well, I'll tell you.

John Thomas Scopes was a quiet, unassuming twenty-four-year-old biology teacher. He had no idea what a hornets' nest he was unleashing when he taught his pupils Darwin's theory of evolution. Indeed, what Scopes considered to be nothing more than performing his duties as a teacher precipitated one of the most widely publicized trials in U.S. history. Children told their parents they were being taught that the biblical account of creation was not to be taken literally; in reality, the teacher had told them, animal life on earth had evolved through a long and gradual process of development from single cells. God had not created it all in six days. The simple farm folk around Dayton were appalled. The area was inhabited by Christian fundamentalists, who believed without question in the word-for-word interpretation of the scriptures. News of the schoolteacher who taught that humans had descended from monkeys spread throughout the state.

In time, a member of the state legislature, John Washington Butler, introduced a bill making it unlawful for any teacher in the public schools of Tennessee to teach a theory denying the biblical account of man's origin. The bill specifically stated that public schools were not to teach that man had descended from a lower form of animal. On March 21, 1925, the Butler Bill became law. But Scopes continued to teach the theory of evolution. In so doing, he was breaking the state law. He was duly arrested and charged with "undermining the peace and dignity of the state."

The rather silly incident in the sleepy little town took on national significance with the entry into the case of two of the most prominent men in the United States. William Jennings Bryan, an ardent fundamentalist, was appointed special prosecutor. The fiery old orator had three times been the Democratic candidate for president of the United States. He lost on all three occasions. Bryan saw the trial as a double opportunity—a chance to strike a blow against the godless and, at the same time, garner favourable publicity which might catapult him into the White House. With the aid of the American Civil Liberties Union, Scopes was able to counteract the prosecution's heavy gun with one of the most prominent defence attorneys in the United States, Clarence Darrow. Only a year before, Darrow had saved Nathan Leopold and Richard Loeb from death in the electric chair for the thrill murder of fourteen-year-old Bobby Franks in Chicago.

The die was cast. It was as if fate had brought these two totally opposite men to do battle in a little town in Tennessee. Avowed atheist Darrow, defender of lost causes, was a sloppy, informal man, given to spinning down-home yarns. Bryan was a fundamentalist through and through and had been in great demand as a speaker, lecturing on the literal interpretation of the Bible.

The Monkey Trial began on Friday, July 10, 1925. In essence, the trial boiled down to science versus religion; some said enlightenment versus ignorance. Reporters came from all over the United States and several foreign countries. A blanket of heat descended on Dayton, Tennessee, turning the poorly ventilated courtroom into a steambath. The symbol of the event, the monkey, was everywhere. Hucksters, medicine men and carnival side-show barkers hawked their wares on Main Street. Fundamentalists argued. Some fought with those who didn't share their opinion. In all, the community took on a bizarrely festive air. Inside the courtroom, the two protagonists joined battle. Darrow pointed out that the defendant Scopes readily admitted teaching the theory of evolution. At no time did he disagree with the Bible. In fact, according to Darrow, many people believed in both Darwin's theory and the Bible. It was all a matter of interpretation.

Darrow's address to the court was thought by many to be the finest ever given by a defence lawyer in any court. He pointed out, "The Bible is not one book, but is made up of sixty-six books written over a period of about one thousand years, some of them very early and some comparatively late. It is a book primarily of religion and morals. It is not a book of science. Under it there is nothing prescribed that would tell you how to build a railroad or a steamboat or to make anything that would advance civilization." He went on, illustrating that at the time the Bible was written, there were many universally believed scientific theories which were later proved to be incorrect with the advancement of knowledge. Bryan addressed the jury for seventy-nine minutes and claimed that teaching children evolution was robbing them of their faith in God.

In a surprise move, Darrow had his adversary, Bryan, take the witness stand as an expert witness on the Bible. Bryan admitted that he believed in the King James version of the Bible word for word. Then, for ninety long minutes, Darrow posed embarrassing questions to the squirming Bryan. "Where did Cain's wife come from if, as the Bible states, the earth was inhabited only by his brother, Abel, and his mother and father, Adam and Eve?" Darrow also had Bryan admit it may have taken longer than six twenty-four-hour days to make the earth. The wily old defender had Bryan state that he firmly believed "God punished the serpent by condemning snakes forever after to crawl upon their bellies." Bryan was stymied when asked, "Have you any idea how the snake went before that time?" All in all, his time spent on the witness stand was a humiliating experience for William Jennings Bryan.

In eight days the trial drew to a close. It took only nine minutes for the forgotten man in the case, John Scopes, to be found guilty. He was fined a hundred dollars, the minimum penalty under the statute. An appeal was launched on a technicality. The Supreme Court of Tennessee reversed the judgment of the jury, but ruled that the law itself was constitutional.

Clarence Darrow emerged as the unofficial victor and went on to defend other unpopular causes. The trial and the personal humiliation he had endured took their toll on William Jennings Bryan. He died in his sleep of heart failure while still in Dayton six days after the trial. In 1960, John Scopes was presented with the key to the town of Dayton by the mayor as the entire community celebrated the thirty-fifth anniversary of the trial on Scopes Trial Day. An excellent movie, *Inherit the Wind,* based on the Scopes Monkey Trial was made in 1960. In it, Spencer Tracy portrayed Clarence Darrow, Frederick March played Bryan and Dick York took the part of John Scopes. In 1967, the Butler Act, which had caused all the excitement in Dayton forty-two years earlier, was repealed.

John Scopes outlived all the principals connected with the controversial Monkey Trial. He died of cancer on October 21, 1970.

# O.J. SIMPSON

QUOTE the initials O.J. anywhere in the civilized world and they will immediately be recognized as those of Orenthal James Simpson. The letters have become more famous or infamous, depending on your point of view, than JFK or LBJ, and those two gentlemen were presidents of the United States.

On July 7, 1947, Enice and Jimmie Simpson looked down at their plump new baby boy, never for an instant thinking that the little tyke would one day be considered the finest football player ever to lace on a pair of cleats. The idea of their child growing up to be a movie star and media personality was beyond their wildest dreams. They had no idea that O.J. would become all of the above, as well as the defendant in the most publicized murder trial in the history of the United States.

The Simpson family lived in low-income government housing on Potrero Hill in San Francisco. O.J. had one brother, Leon, and two sisters, Shirley and Carmelita. When he was five years old, his dad moved out of the house. Life in the projects was not easy. O.J. wasn't a saint. He got into scrapes with the law, which at that time and place was the rule rather than the exception. With the help of a strong-willed mother devoted to her children, O.J. managed to stay in school, where he excelled at sports. At Galileo High, O.J. Simpson was the star of the football team. He was named to the All City Team and led the city in scoring in his senior year.

It was at Galileo that O.J. met attractive Marguerite Whitley, who was the girlfriend of his closest buddy, Al Cowlings. Who could predict that these two men would, years later, capture the imagination of the world as they drove in a white Ford Bronco along Los Angeles freeways. When Marguerite and Al had a falling-out, Al sent his good buddy O.J. to patch up the dispute. As things turned out, O.J. and Marguerite fell in love and that's how Marguerite Whitley eventually became Mrs O.J. Simpson.

After high school, O.J. enrolled at the City College of San Francisco, where tuition was free for residents of California. O.J. exploded on the football team, setting junior-college records which still stand. After his first year, so great was his impact that he received scholarship offers from fifty universities. Even at that early stage in his career, O.J. was concerned about his future. He wanted something better and that something better turned out to be the University of Southern California. In his second and last year at City College, he raised his marks to a level that enabled him to enrol at U.S.C.

In the summer of 1967, O.J. married Marguerite and moved into the athletic quarters at U.S.C. Imagine what it must have been like for this naturally gifted athlete, fresh out of the projects, to find himself with the responsibility of a wife and the potential to become a national hero. Everything was paid for the future star. All he had to do was perform, and perform he did. In his second game against Notre Dame, O.J. broke loose. U.S.C. trailed the number one–ranked Irish 7-0 at half time. In the second half, O.J. scored three touchdowns to crush Notre Dame 24-7. In all, that day, he rushed thirty-eight times, gaining 150 yards. In another game that year, U.S.C. was trailing traditional rival U.C.L.A. 20-14 with only minutes remaining in the game. O.J. ran sixty-four yards to pull the game out of the fire 21–20. O.J. amassed 1,543 yards in his first year at U.S.C., which garnered him the national rushing title and second place in the voting for the Heisman Memorial Trophy, awarded to the top university player in the entire country.

Because of his two-year stint at City College, O.J. was only eligible to play football at U.S.C. for two years. Now entering his senior and last year, he received several professional offers. One of the most lucrative came from the Montreal Alouettes, who coveted having the most charismatic and talented university player in the United States come to Canada. But O.J., always looking to the future, correctly figured that one more season at U.S.C. would increase his value.

In his last collegiate year, O.J. was again voted an All-American. The team ended the season with a 9-1-1 record. Although they lost to unbeaten Ohio State in the Rose Bowl, O.J.'s lustre wasn't diminished by the loss. He had twenty-eight carries, ran for 171 yards and caught six passes in the game. Among the awards he received was the grandaddy of them all—the Heisman Memorial Trophy. During the Heisman ceremonies in New York, he was informed that Marguerite had given birth to their first child, a daughter, Arnelle. A second child, Jason, would be born a short time later.

With only a semester left to finish his degree, O.J. decided to leave university and go for the big bucks. The temptation was just too great. For two years he had heard thousands of fans screaming, "Juice, Juice!" Indeed, the man and the name had substantial commercial value. O.J. signed agreements with

Chevrolet, Royal Crown Cola and ABC TV. Those three commitments brought in over $400,000 annually. All this was before he signed a contract to play professional football. The Juice was on his way.

The previous year, the Buffalo Bills had been able to muster just one win and one tie in sixteen games. With the worst record in football, they had the number-one pick of college players in the annual draft. O.J. hated the idea of going to Buffalo. He had never been there, but had heard about the snow and freezing weather. The California boy longed to stay and play in the sun, but eventually agreed to sign with Buffalo for a reported annual salary of $300,000. Added to his commercial income, it is estimated that O.J.'s total earnings were in the one-million-dollar range. Many have put up with the frozen North for less.

For the first time in his life, O.J. wasn't an instant success. For reasons of his own, coach John Rauch didn't use O.J. to best advantage. Instead of lugging the ball up to forty times a game, O.J. often carried no more than ten or twelve times. The fans didn't like it, O.J. hated it and the Bills kept losing. Just before the 1971 season opened, Rauch resigned. Although O.J. carried the ball more frequently, the Bills continued to lose, ending the season with a dismal one win and thirteen losses. The following year, with O.J. in high gear, the team raised its record to four wins, nine losses and a tie. O.J. led the league in rushing. To all intents and purposes, *he* was the Buffalo Bills.

In 1973, the Buffalo team recruited players with the explicit purpose of protecting and, at the same time, showcasing the talents of their star. O.J. didn't disappoint. Despite the fact that rival defensive coaches knew who would carry the ball, O.J. just couldn't be stopped. In his first game, he carried twenty-nine times and rushed 250 yards, breaking the league single-game rushing record. In eleven games, he exceeded rushing a hundred yards. In the last game of the season, he rushed an even 200 yards, giving him 2,003 yards on the season, smashing James Brown's league record of 1,863 yards. O.J. wasn't on his way; he had arrived. The six-foot-one-inch finely tuned handsome athlete was in demand as a spokesperson for national products. The adoration and the money poured in.

While O.J. was away furthering his career, Marguerite stayed at home. Dissension crept into their marriage, which, to the outside world, seemed idyllic. The high school romance, marriage, college hero, professional athlete, celebrity—who could want anything more? Marguerite Simpson wanted more. She wanted a husband she could talk to and touch, not one she could see only on TV. From 1973 to 1978, the Simpson marriage was marred by several separations and reconciliations. In September 1977, the Simpsons' third child, a daughter, Aaron Leshona, was born. The birth did little to solidify the marriage. A few months later, the Simpsons bought a large home at 360 Rockingham Dr. in Brentwood, California. A year later, O.J. and Marguerite separated. He moved out of the large ostentatious home.

His skills now eroding, O.J. was traded to the San Francisco 49ers. Then, disaster struck. Daughter Aaron fell into the Rockingham swimming pool and died a week later. When advised of the accident, O.J. is reported to have rushed through the hospital corridors shouting, "She murdered my child, she murdered my child!" The Simpson marriage, already in trouble, was over. On March 3, 1980, both parties signed agreements dissolving their marriage. Marguerite was granted custody of their two children, Arnelle and Jason. Financial arrangements were finalized, with both agreeing to the division of their assets. O.J. purchased Marguerite's share of the Rockingham home and, after bitter legal disputes, took possession of the luxurious residence.

In 1977, during one of his many separations from Marguerite, O.J. was eating in a Los Angeles restaurant, where he was waited upon by a stunning blonde. Her name was Nicole Brown and she was only eighteen years old. O.J. asked Nicole for a date. The young waitress had taken a giant step up the social ladder. She quit her job and was squired around Los Angeles by this good-looking athlete and movie star. True, there were over ten years' difference in their ages, but that didn't seem to matter. Everywhere they went, O.J. was recognized and adored. He was charming, kind and generous to a fault. Nicole moved out of her apartment into the mansion in Brentwood. In February 1985, Nicole and O.J. married on the lawn of the Rockingham estate. Soon after, she gave birth to their daughter, Sydney. A second child, Justin, was born three years later, the same year that O.J. was inducted into the Professional Football Hall of Fame.

O.J. and Nicole lived in the fast lane. The former waitress had servants, a luxurious beach home at Laguna Beach and took extensive vacations with her husband all over the world. As for O.J., he had acquired a beautiful, intelligent wife. Those close to him felt he took pride in displaying her before friends and acquaintances. The public's adoration of the former football star didn't diminish. Women in particular threw themselves at O.J. He never discouraged them. Nicole, like Marguerite before her, rankled with jealousy at the thought of O.J. spending time with other women. Friends would later claim that around this time they noticed bruises on Nicole's arms and neck. It was an embarrassing subject to bring up. No one took any action. After all, it was a private matter.

The general public received the first hint that anything of a serious nature was taking place between O.J. and Nicole on New Year's Day, 1989. It was still dark when police took a 911 call from Nicole. When they responded to her plea, they found the terrified woman cowering in the bushes, dressed only in sweatpants and a bra. She cried out to them, "He's going to kill me." O.J. roared out of the house, berating the officers for interfering. He shouted, "I don't want this woman sleeping in my bed anymore. I've got two women and I don't want that woman in my bed anymore." O.J. then took off in one of his cars.

O.J. felt that he was immune from the law. He did not see himself as an ordinary citizen. This was the first time in his career that he'd had to cope with adverse publicity. In the past, Nicole had summoned police to the house, but they had always listened to O.J. Nicole had never pressed charges. She didn't this time, either, but it was O.J.'s bad fortune that a city attorney had witnessed Nicole's condition at the time of the altercation. She had a bruised cheek, a black eye and scratches on her neck. The woman had obviously been attacked.

O.J. entered a plea of no contest to the charge of spousal battery. A municipal judge, who may very well have been an O.J. fan, gave the charismatic former athlete two years' probation, a $200 fine, and an order to donate $500 to a battered women's shelter and to perform 120 hours of community service. In addition, O.J. was to seek psychiatric counselling.

Nicole Simpson led two lives. On the surface, outsiders saw Nicole and O.J. dining at the best restaurants and attending important social functions. They were an ideal couple, leading an enviable lifestyle. But to a select few, Nicole was an abused woman with an extremely jealous husband. He beat her up. He beat her up badly, and no one seemed to care. Even the New Year's incident, where his abuse was exposed, did little to tarnish O.J.'s image. Indeed, none of the large corporations thought it serious enough to drop him as their spokesperson. In February 1992, Nicole left O.J. and filed for divorce. They had been married seven years. O.J.'s total worth was determined to be over ten million dollars. Nicole was awarded in excess of one million dollars in cash and property, plus $19,000 a month in alimony and child support.

The beautiful blonde and the charming football hero parted company. O.J. continued to date glamorous women, in particular Paula Barbieri, who was regularly seen at his side. The young model was showered with gifts and attention. Nicole herself didn't exactly stay on the shelf. At thirty-five years of age she had the looks and body of a far younger woman. She maintained an active social calendar and was often seen with friends, both male and female, at trendy restaurants. One of her favourites was the Mezzaluna, where she became acquainted with some members of the staff.

In January 1994, Nicole purchased a condominium for $650,000 at 875 South Bundy Dr., less than two miles from O.J.'s home on Rockingham. She and the two children moved in. Nicole never neglected her children and recognized that O.J. was their father, encouraging him to visit her condo whenever he wanted, which was quite often. O.J. adored the children. Nicole and O.J. dated and attended various functions together. They seemed to get along well, but in hindsight we know that O.J. resented his ex-wife's dating other men. In fact, he was insanely jealous of her male friends. Some say that Nicole was still very much in love with her ex-husband. They often spent entire weekends together. The pair were so thick that close friends talked about a reconciliation. It was apparent that O.J. was pursuing Nicole. Friends thought it a bit strange. Whenever she was out alone, he would unexpectedly appear on the scene. Some claim that he was constantly seen driving past her South Bundy residence.

At 12:10 a.m., Monday, June 13, 1994, a jogger noticed blood near the gate in front of 875 South Bundy Dr. She peered inside and recoiled in horror at the sight of two bodies on the ground. The female was lying on her side, while the male was in a sitting position, leaning against a stone wall beside the gate. Both had been stabbed to death. They were identified as Nicole Brown Simpson and her friend, Ronald Goldman. Beside Ron's right foot was a white envelope containing a pair of eyeglasses.

In life, Nicole had been in the glare of the public spotlight, but not so Ron Goldman. Ron had still to make his mark. The eldest of three children, he hailed from the Los Angeles suburb of Agoura. Tall and handsome, Ron gravitated to the Hollywood scene, where he ran with the beautiful young people who aspire to be the next Mel Gibson or Brad Pitt. He had some successes. In 1992, he appeared on a TV show called "Studs." Occasionally, he picked up a modelling job. Between engagements, Ron hung around Starbucks during the day and partied at night. At twenty-five years of age, he had time to wait for his big break. Meanwhile, like so many other aspiring actors, in order to keep the wolf from the door, he worked as a waiter—at Mezzaluna Restaurant.

Ron didn't drink or take drugs. He was friendly and obliging, and loved the entire Hollywood scene, especially the beautiful women who seemed to be attracted to him. One such woman was Nicole Simpson. Ron often danced with her in trendy Hollywood clubs. Sometimes, she had him drive her to clubs in her sleek Ferrari convertible. Ron liked Nicole. He told friends that the relationship stopped at friendship. After all, as Ron was quick to point out, if he ever became more seriously involved with Nicole, O.J. would kill him. The in crowd knew about O.J.'s jealous rages.

Now Ron's body lay beside Nicole's in front of her home. The natural question police were asking, considering that they had been called to this very residence by Nicole on several occasions, was, "Where is O.J.?" Police traced O.J.'s movements. On Sunday the twelfth, O.J. played golf at the Riviera Country Club. That afternoon, he accompanied Nicole to daughter Sydney's dance recital at Paul Revere Junior High. After the recital, they went their separate ways. Nicole had dinner at the Mezzaluna Restaurant with her family and friends. At around 8:30 p.m., they left the restaurant. Nicole returned to her home and put Sydney and Justin to bed. Later, she received a call from her mother advising her that she had left her glasses at the restaurant and would Nicole see that they were picked up. Nicole phoned the restaurant. It was Ron Goldman's misfortune to volunteer to run them the short distance to Nicole's condo. It was this pair of glasses that was found in the envelope beside Ron's body.

As dawn broke, police found out why O.J. was nowhere to be seen. He had previously made reservations to fly to Chicago to attend a Hertz function. O.J. was the company's extremely successful spokesperson. He had been picked up by limo at his Rockingham address and driven to the Los Angeles International Airport, where he arrived approximately ten minutes before takeoff at 11:45 p.m. on American Airlines Flight 668. O.J. relaxed on the flight. He had the entire first-class section to himself. At 5:34 a.m., the plane landed and O.J. went to O'Hare Plaza Hotel, checking in at 6:15 a.m. Recognized wherever he went, he signed autographs for fans before retiring for a few hours of much-needed sleep. O.J. didn't sleep long. He was soon advised by phone that his ex-wife Nicole and an acquaintance of hers had been murdered. Police requested that he return home. O.J. caught a flight and was back in L.A. at 11:08 a.m. That same day, he was questioned by detectives for several hours.

There was little doubt in anyone's mind that O.J. was the prime suspect in the double murder. O.J. stayed put in his Rockingham estate and said little. Occasionally, friends arrived at the mansion to lend their support and express their sympathy at his great loss.

Back in Chicago, police searched the hotel room in which O.J. had stayed so briefly. They found a bloodstained towel and a broken glass. O.J.'s counsel issued a statement explaining that when O.J. was informed of his former wife's death, he'd slammed his hand down on the sink, causing the mishap. Rumours fed upon rumours. Tidbits of O.J.'s past abuse of Nicole made the rounds. Many thought he had plenty of time to commit the murder and still make the flight to Chicago, even though the time of death had not been established.

Little by little, the gruesome nature of the murders were revealed. Nicole had been slashed across the throat so severely she had almost been decapitated. She also had four other stab wounds about the neck and three cuts to the back of her head. Defensive wounds on Ron Goldman showed that the young man had fought desperately for his life. Two deep stab wounds had pierced his lungs. Another stab wound had severed the abdominal aorta. Like Ron, Nicole had also sustained several defensive wounds as she'd attempted to ward off her attacker.

O.J. attended Nicole's funeral with his children and members of her family. The next day, his lawyer, Robert Shapiro, was notified that O.J. was being charged with murder. He was ordered to surrender his client by 11 a.m. Shapiro, who knew O.J. was waiting out developments at the San Fernando Valley home of a close friend, Robert Kardashian, sped there to break the news. After speaking with his lawyer, O.J. made phone calls and wrote a few letters.

Then the unexpected happened. The eleven o'clock deadline came and went. While the media waited for this famous personality to be taken into custody, police had to announce that O.J. Simpson had mysteriously disappeared. More drama was to follow. O.J. had jumped into the back seat of his dear friend Al Cowling's white Ford Bronco and the pair had taken off. O.J. was armed and talking suicide. He had left a letter with Kardashian, which Kardashian read on TV to the waiting world:

> To whom it may concern:
>
> First, everyone understand I had nothing to do with Nicole's murder. I loved her, always have and always will. If we had a problem, it's because I loved her so much. Recently, we came to the understanding that for now we were not right for each other—at least for now.
>
> Despite our love, we were different, and that's why we agreed to go our separate ways.
>
> It was tough splitting the second time, but we both knew it was for the best. Besides, I had no doubt that in the future we would be close friends or more.

Unlike what has been written in the press, Nicole and I had a great relationship most of our lives together. Like all long-term relationships, we had a few downs and ups.

I took the heat New Year's 1989 because that's what I was supposed to do. I did not plead 'no contest' for any other reason but to protect our privacy and was advised it would end the press hype.

I don't want to belabor knocking the press, but I can't believe what is being said. Most of it is totally made up. I know you have a job to do, but as a last wish please, please leave my children in peace. Their lives will be tough enough.

I want to send my love and thanks to all my friends. I'm sorry I can't name every one of you, especially A.C.—man, thanks for being in my life.

The support and friendship I received from so many, Wayne Hughes, Louis Marx, Frank Olsen, Mark Packer, Bender, Bobby Kardashian. I wish we had spent more time together in recent years.

My golfing buddies—Alan Austen, Mike, Craig, Bender, Wyler, Sandy, Jay, Donny—thanks for the fun.

All my teammates over the years, Reggie—you were the soul of my pro career. Ahmad, I never stopped being proud of you. Marcus, you got a great lady in Catherine—don't mess it up. Bobby Chandler, thanks for always being there. Skip and Cathy, I love you guys—without you I never would have made it through this far.

Marguerite, thanks for the early years. We had some fun. Paula, what can I say? You are special. I'm sorry, I'm not going to have, we're not going to have our chance. God brought you to me, I now see. As I leave, you'll be in my thoughts.

I think of my life and feel I've done most of the right things. So why do I end up like this? I can't go on. No matter what the outcome, people will look and point. I can't take that. I can't subject my children to that. This way, they can move on and go on with their lives.

Please, if I've done anything worthwhile in my life, let my kids live in peace, from you, the press.

I've had a good life. I'm proud of how I lived. My mama taught me to do unto others. I treated people the way I wanted to be treated. I've always tried to be up and helpful, so why is this happening?

I'm sorry for the Goldman family. I know how much it hurts.

Nicole and I had a good life together. All this press talk about a rocky relationship was no more than what every long-term relationship experiences. All her friends will confirm that I have been totally loving and understanding of what she's been going through.

At times I have felt like a battered husband or boyfriend, but I loved her, make that clear to everyone. And I would take whatever it took to make it work.

Don't feel sorry for me, I've had a great life, great friends. Please think of the real O.J. and not this lost person.

Thanks for making my life special. I hope I helped yours.

Peace and love.
O.J.

Meanwhile O.J. was a fugitive from justice. It seemed as if everyone in California was on the lookout for the state's most wanted man, but it wasn't until early evening that a couple driving on the freeway in Orange County spotted the white Bronco. Police were notified and in a matter of minutes the strange, slow-paced chase televised throughout the world showed a galaxy of police cars following O.J. with Al Cowlings at the wheel. Eventually, Cowlings phoned authorities, beseeching them to keep their distance and informing them that O.J. had a pistol. Police complied. They cleared traffic off the freeway and the unusual caravan continued. Approximately an hour later, O.J. gave himself up to officers outside his Rockingham home. It is estimated that 100 million viewers had watched the dramatic slow-speed chase and surrender.

On July 22, 1994, O.J. Simpson pleaded "absolutely 100 percent not guilty" and the most public of all trials was under way. O.J. purchased the best legal talent money could buy. Dubbed the Dream Team by the press, O.J.'s battery of lawyers included F. Lee Bailey, Johnny Cochrane and Robert Shapiro. In addition, he had in his corner Barry Scheck and Peter Newfield, both experts in disseminating DNA evidence. The state was represented in the main by Marcia Clark and Christopher Darden. Presiding over the court was Judge Lance Ito, who began the trial as a pleasant, personable individual and ended it as a disgruntled judge desperately attempting to retain control of his courtroom. All were to become media stars as the televised trial dragged on.

The Simpson trial was like no other. Both defence and prosecution meticulously examined every piece of evidence. Witnesses' past histories were delved into extensively. Accusations of evidence tampering were commonplace by both sides. The latest in high-tech was used to present the evidence.

After all the evidence was revealed, the case came down to four crucial points: the time element, the blood evidence, police integrity and race.

It was brought out at the trial that a neighbour of Nicole's heard a dog barking and wailing outside her South Bundy condo at 10:15 p.m. Most believe the dog was witness to the double murder. An hour later, O.J. left by limo from his Rockingham home for the airport. The defence contended that he didn't have time to kill two people, dispose of the murder weapon and bloody clothing, return home, wash himself clean and change before leaving his home via limo to the airport. The prosecution claimed he had time to spare.

Blood evidence indicating that O.J. had been at the crime scene pointed to O.J.'s guilt, but, by the time the Dream Team finished with prosecution expert witnesses, such was not the case. Some of the blood samples, it turned out, had been handled in a cavalier manner. The defence claimed that the samples had been contaminated.

Perhaps no other single incident weighted the outcome of the trial more than the questioning of one man, Detective Mark Fuhrman. One of the first detectives at the crime scene, Fuhrman discovered a bloody glove and then found a matching one at O.J.'s residence the next day. The Dream Team painted Fuhrman as a racist cop, capable of planting evidence to gain a conviction. His credibility was scuttled when F. Lee Bailey asked him if he had ever used the derogatory term "nigger" in the past ten years. Under oath, Fuhrman responded that he had never used the word. A tape was later played, featuring an interview with Fuhrman in which the detective constantly used the derogatory word and spoke freely of planting evidence to gain convictions. Other witnesses related incidences of Fuhrman's obvious racist leanings and testified that he had advocated killing all blacks.

And so, after over a year of substantial scientific evidence and a total of 126 witnesses, the trial came to a close. It had cost the state of California $8.9 million. The jury took only four hours to acquit O.J. Simpson of murdering Nicole Brown Simpson and Ronald Goldman.

The chances that a drop of blood found at the scene of the murders was left by a person other than O.J. Simpson is less than one in 170 million.

# ISAAC MERRITT SINGER

ISAAC Merritt Singer is remembered for two very different activities. He was the founder of the Singer Sewing Machine Co., the giant worldwide sewing empire, and was also one of the most prolific studs of all time. We'll let you decide whether or not he committed any crime.

Isaac was born in 1811 in the village of Pittstown, New York, of fine old German stock. As a young man he distinguished himself as a better-than-average machinist and actor. When the machinist racket softened, he took to the road in travelling shows up and down the eastern seaboard. In his spare time he chased girls, more often than not making dishonest women of them. It was in this latter pursuit, while performing in Palmyra, New York, that he spotted sixteen-year-old Catherine Haley. Catherine was an early bloomer. She had luxuriant blond hair, blue eyes and a variety of other attributes normally associated with girls a few years older, all stacked in just the right places.

Isaac introduced himself. Catherine took one look at the six-foot-tall, barrel-chested young man with the side whiskers and booming voice and decided she could do worse. Before you could say catchstitch, Isaac and Catherine were seeing each other on a regular basis. One fine evening, when the moon hung low over Palmyra, they were doing what folks had been doing since Adam and Eve were an item. In walked Catherine's daddy. You've heard of shotgun weddings. Next day, Catherine became Mrs Isaac Singer. With little more than looks and personality, Isaac took his bride to New York, where they rented a flat on Third Avenue. Within two years, the union was blessed with two little Singers.

To make ends meet, Isaac took to the road, using the stage name Isaac Merritt. In Baltimore he stayed with a family named Sponsler. Mr Sponsler was in the oyster business, which might in some small way explain future events. Son of a gun, didn't Mr Sponsler have a knockout of a daughter, eighteen-year-old Mary Ann. Isaac suggested he and Mary Ann get to know each other in a more personal way, but Mary Ann had her principles. She simply wouldn't associate with a married man. Lucky you, exclaimed Isaac, telling Mary Ann he was single, unattached and free as a bird. What's more, the lying devil told her that the reason for his single status was simple: he had never met anyone as pretty as Mary Ann.

Now, that was a different basket of oysters. Isaac Merritt and Mary Ann Sponsler jumped into bed. When Isaac's show moved out of Baltimore, he tearfully kissed Mary Ann goodbye and that should have been that.

A little over a month later, Mary Ann made a startling discovery. Certain biological functions which normally were as regular as clockwork were conspicuously absent. She wrote to Isaac, advising him that she was pregnant. What was a fellow to do? Isaac told Mary Ann to come on over to little old New York. Once she arrived, with thoughts of wedding bells dancing in her head, Isaac confessed. He was married and had not bothered to obtain a divorce. Poor Mary Ann. This was a complication for which she was totally unprepared. Did Isaac have any suggestions? Our boy suggested a nice flat on Third Avenue. Mary Ann agreed. And that's how Isaac Singer had two wives, one common-law and one legit, living directly across the street from each other, neither having any idea of the other's existence. Catherine soon tired of living in poverty. She complained continually. Isaac couldn't take it any longer, so he moved, but not too far—just across the street to the waiting Mary Ann.

In the years that followed, Isaac managed to make a living as an actor. He gave up the flat and travelled with Mary Ann. This cosy arrangement resulted in the birth of four more illegitimate children. In 1848, he came off the road and once again settled in New York, in a flat on Third Avenue. Just for fun, he dropped in on his deserted wife, Catherine, after an absence of many years. It's a tribute to Isaac's gift of gab that he managed to cajole his long-suffering wife into the bedroom. It was just like old times. Isaac took up where he had left off years earlier. Once more, he had two complete families living on Third Avenue.

One day, while walking the streets of Boston, Isaac spotted a sewing machine on display in a store window. His old machinist's instincts were aroused. It didn't bother him much when he discovered that Elias Howe held the patent on the machine. Isaac took apart the machine and improved various aspects, giving it universal appeal. He advertised extensively and hired salesmen to sell door to door. Within a year, money was flowing into the Singer Sewing Machine Co.

Never one to let business interfere with pleasure, Isaac took up with Mary Eastwood Walters. He presented himself as Isaac Robbins, travelling salesman. Soon he and Mary were doing what comes naturally between the sheets. Isaac set up his new lady friend in a comfortable flat on Third Avenue, not far from wives number one and two. Nine months later, Mary Walters gave birth to a healthy daughter.

Three months after this latest illegitimate daughter was born, Isaac met Mary McGonigal, a passionate Irish lass who knew better and liked it a lot. Using the name Isaac Matthews and posing as a salesman, he soon was sleeping with his third Mary. As was the custom with Isaac's lady friends, Mary McGonigal was soon pregnant.

Let's review. Isaac was legitimately married to Catherine. He had Mary Ann Sponsler and Mary Walters living close to each other on Third Avenue. In addition, Mary McGonigal lived within an easy walk on Christopher Street. The women knew him as Singer, Merritt, Robbins and Matthews. They kept having babies, but not one of them knew of the others' existence.

Isaac's business was booming, giving him the excuse that he had to travel. He made sure never to have his picture in the papers and shunned personal publicity of any kind. While Isaac spread good cheer in the bedroom, his sewing machines chugged away. He opened plants in Bridgeport, Connecticut, and Elizabethport, New Jersey. Isaac became a bona fide multimillionaire. When Elias Howe sued, Isaac was wealthy enough to settle the claim to everyone's satisfaction.

Out of fairness to Isaac, it should be pointed out that he took good care of all his women as his wealth grew. They now lived in fine homes and enjoyed liberal allowances. Of course, it was bound to happen. One day he was driving in an open carriage with Mary Ann Sponsler (Mrs Merritt), when he was spotted by Catherine, the legitimate Mrs Singer. The bobbin hit the fan. Catherine made a scene after being informed by Mary Ann that she had borne her Isaac ten, count 'em, ten children.

Mary Walters didn't seem to mind the deception much. Mary Ann Sponsler was another story altogether. With ten children, she felt she should have some sort of rights. She wanted Isaac to divorce Catherine and legitimize her brood.

Catherine wouldn't hear of it, but Isaac had a plan. He found a gentleman who, for a price, would swear that he had had an adulterous relationship with Catherine. In this way, Isaac was able to divorce Catherine and live with Mary Ann Sponsler. He steadfastly refused to marry the mother of his ten children.

What with one thing and another, Isaac decided to divest himself of the everyday running of the business and live like a multimillionaire without all the hassles. At age fifty-one, he set out for Europe to take it easy. Instead, he met Pamela Lockwood Boyer and her gorgeous twenty-year-old daughter, Eugenie. Isaac bedded both mother and daughter, in that order. He used an alias, but when Eugenie became pregnant, Pamela informed him that she knew he was the American multimillionaire Isaac Singer. She threatened him with an international scandal if he didn't marry pregnant Eugenie.

Isaac and Eugenie were married in New York City. He purchased a mansion along the Hudson for his new bride. A month after the marriage, little Mortimer was born. Ten months later, Eugenie bore a second child; a year later, a third. Eugenie had six children in less than seven years. The Singers moved to Paris and then to Paignton on the Devon coast of England.

In 1875, at the age of sixty-four, the old stud took to his bed and died of natural causes. With an array of wives, mistresses, legitimate and illegitimate children, there was some speculation regarding his will. Isaac satisified most of his loved ones. About half his wealth was left to his widow and their six children. The balance was divided between the other four women in his life and their children.

In all, Isaac Singer, who gave us the sewing machine, also gave the world twenty-four children, mothered by two legitimate wives and three mistresses.

# DAVID C. STEPHENSON

THERE is little doubt that the most powerful man in the state of Indiana in the roaring twenties was David C. Stephenson. His source of power emanated from his association with the Ku Klux Klan, at that time the most influential organization in the state.

Stephenson was appointed the Klan's Grand Dragon of the Realm of Indiana. Plain in appearance, but a charismatic perspicuous orator, Stephenson became the official Klan organizer for nineteen states. He was in charge of several little goodies such as initiation fees and uniforms. Stephenson kept four dollars of ever ten dollars initiation fee he collected. He purchased the Klan's hoods and sheets for $1.75 a set and sold them to new members for six dollars. Within eighteen months he was worth over a million dollars.

With wealth and position came political power. Using his money and influence, there was little doubt that Stephenson could deliver the Klan vote. Scores of municipal, county and state officials owed their jobs to their Ku Klux Klan affiliation and D. C. Stephenson. The Grand Dragon reaped his rewards. If he sponsored a bill in the state legislature, it passed. If he opposed the bill, it was defeated. Stephenson relished his position as unofficial dispenser of patronage. He lived like a king. His servants, bodyguards and chauffeur were all housed in a mansion in Indianapolis.

It is difficult to pinpoint when Stephenson met twenty-eight-year-old Madge Oberholtzer. Possibly it was at a banquet held for Governor Jackson in January 1925. Madge was single, attractive and lived with her parents only a few blocks from Stephenson's imposing home. She was employed by the state's public welfare department. Stephenson often invited Madge to his home for dinner, but always in the company of others. Later, Madge was to state that on these occasions he behaved like a perfect gentleman. This pretence was to change in a dramatic way on Sunday, March 15, 1925.

On that Sunday afternoon, Madge's mother received a phone call from Stephenson. He wanted to speak to Madge, who was not in at the time. When she returned home shortly after 10 p.m., Madge called Stephenson, who urged her to meet with him immediately concerning a matter of great importance. In minutes, Stephenson's chauffeur picked Madge up and brought her to his home. Stephenson met her at the door. He was drunk. Bodyguards Earl Klinck and Earl Gentry, as well as chauffeur Shorty De Friese, were present. Madge took one look at the situation, realized Stephenson's female servants were nowhere to be seen and declared that she was going home. Without warning, Gentry and Klinck pinned Madge's arms to her sides and forced her to drink from a glass containing some kind of liquid. She immediately became ill, vomited and almost fainted.

Under Stephenson's instructions, Gentry made arrangements for a train trip. Madge told the men that she had left her home in such a hurry that she didn't have a hat or even a purse. No one paid any attention to her pleas. With the two burly bodyguards on either side of her, Madge was taken to the railway station and accompanied to a Pullman car. Gentry climbed into an upper berth. Dizzy and weak, Madge was shoved into the lower berth. Stephenson climbed in with her. The train left the station. Stephenson then viciously attacked and continually raped her. Not content with ravishing the hapless girl, he proceeded to bite her. Later, teethmarks were found on her arms, neck, back, legs and breasts. Madge lost consciousness and only came to when Gentry awakened her at Hammond, Indiana.

The two men dressed the helpless girl and led her to the Indiana Hotel, a few blocks from the railway station. Two rooms, 416 and 417, were assigned to the party. Knowing that Madge would be missed by her parents, as she had never stayed out overnight in her life, they sent off a wire: "We are driving through to Chicago. Will be home on night train." It was signed Madge. By midday, chauffeur Shorty De Friese joined the group at the hotel. He had driven up from Indianapolis. As soon as he arrived, he was instructed to go with Madge to buy a hat. Stephenson tossed Shorty fifteen dollars for the purchase. After buying the hat, Madge pleaded with Shorty to let her get some rouge at a drugstore. While Shorty's attention was directed elswhere, Madge managed to purchase a box of bichloride of mercury tablets.

Back at the hotel, Madge swallowed six of the eighteen tablets. She immediately became violently ill, vomiting blood all day. By four in the afternoon, she told Shorty what she had done. He immediately informed Stephenson. The four men realized the gravity of the situation. Stephenson made Madge drink a quart of milk. Then they hustled the drastically sick woman out of the hotel and into their car for the 175-mile trip back to Indianapolis. Madge writhed in agony for every one of those 175 miles.

Once back in Indianapolis, the men carried Madge into a loft above Stephenson's garage. Next day, fearing that Madge, who was lapsing in and out of consciousness, would die right there, Stephenson decided to return her to her home. Earl Klinck carried her down to the car, drove her home and carried her directly into her bedroom.

Madge's parents were aghast at their daughter's condition. They immediately brought in medical assistance. As the days passed, the minor bruises and cuts on Madge's body responded to treatment, all except a deep bite to one of her breasts, which had become infected. Her general condition slowly deteriorated.

Meanwhile, Stephenson, Gentry and Klinck were charged with assault and battery with intent to commit a criminal act, malicious mayhem, kidnapping and conspiracy to kidnap. Stephenson was freed on $25,000 bail. He also put up $5,000 bail for Gentry and Klinck. Chauffeur Shorty De Friese had fled.

Madge's condition worsened. She was informed she was going to die. In consultation with her father, she decided to relate her ordeal to a lawyer to be used against her tormentors in the event of her death. This statement was taken down in meticulous detail in front of witnesses. Twenty-nine days after the initial attack on the train, Madge died. Stephenson, Gentry and Klinck were charged with her murder. All three were taken into custody and held without bail.

On October 12, 1925, the three men stood trial for murder at Noblesville, Indiana. Madge's dying statement was entered into evidence. Prosecution attorneys had no trouble corroborating her carefully related statement with eyewitnesses. The defence argued that the Klan and possibly others were out to get Stephenson and had framed him. This argument didn't hold water, but another approach had legal ramifications of interest to lawyers to this day.

It was proven by doctors who treated Madge, and by the post-mortem examination, that she had died from bichloride of mercury poisoning. Did she not commit suicide? If so, despite her dastardly treatment at the hands of the three men, particularly Stephenson, could murder be proven? To counteract this argument, the prosecution claimed that it was the prior actions of these men which had caused the victim to take the poison.

After deliberating six hours, the jury found Gentry and Klinck not guilty. Stephenson was found guilty of murder in the second degree and was sentenced to life imprisonment. D. C. Stephenson, once the most powerful man in Indiana, entered Michigan City Penitentiary in 1925. He remained there for twenty-five years before being paroled to his daughter and given permission to live in

Carbondale, Illinois. Three months later, he disappeared and was found working as a printer in Minneapolis. He was returned to prison as a parole violator and remained there for an additional seven years.

On December 22, 1957, after serving thirty-two years in prison, Stephenson made Governor George Craig's Christmas executive clemency list and was released. Stephenson lived in Indiana until 1970 when, at the age of eighty, he left the state. He has not been heard of since.

# DR HERMAN TARNOWER

DR Herman Tarnower, the son of Russian-Jewish immigrants, graduated from Syracuse University to beome a successful suburban physician. He owned his own medical clinic in Scarsdale, New York, and a large home in nearby Purchase. Two servants, Suzanne and Henri van der Vrekens, lived at the doctor's Purchase estate and took care of his day-to-day needs. In 1979, Dr Tarnower received worldwide recognition when he published his best selling book, *The Complete Scarsdale Medical Diet*. Tarnower had been a wealthy man for years. With the acclaim his book received, he achieved celebrity status.

In 1965, Jean and James Harris were divorced. James later died, leaving Jean to raise two young sons. An honours graduate of prestigious Smith College, Mrs Harris embarked on a teaching career which culminated in 1977 with her appointment as headmistress of exclusive Madeira School in McLean, Virginia. Cultured, witty, pleasing to the eye, Jean Harris appeared to be the consummate career woman who had carved out a happy, interesting life for herself.

Mrs Harris met Dr Tarnower in 1966 at a party in New York. Soon she became lover and companion to the urbane, cultured doctor. Their relationship involved more than pillow talk. Herman Tarnower and Jean Harris travelled the world for months at a time. Jean held court as the doctor's hostess at intimate dinner parties. She often stayed at the Purchase estate for weeks. Mrs Harris was then and is today, by her own admission, madly in love with Hy Tarnower. The relationship over the years, while it appeared idyllic, was a fragile thing. Tarnower, a confirmed bachelor, was a completely self-centred man. Jean knew deep down that she would be his lover and companion only as long as she complied with his every whim.

There is nothing new about the love triangle which slowly but insidiously developed. The other woman was Lynne Tryforos, a good-looking nurse-secretary at Tarnower's Scarsdale Clinic. Tarnower did little to conceal his intimacy with the younger woman. Mrs Harris would find Lynne's nightclothes hanging in what she considered her closet at the doctor's home. The servants would volunteer that Lynne had spent several nights with the doctor. In 1979, Dr Tarnower vacationed with Mrs Harris in Palm Beach. When he returned, he took Lynne Tryforos on vacation to Montego Bay.

On the March night in 1980 when violence erupted to change the lives of all the members of our triangle forever, Jean Harris was fifty-six, Lynne Tryforos was thirty-seven, and Dr Tarnower was a healthy, vigorous sixty-nine.

There was nothing unusual about the beginning of Hy Tarnower's last evening on this good earth. Dinner was served by Suzanne van der Vrekens. Lynne and an acquaintance, Debbie Raizes, were guests. The meal broke up early and the women left at approximately 8:30 p.m. Dr Tarnower retired. Henri van der Vrekens, who had prepared the evening meal, also went to bed. Suzanne chose to watch television and paint a watercolour. That afternoon, Dr Tarnower had received a rather annoying call from Mrs Harris in Virginia. She had asked to visit with him that very night. He tried to shake her off: "It would be more convenient if you came tomorrow." Mrs Harris pleaded, "I can't talk to you tomorrow, Hy. Please, just this once let me say when." Tarnower replied, "Suit yourself."

Jean Harris left for Purchase, New York, in the Madeira School's blue Chrysler. It was a five-hour drive. Beside her on the front seat lay a loaded .32-calibre Harrington and Richardson revolver she had purchased over a year earlier. As she drove through a storm, Mrs Harris might have been thinking of the lengthy letter she had written Tarnower earlier that day. The letter, which belittled Lynne Tryforos in no uncertain terms, would later be used to provide the motive for what was to follow.

Mrs Harris arrived at Tarnower's Purchase estate after a tedious drive. She let herself in through a garage door which she knew was always open and made her way to the doctor's bedroom, a room she had shared with him many times over the past fourteen years. Five shots were fired. Four found their mark. Tarnower was hit in the hand, right shoulder, right arm and downward through the back, puncturing his lung and kidney. Suzanne van der Vrekens ran to the doctor's bedroom and found him in his blood-spattered tan pyjamas. She raised the alarm, but by the time Tarnower reached hospital he was pronounced dead.

Mrs Harris was arrested and stood trial for her lover's murder. Initially, as the facts of the case were revealed, there was a great deal of sympathy for the defendant. It was obvious that she had felt threatened when Tarnower turned from her in favour of a younger woman. It was also apparent that the famed doctor had treated her in a cavalier fashion. Perhaps Mrs Harris should not have taken the witness stand in her defence. Many believe she was responsible for her own undoing. She stated that she had not intended to shoot the doctor. It had all been a horrible mistake. She had travelled to Purchase to talk to him one more time before taking her own life. As she said, "I hoped it would be a quiet, pleasant last few minutes." But it was not to be.

Tarnower was asleep when Mrs Harris entered his bedroom, she told the court. When he awakened, he was in no mood to chat. Frustrated, Mrs Harris picked up a box of curlers and threw them through a window. Tarnower, in a rage, struck her across the face. She threw a cosmetics box. He struck her a second time. Sarcastically, she invited him to strike her again. He walked away.

Calmly, Jean Harris opened her purse and took out her .32-calibre revolver. She raised the gun, pointed it at her head and pulled the trigger. At that exact moment, "Hy came at me and grabbed the gun and pushed my hand away from my head and pushed it down, and I heard the gun explode." This first shot went through the doctor's hand. The gun dropped to the floor. Tarnower went to the bathroom to tend his hand. Mrs Harris found the revolver on the floor, just as Tarnower reappeared. He lunged at her as she picked up the revolver. Once again, it fell to the floor. Tarnower picked it up. Mrs Harris then begged for the gun, "Hy, please give me the gun or shoot me yourself, but for Christ's sake, let me die." He replied, "Jesus, you're crazy, get out of here." Mrs Harris grabbed the revolver now resting on Tarnower's lap. Tarnower jumped on her as she fell back on the bed. Mrs Harris felt the muzzle against her stomach. She pulled the trigger but felt no pain as the gun exploded. Tarnower fell back. Mrs Harris claimed that she placed the gun to her head, but despite continually pulling the trigger, the revolver didn't go off, although it did fire once more when she tested it away from her head. Her wish to die was not due to Tarnower's attention to other women, Mrs Harris claimed, but because of a deep personal and career trauma which made death more attractive than a truly exhausting life.

At her trial, the prosecution attorney stated that Mrs Harris was the typical study of the woman scorned. Her motive was there for all the world to see in her poorly timed letter to Dr Tarnower, in which she obviously illustrated her hatred toward her younger rival for the diet doctor's affection. She had five hours of driving with a revolver in her possession before she entered Tarnower's house, plenty of time for a calm mind to take hold of the situation.

Mrs Harris was found guilty of second-degree murder and sentenced to a minimum of fifteen years imprisonment. She has recently been paroled.

# SHARON TATE

ALMOST thirty years have passed since that night of horror, that night when the rage within Charles Manson's soul was unleashed inside the home of director Roman Polanski and his pregnant wife, movie actress Sharon Tate.

When small-time thief and pseudo–folk singer Charlie Manson was paroled from Terminal Island in San Pedro, California, in 1967, no one was aware that the five-foot-two-inch misfit with the magnetic personality would commit crimes so horrible they are still remembered thirty years later.

There was Charlie, thirty-two, free at last, after serving almost seven years in prison. It was the sixties—the era of love and peace, the drop-in drop-out syndrome, homeless young people wandering the country in search of a meaning to life. LSD helped. It was an era custom-made for Charlie Manson, with his guitar and charismatic personality. Gravitating to San Francisco, Charlie's inner circle of subculture followers grew in number. Mary Brunner, Lynn "Squeaky" Fromme and Patricia Krenwinkel became known as Charlie's girls. They slept, travelled, stole and begged together. They purchased an old bus and scoured the countryside. They were family.

New recruits joined Charlie's family. Susan Atkins, a nineteen-year-old hellion, came aboard. Robert Beausoleil, a twenty-year-old actor, who sometimes lived with thirty-year-old music teacher Gary Hinman, became a Manson follower. Diane Lake, fourteen, who was later renamed Snake because of her distinctive movements during intercourse, joined the family in their nomadic existence. Tex Watson was an avid Manson disciple, who would prove to be a valuable and loyal member of the family. Growth in the family was not derived solely from outsiders. Some of the girls became pregnant. Susan Atkins had a baby. Mary Brunner gave birth to Charlie's baby.

In 1968, Charlie and his followers made their headquarters at the Spahn movie ranch, a dilapidated group of buildings near Los Angeles. The sect had evolved from love and peace to Satanism, hate and revenge. Charlie would send out groups of his followers to "change the world," make it a better place to live in.

In July 1969, Gary Hinman had a falling-out with Charlie. Although Gary had always allowed members of Charlie's family to crash at his house, he was never a committed member of the sect. When Gary, who reputedly had money hidden in his house, steadfastly refused to devote himself to Charlie and his children, he signed his own death warrant. Robert Beausoleil and a couple of the girls paid Hinman a visit. Gary wouldn't give them the time of day. Charlie showed up and, in a fit of rage, stabbed Hinman in the head with a sword, almost severing his ear. Then he left. Beausoleil and the girls bound Hinman with rope. When they phoned Charlie for instructions, they were told to kill their captive. Hinman was stabbed twice in the chest and died on his living-room floor from loss of blood. Charlie's girls wrote "Political Piggy" on the wall in Hinman's blood, after which they returned to the Spahn ranch and sang songs. Within two weeks, police had matched a fingerprint in Hinman's home to Robert Beausoleil. He was picked up and charged with murder.

On the night of August 8, 1969, Charlie's followers went on a mission. They were well equipped. Inside their vehicle they had placed a pair of bolt cutters and a quantity of nylon rope. Linda Kasabian, Susan Atkins and Patricia Krenwinkel jumped in. Tex Watson drove. Charlie instructed, "Leave a sign. You girls know what to do. Something witchy." On the way, Tex told the girls they were going to kill everyone in a house once owned by Doris Day's son, Terry Melcher.

Tex drove up to 10050 Cielo Dr., now leased by director Roman Polanski. Polanski was on a roll. His movies in the sixties included *Repulsion* and *The Fearless Vampire Killers,* as well as the runaway hit, *Rosemary's Baby*. On this night, he was in Europe. His wife, actress Sharon Tate, eight and a half months pregnant, was at home entertaining friends, coffee heiress Abigail Folger, hair-stylist Jay Sebring and family friend Voityck Frykowski.

It was Steve Parent's misfortune to have picked that particular night to visit the Polanskis' caretaker, Bill Garretson, in a separate dwelling on the estate. Steve was in his car, just about to pull away, when he spotted Tex Watson. According to later testimony, Steve said, "Hey, what are you doing here?" Tex thrust his .22-calibre revolver into the open window on the driver's side. As Steve said, "Please don't hurt me," Tex pulled the trigger five times. He probably thought he had killed the caretaker. Inside his house, Bill Garretson heard nothing. He would not hear a sound the rest of the night.

Once inside Polanski's house, Tex accosted Frykowski. He shouted, "I'm the devil. I'm here to do the devil's business." The girls were instructed to secure Frykowski with nylon rope. Abigail Folger was found reading in bed in her room. Sharon Tate was lying in bed in another room. Jay Sebring, fully clothed, sat on the bed talking to Sharon. All the occupants of the house were made to gather together in the living room. It was killing time. Jay Sebring was shot by Tex for suggesting that the gang should allow Sharon to sit down. After all, she was pregnant. While Sebring lay on the floor, unconscious, Tex kicked him in the head.

Abigail and Sharon were tied around the neck with nylon cord. One end of the cord was tossed over a beam. Susan Atkins pulled the rope taut. Abigail and Sharon had to stand straight up or strangle to death. Tex announced that they were all about to die. He ordered Susan to kill. She complied, stabbing Voityck Frykowski repeatedly. When Frykowski continued to struggle, Tex clubbed the wounded man with his gun and shot him. Frykowski made it outside before being killed on the lawn. Fifty-one separate wounds were later found on his body. Sharon and Abigail frantically struggled to free themselves. Abigail was successful. She ran to the back door. Patricia Krenwinkel stabbed at her wildly, but Abigail warded off the blows with her badly cut hands and arms. Tex spotted the melee. He ran over and slashed Abigail's throat and abdomen.

Outside the house, Linda Kasabian stood watch. She observed Steve Parent's body in his vehicle. She saw Frykowski stagger out, screaming for help. It certainly was an action-filled night. Linda wondered how much money would be taken from such a nice home.

Inside, the killing continued. Sharon Tate, unattended for a few moments, freed herself. She started towards her front door, but was seen by Patricia Krenwinkel. Patricia solicitously assisted Sharon to a chair. Then Susan Atkins held her, while Tex Watson stabbed her to death. The three members of Charlie's family took turns stabbing the body. After a while, all was quiet. Tex decorated the bodies with nylon rope. Susan wrote the word PIG in blood on the door. Only thirty minutes had elapsed. It was so very quiet. Everyone was dead. Sharon's black kitten miaowed forlornly amidst the silent carnage.

Charlie would be delighted. As they drove away, the family members changed out of their bloody clothing. Blood-soaked garments rolled into a ball—tossed out of the car—knives out the window—Tex's revolver thrown into a ravine.

Back at the Spahn ranch, the children of evil reported to Satan. He was pleased. They were tired. Everyone slept well.

Next morning, the scene of death was discovered. Horror swept Los Angeles. The nation, and ultimately the entire world, was made aware of the ritual-style slaying that had taken place in exclusive Benedict Canyon. Charlie and his children were ecstatic at the publicity their crime was receiving. It had been a commendable job, but messy. That very night they would do it all again, but Satan himself would lead the way.

Linda Kasabian drove the '59 Ford to the home of grocery chain-store owner Leno LaBianca, forty-four, at 3301 Waverly Dr. His wife, Rosemary, thirty-eight, was in bed when Charlie Manson appeared in the living room, waving a sword at her husband. Charlie tied the LaBiancas standing up back to back, then walked out of the house. His family, waiting in the car, was ready for action. It was killing time again. Tex Watson, Leslie Van Houten and Patricia Krenwinkel were given their instructions. After the job was completed, they were to hitch-hike back to the ranch. Linda Kasabian and Charlie sped off.

The killing squad did their work efficiently. They led Rosemary into the bedroom, where they stabbed her to death. Leno was killed in the living room. Neither victim panicked until the very end. Tex carved the word WAR on Leno LaBianca's chest. Using the dead man's blood, they wrote DEATH TO PIGS on the walls. On the refrigerator door, Patricia wrote HELTER SKELTER. The killers bathed and raided the fridge. Killing was hard work, but it was worth it.

Rosemary's children by a previous marriage called on the house of death and the second night of horror was made known to the world. The ritualistic aspects of the two killing sprees linked them together forever. They became known as the Tate-LaBianca murders.

As the days turned into weeks without the murderers being apprehended, famous movie actors such as Warren Beatty, Peter Sellers and Yul Brynner established a reward of $25,000 for the arrest and conviction of the killers. Weeks turned into months. The family kept busy. They stole gasoline and robbed indiscriminately. One man, forty-year-old Shorty Shea, somehow found out details of the Tate-LaBianca killings. Charlie's clan, led by Steve Grogan, tortured, killed and buried Shorty in the desert.

By the end of September, members of the Manson family were being rounded up for minor crimes. Many were in and out of jail on various charges. Fingerprints recovered at murder scenes were checked against suspects. Snitches were placed in cells. A myriad of evidence pointed to the family as perpetrators of the Tate-LaBianca murders. Finally, the family's leader was taken into custody. The world was shocked. These suspects were from middle-class American families. They likened their leader to Jesus Christ and displayed no remorse for what they had done. Tex Watson was an all-star high-school track star from Texas. Leslie Van Houten had been a small-town high-school princess.

Yet these same young people had stabbed a pregnant woman and had stuck a fork in the stomach of a man they had just killed.

Somewhere in the deep recesses of his disturbed mind, Charlie Manson believed that the blacks of the world would rise against the whites. He would be the catalyst, the trigger which would change the world. Instead, his madness was directly responsible for nine known deaths.

The family leader and his flower children are now thirty years older.

Charles Manson resides in the maximum-security wing of San Quentin Prison, serving several life sentences. From time to time, Charlie comes up for parole. He has been refused seven times. Still defiant, still wild-eyed, the madman who carved a swastika in his forehead may never be paroled.

Susan Atkins pleaded guilty to the murder of Gary Hinman. Her testimony helped indict other members of the family. Sentenced to life imprisonment, Susan is presently confined at the California Institute for Women in Frontera.

Lynn "Squeaky" Fromme went on to gain fame for her attempt to assassinate President Gerald Ford in 1975. She is presently serving a life sentence and has been refused parole since 1986.

Robert Beausoleil is serving a life sentence for the murder of Gary Hinman. He is presently confined at the medium-security California Men's Colony at San Luis Obispo.

Leslie Van Houten is still serving a life sentence for the LaBianca murders. She was not present during the Tate massacre. Leslie has obtained a university degree in psychology and literature while in prison.

Tex Watson was the actual killer of many of the victims. He is presently confined at the California Men's Colony. In 1987, he was turned down for parole for the tenth time. Watson has sired three children via conjugal visits. He claims to have found religion and sometimes acts as chaplain at the prison.

Patricia Krenwinkel is serving her life sentence at the California Institute for Women.

Linda Kasabian, who was outside both the Tate and LaBianca residences on the nights of the murders, testified against her friends in exchange for immunity from prosecution. She is the mother of four children, has changed her name to Christian and lives with her husband in New Hampshire.

Diane Lake, better known as Snake in her Manson family days, also testified for the state. When last heard of, she was working for a large corporation in California.

# WILLIAM DESMOND TAYLOR

BIZARRE is the only word which comes close to describing the life, loves and death of Hollywood director William Desmond Taylor. Even the man's name was phoney. On the other hand, his murder was real enough, but let's start at the beginning.

Taylor was born William Cunningham Deane-Tanner in 1868, County Cork, Ireland. He had a younger brother, Dennis, who was one year his junior. When both lads were in their late teens, their father, a major in the British army, insisted that they follow a military career. When they refused, he tossed them out of his home and thereafter had nothing to do with his two sons.

The boys made their way to America. There is some evidence that William unsuccessfully prospected for gold in the Klondike and later in Montana. Back in New York at the turn of the century, he became manager of a shop called The English Antique Shop at 240 Fifth Ave. Never shy when it came to members of the opposite sex, William dated several girls, but fell in love with one particular beauty, Ethel May Harrison, the daughter of a stockbroker. In December 1901, Ethel became Mrs William Cunnigham Deane-Tanner in the famous Little Church Around the Corner. The happy couple moved into a comfortable home in nearby Larchmont. In 1903, their union was blessed with a daughter, Ethel Daisy.

On October 23, 1908, after seven years of marital bliss, William strolled out of the antique shop, nonchalantly telling his clerk that he was breaking for lunch a bit early. William didn't return to the shop that day or any other day, but next morning phoned and advised a member of his staff to send $600 to him at a down-town Manhattan hotel. The money was delivered and William Cunningham Deane-Tanner promptly disappeared, not only from the antique business, but from his wife and daughter, as well. Four years later, his wife obtained a divorce.

In a case fraught with strange twists, William's brother Dennis, who had a wife and two children and who also managed an antique shop on Fifth Avenue, walked out of his shop and was never heard from again. When it was obvious that Dennis had skipped, a thorough inventory of the shop was conducted, but nothing was missing. Whatever Dennis was, he was not a thief.

The next we hear of William is five years later when he showed up in Hollywood as William Desmond Taylor. No one in the movie capital was ever to know him by any other name. Tall, slim William discovered that he could get small acting jobs in the movies.

Back in New York one fine day, William's ex-wife, Ethel, decided to take in a movie. You can imagine her surprise when there on the screen was her long lost husband. Ethel didn't know what to do, so she called up Dennis's former wife, who by coincidence now lived in California. Like Ethel, she, too, had obtained a divorce. She contacted William and told him her story of having been deserted by Dennis, who left her with two small children to raise on her own. Never for a moment did William admit that she had been his sister-in-law, but he must have sympathized with her situation. He sent her $50 a month for the rest of his life.

William rose rapidly in the film industry to become a full-fledged director and, in a relatively short time, the senior director in the Famous Players–Lasky Co. Because he had never taken out U.S. citizenship, he joined the Canadian army during the First World War, rising to the rank of major. Just before the war ended, he was shipped to England, but was soon returned to Canada, where he received his discharge.

William took up where he left off in Hollywood. A successful director, he could have led the fast life favoured by many of his colleagues. Instead, he preferred to live simply. He purchased a conservative home on South Alvarado Street. One of his immediate neighbours was Edna Purviance, who had achieved a measure of fame as a feature actress in several of Charlie Chaplin's comedies. William's other next-door neighbour was actor Douglas MacLean and his wife.

William always employed one full time servant. Edward Sands performed all the household tasks. He maintained two cars, as well as acting as chauffeur and bartender. William seems to have been well satisfied with Sands's work habits until 1921 when he took a trip to England. Sands had a field day. He pawned William's jewellery, forged his boss's name on a series of cheques, wrecked one of William's two cars and made off with a few good suits. Sands was never seen or heard of again. An investigation into his past revealed that he had once served in the British army under the name Edward Fitz-Strathmore.

What's a gentleman to do without a manservant? William hired Henry Peavey, an efficient homosexual, to replace Sands. Henry was a caution, as they used to say back then. He had the most disagreeable habit of dunking himself in cologne so that anyone in close proximity to him felt they were touring an Estée Lauder factory. Henry also painted his fingernails bright red. To pass the time, he crocheted and embroidered. Each evening after dinner, Henry left the Taylor residence and returned each morning at about 7 a.m.

Let's home in on the day of February 1, 1922. It would prove to be the last day of William Desmond Taylor's life. William had met Mabel Normand on the rebound, so to speak. The comedic star had been the favourite squeeze of studio boss Mack Sennett right up until she walked into his apartment unannounced to find Mae Busch with nothing on but her watch and the radio. You can still see Mae strutting her stuff in old Laurel and Hardy movies. Alas, she wore more clothing in the movies than she was wearing when Mabel caught her in that most embarrassing of positions.

Mabel teamed up with William shortly after the incident. They did the Hollywood scene together and were considered a couple by the gossip columnists of the day. Mabel was to tell investigators that on that fateful February 1, she rose about midday, as she always did when she wasn't working. She read some books William had loaned her. Evidently, Mabel had illusions of graduating from comedy to more serious roles and William was providing her with intellectual reading material. She then gathered up unwanted Christmas presents and had her chauffeur, William Davis, carry them out to her car. Together, they sped away to get refunds or exchanges for the gifts.

At 7 p.m., Mabel had finished returning gifts. She checked in with her maid for telephone messages. There were two. Her studio wanted her to report early the next morning for work and William had more books to lend her. Mabel decided to drop into William's home to pick up the books. En route, she picked up two bags of peanuts, which she consumed in the back seat of the car. Once at her destination, she told her chauffeur to clean the shells out of the vehicle while she went in to get the books. Just as she was about to ring the bell, she heard William talking on the phone. She paused until the conversation ended, rang the bell and was warmly greeted by the director.

Henry Peavey rustled up a couple of cocktails while William explained to Mabel that he was making out his income tax and was attempting to clean up the mess left by his former servant, Edward Sands. At 7:20 p.m., Henry said his goodbyes and left for the day. A short time later, William walked Mabel to her car and the pair kissed goodbye.

At seven the next morning, Henry Peavey reported for work as usual. There was William lying on the living-room floor with an overturned chair straddling his legs. Henry did what every self-respecting servant should do when he finds his boss dead on the living-room floor. He ran out to the street and commenced to yell at the top of his voice. In minutes, neighbours were alerted and someone called a doctor and the police. A cursory examination of the body revealed that William had been shot with a .38-calibre bullet in the left side of the back. A minor mystery arose when it was noted that the bullet hole in William's jacket was a few inches lower than the one in his shirt.

Neighbour Edna Purviance got on the phone. In minutes, word was out that one of Hollywood's most talented directors had been ventilated with a .38 slug in the back. Among those advised of the murder was Mabel Normand, who immediately became hysterical. Mabel had her chauffeur whip her over to William's house without delay. Another call made by Edna that night was to Mary Miles Minter who, while only seventeen years of age, was one of Hollywood's brightest stars. Evidently, Mary knew William extremely well.

Detectives rummaging through William's belongings came up with a darling silk nightgown monogrammed MMM. Love letters on stationery similarly monogrammed were found written by Mary to William. In order to combat the risqué, uncomplimentary rumours whirling about her connection with William, Mary held a press conference, advising those in attendance that she was secretly engaged to William. The juicy publicity affected Mary's career to such an extent that her studio bought out her contract for a sizeable amount of cash. Mary never recovered from the bad publicity and to all intents and purposes her movie career was over.

Quite unlike Mary, Mabel emerged from her association with William relatively unscathed. She told her story in a straightforward manner which was believed by all. A neighbour had seen her and William walk to her car at around seven-thirty the night before. Police even noted the peanut shells on the street where William Davis had swept them out of Mabel's car.

Douglas MacLean told police that he and his wife had heard what he described as a loud report at 8 p.m. Mrs MacLean had gone outside to investigate and had seen a stocky man with his cap pulled down over his eyes leaving William's home. Her statement, combined with Mabel's story, established the time of the murder as being no earlier than 7:30 p.m. and no later than 8 p.m.

During their investigation, police learned that the Taylor residence had been robbed on two occasions during that winter. Some time after the robberies, William had received pawn tickets in the mail for some of the stolen goods. The tickets were made out to William Deane-Tanner. This led investigators to believe that someone out there knew of William's past life, unless the burglar had discovered his real name on a document while robbing the house. Then again, why send the pawn tickets in the first place? It was a real mystery.

There were scores of theories. Some believed that the killer was Edward Sands, who had returned to seek revenge for some wrong done to him by William in the past. Others believed that the stocky man seen by Mrs MacLean was a woman in disguise. One must remember that, other than Mabel and Mary, our William had a ready-and-willing stable of lovelies at his beck and call. Despite the theories, months passed without the case being solved. For some reason, everyone wanted to be involved in the high-profile murder. Over 300 individuals confessed to the crime, but all proved to be cranks.

Who in the world killed the director? Some say it was Mary Miles Minter who, while claiming to have been betrothed to William, could have secretly been furious with him for his open liaison with Mabel Normand. After Mary's contract was bought out by her studio, she purchased a mansion in Santa Monica, where she led a more or less reclusive life. In 1957, she married a businessman and lived until 1984, when she died of a heart attack at age eighty-two.

There are those who believe that William really was engaged to Mary, which was cause for Mabel to return to the house dressed as a man and kill him. They feel that the stocky man seen by Mrs MacLean was really Mabel.

Mabel Normand eloped in September 1926. In her usual flamboyant manner, she and her beau, Lew Cody, woke up a justice of the peace at 3 a.m. to tie the knot. Three years later, Mabel contracted tuberculosis. She died in a sanitorium in 1930. She was thirty-six years old.

No one has ever discovered who murdered William Desmond Taylor.

# HARRY K. THAW

WHEN Harry K. Thaw walked over to Stanford White's table at New York's Madison Square Roof Garden on June 25, 1906 and shot him three times, he had no way of knowing that years later his every move that evening would be studied by students of unusual crimes.

Mad Harry, as he came to be called, was a multimillionaire by the time he was twenty-one, having been left millions by his father, who had made it big in the railroad business. Harry did it all. Once, he rode a horse down Fifth Avenue and up the steps of his private club. Another time, in Paris, he threw a private party for one hundred guests and delighted all the females with a piece of jewellery placed beside each of their dinner plates. That little caper was reported to have set Harry back $50,000. Fun and games were Harry's specialty.

Evelyn Nesbit and her mother arrived in New York in 1901. The object of their trip was to further Evelyn's fledgling modelling career and at the same time seek her fortune. By any terms of reference, Evelyn was a beautiful girl. She had angelic good looks and a demeanour that oozed innocence. She had no difficulty landing a part in the chorus line of the hit musical *Floradora,* then playing on Broadway.

Evelyn had just turned sixteen when a member of the cast introduced her to Stanford White. Now, Stanford was not your average rascal hanging around stage doors trying to pick up chorus girls. Not by a long shot. He was America's most eminent architect, responsible for creating such structures as the Hall of Fame at New York University, the Memorial Arch at Washington Square and Madison Square Garden.

Both Mama Nesbit and innocent Evelyn were thrilled when the distinguished architect asked permission from Mama to accompany Evelyn to dinner. White, who had a bit of a reputation as a womanizer, didn't take long to suggest that life in New York was having an adverse effect on Mama's health. In fact, she looked downright peaked. Mama Nesbit reluctantly accepted Mr White's kind offer to finance a trip back home to clean healthy Pittsburgh.

According to Evelyn, that's when the fifty-two-year-old Stanford asked her to a party at his studio. Would you believe it—there were no other guests, but obliging Stanford suggested they party anyway. After much champagne, the sly old dog thought that Evelyn should try out his red velvet swing. The swing, installed in the studio for just such occasions, allowed Stanford a rather vivid view of his lady friends' legs as they swung through the air. After champagne, swinging and heaven only knows what else, Evelyn later swore that she felt a throbbing in her head. She lay down on Stanford's bed, which naturally enough was surrounded by mirrors.

Next thing the poor child remembered was waking up nude. Even worse, beside her was America's most distinguished architect, also very nude. Evelyn claimed she screamed. Then she cried. Stanford put on a robe. He confessed that while Evelyn may have been many things, she was no longer a virgin. Stanford did the gentlemanly thing. He elicited a promise from Evelyn that she would not tell her mother what had happened and then he drove her home. Evelyn was so distraught that she continued to accompany Stanford to plays, nightclubs and restaurants from that night on.

In the meantime, who should start showering Evelyn with dozens of American Beauty roses with fifty-dollar bills entwined in their stems but mad Harry Thaw. Now, a girl couldn't help but take Harry seriously, even though it was rumoured that, at thirty-four years of age, he was more often in the sauce than not. He also wasn't averse to cocaine. In fact, Harry pretty well tried everything. Despite all this, there was one thing Harry had going for him that couldn't be ignored. He stood to inherit forty million dollars.

By the time she was eighteen, Evelyn was Harry's mistress, having travelled as his live-in companion throughout the United States and Europe. All during their relationship she continued to see Stanford White. In the end, Harry and his millions won out. In April 1905, he and Evelyn became husband and wife. While on a trip to Paris, Evelyn told Harry about the night Stanford White had defiled, disgraced and had good old-fashioned intercourse with her. She even threw in the red velvet swing for good measure. Harry was furious. Evelyn's recitation of how she had lost her virginity to Stanford White preyed on Harry's mind. From that moment on, he taunted White at every opportunity and did everything in his power to ruin the architect's reputation.

The whole mess came to a head on that fateful June night at the Madison Square Roof Garden. After finishing dinner, the Thaws rose to leave. As Harry walked by White's table, he abruptly turned, drew a revolver and shot him twice in the head and once in the body. The architect was very dead. Harry held his revolver high in the air, grasping it by the muzzle to indicate that he was through shooting for the night.

Evelyn ran toward Harry, shouting, "My God, Harry, what have you done? What have you done?"

"I have probably saved your life, dearie," he replied.

"Harry, I'll stick by you," said dear Evelyn. As an afterthought, she added, "My, you are in an awful mess."

A policeman then disarmed Harry and took him away. No sooner was Harry in custody than the Thaw money was at work to gain his freedom. Harry's mother declared that she would spend a million dollars to free her son. She meant every word. Entire law firms were retained to defend Harry. A public relations company was hired to paint Harry's image in the best possible light. In Brooklyn, a play depicting the entire melodrama was enacted at the Amphion Theatre. In it, the hero's name was Harold, the heroine Emeline, and the villain, Stanford Black. The Thaw millions were at work.

One of the most publicized trials ever to take place in New York began on January 21, 1907. Representatives of the press from all over the world congregated to devour every juicy tidbit. They were not disappointed. Evelyn told all. Advised that the main thrust of the defence would be to illustrate that Harry was insane at the time of the murder and did not know that what he was doing was wrong, Evelyn recounted every sordid detail of her deflowering and the effect the story had on Harry. She also revealed that Harry had once taken her to a castle in Austria where he'd beaten her unmercifully with a horsewhip. She wept on the stand. There were those who said that her act was better than anything appearing on the stage at that time. Rumour had it that Evelyn received $200,000 for her testimony. She had to be good. A guilty verdict meant the death sentence for Harry. We must remember that this all took place at a time when the death sentence meant going to Sing Sing, sitting on a chair and having the current turned on.

The jury was split. Seven favoured a guilty verdict and five felt that Thaw was insane and therefore innocent. A second trial was held in January 1908. This time around, Harry was judged to be innocent of murder by reason of insanity. The presiding judge confined him to the Asylum for the Criminally Insane at Matteawan.

No sooner had the doors of that institution closed upon Harry than his family commenced to do everything in their power to have him set free. Finally, in 1915, after several court actions, Harry was judged to be sane and was released from Matteawan. One of the first things he did was to obtain a divorce from Evelyn, who was more than eager to oblige. During Harry's confinement, Evelyn had become somewhat of a hot property, appearing in several stage plays. After the divorce, she promptly married her dancing partner.

Harry continued to get into trouble with the law for the rest of his life. He was arrested several times for disturbing the peace and was fair game for his lady friends, whom he pursued with a passion to the end of his days.

Harry Thaw died in Miami in 1947. He was seventy-six.

# TOM THOMSON

TOM Thomson is considered one of the greatest landscape painters in Canadian art. Since his untimely death in 1917, his work has gained recognition throughout the world. His death has always been a mystery. Did he die as a result of a freak accident or was he murdered?

Tom was born on August 4, 1877, in Claremont, Ontario, approximately fifteen miles from Toronto. Shortly after his birth, his family moved to Leith, near Owen Sound. Here young Tom led a typical rural Ontario life on the family farm. He gave no indication of the artistic talent he would later display. Tom attended high school, worked as a machinist's apprentice and enrolled in a business course. He never finished any of these early endeavours.

At age twenty-four, Tom moved to Seattle, where he obtained a position with a commercial art studio operated by his brother George. In 1905, he returned to Toronto and again found a job with a commercial art studio. In 1911, he switched to another studio, Grip Ltd. It was while employed there that Tom first came in contact with A. Y. Jackson, Arthur Lismer, Fred Varley and Frank Carmichael, all of whom would later achieve fame as members of Canada's Group of Seven. It was probably under the influence of these men that Tom began painting as a hobby. For fun, he sketched around the Toronto area with his new friends.

In 1912, Tom visited Algonquin Park and fell in love with the vivid colours and raw beauty of the Canadian landscape. By 1913, he was seriously painting in the park and managing to eke out a living as a guide. He became well known, particularly around Canoe Lake. Tom was an excellent woodsman and canoeist. Sometimes he would be gone from the shores of Canoe Lake for weeks at a stretch, rowing and hiking deep into the interior of the park on painting trips. Those who knew him then attested to his prowess as an independent spirit in the woods, who was an expert at rowing, hunting and swimming. Thomson painted the wild Canadian scenery he found in Algonquin Park from 1913 to 1917. During this time, he produced such well-known paintings as *Jack Pine, Northern Lights, West Wind* and *Spring Ice*. Many of his works are part of the McMichael Canadian Collection at Kleinberg, Ontario, and appear in private collections throughout the world.

On the evening of July 7, 1917, some guides, tourists and fishermen met at one of the cabins skirting the lake. Tom was there with friends. A few drinks were passed around and the conversation turned to the main topic of the day, the First World War, which was raging in Europe. Many of Tom's artist friends were overseas, but because of his flat feet, his attempts to enlist had met with failure. One American cottager, Martin Bletcher, was of German extraction and many felt he was in Canada to avoid serving in the U.S. army. He and the intensely patriotic Thomson did not get along. Bletcher became loud when drinking. On this occasion, he expressed views sympathetic to the German war effort. Tom was furious and the two men nearly came to blows. Such outbreaks among grown men having a few drinks are usually forgotten the next day, but in this case, as events were to unfold, this particular quarrel remained indelibly impressed in everyone's memory.

The next day, Tom was seen by his friend, park ranger Mark Robinson, peacefully fishing from the shore. Tom spotted Robinson some distance away. "Howdy, Mark," Tom shouted. Robinson waved in acknowledgement. It was the last time the ranger was to see his friend alive. Tom got into his canoe and paddled out on Canoe Lake and to his death. Bletcher and his sister, Bessie, went out on the lake that afternoon. The following day, Bletcher told some people at a lakeside lodge that he had observed an overturned canoe on the water the day before. Uncharacteristically for an experienced cottager along the lake, he hadn't bothered to investigate. Another guide quickly retrieved the overturned canoe. It was Tom's. It still contained his ground sheet, food and one paddle, which was lashed to the canoe in the common carrying position. Missing were his gear, fishing pole and the small axe he always had aboard. Park ranger Robinson immediately instituted an official search for his friend.

On July 15, seven days after he was last seen alive, Tom Thomson's body was found afloat on Canoe Lake. The body was in an advanced state of decomposition. One of the cottagers along the lake was a doctor named Howland. Due to the heat and the state of the body, Dr Howland was ordered not to wait for the coroner who had to travel from North Bay. Instead, he was asked to examine the body and to have an undertaker bury it immediately. Robinson assisted the doctor in removing Thomson's clothing for the examination. While doing this, he discovered fishing line wrapped around Tom's left leg. In his report, the doctor mentioned another strange fact. On Tom's right temple there was a four-inch-long bruise. He attributed the cause of death to drowning. And so Tom Thomson was buried without the benefit of a coroner's inquest two days after his body was found floating on the lake.

The hastiness of the burial generated many questions, which to this day have not been answered. Would an expert canoeist accidentally fall out of a canoe in calm waters which he knew like the palm of his hand? What happened to Tom's second paddle? How did he get the severe bruise on his temple? Why did water-wise Martin Bletcher not investigate an overturned canoe? How did fishing line get wrapped around Thomson's left leg?

Undertaker H. W. Churchill arrived at Canoe Lake with instructions from the Thomson family to have the body exhumed and transported to the family plot in Leith. The undertaker, outfitted with metal casket and lantern, insisted on exhuming the body in the darkness of night by himself. He was dropped off at the freshly dug grave at 9 p.m. and picked up at midnight. Churchill claimed that during those three hours he dug up the grave by himself by lantern light and transferred the decomposed body to a metal casket. Later, the men who picked him up at midnight and assisted him in transporting the casket wondered about his speed. They also wondered at the light weight of the casket. A couple of the men doubted if there was anything in the casket at all. Tom Thomson's body was transported to Leith where it rests today. The casket has never been opened since the night Churchill completed his macabre task.

From time to time there have been groundswell movements to have the casket in Leith examined to ascertain if Thomson's body was really buried there. Nothing has ever come of these efforts and so we are left with two mysteries. Was one of Canada's foremost landscape artists murdered? And does his body repose in the family plot in Leith, Ontario?

# THELMA TODD

WHEN Thelma Todd entered a beauty contest and was crowned Miss Massachusetts, she had no way of knowing that she would be catapulted into fame as one of the leading movie stars of her era.

Thelma's daddy was so impressed with his daughter's beauty that he sent her photo to Paramount Studios. Some-one at Paramount agreed with daddy. Thelma was invited to enter an acting school for a six-month course. In March 1926, at the conclusion of her studies, she signed a one-year contract with Paramount. Thelma was on her way. She received small parts that showed off her natural comic flair. As a result, she appeared in several Laurel and Hardy flicks, as well as a few Marx Brothers comedies. By 1932, Thelma Todd had graduated to big-budget films and was considered a bona fide star. Along the way, she married her agent, Pasquale Di Cicci, but the marriage didn't last. The pair was divorced two years later. Never one to stay on the shelf for long, Thelma commenced to keep company with Roland West, a one-time director who, at forty-seven, was considered past his prime. The pair was inseparable. They were seen around town constantly.

Always a bit of a self-promoter, Thelma, attempting to cash in on her fame, opened a restaurant in Santa Monica called Thelma Todd's Roadside Rest. Roland West was installed as manager. The layout of the place requires a little explaining. Thelma and Roland lived on the ground floor of the restaurant in separate apartments. Roland also had a cottage on a hill about 400 feet above the restaurant. The cottage could only be reached by foot from the restaurant by climbing 270 steps cut into the steep hill. The steps were rather treacherous, particularly in wet weather when they became muddy. However, the cottage on the hill came complete with a garage, which could be reached directly by road. It was in this garage that Thelma kept her Pierce-Arrow convertible. Why Thelma would put up with the inconvenience of having to walk up the steps from the restaurant to reach her car is hard to fathom. Equally inexplicable is the inconvenience incurred when she drove her Pierce-Arrow into the garage. She then had to walk down the hill to her own apartment. Difficult as it is to understand, this is the set-up which existed after Thelma opened her restaurant.

By 1935, Thelma was an established star earning $1,500 a week, a veritable fortune over sixty years ago. In addition, her restaurant was profitable. She worked at the business, often entertaining guests and in general making herself visible to her hordes of fans.

On Saturday, December 14, 1935, movie actress Ida Lupino's father was visiting from London, England. He was a great fan of Thelma's. In keeping with the movie capital's reputation for doing things in the grand manner, Miss Lupino decided to throw a party at the elegant Trocadero Restaurant with Thelma as guest of honour.

The party would have gone unnoticed were it not for the events which were to unfold. Later, every incident that occurred at the party was studied and rehashed in order to discover a motive for murder. A few days before the party, Ida Lupino bumped into Thelma's ex-husband, Pasquale Di Cicci, who commented on how badly he felt at not being asked to the party. Somewhat embarrassed, Miss Lupino invited him to attend on the spot. On the night of the great event, Di Cicci showed up with actress Margaret Lindsay. Thelma thought the whole deal was in extremely poor taste and expressed her feelings to her ex-husband. The incident caused a few tense moments for the party-goers, but nothing more. For the rest of the early evening, Thelma was her usual charming attentive self.

At 2:30 a.m., Thelma's attitude abruptly changed. Sidney Grauman of Grauman's Chinese Theater fame, beckoned Thelma to his table. After a short chat, Thelma's demeanour changed from good cheer to depression. Several guests noticed that she had become very depressed after her talk with Grauman. When the party was over, Thelma took a taxi home. The driver, Ernest Peters, later swore that Thelma told him not to spare the horses, because she was in danger of being kidnapped or slain by gangsters. Peters, accustomed to the weird behaviour of the Hollywood set, paid scant attention, but did as he was told. He sped to Thelma's restaurant and let her out in front of the establishment.

In hindsight, those who chatted with Thelma at the party felt that someone had imparted distasteful news to Thelma during the course of the festivities. While still in a good mood, she had invited four of the guests to a complimentary meal at the Roadside Rest the following evening, a Sunday. The four guests drove up to the restaurant as planned, only to find it closed. They peered in windows, knocked on doors, but try as they might, they couldn't get a response. Disappointed, they left, commenting that Thelma was inconsiderate not to have let them know that she wouldn't be there.

On Monday morning, maid May Whitehead showed up for work at Thelma's apartment on the first floor. She found the apartment empty and was a bit apprehensive when she discovered that Thelma's bed was undisturbed. Obviously Thelma had not slept in the bed since it had been made up two days earlier. May glanced up the hill to Roland West's cottage. She noticed that the garage door was slightly open. Thinking that Thelma was with Roland, May decided to climb those 270 awkward steps to confer with her boss. Growing angrier with each step, May finally reached the garage and looked inside the Pierce-Arrow. There was Thelma, quite dead. Her bloodied head rested against the steering wheel. She was dressed in the evening gown and satin shoes she had worn to the party Saturday night. There was blood on the car seat and the running board. May called police post-haste.

The apparent accident made big news. Here was a rare beauty, loved by thousands of fans, dead due to a tragic accident. An autopsy confirmed investigators' initial suspicions. The dried blood on Thelma's face, which appeared to have come from a wound to her head when she fell into the steering wheel, was estimated to have been there since 5 a.m. on Sunday. In addition, the autopsy indicated that Thelma had died due to carbon monoxide poisoning. She had either gone to sleep with the engine running or had simply been overcome by the fumes. It was a freak accident, and there matters might have stood forever had not the Hollywood rumour mill begun to grind out other theories.

William Persson, a tobacco-store owner, stated positively that Thelma had entered his store at 9 a.m. Sunday morning. She was in her evening gown and blue shoes, which Persson said were a bit muddy. Thelma gave the store owner a nickel and asked him to make a phone call. Persson made the call, but couldn't remember the number. According to Persson, a gentleman entered the store a few minutes later and he and Thelma left together.

The wife of actor Wallace Ford also disputed the official time of death as being 5 a.m. on Sunday. She swore to anyone who would listen that she had spoken to Thelma on the phone at four-thirty Sunday afternoon. She claimed she couldn't be mistaken. She had invited Thelma to attend a cocktail party celebrating her wedding anniversay that day. She recalled that Thelma had asked if it would be alright for her to bring along a companion. Mrs Ford said it would be fine and the two friends joked about it when Thelma wouldn't tell her the name of her friend. Rather sheepishly, Thelma told Mrs Ford that she was still in the evening gown she had worn the night before and asked if she could come as she was. Mrs Ford, accustomed to the strange behaviour of many of her acquaintances, agreed, "Come as you are," she shouted over the phone. Later, she was surprised when Thelma failed to attend the cocktail party. Still others swore they had seen Thelma in a car with a strange man late Sunday night.

Discounting the eyewitness reports of sightings of Thelma after her supposedly official time of death, one of the major mysteries of the Thelma Todd saga which remains to this day is the question of why Thelma made her way to the parked Pierce-Arrow. She had been driven home from the Lupino party and deposited in front of her restaurant apartment by taxi driver Ernest Peters. May Whitehead said she was sure Thelma had a key to the place and could have let herself in. Why would she climb those hazardous 270 steps to the garage?

Police conducted an experiment. A woman of the same height and weight as Thelma and wearing the same type of shoes was made to climb the steps from the restaurant to the cottage. At the end of her journey, her shoes were in far worse shape than Thelma's, which seemed to indicate that Thelma had not made the hike to the cottage.

There were those who were obviously concerned for Thelma's safety. Sid Grauman had phoned Roland West in the wee hours of the morning to tell him Thelma was on the way. Roland waited over half an hour before locking up and going to bed. If Thelma had knocked or had made any noise around the cottage, he hadn't heard her.

The investigation was in full swing when an enterprising detective thought to ask Roland West an obvious question. Did anyone else live in the cottage? Imagine their surprise when they learned that a seventy-year-old bookkeeper, Charles Smith, occupied a room directly above the garage where Thelma had met her end. Smith, who had escaped the initial round of questioning because he had been away visiting relatives, told police that he had slept sound as a drum on Saturday night and had heard nothing. There wasn't anything unusual about that. He always slept as if there were no tomorrow.

On December 18, an inquest jury returned their verdict: "Thelma Alice Todd came to her death on December 15, 1935, in a garage at 17531 Posetano Rd. near Santa Monica, California, and from evidence submitted, death appears to have been accidental—but we recommend further investigation by the proper authorities."

Thelma's body was cremated. A grand jury investigation attributed death to carbon monoxide poisoning. In the end, we are left with the same dilemma detectives faced sixty-one years ago. What set of circumstances fit most of the details surrounding Thelma's death? It seems to me that at the time of the tragedy, students of the case were split between accepting the official medical time of death and the testimony of the many witnesses who claimed to have seen or spoken to Thelma after the official time of death.

I am inclined to believe that the estimation of the medical time of death, based mainly on the condition of dried blood, was an honest error. With a key to her own apartment in her purse, it would have been unnatural for Thelma to make her way up those treacherous steps to Roland West's cottage. The police experiment indicated that she didn't make that trek. It is my opinion that Thelma, conspicuously dressed in an evening gown and fur coat, was seen and spoken to by witnesses long after 5 a.m. on Sunday morning. And remember, scientific calculations were not as precise sixty years ago as they are today.

After Thelma was let out of the taxi by Ernest Peters, she could have been picked up by a friend or acquaintance with whom she spent most of Sunday. This same person may have eventually driven her to the garage to pick up her Pierce-Arrow. Here she was rendered unconscious by a blow to the head. The perpetrator then turned on the ignition, asphyxiating Thelma with carbon monoxide. He quite possibly was attempting to simulate a suicide.

That's the best I can come up with. After all, no one has been able to prove to this day whether Thelma Todd committed suicide, died by accident or was murdered.

# CLAUS VON BULOW

TAKE an aristocratic Dane, mix well with an American heiress, throw in a beautiful mistress for spice and you should come up with enough intrigue to last a lifetime. The aristocratic Dane was Claus von Bulow, the American heiress was Martha "Sunny" Crawford von Auersperg von Bulow and the beautiful heiress was Alexandra Isles.

Claus von Bulow was born in Denmark in 1926 into a wealthy cultured family. His grandfather, Fritz von Bulow, was Denmark's minister of justice from 1910 to 1913. Claus obtained his early education at private boarding schools in Switzerland. He eventually enrolled at Trinity College in Cambridge, where he earned his law degree. After graduation, Claus held a series of positions in the banking field before being employed by J. Paul Getty, then considered the richest man in the world. Claus rose within the Getty empire to become the billionaire oilman's executive assistant. He travelled the world making deals for the Getty organization. His position was so exalted that, when in London, he lived at Getty's palatial estate.

It was while globetrotting on behalf of the eccentric tycoon that Claus met beautiful Martha "Sunny" Crawford, who was then married to an impoverished Austrian prince, Alfred von Auersperg. Sunny and the prince had two children, Prince Alexander and Princess Annie Laurie. Sunny von Auersperg was not a poor little rich girl. She was just plain rich. Her father, George Crawford, the Pittsburgh utility king, died when Sunny was three. When she met Claus, her wealth was estimated at between thirty and one hundred million dollars.

In 1964, four years after their first meeting, Claus and Sunny met again. She and the prince were no longer married. Suave and cultured, the six-foot-four-inch Claus von Bulow took two years to woo and wed the attractive and wealthy Sunny. Claus left the Getty organization to spend all his time with his wife. (Rich people can do that.) Initially, as such things are measured among the very rich, the von Bulow marriage appeared to be an ideal one. A daughter, Cosima, blessed the union. Homes were maintained in London and New York. Sunny purchased Clarendon Court, a mansion on Millionaires' Row in Newport, Rhode Island.

For years the von Bulows mixed with the cream of society. In fact, their home in Newport was used as the locale of the 1956 movie *High Society*. Gala parties were given by the von Bulows. The beautiful Sunny and the very proper Claus were the perfect hosts. For diversion, Claus took on the Vice Presidency of the Preservation Society of Newport, an organization that maintains and runs the huge homes along Millionaires' Row then being used only as tourist attractions. He associated himself with the proper charities. At the same time, he wasn't above dabbling in investments for pin money. One of his investments, the Broadway play *Death Trap,* was an enormous hit. Ironically the play's central plot dealt with a husband's attempt to murder his wife for her fortune.

By 1978, Claus was intimately involved with Alexandra Isles, a beautiful former soap opera actress. They saw each other several times a week. Later, Alexandra would testify that von Bulow told her he was about to divorce his wife. When he vacillated about the divorce, she gave him an ultimatum to obtain the divorce in six months or they would part forever. The expiry date of the ultimatum was the end of 1979.

The von Bulows spent the 1979 Christmas holidays at Clarendon Court. On December 26, as was their custom, they all partook of Sunny's rich homemade eggnog. Sunny, who for years had indulged her craving for sweets, also ate large amounts of ice cream covered with caramel sauce. Next morning, Claus told his wife's personal maid of twenty-three years, Marie Schrallhammer, that Sunny was sleeping and was not to be disturbed. For some time, Marie had been suspicious of von Bulow's nervous commands. Despite his orders and his return to his wife's bedroom, she unceremoniously entered the room. Sunny was unconscious. Von Bulow was lying on the bed beside her. Marie tried in vain to wake up her mistress. She pleaded with von Bulow to call a doctor. Finally, she turned to twenty-year-old Alexander, who looked in at his mother and was appalled at her condition. He insisted that von Bulow call a doctor.

Dr Janis Gailitis responded to the call. He found Sunny von Bulow in a comatose state. As he proceeded to examine the gravely ill woman, Sunny stopped breathing. Only by administering mouth-to-mouth resuscitation was the doctor able to revive his patient. Sunny was rushed to Newport Hospital, where her blood sugar was found to be extremely low. She was given glucose and slowly recovered. From information supplied by von Bulow, Dr Gailitis felt that Sunny's condition had been caused by alcohol combined with large quantities of barbiturates.

Before being released from the hospital, Sunny denied having a drinking problem and swore she never took barbiturates. The doctor didn't believe her until some time after her release when he received reports that tests, taken upon her admission to the hospital, indicated that her blood alcohol level was zero and that she had no trace of barbiturates in her system.

The following year, Sunny's health steadily deteriorated. So did the relationship between Sunny's maid, Marie Schrallhammer, and von Bulow. Marie would later state that she was aware of von Bulow's affair with Alexandra Isles and was dismayed at Sunny's complete dependence on her husband. One day, Marie found a black bag in von Bulow's closet. Inside were syringes and drugs. Every so often, she surreptitiously inspected the bag. When she discovered a bottle of insulin in the bag, she showed it to Alexander before returning it to its hiding place.

The von Bulows left New York for Newport in December to spend the Christmas season of 1980 at Clarendon Court. Marie did not accompany them. On December 21, von Bulow arose as usual. At 11 a.m., he indicated mild surprise that his wife was not up and about. He told Alexander he would look in on her. Von Bulow returned to the dining room in fifteen minutes with the news that he had found Sunny unconscious on the bathroom floor. Sunny von Bulow once again was in a deep coma. She was again rushed to hospital. This time her life was sustained with the aid of life support systems. When Claus was told that his wife's case was hopeless, he implored her children, Alexander and Annie Laurie, to mercifully withdraw the life support systems and let their mother die. Alexander, now twenty-one, was deeply suspicious of his stepfather. The black bag, the insulin and now his insistence to let Sunny die were too much. Alexander hired a private detective to look into his stepfather's affairs.

Meanwhile, the cause of Sunny's coma was determined to be the result of insulin overdose. Alexander and the detective searched von Bulow's room and found his mysterious black bag. Inside was a used syringe. When analysed, the needle of the syringe revealed traces of insulin. Alexander turned over the information he had garnered to the Rhode Island state police. On July 6, 1981, Claus von Bulow was indicted on two counts of attempted murder. At his sensational trial, it was revealed that upon his wife's death he stood to inherit a cool seven million dollars in cash and the interest on $7.5 million for life. Doctors testified that Sunny's condition could only have been brought about by the injection of insulin administered either by herself or someone else.

Claus von Bulow was found guilty on both counts of attempted murder and was sentenced to a total of thirty years' imprisonment. He was set free on one million dollars bail while he appealed his conviction. Von Bulow was granted a second trial in 1985 and was acquitted of the attempted murder of his wife. Upon his acquittal, his two stepchildren filed a $56-million civil suit against him. However, their suit was settled out of court when von Bulow agreed to divorce Sunny and give up all claims to his wife's estate upon her death. As you read this, Sunny von Bulow lies in an irreversible coma in New York's Columbia Presbyterian Hospital.

# OSCAR WILDE

THE Marquis of Queensberry will always be remembered as the man whose name is closely associated with the rules that govern the sport of boxing. The manly art of self-defence needed a nobleman to lend his name to this sport in order to give it respectability.

The marquis achieved another sort of fame. He was the trigger that ignited the spark which was to rock England to its very foundations in 1895. Seldom has that ancient island been witness to a juicier scandal. It seems the marquis's son, Alfred Douglas, was constantly in the company of Oscar Wilde, the famous playwright, and the old marquis didn't like it one little bit. He felt it wasn't natural for two men to be so close. As things turned out, he was right about his son and Wilde.

Now, Oscar was not your average man about town. His parents were, as they used to say in Merrie England, of literary genteel stock. Oscar outdid his parents. Born on October 16, 1854, he had an uneventful childhood. He attended a boarding school in Ireland with the grandiose name of Portora Royal School. In his final year he won a gold medal in classics and led the entire school in Greek. He also won a scholarship to Trinity College in Dublin. In 1871 when he entered Trinity he wasn't yet seventeen years old. Three years later, he graduated first in his class, again achieving awards for excellence in Greek and the classics. In addition, he won another scholarship to Magdalen College in Oxford University. Here he excelled in everything he studied and was considered one of the brightest young intellectuals on campus. After Oxford, he made his way to London. In 1880, he wrote his first play, *Vera,* and a book of poetry appropriately entitled *Poems*.

In January 1882, Oscar accepted an invitation to go on a lecture tour of the United States. From the time the immigration officer asked him, "What have you to declare?", Oscar was a huge success. In all humility, he answered, "Nothing except my genius." Oscar made a quick 1,200 pounds on the tour and returned home in triumph. He took a vacation in Paris, where he became closely associated with such notables as Victor Hugo, Emile Zola, Edgar Degas and Camille Pissarro.

On May 9, 1884, Oscar married Constance Lloyd in St. James Church, Paddington. After a brief honeymoon, they set up housekeeping in London. Constance had an income of a few pounds a year and this, added to what Oscar picked up as a critic, was the couple's total income for the first three years of their marriage. In 1887, Oscar became editor of a well-known magazine, *The Woman's World.* He seems to have excelled in this position, but resigned after two years.

The genius that was Oscar Wilde started to write seriously in 1888, and by 1892 he had reached the peak of his popularity. His play, *Lady Windermere's Fan,* was breaking records at St. James Theatre. This success was followed by three others, *Salome, A Woman of No Importance* and *An Ideal Husband,* all hits. Then came his greatest success of all, *The Importance of Being Earnest,* which many critics believe to be the best light comedy written in the English language.

There was one rather startling fact about Wilde which was generally unknown. Oscar was a practising homosexual and had been for some time. Not only was he a homosexual, but he was a homosexual at the wrong time in history. In the England of the 1890s, the practice was not only illegal, but was considered so despicable that no one of substance would even speak to a known homosexual. Oscar was thirty-eight and had had several adventures with young boys, when he met twenty-two-year-old Alfred Douglas. Oscar was a large, unattractive man, while Alfred had the physique of an Adonis.

Oscar was on the way up when he met Alfred, but had not yet reached the pinnacle of his acclaim. The two men entered into a relationship and one was seldom seen without the other. They became ardent and passionate lovers. Rumours got back to the Marquis of Queensberry, who continually warned his son to break off with Oscar. He faced Oscar and pleaded with him to leave his son alone. Finally, when nothing else worked, he performed the deed that instigated one of the most sensational scandals ever to take place in England.

One fine morning, the marquis walked into Wilde's club and gave the porter a written message for Oscar. The message read, "To Oscar Wilde, posing as a sodomite." When the note was delivered, the playwright realized things had gone too far. He decided to seek the legal advice of Sir Edward Clarke, one of the best-known and most respected lawyers in England. Clarke realized that in Oscar Wilde he had no ordinary client. He considered Wilde a literary genius. Sir Edward asked his client one important question and that was whether he was innocent or guilty. Oscar swore he was innocent and so the decision was made to prosecute the marquis for libel. In taking this step, Sir Edward pointed out to

Oscar that the only way to establish libel was to prove that he was not a sodomite. Should they not be successful, Oscar could be arrested immediately, as indecent behaviour was a serious criminal offence. No wonder Sir Edward wanted to make sure his client was innocent before pressing on to prosecute the marquis.

The trial took place at London's famed Old Bailey to a packed house, with thousands more crowding the streets outside. From the outset, the defence produced several young boys who testified that they were on intimate terms with Oscar. The jury listened to this damaging evidence. It became increasingly clear they would not convict a father who was attempting to save his son from the clutches of a refined, cultured genius with unnatural tendencies. Sir Edward decided to withdraw. The judge instructed the jury that the only verdict was one of not guilty. The jury returned a verdict of not guilty, and Oscar was arrested. The next time he entered the Old Bailey was as the defendant. He was unmercifully exposed and held open to ridicule as witness after witness told of illicit relations with him. He was charged with twenty-five counts of gross indecency and "conspiracy to procure the commission of such acts." The jury failed to reach a verdict and a new trial was ordered.

During the few weeks between trials, while Oscar was free on bail, he was ridiculed wherever he went. He was so infamous that no boarding house would take him in and he ended up living with an alcoholic brother. Finally, on May 22, 1895, the third trial began. It was a disaster for Oscar. A ring of what amounted to male prostitutes was uncovered, and corroborating evidence was produced proving beyond doubt that Oscar was guilty of indecent acts.

When we look back at what happened to Oscar Wilde, we realize that a genius was ruined for an act which is no longer unlawful. Today, Wilde and Douglas would be living together openly. Surely the public was the loser, for we can only guess what literary gems were never written.

Oscar Wilde was sentenced to two years in prison, where he wrote the much-quoted poem *The Ballad of Reading Gaol*. This beautiful poem did much to expose the cruelties of prison life. After his release from jail, Oscar lived in France. The harshness of life in prison had taken its toll. In a few years, he was a dying man. On November 30, 1900, Oscar Wilde was received into the Catholic Church and died a few hours later.

# EDWARD ARTHUR WILSON—BROTHER TWELVE

BROTHER Twelve always claimed that he was born in India of a Hindu father. Actually, he was born Edward Arthur Wilson in Birmingham, England. Folks called him Eddy. Young Eddy made his way to Victoria, British Columbia, where, for a time, he was employed by the Dominion Express Co. In 1903, he succumbed to the lure of the sea and remained a sailor for the next two decades. Along the way, he earned his masters mariner's papers. Eddy's long sojourn at sea is important because on his voyages he presumably studied occult religions. He read extensively about black magic, voodoo and any other hocus-pocus he could lay his hands on.

In 1925, during one of his periodic spells on dry land, Eddy wrote a book called *The Three Truths*. He sent the manuscript to an English publisher with a letter of explanation: "I visited the higher planes, where I met The Masters of the Wisdom. The Masters dictated the book to me. I am, therefore, the twelfth member of the White Circle of the Other Worlds' Wise Men." The book was published. Eddy received an advance and forever after called himself Brother Twelve.

The man of religion made his way to Southampton, where he was pleasantly surprised when readers of his book called on him for further explanation of his doctrines. Brother Twelve was positively overjoyed when these suckers pressed coin of the realm into his bony hands. And speaking of bony hands, the rest of Brother Twelve did not add up to an impressive figure. He was of below-average height, scrawny, and sported a scraggly beard, but he did have oodles of that much-sought-after commodity known as charisma.

Over and above the riff-raff who beat a path to Brother Twelve's flat were a few heavyweights of note. Alfred H. Barley, a well-known London professor, and his wife, Annie, were positively enthralled with the "holy man" and his theories of brotherly love. So was P. J. Fisher, a prosperous businessman who, appropriately, made his fortune in the fish-and-chip game. Brother Twelve showed the heavyweights a map and pointed out one little island, which he called the Place of Refuge. When the world was destroyed by a vengeful God, he told them, his followers in the Place of Refuge would be the sole survivors. And where was this place of peace and tranquillity? Was it located in the Indian Ocean? The China Sea? No, the Place of Refuge was one of the De Courcey Islands close to Nanaimo, British Columbia. And so it came to pass that Brother Twelve talked his well-heeled friends into financing a 300-acre tract on one of the larger islands. He called the place Cedar-by-the-Sea.

Right off, Brother Twelve set up the pecking order. Rich followers could purchase homesites. The filthy rich were given the choicest locations near Brother Twelve's estate, which was called the House of Mystery. Brother Twelve often sat under a huge tree on his estate, extolling those beliefs which would lead his followers to the light. Certain carefully selected females were allowed access to Brother Twelve's private home. The good brother partook of the flesh, as they used to say in the late twenties. I mean, a lot.

By 1929, the faithful numbered well over 2,000, all of whom paid varying amounts for the privilege of listening to Brother Twelve. The self-appointed religious leader surrounded himself with the trappings of wealth. He loved jewellery and perfume and sometimes resembled a sweet-smelling Christmas tree. At other times, he made do with a white shirt, tie and Stetson.

Brother Twelve ran a tight ship. His followers were not allowed to smoke, drink or take snuff. Men and women had separate sleeping accommodations. Wives were separated from husbands. Of course, these stringent rules didn't apply to Brother Twelve himself. He selected choice young lovelies, explaining to them that he wanted to produce a son. He often called himself the god Osiris and his latest lady friend the goddess Isis. Unfortunately, or fortunately, Osiris and his several Isises never did produce a child. When Brother Twelve tired of a bed companion, he banished the unfortunate girl to another island. Sometimes, even further afield. Elsie Fenwick was banished right across the country to, of all places, Toronto. Brother Twelve purchased islands like a drunken sailor. He called his mini empire the Aquarian Foundation.

From 1927 to 1932, Brother Twelve lectured, made love and lived like a king. When he began treating troublesome followers like slaves, he unwittingly initiated the beginning of the end. He also had to cope with those husbands and wives who had been separated. Many thought that just wasn't fair. When Brother Twelve purchased Valdes Island and scampered over there with his latest amour, there was a great hue and cry from those less fortunate followers who had been banished to hard work in the fields. He told the discontented that his love tryst was divinely ordained.

Robert England was treasurer of the Aquarian Foundation. As a former U.S. Treasury agent, he should have known better. England said, "Hold on, there, Brother Twelve," and charged him with the misuse of the foundation's funds.

On the day the charges were aired in court, Brother Twelve is reported to have wished everyone concerned all the bad luck in the world. Son of a gun, if the judge didn't fall sick right there and then. Several members of the jury complained of headaches and two lawyers fell sick without warning. A few followers sitting in the courtroom smiled evil smiles. What did everyone think of their Brother Twelve now? Nasty Mr England, who had started all the trouble, was nowhere to be found.

Brother Twelve produced several witnesses who swore that although they contributed thousands to the foundation's coffers, they had received in return such intangibles as the opportunity to assist the brotherhood. Besides, many said they had turned over their cash to "the spirit" and not to Brother Twelve, the human being. Brother Twelve beat the rap. The charges against him were dropped.

The guru's next move was to purchase the remaining five islands of the De Courcey group. He built a House of Meditation in which he and one of his shapely followers, with the great name of Mabel Rowbottom, did more than meditate. Brother Twelve called her Zee, for short. Nothing seemed to faze the good brother. He and Zee slipped away for several months' vacation in England. Upon his return, he purchased a yacht, which he named the *Lady Royal*. The walls came tumbling down when Brother Twelve tired of Zee, or Mabel, if you like. He invited a Seattle astrologer, Carlin Rudy, and his pretty twenty-five-year-old wife, Sandra, to visit his island Shangri-La.

Soon after their arrival, Brother Twelve talked gullible Sandra into ditching her husband when they returned to Seattle. He suggested she double back to his side to be made a goddess. Sandra thought the entire scheme was a capital sugggestion. She did as she was told. However, hubby Carlin wasn't so easily shunted aside. He returned to the island paradise and was taken prisoner by Brother Twelve's guards. Carlin was held overnight. When he was released, he went directly to the B.C. provincial police.

Accompanied by an officer, Carlin confronted Brother Twelve and wanted to know where the holy man had stashed his wife. Brother Twelve swore he knew nothing about any Sandra. His followers also swore they knew nothing of the mysterious Sandra, who seems to have disappeared from the House of Meditation forever. Most believe she was quietly sent home with the warning not to make trouble.

In 1932, a group of disenchanted followers rowed to the mainland and returned with police. Brother Twelve had been warned in advance. The police found the yacht *Lady Royal* scuttled, buildings demolished and farm machinery ruined. They also found an empty treasury. Brother Twelve and Zee, who was back in favour, had flown the coop. Several followers, who had been swindled out of large sums, sued and were awarded what was left of the islands. Brother Twelve and Zee were traced to Switzerland. Eddy Wilson, alias Brother Twelve, died of natural causes in November 1934. Mabel Rowbottom, alias Zee, took off and has never been heard of again.

# JOHN WILSON

THIS is the story of a man who stood trial for murder in Ontario and returned to the very same courtroom years later as a judge.

In the 1830s, Perth, Ontario, was quite unlike other frontier towns of Canada. Perth had been settled around 1816 through land grants. It became home to members of disbanded military regiments who had fought in the Napoleonic Wars. At the same time, dirt-poor Scottish and Irish immigrants arrived in the area and were consigned to the bottom rung of the social ladder. For the following fifteen years, the town developed a class structure just as stringent as the one they had left back home.

Robert Lyon was probably the most eligible single young man in town. Tall, handsome, athletic Robert, nineteen, was the son of a wealthy, socially prominent family. He was studying law, as was his friend Henry Lelievre, the son of a French frigate captain. Another of Lyon's close friends was John Wilson. Today, we would say John came from the wrong side of the tracks. In reality, his parents were honest, hard-working farmers who had made many sacrifices so that their son could study law.

The following scenario, which was to find a place in the history of our country, began innocently enough. In 1933, Lyon and Wilson were dispatched by their respective law firms to Ottawa, then called Bytown, on business. The two law students met often, had a few drinks, and, like young men everywhere, talked about the girls back home. They knew many girls in common. Wilson had once squired Elizabeth Hughes, who had recently arrived in Perth from England to teach school. Elizabeth was alone in the world, having lost her father to a bout of cholera on the way over. She was a good-looking girl and had several of the town boys doing flip-flops for her affections. Lyon had no way of knowing that Wilson no longer cared for Elizabeth. He had fallen hard for another Perth girl, pretty Joanne Lees. Lyon himself had no sincere interest in Elizabeth, as he was engaged to still another Perth belle, Caroline Thom.

Now, if you follow all this, fine. If not, it is enough to know that as these two young law students from such different backgrounds chatted over drinks, neither was particularly concerned with the affections of Elizabeth Hughes.

Lyon decided to have a bit of fun at Wilson's expense. He told Wilson that Elizabeth was in the habit of "allowing men to indulge in unbecoming freedoms." He told Wilson that their mutual friend, Henry Lelievre, "had sat alongside her with his arms about her in a position which no woman of spirit would permit."

Folks, back in 1833, those were fighting words. However, they didn't have the desired effect because Wilson had shifted his affections to Miss Lees.

John Wilson then did a rather foolish thing. He sat down and wrote a letter to Elizabeth's guardian, a Mr Acland. He quoted Lyon word for word. Later, Wilson revealed that he wrote the letter to finally end his relationship with Elizabeth. Acland was a blabbermouth. He spread the word that Robert Lyon had made a "dishonorable remark about an unprotected female." Lyon returned from Bytown to find half of Perth giving him the cold shoulder. What a cad to have said such things about a defenceless woman. Even his betrothed, Caroline, wouldn't have anything to do with him. Lyon checked with Lelievre, who was furious at Wilson for writing such a letter. Lyon went looking for John Wilson.

Robert Lyon and John Wilson met in front of Perth's courthouse on June 6 that summer of 1833. Lyon didn't waste time with formalities. Did Wilson write that letter? Wilson admitted that he had, but before he could offer any explanation, Lyon hauled off and punched him in the face. Lyon then turned, shouting over his shoulder, "You're a damn lying scoundrel, Sir, and I'll treat you as such every time I meet you." Wilson realized that to do nothing about the insult would be tantamount to ostracization in Perth. He issued a duelling challenge to Lyon, firmly believing that Lyon would accept his explanation of why he had written the letter. Initially, Lyon did show an inclination to seek a peaceful solution but, under the urging of Lelievre, became convinced the dispute could only be solved on the field of honour. Lyon was a crack shot, while Wilson had probably held a gun in his hands only once or twice in his life.

The time and place for the duel was set. It was drizzling rain at 6 p.m. on June 13, 1833, when the asembled entourage walked about one mile outside Perth to a ploughed field. The locale was carefully chosen to be outside the jurisdiction of the local sheriff, whom both men knew well. Lyon's second was Henry Lelievre. Wilson was seconded by Simon Robertson. Official medical representation for the event was Dr William Hamilton. At the count of five, both men fired. Wilson missed. Lyon's bullet barely creased Wilson's skull. Both men were unhurt. Wilson was to state later that at this point he was surprised to be alive. It was the custom of the time that double misses called for apologies all around. However, Lyon and Lelievre wouldn't hear of calling off the duel in midstream, so to speak.

The duellists reloaded. As Wilson stood waiting for the signal, he noted that a ploughed furrow connected him to his adversary in a perfectly straight line. He used it as a point of reference to aim. Wilson shifted his weight slightly, turned his head away and fired on signal. Lyon fell to the ground. The fluke shot had pierced his lungs. He was taken to a nearby home, where he died within minutes. Wilson stood unharmed, amazed at his accuracy and thankful to be alive.

Henry Lelievre left Perth immediately after the shooting and is variously reported to have spent the rest of his life in the United States and Australia.

Wilson and Robertson turned themselves in to the authorities. Wilson was charged with murder, while Robertson was charged with being an accessory.

The two men stood trial in nearby Brockville. Both took the witness stand in their own defence and made impassioned pleas, stressing that at no time did they have any malice towards Lyon. They also pointed out that during the events leading to the duel, they had made repeated attempts to have the whole thing called off. The jury found both defendants not guilty.

John Wilson attempted to pick up the remnants of his life after his acquittal. He tried to renew his relationship with Joanne Lees, but her parents would not let their daughter have anything to do with someone who had been dragged through such a scandal. Wilson moved to London, but kept in contact with Elizabeth Hughes. Following a script which would be unbelievable if written in Hollywood, he returned to Perth two years later and married Elizabeth.

Wilson went on to have a distinguished legal and political career. In 1847, he became a member of Parliament, succeeding William Draper, who had been the prosecuting attorney at his murder trial fourteen years previously. In 1863, Wilson was appointed a judge of the Supreme Court of Ontario. Ironically, the first case he presided over was in the very same Brockville courthouse where he had stood accused of murder thirty years earlier.

John Wilson's public life was successful, but not so his private life. It is said that the former Elizabeth Hughes was an inconsiderate nagging wife. Wilson died in London in 1869. Elizabeth outlived her husband by many years. She died in 1904 in Toronto at age ninety-three.

If you ever visit Perth, you might enjoy a walk through the local park. It has the fitting name of Last Duel Park to commemorate the last duel ever fought in Canada.

# PART 2

## MURDERS STRANGE BUT TRUE

# URSULA ADOMEIT

## VILLAGE VICE

GEORG Richer, 19, made a big play for the most attractive girl in the village. Thirteen-year-old Ursula was one of those blond, blue-eyed German girls who caused pulses to race and heads to turn. The little village of Emslage-Ruehlerfeld, located near the German-Holland border, was home to other pretty girls, but Ursula was different. She looked 21 and had the figure of a silicone-enhanced movie star.

Once Georg was successful in seducing Ursula, she took to sex like Moll Flanders took to haymows. Soon Ursula found herself checking and rechecking her calendar. There was no doubt about it—she was more than somewhat pregnant.

Little Anja came into the world only a few months after her parents married. Within the next four years, three more daughters blessed the union. Anja was followed by Kathi, Alexandra and Petra.

The expanding family did not come about by accident, nor was Georg the instigator. No, Ursula was the aggressive lovemaking partner of the pair. In fact, Georg was tired most of the time. The poor man hardly got any sleep.

While having a schnapps in a bar one night, Georg met 19-year-old Kurt Adomeit. We will never know exactly what Georg had in mind when he invited Kurt, a truck driver, to move into the Richer home. Now, I would be remiss not to point out that Kurt had the looks of a Greek god, complete with muscles and, we can only assume, the necessary auxiliary equipment.

Georg may have invited his new roomer into his home for financial reasons, but there was some suspicion that he welcomed what he suspected would inevitably happen. Sure as God made little green apples, Ursula and Kurt commenced doing it at every opportunity. Tongues wagged in the village.

You can just imagine the gossip when, on June 6, 1972, Ursula travelled to Meppen, the closest town, and reported her loving husband missing. The local police didn't have to be staffed with a Hercule Poirot to come to a couple of conclusions: Ursula and Kurt were lovers; and Georg Richer loved his four daughters and would never desert them. Once the little grey cells started percolating, police felt that it was quite possible that murder most foul had taken place, but, darn it all, they had no proof that any crime had been committed.

Two days after the missing persons report was filed, Meppen police received word that a vehicle belonging to Georg Richer had been found submerged in a pond in the village of Neuringe right on the Dutch border. Was it possible that he was alive and had attempted to get rid of his car before crossing the border into Holland? On the other hand, had his killer planted the car to make it appear that Georg had fled the country? The vehicle was returned to Meppen, but the only information garnered from the auto was that Georg hadn't been submerged with it.

Months passed. Police explored every avenue which could connect Ursula and Kurt to the missing Georg Richer. Despite their strong suspicions, however, authorities could find nothing concrete to connect the pair to the missing man. A year passed before Ursula filed for divorce on the grounds of desertion. The divorce was granted without delay.

Police made a habit of keeping tabs on the two suspects. The lovers were discreet in public. And it was rumoured that Ursula's four young daughters had accepted Kurt as their father. A year after the divorce and two years after Georg's disappearance, Kurt and Ursula officially tied the knot. The four Richer children, now ranging in age from four to nine years, were bridesmaids.

Another year passed. Rumours reached police that Ursula was stepping out at night when her truck-driver husband was out of town. While on one of his trips, Kurt was arrested in Osnabrück for peddling drugs. He confessed to selling the drugs in several judicial districts and was brought back to Meppen where he was jailed.

Detectives, who well remembered the disappearance of Georg Richer, decided to take advantage of Kurt's one weakness. Unlike husband number one, Kurt was extremely jealous of his overactive wife. Police decided to place a detective, posing as a drunk, in Kurt's cell. He would attempt to elicit incriminating information from the suspect. It didn't take long. The undercover detective bragged that he had met one of the sexiest women in the country in the village of Emslage-Ruehlerfeld at a bar called the Black Lamb. Kurt asked about the woman's name. The detective said he didn't know her last name, but was sure her first name was Ursula. Kurt saw red. He became violent and had to be restrained by guards. Then he blurted out the entire story of his unfaithful wife. He claimed that he shouldn't have expected anything better, because Ursula had cheated on her first husband so that she could bed down with him.

The time was ripe. His interrogators told Kurt that they knew that he and Ursula had killed Georg and buried his body, and urged him to unburden his guilty conscience. Kurt turned pale. He didn't realize that the police had nothing on him; all he had to do was keep quiet and Georg's murder would remain unsolved forever. Kurt slumped into a chair and exclaimed, "I'll show you where the body is buried."

On July 1, 1975, Kurt led police to the skeletal remains of Georg Richer. He told investigators that Georg had not been a jealous man and had probably known that his roomer and Ursula were having a prolonged affair.

Kurt told police that Ursula had put sleeping tablets in Georg's tea. The pills, however, didn't even make the victim sleepy. Frustrated, Ursula put a whole jar of tablets in Georg's tea. Strangely, they had absolutely no effect. Undaunted, Ursula purchased rat poison. She put large quantities of poison in Georg's food, only to be told that her cooking was greatly improved.

Kurt claimed that he told Ursula to give up. Georg was proving to be too difficult to kill. Besides, he thought she should attempt to obtain a divorce, but Ursula was adamant—Georg had to go.

On May 13, 1972, Kurt had returned home at around 10 p.m. The girls were already in bed. Ursula had used adhesive tape to wrap a hatchet. She gave the hatchet to Kurt with the pointed suggestion, "Now is the time to do it. He's asleep." Kurt did as he was told. He struck the sleeping man with all his might. "His head sort of exploded," Kurt said.

Ursula cleaned the blood from the bedclothes and the floor of the bedroom. Together they drove the body into the forest and buried poor Georg. Kurt admitted he had driven Georg's car to the Dutch border and into a pond to lead police to believe that Georg had left the country. He had then caught a bus back to Meppen.

Ursula was advised of Kurt's confession. Initially she denied any involvement, but soon broke down and told all. She added that lust and sin had not been the motive behind the crime and was able to prove that Georg had often beaten her severely.

The evidence of wife beating had some effect on the German court. Ursula and Kurt Adomeit were both found guilty and were each sentenced to the relatively light term of 10 years in prison.

# CHARLES ALBANESE

## CUNNING CHARLES ON DEATH ROW

I have always believed that poisoners are the most reprehensible type of killer. Certainly this story's vile dispenser of deadly white powder had little to recommend him. But let's start at the beginning.

Mary Lambert was an 89-year-old live wire who lived with her 69-year-old daughter, Marion Mueller, in the retirement community of Leisure Village located about 50 miles outside Chicago. Both women were healthy and took part in most of the physical activities the village offered.

Marion's daughter Virginia and her husband, Charles Albanese, visited the two women every week. Virginia was extremely devoted to her mother and grandmother and regularly brought them for visits to her home in nearby Spring Grove.

On August 3, 1980, Virginia and Charles had the two women over for Sunday dinner. That very evening, Mary Lambert commenced retching and vomiting. She was rushed to hospital, where she died three days later. The death was sudden, but since Mary was 89 years old, no one thought her demise that unusual. Officially her death was attributed to cardiac arrest.

Twelve days later, Mary's daughter, Marion, died after suffering from much the same symptoms. While no one suspected foul play, the residents of Leisure Village thought it most unusual for two healthy women to die within 12 days of each other. They urged officials to check local restaurants for botulism. The retirement community's water supply was tested. Charles Albanese requested that authorities investigate further. After all, his wife had just lost her mother and grandmother within a two-week span. Charles, who with his father and brother headed his family's large trophy-manufacturing firm, eventually was satisfied that the deaths were the result of a horrible coincidence.

Nine months passed before the subject of the strange deaths again came to the attention of officials. This time the local coroner was informed that a doctor had found traces of arsenic in blood serum taken from one of his patients who had died suddenly. The patient was Mike Albanese Sr., the father of Charles Albanese. Mike was 69 years old at the time of his death. Not only had he died suddenly, but another son, Mike Jr., had also fallen seriously ill, but did not die.

Doctors reported to the coroner that traces of arsenic had also been found in the younger Mike's blood.

Initially, authorities felt there was a possibility that the two men had come in contact with arsenic used for industrial purposes. The Albanese family owned the Allied Die Casting Co. Mike Sr. had founded the company and, together with his two sons, Mike Jr. and Charles, ran the prosperous business. However, arsenic wasn't used in the manufacturing process. Hair and fingernail samples were taken from Mike's body before burial and tested for arsenic. Both tested positive. It was as if some evil force had descended upon Charles's in-laws and now his own father and brother.

Although no concrete connection was found between the deaths, the circumstances were under investigation by law enforcement authorities. Virginia and Charles were questioned. Now that his father was dead and his brother confined to a wheelchair, Charles was running the family business. The police received permission from Virginia to exhume the bodies of her mother and grandmother. Both bodies contained large quantities of arsenic; in fact, 370 times the normal level.

The investigation shifted gears. Nurses and doctors who had attended Mary Lambert and Marion Mueller in hospital were questioned. Several nurses remembered that Virginia and Charles had visited the two women on a regular basis. They also recalled that they often brought them cookies and doughnuts.

Detectives delved into Charles Albanese's background. They learned that Charles was a family man who devoted much of his time to his wife and children. Their home was a large sprawling one, complete with swimming pool. Charles had been married three times. His two previous marriages had ended in divorce. He and Virginia had been married since 1972. Although Charles had never committed a violent act, he did have a police record. In 1965, while working as an automobile salesman in Chicago, he was arrested for armed robbery. He had stolen $160 from a suburban home. Since entering the family business, his fortunes had changed for the better. He drew a large salary from Allied Die, owned his own home and drove a Cadillac. In addition, he split the firm's profits with his mother, Clara, and his brother, Mike Jr.

Detectives learned that Charles had been extremely attentive to his in-laws. He had been so successful in ingratiating himself with Mrs. Lambert that he had convinced her to change her will, leaving everything to her daughter, Marion, bypassing a son, Francis. To the elderly lady, this advice seemed reasonable. Her daughter, Marion, lived with her and was a great comfort to her in her declining years. When both women died within a period of 12 days, the entire estate passed to Mrs. Lambert's grandaughter Virginia Albanese. In this way, Charles came to control around $150,000 in cash, as well as a home valued at $95,000. He quickly sold the house for cash.

Nine months later, down at Allied Die, cunning Charles began taking his coffee break with his father and brother. He often brought cookies and doughnuts from home. After one of these coffee klatches, both Mike Sr. and Mike Jr. became violently ill and were hospitalized. Mike Sr. recovered and was released, but each time he nibbled something with Charles, he ended up back in hospital. On May 16, 1981, he died. Mike Jr. remained in hospital, unable to walk.

Police learned that Mike Sr. had left a personal estate of over half a million dollars to his wife. If Mike Jr. had died, and in due course, Charles's mother, Charles would have wiped out his entire family. Not only would he have inherited all their personal fortunes, he would also have full control of the lucrative family business. It is one thing to have suspicions, however, and quite another to develop proof. Police went about uncovering the evidence they needed. All suppliers and customers of Allied Die were canvassed in an attempt to learn if arsenic, in any shape or form, had found its way into the company's hands. They learned that Allied Die sold scrap zinc to a metal-plating firm in Elkhorn, Wisconsin. The manager of the firm, Joe Reichel, told police that he had had a conversation with Charles concerning arsenic. Charles had told Reichel that he was having trouble with insects around his home and wanted advice on how to get rid of them. Joe suggested arsenic and gave Charles two pounds of the poison, which he used in his own manufacturing process.

Police were forced to move quickly. They found out that Charles was planning a trip to Jamaica with his wife and mother. Investigators were convinced that he intended to murder his mother. Charles was apprehended and charged with three counts of murder and one charge of attempted murder.

On May 5, 1982, the accused man stood trial for the murder of his father and his wife's grandmother. He was found guilty on both charges and sentenced to death. Six months later, he was found guilty of his mother-in-law's murder and again sentenced to death. Between trials, Virginia obtained a divorce.

Today, Charles Albanese resides on death row in Illinois's Menard correctional facility. Gone are the loving wife, prosperous business, caring family, large home, Cadillac and swimming pool. Greed has taken it all away. In May 1989, the U.S. Supreme Court refused to hear Charles's last appeal.

Inmate number N22283 has no future other than his pending date with a lethal injection.

# WILLIAM ARCHERD

## ANGEL OF DEATH

WILLIAM Dale Archerd was born in Arkansas. He left his father's ranch at the age of 15 to wander the Midwest, taking odd jobs to keep body and soul together. By the time he was 17, he had gravitated to hospital work, obtaining employment as a hospital attendant. At that early age, he married the first of his seven wives. The marriage lasted four years. His second marriage was even less successful and was terminated after two years.

While employed in Oakland, California, in the 1940s, Archerd met another young lady, who quickly became wife number three. Unfortunately, he and his new bride encountered some difficulty when they were apprehended with heroin in their possession. This little caper resulted in Archerd spending three years in San Quentin after his good wife testified against him.

Upon his release from prison, Archerd drifted from job to job. It is believed that for the next 20 years this tall, handsome man with the shock of thick white hair became a killing machine. His implements of death were insulin and a hypodermic needle. Archerd had become something of an expert on the effects of insulin while working as a hospital attendant.

In 1947, Archerd was employed at the Kaiser Hospital in Fontana, California, when a friend of his, 34-year-old William Jones, was rushed to hospital in a coma. Ten hours later, Jones died of insulin shock, although insulin had not been prescribed for him. At the time, the death was considered puzzling, but no official action was taken. It would be 20 years before authorities would delve into Jones's death and discover that Archerd had profited by $10,000 from his friend's demise.

On May 14, 1956, Archerd's marriage to wife number three was annulled. The very next day he married Zella Winders. Within a week he was looting his new wife's bank account. It took only a few days for the well to run dry. Archerd called police and told them a fantastic story. He claimed that two robbers had entered his home and injected him and Zella with some mysterious substance, after which they took off with about $500 in cash.

Police investigated but could find no evidence that intruders had been in the home. Archerd insisted that he and his wife had been bound and injected with a hypodermic needle. Next day Zella went into a coma and died before she could be removed to hospital. Official cause of death was listed as pneumonia. Archerd collected $619 in life insurance. The marriage had lasted only 12 days. Zella had more than $10,000 in the bank the day she married. The day she died, her account was down to a few hundred dollars.

Soon after, Archerd married again. If you are keeping track, we are now up to wife number five. It would be a brief liaison. Juanita Plum had recently divorced. Under the terms of her divorce, she came into possession of property that included a $40,000 home. In addition, she received $500 a month in alimony payments. No question about it; Juanita was a fine catch. On March 10, 1958, the happy pair were married in Las Vegas. Two days later, Juanita fell into a coma and died. Her death was attributed to cardiac arrest.

One can only imagine Archerd's surprise—and chagrin—when Juanita's will was read. She left her lady-killing husband exactly one dollar. The balance of her estate was bequeathed to members of her family.

Wife number six was something of a novelty since she survived and lived to testify at her former husband's trial. Not all of Archerd's wives were as fortunate.

In 1960, Archerd and a friend, Frank Stewart, flew to Las Vegas. Just before boarding, Frank took out an insurance policy for $80,000. It covered any accident which might occur on the plane or in the two airports involved. Once in Las Vegas, Frank supposedly fell in the men's room and struck his head. He was rushed to Southern Nevada Hospital, but doctors there could find no physical evidence that a fall had taken place. Next day, Frank's buddy, William Dale Archerd, visited him in hospital. That night, Frank died.

Archerd attempted to collect the insurance money, but the insurance boys balked, and with good reason. They produced a young lady who had visited Frank in hospital and had witnessed Archerd open a parcel containing a hypodermic needle and insulin. Archerd had told the girl he was going to inject Frank with the insulin so he would display the symptoms of a bad fall. Archerd had assured her that, other than rendering Frank unconscious for a short while, there would be no lasting effects from the injection. Archerd didn't collect the insurance and although he was questioned by the police, no charges were laid against the suave charmer.

The year 1960 proved to be a busy one for the angel of death. His divorced brother, Everett, was killed in an industrial accident. Archerd was granted custody of Everett's 15-year-old son, Burney. As official guardian, he was issued a workman's compensation insurance cheque in the amount of $7,000, to be held in trust until Burney reached the age of majority. That cheque was tantamount to a death sentence for the boy. On the day Archerd cashed the cheque, his nephew was admitted to Long Beach Memorial Hospital. The boy had supposedly been struck by a hit-and-run driver. Three hours later, after a visit from Uncle William, Burney's left eye dilated. He lapsed into a coma and was taken to an operating room. The dilated eye indicated pressure on the brain or intercranial bleeding. Doctors drilled burr holes into the skull to relieve the pressure. They were surprised to see no evidence of bleeding or damage of any kind. Thirteen days after being admitted to hospital, Burney Archerd died. Death was listed as terminal bronchopneumonia.

In February 1965, Archerd met 60-year-old Mary Brinker Post. Miss Post was assistant director of publicity for Claremont College and author of the best-selling novel *Annie Jordan*. Two months later, on April 18, they were married. It took our boy 18 months to spend the $21,000 his wife had brought to the marriage, as well as $14,000 she didn't have. On October 15, 1966, Mrs. Archerd the seventh filed for bankruptcy.

On October 28, Mrs. Archerd was involved in a minor traffic accident as she drove to the college from her home. Archerd was in San Francisco at the time, but returned to Los Angeles as soon as he received the news. On the day after the accident, he had photos taken of the vehicle and his wife's minor injuries. He put in a claim that same day to the college's insurance company.

On October 30, two days after the accident, Archerd knocked on a neighbour's door to say that his wife wouldn't wake up. An ambulance was summoned and the stricken woman was taken to Pomona Valley Hospital. The next afternoon she died without regaining consciousness. Although no insulin had been prescribed, an autopsy indicated she had died from bronchopneumonia secondary to hypoglycemia.

Seven was not a lucky number for Archerd. Maybe it was because of the prominence of his victim or because the death was so obviously the result of an insulin injection that authorities decided to put William Dale Archerd's life under a microscope. It didn't take long for detectives to uncover Archerd's past, including the fact that not only had he worked as a hospital attendant, he had been employed in an insulin-shock ward for over a year.

A team of eight detectives dug and sifted through the killer's life for the previous 20 years. It is believed that he murdered two friends, a nephew and three wives. Authorities decided to prosecute on the three strongest cases, those of Zella Winders, Burley Archerd and Mary Archerd.

William Archerd was tried and found guilty of murdering all three. It was the first time anyone in the United States was convicted of using insulin as a murder weapon.

On March 6, 1968, Supreme Court Judge Adolph Alexander sentenced Archerd to death in California's gas chamber. For nine years he resided on death row at San Quentin, but in the end he cheated the gas chamber. William Dale Archerd died of natural causes while still in prison.

# NORMA ARMISTEAD

## ROBBING THE CRADLE

THERE was a degree of inevitability drawing Mary Childs into the life and obsessions of Norma Jean Armistead. You see, Mary was having a baby and Norma, an obstetric nurse, desperately wanted one.

Mary was a 26-year-old grocery-store employee in Los Angeles, California. Her pregnancy had been routine in every way. On September 20, 1974, she entered the Kaiser Foundation Hospital in Hollywood to have her baby. Mary's doctor estimated the baby would weigh about eight pounds. In the hospital, Mary met Norma Armistead and instantly liked the friendly, outgoing 47-year-old nurse.

That night, Norma administered several drugs to her patient before Mary dozed off. When she woke up in the wee hours of the morning, Mary felt that something was drastically wrong. She had no control over her limbs and was unable to get her mind to focus. She peered at her stomach and was shocked to see that she wasn't big anymore. Was this some kind of fantastic dream? No, there were doctors and Nurse Armistead at her bedside. They were all so serious. Mary tried to concentrate and listen as Norma spoke to the doctors. She told them she had visited the ward minutes earlier to find Mary unconscious with a stillborn baby between her legs. When Mary came to fully, she screamed and kicked until Norma managed to calm her down.

In the next few hours, doctors told Mary that blood tests indicated that her body contained large quantities of narcotics, none of which had been prescribed. Mary was stunned. She had never taken any drugs on her own and informed the doctors of this fact. The medics didn't answer. After all, it was quite customary for women to deny they had anything to do with the death of their own baby.

The stillborn child weighed slightly more than three pounds and had been dead for a week. Something was strangely amiss. The admitting doctor had told Mary that her baby had a strong heartbeat and she could expect a healthy baby. There followed more denials. The consulting doctors didn't bother to check with the admitting physician what they felt were this woman's obvious falsehoods. They suggested she go home and try to forget the whole unpleasant experience. Heartbroken and depressed, Mary did as she was told.

In the following months, Norma Armistead became the very dear friend of Kathryn Viramontes. What a coincidence. Kathryn, who already had three children, was once again pregnant and Norma was an obstetric nurse. The father of Kathryn's unborn child had left her during her pregnancy and she needed a friend. Norma more than fit the bill. She was kind, gentle and caring. She also took a great interest in Kathryn's health, insisting she see her doctor on a regular basis. Kathryn assured her friend that her doctor had told her throughout her term that her pregnancy was normal. She could expect a healthy baby. In mid-May, on her last visit to her doctor, Kathryn was told to expect the birth of her child during the first week in June.

Four days later, Kathryn's nine-year-old son, Richie, ran to a neighbour's house crying that something was wrong with his mother. The neighbour found Kathryn's body on the bedroom floor in a pool of blood under a mattress. Bedsheets and clothing were strewn about the room. The neighbour called an ambulance.

Across town, Norma walked into Kaiser Foundation Hospital carrying a newborn baby. Norma told a physician that she had given birth to the baby on the way to the hospital. The doctor was mystified. This woman, whom he had never seen before, seemed to be past childbearing age. After seeing to it that the baby was cared for, he proceeded to examine Norma. His suspicions turned to amazement when he discovered his patient had no cervix or uterus. The doctor realized Norma had had a hysterectomy.

Authorities were notified. The strange-but-true tale soon unfolded. Norma, who was living common law with Charlie Armistead, felt she was losing him because of her inability to have a baby. As an obstetric nurse, she had the opportunity to steal a live baby and replace it with a foetus available to her from the hospital morgue. She had given massive doses of drugs to Mary Childs to induce labour and render her helpless. At the time, Mary's doctors had believed their obstetric nurse rather than the confused patient. If they had taken the time to check out Mary's story, the evil that was Norma Jean Armistead would have been stopped then and there. As matters turned out, Norma had walked to another hospital with Mary's baby to try to obtain a birth certificate, telling the nurses she had given birth on the way to the institution. She had refused medical help and left the hospital with the baby. She later procured a birth certificate in the name of Carrie Armistead.

Shortly after, Norma ingratiated herself into the life of Kathryn Viramontes. At the same time, she gained weight in order to appear pregnant. All the while she posed as a caring, concerned friend, more than willing to assist Kathryn through her pregnancy.

On May 16, 1975, while visiting Kathryn, the obstetric nurse injected her friend with various drugs, rendering Kathryn unconscious. To make sure there would be no outcry, Norma placed tape over her victim's mouth and slit her throat, killing her immediately. It is not necessary to go into detail here. Suffice it to say, Norma performed a Caesarean section on the dead woman.

Within 24 hours, the relationship between Norma and Kathryn was known to police. Norma confessed her terrible crimes and gave her reasons. Her common-law husband, she told police, had threatened to return to his wife and children. Norma was convinced that only by producing babies could she prevent Charlie from leaving her.

Despite Norma's strange behaviour, psychiatrists found she knew the difference between right and wrong and had acted with full knowledge of the consequences of her actions. In March 1976, she was found guilty of murder and sentenced to life imprisonment.

A postscript to this strange case was provided when Mary Childs's eight-month-old baby, who had been living with Norma and Charlie, was returned to her. Mary sued the hospital and the attending physicians for $24 million. She was awarded $375,000, a large portion of which went to pay legal fees.

# RONALD BENNELL

## NOTE PROVED TO BE HIS DOWNFALL

LINDA Stewart found herself in the wrong place at the wrong time.

Attractive, 22-year-old Linda lived at 285 Kingsway in Manchester, England, with her mother, grandmother, a married brother, his wife and baby daughter. Linda had her problems. A rather shy, quiet girl, she had never dated much, but was keeping company with one steady boyfriend. The two young people saw each other several times a week.

In 1970, when Linda became pregnant, it was a foregone conclusion that the couple would marry. Unfortunately, the engineering firm where Linda's boyfriend was employed was being liquidated. When the young man found out that he would shortly be unemployed, he informed Linda that they would be unable to wed. Understandably, Linda didn't take the news well, but the two lovers continued to date regularly.

When Linda wasn't out with her boyfriend, she usually spent her evenings with her best friend, Jennifer Earl, who lived about a half mile from her home. On Friday, November 27, 1970, Linda called Jennifer at about 8:30 p.m. She suggested a walk and perhaps a drink at a local pub. Jennifer called for Linda and the two friends walked for a while. Shortly after 10 p.m. they dropped into the Princess Hotel. They consumed two beers each before leaving at around 11 p.m. for the walk home. Linda and Jennifer chatted for a while at the junction of Mauldeth Road and Kingsway before separating to walk the remaining distance to their respective homes.

Just before they parted company, Jennifer noticed a man peering into a store window nearby. Slightly apprehensive, she asked Linda if she wanted her to walk with her. Linda laughed at the suggestion and walked off alone.

Next morning, 72-year-old Gwen Hughes woke up, put the kettle on and took some trash to the dustbin. She remembered to be careful because the path leading to the garden area of her Kingsway duplex had been paved the previous day. As she walked to the edge of the property, Gwen sighted a bundle of clothing on the path. Drawing closer, she saw long red hair flowing from the clothing. Gwen and a neighbour called police.

The body of the young girl bore bite marks on both breasts and the impression of boot marks across her chest. She had been raped and beaten to death. Although the girl's body had been found on the newly paved path, there was evidence of a struggle in an adjoining flower bed. The earth in the flower bed was disturbed and there was a wide opening in a hedge beside the path. Apparently the victim had been accosted on the other side of the hedge and had been dragged through the flower bed and hedge to where the body was found.

Gwen Hughes stated that she had been awakened the night before by a thumping noise. She had gotten out of bed and peered out a window. Although the noise continued, she hadn't seen anything unusual. When the noise stopped, she went back to bed. Other neighbours reported that they had heard the piercing scream of a woman around 11:30 the previous night, but because they often heard strange noises from the busy Kingsway, they had not taken any action.

The area around the body was closely examined. Boot prints taken from the flower bed matched those on the victim's chest. A man's crude metal ring was found in one of the flower beds. Near the path, detectives found a half-eaten meat pie. Investigators initially felt that the meat pie and the ring could have been dropped there days earlier and might have nothing whatever to do with the murder. But these two items took on new significance when Gwen Hughes's handyman told police that on the day of the murder he had cleaned the flower beds and swore that he had left the earth smooth and clean. He took great pride in the hedge and he insisted that there was no opening in it when he finished his work.

When Linda's family reported her missing, the identity of the body on the footpath was quickly established. Detectives went about tracing Linda's movements on the previous night. Linda's friend, Jennifer Earl, related their visit to the pub on the night of the murder. Linda's boyfriend was questioned extensively. He told police that he was supposed to go out with Linda that night, but had called off the date. He and a group of his colleagues from the engineering plant had gone pub crawling to bury their sorrow at joining the ranks of the unemployed. They had been very intoxicated and were remembered at each pub they visited. Police carefully checked the group's movements and were convinced that Linda's boyfriend could not have been the killer.

With the elimination of the most logical suspect, police fanned out, questioning known sex offenders, customers who had been at the Princess Hotel on the night of the murder and anyone who had been near the scene of the crime.

One thing puzzled them. The killer had taken away Linda's shoes and purse. Many sex offenders rob their victims but none of the officers involved in this investigation could remember a rapist who carried away his victim's shoes.

Detectives were convinced that the killer lived within a mile of the murder scene. They decided to search all the garbage within a square mile of the tragedy. The city of Manchester cooperated by delaying garbage pickup for a full week so that police could search individual garbage bags. The distasteful task bore immediate results. On Tuesday morning, a pair of ladies' shoes were found in a garbage bag. In the same bag, police found letters addressed to Linda as well as her photograph. Linda's family identified the shoes. A hundred yards down the road, in another bag, investigators found the contents of Linda's purse. It was apparent that the killer had disposed of Linda's belongings in nearby garbage bags as he fled the scene of the crime.

The ring found in the flower bed was sent to the Metallurgy Department of Manchester University. A report came back stating that the ring was made of stainless steel and had been manufactured at an engineering plant by an amateur who had most probably used a piece of scrap metal to fashion the crude ring. Police then systematically canvassed engineering firms that used such metal. The description of the ring and the description of the man seen by Jennifer Earl were widely publicized.

Detectives knocked on doors and asked the following four questions: Are you acquainted with a man in his early twenties with long blond hair who wears a tan car coat? Do you know a man who hasn't been to work since last Saturday? Have you seen a man with blood or tar on his clothing? Do you know a man missing from home since last Saturday?

Authorities hoped that if their theory was correct, the killer would succumb to the pressure and act in an erratic manner. Their ploy worked. While interviewing employees at the Renold Engineering Works, police were interrupted by one of the company's officers, who gave them a note that had been slipped under a locker door by an employee. It read: "Andy, I want you to tell the firm to send my wages home to my parents, I think I killed that girl, but I'm not sure, but it's my ring they found, so it must be me, tell the cops not to look for me because I will kill myself." The note was signed "Ron."

The writer of the note was well known. His name was Ronald Bennell, an 18-year-old apprentice who lived with his parents and four brothers and sisters close to the plant. Police located Ron at his girlfriend's apartment in Benchill, a suburb of Manchester.

The suspect was taken to the police station, where he related how he had spent the night of the murder. He claimed he had gone to a dance with his girlfriend, had had too much to drink and had become belligerent. After he dropped off his girlfriend, he had picked up a meat pie and chips, which he started to eat as he walked along the Kingsway. He saw Linda walking by and said, "Hello, love." She replied, "Get lost."

Ron had grabbed the unwary girl and pushed her through the hedge. Linda had screamed as he put his hand around her neck. It was then his ring must have slipped off, he told authorities. He felt the girl go limp, so he dragged her to the path and had sexual intercourse with her while she was unconscious. As she regained consciousness, he'd struck her over the head again and again. Ron claimed that as he ran from the scene, he stepped on the body with his tar-stained boots. On the other side of the hedge, he picked up Linda's shoes and purse. He could give no reason for having picked up these items. He disposed of them in nearby garbage bags.

Bite marks on the body matched plaster casts taken of Ron's teeth. Even the meat pie tossed away at the scene bore the impression of Ron's teeth. His boots had made the prints found on the body. He told police that the coverage given the case by the press had caused him to lose his nerve and write the note which proved to be his downfall.

On March 1, 1971, Ronald Bennell pleaded guilty to murder and was sentenced to life imprisonment.

# ANTONIO BENTO AND MARIA NEUBAUER

## PLAYBOY OF BRAZIL

THE year was 1941, and while the rest of the world was busy shooting at one another, life was pleasant enough in Brazil, particularly if you were the son of one of the richest men in the country.

Antonio Bento, at the age of 21, had it made. His daddy was loaded, and Tonio lived the charmed life of a playboy. He drank the finest wines, ran around with the most beautiful women and is purported to have sung riotous songs. Life was one party after another.

One night in February, Tonio was carousing in the neighbouring town of Niteroi when he took a fancy to a singer in an exclusive nightclub. Irene Romero had whatever it is you are supposed to have in all the right places. She was cute as a button, with large eyes and long black hair. Tonio, no novice when it came to the opposite sex, fell hard for Irene. The pair talked that night for two hours at a secluded corner table and struck up a deal.

Fast worker that he was, Tonio offered Irene a rent-free apartment in Santa Teresa, one of the classiest sections of Rio de Janeiro. Before you could say "coffee beans," Irene accepted the offer, and one week later was ensconced as Tonio's mistress in a luxury apartment.

Darn it all, Tonio should have stopped right there: for a lad of 21 he had the world by the tail. Unfortunately, he spoiled everything by actually falling in love with Irene. They got along so well together that in the next two years Irene gave birth to two sons, Marco and Isaias. Tonio even gave up the life of a playboy. His daddy bought him a rundown hardware store to get his feet wet in the world of business. He started getting up at seven-thirty in the morning, going to work and returning late in the evening. He kept mentioning things such as maturity, fulfillment and the like, to Irene.

Well, this was ridiculous. Irene became furious. It was unheard of for the son of one of the richest men in Brazil to be working like a dog—too tired to have parties. Irene started to nag Tonio; the nagging soon turned to fighting. One day she went too far, accusing Tonio of being unfaithful to her. Tonio, who had been a good partner to Irene, couldn't forgive her for the insult. He stormed out of the apartment and headed for a bar he knew in Niteroi.

As the night wore on and Tonio proceeded to tie one on, a 32-year-old lady named Maria Neubauer took on the part of consoling, sympathetic listener. She was good company, and Tonio poured out his story of his crushed home life and his love for his two sons.

The couple spent the night together and became close friends. In fact, they became so close that next morning Tonio would have been happy enough to spend the rest of his days with the experienced Maria, but he truly loved his sons and in order to see them he had to call on Irene. Now his life became a topsy-turvy round of going to work, then to Irene's and then to Maria's. It was enough to wear out a man; something had to give.

Well, Maria had the perfect solution. She told Tonio to kill Irene, poison her, simple and neat. He would then have his Marco and Isaias, and above all, he would have Maria. At first, Tonio thought the idea preposterous, but with Maria working on him he started to change his mind. Finally he decided to go through with it.

One night, when Tonio knew his two sons were away visiting relatives, he called on Irene. While they were drinking a bottle of beer, he slipped a vial of poison into her glass. Not waiting for the poison to take effect, Tonio left the apartment and rushed to Maria.

When Maria heard his story she was far from pleased. She pointed out to Tonio that he had forgotten to clean up the glasses. Tonio killed a half bottle of whiskey to get up enough nerve to go back to Irene's apartment. When he opened the door he found Irene sprawled across her bed, unconscious. He washed the incriminating glasses and the beer bottle.

Poor Tonio was not an experienced killer. In fact, exhausted from the tension and the liquor, he sat down in a soft armchair and fell asleep. In the meantime, Irene started vomiting in the bedroom. She brought up the entire contents of her stomach and then fell asleep, exhausted. When she woke up in the morning, she felt terrible. She staggered into the kitchen and found two washed glasses and a washed beer bottle. (Tonio may have made history by becoming the only person outside of a brewery to wash out a beer bottle.) Irene then discovered Tonio asleep in the chair. She put two and two together and came up with poison.

Irene saw red. She started clawing at Tonio before he was awake. Like a madwoman, she was now screaming at the still-drowsy Tonio. "You will never see the children again. Instead, you will go to prison, and your father will disinherit you for dragging his name into the mud."

In one outburst Irene had vividly described the destruction of Tonio's life. Tonio retreated to the kitchen, grabbed a rolling pin and swung viciously at Irene's head. The first blow knocked her down and Tonio kept swinging until there was very little left of her head. Both he and the kitchen were covered with blood.

Back Tonio went to Maria. When Maria heard this latest development, she put Tonio to bed for a few hours' rest. While he was asleep, she burned his bloodstained clothing. Then she woke Tonio up and explained to him that they couldn't leave Irene's body in the apartment. He would be sure to be suspected. They both went back to Irene's apartment, Tonio for the third time.

Maria took one look at the condition of the kitchen and sent Tonio out to purchase a large wooden crate. While Tonio was out picking up the crate, Maria realized that she had missed her breakfast. She prepared a substantial meal, getting the necessary ingredients from the refrigerator. Each time she went to the refrigerator, she had to step over Irene's battered body.

When Tonio, who was by now a walking zombie, returned with the crate, Maria informed him that they would have to dismember Irene's body. Tonio felt things had gone far enough. He just couldn't do it. Maria said that she would do the nasty job herself.

It seems she had thought of everything, having brought along a saw just for the purpose at hand. Hard-working Maria managed to sever Irene's arms, legs and head. The crate was too small for all the body parts, so Tonio ran out and purchased a suitcase, solving that particular problem. Then the industrious Maria scrubbed the kitchen until it was spotless.

Maria and Tonio had a heart-to-heart talk. She told him that she had a sister, Virginia, who lived in Niteroi, and whom she could trust with their peculiar luggage. Her sister lived with a boyfriend, Waldema, and an 18-year-old son, Eurico, both of whom could also be trusted. The "luggage" was duly stored at Virginia's house.

Now, completely under the domination of Maria, Tonio told neighbours and friends that Irene had fallen ill and was at a sanitorium for an indefinite stay. He moved out of the apartment and placed his two children with relatives.

Irene effectively had disappeared off the face of the earth. Seven months went by, and to all intents and purposes Tonio and Maria had managed to commit the perfect murder.

Well, not quite. Back at Virginia's home, Irene's body had been buried in a tiny courtyard. Virginia was haunted by the fear that as the body decomposed it would create an odour that would lead to its discovery. Each night she sprinkled chloride of lime over the courtyard. But the solution itself started to give off an odour, and neighbours complained.

Finally someone called the police, and the jig was up. Soon the whole entangled web of intrigue was unravelled and Virginia, her lover and son, as well as Maria and Tonio, were taken into custody. Because of the wealth and prominence of his father, Tonio's involvement caused a national sensation.

When the series of trials that followed the arrests were concluded, the three who had disposed of Irene's body each received 18 months in prison. As they had spent more time than that in jail awaiting trial, they were released.

Maria Neubauer was sentenced to nine and a half years' imprisonment. Tonio, the millionaire's son who a few short years before had had everything a man could want, was sentenced to 21 long years in prison.

# MAGGIE BOO

## LOVE HANDLES

MARGARET Crump felt life was passing her by. There she was, decidedly plump, with ever so tiny crow's feet making their unattractive appearance beside her eyes, which in recent months had developed an involuntary squint.

One day, Margaret, who had seen four decades come and go, looked across the breakfast table at her husband of 14 years. Wasn't he a prize? she thought. David spent most of his time collecting money for worthy causes in and around Folkestone, England. When he wasn't complaining about the state of the Commonwealth, he was moaning about his ulcerated leg. Among David's more disagreeable traits, Margaret felt his bouts of depression ranked right up there as the most annoying. Sometimes David was so low he threatened to commit suicide. No one, least of all Margaret, took his threats seriously. It was a loveless marriage that had produced no children.

Year after dreary year, David collected funds for charity, while Margaret pursued her hobby of citizens' band radio. Each evening, after David took his sleeping pills and she could hear him snoring, she would plug in her equipment. Her CB handle was Maggie Boo. Her hobby was her one escape from her boring, loveless marriage.

One fog-enshrouded night in 1986, Maggie Boo received a response from Hawaiian Cruiser. It was like no other response she had ever received. Hawaiian Cruiser had a melodious sexy voice. He flattered Maggie Boo. What's more, he was suggestive. Maggie Boo said nothing to discourage the naughty boy. Each night she would wait to hear David snoring so she could exchange sweet sly insinuations with her Hawaiian Cruiser.

It was agreed. The pair had to meet. Margaret hid those crow's feet as best she could and pulled out the few invading gray hairs. She and Hawaiian Cruiser met in a restaurant. The sexy voice belonged to 20-year-old David Belsham, a skinny young man with a severe case of acne. If you can imagine Ichabod Crane, you pretty well have the picture.

Despite their physical deficiencies and the discrepancy in their ages, Maggie Boo and Hawaiian Cruiser got along famously. They met often and soon became lovers. Juices dormant these many years once again flowed freely within Margaret Crump. Life was worth living, after all. Belsham was attentive, polite and, above all, terrific in bed.

In time, Margaret introduced Belsham to her husband. Crump never suspected for a moment that this young lad was anything more than a fellow citizens' band enthusiast. Eventually Margaret met two of Belsham's friends, Stephen Farthing and Paul Thompson. When Belsham requested that the two men, who had recently been asked to leave their rooming house, move in with the Crumps, Margaret agreed it would be a good idea. Even her husband liked the arrangement. They could do odd jobs around the place, allowing him more time for his charity work.

For a while, all went well. Farthing and Thompson had a roof over their heads, Crump had two built-in handymen, Belsham had done a favour for two friends and, of course, we all know what Margaret was receiving in quantities she had once only fantasized about.

In the deception business, one must realize that things can't go on forever. In 1987, David's ulcerated leg so bothered him that he had to be hospitalized. Belsham moved into the Crump house to keep Margaret company.

Playing house appealed to Belsham. There is good evidence he had fallen in love with Margaret and dreaded the fast-approaching day when her husband would be released from hospital. He and Margaret discussed their predicament. They would do the honourable thing. They would tell her husband of their love for each other. No doubt, he would be civilized and drop out of the picture. After the divorce, they would marry and live happily ever after.

Well, folks, David did come home from the hospital. Margaret and Belsham told him their intentions. Rather than take the news calmly, David said he would rather die than grant his wife a divorce. In addition, loud and clear, he ordered Belsham and his two buddies out of the house.

No one left the Crump residence. In the next few days, you could cut the tension with a knife. Each evening, Crump went to his room, took his sleeping pills and went to sleep alone. Downstairs, Belsham, Margaret, Farthing and Thompson plotted his demise. They would make the murder appear to be a suicide. After all, David had suffered from depression for years and had often mentioned suicide to anyone who would listen.

On July 16, 1987, David went to his room, extracted several sleeping pills from a bottle on his night table and took them with a glass of water, as was his custom. Margaret, realizing that he would take his usual large quantity of sleeping pills as he read his Bible in bed, brought him a cup of coffee. She had solicitously dissolved several sleeping pills in the coffee before taking it upstairs. David grumbled a thanks and drank his coffee.

Next morning, Stephen Farthing found David dead in bed. He called an ambulance. The ambulance attendants noted the empty medicine bottle, observed the room was otherwise neat and tidy and concluded that David had committed suicide by means of an overdose.

Nothing would have been done about the open-and-shut case had a relative of David's not called the Folkestone Police Station the day following his death with the information that David had written to her two weeks before, informing her that he believed the four conspirators living in his house planned to kill him. He had also told her of his wife's ongoing affair with Belsham. Evidently, Crump had sneaked downstairs one night and had overheard the entire plot. Although he was alarmed, he couldn't bring himself to believe that his wife and her friends would actually kill him. David was wrong.

An autopsy was performed. The results indicated that David had taken a large quantity of barbiturates, about 12 pills, several of which had not been absorbed into the bloodstream by the time death occurred. The attending pathologist also discovered cotton fibres in David's nose, mouth and lungs, indicating that the victim could have been suffocated with a pillow.

The investigation might have bogged down at this point had David Belsham kept his mouth shut. However, like so many killers before him, he had an irresistible urge to tell someone that he had committed the perfect murder. Belsham chose a buddy in a pub. He related in detail how Margaret had laced the coffee with sleeping pills. They had waited awhile before climbing the stairs and finishing the job with a pillow. Belsham's drinking buddy scampered down to the Folkestone police station to tell what he had heard.

All four conspirators were arrested, tried and found guilty of David Crump's murder. Because of his youth, Paul Thompson received an indefinite prison term, while Stephen Farthing, Maggie Boo and Hawaiian Cruiser were sentenced to life imprisonment.

# TYRONE BORGLUND AND ERIC PEEVER

## THE AXE MASSACRE

THE murders were atrocious, cold-blooded acts committed by boys not old enough to vote.

In January 1988, seven individuals lived in the three-bedroom bungalow on Fourteenth Avenue in Mission, B.C. The residents of the house had experienced diverse upheavals en route to the small town located about 65 kilometres east of Vancouver.

Karsten Madsen met Leny van Rikxoort in 1977 in Vancouver. Karsten, at 27 years of age, had been married, divorced and deeply involved with another woman before meeting Leny. His marriage to Sharon Peever had brought two children into the world, Eric and Michael, who remained with their mother after the divorce. When he met Leny, he was also the father of Jason, a bouncing eight-month-old, the result of his last involvement.

Leny and Karsten married in 1978. Their daughter, Michelle, was born that same year. Little Jason was also a part of their family. The Madsens relocated often in the following seven years, eventually settling in Mission. Like many Canadian families with young children, they required two incomes to keep a roof over their heads. Karsten made a precarious living as a drywall installer. Despite the ever-present need for more money, the Madsens appeared to be happy. They were outgoing and well liked. The family consisted of four individuals living in the bungalow on Fourteenth Avenue. They would all become victims.

In 1985, the Madsens applied to become foster parents. Their motives have come under close scrutiny. Certainly the $500 they would receive monthly from the B.C. Ministry of Social Services was a factor. There is some evidence that the money enabled them to purchase a new car. Whatever the motivation, 14-year-old Tyrone Borglund moved into the Madsen home. The addition of Tyrone to the household brought the number of residents in the bungalow on Fourteenth Avenue to five.

Initially, things went well, but it wasn't long before Tyrone became disruptive around the house. From time to time, Leny reported his behaviour to the ministry. On more than one occasion, Tyrone was removed and placed in another foster home, but was taken back by the Madsens when he promised to mend his ways.

As the years passed, Eric and Michael, who were living with their mother, Sharon Peever, grew to be teenagers. Eric, the older of the two, was thrown out of his home by his mother's common-law husband when he was caught stealing from the house. Eric contacted Karsten, his biological father, and moved in with the Madsens in Mission. Eric and Tyrone seemed to get along well. They were approximately the same age and soon became close friends.

The sixth player in the tragedy that would follow was on stage. One more player was required to complete the cast. Eric's younger brother, Michael, contacted Karsten and moved into the bungalow in Mission. The full complement of seven individuals was now gathered in the house on Fourteenth Avenue.

Karsten and Leny knew they had problems. Michelle and Jason behaved like normal youngsters, but the three older boys were a handful. On more than one occasion, the police contacted Leny. The boys had become petty thieves. They even stole from their own home. Karsten had to keep a careful eye on his liquor. Small items often went missing. Leny gave the boys severe tongue-lashings, which seemed to sink in at the time, but which had little lasting effect.

Tyrone and Michael shared sleeping quarters in the basement and it was there that the three boys planned the murder of the other four members of the family. Karsten, Leny, Michelle and Jason would all be murdered. The boys would take money from the master bedroom, steal Leny's Toyota and take off for Fort Saint John.

On the night of January 17, 1988, the stage was set. Tyrone suggested the axes. They were weapons of opportunity, just lying there in the house. The boys practised swinging the axes down there in the basement. Upstairs, the house was quiet. Everyone was asleep. Eric sneaked upstairs and returned with some wine and pear brandy. The boys took long swigs from the bottles. Tyrone and Eric, equipped with the axes, slowly climbed the stairs. Michael carried a maul. He would later testify that when the reality of what they were about to do came to him, he couldn't go through with the plan. He left his fellow conspirators and returned to the basement.

Tyrone and Eric continued to the master bedroom. Karsten and Leny were sleeping soundly. The moves had been well planned. Tyrone would kill Karsten while Eric took care of Leny. Tyrone lifted the large axe above his head and brought it down with all his might on the sleeping man's skull. The force of the blow split open Karsten's head. Leny awoke with a start. She screamed, her hands instinctively shielding her head, but there was no escape. Eric brought the axe down. Her arms may have deflected the initial blow so that the first swing didn't render her unconscious. We will never know how many times Eric swung that axe, but at some time in the midst of the blood and the passion, he dropped the weapon and ran to the refuge of the basement. Tyrone finished the gruesome task in the bedroom.

Eleven-year-old Jason was awakened by the noise. Rubbing sleep from his eyes, he strolled into the master bedroom. Only half-awake, he couldn't quite absorb the scene he was witnessing. He said, "What are you doing to my mum?" Three vicious swings from Tyrone's axe and the little boy lay dead on the bedroom floor.

The next to wake up was nine-year-old Michelle. She too was drawn to the source of the noise. Tyrone intercepted her at the doorway. She met the same fate as Jason. There was no more noise from upstairs in the house on Fourteenth Avenue in Mission, B.C.

Down in the basement, there was plenty of excitement. They had actually done it. True, Tyrone was the ringleader, but they had all been involved in one way or another. Now that it was over, Eric felt he owed Tyrone an explanation. After all, he had retreated during the height of the attack. Tyrone assured him there were no hard feelings. In the end they had accomplished what they had set out to do.

The three boys entered the room of carnage. Their plan was working. In minutes they removed all the bills from Karsten's wallet and Leny's purse. The keys to the Toyota were there in her purse just as they had expected. It didn't take long for them to get out of the house, leaving behind four bodies hacked to death in the bedroom. The teenagers wheeled the Toyota out of the driveway and headed toward Fort Saint John, 790 kilometres to the northeast. Good times lay ahead. Only then did Tyrone and Eric notice that their clothing was spattered with blood.

Once in Fort Saint John, the boys purchased booze, called friends and partied. Two days after the killing spree, Tyrone was picked up for drunk driving. The Toyota was soon traced to Mission, B.C., the bodies discovered and the bloody multiple murders exposed.

What had triggered the vicious attack that had taken four lives? According to Tyrone, they were angry at Leny because she had given them another one of her patented tongue-lashings and had forbidden them to watch TV. All charges against 15-year-old Michael Peever were dropped in exchange for his testimony.

After the murder trial, in which he appeared as the Crown's star witness, he was placed anonymously in a group home somewhere in British Columbia.

Tyrone and Eric stood trial for murder in adult court. Their claim that they had taken the axes into the Madsens' bedroom solely to frighten them was not believed by the jury. It took only three hours' deliberation to find both boys guilty of murder.

Tyrone Borglund, 16, and Eric Peever, 17, were sentenced to life imprisonment with no possibility of parole for 25 years. They are presently serving their sentences.

# ERNIE BROWN

## GROOMED TO KILL

SINCE time immemorial, certain married women have scorned their legal mates for butlers, chauffeurs, gardeners, cooks and other assorted gentlemen in the employ of their well-heeled hubbies. You would think busy husbands would be wary of the hired help, especially if they are what is commonly called hunks.

Ernest Brown was a hunk. He stood a tad over six feet and had a chiselled countenance complete with two attractive dimples, which served to light up his face when he smiled that seductive smile of his. And as for Ernie's muscles, they had muscles of their own.

In 1929, Ernie hired on as a groom-gardener with Cattle Factors Ltd. of Saxton Grange, Yorkshire. The isolated farm was a thriving business operated by Fred Morton. Now, Fred wasn't a bad guy. It was just that he was terribly busy and had precious little time for his wife and two-year-old daughter.

Let me tell you about Dorothy Morton. There is no other way to put it—Dorothy was stacked. She was a gorgeous woman with an outstanding figure. When she went into Sherburn-in-Elmet to shop, heads turned to gaze upon what many considered to be the most beautiful woman in all of Yorkshire.

It was Dorothy's love of horses that placed her constantly in the company of groom Ernie Brown. Fred Morton was often away on business. And Ernie had monkey business in mind. Initially, Dorothy didn't fall into Ernie's arms. No sir, he had to work for her affection, but eventually nature took its course. The two handsome young people bedded down at every opportunity and thus formed two angles of a very dangerous triangle.

Dorothy attempted to break off the affair but Ernie wouldn't hear of it. When she forced the issue, he threatened her. Poor Dorothy. What had once been a thrilling experience had become a vulgar, risky game. She wanted out. She even thought of telling her husband about the entire sordid affair, but she was too afraid.

In June 1933, Ernie threw a snit when Fred asked him to perform some menial task around the farm. He quit his job and left. Dorothy drew a sigh of relief. After four years of threats and intrigue, it was over. Her relief was short-lived. Ernie either changed his mind or found that jobs were not that easy to come by. He also may have missed the sex he had grown accustomed to for the past four years. Whatever the reason, Ernie showed up back on the farm one day when Fred was away on business. He threatened to tell all unless Dorothy phoned her husband and succeeded in having Ernie rehired. Dorothy did as she was told. Fred took Ernie back into the fold as an odd-job man. Resenting his new lowly status, Ernie became a surly lurking presence, forever bad-mouthing Fred Morton.

On September 5, Ernie went over the brink. Knowing that Fred was away on business, he entered the farmhouse and struck Dorothy in front of Ann Houseman, her daughter's nurse. Ernie picked up a shotgun and ordered Ann out of the house. Although terrified, the nurse refused to leave. Ernie calmly sat down and cleaned the weapon in front of the two frightened women.

At 11:30 p.m., Ann and Dorothy were relieved to hear Fred's car chugging into the farmyard. Ernie left the house, apparently to get out before the boss arrived. He took a kitchen knife with him. The women were shocked when Ernie re-entered the house a few minutes later, exclaiming, "The boss has been here and gone out again."

Desperately, Ann and Dorothy engaged Ernie in conversation. Around 2 a.m., Ernie left the house once more. A few minutes later, the women heard a strange crackling sound. Dorothy peered outside. The garage was a blazing inferno. She attempted to use the telephone but found that it was out of order. No doubt Ernie had cut the wires. Hurriedly, the women dressed Dorothy's daughter and rushed outside. Fearful of being sighted by Ernie, they hid in a ditch, spending the rest of the early-morning hours huddled there. When they saw Ernie leave in a wagon, they made their way to Towton, about a half mile away, and told authorities about their terror-filled night.

The local fire brigade arrived, closely followed by Ernie Brown. The fire was extinguished and the Mortons' gutted Chrysler was examined. In the front passenger seat were the charred remains of what had once been a human being. The head, arms and legs had been burned into cinders, but keys and a diamond ring left no doubt that the body was that of Fred Morton.

The ensuing investigation revealed that the farm's telephone wires had been cut with a knife and that Fred had been shot to death before the car and garage had been set on fire. Shotgun pellets had entered Fred's heart. Apparently the weapon had been held directly against his stomach. It was quite amazing that although all of Fred's upper body had been consumed by the fire, investigators found a few square inches of flesh that miraculously had not been burned. Shotgun pellets and gun wadding were found in this small portion of flesh.

Ernie Brown was taken into custody and charged with Fred Morton's murder. His trial fascinated England, not because of the rascal himself, but because of Dorothy Morton, who was the Crown's star witness. The 30-year-old Dorothy, as beautiful as any movie star, took the witness box and revealed all the juicy details of her affair with the family groom. She even admitted that, on one occasion only, she had been intimate with another chap while carrying on with nasty Ernie and living with her husband. For shame! Such things just didn't happen in Yorkshire.

The prosecution proved that Fred Morton's shotgun, which Ernie had taken from the farmhouse on the night of the murder, was the murder weapon. They also proved that the kitchen knife found in Ernie's possession had been used to cut the telephone wires.

It was all too much. The Yorkshire jury found Ernie guilty of murder. He listened unmoved when the presiding judge sentenced him to death by hanging. As he was led from the courtroom, he took one fleeting glance at Dorothy. An angry crowd of 1,000 hurled insults at Dorothy as she walked to a waiting vehicle.

On February 6, 1934, Ernie Brown was hanged at Armley Prison, Leeds.

# EUGENE CHANTRELLE

## HE WASN'T GRANTED HIS LAST REQUEST

ELIZABETH Dyer fell hard for her schoolteacher. While this is not an uncommon phenomenon, Lizzie took her infatuation far too seriously. Then, again, who can blame her; she was only 15. Her teacher, Eugene Chantrelle, who should have known better, was a mature 34.

Chantrelle had been educated in Strasbourg and Paris. He claimed that he had attended medical school, but for reasons of his own had not bothered to obtain his medical degree.

In 1867, we find suave, aristocratic Eugene teaching Greek, French and Latin in Edinburgh, Scotland. The handsome teacher stood straight as an arrow and sported a shock of wavy brown hair.

Lizzie pursued Chantrelle with dogged determination, using all her wiles, which even at 15 were appreciable, to land her teacher. She succeeded to such an extent that certain expected lunar regularities became uncharacteristically absent and Lizzie found herself pregnant. This rather embarrassing state of affairs was made more difficult by the fact that her mother despised Chantrelle with a passion.

When Lizzie's parents heard of their daughter's delicate condition, they agreed that a marriage was an absolute necessity. In August, the pupil and her teacher tied the knot.

The marriage was not a happy one. In the following years, Chantrelle displayed a vile temper, which erupted at the least provocation. In 1876, the couple had three children, Jack, Louis and a newborn baby. They lived in a double flat on George Street, which consisted of a kitchen, parlour and a classroom on the lower floor, and three bedrooms on the top attic level.

By 1877, Chantrelle was guzzling a bottle of whiskey every day at home. Every afternoon he could be found at his favourite watering hole, the Hanover Hotel. Just to complete the picture, the suave teacher of foreign languages liked to frequent the local house of ill repute only a block away on Clyde Street. Let's face it, Chantrelle was not what you would call a good family man.

The Chantrelles retained a servant, Mary Byrne. It is from her that we learn that the master of the house belittled his wife in front of the children, often referring to her as "that bitch." Sometimes he struck her. On those occasions, Lizzie retreated to her mother's home, but she always returned, determined to make a success of her marriage.

Life went on in its turbulent way. Once Lizzie went as far as to have her husband jailed for striking her, but when it came time to press charges, she relented. The family managed to have an almost peaceful Christmas in 1877, despite the head of the household being sloshed to the gills most of the time.

Chantrelle's drinking and carousing had caught up to him in a financial way. Although at one time he had given private language lessons, he found his pupils dropping off one by one until the classroom in the flat was a quiet, deserted place. A loan from the bank kept the wolf from the door for a while, but as time passed the bank began pressing Chantrelle to pay back the loan.

In desperation, the teacher attempted to supplement his income by working as a part-time insurance agent for the Star Accidental Assurance Co. He sold only one policy to a personal friend, but while employed as an agent, he inquired extensively as to what legally constituted an accidental death which would be paid off by an insurance company.

Instead of continuing with Star Accidental, Chantrelle called as a customer on the Accidental Assurance Association of Scotland. Here he purchased three policies. He insured maid Mary Byrne's life for £100 pounds. He also insured his own life and Lizzie's in the event of death by accident for £1,000 each. Lizzie, who was well aware of the insurance policies, told her mother, "My life is insured now. Momma, you will see that my life will go soon." Although Mrs. Dyer was alarmed at hearing her daughter utter such ominous words, she assured Lizzie that she had nothing to worry about. Momma was dead wrong.

On New Year's Eve, 1877, the family had a pleasant evening meal, after which the children were put to bed. Lizzie and Eugene sat in the parlour for the rest of evening until midnight, when the sound of the bands playing at Edinburgh Castle swept over the city. Mary was invited into the parlour to enjoy the music through the open window. Shortly after midnight everyone went to bed.

Next day, the family woke up and proceeded with their usual routine. At eleven o'clock, Mary was given the rest of the day off. She spent the day at the home of a friend, returning at 9:45 that night. Chantrelle greeted Mary, informing her that Lizzie wasn't feeling well and had gone to bed. Mary went directly to her mistress's bedroom and chatted with Lizzie, who assured her that she was feeling better than she had earlier in the day. Lizzie asked Mary to peel an orange for her. Mary did so and gave her mistress one wedge, leaving the balance of the orange on a plate. She then retired for the night.

According to Chantrelle, he had polished off a bottle of whiskey in the parlour before looking in on Lizzie at about midnight. He also claimed that he and his wife had made love, but considering Lizzie's illness, most believe the claim to be a fabrication. Chantrelle then retired for the night.

Next morning, while Mary was busy heating water in the kitchen for tea, she heard a loud moan from the bedroom. She ran to Lizzie's side and found her very pale, lying in bed as if unconscious. She also noticed stains on the pillow and bedclothes which she assumed was vomit.

Mary ran from the room, woke Chantrelle and told him to call a doctor immediately. He entered his wife's room, followed in a few moments by Mary. Chantrelle asked Mary if she smelled gas. She told him she didn't think so, but after a little while detected an odour she took to be gas.

Chantrelle left the house in search of medical assistance. Dr. James Carmichael, who knew Chantrelle, accompanied him back to the house. The doctor smelled gas immediately and had Lizzie moved to another bedroom. He sent for Dr. Henry Littlejohn, who arrived in minutes. Dr. Littlejohn came to the conclusion that Lizzie was near death and would not recover. He too decided that gas was responsible for her condition. He ordered that the patient be removed to the Royal Infirmary and that the gas company be called to inspect the house.

Lizzie's mother was informed of her daughter's serious illness. She showed up with her family physician, Dr. Gordon. The doctor checked Lizzie's symptoms and came to the conclusion that her condition had not been caused by escaping gas. He believed that her illness was the result of narcotic poisoning. Dr. Douglas MacLagan at the hospital also figured Lizzie was suffering from opium or morphia poisoning.

When Chantrelle arrived at the hospital, he became furious on learning that doctors thought Lizzie had been poisoned with a narcotic. He stormed out of the hospital in a rage. When he cooled off and returned to see his wife, he was informed that Lizzie was dead. Throughout the excitement and the tragedy, Chantrelle stayed well oiled.

The doctors were on the horns of a dilemma. They believed Lizzie had been poisoned by opium because of the symptoms she had displayed. However, many of those same symptoms were consistent with gas poisoning. The gas company found that a gas pipe had been purposely loosened. A gas company employee stated that the pipe could have been wrenched loose in the matter of a second or two.

Police investigating Lizzie's death concluded that someone had poisoned her with opium. They felt that when Chantrelle was summoned by Mary and entered the bedroom, he instantly decided, in a drunken sort of way, that his wife's death would not be considered accidental and he would therefore not be able to collect the £1,000 insurance. To make certain that her death appeared accidental, he loosened the gas pipe, figuring a leaking gas pipe would be accepted as a bona fide accident.

It was also believed that Chantrelle had fed Lizzie opium so that she would be totally out of it when he turned on the gas. But why did he go to the trouble of loosening a pipe rather than just turning on the gas? Detectives felt that Chantrelle, despite his hateful ways towards his wife, was attached to his children. He didn't want to harm them or himself. Still tipsy from his previous night's drinking, he was awakened suddenly by Mary and knew he had to fake gas poisoning to collect that insurance. A quick pull of the pipe while Mary was out of the room solved all his problems.

An autopsy did little to clear up the situation in that it failed to establish the cause of death. The presence of opium could not be proven as it disappears rapidly in the system. However, traces of opium were found in the vomit stains recovered from Lizzie's pillow and bedclothes. One must remember that Chantrelle had medical training. He maintained what amounted to a small apothecary on the premises, which contained a large supply of opium.

Eugene Chantrelle was taken into custody and tried for the murder of his wife. He was found guilty and sentenced to death.

On May 30, 1878, Chantrelle made his mark in criminal history. When asked if he had a last wish, he replied, "Send in three bottles of champagne and a whore." Next morning he was hanged as a chaplain recited the Lord's Prayer. Eugene Chantrelle went to his death without being granted his last request.

# STYLLOU CHRISTOFI

## ONE MEAN MUMMY

IT is my opinion that sons should treat their mothers with respect, no matter what the circumstances. This is especially true if you happen to have a mean mummy who doesn't like your wife. Sound like the beginning of a Greek tragedy? Well, that's exactly how it turned out. Mrs. Styllou Christofi was a mean mummy extraordinaire.

Mrs. Christofi hailed from Cyprus. The 53-year-old peasant woman had been born to poverty and remained illiterate all her life. She had never left her home village until she travelled to London, England, to visit her son, Stavros.

Rather than being proud of her son's accomplishments, Mrs. Christofi was furious that he had abandoned the way of life she cherished back in Cyprus. The truth of the matter was that Stavros had carved out a new and comfortable life since emigrating to England in 1937. He was a wine waiter in a fashionable restaurant in London's West End. Along the way he had married Hella, a pretty German girl whom he loved dearly. The Christofis had three young children and a comfortable home. All in all, the ambitious Greek boy had done very well for himself and his family.

Stavros's mother simply didn't see it that way. She watched with steely eyes, hatred oozing out of every pore. How dare this interloper Hella poison her son's mind so that he had become more English than Greek? Each evening he went off to his soft job, a far cry from the sun-drenched days in the fields back home. And the children? Were they to grow up in this prosperous society, never understanding the work ethic which was such an important part of their heritage? Mrs. Christofi was further frustrated by not being able to speak English. She was effectively cut off from conversing with her daughter-in-law and her grandchildren.

On July 29, 1954, at precisely 8 p.m., Stavros left his home for work as he did every evening. His mother had been living with him now for the better part of a year. It just hadn't worked out. On three different occasions, she had moved out, and three times she returned. The incessant insinuations about casting aside his roots had started all over again.

Mrs. Christofi blamed Hella for all the discord in the family. The venomous feeling directed towards Hella didn't go unnoticed. Hella, who couldn't converse with her mother-in-law, often became depressed because of the obvious animosity displayed by the older woman. Finally, it was unofficially agreed that Hella would take the children and visit her family in Germany. When she returned, Mrs. Christofi would leave for Cyprus. In Mrs. Christofi's mind, she was being tossed out of her own son's home. What's more, the expulsion was tantamount to being removed from his life.

This night would be different. Stavros kissed Hella goodbye, unaware that he would never see his wife again. Once he was out of the house, Hella put the children to bed. The two women busied themselves cleaning the kitchen. Without warning, Mrs. Christofi picked up a heavy metal plate used to collect ashes from the stove and struck Hella on the back of the head. The unconscious woman fell to the floor. Mrs. Christofi proceeded to strangle Hella with a scarf belonging to one of the children.

The house was deathly quiet. For the next few hours, Mrs. Christofi was a busy mummy, but her deeds were performed with a singleness of purpose.

At 11:30 p.m., John Young, the Christofis' next-door neighbour, took his dog for a run in the backyard. He noticed a bonfire in the adjoining yard. John shouted but received no response. He peered over the brick wall separating the two properties and observed what he thought was a mannikin burning in the fire. As he turned to go back into his home, he saw someone leave the Christofi house and walk towards the fire. Young later stated, "I left when I saw someone I recognized. I thought all was in order." John Young was wrong. Mummy dearest had just come out to stoke the fire. She was burning her daughter-in-law.

About 1 a.m., Mr. and Mrs. Burstoff were driving to their home in Hampstead when they were hailed by Mrs. Christofi. In broken English, she said over and over, "Fire. Burning. Children sleeping." The Burstoffs accompanied Mrs. Christofi to her home and discovered the badly burned body in the backyard. They called police. While they waited, Mrs. Christofi told the Burstoffs, "My son marry Germany girl he like. Plenty clothes, plenty shoes."

Police were quickly on the scene. They found bloodstains on the kitchen floor which had been partially cleaned. Beside Hella's body they found paper which had been soaked in paraffin. Hella's wedding ring was not on her finger, but was recovered from Mrs. Christofi's room. In a dustbin were three portions of a child's scarf. The scarf had been cut into pieces in order to remove it from Hella's neck.

Police questioned Mrs. Christofi. She told them, "I wake up, smell burning, go downstairs. Hella burning. Throw water, touch her face. Not move. Run out, get help." Through an interpreter, Mrs. Christofi claimed that she and her daughter-in-law had been on perfect terms. She had gone to bed that night, leaving Hella in a good mood doing household chores.

In due course, Mrs. Christofi was arrested and charged with Hella's murder. Her trial was unique in that every word was translated into Greek. The English jury took only a matter of hours to find Mrs. Christofi guilty of murder. She was sentenced to death. All appeals failed. The execution was to proceed as scheduled.

On the day before the execution, it was revealed, via the British press, that the chief medical officer at Holloway Prison had filed a report before the trial, stating, "The clinical picture is that of a nonsystemized disillusional mental disorder." The doctor had insinuated that Mrs. Christofi was incapable of realizing that what she had done was wrong.

This caused quite a disturbance, and great efforts were made to commute the condemned woman's sentence at the last minute. All these efforts were doomed to failure and Mrs. Christofi was hanged as scheduled.

Only after her execution was it revealed that Mrs. Christofi was no amateur in the not-so-gentle art of murder. Back in 1925, in Cyprus, she had killed her mother-in-law by ramming a burning torch down her throat. The crime had been one of hate and jealousy involving her husband and his mother. Inexplicably, on that occasion, she had been acquitted. As I said, Mrs. Christofi was one mean mummy.

# GORDON FREDERICK CUMMINS

## WARTIME RIPPER

THE winter of 1942 was one of fear and chaos in war-torn London, England. Thousands of allied servicemen stationed there worked hard and played hard, while each night Hitler's Luftwaffe rained bombs on the streets of the city.

Normal criminal activity took a back seat to the larger task of protecting the country from a common enemy. It required an extraordinary series of events to capture the population's interest in anything other than war news. Such a series of events began on the night of February 9, 1942.

Evelyn Hamilton was a respectable 42-year-old pharmacist who had recently moved to London from Hornchurch, Essex. An electrician found her body lying on the floor of an air-raid shelter in Montagu Place, Marylebone. Evelyn's silk scarf was wrapped around her mouth and nose. Her clothing was in disarray and her open handbag was found beside her body. It had been rifled and some of the contents had spilled out on the floor. Police also found a flashlight nearby. No fingerprints other than those of the victim were found on any of the items. Evelyn had been manually strangled to death. From the bruise marks on her neck, police believed that the killer was left-handed.

While murder can never be said to go unnoticed, Evelyn Hamilton's murder would not have received the notoriety it did in war-ravaged London but for one fact. She was the first victim of a maniac who was to become known as the Wartime Ripper.

The very next morning, the body of Evelyn Oatley was found in her flat on Wardour Street, Soho. Evelyn was a prostitute who often had clients visit her in her flat. She was found naked on her bed. Her killer had strangled her with his bare hands. Once again, the open purse was found close by the body. The killer had dumped out most of the contents of the purse and, as had been evident in the Hamilton murder, had taken whatever money the purse contained.

Evelyn Oatley's body had been horribly mutilated around the lower stomach with a can opener, which the killer had thrown onto a couch. Because some of the mutilations resembled those inflicted by the infamous Jack the Ripper before the turn of the century, the British press dubbed the killings the work of the Wartime Ripper.

Police noted the similarities between the two murders committed a day apart. Both women had been strangled; both had been robbed; and both appeared to have been killed by a left-handed person. In the Oatley case, the murderer had left fingerprints on the can opener, but a check with Scotland Yard failed to match the prints with any on file. Apparently the Wartime Ripper had never been arrested.

Three days later, neighbours grew concerned when Margaret Florence Lowe failed to follow her usual routine. Police were called to her one-room apartment on Gosfield Street off Tottenham Court Road. They forced the door open. Inside, on the bed, lay Margaret's nude body under a quilt. A scarf was wrapped around her neck and the lower portion of her stomach had been mutilated. The killer had left several clear fingerprints in the room. These were checked against those lifted from Evelyn Oatley's can opener. They matched. The Wartime Ripper had struck again.

While Scotland Yard was actively investigating this latest murder, they received another urgent call. Unbelievably, the Wartime Ripper had struck for the fourth time in four days. The body of Doris Jouannet, 32, the wife of a hotel owner, was found in her two-room flat in Paddington approximately one hour after she was strangled to death. A silk scarf was wrapped around her neck and she had been mutilated in the same manner as the other victims.

The killings had taken place with such rapidity that Scotland Yard was having difficulty correlating all the information garnered from the four crime scenes. They knew they were dealing with a sex maniac who robbed, strangled and mutilated his victims. There was little doubt in anyone's mind that he would continue to kill until he was either apprehended or dead. Authorities didn't have long to wait.

On the same night as the Jouannet murder, another woman was attacked. Greta Heywood was different from the previous victims of the Wartime Ripper. She survived. Greta was in a Piccadilly bar when a good-looking young airman joined her. He seemed friendly enough and proved to be a pleasant, charming companion. When he suggested that they drop into another bar located nearby, she agreed but pointed out that she had to return to the original bar to keep a prior date for dinner.

Everything was totally in order until they stepped out onto the streets of blacked-out London. Without warning, the airman pulled Greta into the doorway of an air-raid shelter. No words were spoken. He clamped his hands around Greta's neck and proceeded to strangle her. Greta grappled with her attacker and dropped her flashlight. It fell to the sidewalk, attracting the attention of a passerby. Greta's assailant heard the man approaching and immediately ran away. In his haste he dropped his service gas mask. The moment that gas mask fell to the sidewalk, the Wartime Ripper's brief but horrific career came to an abrupt end.

The young man who heard Greta's flashlight fall to the sidewalk picked up the gas mask and turned it over to police. Inside was the service number of its owner—525987. A check of RAF records identified the owner of the gas mask as Gordon Fredericks Cummins. Before Cummins could be located, he struck again. Minutes after his attack on Greta Heywood, he picked up Catherine Mulcahy, who drove with him in a taxi to her apartment. Once inside, he immediately attempted to strangle her. Catherine screamed and desperately fought for her life until finally Cummins fled.

Within hours, the wanted man was located and arrested. Initially, Scotland Yard was stunned to learn that Cummins had apparently been in his dormitory asleep when two of the murders had taken place. The billet passbook indicated that he had been in the barracks at the time two of the women had been strangled. Several roommates said they had seen him go to bed and get up in the morning. This mystery was solved when police questioned two fellow airmen who had witnessed Cummins sneaking out of his quarters after he thought everyone was asleep. They even located one man who had sneaked out with Cummins.

Cummins's fingerprints matched those found at the scene of the crime. To further solidify the Crown's case, a fountain pen and cigarette case belonging to two of the victims were found among Cummins's personal effects.

Strangely, the accused man denied killing anyone. Adjudged sane, Cummins stood trial in the Old Bailey. His wife appeared in court every day. She believed completely in her husband's innocence. No one else did. The English jury took less than an hour to find him guilty of Evelyn Oakley's murder.

On June 25, 1942, Gordon Frederick Cummins walked unwaveringly to the gallows. No one will ever know why this man, who had never been in trouble in his life, turned into a maniac for four days in February 1942.

# GEORGE CVEK

## HITCHHIKER FROM HELL

IT didn't take long for the police of several states to realize that they had a diabolical sneak thief, rapist and killer on their hands.

In November 1940, a Bronx couple picked up a hitchhiker on the Pulaski Skyway in New Jersey. The young man, who introduced himself as John Mitchell, was polite and charming. He told the couple that he had spent some time in Boys Town, Nebraska, and was hitchhiking to Maine to visit his sister. Boys Town, the home for troubled boys founded by Father Edward Flanagan, was well known, depicted in many movies and magazine articles. When Mitchell related how he had lost all his money and his suitcase in a lavatory, the Bronx couple offered him a small amount of money to tide him over. Initially, John refused the offer, but gradually let the money be forced into his hands. He insisted on getting the young couple's name and address so that he could repay their kindness.

Five days later, John Mitchell showed up at his benefactors' Bronx apartment. The woman of the house was alone, but when she recognized John, she immediately let him in. He explained that he had been successful in obtaining employment, but needed a few dollars to tide him over until pay day. The woman had no cash in the house and told him that her husband would be home in a few hours. She prepared a sandwich for John, who complained of having a headache.

While she was placing a bottle of aspirin on the kitchen table, John sneaked up behind her, grasped her neck in a headlock and dragged her into the bedroom. He tied the woman's hands with one of her husband's neckties and thrust a handkerchief into her mouth. After raping her, John stripped the apartment of valuables.

Three months later, the thief struck again. This time he introduced himself as Joe Mitchell of Boys Town. He told a woman that he had met her husband while hitchhiking and would wait until he returned home from work. He stayed for two hours before requesting aspirin. Using the same method as he had employed in the first attack, he tied his victim, shoved a handkerchief into her mouth and looted the apartment of valuables. Fortunately, the woman was not raped.

On February 4, 1941, John Pappas, a wealthy importer, returned to his third-floor apartment on Grand Concourse in the Bronx to find his wife lying dead on her bed. She had been strangled.

John had been married a year earlier in Alexandria, Egypt. His wife was a rare beauty, but was extremely shy in her new surroundings. He told police that she never left the apartment alone. Groceries were delivered once a week by one of his friends. His wife had no relatives or friends living in the U.S.

John was amazed that the crime scene indicated that his wife was acquainted with her killer. Two partially filled wineglasses and two empty coffee cups were on a table. Beside them was a tray of cookies and a water goblet. Nearby, on another table, was a bottle of aspirin. A lamp was overturned on the floor. Mrs. Pappas's rings had been torn from her fingers and other jewellery was missing from the apartment.

The killer had stuffed a handkerchief into his victim's mouth and had used his own necktie to tie her hands. He had knotted a towel around her throat. She had not been raped.

A wedding photograph, normally kept in the bedroom, was found in the living room. Mrs. Pappas had used her very best china to serve her guest. Her husband told detectives that she only took out her good china for special guests. He could offer no explanation as to why his extremely shy wife had obviously played hostess to her killer.

Fingerprints lifted from the water goblet didn't match those of anyone who had normal access to the Pappas apartment, nor did the FBI have any records of these prints.

Detectives were sure that the reported rapist and thief had graduated to murder. There were simply too many similarities in the three cases under investigation—the aspirin bottles, the handkerchiefs and the neckties. Because one victim had been raped and the others spared, it was theorized that the prime motive for all three crimes was theft. The rape had been an afterthought. Mrs. Pappas may have been killed because she didn't comply with the intruder's demands. The day after her murder, investigators learned that a man had attempted to gain entrance to three other apartments in the neighbourhood, but had been turned away.

Father Flanagan of Boys Town was contacted concerning anyone named Joe or John Mitchell who had been a resident of his well-known home for boys. The beloved priest replied that their man was an impostor. He added that several individuals had written him about a boy named Gerry Mitchell who claimed to be from Boys Town. It was obvious that someone was using the good name of the home to obtain money from unwary strangers.

Father Flanagan enclosed a postcard sent by the impostor to Boys Town. No doubt the card had been written to impress a potential victim. It read, "Dear Father Flannigan, Just a few lines to let you know that I am well and hope you and the rest of the boys are the same. Please don't worry about me, because I am being taken care of by the nicest people I ever met. Am writing the details in a letter which will follow this. So long." The card was signed "Gerry." Father Flanagan, anxious to have the impostor out of circulation, pointed out that his name had been misspelled and that each time the letter "r" had been written, it had appeared as an inverted "v."

Eight days after Mrs. Pappas's murder, the man with the convincing hard-luck story struck again with tragic consequences. An unwary motorist picked him up hitchhiking between Newark and Trenton. He told the man he was John Mitchell from Boys Town. Mitchell later showed up at the man's house in Philadelphia when only his pregnant wife was at home. Once inside, he raped her, stole anything of value he could carry and left. As a result of the violent rape, the woman lost her baby.

On March 3, 1941, Mrs. Elizabeth Jensen, 34, was found dead in her Bronx apartment. She had been tied with a necktie and a handkerchief had been forced into her mouth.

Because the two cases where murder had been committed were located not more than a mile apart, detectives began canvassing hotels and rooming houses in New York, looking for every name used by the Boys Town impostor.

It was a mammoth task, but it paid dividends immediately. The very day officers began canvassing the area, they discovered that a man fitting the killer's description had often stayed at the Mills Hotel on Seventh Avenue. The hotel was staked out on the chance that the suspect might show up. Sure enough, he walked into the lobby and checked into a room using the name G. Kolosky of Harrisburg, Pennsylvania. When detectives checked the registry, there were the telltale inverted "v"s in the word "Harrisburg." Police knew they had their man.

Kolosky was taken to a police station and searched. An ID card was found on his person, revealing his real identity to be George Joseph Cvek. He admitted his identity, but denied all knowledge of any crimes. When he was informed that his fingerprints matched those found on the water goblet in the Pappas apartment, he broke down and confessed to the Pappas murder. Mr. Pappas remembered that he had once picked up Cvek, who was hitchhiking into New York City.

Cvek refused to discuss the Jensen murder or any of his other crimes, although he agreed that he was the culprit in all these cases.

In May 1941, Cvek was tried and convicted of the murder of Mrs. Pappas. The following year he was executed in Sing Sing's electric chair.

# JOHN DIETZ

## OUTLAW COUNTRY

LITTLE disputes sometimes lead to big disputes and on occasion big disputes lead to bloody murder. That's what happened in the backwoods of Wisconsin at the turn of the century.

Our tale of woe began in 1904 when John Dietz left his watchman's job at Price Dam and, together with his wife, Hattie, purchased a section of land along the Thornapple River. One end of another dam, known as Cameron Dam, rested on Dietz's land. Both dams were owned by the Chippewa Lumber and Boom Co.

John left his job at Price Dam on the Brunnette River under bitter circumstances. He claimed he was still owed wages, while the company insisted that he had been paid in full. The matter became an obsession with John. He truly felt he had been cheated by the company and that there was very little he could do about it.

John and his two robust sons, Leslie and Clarence, built a substantial house and barn. He watched as millions of feet of logs roared down the river through Cameron Dam. In time, he got a bright idea. He posted a sign forbidding trespassers from setting foot on his land. This effectively shut down Cameron Dam, which meant that no head of water could be established to allow the flow of logs to the waiting sawmills downriver. In addition, John let it be known that the dam would remain inoperable until he was paid the sum of $8,000 for the 80 million feet of logs that he estimated had already gone downriver since he purchased his land. When John took this bold and, at the time, unheard-of move, there were six million feet of logs behind the dam.

The company obtained an injunction forbidding John from interfering with the transportation of their logs. John chose to ignore the injunction. As a result of this latest development, a warrant was issued for John's arrest. Two armed deputies were dispatched the 60 miles from the county seat at Hayward to John's backwoods home to make the arrest. Three company men joined the two deputies.

The horse-drawn wagon carrying the five men made its arduous way to John's enclave. As they approached Cameron Dam, they were greeted by John's not too friendly welcome, "Hands up, you sons of bitches!" he shouted. He then commenced to shoot. So did a friend and neighbour Valentine Weisenbach, who was hidden from view. One deputy fell off the wagon as the horses, startled by the gunfire, reared and galloped away. Just for fun, John and his friends took shots at the deputy as he ran for his life. The man had no way of knowing that John and Val had no intention of killing him. They were just having a little sport, backwoods style. In due course, Val Weisenbach was arrested and charged with attempted murder. He was found guilty and received a term in the penitentiary. No one dared bother big bad John Dietz.

Friends pleaded with John to give up his battle with the lumber company, as well as with the county and the state. They felt he couldn't win. John thought otherwise. His family, including his beautiful wife, Hattie, and two eldest sons, Leslie and Clarence, were totally loyal. So were his two daughters, Myra and Helen. For five years, this remarkable family didn't allow a trespasser on their property. All attempts to operate the dam failed.

From time to time, authorities attempted to arrest John, but each time they tried they were met with a barrage of bullets. On one occasion Clarence was wounded by a lawman's bullet. A deputy was also wounded in one of the mêlées.

In order to end the feud, the company paid John's claim for back wages. The amount was $1,717, a veritable fortune in those days. John refused to be pacified. He insisted they pay him that $8,000 before everything could be settled.

In isolated areas of Wisconsin, it was customary for teachers to live in their students' homes. The teacher would be paid by the parents, who would later collect their outlay from the local school board, which in this case was the Winter School Board located some 10 miles from the Dietz home. John, who believed strongly in education, hired a tutor for his children.

On September 6, 1910, John and son Clarence drove into Winter. He not only wanted the money he had paid the tutor, he also wanted reimbursement for rent and heat. The school board balked and a fist fight broke out. John pulled out a pistol and fired at a clerk of the school board, Bert Horel. Horel was wounded, but survived. For the umpteenth time, a warrant was issued for the arrest of John Dietz.

Sheriff Mike Madden, relatively new to the area, had heard all the stories of the Dietz family and had made it his mission to bring John to justice. The sheriff deputized two local men. They made their way to a point in the woods where they could keep the Dietz home under surveillance. When they observed members of the family hitching up a wagon, they correctly figured their quarry was preparing for a trip into town. The sheriff and his deputies placed themselves in an advantageous position to intercept the Dietz wagon.

Unknown to the the sheriff and his men, only Clarence, Leslie and Myra were in the wagon. Instead of meekly surrendering, they started shooting in typical Dietz fashion. Clarence took a bullet in his left arm. Myra suffered a flesh wound in the back. Leslie got away through the thick woods. The sheriff and his party drove the wounded Dietz offspring to the hospital in Winter, where both quickly recovered.

The story of young people being ambushed by lawmen in the backwoods of Wisconsin made the big-city newspapers. There was tremendous sympathy for the youngsters, who were depicted as babes in the woods rather than the stubbornly loyal offspring of the growing legend that was John Dietz. Major newspapers sent reporters to Wisconsin to cover the ongoing story of obstinate John and his family.

The governor of Wisconsin, J.O. Davidson, realizing that a bloodbath could take place in his state, decided to personally intervene. He sent an envoy to the Dietz home. Waving white handkerchiefs, the governor's party carried written documents from the governor, guaranteeing that all criminal charges against John and his brood, except for the wounding of Bert Horel, would be dropped. Once again, John said thanks but no thanks. He wanted the Horel charges dropped and full payment for all the logs that had gone through Cameron Dam. The governor couldn't acquiesce to John's requests. The official party told John that both sides were now at an impasse and that he would be well advised to have his family leave while the going was good. John's wife and children wouldn't hear of such a thing. They would stay to the bitter end. As the governor's party left the Dietz home, John raised the American flag and prepared to do battle.

That fall, an official posse of 60 armed men surrounded the Dietz property. The entire episode had captured the imagination of the public. Forty newspaper reporters were on hand, as were 1,000 hearty individuals from nearby towns. It didn't take long for the deputies to fire at anything that moved in John's house or barn. The Dietzes responded in kind.

One of the deputies, Oscar Harp, was shot in the head and died on the spot. The shooting continued all day. The house was a shambles, literally destroyed by gunfire. John was badly wounded in the left hand and bled profusely. Late in the afternoon Helen, barely a teenager, realized that her entire family would sooner or later be annihilated. She came out of the house waving a white flag. Helen wanted a doctor for her father, who she felt might bleed to death. She returned to the house accompanied by a doctor and a priest. At the urging of his wife, John was talked into surrendering. The battle was over. It has been estimated that over 2,000 shots were fired by the opposing sides. The entire family was taken to Winter, where John revealed that he had given in because Hattie was pregnant.

A year later, John stood trial for the murder of Oscar Harp. He defended himself and received commendations from lawyers and judges on the manner in which he conducted his defence. Despite his eloquence, he was found guilty and sentenced to life imprisonment. Ten years later he was pardoned by the governor of Wisconsin.

John Dietz died of natural causes in 1924 in a Milwaukee hospital. At his side when he breathed his last were his wife, Hattie, and his six children.

# DIANE DOWNEY AND LINDA PRUDDEN

## LESBIAN KILLERS

IT has been said that no one is aware of what goes on in the privacy of other people's homes. Certainly the outside world had no idea of the turbulent life being led by Robert and Diane Downey of Piscataway, New Jersey.

Robert was a mild-mannered, pleasant man who worked at two jobs to support Diane and their three young children, ages 7, 5 and 3. She was forever after Robert to spend more time at home with her and the children. This minor bone of contention was overshadowed by a car accident involving Diane which took place in March 1980. Diane recovered from her severe injuries, but was unable to take part in normal sexual activity from then on. Robert was understanding and supportive. He loved his wife and declared that he would allow no physical injury to come between them. Diane felt that now, more than ever, she required her husband's companionship. Robert tried to be home more often, but the pressure of his two jobs didn't allow him that much time away from his places of employment.

It was while convalescing from her injuries that Diane met Linda Prudden, a married woman in her thirties who was herself the mother of two boys. The women became close friends. They saw each other every day and, on many occasions, Diane and her children slept over at Linda's house.

In time, Diane and the kids were spending more time at the Pruddens' than at their own home. By November 1981, Diane was, to all intents and purposes, living full-time at Linda's. Robert was understandably miffed. He had been a good and faithful husband and father. Why was his Diane behaving this way? With Christmas just around the corner, he wanted his wife and children to return home. That's when Diane informed Robert of her little secret. She and Linda were lesbian lovers. Well, you could have knocked Robert over with a feather but, after giving the matter some thought, he accepted a situation he could do little about. He told Diane that he still loved her and pleaded with her at least to bring the children home for Christmas. Diane promised to do so.

Two days before Christmas, a neighbour was working in his garage when Diane Downey ran across the street and told him her husband had received a terrible beating. He was lying on the kitchen floor. The man summoned police, who rushed to the scene. They met Diane and Linda sitting in a car parked in the driveway of the Downey home.

The officers were surprised at the sight that greeted them inside the house. It looked as if someone had literally spattered blood over the entire floor and walls of the kitchen. The living room and kitchen were in total disarray, with furniture overturned and drawers pulled open. In the middle of the blood-spattered kitchen lay Robert Downey. He had obviously put up a terrific struggle for his life. Later, an autopsy would reveal 48 stab wounds all over his body.

The two women were questioned. Diane told detectives that she had last spoken to her husband the previous night. That morning, she, along with her three-year-old daughter and her friend Linda, was delivering Christmas presents to Robert. Upon entering the house, they discovered Robert's body. When asked where the three-year-old had been when they had gone inside with the presents, they both said they had left the youngster in the car. They couldn't give any reason why the little girl hadn't accompanied them into the house.

Detectives firmly believed they were investigating a murder that had taken place during the course of a robbery. They were gentle and respectful to Mrs. Downey, assuming she had just suffered a great loss.

One of the investigators noticed that Diane had several Band-Aids on her hands. He idly inquired how she had hurt herself. Diane replied that when she had first sighted her husband's body, she had clutched a glass off the kitchen counter. She had dropped the glass, breaking it on the counter. To steady herself, she had placed her hand on the counter and had cut herself.

The detective recalled having seen the broken glass, but the kitchen counter was at the far end of the room, away from the doorway. Surely Diane would have seen her husband on the floor long before making her way across the room to the counter. Now aware that there might be more to this murder than originally met the eye, the detective inquired where the Band-Aid packaging had been discarded. Diane told him that she had gone to the car to fetch and apply the bandages, but couldn't recall what she had done with the packaging.

The door of the Downey home was examined. It had been jimmied to appear as if an intruder had gained entrance. However, it was an amateurish job and had obviously been forced open from the inside.

Within the next 24 hours, a team of detectives learned that Diane had been seen the night before in her distinctive white station wagon in front of her home at around the time the murder had taken place. A thorough search of the Prudden home uncovered a hunting knife. Laboratory tests indicated that this knife matched wounds on Robert Downey's body and fit rips and tears in his clothing.

Both women were arrested and charged with Robert's murder. The details of their lesbian relationship came out at their trial. Each claimed that the other had wielded the hunting knife. They admitted to their deep love for each other and stated that Robert, who refused to give up his wife, had to be put out of the way. While he'd appeared to condone his wife's actions, he was forever pleading with her to return home. The lovers had decided to kill him and in the eyes of the law were equally responsible for his death.

Diane Downey and Linda Prudden were found guilty of the murder of Robert Downey. In 1983, both were sentenced to life imprisonment.

# LAURA FAIR

## SHE WASN'T LUCKY IN LOVE

YOU would have to say that Laura Fair was not lucky in love. At the tender age of 16, Laura married William Stone, a liquor salesman from New Orleans. A year later, he died of cholera.

Laura, a blond, blue-eyed Southern beauty, returned to school, but soon gave up her quest for a higher education in favour of marriage to one Thomas Grayson. Where Stone had been preoccupied with selling the demon rum, Grayson was intent on drinking Louisiana dry.

When sloshed, which was most of the time, Grayson had the distressing habit of joining Laura in bed with a pair of six-shooters, which he would fire at the most inopportune times. Laura fled to California, where she obtained a divorce.

Never one to let the grass grow under her feet, Laura strolled down the aisle for the third time in 1859. Lawyer William Fair stayed married to Laura for two years, during which time Laura gave birth to a bouncing baby girl, Lilliam. Unfortunately, William blew his brains out in a doctor's office in San Francisco, which had the effect of terminating not only his marriage, but his life, as well.

William left his wife and daughter with little in the way of worldly goods. Laura had one asset—a diamond ring given to her by her late husband during happier times.

In 1863, Laura took her daughter and moved to Virginia City, Nevada, to seek her fortune. She raised some cash on her ring and managed to rent a large rooming house called Tahoe House. The 50-room establishment was a success from the very beginning.

One day, lawyer Alexander Crittenden took a room at the Tahoe House. The lives of Laura and Alex would never be the same again. Alex was no ordinary legal beagle. He was a blue blood from Kentucky whose family was on a first-name basis with generals and senators.

Alex fell hard for Laura. The old rascal should have known better. There he was, well into his fifties, with a wife, Clara, and seven children. When he met Laura, he had already celebrated his silver wedding anniversary. But love does not always take age or circumstances into account. Laura and Alex met clandestinely for about a year before they grew careless, or simply didn't give a damn. It matters little. The results were the same.

Clara, who still lived in San Francisco, came to Virginia City to visit one of her daughters. She quickly learned of her husband's prolonged romantic entanglement. Stories of the love affair between the influential lawyer and the successful businesswoman had been making the rounds for a full year. The pressure was too much for even randy Alex. He and Laura took a trip to San Francisco, where he did the unthinkable. He arranged a dinner date with his wife and his mistress.

Laura found Clara a real charmer, if a little on the plump side. In fact, the two women got along famously, considering their respective relationships to the man sitting between them. Clara gingerly suggested that Laura drop out of their lives. Laura replied that she would never give up Alex. So much for the pleasant dinner party.

For the next few years the affair between Laura and Alex continued unabated. They often talked of Alex divorcing his wife, but the wily lawyer always hedged. Like many a middle-aged Casanova, he wasn't quite willing to leave the mother of his seven children. Of course, he didn't want to give up the thrills and spills of his lovemaking with Laura either. It took a long while, but eventually it got through to Laura that Alex would never leave his wife. She became extremely jealous of her rival.

There were scenes. On one occasion, Laura lost her cool and marched into the Crittenden home in the middle of the night, demanding to talk to her lover. Alex showed up at the top of the stairs and shouted down, "I am utterly disgusted with you." Laura left in a huff, but received some measure of satisfaction when, a few months later, Alex forced his way into her room with the same general demands. Things were heating up.

During this tense and turbulent period, Laura met and married Jesse Snyder. Jesse was well aware of the relationship between Laura and Alex. At the time, a rumour circulated that Laura had paid Jesse $10,000 to go through with the marriage. She may have felt that once married she would be more desirable to her true love, Alex. Her plan didn't work. Alex informed her that nothing much had changed. Instead of requiring one divorce, they now needed two. Clever as a fox, Alex told Laura to get her divorce first. Just as Jesse had agreed to marry Laura, he now quickly consented to divorce her. Some said that Alex paid him $10,000. If this was the case, Jesse was no fool. He'd managed to make $20,000 for a few months of not-unpleasant employment.

Laura pointed out to Alex that it was his turn to divorce. Instead, Alex said that his wife was taking one of her many trips to Virginia City and it would be in poor taste for him not to meet her. (Clara was in San Francisco.) Laura was livid. It finally dawned on her that her lover never intended to leave his wife.

Laura learned that Alex was to meet his wife aboard the ferry *El Capitain*, at the Oakland dock. Unknown to her lover, Laura planned to be aboard that ferry. On a cool fall day in November, Alex and Clara were united aboard the *El Capitain*. Laura found them on the crowded deck, sitting arm in arm. Their eldest son, Parker, stood nearby. Laura pulled out a chrome-plated pistol and fired at her lover. Alex slumped to the deck. Laura disappeared among the passengers on the crowded ferry. Parker and a harbour police officer searched the ferry and soon located the desperate woman. Parker turned to the police officer and said, "This is the woman who murdered my father." Parker was wrong. Laura wouldn't become a murderer until two days later, when Alex expired. Laura replied, "I do not deny it. He ruined me and my child."

On March 27, 1871, Laura Fair stood trial for murdering her lover. The proceedings lasted a month, with the outcome never in doubt. Laura had planned the murder down to the last detail. She had purchased the murder weapon and had followed Alex onto the ferry. She had even visited the boat the day before the murder to study the layout. To these accusations, Laura's counsel could only plead that she had purchased the pistol for protection and had been insane at the time of the shooting. To establish that Laura was madder than a March hare, her lawyers claimed that she had told them God had married her to Alex and that she was really his wife, not that interloper Clara. This line of defence didn't work. The jury took only 45 minutes to find her guilty.

All was not lost, however. In February 1872, the Supreme Court of California reversed Laura's conviction on two technicalities which had absolutely nothing to do with her innocence or guilt. In September of the same year, Laura stood trial for the second time. This time the jury retired for three days before returning the surprising verdict of not guilty.

Laura then embarked on a lecture tour and for a while was something of a celebrity. After all, it isn't every day that a woman kills her lover in front of his son and wife, admits it and then walks out of the courtroom a free woman. But Laura's prosperity was short-lived. Her lawyers sued her for large legal fees and collected.

In 1913, Laura's only daughter, Lilliam, was found dead in an empty room in New York City. She had starved to death. Laura Fair lived until 1919, when she too died in poverty in San Francisco. She rests today in that city's Woodlawn Cemetery.

# JOHN FIORENZA

## THREE GRAVE MISTAKES

KILLERS, for reasons known only to themselves, seem to have an affinity for bathtubs. Many infamous murderers down through the checkered history of crime have positioned their victims in tubs. Canada's Terrence Milligan killed his wife in her bath. England's George Smith placed so many of his wives in the tub that he will forever be known as Brides-in-the-Bath Smith.

On April 10, 1936, two upholsterers, Theodore Kruger and his assistant, John Fiorenza, attempted to deliver a love seat which had been re-covered to the apartment of Mr. and Mrs. Lewis Titterton at 22 Beekman Place in New York City. The two men arrived at 4:30 p.m. to find the door to the Titterton apartment ajar. Receiving no response to their knocking, they walked in. They found Mrs. Titterton quite dead in the bathroom, lying in a half-filled tub of water. She was wearing only a pink pyjama top, which was fastened around her neck and had been used to strangle her.

Detectives were soon on the scene. From the condition of the interior of the apartment, they ascertained that Mrs. Titterton had been raped and murdered in her bedroom, after which the killer had placed her body in the bathtub. They ruled out robbery as a motive since there was no sign of a search and nothing had been taken from the apartment.

Mrs. Titterton's wrists bore signs that they had been bound with cord, which was verified when police found a 13-inch piece of five-ply cord under her body. The killer had obviously cut away a much longer cord and removed it, inadvertently leaving behind the smaller piece of cord found in the tub. The cord was examined closely. It appeared to be of a type used in Venetian blinds. The Titterton apartment had Venetian blinds, but none had been cut away. Apparently the killer had brought the cord with him, which led detectives to believe that the rape had been premeditated. The bed upon which the rape had taken place was dismantled and carted away for laboratory analysis.

It was established that the murder had occurred between 10:30 and 11:30 a.m. on the day the body was discovered. Mrs. Titterton had talked to a friend on the phone at 10:30 a.m. At eleven-thirty, a boy delivering dry cleaning had received no answer when he knocked on the door. He had heard the phone ringing inside the apartment, and when no one responded, he figured there was no one at home and left.

Mrs. Titterton was an attractive, 33-year-old woman, who was happily married to an executive of the National Broadcasting Company. Lewis Titterton initially came under some suspicion. Although he had been at work in the NBC building all day, he had left the building on several occasions, which would have enabled him to travel to his apartment, kill his wife and return to work. When questioned, he pointed out that husbands usually don't rape their wives before murdering them. His interrogators tended to agree with him.

During the one-hour interval when the murder had taken place, W. A. DeWitt, a writer, was in his study overlooking the roof of the Tittertons' building. He watched as a fat man in blue overalls walked slowly across the roof of 22 Beekman Place. The mystery man turned out to be Dudley Mings, the janitor of the building. Mings explained that he had gone to the roof to repair a door. The door had been repaired, but it was impossible to verify when Mings had performed the job. He, like Lewis Titterton, remained a possible suspect.

Meanwhile, the boys down at the lab had tested the bedspread taken from Mrs. Titterton's bed. They came up with a length of gray horsehair and a dab of orange paint. Hot to trot, they went about extracting samples of horsehair from the padding of every suspect's clothing. The single strand of hair didn't match samples taken from the clothing of Lewis Titterton, Dudley Mings, the boy who claimed he had attempted to deliver dry cleaning on the day of the murder, or other tradespeople who had called at the building.

The orange paint matched paint recently applied to the Tittertons' fire escape. The painters turned out to be real characters. They admitted that one of the perks of their chosen profession was the opportunity to gaze at assorted women in various stages of undress. Several stated that Mrs. Titterton often strolled around her apartment scantily clad. They had looked, but swore they had never touched. The painters were eliminated as suspects when detectives learned that the bedspread had been placed on the fire escape to be aired.

In desperation, police sent samples of the cord found under the body to cord manufacturers and samples of the horsehair to companies using horsehair in the manufacture of their products. They struck pay dirt. The cord that police thought was Venetian-blind cord turned out to be the kind used in the upholstery business to bind padding. They also learned that horsehair was used in the upholstery trade.

A light went on. Weren't those guys who found the body in the first place delivering a recently upholstered love seat to the Titterton apartment?

Theodore Kruger, the owner of the upholstery shop, had a clean record, but such was not the case for his assistant, John Fiorenza. John had served time for stealing automobiles and was currently on parole. Kruger, who knew of his employee's criminal status, recalled that on the day of the murder John had phoned in advising him that he had to report to his parole officer that morning. He had arrived for work at the upholstery shop around 12 noon.

John was taken into custody, although police knew they scarcely had enough evidence to gain a conviction. They were counting on a confession and they got it. Cunning rascals that they were, the New York cops obtained a sample of John's semen. They told him they were comparing it to semen found on Mrs. Titterton's bedspread. John had no way of knowing that no identifiable semen had been found. When detectives informed him they had a match, John panicked and told all.

Some months earlier, John had called on Mrs. Titterton to perform some repair work on her furniture. She had been scantily clad and the thought of having her preyed on John's mind. It got so that she was all he could think about.

On the night before the murder, John thought up the excuse to tell his boss. He made his way to Mrs. Titterton's apartment, knowing full well that her husband would be at work. He had no trouble gaining entry as Mrs. Titterton recognized and trusted him. He tied her up with cord he had taken from the upholstery shop, then raped and killed the defenceless woman before placing her in the bathtub in a crude attempt to simulate suicide.

John made three grave mistakes: he dropped that incriminating piece of cord; forgot to remove the pyjama top from around his victim's neck; and shed a piece of horsehair from his clothing onto Mrs. Titterton's bed.

John Fiorenza pleaded guilty to murder and was sentenced to life imprisonment.

# LAWRENCE FOYE

## HOTEL HORROR

LENORE Gilbey had once been married to Anthony Gilbey, heir to the Gilbey gin fortune. In those days, she had travelled the world, attending the premier social events of the various countries she visited. In the early 1980s, the middle-aged mother of three devoted her time to charitable causes, both in Europe and the United States.

Through no fault of her own, Lenore was to cross paths with Lawrence Foye. While Lenore was at home in the fine salons of Europe, Lawrence hailed from that section of the Bronx known as Fort Apache, one of the toughest areas in the entire U.S.

On August 5, 1983, Lenore was registered at the Gorham Hotel in New York City. The Gorham is a small, well-appointed establishment located close to the downtown Manhattan action. On this particular night Lenore was alone in her suite on the sixteenth floor, unaware of the various events going on in the hotel which would affect her life.

Nothing was heard from Suite 1603 until the next day when, a little after 4 p.m., a maid discovered Lenore Gilbey's body. She had apparently been suffocated with a pillow. Her bedroom was in total disarray. Lenore's clothing and personal effects were strewn around the room, but it was impossible to tell what, if anything, was missing. The suite yielded Lenore's fingerprints, but no others, which indicated a clever or extremely fortunate killer.

Detectives examining the suite were attracted to the balcony. They noted that drapes from the penthouse suite above hung down the side of the building to within several feet of the balcony. It was conceivable that the killer had gained entrance to Lenore's suite via the balcony. He would have had to have been an agile and daring man to have climbed down the outside of the building holding on to drapes which could give way at any time.

Investigators questioned hotel staff for any strange or unusual events which may have taken place in the hotel on August 5 or 6. A desk clerk told them that two female guests reported that they had been frightened out of their wits when they had walked smack-dab into a nude black man in the hall outside their rooms. The man had said nothing and had hastily walked away. The women had checked out of the hotel but were easily located. They felt that they could identify the man if they saw him again. Police learned that one of the two women had told a porter that she had seen a man in drag leaving the hotel sometime on the morning of August 6. She described the man as black and wearing a pair of women's blue shorts, a red blouse and slippers. To top off his strange appearance, the weird-looking individual was wearing a shower cap. The woman felt that this man and the nude man she had encountered in the hall were one and the same.

Detectives canvassed all the occupants of the hotel. One man who claimed that he possibly had useful knowledge agreed to tell all in exchange for anonymity. On the afternoon of August 5, this guest—a businessman—met a black man, Lawrence Smith, in a downtown bar. The two men drank all day and ended up in his suite. At one point he and Smith had an argument, which culminated with him throwing Smith out of the suite into the hall. There was one thing—Smith had been stark naked. Convinced that Smith must be the man who had startled the two women in the hall, detectives felt that he was also the man who had so conspicuously left the hotel in drag the following day. Could he be Lenore Gilbey's killer?

The embarrassed businessman turned over everything Smith had left in his suite. This consisted of a sweatsuit, a book, a pair of football tickets and some photographs, but no identification. The businessman stated that Smith had told him that he worked in a downtown print shop not far from the hotel. The two women involved identified the photographs as the man they had seen in the hall.

The hunt was on for Lawrence Smith, although investigators were certain that their suspect had used a false name. The crime was reconstructed. Smith had accepted an invitation to take part in a homosexual encounter with the visiting businessman. They had argued. Smith had been thrown out of the ninth-floor suite into the hall, stark naked, where he had encountered the two women. He had hastily made his way to the stairway exit and had walked up to the roof, looking for a way out of his dilemma. Finally, at the front of the hotel, he had seen the exposed drapes leading partway down to the sixteenth floor and Lenore's balcony. He had climbed down the drapes and had jumped the remaining distance to the balcony, never knowing or caring who occupied the suite.

Smith's initial intent was to obtain clothing and any money he happened to come across. Suddenly he was face-to-face with Lenore Gilbey. How horrified this woman must have been. Here she was, 16 storeys up, yet there lurking in front of her as if he had flown in the window, was a desperate nude man. Smith's idea of obtaining clothing took a back seat to the sexual assault which followed. Then, in order to conceal his crime, he placed a pillow over Lenore's face until she died of suffocation. There is some evidence that he slept with the body. Next morning, Smith found some clothing he could get into and left the apartment. It was then that he was seen leaving the hotel.

Police canvassed print shops located near the hotel, asking employees if they recognized Smith's photograph. It wasn't long before they located their man. His real name was Lawrence Foye, a bad actor who was convinced that he had gotten away with murder. At first he denied having had anything to do with the killing, but when faced with his own photographs, he admitted to the homosexual liaison with the businessman. After he was told that he had been identified as the man who had been seen wearing Lenore Gilbey's clothing on the day after the murder, he confessed.

It had all happened just as the police had theorized. He hadn't entered Lenore's suite with the intention of assaulting and killing her, but simply to get something to wear. Things had gotten out of hand. In addition to the items the police already knew were taken from the murder scene, Foye confessed to having taken a cosmetics case which he had later thrown away. This case was located in an alley described by Foye.

The accused man was tried for the murder of Lenore Gilbey. His attorneys came up with a rather unusual defence. They claimed that their client had been subjected to a homosexual attack which had caused him to run out of the businessman's room. A psychiatrist testified that the attack, coupled with the alcohol Foye had consumed, had rendered him temporarily emotionally disturbed and not responsible for his actions.

The New York jury didn't buy Foye's story. He was found guilty of felony murder, robbery and burglary. The presiding judge, Sybil Hart Kooper, described his crime as one of the most vicious cases ever placed before her. She sentenced Lawrence Foye to 25 years to life with no possibility of parole.

# AUGUST FRANSSEN

## DETECTIVE'S AD STRUCK PAY DIRT

---

BEFORE the turn of the century it was not unusual for small towns to enlist the assistance of private-detective agencies to solve major crimes. Let's face it, local sheriffs often did little more than shove the town drunk into the hoosegow every Saturday night. They were ill equipped to deal with murder most foul.

It was only natural for the good folks of the tiny village of Edgeville, just outside New York City, to elicit the aid of the famed Pinkerton Detective Agency when one fine morning they woke up to find an almost nude male body in their midst.

The local coroner carted away the body and soon related his findings. The victim was a stranger to the village. He had been struck a vicious blow to the back of the head with a barrel stave, which had been found beside the body. The single blow had killed the man, but the killer had made sure that he was dead by stabbing him with a penknife just below the heart. The body had been stripped of all clothing with the exception of socks, a shirt and underwear.

Nothing like this had ever happened in Edgeville before. The townsfolk were incensed. They called on the Pinkertons to solve the case and bring the culprit to justice.

Detective George Bangs took over the investigation. He viewed the body and, in the style of that other great private eye, Sherlock Holmes, came to several conclusions. Facial features indicated to Bangs that the victim was of Teutonic extraction. His fingers were long and uncalloused, with well-trimmed nails. Bangs guessed that the man may have been an artist. His socks were knit from very fine wool often favoured by German manufacturers. The man's shirt had tiny holes in the chest area. Bangs surmised that a monogram had been ripped from the shirt in order to conceal the victim's identity. When Bangs connected the little holes, he came up with the letters A.B.

The clever detective knew he was in on a tough one. He decided to try a long shot by inserting the following advertisement in the *New York World:* "Information wanted about German artist, aged about twenty-eight, initials

A.B., who came to this country within the past few months and who has for more than a week been missing from usual haunts."

The ad struck pay dirt. Bangs was contacted by Jacob Kuenzle, who claimed that he not only knew the man described in the ad, but roomed with him in the German district of New York. Bangs called on Kuenzle immediately. In the room the two men shared, he found several shirts monogrammed with the initials A.B Jacob told Bangs that his roommate's name was Adolph Bohner. In return, Bangs informed Jacob that his buddy was most probably a murder victim.

Adolph Bohner turned out to be an artist just as Bangs had suspected. His work wasn't being well received and he was always short of funds. He had left his fiancée, Rosa, back in Strasbourg. It was she who had embroidered his initials on his shirts.

Bangs contacted the Pinkerton Agency in Germany and told them to check out the Bohner family, as well as Adolph's fiancée, Rosa. He soon had a report back that Adolph came from a well-respected family. Rosa was playing the field in her fiancé's absence. In particular, she was seeing one August Franssen, the son of a shoemaker. Shortly after Adolph left for New York, August was suspected of stealing money from his father and had disappeared.

Bangs procured a photograph of Franssen and showed it to Jacob. A few male friends had visited Adolph in their room, but Jacob was uncertain whether Franssen was one of them or not. The only outstanding thing Jacob could remember about one of the visitors was a distinctive leathery smell about his person. Bangs knew that Franssen had followed his father's profession of shoemaker in Europe and was now certain that his man was in New York working in the shoe trade. His theory received a setback when Rosa was questioned further and revealed that Franssen was in Alsace and visited her often.

The Pinkertons descended like bloodhounds in and around Edgeville seeking out shoemakers or anyone who worked in leather. They located a shoemaker named Heinkel who had hired an Arthur Frances, whose description fit that of August Franssen. The man no longer worked for Heinkel.

Bangs was in a quandary. He was firmly convinced that Arthur Frances was August Franssen, but his theory didn't hold water if Rosa was to be believed. An agent was sent to question Rosa for the third time. She now admitted that she had lied earlier. In fact, she felt certain that Franssen had skipped to the United States.

Although the Pinkertons had identified a major suspect, they still had not located him. It was decided to place one of their agents, German-speaking

Wilhelm Mendelsohn, in the German area of New York City. The Pinkertons believed that this would be the most logical location for the fugitive to settle.

Mendelsohn canvassed shoe manufacturers, ostensibly looking for employment. He didn't locate Franssen, but he did find a factory where his quarry had previously been employed. A co-worker of Franssen's gave the detective the name of a bar where Franssen often spent his evenings. Mendelsohn became a regular at that bar. Sure enough, one fine evening, Franssen strolled through the swinging doors.

Detective Bangs knew they had their man, but realized he didn't have enough evidence to gain a conviction. He was positive that Franssen had been in love with Rosa and had followed Bohner to New York to kill him and eliminate him as a rival for Rosa's affection.

The Pinkertons decided to play out the string. Influence was used to secure a position for Mendelsohn in the shoe factory where Franssen was employed. The two men became bosom buddies. In the following weeks, Franssen received small loans from Mendelsohn. The two men met every day at the saloon.

Gradually, Franssen confided in the detective. He was an artist who hated his job in the shoe factory. He simply had to get away from New York, but didn't have the money to move to California. Maybe his friend Mendelsohn could help him out. He really didn't want a loan. He would sell some of his belongings. He had a suit in hock which he would sell to Mendelsohn really cheap. Mendelsohn said he would purchase the suit if it fit him. Franssen handed over the pawnshop ticket.

Accompanied by Detective Bangs, Mendelsohn retrieved the suit and showed it to Jacob Kuenzle, who positively identified it as belonging to his former roommate, Adolph Bohner.

That did it. Franssen was picked up and charged with murder. All the evidence against him was circumstantial, but it was extremely strong evidence. Franssen was found guilty and sentenced to death. His lawyers won him a second trial on a technicality and this time succeeded in securing a guilty verdict with a recommendation for mercy.

August Franssen had come within an ace of getting away with murder. Only dogged detective work by an independent agency proved his undoing. He was sentenced to life imprisonment.

# RICHARD FREDERICKS

## BODY DOUBLE

IT'S rather distressing to all concerned when a supposed murder victim walks into a police station. It doesn't happen every day.

A Mexican rancher discovered the body one day in 1953 as he walked through one of his fields. It wasn't a pleasant sight. The woman had been beaten about the head so severely that her features were beyond recognition. Most horrific of all was the absence of the victim's hands.

Mexican police were soon at the crime scene. A cursory examination of the clothing worn by the dead woman indicated that she was American. Because the body was found near Ensenada, about 50 miles south of the California-Mexican border, the Los Angeles police were notified. An American detective was dispatched to assist in the investigation.

There was precious little to help the officers identify the dead woman. She had been dead for weeks and the body had been ravished by the elements. Obviously her killer had cut off her hands and had picked the isolated area to dump the body in order to make identification difficult, if not impossible.

A description of the murder victim was widely distributed in California and Mexico. She was five feet six inches tall and weighed 115 pounds. She had a mole on the right side of her neck. When found, she was wearing a red blouse and jeans.

The publicity soon brought practical results. A distraught woman drove down from San Diego, deeply concerned that the murdered woman could be her daughter. She viewed the body and burst into tears. "It is Olga," was all she could say between sobs. After giving the woman time to compose herself, detectives asked her how she could be sure, considering the condition of the victim's face. They were assured by the victim's mother that Olga had worn an identical red blouse and jeans. The mole on the corpse's neck was further proof, the woman told them.

During this discussion, a police doctor informed the woman that the victim had three gold teeth and indicated their position in her mouth. Sadly, the woman nodded. Now she was absolutely positive. Her Olga had three gold teeth in exactly the same positions.

Next day, the same newspapers that had solicited information to help identify the handless body in the field revealed that the victim's name was Mrs. Olga Carrino, a San Diego mother of two young sons, aged five years and nine months.

Four days passed before an attractive young woman walked into a San Diego police station. She told the officer in charge, "I am Olga Carrino and I am not dead. What's more, I have my two hands." With that declaration the woman pushed her hands forward to make sure the startled officer saw what she was talking about.

Olga had quite a story to tell. Her husband, Fernando, was employed on a tuna clipper fishing in the Pacific. Because he would be away for some time, she and her two young sons had moved in with her in-laws. The arrangement hadn't worked out. They had fought and she had stormed out of the house and had gone to live with a girlfriend.

Olga had heard of her "death" only about an hour before walking into the police station. Her girlfriend had shown her details of her demise in a four-day-old newspaper. Olga had immediately informed her family that she was alive and well and then had gone directly to the police station. Yes, she wore an identical red blouse and jeans as the dead woman. Yes, she had a mole in exactly the same location on her neck as the murder victim. Most amazing of all, Olga had three gold teeth in the same places as the handless body. She opened her mouth and showed the detectives her teeth. There was no question about it: whoever had been murdered and dropped into that Mexican field was not Olga Carrino.

Detective Charles F. Stewart of the Los Angeles Police Department was studying missing persons reports in a routine manner when information on one of the documents rang a bell. He had recently read the facts and figures about a woman's body found in Mexico that were startlingly similar to the missing persons report he was scanning.

The missing woman was Ruth Fredericks. She had been reported missing by two friends who hadn't seen her for more than a month. The women had made a date with Ruth to go to the movies. The three had made arrangements to obtain a babysitter for their children. Ruth simply hadn't shown up.

The two friends had inquired as to her whereabouts from her husband, Richard. He didn't volunteer any information and seemed extremely cavalier about the whole thing, which is why they took it upon themselves to report her missing. They felt that Ruth would never voluntarily leave her three children. Ruth was five feet six inches tall, weighed 115 pounds, had a mole on her neck and often wore a red blouse and jeans. She also had three gold teeth.

Stewart believed the handless body found in Mexico was Ruth Fredericks. He interviewed the two women who had reported Ruth missing and got an earful. They had known Ruth for two years. During that time, her husband, Richard, was a holy terror. He continually screamed at his wife. Often Ruth would show up with a black eye or a bruised arm. When Ruth disappeared, they figured she must be dead, because there was no way she would leave her five-year-old son and the two younger children.

They informed Detective Stewart that the five-year-old had stopped attending school. Upon learning this, one of the women had gone to the Fredericks' home and found it vacant. She checked with the Fredericks' immediate neighbour and was told that Richard had sold his car, packed his belongings and had flown to New Jersey with the three children. Richard had worked in New Jersey before moving to California.

Detective Stewart called on the insurance company where Richard had been employed. He learned that his man had been transferred from New Jersey and for a while had been a friendly valued employee. In the past year, he had undergone a remarkable change in personality. He consistently harped about his wife being unfaithful, although, as far as anyone at the insurance company knew, Ruth Fredericks was a faithful wife and loving mother.

When an employee found a gun in Richard's locker, he had informed Ruth of his discovery. Ruth had told her husband's colleague that Richard's behaviour was so bad she was considering having him confined.

Evidently, Ruth was able to talk Richard into entering a psychiatric hospital for observation. He stayed only a week before signing himself out. After his short spell in hospital he became moodier than ever and hardly communicated with fellow employees at the insurance company. Finally, Richard confided to a co-worker that his wife was a tramp and had run away with a sailor. He said he wasn't sorry and that he was better off without her.

After tracing Richard to Maplewood, New Jersey, Detective Stewart flew there for a face-to-face confrontation with his suspect. Stewart knocked on the front door of the man who he believed had brutally killed his wife and chopped off her hands. He introduced himself and was graciously invited into the house by Richard. Stewart gingerly inquired, "Your wife's name is Ruth, isn't it?"

Homicide investigators claim to have heard it all, but it is doubtful if Detective Stewart was prepared for Richard's reply. "Her name's Ruth and I killed her."

Richard went on to explain that on the previous January 6, he and Ruth were in the backyard of their Van Nuys residence. He had accused her of being unfaithful. She became furious, screaming that he was wrong and that he must be crazy. When he retreated to the garage, she followed. He saw red, picked up a mallet and struck her on the head. He couldn't stop swinging until his wife's face was nothing more than a mass of flesh. He carried her body to his workbench, where he chopped off her hands with a hatchet. He then buried the hands in the backyard and placed Ruth's body in the trunk of his car. In an effort to dispose of the body, he drove to Mexico, crossing the international border at Tijuana. No one searched the interior of his vehicle or asked him to open his trunk. Relieved, he drove to Ensenada and dumped his wife's body in an isolated field.

Richard told Stewart that he thought he was home free when he read that the dead woman had been identified as Olga Carrino. When he learned that the error had been discovered, he panicked and fled to New Jersey.

Stewart had Los Angeles detectives dig in Richard's backyard. Sure enough, right where Richard said he had buried them, they discovered the hands of Ruth Fredericks.

Richard Fredericks waived extradition and was returned to California to stand trial. He was found guilty of murder in the second degree and received the strangely lenient sentence of one to 10 years' imprisonment.

# PAT AND WILLIAM GIL

## KILLER WITH A PENCHANT FOR TRAVEL

CERTAIN murderers firmly believe that their victims' bodies should be transported great distances in order to avoid detection. Who can forget Winnie Ruth Judd who shipped one of her victims halfway across the United States? Considerate Winnie accompanied the body on the train. Canadians tend to send unwanted bodies to Newfoundland, for reasons known only to themselves.

In this story, the killer with a penchant for travel is Patricia Gil, a fine cut of a woman, who stood a lofty five foot two inches tall and weighed in at a pudgy 220 pounds. Pat lived with Jose Ramos for nine years. The pair had two children before calling it quits. Shortly after the breakup, Pat married William Gil and moved into a home on Chicago's West 47th Street. The house had once been Saint Christopher's Rectory.

A year later, Jose learned of the marriage and was furious. After all, the substantial Pat was the mother of his two children. It didn't matter to Jose one little bit that for six of the nine years he had lived with Pat, he himself had been legally married to a woman named Juanita.

On the evening of May 25, 1980, William Gil and 17-year-old Danny Anderson, a boyfriend of Pat's younger sister, were listening to the car radio in the Gils' backyard, while Pat, inside the house, was on the phone with a furious Jose. Jose told her he was coming over to give her a piece of his mind. She said, "No way, Jose," but Jose wasn't deterred. Scared sick of her former lover, she went out to the backyard and asked William for moral support and the use of his .38-calibre pistol. William fetched his weapon from the glove compartment of his vehicle and passed it over to his wife.

Jose arrived and told Pat in no uncertain terms that he thought it downright inconsiderate of her to have married William behind his back. To illustrate his displeasure, he'd brought along a baseball bat, which he swung with reckless abandon against a door. Certain that her head was about to be Jose's next target, Pat pulled the trigger of the .38, propelling a bullet directly through Jose's neck. This latter move by Pat definitely discouraged Jose from inflicting further abuse. He slumped to the floor, deader than a mackerel.

William and Danny ran into the house. Danny's first reaction was to call police, but William made him put down the phone. He counselled his distraught wife. Well, "counselling" may be too strong a word. Actually, he said, "Get the hell out of here." Pat gathered up her children and took them to her mother's. When she returned to the former rectory, she found that Jose's blood no longer soiled the kitchen floor. What's more, his body was nowhere to be seen.

While gazing at the sanitary condition of her kitchen, Pat was interrupted in her reverie by police officers who were responding to a neighbour's complaint that they had heard a shot. Pat swore that there had been no gunfire. Someone was obviously mistaken or playing a prank on the police. Satisfied that that was the case, the police left the Gil residence.

William confided his little secret to Pat. He had deposited Jose in the trunk of the dead man's own car, a 1973 Chevrolet. It remained there for four days. On May 29, William, with Jose in the trunk, headed south. Pat and Danny Anderson followed in Pat's car. They drove and drove until Jose's old heap broke down in Ashland, Kentucky. The conspirators hired a tow truck and had the vehicle hauled into the West Virginia hills. Once there, they temporarily abandoned the Chevy and spent a few hours visiting Pat's uncle and aunt, Lucy and Herbert Dancy, in Coal City. After leaving her relatives, Pat and the two men purchased a large can of gasoline. They returned to the abandoned Chevy and doused it with gas. A match did the rest. The West Virginia sky lit up like a home run at SkyDome. Pat, William and Danny jumped into Pat's brown Plymouth and headed back to the friendly confines of Chicago.

On June 10, the odour emanating from the abandoned car came to the attention of the police. They pried open the trunk. Voilà, there was what was left of Jose.

The state medical examiner prepared a dental chart of the man in the trunk. He was able to tell authorities that the hands of the victim had been bound with a leather belt. The man had been dead for two to three weeks. Although the body was badly decomposed, the victim had kept one hand firmly closed, enabling authorities to obtain fingerprints.

Meanwhile, the Chevy was undergoing forensic examination. The car's licence plates had been removed, but police were able to obtain the vehicle's serial number. The ownership was traced to one Jose Ramos of Chicago.

Chicago detectives were contacted. They quickly located Juanita Ramos, who informed them that her husband had left home on May 25 and hadn't been seen or heard from since. She added that Jose drove a 1973 Chevy and gave the investigators the name of her husband's dentist. The dental chart from West Virginia was forwarded to Jose's dentist, who positively identified the victim as his patient, Jose Ramos.

Now that the body in the trunk had been identified, police were left with the taxing problem of who in the world would take the trouble to transport a dead man into the hills of West Virginia. Juanita could give no logical explanation as to why her husband's body had been carted over 500 miles from their home in Chicago. Several individuals had seen the wreck being towed to the spot where it was found. No one thought it that unusual. Evidently, cars are often abandoned in the hills of West Virginia.

Detectives interviewed Jose's friends and relatives. They learned about his relationship with Pat Gil. Pat was contacted and admitted that she had lived with Jose, but swore up and down that she had had nothing do to with his murder. During their investigation, detectives learned of Pat's relatives in West Virginia, Lucy and Herbert Dancy. They lived in Coal City, only a couple of miles from the abandoned Chevy. The Dancys were located and, without hesitation, told police about Pat's sudden visit. Herbert remembered the day—May 29. In fact, Herbert remembered quite a bit. He told detectives he had received a phone call from his niece, Pat, advising him that her car had broken down in Pemberton and that they were travelling in two vehicles.

Herbert had driven to meet her, after she had made her way to Coal City in a Plymouth. Pat was accompanied by two men, her husband, William, and her sister's boyfriend, Danny Anderson. All three followed him back to his place in the Plymouth. They had a short but pleasant visit. Pat said they had to leave to attend to the broken-down vehicle. That's the last Herbert saw of the Chicago branch of the family.

In due course, the tow-truck operator was located. He well remembered towing the car into the hills. How could he forget? That car gave off the most peculiar odour.

As they say in the murder business, enough is enough. Chicago detectives paid one last visit to Pat. She sensed the jig was up. Pat told the officers about the funereal trip to West Virginia. She maintained that Jose would have killed her with the baseball bat had she not plugged him in the neck.

In November 1982, Pat and William Gil were convicted of voluntary manslaughter. Both were sentenced to 18 years' imprisonment. Danny Anderson received a suspended sentence.

Ironically, when the state of Illinois overhauled its crowded prisons in 1987, two of the prisoners who received early releases were Pat and William Gil. Both were released after serving less than five years behind bars.

# ED GRAMMER

## A BURR UNDER HIS SADDLE

ED Grammer was office manager of the Climax Molybdenum Co. in New York City. He had a good job, a loving wife, Dorothy, three children and a nice home in the Bronx. There was one burr under Ed's saddle and that was his penchant for playing the field. I'm not talking horses here.

Her name was Mathilda Mizibrocky, a winsome lass who worked for the United Nations. She met Ed at a bowling alley and soon found herself engaged in a more horizontal activity, which many categorize as not only pleasant, but athletic as well. Mathilda had no idea that her Ed was already married. She often mentioned that he should make an honest woman of her. Ed came up with excuse after excuse, but finally hung his hat on their different faiths. He was Protestant; she was Roman Catholic. But who knows, if they stayed in bed long enough, the rules might change.

When Ed's father-in-law died, Dorothy dashed off to Baltimore to care for her mother. Ed was delighted. Dutiful husband that he was, he wrote Dorothy to stay as long as she liked. She stayed several months. Ed took the opportunity to spend a pleasant two weeks with Mathilda in Chicago during his wife's absence. Ed was so obsessed with Mathilda that he neglected to write to his wife in Baltimore.

Dorothy was concerned. She phoned Ed's office and spoke to Jean Bilelo, his girl Friday. Like all good secretaries, Jean was cool. She wired her boss to get in touch with his wife. Ed phoned Dorothy and assured her that his letters must have gone astray. Despite his protestations, the seed of suspicion had been planted in Dorothy's mind.

Meanwhile, Mathilda continued to apply marriage pressure. Ed continued to hide behind their religious differences, but was having an increasingly hard time keeping Mathilda at bay. Then there was Dorothy with her snide insinuations. She was even threatening to leave her still-grieving, ill mother and return to hubby's ever-loving arms. It was enough to make any self-respecting adulterer cringe.

Ed took a trip to Baltimore to placate Dorothy. He may also have taken the trip to murder her. The results were exactly the same for Dorothy. She ended up dead.

On August 19, 1952, Ed spent the day with Dorothy. That evening they stopped for drinks on the way to the train station, where Ed would catch the train to New York. He later claimed that he had had five or six slugs of Scotch and water. Dorothy had nursed one.

It was after midnight when two policemen, Officer Paul Hardesty and Sergeant John Eurite, stood in amazement as a blue driverless Chrysler sped down the street, caromed off a telephone pole and drove out of control up an incline, finally coming to a standstill as it rolled on its side. The two men were no more than 10 metres from the vehicle when it came to a full stop. Inside was the body of Dorothy Grammer.

The officers noted that the car's engine was still running. They extracted a pebble from under the front of the accelerator pedal, which had kept the accelerator pressed down and had enabled the car to run without the aid of a foot on the pedal.

Dorothy had been bludgeoned about the head. The officers didn't have to be Einsteins to come to the conclusion that she couldn't have sustained her injuries in the car crash. The vehicle's interior wasn't damaged in any way. The dead woman's purse and eyeglasses were missing. It appeared that the person who stuck the pebble under the accelerator pedal believed that the vehicle would plunge over an embankment on the other side of the street, burst into fire and obliterate the evidence of murder.

Next day, Dorothy was identified and her husband was advised of the tragedy. He returned immediately to Baltimore. As soon as it was learned that Ed had been with Dorothy about an hour before the murder, he was taken into custody and questioned.

After several hours of questioning, Ed confessed, but gave no reason for killing his wife. He told officers that he had been high on the Scotch he had consumed and had stopped the car on the way to the station. He had stepped out of the vehicle, picked up a small pipe conveniently lying at his feet and had beaten his wife to death. Ed claimed he couldn't remember anything after that. He stated that he didn't even know if he had started up the car of if he had put the pebble under the accelerator. He had staggered down the road and caught the train to New York. Ed signed his confession and that should have been that, but it wasn't.

Ed had remembered to take the train and remembered to take from the murder vehicle documents pertaining to his work and turn them in to his office upon his arrival in New York. He remembered to have his suit dry-cleaned the first thing next morning. In fact, Ed had a selective memory. He remembered to leave Mathilda out of his confession, thereby denying authorities an obvious motive.

When Ed retained the services of a competent lawyer, things changed appreciably. He maintained that he had not killed his wife. He said he would have confessed to anything in order to get some sleep.

Ed pleaded not guilty. Other than the revealing confession he'd given earlier, the prosecution had precious little concrete proof to connect Ed directly to his wife's death. The murder weapon was never found and no one had seen Ed commit the foul deed. The prosecution traced Mathilda, who told of her undying love for Ed and his reluctance to marry her because of their religious differences. Of course, Mathilda now knew that Ed, the snake in the grass, had been married all the time.

Defence attorneys pointed out that if Ed had actually taken his wife's life, he had done it on the spur of the moment. After all, he could have obtained a divorce in order to marry Mathilda. Then there was Mathilda's statement that she had asked Ed to marry her; he had never proposed to her. Had he divorced his wife, she would have married him in spite of the fact that her religion forbade her to marry a divorced man.

Did Ed have a real motive to plan the death of his wife? Did that pebble lodge under the accelerator by accident, as Ed claimed? Did he kill Dorothy during a domestic dispute while under the influence of alcohol as he had originally claimed in his confession? Conviction of premeditated murder meant a mandatory death sentence. Murder in the second degree was punishable by life imprisonment.

Ed had elected to be tried by a judge only. His decision predicated whether Ed would live or die. The presiding judge found him guilty of first-degree murder. The Court of Appeals unanimously rejected Ed's appeal in the fall of 1953. On June 11, 1954, Ed Grammer was hanged for the murder of his wife, Dorothy.

# CHARLIE AND LIONETTI HAYNES

## A TALE OF HORROR

THE nature of the crime that follows might not be for those with weak stomachs. They should consider reading these pages well after breakfast. Forewarned is forearmed.

On February 24, 1978, two derelicts were searching for anything of value in a dumpster in Eugene, Oregon. They opened a garbage bag and found more than they bargained for—a female thigh and breast. Police were called, the area was secured and the body parts were removed for analysis. Forensic scientists were able to ascertain that the body parts had belonged to a woman between 20 and 30 years old, weighing approximately 140 to 160 pounds. The body had been dissected with a knife, and the breast bore several teeth marks.

Detectives scanned reports of missing women and came up with Pamela Bruno, 24, who fit the description. Pamela had been reported missing by her husband on February 22, two days before the gruesome discovery in the dumpster.

The Brunos lived in a rundown apartment building in nearby Springfield. Johnny Bruno claimed that his wife had disappeared on February 17. He had awoken to find her gone, but hadn't notified police until February 22 because Pamela had often disappeared for a few days at a time. She was a heavy drinker, frequented local bars and, to put it kindly, was extremely promiscuous. Bruno admitted that he himself was not a candidate for canonization. He had been convicted in Washington State, together with Pamela, for contributing to the delinquency of a minor. Both had taken part in lewd sex acts with 15-year-old girls. They were not the salt of the earth.

Police felt that the victim was Pamela Bruno when they had her blood type checked from records in Washington. It matched the type taken from the body parts found in the dumpster. Johnny was advised that his wife might have been a murder victim. He didn't act surprised. A search of the Bruno apartment failed to uncover any trace of blood. If Pamela Bruno had been butchered, it had not been done in the Bruno apartment.

Johnny was taken to police headquarters for further questioning. When it was suggested that others might have been involved in Pamela's murder,

Johnny opened up. He implicated Charles Haynes, 31, a colleague of his at a tree-planting company, and Haynes's wife, Lionetti.

Johnny told an unbelievable tale of horror. The murder had taken place at the Haynes residence on West Fifth Avenue in Eugene. On February 21, the Brunos had visited the Hayneses for a day of drinking and smoking pot. Everyone agreed that a session of group sex would nicely break up the day. At the last moment, Pamela decided not to participate. The two men tied her up and that's when things got out of hand. Johnny told detectives that Lionetti had inflicted the initial stab wound, after which Charles had stabbed Pamela several times. Johnny claimed he had stabbed his wife only once.

The three participants suddenly realized that Pamela was dead. Charlie blurted out, "We got to do something about this now. We're going to have to cut her up." His suggestion was met with unanimous approval. Pamela's body was lugged to the bathtub. Johnny Bruno told detectives in graphic terms not necessary to repeat here how he helped to drain the blood from his wife's body and to butcher her. The body parts were placed in plastic bags and deposited in various dumpsters around Eugene. The only portions ever found were the thigh and breast discovered by the two derelicts.

Charlie and Lionetti Haynes were located at their home and taken into custody. On May 23, 1978, Johnny Bruno stood trial for his wife's murder. His statement given to police detailing the horrible crime had been taped and was now played back to the jury. Understandably, it had a devastating effect. In addition, medical experts testified that the severed breast had been mutilated extensively by human teeth. They also confirmed that the body parts contained minuscule amounts of blood, lending credence to Bruno's testimony that the body had been strung up and drained of blood for some time before it was dissected. These facts pointed to a deliberate murder and cover-up to avoid detection rather than a wild sex orgy that had gotten out of hand. Defence lawyers paraded an array of experts who attempted to cast doubt on Johnny's sanity. They had a difficult time overcoming the defendant's own statement that he definitely knew right from wrong.

The jury also heard that Johnny had been so drunk at the time of the murder that he could hardly remember what had transpired. His lawyers insinuated that he was afraid of Charlie Haynes and would do whatever his dominant colleague suggested. The jury didn't buy the defence arguments. They deliberated only three hours before finding Johnny guilty of felonious murder. He appealed the verdict but his conviction was upheld. Johnny Bruno was sentenced to life imprisonment, a sentence he is presently serving. He will be eligible for parole on March 13, 1998.

Charlie Haynes chose a rather complicated move called a "trial by stipulated facts," which is the next thing to pleading guilty. It differs in that it enables the accused to appeal the verdict. Charlie was sentenced to life imprisonment. He appealed on a technicality, but his appeal failed and his sentence stood. His lawyers took his case all the way to the Oregon Supreme Court and won their client a new trial, but it was all for naught. In May 1981, Charlie stood trial for Pamela Bruno's murder. He was found guilty and again sentenced to life imprisonment. He too is presently serving his sentence in the Oregon State Penitentiary. Haynes was paroled in January 1997.

After almost two years of delays and postponements, Lionetti Haynes was tried and convicted of first-degree manslaughter. Throughout her trial, she maintained that she was innocent of the charge. Despite her protests, she was found guilty and sentenced to 20 years' imprisonment, with the two years already spent in jail to be applied against her sentence. Lionetti Haynes was paroled from the Oregon Women's Correctional Center on March 11, 1985.

# GEORGE HLADY

## TRAGIC END TO A NEW LIFE IN A NEW LAND

IT was just another working day for Eino De Witt and Wally Sempke on the McIntyre River. The two men were perspiring under the hot August sun that day in 1952 when Eino spotted a strange-looking object in the water near the south side of the McIntyre. The men lowered a skiff off their big derrick scow and rowed across the river to investigate.

The strange-looking object was the body of a man floating face down. A half-inch rope was looped tightly around the man's neck with one strand wrapped across his mouth like a gag. In addition, there was a two-inch gash on the right side of the victim's head. Two heavy steel plates were tied to the dead man's neck and feet with wire. These plates were risers used under railway tracks at switching points. They could be found stacked anywhere along the rail line and, in fact, these two plates were stamped as being the property of the Canadian Pacific Railway.

Back in 1952, the twin cities of Fort William and Port Arthur were separate entities, which were eventually united to form what we now know as Thunder Bay. At the time of the murder, railway officials had become concerned about the high incidence of grain thefts from CNR and CPR railway cars. Thieves were breaking boxcar seals and carting away bushels of grain. Others were even more brazen, drilling through the boxcars and letting the grain run directly into bags outside the cars. Because of the proximity of the parked railway cars to the point where the body was taken out of the water, officials believed that the murder could, in some way, be connected to the theft of grain.

An autopsy indicated that the unidentified man had already been dead when he was submerged in the McIntyre. In addition to the blow on the head, he had been manually strangled. His clothing proved to be untraceable and there was no documentation found on the body to assist in identification. Callouses on the victim's hands indicated that he worked at physical labour, but decomposition made fingerprinting impossible. He wore a ring engraved with the initials W.H.

Dr. A.E. Allin, chief pathologist for the attorney-general's department, informed police that the dead man had a long scar along the back of his body.

The scar was the result of a lung operation in which a rib had been removed. Once seen, it is doubtful anyone would forget that livid scar.

Police received a hot lead when Ignace Hyriciuk reported that a tenant of his, Josef Panok, had been missing for some weeks. Ignace explained that his tenant had recently immigrated from Europe with his wife and young daughter. They had rented a tiny house on dilapidated Simpson Street in Fort William. Ignace went on to tell investigators that the Panoks' friend, George Hlady, lived with them. Ignace was taken to the morgue to view the body but couldn't say with any degree of certainty that the dead man was his tenant.

Detectives drove to the tiny house on Simpson Street. Once there, they learned that the Panoks didn't rent the entire house, but occupied two cramped rooms on the second floor. Mrs. Panok, an attractive brunette, couldn't speak English. The officers' questions were translated by well-built blond George Hlady. George explained that he and Panok were friends from the Ukraine.

With George translating, Mrs. Panok told the officers that she wasn't worried about her husband. He was in Winnipeg visiting a family named Kummel, who lived on Bannerman Street. Police suggested that she and George view the body in the morgue to assist them in their identification attempts. Mrs. Panok readily agreed.

When she looked down at the horrible sight of the decomposed corpse, Mrs. Panok cried out, but after settling down she stated that the dead man was definitely not her husband. George Hlady agreed. Both swore they had never seen the initialled ring before.

Investigators, under the direction of Port Arthur police chief Tom Conner, learned of a missing man, a lumberjack, whose initials were W.H. Several individuals identified the ring as belonging to the missing man. After viewing the body, they all agreed that the dead man was not the elusive W.H.

This minor mystery was solved when W.H. showed up. A giant of a man, he had been on a drunken spree to end all sprees, and had found himself in Copper Cliff with a monumental hangover and no money. He had not heard of the murder until he returned to Port Arthur. W.H. stated that the ring had belonged to him and that he had given it to a man named Panok as a reward for helping him out once when he was in a fight in a beer parlour.

W.H. accompanied police to the morgue and positively identified the dead man as Josef Panok. He recognized the long scar, explaining that he had worked with Panok many times under the hot sun when both men had been stripped to the waist. But how could this be? Panok's wife and best friend had already viewed the body and had sworn they didn't know the identity of the dead man.

Police, now wary of Mrs. Panok, checked out the Kummel family who supposedly lived on Bannerman Street in Winnipeg. There was no such family. When Chief Connor called on Mrs. Panok this time, he brought along his own translator. He asked his suspect, "Why didn't you identify your dead husband at the morgue?" Mrs. Panok replied, "Hlady told me not to. He threatened to kill me if I did. He and Josef went out to steal wheat and only George came back."

Mrs. Panok went on to tell the officers that her husband and George had known each other in Germany, where they dabbled in the black market. When their illicit business dried up, George made his way to Canada, promising to arrange for the Panok family to follow him. True to his word, he made arrangements for the Panoks to emigrate and was successful in getting Josef employment on a CPR work gang.

Living conditions were primitive. She, her husband and George all slept in the same bed. Daughter Karen slept alone in the only other room, the kitchen. According to Mrs. Panok, George had asked her to leave her husband and go to Toronto with him. She had refused his offer and the tension had become unbearable in the enclosed living space.

George was picked up at his place of employment on the railway. When presented with Mrs. Panok's statement, he agreed to it all, but he swore he had not killed Josef Panok. Lodged in jail, George made another statement to police. He said that he and Josef had gone out on the night of the tragedy to steal wheat from the boxcars. Just as George was about to break the seal and open the boxcar, Josef sneaked up behind him and put a rope around his neck. George said he grabbed at the rope with one hand and swung around with the other, striking Josef a blow to the head, which sent him reeling against the side of the boxcar. He then related that he had tied the rope and the steel risers to the body and tossed it into the McIntyre River.

Mrs. Panok filled in the rest of the evening by telling investigators that George had returned to the house around midnight, pale and shaken. Later, she would testify in court, "I couldn't sleep and I asked him again where Josef was. He told me he had killed my husband and thrown him in the river."

George stood trial for the murder of Josef Panok. He pleaded self-defence, but couldn't account for the tiny broken bones in the victim's neck which indicated manual strangulation. The jury could not dismiss the obvious motive, that of a love triangle. They chose to believe that George had killed Josef in an attempt to possess his wife.

George Hlady was found guilty of the murder of Josef Panok. On April 28, 1953, after all appeals were exhausted, he was hanged at the Port Arthur jail.

Mrs. Panok, accompanied by her five-year-old daughter, returned to Germany shortly after the conclusion of George's trial, her dreams of a fresh start in the new world shattered forever.

# JACK HOLMES AND HAROLD THURMOND

## SAN JOSE MOB LYNCHED KIDNAPPERS

WE like to believe that lynching has become unfashionable. It is distressing to learn that this unsavoury, if not downright nasty, practice was very much in vogue well into the twentieth century in many areas of the United States.

In 1933, Alex Hart owned one of the largest department stores in San Jose, California. His 22-year-old son, Brooke, had just graduated from Santa Clara University and had been made a junior partner in the prosperous business.

At six o'clock on November 9, 1933, Brooke, his father and sister were the last to leave the store. They locked up and waited while Brooke walked the three blocks to a parking lot to pick up the family's Studebaker.

Alex Hart and his daughter waited for some time before deciding that Brooke must have misunderstood that he was to pick them up. They made their way home, but still there was no sign of Brooke. After calling his friends, they decided to inform police. By ten o'clock that evening, the terrible thought that Brooke could have been kidnapped coursed through the minds of the missing man's family. At ten-thirty, their worst fears were realized. Alex received a phone call: "We have your son. We want $40,000 for him. Keep the police out of this if you want to see him alive."

Alex informed police of the call, but nothing further was heard from the kidnappers for a few days. Quite unexpectedly, a young girl knocked on the Harts' front door with a note she claimed had been given to her by a stranger who had asked her to deliver it to the Harts. On the scrap of paper were the words "We have Brooke and are treating him right."

Another day passed before the Harts' Studebaker was found outside San Jose. The vehicle provided no clues leading to the location of the missing man. The kidnappers kept in touch. They again contacted Alex by phone on November 15, giving detailed instructions as to where to drop off the ransom money. This time Alex was able to keep the kidnapper on the line long enough to have the call traced. Police sped to a San Jose garage and picked up Harold Thurmond.

Now, Harold wasn't your average run-of-the-mill lowlife. He came from a respectable family and had never been in any trouble before he tried his luck at the kidnapping game. When questioned, he told police that he had an accomplice, Jack Holmes, who was also taken into custody.

The two men confessed and told authorities the same story. Both were unemployed and had had time on their hands to hatch their amateurish plot. They had plucked Brooke off the streets of San Jose as he was getting into his Studebaker. Together with their captive, they drove in his car to the San Mateo–Hayward Bridge. Once there, one of them knocked Brooke out with a brick brought along especially for that purpose. Both men had a hand in tying Brooke up with wire and weighing him down with a slab of concrete.

Just as they were about to toss him off the bridge, Brooke regained consciousness and started screaming. It was dark and no cars passed by during the interval it took to complete the job. Brooke, screaming hysterically, was tossed off the bridge. For good measure, Harold took a few potshots at Brooke, but didn't think he hit his target. Brooke quickly disappeared from sight.

It was a heartless, cold-blooded recital of murder of a well-liked, well-respected member of the community; consequently, there was great concern for the safety of the two confessed killers. They were placed in the San Francisco Prison for safekeeping. Inexplicably, six days later, they were removed to the less secure Santa Clara County Jail and lodged in separate cells on different floors.

On Sunday, November 26, 17 days after the abduction, Brooke's body was found. Two duck hunters came across the partially decomposed body about a mile south of the bridge. The concrete used to weigh down the body had come loose, allowing it to surface.

In San Jose, word of the cold-blooded cruelty displayed by the two men in custody spread throughout the community. The Hart family was respected; Brooke had been well liked. It was as if the city was waiting for an excuse to spring into action. The recovery of Brooke's body confirming the terrible rumours was that excuse.

A crowd, estimated at 15,000, congregated in front of the jail. Many were young men in their twenties, the same age as Brooke and the two men in custody. Some were former school chums of the murdered man. Children were held high in the air so they could get a better view of what was about to take place.

Sheriff Bill Emig was aware of the community's ugly mood. He had prepared for just such an eventuality, having enlisted the assistance of 20 county officers and state highway patrolmen. Equipped with shotguns and tear gas, they covered every window and door. Alex Hart, devastated at the news that his son's body had been recovered that day, still summoned enough strength to make an impassioned plea in front of the jail, imploring the crowd to go home. He was hardly heard over the din of the mob.

Sheriff Emig had set up barricades at the front of three alleys beside the jail. Sixty men charged the barriers and were repulsed by tear gas. On the fourth try, they crashed through. Using planks and pipes from a nearby construction site, they broke down the doors of the jail. Inside there were only three officers between them and the killers. These officers were quickly disarmed.

Deputy John Moore was forced to lead the mob to Jack Holmes's cell. Holmes, frightened out of his wits, begged, "For God's sake, give me a chance." The mob laughed and proceeded to inflict a severe beating on their quarry. On they went, up to Harold Thurmond's cell. It was empty. Terror-stricken, Harold had managed to find a hiding place among pipes in the ceiling. He was spotted, pulled down, tied with rope and dragged down the stairs headfirst.

The two murderers, now almost unconscious, were taken to Saint James Park. Harold was strung up on a large tree. His execution didn't go well. He choked to death at the end of the rope. Jack was made to look at his friend's body before he too was hanged. Someone in the mob knew how to make a proper hangman's knot, so Jack didn't suffer as much as his companion.

It was over. The mob pressed forward, ripping and tearing at the clothing of the dead men for souvenirs. Citizens boasted that they had taken part in the lynching. For years after, souvenirs of the event could be purchased in and around San Jose.

An inquest was held into the two deaths, but no indictments were issued and no one was ever prosecuted for the lynching. The governor of California expressed the mood of the city when he stated, "I would pardon those fellows if they were charged. I would like to parole all kidnappers in San Quentin and Folsom to the fine patriotic citizens of San Jose."

# BRIAN HOOD AND JENNIFER REALI

## POSSESSED BY PASSION

---

ATTRACTIVE Jennifer Vaughan did all the proper things. She attended the University of Washington, made the varsity rowing team and dated often. They were great, carefree days in the early eighties. Jennifer thought they would last forever. She was sure of it when she met Ben Reali, a career army man. In 1984, they married and were soon the proud parents of two daughters, Tinneke and Natasha.

Despite the appearance of tranquillity, Jennifer was not happy. Although her marriage was stable and her lifestyle secure, she longed for something more. Her existence in Colorado Springs had become routine—housework, the kids, and above all, staid, boring Ben. There was definitely no excitement in Jennifer's life; that is, until Brian Hood came upon the scene.

Brian hailed from Houston, Texas, where his dad was big in the insurance game. After graduating from Angelo State College in 1986, he married Dianne, who had been his steady girlfriend throughout his college years. The young couple moved to Colorado Springs, where Brian, like his father, pursued the insurance business. He also joined the Fellowship Bible Church and became deeply involved in the religious life. Following her husband's advice, Dianne joined the church as well. Both devoted much of their time to ecclesiastical pursuits and led a strict, devout life. They had three children: Jerrod, 7, Leslie, 5, and baby Joshua.

In 1989, Dianne was told she had contracted lupus. Although her form of the disease was not life-threatening, she had to take extremely good care of herself and lead a quiet life. Sexual activity had become a thing of the past. Brian, stout-hearted fellow that he was, told his wife not to worry about their lack of intimacy. His religious beliefs would see him through the crisis and would fill the void left in their sex life.

Wouldn't you just know it—Brian met Jennifer Reali at Bally's U.S. Swim and Fitness Club. He took one look and religion flew out the window. As for Jennifer, she thought she had died and gone to heaven. A hunk had dropped into her lap, so to speak. The pair had lunch. A few days later, Brian called on

Jennifer when hubby and kids were absent, ostensibly to discuss her insurance program. We know for a fact they discussed other things, because they had intercourse on top of a convenient washer-dryer in the laundry room.

After this initial exhilarating experience, Brian became a rather demanding lover. He seemed to require sex practically all the time. Jennifer loved every minute of it. She insisted that Brian accommodate her with a variety of methods and positions. It was all great fun, but wouldn't it be wonderful if they could be together all the time without sneaking around the sickly Dianne and boring Ben?

Brian racked his brain and came up with the rationalization that satisfied his morals. He explained to Jennifer that they could kill Dianne, which would be no more of a sin in the eyes of God than if he divorced her. Besides, all things considered, God would forgive them. Jennifer, now totally dominated by her lover, agreed. Dianne had to go.

Brian advised Jennifer that the opportunity to kill Dianne would present itself in two weeks when his wife would be attending a lupus support-group meeting and would be vulnerable as she returned home. According to Brian, the entire adventure would be akin to a religious experience. They would be free to fulfil their every desire. Jennifer heartily agreed.

In preparation for the great event, Jennifer had her husband Ben take her out to a shooting range, where she practised shooting with one of the guns from his collection. While Jennifer was busy practising, Brian and Dianne went away on a three-day marriage-encounter weekend. On the very date the murder was supposed to take place, Brian informed Jennifer that their affair was over. He was returning to his wife and that was that.

Undaunted, and maybe more possessed than ever, on the designated night, Jennifer took her husband's gun, donned a black mask and camouflage fatigues and headed for the Otis Park Community Center. Inside, Dianne was attending her lupus support-group meeting. Jennifer hid in some bushes and waited for her victim. When Dianne emerged from the centre with a friend, Karen Johnson, Jennifer caught up to the pair and attempted to grab Dianne's purse. Dianne threw her purse at her attacker, shouting, "Take it!" Instead, the disguised figure shot Dianne in the back. As Dianne spun away to run back into the centre, she fell to the ground.

Karen watched in terror as the assailant ran to Dianne's side. Then, as the wounded woman begged for mercy, Jennifer shot her through the heart. She then drove home. Karen's screams soon brought assistance, but it was too late for Dianne. She lay dead on the sidewalk.

Investigating officers were not fooled by the attempt to make the attack look like the work of a mugger. Muggers do not usually remain at the crime scene to execute a wounded victim. No, it looked like a deliberate, planned assassination. Brian was informed of his wife's death and was devastated. However, it didn't take detectives long to learn through the army grapevine that Ben Reali's wife, Jennifer, was doing what comes naturally with the husband of the dead woman.

On the day of Dianne's funeral, Brian was arrested and charged with her murder. Two weeks later, Jennifer was charged with first-degree murder and conspiracy. The trials of the accused were sensational. Sexual revelations liberally sprinkled with religious beliefs made for juicy testimony. Jennifer confessed that she had shot Dianne, but claimed that Brian had ordered her to do the job. Captain Ben Reali bowed out of the scenario by filing for divorce and gaining custody of his two daughters.

Brian was the first of the pair to stand trial. His lawyers put all the blame on Jennifer, painting her as a woman who saw her lover returning to his wife. Solution—do away with the wife. The ploy didn't work. Brian was found guilty of conspiracy to commit murder. He was sentenced to 37 years in Colorado State Prison.

In March 1992, Jennifer stood trial. She was found guilty of murder in the first degree, as well as conspiracy to commit murder, and was sentenced to life imprisonment with no possibility of parole. Brian Hood and Jennifer Reali are presently serving their sentences.

# DR. JAMES HUDSON

## SWINGER KILLED WIFE AND DAUGHTER

THE first 12 years of James and Kay Hudson's marriage went along famously. Of course, for 10 of those years, Kay had no idea that her dentist husband was a real swinger. Dr. Jimmy was careful. He loved to travel and only dated women when he was out of town.

Jimmy wasn't averse to taking part in group sex. When he approached Kay with the great idea that she join him in fun and games, she was appalled and refused to have anything to do with her husband's jollies. That's when she realized that her marriage was in trouble. Kay felt that adopting a child might be the solution to straightening out her rocky union.

In April 1983, the Hudsons had no trouble adopting a baby girl, Wilma Dale. They were prime adoptive parents. After all, Jimmy was a partner in a prosperous dental practice and Kay had recently attended the University of North Carolina, where she had finished a master's degree. To the outside world, the Hudsons, with their impressive home in Oak Ridge, North Carolina, were a respectable, well-educated couple. Kay knew better.

For a while after the adoption, Jimmy seemed to settle down. He was more attentive to Kay and doted on his new little daughter. His solicitous attitude didn't last. When Wilma Dale became ill, Jimmy dropped her like a hot potato. He complained that Kay paid too much attention to their daughter and neglected him. After Kay found letters from strange women describing specific sex acts they had enjoyed with her husband, she knew the end of her unstable marriage had come. She also realized that her husband had turned into a sexually aggressive man who bore no resemblance to the young man she had married.

In March 1986, Kay wrote a long letter to Jimmy outlining the reasons she was leaving him. She pleaded with him not to attempt to find her and assured him that she and Wilma Dale would make out fine on their own.

Jimmy read the letter left for him by his wife. He called police, but was told there was little they could do. There was no law preventing a mother from leaving her own home with her daughter. A few minutes later, Jimmy had a bright idea. He called police a second time, advising them that he was in hospital after having suffered a heart attack. He begged them to bring Kay to the hospital.

The fake heart-attack ploy worked. Kay was driven to the hospital, where the estranged couple had a meeting. During the course of the conversation, Jimmy wheedled Kay's address out of her. In return, he promised to receive help from a psychiatrist. Kay insisted on living separately from her husband, at least until he renounced his kinky lifestyle.

A few days later, on March 24, a blood-spattered Jimmy drove to a police station and told the first officer he met, "I think I killed my wife and daughter." According to the dentist, his wife had attacked him with a knife. Further than that he couldn't remember. Jimmy was hustled off to hospital to take care of wounds to his chest and hand. They proved to be little more than superficial.

Police entered Kay's apartment and found her body and that of her three-year-old daughter, Wilma Dale. Both had been stabbed repeatedly. Jimmy was arrested and immediately underwent a battery of psychiatric tests to ascertain if he was fit to stand trial. Tests indicated that he was sane, which gave the state the right to impose the death penalty if the accused was found guilty of murder.

Jimmy's trial did not focus on whether he committed the murders, but whether or not he should receive the death penalty. The prosecution revealed that the two victims had been the recipients of vicious beatings before being stabbed to death. The jacket and T-shirt Jimmy was wearing on the night of the murders were introduced as evidence. Both were devoid of slashes and cuts, although Jimmy swore he was wearing them when he received the wounds to his chest as he and Kay struggled for possession of a kitchen butcher knife. The prosecution's implication was clear. Jimmy could have inflicted the superficial wounds to his own chest after he murdered his wife and daughter.

Statements given to the police by Jimmy were read into the record. He confessed to having had several affairs, but always with women from out of town because of his prominence in the community. On the day of the murder, Jimmy had been with Wilma Dale all day. He had dropped off his daughter at Kay's apartment at 6 p.m. and had lingered for some time. Kay had asked him to leave, and that's when the trouble had started. She had become violent and Wilma Dale had started to cry. Kay had slapped his face and had come at him with a butcher knife. That's the last thing Jimmy said he remembered. He had no recollection of the actual stabbings, but did recall washing the blood off his hands and face in the kitchen. He claimed that was when he took off his jacket and T-shirt.

Jimmy admitted that both his marriage and his dental practice had deteriorated because of his unusual sex life. For example, he told of his attempt to make Kay join a nudist colony with him. She would have no part of any of his sexual activities. As the years passed, she more or less consented to his going his own way. The letters she found were the straws that broke the camel's back.

Defence attorneys paraded an array of psychiatrists to the witness stand who stated that Dr. Jimmy was a severely disordered personality. They related that in previous times in his life he had suffered from amnesia and had blanked out distasteful episodes. They claimed that he'd suffered from emotional shock on the night of the murders and truthfully couldn't remember the killings.

The prosecution wasn't through. A fellow prisoner of Jimmy's gave testimony. This man, who was the prison librarian and a three-time killer, had volunteered to give testimony after seeing photographs of Wilma Dale's body. He informed the court that Jimmy told him he had killed his wife and had then waited 20 minutes before stabbing his daughter. This threw some doubt on Jimmy's claim that he had operated in a state of emotional shock and had no knowledge of the crime. Although the defence attempted to discredit the librarian, who had already spent 20 years in prison, it was clear to the jury that he had nothing to gain and had put himself in considerable jeopardy by coming forth to testify.

On April 11, 1987, the North Carolina jury found Jimmy guilty of first-degree murder in the case of his daughter and second-degree murder in the case of his wife.

Dr. James Hudson, the once-prosperous dentist with the attractive wife and ostentatious home, managed to save his life. He was sentenced to life imprisonment for the murder of his daughter and 50 years for the murder of his wife. He is presently serving his sentences.

# RICHARD IVENS

## KILLER MOVED BODY FROM PLACE TO PLACE

IT takes more than your average riot, murder, or stuffed ballot box to gain the attention of the Chicago police. Despite past indiscretions perpetrated by the good citizens of Chicago, the year 1906 started off nastier than most. Three women, Mrs. E.F. Mize, Mrs. Maude Reese and Mrs. A.W. Gentry had been murdered in the last three months of 1905. The city's finest had no idea who had committed these crimes.

Understandably, the police force was under increasing pressure to solve the murders. They were totally demoralized when Fred Quimba walked into a police station and told the desk sergeant in a stage whisper, "There's a dead woman in my front yard."

Fred lived on the corner of Fullerton and Orchard Streets. Within minutes, police officers were speeding to the area to secure the crime scene. The boys back at the station house, now certain that they were dealing with murdered woman number four, were somewhat miffed when they received word that there was no body in Fred's front yard.

Fred couldn't explain the absence of his very own personal corpse. Police looked at him skeptically, thanked him for being such a public-minded citizen and told him to be sure to give them a call if he found any more bodies.

An hour later, the very same desk sergeant who had been both aggravated and amused by Fred Quimba, received a phone call from one J.H. Rush, who exclaimed, "There's a dead body in my yard." Mr. Rush went on to explain that he lived on the corner of Fullerton and Orchard. Once again, police officers were dispatched to the now-familiar area. They located Rush, but surprise of surprises, for the second time on the same day they failed to find a body.

Mr. Rush and his wife were escorted to the police station. They described the dead woman in detail. There was no doubt in their minds that they had seen the woman and she had definitely been dead. Someone must have removed the body when they left to telephone police. So insistent were the Rushes, the police agreed to return to the scene. The Rushes' credibility escalated when detectives discovered bloodstains on the ground where the couple had allegedly seen the body.

Chicago flatfeet were now convinced that they were investigating the case of a body which, in some mysterious way, had become mobile. Any doubts were dispelled when Frank Hollister walked into a police station. Unlike Fred Quimba and J.H. Rush, Frank's approach was quite different. He said, "I'm Frank Hollister and I want to report the disappearance of my wife."

Frank turned out to be somewhat of a heavyweight. He was the owner of the Hollister Printing Co., one of the largest printing firms in Chicago. According to Frank, his wife had left their home early the previous morning. She had visited a grocery store where she left instructions for her groceries to be delivered. The groceries had arrived at the Hollister residence at 10 a.m. She had then ordered flowers to be delivered to the Methodist Episcopal Church, where she had a 3 p.m. appointment to take part in choir practice. She hadn't shown up.

On January 13, 1906, Edward Ivens walked into a police station to report that his son Richard had found the body of a woman. Edward explained that he owned a carpentry shop on Belvin Avenue and a livery stable next door. He kept horses and wagons at the stable. His son Richard fed the horses and cleaned out the stable every morning at 5 a.m. Richard had found the body in the vicinity of the stable.

This time there really was a body, that of Mrs. Bessie Hollister. She had been beaten about the head and had been strangled to death. A 48-inch length of wire had been wound around her neck. Near her body, police recovered a 12-inch length of green string.

Detectives soon learned that the wire was used by florists and the green string was of a type often used by upscale grocery stores. The Hollisters' maid was questioned. She volunteered that when Mrs. Hollister left the house that morning, she had taken along a beautiful gold clock for repair. The maid had wrapped the clock in white tissue paper and had secured it with green string she had saved from the grocer's.

A thorough search of the crime scene and adjoining areas failed to turn up the clock, but police did find a muff and purse belonging to Mrs. Hollister. The killer had obviously covered these items with leaves which had blown away.

When blood was found on the floor of one of Edward Ivens' wagons, police were convinced that someone had killed Bessie Hollister and had moved her body, for some unknown reason, from place to place, possibly using the horse and wagon in Ivens' stable. Everyone who had reported seeing the body was questioned again and, this time, believed.

Police decided to interrogate the individual who had actually come up with Bessie Hollister's body, namely, Richard Ivens. They knew that Richard's brother owned a florist shop and that Richard had access to the type of wire used to strangle Mrs. Hollister. Armed with this information, they had Richard relate his every move on the day of the murder. Business had been slow and he claimed that he had spent much of the day and night alone. When a search of his premises uncovered a jackknife with a small length of green string adhering to the blade, Richard was arrested and taken into custody.

Richard broke down. He told police, "I've got the clock. I found it beside Mrs. Hollister. I was going to pawn it. But I didn't kill her. I had nothing to do with that." He turned the clock over to police.

After only one day in custody, Richard confessed to Mrs. Hollister's murder. In his own words, he said, "I killed her. I chased her and slugged her. I took her money. She pleaded with me to take her home, said I could keep the money and she wouldn't tell anybody. I hit her again and again and then we came to Fullerton and Orchard. I saw a piece of wire in the gutter and twisted it around her neck and pulled it tight. As I walked away, I saw a man hovering over the body. When he went away, I went back. I thought she was dead and threw her over the fence and into the yard. I went away a couple of blocks and then got to worrying that she wasn't dead. I saw another man running away from the yard and figured he'd found her. I went back. I thought her leg moved and figured I'd better move her. I went back behind the fence and threw the body over my shoulder and carried it to the stable. I hitched up a team to a wagon and drove out, but didn't go far. I returned and dumped the body close to the stable."

Richard stood trial for the murder of Bessie Hollister. He recanted his confession, claiming that he had been beaten by police to extract it from him. Throughout his trial he professed that his only crime was finding the body and stealing the clock. No one believed him.

Richard Ivens was found guilty of first-degree murder and sentenced to death. He was hanged on June 22, 1906. No evidence was ever brought forward implicating him in the murders of the three Chicago women killed in late 1905. These crimes remain unsolved.

# BAHAR KANDLBINDER AND WOLFGANG GRUNWALD

## HUBBY WOLF AND MISTRESS BAHAR

INGE Hermann was only 19 years old when she fell in love with Wolfgang Grunwald. Her mother was fit to be tied. Mrs. Hermann simply didn't understand how an attractive girl like her daughter could fall for a no-goodnik like Wolf. The boy had no job and no prospects. Besides, he had an atrocious complexion. Surely, with all the eligible boys in Munich, Germany, her Inge could do better.

Mrs. Hermann's opinion became academic when Inge, due to an unfortunate miscalculation, found herself definitely pregnant. Quick as a bunny, she and no-goodnik Wolf became husband and wife.

The marriage, born out of necessity, was not a happy one. The responsibilities of married life didn't change Wolf one iota. Two years after he and Inge tied the knot he still had no job and no prospects. When he chose a mistress, Inge felt it prudent to pack up her baby and go home to Mama.

Wolf's mistress, a 32-year-old Turkish woman, was gainfully employed as a masseuse in a shop that featured massages of a specialized nature. Folks, you know what I mean. Living with Bahar Kandlbinder had one positive effect on Wolf. He got a job in a manufacturing plant. When Inge filed for divorce, Wolf didn't oppose the action. In fact, considering that he was the recipient of all those massages on a regular basis, we must assume that he was rather pleased with the way things were working out.

On June 19, 1974, Inge failed to arrive home from her job at a gas station at her regular time of 4 p.m. Her mother immediately reported her missing to police. Inge had always arrived home promptly since she and her baby had moved in with her mother.

Police located Wolf at home watching television with Bahar. He told detectives he had no idea where his estranged wife could be. There where no new developments for two days.

The possibility that Inge might have run away was eliminated when a lock tender on the River Isar in Munich found a woman's purse containing some money and identification papers belonging to Inge Grunwald. The river was dragged but nothing further was uncovered.

The next day, a man, walking in the woods about nine miles from the city, came across Inge's body lying below a steep incline. He ran to the nearest telephone, which was some distance away, and called the police. Inge had been hacked to death with a hatchet. Her scalp was virtually split open. The blows had been struck from behind. She was fully clothed and had not been sexually interfered with in any way. An investigation of the crime scene indicated that Inge had been killed beside a logging trail at the top of a steep incline. Her body had been rolled down the incline to where it was found.

The logging trail was closely examined. Casts were made of tire tracks and footprints leading to the edge of the incline. One set of footprints belonged to the victim. The other two had been made by a man and a woman.

Detectives were able to reconstruct the circumstances of Inge's murder. Accompanied by a male and female, she had walked 25 yards from the car that had made the tire tracks. Here she was struck several times from behind with a hatchet. Inge had fallen, bleeding profusely. She was then dragged the rest of the way to the steep slope and pushed over the edge. The body rolled some distance, finally coming to a stop. A list of clothing worn by the murdered woman when she went missing was given to authorities by her mother. The body was dressed in all the clothing listed, with the exception of a red velvet jacket.

The logical suspects were hubby Wolf and his mistress Bahar. The tires on Wolf's Opel Kadet were checked against the cast made of the tire tracks at the scene of the murder. Much to investigators' surprise, they didn't match. Although the suspects' shoes were the correct sizes, they did not match the prints taken near the logging trail. The suspects' clothing was examined for blood, but none was found.

Munich police had no idea why Inge had been murdered, but they were sure her husband and his mistress were the culprits. They set up investigative procedures, which lack the glamour of the fictional murder investigation, but which more often that not snare the killer in real life. Dry-cleaning establishments were canvassed in an attempt to find out if Wolf or Bahar had deposited any bloodstained clothing. Hardware stores were checked for the purchase of a hatchet before the date of the killing. It was theorized that Wolf may have been cunning enough to purchase new tires immediately after the murder.

Sometimes one connecting clue is uncovered in a massive investigation. On this occasion, everything attempted by the police came up aces. The hardware store where Wolf had purchased a hatchet on June 13 was found only four blocks from his apartment. The clerk who had sold him the hatchet knew him by sight. Police also located the tire shop where Wolf had purchased new tires. Inge's missing red velvet jacket was not located in a dry-cleaning establishment, but the bloodstained jacket was found in a playground near the River Isar.

Wolf was informed of the evidence pointing to his guilt and immediately confessed to his involvement. He vehemently denied that he had killed Inge, claiming that Bahar had struck the fatal blows. According to Wolf, his wife had threatened to commence proceedings to have Bahar confined to a mental institution. Although Inge had no legal right to take such action, Bahar believed it was possible and decided to kill her antagonist. The pair picked Inge up and drove out to the woods, ostensibly to discuss the impending divorce. Wolf had purchased the hatchet at Bahar's instructions. He had waited in the car while Bahar struck the fatal blows. His mistress had then summoned him to help drag the body to the edge of the slope and push it over. Wolf admitted that he should have informed police of the murder, but by the next morning he believed that it was too late. That's when he went out, changed the tires of his Opel Kadet and threw away both his and Bahar's shoes.

Now it was Bahar's turn. She too confessed involvement, but named Wolf as the killer. According to Bahar, the reason for the killing was Inge's threats to inform Wolf's employer that he had stolen goods and money from the plant. To complicate matters, Bahar had attempted to break off her relationship with Wolf. For her trouble, he had beaten her black and blue. After that little episode, Bahar never again mentioned leaving him. She claimed that it was she who had stayed in the car at the time of the murder and Wolf who had inflicted the blows with the hatchet.

Police believed Bahar's story. She was a short, tiny woman. Tests indicated that it would have been impossible for her to have inflicted the fatal blows without standing on something like a box or step stool.

Bahar Kandlbinder was found guilty of being an accessory after the fact of murder. She was sentenced to two and a half years' imprisonment. Wolfgang Grunwald was found guilty of murdering his wife and was sentenced to life imprisonment.

# ERNST KARL

## MURDERED WOMAN'S BODY DISSECTED

ON May 10, 1973, a garbage man in Vienna, Austria, took the cover off a trash can outside a retail store and stared directly into the lifeless face of a young woman. Within minutes, a horde of officials were swarming the area. The murdered woman's body had been dissected. Body parts were found in other trash cans close by. It was sheer luck that the contents of all the cans had not been taken away by a garbage truck and disposed of in the city dump.

The body was taken to the morgue where an autopsy revealed the following facts. The victim had been between 18 and 22 years of age, had stood 5 feet two inches tall and had weighed 102 pounds. She had been dissected by someone with no medical skill who had used a common butcher knife and hacksaw. Sexual intercourse had taken place shortly before or at the time of death, which had taken place two days previously in the afternoon or early evening.

It was obvious that other than the girl's body parts, the contents of the trash cans had come from the nearby shops. Police believed that the killer would not have disposed of the body outside his own shop. Questioning of the shop owners in the area proved that this was the case. All were cleared of any involvement in the murder.

Reports of missing girls in Vienna were checked out. None matched the girl found in the garbage can. Photographs of the dead girl were widely distributed and featured in local news-papers. This effort bore fruit. Martin Katz of the Albo Manufacturing Co. called police. He was sure the dead girl was Ilse Morscher, a clerk at Albo. Martin had taken it upon himself to check out the Human Resources Department of his company. He was told that Ilse had simply failed to show up for work one day and had never inquired about salary due to her.

Police were told by Albo's personnel staff that Ilse was 21 years old and lived alone in an apartment. She had no casual or steady male friends and had worked in Vienna for only three months. Ilse was a shy girl, well liked by everyone. A newcomer to the city, she spent most of her spare time taking in the sights that Vienna had to offer. The woman's apartment was searched, but yielded nothing that would lead to the identity of the killer.

Girls at Ilse's office informed detectives that Ilse had told them she planned on visiting the Prater, Vienna's famous amusement park, on the Friday evening she disappeared. As the autopsy had revealed that Ilse's last meal had consisted of sausage and candy, typical amusement-park fare, police surmised that she could have met her killer at the park.

A canvass of sausage sellers at the Prater turned up the vendor who had sold Ilse her last meal. He positively identified her from her photograph and swore that she had been alone. Next, police conducted a door-to-door search for anyone who had seen the young woman leave the park. Several people who lived in the area came forward, informing police that they had seen Ilse walking alone. From that point on, she simply vanished. Detectives believed that somewhere along the route, Ilse had been either dragged or lured inside an apartment by a rapist who killed her and dissected her body. Each apartment building-dweller in the area was questioned. Many were eliminated as suspects. Others had their apartments searched from top to bottom.

It was in this way that Johann Rogatsch became a prime suspect. For starters, Johann had been previously convicted of minor sex offenses. Blood was discovered in his bathroom. The blood was not his type, but was the same type as that of Ilse Morscher. Police dismantled the plumbing in the apartment and discovered bone chips and hair in the drains. Charred bits of women's clothing were found in the basement furnace.

Johann was questioned for hours. Initially he denied any involvement, but eventually he broke down and confessed. According to Johann, he had lured Ilse into his apartment, wanting nothing more than a friendly kiss. When she repulsed his advances, Johann said he panicked and gave the girl a karate chop, a martial art he had only recently taken up. He must have hit her too hard because she crumpled to the floor, dead.

Johann conveniently omitted the rape from his confession, but it did him little good. On January 4, 1974, Johann Rogatsch was found guilty of rape and first-degree murder. He was sentenced to life imprisonment at the federal prison at Stein.

All things being equal, when the cold steel bars of the ominous prison closed behind Johann, that should have been the last heard of the rapist/killer. But such was not to be the case. His path crossed that of prisoner Ernst Karl.

Ernst, an inmate since 1968, wasn't rowing with both oars in the water. He had been a rookie police officer in Vienna in 1968 and had been on the force only four months when he made headlines. In the wee hours of April 4,

Patrolman Ernst Karl radioed headquarters that he had just been in a shootout with two gangsters inside a public garage. Fortunately, he had shot the two men dead.

Detectives were at the scene in a matter of minutes. Sure enough, the rookie had plugged the two hoods in the head. They lay on the floor of the garage in pools of blood. Both had weapons clutched in their hands. Next morning, newspapers hailed Ernst as a hero. The public ate up the story. Here was a police officer of whom everyone could be proud. Everyone, that is, except the police.

Police felt that there was nothing of value in the garage. Why were the men there at 1:30 a.m.? Upon checking out the dead men, Walter Poettler and Johann Khisl, police learned that they were small-time hoodlums who pulled off the odd swindle and rolled the occasional drunk; hardly big-time gangsters.

Detectives took another look at their own man, Ernst, who obviously had a fantastic aim to have shot two armed men in the head before either one could get off a shot. Someone got the bright idea that if the two hoods were blackmailing Ernst, he might have decided to kill them.

A full investigation was conducted into the patrolman's background. It was discovered that he was a homosexual. Ernst was confronted by his superiors and admitted that he was being blackmailed. He was turning over almost all his salary to the blackmailers in return for their silence about his sexual orientation. Finally, he decided to kill them. According to his reasoning, he would rather kill them let them blackmail him into committing crimes in order to provide them with more money. To Ernst's way of thinking, they were criminals who deserved to die.

The Austrian court didn't see Ernst's point of view. He was found guilty of murder and sentenced to 20 years' imprisonment at the federal prison in Stein. Once incarcerated, our Ernst soon gained a reputation as a law-and-order nut. If a prisoner committed the smallest infraction, Ernst held a mock trial and meted out what he felt was appropriate punishment. He soon came to be the most feared man in the institution.

This was the man whom Johann Rogatsch met when he first entered prison to serve his sentence. Johann didn't notice that the other prisoners stayed clear of Ernst. He had only one thing in mind, escape. He approached the former police officer with a scheme. He needed a partner and told Ernst that the best way to escape would be to take one of the warden's children as a hostage. Little did Johann know that he was talking to a man who was a stickler for law and order, a man who punished others for stealing a cigarette; in short, a real fanatic.

One day the two men were alone in the yard when Johann went over his plan with Ernst in detail. That was enough for the one-time cop, who decided that Johann was about to commit a crime and had to be punished. Without warning, Ernst clasped Johann's neck in his huge hands and squeezed the life from the unsuspecting prisoner. Guards ran to the scene of the attack, but it was too late. Johann was dead and Ernst was proud of what he had done.

When he stood trial for murder, Ernst made an impassioned plea for law and order in prison. He told the court he would do everything in his power to see that justice was served efficiently and swiftly.

Ernst Karl was found guilty of murder and given a life sentence. Since his incarceration for the second time at Stein, there has been a marked decrease in crime within the prison.

# YVONNE KLEINFELDER

## OPPOSITES ATTRACT

IT has been said that opposites attract.

Yvonne Kleinfelder was 39 years old back in 1975 when she met John Comer, who was three years her senior.

Yvonne was born and grew up in Chicago. Never one to aspire to higher education, she dropped out of high school and became a drifter, one of those rootless girls who jump from bar to bar, sometimes serving hooch to eager customers, sometimes performing as a stripper. In the 1960s, she was arrested three times for being an employee of a house of ill repute.

In the early seventies, Yvonne delved into the shady world of witchcraft, gravitating to a group known as the Foundation Faith of God. Sometimes she sold the organization's literature on the street corners of Chicago. Often she toiled in the group's kitchens.

Yvonne, who weighed around 125 pounds and stood only five feet, one inch tall, discovered that she had the extraordinary ability to dominate weaker personalities. Enter John Comer, a six-foot, 180-pound, good ol' southern boy. John had attended the University of Alabama, leaving that institution to work with a large manufacturer of pinball machines in Chicago. In time John was promoted to foreman. From all accounts, he was a regular fellow who got along well with employees and acquaintances.

Not long after the Satan worshipper and the pinball-machine foreman met in 1975, they became lovers. John moved into Yvonne's apartment at 745 West Gordon Terrace. Initially, their relationship might have been normal, but we do know that before many months had passed, John was showing fellow employees strange injuries to his body. One co-worker would later state that when John removed his shirt, he observed welts on his back that resembled ugly streaks left by a lash.

In 1978, John was admitted to hospital on three different occasions, suffering from injuries to his back and face. He was no longer the robust specimen he had been when he had first moved in with Yvonne. He was now 30 pounds lighter and was forever showing up with strange and unaccountable injuries, such as a cut ear or a rope burn around his neck. Toward 1980, John's acquaintances noticed that he was always broke, even though he was earning a good salary.

Friends guessed that John's girlfriend, Yvonne, had a strange hold over him and that it was she who was inflicting the damage to his body. It was difficult to fathom why John didn't simply walk away from his nemesis as his friends suggested, but he never did heed their advice.

At 9:30 a.m. on May 1, 1980, Shemia Brewer, a 24-year-old acquaintance of Yvonne's, was surprised when Yvonne called at her apartment in a rather agitated state. Yvonne told Shemia that her roommate was hurt and asked her to accompany her back to her apartment.

Shemia was astounded when she entered Yvonne's apartment and saw John under a table. His hands were tied to two of the table legs and his body was covered with a blanket. Yvonne told her that John had been burned while trying to extinguish a fire. Because Yvonne didn't have a phone, the pair made their way to a restaurant, where Shemia called police and an ambulance.

While the two women discussed the entire matter, Yvonne related that she had told a little white lie. John hadn't put out a fire at all. She had burned him by throwing boiling water on him. And why had she done such a thing? Yvonne explained that John had talked out loud and in general had misbehaved at a prayer meeting the previous Friday. He simply had to be punished.

Shemia returned to Yvonne's apartment while Yvonne made a side trip to visit her pastor. In minutes, police and ambulance attendants were undoing the ropes which bound John's hands to the table legs and those which tied his ankles together. Although badly burned, John was alive. As the paramedics carried him away on a stretcher, he was able to say only three words, "Yvonne boiled me."

Police took a statement from Shemia. They couldn't believe that John Comer had been lying on his back in that horrible condition for six days since the previous Friday. Shemia was able to fill in the police with more details which had been related to her by Yvonne. Evidently, beating up on John was an almost daily occurrence. Yvonne had beaten John with a whip and had kicked him about the head. When he attempted to attack her, she had doused him with boiling water. Yvonne had confessed to Shemia that she had planned the fight and had boiled the water expressly to throw at John.

Detectives located Yvonne at the Church of the Good Shepherd (she wanted to cover all the bases), where her pastor, Brother Edward Bartus, turned her over to police. Yvonne was charged with aggravated battery. The day after her arrest, she was questioned by detectives. She had an amazing story to tell.

Yvonne and John had been living together for five years. As the years passed, John showed less and less respect for her. As a result, she gradually inflicted more severe punishment on him. She started off beating John with a belt. He never objected and never fought back. In time, Yvonne bought a whip and often flogged him until he bled. On the night she lost her cool, she waited until John was dressed only in his shorts. She boiled a large pot of water and liberally doused the shocked man with it.

In the midst of the interrogation, two unusual events took place. Yvonne abruptly asked the detectives to hold her hands and pray with her. While thus engaged, they received a message from the hospital that John Comer had died. Yvonne Kleinfelder was charged with his murder.

A post-mortem revealed a major flaw in Yvonne's story. The area of John's wrists that had been protected by rope had not been scalded, indicating that the boiling water had been thrown on him after he had been bound to the legs of the table. When faced with this information, Yvonne confessed that she had broken John's spirit. He would obey her every command. On the night of the tragedy, she had ordered him to take off his clothing. He complied like a child. She kicked and beat him unmercifully before tying him to the table. Just as the post-mortem revealed, she doused him with the boiling water after he was tied to the table. John was left there to suffer for six days before Yvonne sought help. During that time she did a lot of praying to the devil.

On December 10, 1980, Yvonne Kleinfelder was found guilty of murdering John Comer. She was sentenced to 25 years' imprisonment. After serving 11 years in Illinois's Dixon Correctional Facility, she was paroled on January 14, 1992.

# MARC LEPINE

## MISOGYNISTIC MADMAN

THE Ruger Mini-14 semi-automatic .23-calibre rifle is manufactured in the United States. Each year the Connecticut firm that produces the weapon exports about 2,000 units to Canada. The Ruger has several advantages over other weapons. It weighs only six and a half pounds, is extremely accurate and can hold 50 rounds of ammunition in its magazine. Each one of those 50 rounds contains enough explosive power to hurl a lead slug towards its target at over 3,000 feet per second. The Ruger is an excellent rifle for hunting deer and other game.

On December 6, 1989, Marc Lepine used the rifle to kill fourteen innocent young women in Montreal.

Marc was born Gamil Gharbi to a French-Canadian mother and an Algerian father, Rachid Liass Gharbi. His parents married in 1963, but separated in 1971 when Gamil was seven. There is evidence that the boy was abused by his father, whom he grew to detest. As a teenager he had his name legally changed to Marc Lepine, taking his mother's maiden name. He and his younger sister, Nadia, were raised by their mother.

In school, Marc gained the reputation of being a loner who achieved excellent grades. In reviewing Lepine's history, it appears that he made only half-hearted attempts at carving out a career. He enrolled in a junior college, but didn't complete his studies. He subsequently took a computer course and a course in chemistry, giving up on both these endeavours. He attempted to enlist in the Canadian army, but was turned down. The reason given by army personnel was "anti-social behaviour."

Along the way, Marc Lepine built up a hatred towards women. He rationalized that the army had turned him down because they had relaxed their rules regarding female recruits. In Marc's mind, his rejection by the army was directly caused by women. This phenomenon was nothing new to Marc. His warped reasoning laid all his rejections at the feet of one group—women.

The hatred in Marc's psyche festered until the thought of women taking what he considered men's rightful place in society became his all-encompassing focus. Slowly, a plan took form. Marc began dropping in to a north-end Montreal gun shop. Store employees say he made the usual customer inquiries and didn't appear strange or different in any way. He applied for a firearms-acquisition certificate from the police department. Since he had no criminal record, the permit was duly issued. The Ruger semi-automatic was purchased for $600.

Fifteen days later, unemployed 25-year-old Marc Lepine had chosen his target. This was no spur-of-the-moment decision made by an impaired individual. Marc neither smoked, drank nor used drugs. He had targeted the University of Montreal's L'École Polytechnique. Marc believed that engineering, traditionally a male occupation, was being infiltrated by women, who he perceived to be his personal enemies.

On a cold December day shortly after 5 p.m., Marc Lepine walked into the university building carrying a parcel wrapped in a green garbage bag. Only two days remained before the Christmas vacation would commence and this building would be virtually deserted. Now it was teeming with students, many of them chatting about the imminent Christmas recess.

Marc made his way to the second floor, where he met Maryse Laganière, a 25-year-old employee of the university. Marc shot her dead on the spot. Within a moment, wearing a wry smile across his face, he entered Room 303. Speaking in French, he requested that the women be separated from the men. No one paid much attention. Maybe this was someone's idea of a prank.

Marc, likely sensing that he wasn't being taken seriously, fired two shots into the ceiling. He shouted, "You're all a bunch of feminists and I hate feminists." He went on to instruct the men to leave the room. Over 40 male students walked out of Room 303. As one of the women attempted to reason with Marc, he opened fire with the deadly Ruger. In minutes, the classroom was transformed into an enclosure of carnage. The wounded moaned. Six young women lay dead in crumpled heaps. Operating with cool determination, Marc descended to the first floor, entered the school cafeteria and opened fire. In an instant, three women were murdered.

The gunman's mission was still not complete. He climbed two flights of stairs to the third floor. Students and professors alike were unaware that a man with a rifle was on a rampage. When Marc entered Room 311 and opened fire, the terror-stricken occupants desperately attempted to find some protection under desks and behind anything that would afford them cover. There was no escape. Marc sought them out. Leaping from desk to desk, he kept on shooting. Four more young women lay dead among the wounded.

Then, according to those close by, Marc uttered an expletive and shot himself in the head, killing himself instantly. In his wake he left 14 young women dead and 13 wounded. The carnage he wreaked that day took the lives of Geneviève Bergeron, 21; Hélène Colgan, 23; Nathalie Croteau, 23; Barbara Daigneault, 22; Anne-Marie Edward, 21; Maud Haviernick, 29; Maryse Leclair, 23; Annie St. Arsenault, 23; Barbara Marie Clueznick, 31; Maryse Laganière, 25; Anne-Marie Lemay, 27; Sonia Pelletier, 28; Michèle Richard, 21; and Annie Turcotte, 21.

With the exception of Albert Guay, who was instrumental in placing a bomb on an aircraft in 1949, killing all 23 aboard, the Lepine rampage was Canada's worst mass murder. The city of Montreal and the entire country were aghast at the cold-blooded killings.

As the bodies were removed and the wounded were attended to, no one could even guess at the killer's motive. But Lepine had taken care of that detail. He had left a three-page letter outlining his reasons for the mass killings. His last message to the world blamed feminists for all his personal ills and indeed the ills of the world. It also contained a chilling future hit list of 15 women who had achieved acclaim, many of them in occupations traditionally held by men.

And so it was left for survivors to bury their dead—young talented women with a lifetime ahead of them, whose lives were so tragically taken away while attending school.

At Notre Dame Basilica, Paul Cardinal Gregoire described the horror best as his voice rained down over nine of the coffins of the slain. "Fourteen youths were brutally mowed down in the beauty of their youth. In a few moments, a hopeless and vicious act of another young person was sufficient to destroy all the dreams and all the promises. Your daughters, your sisters, your friends, the future engineers over whom we weep, chose to be builders of society—in memory of them, in solidarity with them, you must strive to build a world of friendship. I ask God to give them peace."

Among the thousands overflowing the basilica were the mayor of Montreal, the premier of Quebec and the prime minister of Canada.

# ELMER LORD

## THEY FOUND THE KILLER IN THE TRUNK

MURDERERS never seem to learn that steamer trunks are cumbersome things designed to carry clothing rather than bodies.

Aletha Patterson stared down at the ominous trunk giving off the strange odour. It had been a busy day for Aletha. She had received notice months earlier that one of the rooming houses she managed, a four-storey brick structure on Third Street in Washington, D.C., was to be demolished to make room for a parking lot. All the tenants had been given notice weeks earlier. Some had decided to move to another building Aletha oversaw, while others had informed her that they would be seeking accommodation elsewhere.

With the help of superintendent Elmer Lord, Aletha supervised the professional movers who were busily loading furniture to be removed to the new building on Twelfth Street. Elmer, who hailed from England, was an efficient, conscientious employee.

It was the movers who brought the trunk to Aletha's attention. She couldn't remember having seen the trunk before. It bore no tags, but had the words "This Side Up" printed on the top in white chalk. Aletha called police. At around 11 a.m., September 12, 1952, two officers arrived at the rooming house. They pried open the trunk and peered inside. There reposed the decaying body of an adult male.

The body was immediately transferred to the morgue, where an autopsy was performed. The dead man had been about 60 years of age. He had received three powerful blows to the head with a blunt instrument. Any one of the three blows could have caused death. There was nothing in the man's pockets to assist in identifying him. He had been dead for about three months.

Detectives questioned Aletha and Elmer. Both stated that none of their roomers had disappeared, but there were a few who had not made the move with them. These roomers were traced and cleared of any complicity in the crime. Aletha and Elmer viewed the body, but claimed they couldn't identify the badly decomposed corpse. They were asked to search their memories for any unusual event which had occurred three months earlier.

Elmer remembered a Marine, accompanied by his wife, who had inquired about a room about three months earlier. The Marine had required a room for one night only and had lugged along a trunk. This type of inquiry may be considered odd in other cities, but in Washington, where servicemen and government employees are constantly on the move, it is rather routine. Elmer recalled the Marine's name, William Schmidt, because he once had an employee by that name. Schmidt had left his trunk in his room and had told Elmer that he would send around a mover for it the next day. That's the last Elmer saw of the Marine or his trunk.

Detectives elicited the assistance of the military. They were soon informed that there were 11 William Schmidts in the Marine Corps and that two lived near Washington. Both these men were checked, but were able to establish their innocence. Neither matched the description of the William Schmidt who had rented the room from Elmer.

The empty house on Third Street was thoroughly searched. Police found a locked closet door on the third floor. Someone had nailed the door shut with new nails and sealed it with putty. Investigating officers had the premonition that more bodies would be uncovered behind that door, but such was not the case. When the door was broken down, the closet was empty, but a sickening odour similar to the one that had emanated from the trunk was evident.

Detectives were stymied. Why would someone go to so much trouble to secure an empty closet? Had the closet provided a hiding place for a body which had been removed? If so, why nail it shut and seal it with putty?

Once more, Aletha and Elmer were asked to try to remember anything out of the ordinary. Aletha mentioned that the man who had previously held Elmer's job had left suddenly three months earlier. Retired pensioner Frank Moore had told Aletha he was going to Baltimore. Moore had left without turning in some of the rent money he had collected.

A short time after Moore's departure, Elmer Lord had asked Aletha for the man's job. She was more than happy to have the rather aristocratic Elmer look after the place and collect the rents.

Was it possible that Frank Moore had killed someone and left for parts unknown? Moore was checked out. He had never been in any trouble and had been an upstanding citizen, well liked by all. His sister, living in Arlington, Virginia, was appalled that anyone would think her brother would steal rent money, let alone commit a murder. She had another theory. Her brother had been in the habit of phoning her every week, but had stopped abruptly about three months earlier. Maybe, he was the victim rather than the murderer.

Frank Moore's sister viewed the body. She positively identified her brother. She even recognized his shirt, which she had given him as a gift.

The murder victim had been identified, but police were no closer to solving the crime. They were convinced that the killer had lived in the Third Street rooming house. Every roomer who had lived in the house three months earlier was found and questioned again without concrete results.

At a police meeting concerning the case, one detective theorized that if the killer had been an occupant of the house, he may have purchased the putty and nails from a nearby store. It was decided to canvass every store that sold such items within a 10-square-block area.

It took two days before weary detectives hit pay dirt. An alert store clerk remembered selling nails and putty to a man earlier that summer. She recalled the sale because the man had asked a lot of questions about the relative merits of plaster of Paris and putty. He had wanted to know which product cracked more easily. He had also purchased a small hatchet. She especially remembered the man because he spoke so elegantly, with an English accent.

Bingo! Why had no one thought of him before? Elmer Lord. The man in the case who appeared to be above suspicion.

Detectives obtained a search warrant before speeding over to Elmer's new quarters on Twelfth Street. Elmer greeted the familiar officers in his usual polite way. "Now what can I do for you?" The detectives' reply was a bit of a shock to staid Elmer, "You can tell us why you murdered Frank Moore. That would help a lot."

The flustered man attempted to bluff his way out of his predicament. He accused the officers of being lunatics to even suggest such a thing, but they produced a search warrant and proceeded to search Elmer's rooms. From a cardboard box, they extracted what was left of a can of putty, some new nails, a pair of bloodstained cotton gloves and a blood-caked hatchet.

Elmer slumped into a chair, sighing, "I'm not an accomplished killer, I guess." He went on to confess that on June 2, he had gone to Moore's room to join him for breakfast, which he did often. According to Elmer, the two men had argued over a trivial matter. During the argument, Frank had thrown a hatchet at him, but missed. Elmer threw it back at Moore, striking him in the head and killing him instantly. The police listened, but discounted much of Elmer's story, which was not compatible with the autopsy report.

Elmer went on to say that he had dragged Moore's body to the hall closet, where it remained for three months. He had nailed the door shut and had sealed it with putty when the odour became noticeable. He then asked for and got Moore's job. In September, when Aletha informed him that they had to move to another house, he was beside himself with worry. All he could think of was that body in the closet. By chance, he had found an old trunk in the basement. Being superintendent of the building, he knew the times when he wouldn't be seen or disturbed. He had lugged the trunk to the closet, had broken open the door and had placed the body inside. Later, the trunk was put in the hall to be moved by professional movers.

Elmer had nailed back the closet door and sealed all cracks with putty, hoping that this would keep the odour in the closet. Unfortunately for him, the movers became suspicious of the trunk. He had planned on depositing it in the basement of his new home. Had he succeeded, his crime might never have been discovered.

On March 19, 1953, Elmer Lord stood trial for the murder of Frank Moore. He insisted that the killing was not premeditated and evidently the jury believed him. He was found guilty of second-degree murder and sentenced to 7 to 21 years' imprisonment. He has long since been paroled.

# GRACE LUSK

## LOVE TRIANGLE

---

LET me introduce you to Grace Lusk. You will like her. Everyone did in Waukesha, Wisconsin.

Amazing Grace was an attractive schoolteacher who, in many ways, was perfect. She was intelligent, highly educated, a snappy dresser in the style of 1913 and a real looker. She also had the figure to go with her many admirable attributes. There was one thing though. Nearing 30 years of age, our Grace lacked an experience which many girls of far more tender years have taken part in and, yes, even enjoyed. You see, Grace Lusk was a virgin.

Grace was introduced to 50-year-old Dr. David Roberts at a dinner party. The veterinarian, in partnership with L.D. Blott, owned the David Roberts Veterinary Co., a flourishing local business whose main products were a line of medical remedies for cattle in distress. In addition, the doctor owned a breeding farm and a dairy. He also owned Mrs. Roberts. No one had a bad word to say about Mrs. Roberts. Nobody ever does. But let's get back to Grace and Dr. Dave.

The virginal schoolteacher found the handsome doctor nigh on irresistible. One day she required some information about various cattle breeds to impart to her students. She found the doctor most accommodating in this regard. That's how it started—a gently squeezed hand—a stolen kiss, and then that most intimate of all acts took place. I mean, over and over again.

Grace was thrilled and excited with this new sensual experience which had eluded her all of her 30 years. Dave told her he loved her dearly. It would be only a matter of time before he would divorce his wife, marry her and they would live happily ever after. But that time never seemed to roll around.

Dave the Knave was burning the candle at both ends, so to speak. He had no intention of leaving his wife. After all, the Roberts family was well respected. Mrs. Roberts was a wheel down at the church. No, a man of his looks, charm and sexual prowess would service both women; something like the stallions at his breeding farm.

But Grace had been put off for too long. When the sizzling affair was in its fourth year, she decided to have it out with Dave. One evening, while comfortably ensconced in a hotel room, she confronted him, stating that he had to tell his wife, Mary, of their love. Grace wanted to know then and there if she had been deceived. She explained that first her education and then her teaching career had occupied all her time and thoughts until she'd met him. Now her life had been terribly disrupted. If he didn't truly love her, she wanted to know now. If he did love her as he claimed, it was only fair to them all that he inform his wife of the truth and ask for a divorce.

Can't you just see Dave wiping the perspiration off his forehead? Once more, he told Grace he would tell his wife soon. Not good enough, said Grace. She pulled a revolver out of her purse and commanded Dave to put his hand on a Gideon bible and swear he would tell his wife of their love that very night. Dave's hand couldn't wait to spread-eagle on that bible.

Moments later, the lovers embraced and did what lovers do. Now in a somewhat better mood, Grace accepted Dave's latest proposition, namely, that he would tell his wife about them by June 15.

Dr. Dave Roberts had a problem. He had to get rid of Grace, but just how was another matter. Grace moved things along a bit when she wrote a letter to Mary Roberts, insinuating that Mary's husband would be approaching her shortly over a delicate subject involving Grace and the good doctor. Mrs. Roberts received the letter and was somewhat puzzled. She had never in her wildest imagination suspected that her husband had been unfaithful. She confronted Dave, who passed off the letter as being from a girl who was making a bit of a nuisance of herself.

Undaunted, Grace wrote another letter, a much more explicit letter. This time, Mary Roberts had to take notice. She insisted on meeting with this girl whom she thought was chasing her husband. Dave could no longer persuade her that their relationship was nothing more than an infatuation.

On June 21, 1917, Mary Roberts took the bull by the horns and visited Grace at her rooming house. The adversaries stood face-to-face, eyeball-to-eyeball. Mary's opening gambit was simple and to the point. She wanted the younger woman to withdraw. Grace countered with the claim that Dave truly loved her and that should be the deciding factor.

Despite Mary's pious nature, she let fly some very unladylike remarks. Regaining her composure, she suggested that the proof of the pudding is in the eating. She called Dave at home and told him to get right over there and repeat his words about Grace being a nuisance.

As had become his habit, Dave rubbed the perspiration from his forehead. He knew he had to do something. He picked up his business partner, L.D. Blott, and drove over to Grace's place. As they approached, they heard the loud reports of two shots. Dave, scared out of his wits, told Blott to go and see what was happening. Blott, also a tad apprehensive, peeked in through a window. There, on the floor, was Mary Roberts with two bullets in her side. Blott ran back to Dave, who quickly called a doctor and police. Dr. Davies was the first to arrive at the scene. He examined Mary Roberts and declared that she was dead.

The doctor, completely occupied with the dead woman at his feet, looked up to see Grace at the top of the stairs. Not quite grasping the situation, Dr. Davies told Grace that Mrs. Roberts was dead. It was only then that he noticed the trickle of blood seeping from Grace's left breast. Later, he would learn that the wound was self-inflicted, but at the time the doctor had other problems.

Grace, who he now figured had killed Mrs. Roberts and turned the weapon on herself, was loosely holding a revolver in her right hand. He made a gesture forward, as if to approach Grace, but stopped abruptly when she commanded, "If you come up, I'll shoot."

Dr. Davies talked quietly to Grace, attempting to calm her down. He succeeded somewhat as Grace rambled on about her reasons for the shooting. She related that Dave had told her repeatedly that he loved her only and how he had sworn on a bible that he would tell his wife everything by June 15. She even reminded Dr. Davies that it was the twenty-first, making Dave delinquent by six days. Grace said that she had given Dave an out. She had told him that if he really didn't love her, he could call off the whole thing. The cad had sworn that she was his true love and that he had no feelings for his wife.

At the conclusion of her yarn, Grace inquired of the doctor as to the location of the heart. Dr. Davies pointed to the area. Grace then turned and hurried to her bedroom. The doctor heard a shot and rushed to her side. Whatever qualities Grace possessed, accuracy was not one of them. She had missed killing herself for the second time that evening.

The semiconscious Grace was removed on a stretcher. She was able to say, "I am so strange. I love him still."

The love triangle and its tragic conclusion was the most exciting event ever to take place in Waukesha. People took sides. Some felt that Grace deserved the worst for killing churchgoing Mary Roberts, and even expressed disappointment at Grace's poor aim. Others felt that Dave Roberts was the culprit of the entire piece.

Grace stood trial for the murder of Mary Roberts. She was found guilty of murder in the second degree. When the foreman of the jury read out the verdict,

Grace didn't swoon or burst into tears. She sprang from her seat and clutched the neck of the prosecuting attorney until court officials pried her hands from his neck. She had to be forcibly removed from the courtroom.

Grace was sentenced to 19 years' hard labour at the Wisconsin State Prison at Waupun, with the stipulation that every June 21 be spent in solitary confinement.

In January 1923, after serving five years of her sentence, Grace Lusk received a pardon from Wisconsin governor John J. Blaine. She moved to a southern state where she died of natural causes in 1930. As for Dr. David Roberts, he remarried and lived out the rest of his days in relative comfort and contentment.

# LEE ROY MARTIN

## TERROR IN A SMALL TOWN

NO one wanted to listen to Roger Dedmond. It was one of those cases where everyone was convinced he'd killed his wife.

Roger's strange saga began on March 1, 1967, when he and his wife were spending an evening in a nightclub near the town of Gaffney, South Carolina. Twenty-eight-year-old Roger was downing whiskey straight up with beer chasers. He and his wife, Ann Lucille, began quarrelling, which wasn't unusual. It seemed every time the young couple had a few drinks they would sort of agree to disagree.

Ann Lucille became so angry that, at one point, she flailed out at Roger and scratched his face. As the evening wore on, the couple reconciled and decided to get a bite to eat. They drove to a doughnut shop. Roger left his vehicle, purchased doughnuts and coffee and returned to find that his wife had driven off in the car. This might cause the average husband some concern, but Ann Lucille often pulled such capers, especially when she was a bit tipsy or angry or both.

Next morning, Roger Dedmond was informed that his wife had been murdered. Her body had been found in the centre of the highway, between the towns of Union, South Carolina, and Spindale, North Carolina. Roger was picked up as the logical suspect and tried for the murder of his wife.

He stuck to his story of her disappearance at the doughnut shop. It was an unlikely tale, especially since police officers swore that Roger had confessed his guilt to them when he was taken into custody. He admitted that he had argued with Ann Lucille and that she had scratched him, but swore that he had had nothing to do with her death. The jury preferred to believe the police and found Roger Dedmond guilty of manslaughter. He was sentenced to 18 years' imprisonment. Roger was hustled off to the Union County Prison Camp and that, to all intents and purposes, was that.

Two months passed. On February 8, 1968, Bill Gibbons, the managing editor of the local newspaper, the *Gaffney Ledger,* received a most unusual phone call. The caller assured Gibbons that this was not a crank call. He gave explicit instructions, informing the startled newsman where two female bodies could be found. He also stated that he was the killer of Ann Lucille Dedmond. Then the caller hung up.

Gibbons believed that the man was a crank, but stranger things have happened. He called the local sheriff and together they followed the phantom caller's instructions. Sure enough, near a bridge over People's Creek, just as the caller had said, lay the body of a nude female. The body was quickly identified as that of Nancy Parris, a 26-year-old housewife who had been reported missing while walking her poodle the previous day. The back of the body bore signs of having been burned by cigarettes. An autopsy revealed strangulation to be the cause of death.

Additional officers were requested to trace the second body. In the exact location indicated by the caller, police found the nude body of 14-year-old Nancy Rhinehart. She too bore cigarette burns and she too had been strangled. Nancy had been reported missing by her mother 10 days earlier. Both victims had been murdered within 24 hours of the time they had been found. Investigators theorized that Nancy Rhinehart had been held captive for 10 days before being killed.

The news that two female bodies had been found in the Gaffney area spread terror throughout Union County. There was also the distinct possibility that the same man had killed Ann Lucille Dedmond.

Was some maniac on a killing spree and was he now playing a macabre game? Most serial killers distance themselves from their victims and make every effort to escape detection, but there have been exceptions. David Berkowitz, also known as Son of Sam, wrote to a newspaper. Jack the Ripper wrote letters to the police. Did their counterpart in peaceful Gaffney demand recognition for his kills? Had he not made the phone call to the newspaper, the bodies of his two latest victims might never have been found.

Citizens in the area bought locks and guns. In the two days after the bodies were discovered, the main hardware store in Gaffney sold 200 guns, all they had in stock. Five days later, on February 13, 1968, 15-year-old Opal Buckson was walking the quarter mile from her home to the bus stop to catch her lift to school in Gaffney. Her brother and sister, Gracie, had not been as fast as Opal in completing their chores, and as a result trailed along behind their sister.

It was Gracie who noticed the man who grabbed Opal and forced her into the trunk of his blue sedan. Gracie was about 50 yards away. She couldn't believe her eyes. Opal screamed and so did Gracie, but the man managed to slam his trunk closed and drove away with the teenage schoolgirl. Gracie's brother ran home and told his father what had happened.

Emanual Buckson ran down the road and found his daughter's schoolbooks spread across the highway. He also recovered one of Opal's shoes. Investigators interviewed all the principals involved and concluded that this latest abduction was most probably connected to the man who had committed the two previous murders.

Police revealed to the public that Bill Gibbons had received another call from the alleged killer on the day before Opal's kidnapping. Gibbons was certain it was the same voice that had directed him to the two bodies. This time the mystery caller said, "If they don't catch me, there will be more deaths." He also emphatically stated again that he was the killer of Ann Lucille Dedmond. When Gibbons attempted to talk the man into giving himself up, the caller responded, "It's no use. I'm psycho and I'd get the chair. They'll have to shoot me like the dog I am. The only reason I'm telling you all this is to get that other boy out of prison. He's serving my sentence."

Gibbons kept the man on the line. He inquired about the fate of Nancy Parris's poodle. The caller claimed he had killed the dog, but not at the location where the body had been found. He had killed Nancy and her poodle in one location, but had moved her body. He would not say where the dog could be located because he had left tire tracks there that could be traced to him.

During the same call, the killer told Gibbons how he had stopped Ann Lucille Dedmond as she drove erratically down the road. He had been trailing the Dedmonds from the time they had left the nightclub. He also described what she had been wearing and gave several details only the killer could know. Once detectives heard Gibbons's story, there was no doubt whatever that an innocent man was in prison serving time for a crime he had not committed.

On February 15, two days after Opal's kidnapping, hundreds of citizens of Union County were searching for the girl. Two of the searchers, Theodore Lang and Frank Henders, were cruising the back roads of the county looking for anything suspicious. They spotted a man standing beside a vehicle. The stranger quickly drove away. Lang and Henders thought he was behaving suspiciously and managed to obtain the licence number of the vehicle. They passed along the information to the sheriff's office.

That same day, detectives drove out to the spot where Lang and Henders had observed the man standing beside his car. One of the officers noted a quantity of fresh pine needles protruding from under a dead log. To the trained officer, the scene didn't look natural. Debris and branches were removed, uncovering the bare legs of Opal Buckson. Her body bore the tell-tale cigarette burns. Opal, like the other victims, had been strangled.

By the time Opal's body was found, the licence number of the suspect's vehicle had been checked. The car belonged to a local man, Lee Roy Martin, a 30-year-old textile worker. Martin seemed to be an unlikely serial killer. He was a steady, hard-working family man, whose wife refused to believe that her husband was anything but what he appeared to be. But Lee Roy Martin heard voices. He claimed it wasn't him who had killed the four women, but another Lee Roy. Martin led police to the victims' clothing and to the corpse of Nancy Parris's poodle. He was found guilty of four counts of murder and received four life sentences. After serving three years in prison, he was murdered by a fellow inmate.

Roger Dedmond was released from prison after serving one year. Today, he is in the construction business in North Carolina.

# MARCUS MARYMONT

## TORRID AFFAIR LED TO MURDER

MARCUS Marymont had always wanted a military career. As a teenager he was a member of the California National Guard. In 1937, he joined the U.S. Army and later transferred to the air force.

Mark was born in Oakland, California, the product of an average home. He did well in school and was never in any trouble. Mark's decision to make the military a lifelong career appeared to be a wise one. He served in the United States, Japan and Korea before being transferred to the U.S. air force base in Scunthorpe, England.

Mark's career in the service was distinguished. In all, he was the recipient of 13 medals, the most notable being the Soldiers Medal. In 1941, while serving in Alaska, Mark had saved a man from a burning ship without regard for his own safety. Along the way, he married, had three children and received several promotions before achieving the rank of master sergeant.

In 1956, we find Master Sergeant Marcus Marymont, a family man approaching middle age, stationed in England with his stable, rewarding career well established. Wouldn't you just know it, Mark walked into a shop in Maidenhead one day and met Mrs. Cynthia Taylor. Cynthia was a cute 23-year-old with a charming smile and a gorgeous figure.

There stood the sarge, resplendent in his crisp uniform, fit as a fiddle. Thoughts of his 43-year-old wife, Mary, and the three young ones at home didn't enter his head. Whatever chemistry takes place between members of the opposite sex boiled and seethed within Mark and Cynthia on that fateful day. As luck would have it, Cynthia was separated from her husband.

Let me spare you the titillating details. Suffice it to say, Mark, who was 37 when he met Cynthia, should have known better. Within weeks, they were lovers. The opportunities for lovemaking posed something of a problem. After all, Mary and the three kids lived close to the base. Despite this inconvenience, Mark and Cynthia never let two weeks pass without bedding down, either at her digs or at a convenient hotel.

We all know that such a relationship cannot last forever. In the normal course of human endeavour, something usually has to give. The lovers managed to continue their affair for two years before things came to an abrupt end.

On June 9, 1958, Mary Marymont died in hospital. A little over a month later, Mark was charged with her murder. Being a member of the U.S. Armed Forces, he was tried by a U.S. general court martial at Denham, England. It was alleged that he had poisoned his wife with arsenic because he was in love with Cynthia Taylor.

A doctor testified that Mary had been brought to the hospital in critical condition. Mark had told the doctor that his wife had taken ill at about 9 p.m. the previous evening. He had fetched her some medicine from the hospital, but in the morning she was much worse and he had her removed to hospital. Another doctor who had attended Mary before she died was aware that she had been sick off and on for the past year. He suspected that she had been poisoned, but when he mentioned it to another doctor, he was told, "You have been reading too many magazines."

After Mary's death, the doctor spoke to Mark about an autopsy. Initially, he agreed, but later said that in deference to his children he didn't want his wife's body disfigured. Nevertheless, an autopsy was performed. It indicated that Mary had received a large dose of arsenic within 24 hours of her death, as well as quantities of arsenic a month or two before her death. Marcus was arrested and charged with her murder.

Renowned pathologist Dr. Francis Camps was called as an expert witness at the trial. He confirmed that there was no doubt whatever that Mrs. Marymont's death had been caused by arsenic poisoning.

At this stage of the trial, the prosecution had firmly established the cause of death. They then went about proving that the accused had had access to arsenic. Two civilian cleaners at the air force base testified that about a month before the murder, they had seen a master sergeant in the base's chemical lab, where arsenic was kept. According to the cleaners, the sergeant had said, "There's a lot of chemicals on these shelves. There's even arsenic." The cleaners had agreed. The sergeant inquired, "Don't they lock this stuff up?" The cleaners told him that they didn't. They identified the sergeant as Mark Marymont.

A pharmacist in Maidenhead, Bernard Sampson, testified that on May 23, only weeks before Mary Marymont's demise, Mark had attempted to purchase arsenic from him. When Sampson told the sergeant that he had to have a police form made out before he could sell Marymont the poison, the sergeant thanked him and left the shop.

Brick by brick, the prosecution was building a formidable case, but the juicy motive for murder was left for the principals to reveal from the witness box. Mark took the stand and admitted to his prolonged affair with Cynthia. He told the court that he had met and made love to her at every opportunity.

Whatever else Mark said, nothing had the impact of his statement that he had left his wife and children over the Christmas season of 1957 to spend it shacked up with Cynthia. Honestly, folks, you just don't do that. But wait, there was more. After Mary had gone to her great reward, Mark had waited only four days before rushing to the ever-loving arms of Cynthia Taylor. For shame!

Sixty-nine letters written by Cynthia to Mark were introduced into evidence. They smouldered with expressions of undying love. These letters had been found in Mark's desk at the air force base. A prosecution lawyer made much of the fact that Mark hadn't destroyed them. He theorized that the accused had had no reason to destroy the letters because he had firmly believed he would never be accused of murder.

In summing up, the prosecution further theorized that Mark had been feeding arsenic to his wife for months to establish the fact that she was in ill health. On June 9, he had gone to the hospital to procure medicine, into which he had mixed a fatal dose of arsenic.

It must be pointed out that Cynthia Taylor did not know Mark was a married man. They had often talked about marriage, but not too seriously, because her estranged husband wouldn't grant her a divorce. She claimed that Mark had promised to adopt her baby son, Chris, when they did marry.

Defence attorneys acknowledged Mark's affair with Cynthia, but presented another theory in regard to Mary's death. They produced a witness, Marion Conway, the wife of another master sergeant. She swore that Mary had confided in her that she was aware of her husband's affair. Mrs. Conway told the court, "She was under a terrific emotional pressure because, she said, she minded terribly to think of her husband making love to someone else, then coming home and making love to her. She felt she almost couldn't stand it." In this way, defence counsel put forth the theory that Mary Marymont had become despondent and had committed suicide.

Mark admitted to having chatted with the cleaners in the chemical lab, but surely that was not proof of guilt. He swore he had never been in Bernard Sampson's pharmacy and claimed that Sampson must be mistaken. Under cross-examination, the pharmacist admitted that the sergeant had not been in his shop more than 10 seconds.

In the end, Sergeant Marymont was found guilty. He stood at attention and heard the sentence read by Colonel Albert Snider: "It is my duty as President of this Court to inform you that the Court in closed session and upon secret written ballots, three fourths of the members present concurring, sentences you to be dishonorably discharged, forfeit all pay and allowances and be confined to hard labour for the term of your natural life." Master Sergeant Marcus Marymont was returned to the United States and incarcerated at Fort Leavenworth Prison to serve his sentence.

# DONALD MASON

## PROPER YOUNG MAN KILLED HIS WIFE

DONALD Mason was a proper young man raised in a proper religious family. Smoking, drinking and cursing were what other boys did, not Don. The Bible was the word of God and the Good Book was the most influential factor in his life. Sex before marriage was unthinkable.

Don met Ruth Ragatz, a stunning blond, at a church convention. Don was smitten, but there was a complication. Ruth was seeing another boy. However, she and Don continued to see each other at church functions until finally Ruth terminated her relationship with Don's rival. The pair married in July 1983.

The honeymoon preyed on Don's mind. Although he had been a virgin, he discovered that Ruth was not. The thought of his wife in bed with another man festered in his mind. He couldn't get it out of his head. As the months wore on, he began to worry that since Ruth had not been chaste before their marriage, how could he be sure she had been faithful since their wedding day.

Three years of doubts and suspicions passed. Don thought of divorce, but with his religious background that was out of the question. There was another way; he would murder his wife. (Apparently, his religious background didn't hinder that decision.) Lesser men than he had committed murder and avoided detection. Murder was definitely the answer to his dilemma. He would plan the details and he would kill his wife. It would be the perfect murder.

In October 1986, Don took out a life insurance policy for $100,000 and one on Ruth's life for the same amount. The scheme would not only be perfect, it would pay handsomely as well.

Don was 27 years old. He and Ruth lived in a trailer park in Plattekill, New York. Both worked at the AT&T complex in Ramapo. They were well liked, conscientious employees. No one knew what dark thoughts Don Mason harboured in his warped mind.

In March 1987, Don underwent a hernia operation and was off work for a couple of weeks. What an opportune time to put his well-thought-out plan into action. He would use a belt to strangle Ruth. No gun, no knife, no discernible murder weapon. How clever, Don thought. It would look like a robbery with sexual assault as an afterthought. He would receive sympathy from friends and co-workers, even some police officers, whom he knew personally.

On Tuesday, March 24, after Ruth came home from work, Don playfully told her, "Turn around and close your eyes." Ruth may have thought she was about to be given an unexpected present. When she turned her back, he quickly looped a belt around her neck and pulled tight. Ruth, eyes bulging, managed to turn around. She scratched at Don's face, but it was no use. He pulled tighter until Ruth stopped breathing.

Don bent over his wife and ripped jewellery from her body. Then he dragged her out to her car. It was tough sledding. After all, Don had recently had a hernia operation and he didn't want to dislodge his stitches. Soon, he was speeding along the thruway. As far as any onlooker was concerned, it seemed as if Ruth was catching a few winks in the passenger seat. At the toll booths, no one gave them a second glance.

Don pulled into the Caldor Shopping Centre in Ramapo and drove up beside a trash-disposal unit behind the Shop-Rite Supermarket back door. He dragged his wife's body out of the car. Don realized one thing had gone wrong, but there was nothing he could do about that now. Ruth had managed to scratch his face. Systematically, Don went about breaking Ruth's fingernails, knowing that it was his flesh under those nails. It was a tedious task and dangerous, too. Someone could walk out of the Shop-Rite at any moment. Don quit breaking the nails. He ripped at Ruth's blouse and tore away her brassiere. Then he pulled down her pantyhose. Working frantically now, he removed her coat and purse before driving away.

It had all gone smoothly. Don drove Ruth's car to the parking lot of a King Kullen Supermarket in Suffern, where he transferred to a rented car he had previously placed there. As he approached his home at the trailer park, he threw away Ruth's coat and purse along with the belt he had used to kill her.

Don washed his hands and face. It was time to prepare a hot meal for Ruth. After all, since he was recuperating from his hernia operation, he had been in the habit of preparing the evening meal. It was the least he could do.

That evening, Don called a friend, Bob Parks. Don was concerned. Ruth hadn't come home from work. He and Bob drove around looking for Ruth's Chevy Sprint, but couldn't locate it. The folks at AT&T told him she had left the facility at 5:30 p.m. Don called the police, but they said they couldn't do anything for 24 hours.

Next morning, Don Mason was beside himself with worry. Tearfully, he reported his wife missing to the Ramapo police. Within an hour a truck driver making a delivery to the Shop-Rite Supermarket came across the body of Ruth Mason. As soon as she was identified by an AT&T employee, a detective informed Don that his wife had been murdered. He burst into tears.

That night, Ruth's car was found. Nothing of importance was discovered in the vehicle, but its location puzzled investigators. Who would dump a body where it could be found at any moment and then abandon the victim's car some miles away? It appeared to investigators that the killer would have to have had a second car in order to get away from the shopping centre where Ruth's Chevy was found. It just didn't add up. Was rape the motive or was it robbery, or as sometimes happens, a combination of both? Why take the dead woman's purse? Where had she been attacked?

Don Mason, understandably distraught, was requested to visit the Ramapo police station to assist police. Detectives couldn't help noticing the scratch on his face, but didn't comment about it at the time. An autopsy performed that same day indicated that Ruth had not been raped. Death was attributed to asphyxiation due to ligature strangulation. It was believed that the murder weapon was something smooth, like a belt.

One of the detectives mentioned that Don would be wise to have the doctor who had just performed the autopsy take a look at that nasty scratch on his face. Don agreed. The doctor treated the scratch and informed detectives that it had been made by a fingernail and was surrounded by cosmetic makeup. Don told police he didn't remember how he had received the scratch, but admitted that he had applied makeup so the scratch wouldn't be so noticeable.

Detectives believed that Don Mason had killed his wife. They asked him to agree to a polygraph test and were surprised when he quickly acquiesced.

While waiting for arrangements for the test to be finalized, one of the detectives informed Don that his version of his wife's disappearance didn't make sense. Don surprised those present by blurting out, "I killed her. I did it in our trailer as soon as she came home from work." He went on to tell of his obsession that his wife was unfaithful. The thought had eaten away at his mind until he had turned to murder to solve his problem. He told detectives that he had hidden his wife's jewellery and a $100,000 life insurance policy under his bed.

Don wondered out loud whether he would have gotten away with murder had Ruth not scratched him. No one told him that his credit card had already been traced to the agency where he had rented the getaway car.

Don Mason pleaded guilty to his wife's murder. He was sentenced to a term of 22 years to life in prison.

# MARY KAY MCKINLEY

## LITTLE SISTERS

IT'S sort of an unwritten law and is in decidedly poor taste to make love to two sisters at the same time. John Cassidy of the western Pennsylvania town of Monongahela didn't believe in written or unwritten laws. He had known Mary Kay and Bonnie McKinley all their lives. While they were still in their early teens, he had had intercourse with both sisters. John married Mary Kay when she turned 17.

Despite the wedding, complete with whiskey and dainty sandwiches, John simply couldn't get Bonnie out of his mind. Darn it all, what's so wrong about a man bedding down with two women? The more he thought about it, the more it made sense. John sat Mary Kay and Bonnie down and told them his plan. He would stay legally married to Mary Kay, but wanted Bonnie to move into their home and share their bed. Well, son of a gun, the girls didn't think the idea half-bad. Just as they had shared treats as little girls, they would now share a husband. Bonnie moved in and everyone was as happy as a lark.

Both sisters proceeded to have children. Mary Kay had five and Bonnie, four. John, the rascal, fathered an additional child by a third woman who doesn't enter our racy tale other than to provide a tenth child to the Cassidy household. It got so crowded around the house that John purchased a second home, in which he installed Bonnie and their four offspring. John split his lovemaking between the two homes on a time-sharing basis. This rather pleasant arrangement continued for 12 years and might have gone on indefinitely, except for one thing. John committed suicide.

On February 12, 1991, the sisters and the 10 children were saddened by this untimely circumstance. Mary Kay found John with half his head blown off. Evidently he had placed the barrel of a shotgun under his chin and fired away. Both wives, er… sisters, attended the funeral, as did all 10 children. Everyone wept.

The local coroner officially labelled the death as suicide, although he was puzzled after receiving an anonymous call from a woman who insisted John's demise was something more than suicide. Without evidence to the contrary, the coroner stuck to his original cause of death.

A month after the funeral, Bonnie drove to the closest state police office in Belle Vernon with a story to tell. It was she who had called the coroner. She had something on her mind and had to tell someone. Bonnie said that some time before John's death, he and she had purchased a telephone tape recorder and had installed it on his own line in the basement of his and Mary Kay's home. John had told her that he suspected that his 29-year-old wife was having an affair with a 17-year-old local boy, David Bowers. Bonnie passed over the tape, which was played then and there. It was a conversation between young Bowers and Mary Kay in which they expressed undying love for each other and plotted to kill John.

The police well realized that under Pennsylvania law recorded conversations cannot be used as evidence, yet they had no intention of letting a murderer go unpunished. They asked Mary Kay to drive over to the police station. Once there, officers explained the situation to her and played a couple of minutes of the tape. Mary Kay burst into tears and confessed to her husband's murder.

According to Mary Kay, she had often been abused by John, particularly when he was in his cups. On the night of the murder, he had been drunk and had passed out on a couch in the living room. Mary Kay believed that she had only one chance at happiness and that was to kill her abusive husband and latch on to her 17-year-old lover. She would begin a new life. Mary Kay thought of the ramifications, but all things considered, decided to go through with the murder. David had agreed that it was the only sensible thing to do and had instructed her on how to murder her husband.

Mary Kay pulled the trigger. Then she did what many self-respecting killers have done before her. She dialled 911. Based on Mary Kay's story, she and David Bowers were arrested.

The district attorney had a problem. In custody were two individuals who had planned and carried out a cold-blooded murder, yet the prosecution's case was flimsy because the tape recording couldn't be used as evidence. Since the subsequent confession had been given based on the few minutes the tape had been played for the accused, it too might very well be inadmissible as evidence.

It was plea-bargaining time. In the case of Mary Kay, the D.A. agreed that in return for a guilty plea, the charge would be reduced from first-degree murder to third-degree, which carried only a 5- to 10-year prison sentence. In addition, Mary Kay agreed to testify against David Bowers.

She revealed that her romance with David began years before when he used to call early in the morning to go hunting with her husband. A little kiss led to a little hug and a little hug led all the way to bed or a convenient haymow. Mary Kay stated that she never had intercourse with David in her home. She was too afraid of John, and besides, those children were underfoot all the time.

And why did Bonnie turn in her sister? Well, according to Bonnie, Mary Kay had no right to knock off John. After all, he was her man too, and she didn't have a spare like David waiting in the wings to take up the slack, so to speak.

In the end, Mary Kay was found guilty and received the agreed-upon sentence of 5 to 10 years' imprisonment. David Bowers stood trial in January 1993. Mary Kay testified that he had instructed her on how to murder her husband. He had told her the best time to do it would be when John passed out. He allegedly had even told her how to place the shotgun to make it look like suicide.

Despite the damaging testimony given by David's former lover, the Pennsylvania jury chose to believe that the older woman had been the driving force behind the love affair and the murder plot. David Bowers was found not guilty.

David walked. Mary Kay went to jail. Her children now live with their maternal grandfather. Bonnie lives with her brood and no doubt pines for the good old days when she had half a husband.

# THE MENENDEZ BROTHERS

## THE AMERICAN DREAM SHATTERED

ON the night of August 20, 1989, around 10 p.m., Jose and Kitty Menendez sat watching TV, eating vanilla ice cream and strawberries in the family room of their $5-million home in Beverly Hills, California. Two intruders lugging 12-gauge Mossberg shotguns walked into the room through open French doors. One raised his shotgun and fired directly into the back of Jose's head.

It is believed that Kitty rose from the sofa and, for a split second, may have seen her attacker. A shotgun blast tore into her face. The killers stood there amidst the blood and human tissue. They continued to fire shot after shot into the two bodies. Jose was struck six times. Kitty received 10 blasts. Their bodies were literally blown to pieces. The two killers gathered up the 16 casings from the pools of blood on the floor. Officials later stated there was nothing left of the victims' faces to distinguish them as human beings.

Who were these people whose bodies lay in pieces amidst the opulence of their Beverly Hills mansion?

Jose Menendez was born in Cuba in 1944. When Fidel Castro came to power, the affluent Menendez family sent their 16-year-old son to the United States to live with a relative. Jose, an excellent swimmer, entered high school in Hazelton, Pennsylvania, where he soon earned an athletic scholarship to Southern Illinois University. While attending university, the ambitious young Cuban met and fell in love with beauty queen Mary Louise Anderson, known to everyone as Kitty. Kitty and Jose married. Jose was 19, Kitty, 21.

The young couple moved to New York, where Jose completed his education at Queens College. To make ends meet, he held several jobs, including washing dishes in a restaurant. He obtained his first real job with Lyons Container Services. In three years, he was president of the company. Jose moved from executive position to executive position, always advancing and always excelling. By the age of 35, he had become chief operating officer of RCA/Ariola at an annual salary of $500,000.

Jose and Kitty had two strapping sons, Lyle and Erik, a pleasant home in Princeton, New Jersey, and all the trappings of wealth and success. The two boys exhibited the athletic skills inherited from their parents. Tennis became their major sport. Jose saw to it that both boys received private instruction.

In 1986, Jose retired from RCA, walking away with a cool $1 million. He was hired to reverse the sagging fortunes of International Video Entertainment Inc. at the whopping salary of $1 million a year. His new position required the family to move to Los Angeles, the centre of the entertainment industry.

Jose purchased a new home in Calabasas. Kitty busied herself remodelling the house. Erik attended high school, where he was a star on the tennis team. Lyle was accepted at Princeton University, where he too excelled at tennis. Jose characteristically plunged himself into his new job. He was extremely successful at turning around a company that had lost $19 million the previous year into a cash cow producing a $20-million profit two years later.

On the surface, the family appeared to have attained the American dream. But there were bumps. At Princeton, Lyle was caught copying a classmate's assignment paper and was summarily suspended from university. He returned home. His parents were deeply hurt by their son's suspension.

The offspring of the wealthy, born into material riches, often become bored with their lives. So it was with Erik and Lyle. Fast cars and tennis weren't enough. To break the monotony, they burglarized homes together with other wealthy boys, not for the loot, but for the thrill. Erik confessed to being involved in a burglary. Many believe Lyle was also involved. Jose used his influence and managed to have Lyle exonerated, while Erik was put on probation. The court ordered both boys to undergo psychological counselling. Their mother set them up with psychologist Jerome Oziel.

The disgrace of their sons' actions was too much for Jose and Kitty. They decided to move up to Beverly Hills, to the never-never land of the very rich. Jose purchased a $5-million Spanish estate complete with swimming pool and tennis court on North Elm Drive. The family had arrived in every sense of the word.

Lyle, now 21, was accepted back at Princeton, but things didn't go well at university. He often argued with lecturers and other students. Lyle and his roommate, Donovan Goodreau, had a heated argument over some money that Lyle claimed was missing from their room. He threw Goodreau out. Donovan left without his wallet. Later, Lyle showed friends the wallet, which contained Goodreau's California driver's licence. That summer of 1989, Lyle was back in Beverly Hills living with his parents.

About two hours after the roar of the shotgun blasts echoed through the Menendez home, Lyle and Erik allegedly drove home from a movie and discovered the bodies of their parents. Erik, 18, dialled 911 and sobbed hysterically, "They shot and killed my parents." When police arrived, they found Erik curled in the foetal position on the front lawn.

Who committed this terrible crime? For a while there, many believed that the Mafia had been hired to rub out a business competitor. The police had little to go on as nothing incriminating had been been found at the scene of the killings. No murder weapon has ever been found.

In the weeks immediately following the murder of his parents, Lyle is reported to have gone through $700,000, which tended to attract the attention of the police. He rented a limo and hired a bodyguard, ostensibly to protect him from the assassins who had killed his parents. He also picked up a Porsche Carrera and a Rolex watch, as well as clothing costing $40,000. Lyle always favoured a Princeton hangout, Chuck's Spring Street Café. He must have fancied it a great deal. Immediately after his parents' deaths, he bought the café.

Six months passed. The two sons of the victims stood to inherit $14 million. Unexpectedly, Lyle was picked up by Los Angeles police and charged with his parents' murders. Erik, who was attending a tennis tournament in Israel, was taken into custody when he returned home.

Judalon Smyth was a 37-year-old former lover of psychologist Jerome Oziel, the doctor who was Erik's and Lyle's counsellor. Smyth had called Los Angeles detectives with a most amazing narrative. She swore that two months after the murders, she had been in Dr. Oziel's office and had overheard Erik confess to the murder of his parents.

Smyth went on to tell the detectives that when Lyle heard that his brother had confessed he threatened to kill the doctor if he reported the confession to police. She also claimed that Oziel had tapes in which both Erik and Lyle had discussed the murders with him. Smyth said that the murder weapons had been purchased at a sporting goods store somewhere between Los Angeles and San Diego.

Smyth's story was taken seriously. Certain facts revealed by her checked out. Police opened Dr. Oziel's safe-deposit box and confiscated 17 audiotapes concerning the murder. Detectives found the sporting goods store in San Diego where two 12-gauge Mossberg shotguns had been sold to a young man using Donovan Goodreau's California driver's licence for identification two days before the murders. You may recall that Lyle had shown friends Goodreau's licence after he threw him out of his room in Princeton.

Dr. Oziel has claimed that his controversial tapes were discussions between doctor and patient and are therefore confidential. At a closed-door preliminary hearing, a judge ruled that since Lyle reportedly threatened to kill Oziel if the doctor revealed the contents of the tapes, the doctor/patient confidentiality had been broken and the tapes could be introduced at a future trial.

This ruling was appealed and it was left for the Supreme Court of California to decide whether or not the tapes would be admissible. Eventually, the Supreme Court ruled that Dr. Oziel's taped notes, which reportedly relate in detail how the two brothers had killed their mother and father, would be admissible as evidence.

On July 20, 1993, the two brothers were to stand trial, but a week before their date with justice, their lawyer, Leslie Abramson, arguably the best criminal defence lawyer in California, admitted her clients had killed their parents. All the protestations of innocence during the last four years were out the window. Now the defence would go about attempting to prove that Lyle and Erik had been sexually molested for years by their father with their mother's knowledge. They had killed in self-defence.

On the other side of the coin, the prosecution contended that the brothers killed for greed, their motive being to get their hands on a $14-million estate. If found guilty, Erik and Lyle, 22 and 25 years of age, could have received the death penalty.

The trial, carried live on TV, was gripping and emotional, but no one knew if the boys' testimony was true or not. Lyle, complete with choked-back controlled tears, related how his father started massaging him at age six. Eventually, this led to oral sex, which Jose supposedly believed was a true form of father/son love. Lyle claimed that life was a constant round of rapes and other depravities. When the boys complained to their mother, she told them that their father knew best. Yes, they claim they feared for their lives and that led to killing their parents. In California, that can be construed to be self-defence.

Some correspondents who covered the bizarre trial called this the chutzpah defence. It was not easy to believe that two privileged young men, who had lied for years, were telling the gospel truth.

Evidence had been brought forth indicating that Jose was a hard-driving executive who was equally demanding on his sons. He pushed them to excel at tennis and life in general. Did he sexually molest his sons, as Lyle and Erik claimed? Perhaps we will never know. Meanwhile, the family that acquaintances thought exemplified the American dream was certainly something less than that. Mother and father are dead.

In 1994, the two sons stood trial, their lives hanging in the balance. When the jury failed to reach a verdict, the presiding judge declared a mistrial. Two years later, and after a five-month trial, Erik and Lyle Menendez were found guilty of murdering their parents. They were sentenced to life imprisonment, a sentence they are presently serving.

On the day of the sentencing, Lyle married his girlfriend, Anna Eriksson, who he came to know by correspondence. The ceremony was carried out by conference call. Lyle and his best man, Erik, were eight miles away in prison while the bride was in Lyle's lawyer's office in Los Angeles.

# ROLAND MOLINEUX

## A DEADLY GIFT OF POISON

LET'S face it, poison is the most insidious method of disposing of the unwanted. Oh, sure, you can chop, strangle or shoot friends and enemies, but employing these pedestrian methods necessitates being in relative proximity to the victim. Poison allows the perpetrator to put distance and, in many cases, time between himself and the recipient of the fatal white powder or deadly vial.

The Knickerbocker Athletic Club of New York was one of the most prestigious clubs in the Big Apple at the turn of the century. It catered to the sporting crowd, but was also a home away from home where gentlemen could discuss accumulative preferred stocks, the state of the Union and what trinket to pick up at Tiffany's for their current mistress.

In 1898, the club was saddened by the loss of Henry C. Barnet, an executive of the Knickerbocker Club. Henry had suffered a bout of diphtheria and had been confined to bed at the club for a week. Doctors said he had resumed his normal activities prematurely and, as a result, had died of a heart attack.

Six weeks after Henry's demise, a seemingly unrelated event occurred at the club. On the day before Christmas, athletic director Harry Cornish opened his mail and was pleased to see that someone had sent him an attractive Christmas present. It was an ornate silver bottle holder complete with a sealed blue bottle of Bromo-Seltzer. An envelope accompanied the gift, but there was no card inside the envelope. Someone had forgotten to enclose the card, thought Harry. He was curious enough to tear away his name and address from the wrapping paper.

A few days later, he took the gift to his home. Harry was divorced. He lived with an elderly aunt, Katherine Adams, and her married daughter, a Mrs. Rogers. They teased the 32-year-old Harry about a secret female admirer who was sending him anonymous presents.

On December 28, Katherine Adams awoke with a violent headache. She suggested that some Bromo-Seltzer might do her the world of good. Harry remembered his recently acquired gift, broke the seal and poured some of the powder into a glass of water. Katherine drained about three-quarters of the glass and remarked that the potion tasted bitter. Harry took a sip and said that it tasted fine to him.

Minutes later, Katherine took ill and called out for Harry to come to her aid. Harry jumped up, staggered and fell to the floor. He managed to get outside, where he violently vomited, which probably saved his life. Meanwhile, Mrs. Rogers had summoned a doctor for mother, but there was little the doctor could do. Katherine Adams died shortly after his arrival.

The Bromo-Seltzer was analyzed and found to contain cyanide of mercury, a deadly poison. The doctor who ministered to Harry was the same medic who had attended the late Mr. Barnet only weeks earlier. He remembered that Barnet had mentioned something about receiving a gift through the mail.

Katherine's murder was covered extensively in the New York newspapers. Harry provided them with the sample he had kept of the handwriting on the wrapping of his gift. It was reproduced in the paper. Two officials of the Knickerbocker, John D. Adams and Andre Bustanoby, recognized the sample handwriting. After checking some correspondence on file, they came to the conclusion that the man who had addressed the poisonous gift to Harry was club member Roland Molineux. New York's finest were immediately informed of their discovery.

An investigation into Roland's history was most enlightening. Detectives learned that back in 1897 Roland had introduced his girlfriend, Blanche Cheeseborough, to Henry Barnet. Henry had taken a shine to Blanche and had become Roland's rival for her affection. Henry's pursuit of Blanche had come to an abrupt end when he had taken ill and died at the club. Nineteen days after Henry's untimely death, Blanche and Roland were married at the appropriately named Church of the Heavenly Rest.

But why oh why had poor Katherine Adams been poisoned? The poison wasn't meant for her at all. In 1897, Roland had had a bitter argument with Harry Cornish concerning the running of the Knickerbocker Club. The dispute had ended up before a committee of the club's officials, to whom Roland stated, "Discharge Cornish or lose me." Cornish stayed. Roland had no way of knowing that Harry would take home the silver holder and the bottle of poison, nor did he have the slightest idea that Harry's Aunt Katherine would be the victim of his diabolical scheme.

When Henry Barnet's body was exhumed and found to contain cyanide of mercury, Roland was taken into custody and charged with the murder of Katherine Adams and the attempted murder of Harry Cornish.

At the trial the prosecution paraded an array of the obligatory handwriting experts, who had compared the writing on Harry Cornish's poisonous gift to that of Roland Molineux. The two samples were a match. No amount of cross-examination could change the experts' opinion. There was no doubt that Roland Molineux had addressed the fatal parcel.

Investigators traced the bottle holder to a store in Newark, not far from Roland's place of business. One of Roland's employees swore that the paper used to wrap the poison was exactly the same as the kind used in Roland's office. Cyanide of mercury was readily available to the accused at his workplace.

The Molineux trial lasted three months, but the jury took only eight hours to find the rogue guilty as charged. Roland was sent up the river to Sing Sing, where he awaited his execution on death row. Using his father's money, he fought for his life for the following two years. In October 1901, the Court of Appeals reversed the previous court's verdict and ordered a new trial.

The passage of time often has a strange effect on the public's attitude towards a murder suspect. Almost four years after the murder, Roland Molineux again stood trial for murder and attempted murder. This time, no details of Barnet's murder were admissible. Roland was allowed to testify and, all in all, gave a good impression. The defence came up with a witness who swore she had seen another man, not Roland, mail an identically wrapped parcel addressed to Harry Cornish.

The jury deliberated only four minutes before acquitting Roland. Unlike many a man who narrowly escapes an appointment with the electric chair, Roland didn't fade into obscurity. He wrote several books about his experiences and was relatively well known in the New York area.

In 1913, Roland Molineux suffered a nervous breakdown and was confined to the New York State Hospital for the Insane. He died there in 1917.

# DAN MONTECALVO

## A HIGHLY UNLIKELY PAIR

THEY met, wed and, ultimately, one was to kill the other.

Carol was born to hard-working blue-collar parents in Buffalo, New York. She grew up to be an attractive young woman who thirsted for higher education. With the support of her family, she attended and later graduated from State University of New York with a Bachelor of Science degree. In 1970, she earned her master's degree from the same university.

An unsuccessful marriage to a foreign student lasted only one year. Carol's father had been opposed to the marriage, and from that time father and daughter were never on what you would call friendly terms.

Single and alone, Carol remained in her position as a student counsellor at the University of Wisconsin at Madison. In time she became deeply involved in religious life and attended bible classes regularly. One of her religious friends asked her to be a pen pal of bank robber Dan Montecalvo, then serving time at the Federal Correctional Institution in Oxford, and Carol agreed.

Letters flowed between the two very different personalities. Soon Carol was visiting Dan at every opportunity. To her, Dan Montecalvo was a charming, sensitive man who had been led down a path of crime through no fault of his own.

Dan's father had been a small-time thief in Chelsea, Massachusetts. He had been shot to death by police during the commission of a robbery. His mother, a part-time prostitute, often brought clients to their two-room apartment when her little son was at home. Dan started stealing at the age of nine and spent the next nine years of his life in and out of reform schools and foster homes.

As a kid, Dan acquired a lengthy police record. As a young man, he was a hard-drinking, gun-toting gambler who specialized in robbing banks. Whenever he did pull off a successful robbery, he blew his take on gambling. It was a no-win situation. He was caught and stashed away in penitentiary. This was the man whom religious, trusting Carol had taken to her heart.

Dan professed that he too was madly in love. Most of Carol's visits to the penitentiary were spent praying with Dan. Within a short time he converted to

Carol's evangelistic sect. Although he had 10 more years to serve, the lovers thought that prayer would be instrumental in obtaining his early release. In the meantime, they decided to marry. It took some time, but eventually they received permission from prison authorities. On July 14, 1980, they were married in the prison yard. Six months later, their prayers were answered. Dan was released and the happy couple moved to California to begin a new life together.

The Montecalvos settled in Burbank, where Carol obtained a position with a telephone company, selling Yellow Pages ads. Soon after landing the job, it was apparent that she had an unusual aptitude for that type of work. Carol was the ace of the sales staff. Later, she switched to Pacific Bell, where she made a fine living. Things didn't go as well for Dan. He moved from job to job, drank heavily and often lapsed into deep depression. In 1986, a bleeding ulcer made working impossible for him. Dan took to the bottle with a vengeance.

Carol, with her simple faith that prayer could solve all problems, prayed that her husband would turn his life around. Once again, as if by a miracle, she received the good news that she had won a sales contest at her place of employment. The prize was an all-expenses-paid trip to Hawaii. Just what Dan needed: a full week's escape from the troubles of the world. He would return a new man, the charming soft-spoken, considerate Dan she had married years earlier in the prison yard.

On March 31, 1988, Carol was busy preparing for their trip. Next day, they would take off for beautiful romantic Hawaii. That night, around ten-thirty, Carol and Dan went for a walk, as they did most nights that Dan was home.

The call was received by the 911 operator a few minutes after 11 p.m. The caller was a man who implored, "Please help, hurry up. We've been shot." One minute later, the first police car arrived at the scene. From the information given by the desperate caller, there was some concern that an armed burglar might still be in the house or on the premises.

It was nine minutes after the initial call before Dan came out of the house. Only then did police rush to his aid and into the house, where they found Carol on the floor of the hallway. It was too late. Carol was dead, apparently shot to death by a burglar. Dan had been shot in the back by a single .25-calibre bullet, which had lodged in the front of his body near the small intestines. He was rushed to hospital, where he successfully underwent an operation.

Detectives listened as Dan told his story of the shooting. When they left the house for their walk, he and Carol locked up as usual. Upon returning, they strolled up the driveway. Dan noticed that their vehicle licence plates were to expire the next day. He had the sticker to place over the old plates in the glove compartment of the car. He fetched the sticker while Carol went inside to get a wet towel to clean the plates. Suddenly, Dan heard her shout, "What are you doing here?," followed by the sound of two shots. Dan ran into the house, only to be grabbed from behind. He was shot and fell to the floor. He heard a male voice say, "Let's get out of here," or words to that effect. Dan was able to get up. He saw Carol lying in the hall bleeding profusely as he made his way to the den to use the phone. It was then he noticed that their safe had been burglarized. A cash box had been pried open. About $800 in change and loose bills were missing. Dan dialled 911.

Detectives looking for signs of forced entry found a slit in the back-door screen, which had apparently allowed the intruders to reach inside and open the door. There seemed little doubt that Carol and Dan had been unfortunate enough to surprise armed burglars in the process of robbing their home. Dan received the sympathy of investigating officers and his wife's religious friends.

It took only a week for the situation to change dramatically. A check of Dan's past disclosed his criminal record. A man with such a record deserved a closer look, police decided. As they delved deeper, they found out that Carol had been insured for $600,000. Dan had already collected $400,000, but a few of the insurance companies held back their payments when they learned he was a suspect in his wife's murder. Still, $400,000 isn't bad. Dan visited Las Vegas and proceeded to lose thousands of dollars a night. Authorities also learned that before Carol's death, Dan had been gambling on credit at the Las Vegas casinos. When he failed to honour his markers, the casinos threatened to deposit them at his bank, a normal procedure when clients can't pay up. In Dan's case, he had no hope of covering the markers, which would have been treated as rubber cheques. Being a parolee, this offence could land him back in prison. As soon as he laid his hands on Carol's insurance money, he paid off the threatening casinos.

Police were sure they had their man, but one thing bothered them. Carol had been shot with a .38 weapon, while Dan had been shot with a .25. How had he disposed of the two weapons after shooting his wife and himself? A search of Dan's belongings uncovered an empty hollowed-out book, which could have held the two weapons until he was able to get rid of them.

Based on overwhelming circumstantial evidence, Dan Montecalvo was arrested and charged with his wife's murder. He was tried and convicted. Protesting his innocence to the end and acting as his own co-counsel, he was sentenced to 27 years' to life imprisonment. He is currently serving that sentence.

# JOE NAIL

## NAILED

IF ever two people were completely different, they were Carolyn and Joe Nail. Carolyn, 48, was a dark-complexioned brunette with a stunning figure. A graduate nurse, she had risen in the ranks of the Marshall Memorial Hospital in Madill, Oklahoma, to become director of nursing. Her husband, Joe, was an oilfield roustabout who drank heavily between jobs. He was constantly fearful that Carolyn, more often than not the family breadwinner, would leave him.

Joe's fears were well-founded. Carolyn couldn't abide the drunkenness and abusive threats indefinitely. In August 1989, she obtained a divorce. Joe didn't take the divorce well. He drank more than usual and often confided to acquaintances that he would get even with " that bitch."

Carolyn went about restructuring her life. She dated 60-year-old Don Hofferber, a successful contractor. Although Don had divorced his wife in 1976, they continued to have an off-and-on relationship until 1990, when they permanently parted. He liked and admired Carolyn Nail. With both of them free, it was a foregone conclusion among their friends that the pair would eventually marry. Meanwhile, Don was Carolyn's constant companion.

Madill is a small Oklahoma town with a population of about 3,000. Violence is not an everyday occurrence there. Murder and its ugly ramifications are practically unknown in the peaceful little community. That's one of the reasons the desperate call to the hospital received immediate attention.

On Saturday, June 2, 1990, the Marshall Memorial switchboard received an ominous call pleading, "Help me." There followed a fading partial address. In minutes, an ambulance and police were speeding to Carolyn Nail's home.

The first officers at the scene noted the glass patio door at the rear of the house was broken to pieces. Proceeding with caution in case the intruder or intruders were still in the house, police made their way to the master bedroom. There, at the foot of the bed, clad only in shorts, was the body of Don Hofferber. He had been shot in the neck, abdomen and arm. Carolyn lay dead beside the bed. She had managed to dislodge a white telephone from the night table and call the hospital before she died. She had been shot five times. Three bullets had entered her back, causing her death.

It was later determined that both Carolyn and Don had been murdered with the same weapon, a .22-calibre semi-automatic rifle. From the position of the bodies, it appeared the killer had opened fire at the couple from the bedroom doorway. Carolyn's pit bull cowered in a corner amidst the blood and chaos. Police found $1,700 in Don's wallet, which ruled out robbery as a motive for the killings.

An autopsy indicated that the pair had engaged in sexual intercourse shortly before being shot. Don had died instantly, but Carolyn had lived long enough to make her desperate phone call.

Initially, police speculated that one of Don's many competitors in the construction business, envious of his success, may have been responsible for the killings. Don had a reputation for being a ruthless businessman. It didn't take long, however, for police inquiries to turn up the bad feeling Joe Nail harboured for his former wife. It was learned that Carolyn had told Don of her fear of Joe. Don had given her a .25-calibre handgun for her protection and had purchased a .380-calibre weapon for his own use. Both guns were located, but neither played a part in their owners' deaths.

Joe, who lived in a trailer 40 miles from Madill, was questioned. He readily consented to have his trailer searched. Nothing incriminating was found. Joe admitted he hated his ex-wife, accusing her of running around on him before they were divorced. He wasn't sorry someone had blown her away, but swore he wasn't the guilty party. Joe said he had been fishing alone at the Lake of the Arbuckles at the time of the murders. He had last seen Carolyn a few days before her death, when he had gone to her house to pick up the pit bull, which they owned jointly. He had returned the dog the same day. That was Joe's story and he stuck to it.

Investigators believed that Joe Nail, probably intoxicated, had committed the double murder. Despite their suspicions, there was no eyewitness and no murder weapon. Their case had to be built on circumstantial evidence and that's exactly what they set out to do.

In a small town the size of Madill, rumours spread like weeds. Many of these stories reached the ears of the police. Everyone in town realized an aggressive pit bull would never allow a stranger free access to the house without offering some resistance. Surely the killer was well known to the dog. A neighbour of Carolyn's contacted police, saying that on the evening of the shooting, while standing in her front yard, she noticed a white pickup parked in front of Carolyn's house. She went into her home for a few minutes and then came back outside. As she did so, she watched the pickup drive away. When it was directly opposite her, the driver stared at her. Their eyes met. She was sure he was Joe Nail.

Although Joe had stated he had been fishing at the time of the crime, a security guard at his trailer park swore that Joe had driven out of the park in his white pickup about two hours before the murders and had returned about an hour after the murders, allowing him plenty of time to drive the 40 miles to Carolyn's house and back. In addition, several of Joe's acquaintances came forward, stating that he had often verbally threatened to kill his ex-wife. Carolyn's friends volunteered that she lived in fear of Joe.

Detectives believed this was a case of murder without any great intrigue or plot, simply a man enraged at his ex-wife and her lover, enraged enough to kill them both.

In October 1990, Joe was taken into custody and charged with the double murder. The prosecution proved that Carolyn had once given Joe a .22-calibre semi-automatic rifle as a birthday present. They produced a witness who placed Joe in his truck about nine miles from Carolyn's home, as well as the neighbour who placed him in front of Carolyn's home on the night of the murders. The security guard from Joe's trailer camp also gave his damaging evidence.

Joe's defence attorney pointed out that Don Hofferber had business enemies who wanted him out of the way. In addition, several members of his family stood to inherit large sums of money and a prosperous business. Wasn't it just possible that Don was the main target and Carolyn an incidental victim? The Oklahoma jury thought not.

Joe was found guilty on two counts of first-degree murder, placing him in jeopardy of receiving the death penalty. However, his attorney pleaded that the murders were crimes of passion. He was successful in having Joe Nail sentenced to two life terms without possibility of parole.

# HANK NGUYEN

## REJECTED SUITOR

WHEN Saigon fell in 1975, Tina Pham fled her native Vietnam in a desperate effort to find a safe haven. Like many other boat people, she made her way to Indonesia. Tina married and had two children. She and her husband eked out a meagre living for years before deciding to emigrate to the United States. In 1980 they settled in Orange County, California, where their third child was born.

By 1985, Tina's marriage had deteriorated and ended in divorce. However, she and her ex-husband were on good terms. Both contributed to their children's support and spent an equal amount of time with them. Tina worked as a hairdresser. She lived in a comfortable apartment with relatives in Garden Grove, California, not far from Reverend Robert Schuller's famed Crystal Cathedral.

Each morning Tina reported for work at precisely 11 a.m. On October 24, 1990, when she failed to show up or phone in ill, her employer called her home, but received no response. Tina and all her relatives were apparently not in.

That night, one of Tina's relatives tried her bedroom door and found it locked. She assumed Tina was asleep, but when there was no sign of Tina after several hours had elapsed, she decided to unlock the door with a spare key kept in the apartment. The bedroom was in darkness and there was no sign that anything in the room had been disturbed. More important, there was no sign of Tina.

The relative gingerly made her way to the bathroom. There lay Tina Pham on the floor. The 42-year-old woman was on her back, her black dress pushed up around her waist. Her panties were pulled down halfway to her knees. Dried blood had oozed from her mouth onto the bathroom floor.

An ambulance was at the scene in a matter of minutes. Medical attendants confirmed that Tina was dead. A police photographer arrived at approximately the same time and took photos of the body before a relative lifted Tina's panties and rearranged her dress. Later, this relative would explain that she had done so in order to spare the victim unnecessary embarrassment and had no idea she was contaminating a crime scene.

Initially, there was no indication that a crime had been committed. Relatives of the dead woman told police that Tina had suffered from heart disease and was taking medication, which was found in the bathroom. There was no reason to believe that Tina's death was due to anything but natural causes, although police noted that her bedroom window was open about 12 inches. Since nothing was missing from the bedroom, it was assumed that Tina had opened the window herself.

An autopsy was performed to verify the cause of death. Dr. Ronald Katsuyama noted petechial haemorrhages in the eyes, which indicated to him that strangulation was the cause of death. The interior of the victim's throat revealed several bruised areas. Tina had received a blow to the mouth which had split her lower lip. The blood found on the bathroom floor had emanated from this wound. After hearing from the coroner, police realized they had a murder on their hands. In addition, when they scanned the photos taken at the scene by the police photographer, they learned that someone had rearranged Tina's panties and dress.

Police immediately mounted a full-scale murder investigation. Tina's bed was examined. When the bedspread was removed, a small quantity of blood was found on one of the sheets, leading police to surmise that Tina had sustained the split lip while on the bed.

The time of death was established at between 9:45 a.m. and 11 a.m. on the day the body was found. A friend had talked to Tina on the phone at nine forty-five and, as she had not turned up for work at 11 a.m., it was reasonable to assume that she had been murdered between these times.

Police learned that Tina had dated three different men since her divorce. Two of her boyfriends were checked out and eliminated as suspects. The third, Hank Nguyen, was located on the day following the murder. Detectives were shocked when, unlike the other Vietnamese who had been questioned, Hank proved to be most uncooperative. He would not discuss the case without having his lawyer present, but was willing to set up an appointment for the next day. Then, just as the detectives were about to depart, he changed his mind.

Hank told police he had nothing to fear. He had been busy supervising a construction job in Huntington Beach on the morning of the murder. He said he had been on the site until 9:30 a.m. when he left to purchase some supplies at a hardware store, returning to the construction site at 11:20 a.m. For emphasis, Hank used hand movements. That's when police noticed his bandaged thumb. When the detectives suggested they take a photo of his injured thumb, Hank refused.

Next day, Hank Nguyen showed up at police headquarters with his lawyer. He insisted that he had hurt his thumb in the hardware store and consented to remove the bandage. The thumb was examined and photographed. It was noted that the skin was broken on both sides. For all the world, it looked like a bite. Hank was quickly becoming a prime suspect.

Tina's relatives were questioned extensively. Slowly, authorities were able to piece together the relationship between Tina and Hank. One relative reported that she had taken Tina to a doctor to close a cut on her scalp. Tina claimed she had passed out, fallen and cut herself, but the relative believed Hank was responsible for the head wound. It had happened just before they broke up.

Police contacted an odontologist, who examined the photographs of Hank's thumb. He compared the photos with plaster casts of Tina's teeth. They matched. The doctor suggested that the position of the bite mark was compatible with the thumb having been placed over the victim's mouth, but he admitted that the teeth marks, while consistent with Tina's teeth, could also have been made by thousands of other people with the same dental characteristics.

Detectives dusted the window sill of the open bedroom window. They were able to lift a single print, which matched Hank's index finger. While incriminating, it proved nothing, as Hank had often been in the bedroom and could have left the print at any time.

A search of the suspect's home was most revealing. Police found colour photographs of Tina taken in happier times. One picture featured Tina posing with her dress crumpled around her waist and her panties dropped halfway down to around her knees. Police did a double take. The photo matched the first photo taken of Tina's body. Hank had posed Tina's corpse in the exact position she had assumed when she had allowed him to take the erotic photo.

Investigating officers did one final check. At 9:30 a.m. they left the Huntington Beach construction site where Hank had been working. Driving as slowly as they dared, they proceeded to the hardware store and purchased the very items he claimed to have purchased. They then drove to Tina's apartment, allowing time for the murder and time for Hank to return to the construction site. At 11:20 a.m., Hank could easily have been back to work. Their suspect had had plenty of time to commit the murder.

The pieces fell into place. Hank was a rejected suitor. He and Tina had argued. He had probably punched her while she was in bed, splitting her lip, which bled onto the sheet. Tina ran away from her lover into the bathroom. As he strangled her, she bit him. Once she was dead, in a hateful symbolic gesture, he had positioned her body in the same pose as during a previous sexual encounter.

Hank Nguyen was arrested and stood trial for Tina's murder. On May 28, 1991, after deliberating for just five hours, the jury found him guilty of first-degree murder. He was sentenced to 25 years' imprisonment. At a later sentencing hearing, the conviction was adjusted to second-degree murder. The presiding judge ruled that the crime had not been premeditated and reduced the sentence to 15 years to life. Hank Nguyen is presently serving his sentence.

# WILLIE O'SHEA

## IRISH JUSTICE

WILLIE O'Shea was a native of Ballyhane, County Waterford, Ireland. To say that he was a bright lad would be to overstate the case. No, Willie was a young man with below-average intelligence who worked as a farm labourer when the mood struck him, which wasn't often. He much preferred to snare rabbits and sell them for a living. Willie didn't need much to sustain himself, as he lived with his mother and stepfather, Michael Byrne.

In 1940, at age 20, Willie married 17-year-old Maureen Clavin. The marriage wasn't a happy one right from the beginning. Willie and Maureen lived in a three-room thatched cottage, but Willie was hardly ever home. He preferred the company of 16-year-old Thomas White, a fellow aficionado of the rabbit-snaring game. Thomas also had a distinct aversion to manual labour.

Maureen was forever complaining that her husband didn't earn enough money to provide her with the necessities of life. He often left her alone at night without oil for her lamps or even candles. Maureen was afraid to be alone in the darkened cottage at night.

In 1942, when Maureen became pregnant, it was not a joyous occasion in the O'Shea household. Willie didn't change his argumentative, neglectful ways one little bit. In February 1943, Maureen gave birth to a healthy baby boy. Four days after returning home from the hospital, she was awakened by the smell of smoke emanating from the roof of the cottage. As usual, Willie wasn't home.

Maureen had time to dress herself and the baby before making her way to her mother-in-law's home while her cottage burned to the ground. Willie, the no-goodnik, arrived home to his burned-down house a little after 1 a.m. He walked to his mother's home and joined his wife and baby. There was some suggestion that arson had been involved, but nothing came of the rumours.

For three weeks the O'Sheas stayed with the Byrnes. There was a dramatic change in Willie's treatment of his wife. He was more attentive and there was no more quarrelling. Willie even took Maureen out for a walk each evening after tea. They would stroll arm in arm for about a mile down the dark road. The situation became so rosy that Willie actually secured a job working in a quarry.

Then it happened.

Willie and Maureen had gone for their usual evening walk. Suddenly, his mother was surprised to see her son running towards the house. Maureen was nowhere to be seen. Willie was crying and trembling. When Mrs. Byrne could get no information out of him, she ran down the lonely dark road screaming Maureen's name. Unable to locate her daughter-in-law, she returned to her home and implored Willie to tell her what had happened. Finally, Willie blurted out, "Somebody fired a shot at us." Mrs. Byrne ran down the lonely road once more. This time she came across Maureen's body. The young mother had been killed by a single shotgun blast in the back.

What in the world had happened? That's what the police wanted to know. They questioned Willie, who explained that he and Maureen were walking arm in arm along the road when a shot rang out. He felt her slumping to the road and gently lay her down. He saw nothing in the dark, but ran home in fear for his life. He told police he was sure the shot was meant for him.

The police paid a visit to the home of Willie's good friend, Thomas White. While there, they confiscated a shotgun which obviously had recently been cleaned. When Thomas was told of the tragedy, he returned to Willie's home with the police.

Willie was questioned about the fire that had burned down his home. Did he think there was any connection between the two incidents? Willie was confused, but although he swore he had nothing to do with his wife's death, he insinuated that he knew the identity of the killer. When asked if Thomas White was implicated, Willie broke down and told his fantastic story.

Willie had asked Thomas White to shoot his wife. Thomas agreed to do the job. Each night Willie walked with Maureen with the sole purpose of leading her to her death. As an aside, Willie told police that Thomas had set fire to the cottage, as well, in a failed attempt to kill Maureen. Willie knew the exact spot where Thomas would fire the fatal shot. On one occasion, Thomas didn't fire because someone happened along the road, but finally conditions were perfect.

To warn Willie that all was set, Thomas tapped his friend on the shoulder with the barrel of the shotgun. Then he shot Maureen from a distance of about three inches. Maureen said, "Oh, Jesus" as he let her slide to the road. Willie didn't even turn to see Thomas. He explained there was no need; he knew very well who had fired the shot.

The police questioned Thomas, who said he had seen Willie and Maureen walking on the night of the murder. He had ridden past them on his bicycle and had gone straight home. When his mother arrived home, she informed him of the tragedy. Thomas claimed that he hadn't used his shotgun for a few days and always cleaned it after each use.

Detectives confiscated Thomas's boots and socks, which were soaking wet and covered with mud. This was rather strange as the weather had been unusually dry for several weeks. When Willie led police to the exact spot where Thomas had stood to fire the fatal shot, they noticed a bog which never dried out. They made out the faint impression of Thomas's boots in the mud.

Both men were arrested. Willie was the most vocal, admitting his guilt over and over. He explained that he felt as if he was in prison being married. When the baby came along, he couldn't even go snaring rabbits when he felt like it. When he suggested to Maureen that he go away to join the army in England, she wouldn't hear of such a thing. There was no other way. Maureen had to go. Now he was dreadfully sorry about the whole thing.

On June 7, 1943, Willie and Thomas stood trial for murder. On the very first day of the trial, Thomas's lawyer applied for a jury to judge whether his client was mentally fit to stand trial. Renowned Irish doctors testified that, after interviewing Thomas, it was their opinion that he was mentally subnormal and could not follow the judicial procedures, nor could he give instructions to his lawyer. It took the jury only 10 minutes to find him unfit to stand trial. Thomas White was confined to hospital.

Willie wasn't as fortunate. He stood trial and was found guilty of his wife's murder. He too was examined by doctors, who agreed that although he was not a mental giant, he did know right from wrong. On August 12, 1943, Willie O'Shea was executed.

The old Irish trial is a rare example of the unusual circumstances that can take place in a murder case. The man who did not fire the fatal shot was executed, while the man who pulled the trigger never stood trial.

# PELL, ROYAL AND MOREY

## SENSELESS KILLING

VARIOUS studies have been conducted on the home life of men and women who have committed murder. A disproportionate number of these killers seem to come from broken homes, where alcoholism, and child, wife and drug abuse were prominent. None of the above applies to the Morey family of Ypsilanti, Michigan.

The Moreys lived in a white clapboard house on Pearl Street. Bill Morey worked all his life for the United Stove Co. Over the years he had managed to pay off the mortgage on his home. Mrs. Morey taught school for the first six years of her married life. The family attended church every Sunday.

On January 27, 1933, the Moreys were blessed with their first child, a son. Bill was their pride and joy. As he grew up, he achieved good marks in school, sang in the church choir and regularly attended Sunday school. Eight years after Bill's birth, a second child, a daughter, was born to the Moreys. Young Bill was a loving, protective big brother. In high school, Bill's marks seemed to level off. Some of his teachers felt he was an underachiever when it was learned that his IQ was 123.

During his junior year in high school, Bill took his first drink of beer. Soon it became customary for him and his friends to pick up a case of beer a couple of times a week and to cruise the town looking for girls. Bill had no trouble finding girlfriends. He stood an inch over six feet, had a shock of thick black hair and the slim build of an athlete.

When Bill graduated from high school, his marks were below admission standards at the University of Michigan. He was told to apply to another college and reapply in a year's time. Bill was accepted at Michigan State Normal College, located only a few blocks from his home. That summer of 1951 he looked forward to his first semester at Michigan State.

If a cross section of 18-year-old young men had been taken, it is conceivable that Bill would have been hailed as your average all-American boy. He wasn't a slacker; he wasn't outstanding. Bill was an average boy from an average home. Yet Bill Morey would kill before the summer was over.

On September 11, Bill and two friends, Dan Myers and Max Pell, went for a drive in Dan's car. The boys purchased a case of beer and cruised around town looking for girls to pick up. They drove to Ann Arbor, but didn't have any luck finding girls. Finally, they parked near University Hospital.

For reasons never really explained, the conversation centred on how easy it would be to grab a purse from one of the several nurses going to and from the hospital. One of the boys thought it was a crazy idea. Bill thought it would be cool. Evidently he said, "Let's hit someone over the head and rob them." Dan piped up that the whole thing was silly. Bill insisted. He would hit a nurse over the head, rob her and drag her into the car.

Bill picked up a 12-inch wrench and watched for a likely victim. Nurse Shirley Mackley left the hospital. For a few minutes, she was alone on the street. Bill walked hurriedly up behind her and swung the wrench at her head. Shirley felt the glancing blow, screamed and ran for her life. Bill dashed back to the car and the three boys drove away. Max and Bill laughed at the botched robbery attempt.

The boys enjoyed reading about the attack on the nurse in the local newspaper. During the week following the assault, Bill, Max and another boy, Dave Royal, were driving around town. They picked up a fourth boy, a preacher's son, Dan Baughey. Bill bragged to Dan that it was he who had attacked nurse Shirley Mackley. Dan didn't know what to do. Maybe the guys were just pulling his leg. He decided to discuss the matter with his father.

Next evening, Max, accompanied by Bill and Dave, drove to University Hospital. Thirty-four-year-old nurse Pauline Campbell left the hospital after completing her shift. Pauline was a pretty woman, well-liked, quiet. She didn't deserve to die on the streets of the city.

Bill picked up a mallet from the floor of the car. It was a rubber-headed one used to take dents out of cars. He stuffed it into his belt and got out of Max's car. Pauline had no idea that she was being stalked by an 18-year-old student. Bill was wearing moccasins and made very little noise as he closed the distance between himself and Pauline.

Max turned on the headlights of the car and slowly followed. Bill was finally in range. He brought down the mallet with all his might on Pauline's head. Again and again the mallet crashed against Pauline's skull until she was dead. Bill shouted to Dave to come and give him a hand. He was attempting to drag Pauline into the car. Dave jumped out to assist with Pauline's limp form, but Max objected. The interior of the car had just been cleaned. He didn't want blood all over the seats and floor. The boys took Pauline's purse, left her body on the road and drove off.

A few minutes later, Bill examined the contents of Pauline's purse. It contained the usual things, as well as $1.50 in cash. Bill kept the money, but threw the purse and its contents into the Huron River. The three boys stopped for sandwiches and coffee.

Bill returned home at 1:30 a.m., in time to make his curfew. His mother let him in. She noticed nothing unusual in his behaviour and went to bed. Bill went up to his room, crawled out a window and rejoined his buddies. At 4:30 a.m., the three friends returned to their respective homes.

On Monday, Bill registered at Michigan State Normal College. The following day he delivered an address at his high school, advising students on the complications of enrolling in an institution of higher learning.

Over the weekend, Dan Baughey heard about the murder on the radio. He recalled the conversation he had had with Bill about the attack on Shirley Mackley. He wondered if Bill and his friends had had anything to do with the murder, which was the main topic of conversation in Ypsilanti and Ann Arbor. Dan asked his father for advice and was told to go to the police with his suspicions.

Bill, Max and Dave were picked up. Initially they denied any involvement, but when asked to take lie detector tests, they lost their nerve and confessed.

Dan Myers, the boy involved in the first attack, was sentenced to one to ten years' imprisonment for his part in that incident. Dave Royal was found guilty of murder in the second degree and was sentenced to 20 years to life. Max Pell and Bill Morey were found guilty of murder in the first degree. Both were sentenced to life imprisonment.

In the state of Michigan, which has no death penalty, a sentence of life imprisonment means natural life, unless the sentence is commuted. There is no parole granted in the case of a life sentence for first-degree murder.

The murder of Pauline Campbell is remembered not because of its convoluted plot or the evil background of the participants. It is remembered because no one, including the perpetrators, has ever given a logical reason for this senseless killing.

All three men involved have been released from prison. Max Pell had his sentence commuted by the governor of the state in 1967, after serving 16 years. Dave Royal was paroled in 1970 after serving 19 years. Governor W.C. Milliken commuted Bill Morey's sentence in December 1970, after he'd served just under 20 years in prison.

# VALERIE PERCY

## SENATOR'S DAUGHTER MURDERED

CHARLES Percy was in the midst of his campaign for the U.S. Senate. The former president of the Bell and Howell camera empire had retired from the world of business and finance to enter politics.

Percy, a self-made millionaire, was a man who had it all. He and his wife, Lorraine, lived in the small exclusive community of Kenilworth, a suburb of Chicago, on an estate bordering Lake Michigan.

On the night of September 18, 1966, 11-year-old Mark Percy was staying overnight with friends. Roger Percy, 19, was away at university. At home that night were Charles, Lorraine and three of their children, Gail, 13, and the 21-year-old twins, Sharon and Valerie.

Sharon chatted with Valerie in her sister's bedroom at around eleven-thirty after returning from a date. Valerie was sitting on her bed watching TV when the twins bade each other goodnight. Sharon retired to her room. Gail was already asleep. Charles had come home late and had watched TV with Lorraine. The couple retired about 1:30 a.m.

Some hours later, Lorraine woke up. She thought she heard glass breaking but wasn't concerned enough to investigate. Later she said that she thought one of the girls had toppled a glass from a night table. She turned over and went back to sleep. In an instant, another noise disturbed Lorraine. She called out, "Valerie, Val," but received no response.

Lorraine left the master bedroom and opened the door to Valerie's room. There in the dark she saw the form of a man bending over her daughter's bed. She didn't see the man's face, but believed he was wearing a shirt or jacket. He carried a flashlight, which he pointed at the terrified woman as she opened the door. Lorraine Percy later told police, "I took a step backward, turned and ran back to our bedroom. I awakened my husband and pressed the central burglar-alarm button that activated the siren on the roof."

The assailant ran past Lorraine and down the stairs. He fled through French doors and out into the night. At precisely 5:05 a.m., the siren broke through the silence of the early morning. Charles Percy called his neighbour and friend, Dr. Robert Hoft. In a matter of minutes, the doctor was bending over the blood-spattered body of Valerie Percy. The young girl, who had just graduated from Cornell University and had come home to assist her father in his political campaign, was beyond help. She had been bludgeoned about the head and had been stabbed 10 times in the throat and chest.

Charles Percy called the Kenilworth police. Realizing they were ill equipped to handle the first homicide ever to take place in their community, they immediately called Chicago police for assistance.

Detectives ascertained that the assailant had gained entrance through the French doors. He had used a glass cutter to cut away a small section of glass, enabling him to reach in and open the door from the inside. It was this piece of glass falling to the floor that had disturbed Lorraine's sleep.

Due to the prominence of the murdered girl's father, the homicide caused a sensation. The Percys moved out of their home and went into seclusion as police mounted an extensive investigation into the killing.

Several things puzzled investigators. It appeared that the assailant had gone directly to Valerie's room where he had instituted the vicious assault. Yet the dead girl's friends and acquaintances could come up with no one who would want any harm to come to Valerie, let alone kill her. Robbery didn't appear to be the motive as nothing had been taken from the estate. Conversely, some investigators reasoned that the killer had ventured into Valerie's room by chance and had been interrupted by the girl as he cased her room for anything of value.

For a short while police couldn't understand why the Percys' Labrador retriever hadn't barked at a stranger entering their home at five in the morning. However, they soon realized that because Charles was in the midst of a major political campaign, strangers were constantly entering and exiting the house. The dog paid them little heed.

As the weeks passed, it became clear that Valerie's murder wouldn't be quickly solved. For some strange reason, the high-profile murder attracted a series of confessions. In all, 19 men confessed to the crime. Each confession had to be checked out. After time-consuming investigations, all the men were cleared of any complicity in the Percy killing.

In 1967, a professional burglar, Fred Malchow, was drawn into the web of the investigation. Malchow was no ordinary thief. He and other members of a gang would rob a residence, hop a plane and be in another part of the country that same day. He was questioned in the Norristown Pennsylvania Jail. Although he was known to have been in Chicago at the time of the murder, he steadfastly denied that he had had anything to do with Valerie's death.

Later, a fellow inmate informed police that Malchow had confessed the Percy murder to him. Totally unexpectedly, Malchow escaped from jail before he could be questioned further. The desperate career criminal was killed when, surrounded by police, he jumped to his death from a trestle into the Schuylkill River.

Three years after Malchow's death, another convict, Jimmy Evans, who had spent time in jail with him, came forward and told authorities that Malchow had also confessed to him that he had killed Valerie Percy. According to Evans, Valerie had awakened while Freddie was in her room. Freddie had held her down with one hand, while he stabbed her with the other.

Seven years after the murder, the name Fred Malchow came to the forefront once again. Harold Hohimer told detectives that his brother Francis had confided in him on the day after the murder, telling him, "I've been on a score. There was some trouble, and I had to do somebody in. I had to 'off' somebody."

Francis Hohimer, a burglar serving a 30-year sentence in the Iowa State Prison, was questioned by police. He told them that back in 1966 he had headed a gang of robbers. He disagreed with his brother's story. He claimed that he himself hadn't been in the Percy residence on the night of the murder. One of his gang, Fred Malchow, had been the killer. Francis went on to tell police certain details concerning the interior of the Percy home, which he could know only if he'd been there or if the killer had described them to him.

With the chief suspect in the case long dead, authorities felt that the Valerie Percy murder was unsolvable.

In 1966, after staying in seclusion for two weeks, Charles Percy announced that he was continuing his political campaign. He was successful in his bid for the U.S. Senate. In his victory speech, he said, "There is one person who is not here. She would have been happy to be here." Those present knew he was referring to his daughter Valerie.

# PETER QUEEN

## WAS CHRISSIE'S DEATH MURDER OR SUICIDE?

THE demon rum has played a major role in many a murder case. Certainly, Chrissie Gall's alcoholism caused her death. Whether her life ended by means of murder or suicide is another matter.

Chrissie was the daughter of a shoemaker in Glasgow, Scotland. One of six children, she was forced, for financial reasons, to leave school at age 14 and obtain employment as a domestic. For years Chrissie worked to help support her family. In 1925, when she was 21, she was employed by the Queen family. It was while thus employed that she met the Queen's 24-year-old son, Peter. Peter had been married at age 18 to a young girl who was an alcoholic. After two years of marriage, Mrs. Queen was placed in an institution. The couple never lived together from that time on.

Peter fell in love with Chrissie. When she left his parents' employ to take care of her own seriously ill mother, he often called on her. After her mother's death, she stayed on to take care of her father.

Chrissie was a pretty girl of average intelligence. There is little doubt that, as Peter loved her, she in turn loved him dearly. Strangely for one so young, Peter had fallen in love for the second time with a girl who was addicted to alcohol. Peter, who didn't drink at all, was kind to Chrissie and always treated her with affection.

Three years after the death of his wife, Mr. Gall moved in with one of his other daughters and Chrissie left home. Peter saw to it that she was comfortably placed in rooms at the home of two of his friends, Mr. and Mrs. James Burns. By this time, Chrissie was drinking every day and was intoxicated half her waking hours. Three months later, Peter moved in with her and they lived together as husband and wife.

The year was 1931. Peter was 30, Chrissie, 27. Peter was still a married man. Chrissie was extremely sensitive to the situation and went out of her way to make sure none of her relatives knew she was living with a married man. She often said that this guilty knowledge had driven her to drink.

The drinking continued. Mr. and Mrs. Burns were sympathetic to Chrissie's condition and often had long talks with her in an attempt to get her to stop drinking. Chrissie always promised that she wouldn't drink anymore, but always returned to the bottle. She often threatened to commit suicide. Throughout it all, Peter was an understanding companion and lover.

In the summer of 1931, Chrissie turned the gas on in the kitchen and retired for the night in a drunken stupor. It was only by good fortune that Mrs. Burns managed to save both their lives. Shortly after this incident, Peter and Chrissie moved to their own home at 533 Dunbarton Road. Her family was still under the impression that she was a domestic. They had no idea she was living with Peter Queen.

Chrissie continued to drink heavily. Peter came to the conclusion that a change of scenery would do Chrissie good. He made arrangements for her to vacation in Aberdeen with her young niece Nessie. Chrissie would have to look after the little girl and Peter felt that keeping busy might assist her in staying away from alcohol.

On Thursday, November 19, Chrissie met her brother Bert. The two went pub crawling and Chrissie proceeded to get very drunk. When she returned to the house on Dunbarton Road with her brother, a worried Peter was waiting up for her. For the first time Chrissie had brought a member of her family to her home. Drunk as she was, she was able to tell Peter to please let on it was his aunt's house. Peter went along with Chrissie, and her brother left the house believing that she was a domestic to Peter's aunt. He would never see his sister alive again.

Next day, Chrissie woke up and proceeded to drink all day. That evening, two friends, Mr. and Mrs. Johnston, visited and found Chrissie in bed. They stayed some time and helped Peter feed her sandwiches and tea. The Johnstons left at 10:45 p.m. Four hours and 15 minutes later, at 3 a.m., Peter Queen rushed into a Glasgow police station and informed police that Chrissie was dead.

Police officers entered Chrissie's bedroom. She lay dead in her bed with the bedclothes pulled up, covering her chest. A rope, tied in a half knot, was around her neck. Her upper denture was still in place. Chrissie was dressed in her nightclothes. The rope, which proved to be part of a clothesline, was removed by a police officer, who would later state that the knot was very tight. The bedroom itself was eerie, in that nothing was disturbed. There was no sign of a struggle.

An autopsy indicated the obvious, that death was due to strangulation. Within two hours, Peter Queen was taken into custody and charged with murder. When charged, he said only, "I have nothing to say."

Peter Queen's murder trial began on January 5, 1932. A police officer took the witness stand and stated that when Peter first reported Chrissie's death in the police station, he had said, "My wife is dead. I think I have killed her."

The Johnstons were the last people, other than Peter, to have seen Chrissie alive. Mrs. Johnston told the court that in her opinion, when they left the house on Dunbarton, Chrissie had been totally intoxicated. Mr. Johnston didn't quite agree. He thought she was only slightly drunk.

Unfortunately, the pathologists who performed the autopsy neglected to examine the stomach contents or blood for alcohol. The evidence concerning Chrissie's condition was of prime importance to the Crown, who were attempting to prove that the woman was so helpless she could have been strangled without offering any resistance, which would account for the undisturbed state of the death scene.

Peter Queen testified in his own behalf. He stated that he and Chrissie had chatted for some time after the Johnstons departed. Chrissie had been extremely worried whether her brother Bert had swallowed the story about her being a domestic for Peter's aunt. Because Chrissie had been so weak from heavy drinking, he told her he had called a doctor who would be visiting with her the follow morning. Chrissie had told him to fetch their very best pillowslips in anticipation of the doctor's visit.

Peter said he went to fetch the pillowslips, but couldn't find them. He called out to Chrissie. When she didn't reply, he figured she had slumbered off. He sat down and smoked a cigarette. After about 15 minutes, he prepared to go to bed. It was then that he re-entered the bedroom and found Chrissie with the rope around her neck.

Peter shook Chrissie and then rushed from the house to the police station. He disagreed as to what he had said to the police officer. Peter swore he had said, "My wife is dead. Don't think I have killed her." Peter's statement is only one word different from the police officer's version, but the one word makes a world of difference to the meaning.

An expert testifying for the defence stated that Chrissie had definitely managed to strangle herself. He had examined the rope and said that because of its texture it would have stayed firmly fastened around Chrissie's neck even after she lost consciousness and her hands had fallen away.

It was the defence's contention that Chrissie had strangled herself while Peter was out of the bedroom searching for the pillowslips. The Crown believed that Peter had wrapped the rope around Chrissie's neck, thereby ridding himself of a woman suffering from both depression and alcoholism.

After two hours' deliberation, the Scottish jury found Peter guilty of murder with a recommendation for mercy. Peter was sentenced to death, but three days later this sentence was commuted to life imprisonment.

Peter spent over 20 years in prison before being released. He returned to Glasgow and created a new life for himself. None of his new friends knew his true identity.

Peter Queen died in May 1958. To this day, many believe that he was wrongfully convicted.

# PETER REILLY

## UNTRUE CONFESSION

THIS is the story of a mother and her son.

Barbara Gibbons was born in Berlin, Germany, on November 20, 1921. Her father, Louis, was in the import-export business and travelled a great deal.

The family moved to England when Barbara was still a child, and later, when the family business failed, to New York City.

Barbara eventually went to work for an insurance company. The family maintained a cottage in Falls Village, Connecticut, and for several summers Barbara would escape the city and make her way to her parents' summer retreat.

On March 2, 1955, Barbara gave birth to a baby boy. For no apparent reason, she called her baby Peter Reilly. No one other than Barbara was ever to know the identity of Peter's father. Barbara and her baby came to live in her parents' cottage.

As Peter grew up, it became apparent he was a good student and altogether a typical teenager, although there were those who may have thought him overly quiet. Eventually, Barbara and Peter moved into a small cottage that had once been a diner located near the village of Canaan.

Barbara and Peter got along well enough, but Barbara did have the habit of leaning heavily on her son when she thought he was in the wrong. Barbara often entertained rather unsavoury male companions, and thought nothing of drinking heavily in her son's presence.

Friday, September 28, 1973, should have been an ordinary day for Barbara Gibbons. Instead, it was to be the last day of her life. Barbara went shopping in Falls Village. She purchased some groceries and a wallet before returning to her cottage. At two o'clock, after school was dismissed, Peter joined his mother. They played a few hands of gin rummy.

That evening, Geoff Madow, a school chum of Peter's, dropped by in his car. He and Peter left Barbara watching Walter Cronkite on TV and headed for a teen centre meeting in North Canaan. Geoff drove his own car, while Peter, 18, drove Barbara's 1968 Corvette.

At 9:30 p.m. Peter left for home, arriving between 9:50 p.m. and 9:55 p.m. He entered the cottage, but his mother didn't respond to his greeting. He then went into her bedroom. His mother's nude body lay sprawled on the floor.

Barbara's eyes were blackened and her nose was broken. Both thighs were broken, and later it was discovered three ribs were fractured. Her stomach and back had been savagely slashed. Her throat had been cut in such a way that she was nearly decapitated. Barbara's blue jeans and panties were lying near her body. It appeared that she had been sexually attacked.

Within minutes police converged on the murder scene. This was really something. It wasn't every day that the peaceful little village had a homicide. That same night police read Peter his constitutional rights. They took a statement from him describing his activities up to the time he walked into his mother's bedroom. They also had Peter sign a waiver allowing investigating officers to question him without the presence of a lawyer. Peter's clothing was examined but no sign of blood was found on them. Stripped naked, his body revealed no scrapes or scratches.

Next morning, Peter was taken to Hartford and advised he was a suspect in his mother's murder. Peter may have even suggested a polygraph test would clear up the entire matter. Whoever first suggested the idea, the police were all for it. Once again, Peter was read his constitutional rights. He initialled each paragraph.

Sergeant Timothy Kelly was an expert at asking questions and operating his lie detector machine. Kelly and Peter came to an understanding that if Peter told all, the machine would effectively clear him of any suspicion in his mother's murder. Slowly the questions turned to the possibility that Peter may have killed his mother, but no longer could remember. Here are a few examples extracted from tape recordings of the interview.

*Kelly: Now is there any possibility that you came in that yard like a bat out of hell last night and hit your mother?*

*Peter: No.*

*Kelly: And you became frightened and you said, 'Holy Christ, what do I do now?'*

*Peter: No, I'm positive.*

*Kelly: Accidents can happen.*

*Peter: Right.*

A few minutes later.

*Kelly: From what I'm seeing here, I think you got doubts as to what happened last night, don't you?*
*Peter: I've got doubts because I don't understand what happened.*
*Kelly: Are you afraid that you did this thing?*
*Peter: Well, yes, of course I am. That's natural.*

Slowly and methodically, quiet, passive Peter Reilly was led through hypothetical situations illustrating that it was just possible he was the killer. More questions.

*Kelly: Remember you and I were talking and we were talking about your mother's legs. Remember?*
*Peter: Yes.*
*Kelly: What did you do to her legs?*
*Peter: I jumped on them.*
*Kelly: And what else did you do? What's really burning inside of you that you don't want to tell us about, that you did to your mother?*
*Peter: I'm not sure.*
*Kelly: What do you think you did?*
*Peter: Did I—I think I raped her.*
*Kelly: Okay, why do you say that?*
*Peter: I mean, that's what it seems like I did. That's what everything looks like I did.*

After 25 hours of questioning, Peter Reilly signed a statement confessing to the murder and mutilation of his mother. When news of Peter's confession spread through Canaan and the surrounding area, citizens were shocked. No one could believe Peter could harm anyone, let alone brutally murder his mother.

Peter was formally charged with his mother's murder. Bail was set at $50,000. Six thousand dollars was raised by concerned citizens, who formed a Peter Reilly Defense Fund. He was invited to stay with Marion and Meyer Madow, the parents of his friend Geoff.

Peter Reilly's trial began on March 1, 1974. Soon it was established that the police had acted fairly. They advised him of his constitutional rights. He had been fed and had been given time to sleep. At no time had he been threatened. As a result, his confession was admitted as evidence. A doctor took the stand and testified he thought Peter could have inflicted the wounds to his mother without getting blood on his clothing.

The jury was told that it had a choice of three possible verdicts: guilty of murder; not guilty of murder; or guilty of manslaughter in the first degree. After deliberating for several hours the jury found Peter guilty of manslaughter in the first degree. Later he was sentenced to 6 to 16 years in prison. Bail was raised to $60,000 pending an appeal for a new trial.

Again Peter's legion of friends came through with the extra money and again Peter was released from jail. By this time the dogged efforts of the local citizens had come to the attention of famous and influential people willing to assist the Peter Reilly Defense Fund in a material way. Among others, luminaries Arthur Miller, Mike Nichols, Dustin Hoffman, Elizabeth Taylor and Candice Bergen all took an interest in the case.

While his friends fought for a new trial, Peter returned to high school. He managed to graduate while still out on bail.

Finally, the court consented to a hearing in order to ascertain whether there were grounds for a new trial. With a new lawyer and funds to hire a private detective, this hearing progressed very differently from the trial that had preceded it.

During the course of the hearing, it became clear that while police had acted fairly on the surface, at no time did they direct a question towards Peter with the idea of clearing an innocent boy who had just found his mother's mutilated body. Instead, the questioning officers found themselves with a quiet, unsure, exceptionally pliable youngster, who would eventually agree to anything in order to please his interrogators. Doctors testified this extreme pliability was an outstanding feature of Peter's personality.

Peter's lawyer produced another suspect who had the motive and opportunity to murder Barbara. She had taunted him at every opportunity concerning his homosexual tendencies. In fact, the questioning of this witness became so critical that the presiding judge had to warn the lawyers that no one was on trial during the hearing.

On March 25, 1976, the court ruled: "After a long and deliberate study of all the transcripts of the original trial and the present proceedings, together with the pleadings and exhibits in both cases, this court concludes that an injustice has been done, and that the result of a new trial would probably be different."

Peter was not to stand trial again for the murder of his mother. On September 27, 1979, six years less one day from the time he walked into his mother's bedroom, the court ruled that "There was insufficient evidence to warrant prosecution."

No one has ever been convicted of murdering Barbara Gibbons.

# ALICE RHODES

## LOCKED AWAY

IT has been said that all killers are despicable, but even in the murder business there are degrees. The nasties described in this piece rank right up there with the most reprehensible of all time.

The curtain of our horror story rises on the not-so-happy occasion of the marriage of 24-year-old Lewis Staunton to 36-year-old Harriet Butterfield. The nuptials took place on June 16, 1875, in London, England.

Lewis was small, cunning and totally bored with his occupation of clerk in an auctioneer's office. Harriet was a dumpy, ugly creature who, in the language of the day, was considered an imbecile. A year before her marriage, her mother had attempted in vain to have her certified as a lunatic.

One might wonder why Lewis Staunton would marry such an unappealing woman. The answer was cold hard cash. Harriet came complete with £4,000, a veritable fortune in those long-ago days.

The unlikely pair set up housekeeping in Loughborough Road, Brixton. Things didn't go well from the very beginning. A few weeks into the marriage, Mrs. Butterfield visited her daughter. She was coolly received by Lewis and left the Stauntons quite disturbed that all was not right with Harriet and her husband. Next day, she received a letter from Lewis, accompanied by one from Harriet. Both missives contained the same message. She was told in no uncertain terms that she wasn't welcome in the Staunton home and never to call again. I suppose mothers-in-law are accustomed to such treatment, but it still must have been hard to take.

Lewis retired from the clerking business and invested his newfound wealth. He also took up with a former girlfriend, Alice Rhodes. Alice was everything Harriet was not. Besides, she was sort of family, being the sister of his brother Patrick's wife, Elizabeth.

In March 1876, Harriet gave birth to a boy, Tommy. Rather than being pleased, Lewis found the child almost as obnoxious as he found Harriet. He had Alice Rhodes move into his house, ostensibly to look after his wife and his new son. Alice didn't do any of those things. She looked after Lewis.

Two months after Harriet gave birth, Lewis wrote to his brother Patrick relating how repulsive Harriet was and how she didn't take care of her personal hygiene. Patrick responded by suggesting that Harriet might find it pleasant to spend some time at his home, The Woodlands, in Cudham, Kent. The country air would do her good. Lewis shipped off Harriet and Tommy to his brother's home, where mother and child were given a room upstairs in the attic. Initially, Harriet took her meals with Patrick and Elizabeth, but it wasn't long before her meals were delivered to her in her room. Gradually, Harriet and her son were ignored and neglected. The one window in the room was boarded up. Harriet, who hadn't washed herself in the best of times, now totally disregarded cleaning herself or Tommy.

In October, Lewis and Alice Rhodes took up residence about a 20-minute walk from The Woodlands. Alice posed as Lewis's wife. No one had the vaguest idea that a few miles down the road his real wife and son were virtual prisoners, slowly starving to death.

Tommy grew so weak from lack of nourishment that Patrick took him to Guy's Hospital, where he died the following day. The death did not arouse any undue suspicions. When Lewis was notified of his son's death, he was somewhat less than distraught. He told hospital authorities his name was Harris and that the little boy was the son of one of his farm employees. He passed over 25 shillings for the child's burial. In Lewis's warped mind, that was the end of the matter.

By this time, Harriet was being fed leftover scraps from the Stauntons' table. When there were no leftovers, she wasn't fed at all. She had no washing facilities and grew so filthy that the other members of the family avoided the odour when they passed her door. Because she had no shoes, crusts formed on the soles of her feet. In time she lost the power of speech and made only guttural animal-like sounds.

As the months passed, Harriet was something that lived upstairs. She didn't exist to the outside world and was almost nonexistent to the Staunton clan. No great plan was hatched, but individually all three Stauntons and Alice Rhodes were waiting for Harriet to die.

Two things happened. Alice became pregnant and Lewis came to believe there might be an investigation if Harriet died at home. The four schemers decided to move Harriet out of Patrick's house. Lewis located a bedroom and sitting-room arrangement at 15 shillings a week, operated by a Mrs. Chalkins in Penge, London.

Harriet was in terrible shape. After all, she had not left her room all winter. The Stauntons knew they had to come up with a story for Mrs. Chalkins. They told her that the facilities were for Lewis's mother, who was basically healthy, but refused to eat. The concerned Stauntons asked Mrs. Chalkins for the name of a doctor. She recommended a Dr. Longrigg.

Harriet arrived at the rooming house on Forbes Road. Lewis and Patrick assisted her into the house. Mrs. Chalkins was shocked at her new roomer's appearance. She reeked of neglect. That night, Alice and Elizabeth stayed with Harriet. The two men took rooms at a nearby hotel.

Next morning, a Friday, the two women informed Mrs. Chalkins that Harriet had spent a difficult night and appeared to be very ill. Dr. Longrigg was summoned. He examined Harriet and told all concerned that she would be dead within 24 hours. She was placed in a nurse's care. The nurse was startled at the emaciated condition of her patient. At one-thirty that afternoon, Harriet died in her bedroom, while the Stauntons relaxed in the sitting room. No one shed a tear.

Within the hour, Lewis had an undertaker in the house. Dr. Longrigg signed the death certificate and left instructions with the nurse to lay out the body. Lewis attempted to have the burial take place that day, but the undertaker couldn't do the job until Monday.

The Stauntons returned to Patrick's farm. On Monday the annoying Harriet would be nothing but a memory. They would take the boards off the window and give her attic room a thorough cleaning.

Had the Stauntons displayed some emotion at Harriet's death, there is little doubt they would have gotten away with murder. Their callousness caused the nurse at Penge to wonder about the emaciated woman who must have been so neglected in life. She told the undertaker of her suspicions. He in turn spoke to a friend, who happened to be acquainted with Mrs. Butterfield. The acquaintance thought the dead woman might be Harriet. When Mrs. Butterfield learned of the death, she notified police. As a result of her complaint, the funeral was delayed and a post-mortem conducted. Dr. Longrigg immediately withdrew the death certificate.

The post-mortem indicated protracted undernourishment and protracted neglect. At the time of her death. Harriet weighed 70 pounds. A coroner's inquest was conducted. As a result, all four conspirators were arrested and charged with Harriet's murder.

Their trial was closely followed throughout England. Rarely have defendants been more despised by the British public. All four were found guilty of murder and sentenced to death.

Three days before the sentences were to be carried out, Alice Rhodes was given a free pardon. The sentences of Lewis, Patrick and Elizabeth Staunton were commuted to life imprisonment.

# JIMMY RIVA

## DEVIL MADE HIM DO IT

---

JIMMY Riva was a bright little boy, but even as a preschooler he displayed telltale signs of being disturbed. He hurt animals and had an abnormal interest in blood. Later, in school, he showed flashes of brilliance interspersed with periods of depression. His grades suffered. In his early teens he let his hair grow to below his shoulders and wore a necklace of garlic.

The Riva family lived in Marshfield, Massachusetts, about 30 miles south of Boston. Many people in the town knew that Jimmy was one deeply troubled youngster. Sometimes, at night, he prowled the streets. Like some parents of disturbed children, Jimmy's thought that he might outgrow his aberrant behaviour. Several psychiatrists shared their optimism.

By the time he was 18, Jimmy had run away from home several times. Once, his parents found him in Florida. He had little regard for his appearance and rarely bathed. Away from home he lived off the land and broke into unoccupied homes for shelter.

Jimmy received psychiatric counselling and spent several short periods in mental institutions. Despite his history of irrational behaviour and his scrapes with the law, he had never displayed any physical aggression towards members of his family.

On April 10, 1980, Jimmy's grandmother, Carmen Riva Lopez, 74, was found dead in her burned-down bungalow at 19 East Street. Although Mrs. Lopez used a wheelchair, she was able to live alone and take care of her everyday needs. Her grandson Jimmy dropped in every so often to help her with heavier chores around the house.

Grandmother and grandson didn't get along. Mrs. Lopez couldn't stand Jimmy's long hair and dirty appearance. She constantly berated him to cut his hair and bathe. Jimmy didn't take the verbal abuse well. He usually said little, quickly completed his chores and left the house as speedily as possible.

Authorities were at a loss as to the origin of the fire. Initially, they felt that they were investigating an accident caused by an infirm elderly woman. However, an autopsy revealed that the horribly burned Mrs. Lopez had died as the result of two stab wounds to the heart. Her lungs bore little evidence of toxic fumes, indicating that she was dead before the fire started.

In addition, two bullets were found in her body.

Both bullets had been painted gold.

A search of the cooled-down ruins of Mrs. Lopez's house uncovered a tin box that had escaped the ravages of the intense fire. The box, which belonged to Jimmy, contained several bullets covered with gold paint.

Jimmy was now the major suspect in his grandmother's murder. Brought in for questioning, he admitted visiting her on the day of the fire. He even admitted that he had argued with her as usual regarding his appearance, but vehemently denied having anything to do with her death or the fire. When Jimmy was searched at the police station, detectives found a bloodstained fishing knife in his back pocket. There were some hairs adhering to the blade. Jimmy was held in custody and charged with his grandmother's murder.

The case against Jimmy received a severe blow when laboratory analysis of the knife indicated that the blood on the blade was not the same type as Mrs. Lopez's and that the hair was not human hair. Police wondered if they had fallen into the trap of concentrating on one suspect to the exclusion of all others.

The murder investigation was at a standstill, but took a dramatic turn on June 14 when Jimmy's mother walked into the Marshfield Police Station and told detectives that she had just visited her troubled son. He had confessed to the murder of his grandmother in detail. The confession amounted to a horror story.

Jimmy told his mother that he was a vampire. He had shot his grandmother with bullets painted gold because he had been told to do so by voices that had total command over his actions. He had stabbed her with a kitchen knife and had attempted to drink her blood.

The voices of the devil and the vampires had urged him to drive to his grandmother's home. He had taken her washtub to the basement, but all the while had known that he would kill the elderly woman. Acting under the voices' instructions, he had previously painted his .38-calibre revolver with gold paint and had hidden it in the basement. His shots had not been fatal and his grandmother had begged for her life. That's when Jimmy had stabbed her with the kitchen knife. He explained that the voices had insisted and that he had been forced to comply with their wishes.

After Jimmy was sure his victim was dead, he had tried to drink her blood, but found this too difficult to do. He had doused the body with gas and had set it on fire.

Jimmy explained that after the killing he had contemplated suicide, but the voices had told him that would be the act of a coward. He had to obey the voices. Jimmy went on to tell his mother that he knew his grandmother hated him and the only way to satisfy the voices was to kill her and to drink her blood. They told him that he stood to gain many material rewards, such as cars and money, if he went through with his assignment.

Strangely enough, psychiatrists informed the court that Jimmy was competent to stand trial. On October 22, 1981, he was tried for arson and for the murder of his grandmother.

Defence attorneys logically pleaded that their client was insane, while the prosecution countered that Jimmy had planned, executed and covered up the murder knowing full well that what he was doing was wrong.

The defence presented a well-known psychiatrist who clearly stated, "He was insane at the time of the killing of his grandmother and is insane now. He was obviously not responsible for the murder by reason of insanity."

The prosecution scored telling points when their expert testified that Jimmy had taken a well-respected psychiatric test and had achieved marks indicating he was a "normal person." The prosecution agreed that Jimmy suffered from a mental illness, but argued that it did not diminish his capacity to recognize that he was doing something wrong.

A tape of Jimmy being questioned by police the day after the murder was played to the jury. The prosecution pointed out that the answers given by the accused indicated a normal, well-organized mind.

Evidently, this tape swayed the jury. Jimmy Riva was found guilty of second-degree murder and arson. He was sentenced to life imprisonment and must serve a total of 27 years before he is eligible for parole. After spending one month in prison, he was transferred to the state mental hospital at Bridgewater, where he is presently confined.

# PAULINE ROGERS

## POISON PAULINE

---

MORRIS Amos was a big healthy specimen, never sick a day in his life, until he took the miseries in the winter of 1977. Morris would bend over and complain that his bouts of cramp would be the end of him. On a good day, Morris could give Nostradamus a run for his money. He was dead on in regard to his future.

Morris's wife, Pauline, was a rock. Folks from Kentucky are like that. Whenever Morris complained, there was his Pauline with an encouraging word. When he began to lose serious weight, about 30 pounds in a few weeks, ever-loyal, ever-faithful Pauline was there at his side with piping hot chicken soup. It shouldn't have hurt, but it did. Morris complained of a burning thirst that wouldn't go away. Pauline brought him quarts of strawberry ice cream.

Louisville neighbours were amazed at Morris's rapid deterioration. He went from a good old boy with a substantial layer of suet cascading over his belt to a gaunt, feeble man, all in a few months. Diarrhoea on a daily basis will do that to a fellow.

Pauline insisted that Morris see a physician. The doctor took one look at him and agreed that something was drastically wrong with his 46-year-old patient. He prescribed vitamins and a high-protein diet. I would like to report that Morris's condition improved, but such was not the case. His condition worsened to such an extent that he had difficulty walking. The tips of his fingers turned blue and his face took on a grey, pasty look. On a second visit to the doctor, it was suggested that Morris reduce his workload, which was kind of redundant since Morris was now too weak to do much more than breathe.

A week after the doctor's latest advice, Morris was admitted to Suburban Hospital, where his illness was considered somewhat of a mystery. Physicians there couldn't figure out what was causing Morris to waste away to nothing. There were various suggestions, from muscular dystrophy to a virus, but all these conditions were ruled out.

On February 17, 1977, two days after being admitted to hospital, Morris died. Doctors believed that death had been caused by a heart attack, but weren't positive. They approached Pauline to suggest that a post-mortem would clear up any doubts and reveal the cause of her husband's rapid deterioration. Pauline wouldn't hear of it. She told the doctors, "My Morris would never approve of such a thing."

The death certificate was duly signed. Morris was laid to rest, accompanied by the usual formalities. It was sad. Pauline wept into a dainty handkerchief while her husband was lowered into his final resting place. Pauline received the proceeds of a modest life insurance policy as well as social security cheques. Life went on.

Five years later, when Morris's death was little more than a dim memory, Luther Rogers, an assembly worker down at the Ford plant in Louisville, was admitted to hospital. He complained of severe diarrhoea and a burning thirst. Luther tried every treatment his doctors recommended, but he went rapidly downhill. After several days in hospital, his health showed a marked improvement. In fact, Luther was so strong he was released into the loving arms of his wife.

Two months later, Luther, like a bad penny, showed up at the hospital again. He could hardly walk. Tests indicated a drastic decrease of white blood cells, but medics were stumped as to the cause. They met and discussed every possibility. Someone asked if Luther had ever been tested for poison. It was a long shot, but the doctors decided to conduct several tests. In the meantime, Luther's intake of food and drink was being carefully monitored.

Luther's wife visited as usual. She asked her husband's nurse if she could feed him some ice cream. After all, he complained constantly of his extreme thirst. The nurse could see no harm in ice cream. Luther looked up gratefully as his wife spoon-fed him heaping tablespoons of the cooling delicacy. It was strawberry, his favourite flavour. When Luther polished off the ice cream, his wife tossed the empty container into the wastebasket. After she left the hospital, Luther's lab tests were completed and given to his attending physicians. Normal urine tests contain 200 milligrams of arsenic. Our boy had 20,000 milligrams inside him. Someone was poisoning Luther. Doctors called in the police.

Detectives inquired about Luther's intake of food. They were assured that his entire diet was supervised and carefully monitored. Nevertheless, the nosy detectives wanted to question Luther's nurses. The nurses told the detectives that no one, absolutely no one, had fed Luther anything other than his prescribed nourishment, much of which was given intravenously. Of course, his wife was an exception. She had fed him strawberry ice cream. As a matter of fact, she had been there earlier in the day and had tossed the empty ice-cream container into the wastebasket.

The container was retrieved. Large traces of arsenic were found. Luther's home was searched for arsenic but none was uncovered. Finally, his wife's background was investigated. Well, son of a gun. Quicker than you could consume a mint julep, it was learned that Pauline Rogers's previous husband, Morris Amos, had died five years before under exactly the same circumstances that surrounded Luther's illness. Both had been healthy, robust men who had wasted away in a matter of weeks for no apparent reason. In each case, Pauline had fed them strawberry ice cream. It was all much too much.

County coroner Richard Greathouse was made aware of the facts of Morris's death. Since arsenic remains in the hair and fingernails of deceased persons, he authorized the exhumation of Morris Amos's body. In June 1982, the body was transferred to University Hospital. A day later the results were delivered to the coroner's office. Morris had not died of a heart attack. Arsenic had been found in the body: 460 milligrams in hair, 470 in the stomach and 18,000 milligrams in the liver. From the hair it was ascertained that Morris had been systematically poisoned for over a year.

Pauline Rogers was taken into custody and charged with the murder of Morris Amos. Next day, she raised bail of $2,500 and was released from jail. That same evening, she was hospitalized with severe stomach cramps. Pauline had poisoned herself. She recovered, but the incident revealed that she was an avid gardener and had access to arsenic-laced pesticides.

In August 1982, Pauline Rogers was indicted on charges of murdering her previous husband, Morris Amos, and of the attempted murder of her current husband, Luther Rogers. Pauline was found guilty on both charges, although she never revealed the motive for her actions. She was sentenced to 20 years' imprisonment for murder and received the maximum sentence of 20 years for attempted murder. The sentences were to run consecutively.

Today, Pauline resides in the Kentucky Correctional Institution for Women. Officials there tell me she is a model prisoner and gets along well with staff and fellow inmates. She will be eligible for parole in the year 2000 at the age of 64.

# TIMOTHY ROMAN

## THE TRAGIC LIFE OF SUSAN CABOT

WHEN Harriet Shapiro's family moved from Boston to New York, they had no idea that little Harriet would become a Hollywood movie actress. Harriet, who was born in 1927, was an outstanding beauty with her olive complexion and flashing brown eyes. After graduating from Washington Irving High School, she was initiated into the acting profession, playing summer stock in Maine.

At age 23, Harriet changed her name to Susan Cabot and made her first movie, *On the Island of Samoa,* for Columbia Pictures. There followed a series of B-movies, such as *The Battle of Apache Pass, Flame of Araby, Tomahawk, The Wasp Woman* and many more. She appeared on the silver screen with the likes of Tony Curtis, Rock Hudson and Lee Marvin.

In 1959, at the height of her career, Susan made international headlines when she was romantically linked with King Hussein of Jordan. The unlikely pair dated and even arranged a rendezvous in New York before the romance fizzled, much as Susan's career faded, and eventually died. Susan was one of those beautiful women who had made a fine living for years as a budding starlet, but who never quite climbed the ladder to star status. She was quickly forgotten by the movie-going public.

Susan married businessman Martin Sacker, but eventually they divorced. She entered a second marriage to Michael Roman, bringing a son, Timothy, to the union. This marriage also ended in divorce.

Timothy had major health problems, having been born a dwarf, a fact that Susan could not accept. She spent thousands of dollars to save her son's life and to assist him in growing. As a youngster, Tim was subjected to growth-hormone injections over a period of years. While the experimental treatment succeeded in developing the lad's growth until he reached five feet four inches, the injections had severe side effects. When Susan was told that the injections threatened her son's life, she discontinued them, but immediately instituted other treatments. The large quantity of experimental drugs administered to Tim no doubt had a detrimental effect. He suffered from severe psychiatric problems and was considered to be emotionally immature during his teenage years.

Susan lived alone with her son in a luxurious home in the Los Angeles suburb of Encino, overlooking the San Fernando Valley. Years passed. Tim was her one consuming passion. Some said she was a domineering, obsessive mother who completely controlled the boy. Susan pointed out to her critics that when Tim was born it was estimated that he would grow to a maximum height of four feet. Because of her efforts, he was five feet four inches tall.

Acquaintances of Susan claimed that mother and son were emotional wrecks. She neglected her home to the point where they were living in abject squalor, with two large dogs as their only company.

In 1986, Tim was attending Pierce College, but didn't display any career direction. Although he had no friends, he did have a hobby. He was enthralled with the martial arts and read everything he could lay his hands on regarding the topic. In the main, his life revolved around his overprotective mother. Susan rarely let her 22-year-old son out of her sight.

On December 10, 1986, the strained relationship between the possessive 59-year-old Susan and her emotionally disturbed son burst into violence. Tim called police. They found him in the living room, sobbing uncontrollably. Susan Cabot, clad only in a purple negligée, lay dead on her bed. She had been beaten about the head. Tim told police that he had been attacked by a martial arts practitioner, who had overpowered him, cutting him on the arm and striking him over the head with some kind of blunt instrument. Tim said he must have been unconscious for about half an hour. When he regained consciousness, he called for help.

Paramedics attending to Tim noted that the knife wound on his arm was little more than a scratch and the bruise on his head had not even caused swelling. The first detectives at the scene listened to Tim relate how he was in bed earlier in the night, but was accosted when he got up to fix a sandwich. Police found it strange that there was no evidence of forced entry.

A search of Tim's room turned up a blood-smeared barbell, which proved to be the murder weapon. The many posters of martial arts films that adorned Tim's walls revealed the reason why he had picked a martial arts expert as his bogus attacker.

Tim was arrested and charged with his mother's murder. After so many years out of the news, the name Susan Cabot had made the headlines once more. Her old romance with King Hussein was again publicized with the additional juicy tidbit that Tim might have been sired by the king. It was rumoured that because Susan was Jewish, the romance was doomed and broken off by mutual consent.

Tim had more pressing problems. Several legal proceedings were conducted to ascertain if he was fit to stand trial. Eventually he was deemed to be capable. On May 1, 1989, over two years after his mother's death, Tim stood trial for her murder.

The prosecution painted Tim as a cold-blooded killer who knew very well what he was doing. He had planned the killing and had carried it out without hesitation or remorse. They also contended that he had inflicted superficial wounds to his own body in an attempt to invent an intruder. He had hated his mother for years for her domineering and possessive personality.

Tim's defence attorneys didn't see it that way at all, but before the defence had an opportunity to present its case, famed lawyer Chester Leo Smith took ill and could not continue. A mistrial was declared and a second trial set for October.

On October 5, the prosecution presented basically the same evidence as they had at the earlier trial. The defence leaned heavily on Tim's health problems. They pointed out that the boy had received hormone injections in his legs twice a week for 15 years between 1970 and 1985. In addition, they produced medical records indicating that Tim had been born with brain damage. Psychiatrists testified that his mental problems would have made it impossible for him to have formed the intent to kill his mother. It was a strong argument. There sat Tim in the courtroom, acting and looking like a boy of 14, although he had celebrated his twenty-fifth birthday in jail.

Tim took the witness stand in his own defence. He had drastically changed his story in the almost three years since the murder. From the witness stand he related that he and his mother had had a severe argument, which had culminated with her swinging the barbell at his head. Tim remembered trying to push his mother away, but nothing more than that. He admitted hiding the barbell. He admitted lying to police and making up the story about the man who had attacked his mother and himself.

Tim was found guilty of involuntary manslaughter, which carries a maximum sentence of four years' imprisonment. As Tim had already spent three years in jail, the judge sentenced him to a three-year suspended sentence. Because he had not been found guilty of the far more serious charges of voluntary manslaughter or murder, he was entitled to inherit his mother's estate of approximately one million dollars.

Timothy Roman walked out of court with his adoptive grandparents, a free man.

# CHARLEY ROSS

## THE KIDNAPPING OF LITTLE CHARLEY ROSS

---

MOST of us are aware of the details surrounding the kidnapping of the Lindbergh baby from its nursery on March 1, 1932. The discovery of the child's body left the U.S.—indeed the world—in a state of shock. Bruno Hauptmann was eventually tried for the child's murder, found guilty and executed.

Far less is remembered today about the kidnapping of little Charley Ross, but at the time, his abduction caused almost as great an outcry as the Lindbergh tragedy. Charley was the first child kidnapped for ransom in the history of the United States.

Christian K. Ross lived in a large three-storey white house in the Germantown section of Philadelphia. Ross was a well-to-do businessman who devoted a portion of his time to politics and church affairs. He and his wife were considered to be pillars of the community. The happy, contented couple had seven children.

In the latter part of June 1874, Mrs. Ross departed for a vacation to Atlantic City with her eldest daughter, Sara. The two oldest sons, Stouton and Harry, left their home for a visit with their grandmother in Middletown. On Wednesday, July 1, the two youngest sons, Charley, 4, and Walter, 6, were at home with their sisters, Marian and Anne. Also about the home that day were two servants—a cook and a gardener.

Ross left for work in downtown Philadelphia. There was a sense of anticipation about the house, for the children were getting ready to celebrate the Fourth of July.

Charley and Walter went outdoors to play. No sooner were they outside than two men approached them in a horse and buggy. Both boys were unconcerned. They recognized the rig and the men. On the previous Saturday the two men had stopped and chatted with the boys, and had even given them some candy. The very next day the same thing happened. Now, for the third time, it looked as if the boys would get a treat. Incidentally, the familiar admonition "Never take candy from a stranger" is derived from this case.

Sure enough, the rig stopped and the two men offered the boys some more candy. When the men suggested they take the boys for a drive and buy them firecrackers, Charley couldn't wait to be lifted aboard the buggy. Walter scampered up on his own.

That evening, Christian Ross returned home from his business at six o'clock. His two sons were nowhere to be found. Accompanied by some concerned friends, he searched for the boys throughout the neighbourhood. As darkness fell, he was on his way to a nearby police station when he spotted Walter on the street. The boy was accompanied by a man named Henry Peacock, who had found Walter crying on a street corner some eight miles away and was delivering him to his home. Later, Peacock was checked out. He was exactly what he appeared to be—a concerned citizen delivering a lost, bewildered child to his parents.

Ross questioned Walter: "Where is Charley?"

"Why, he's all right. He's in a wagon."

After much questioning, it became apparent that little Charley had been spirited away by strangers.

On July 4, the Ross family received a ransom letter advising them that Charley was being held for a cash payment and that a more detailed letter would follow. With the receipt of the letter, the U.S. had experienced a new type of crime—money for the return of a child. Philadelphia police were at a loss for what action to take. They took none.

Analysts studied the letter and were convinced it was written by someone who was disguising his handwriting and purposely misspelling simple words. On July 6, another ransom letter was delivered, this time demanding $20,000 and warning the frightened parents not to let the police interfere with the drop off of the money.

All through July, the Ross family received notes from the kidnappers. They replied by placing advertisements in the local newspapers as instructed. It must be pointed out that, like the Lindbergh kidnapping, the Ross affair was public knowledge and received headline treatment across the country. The public thirsted for any new developments. Law enforcement authorities realized that if the ransom money ever changed hands successfully, there would be an epidemic of kidnapping throughout the country. All during July, Mr. and Mrs. Ross went through hell, for many of the kidnappers' letters contained details of what they would do to Charley if his parents didn't follow instructions to the letter.

Towards the end of July, the city of Philadelphia offered a reward of $20,000 for the arrest of the kidnappers and the safe return of the child. This reward attracted scores of crank calls and clues, all leading nowhere. Amazingly, the kidnappers kept up their correspondence with Ross.

Finally, the details of turning over the ransom money were worked out. Ross was to board a New York–bound train at midnight in Philadelphia. The kidnappers said contact would be made sometime during the trip. Ross boarded the train as planned, with two plainclothes policemen covering his every move. No attempt at contact was made. A further letter from the kidnappers made no reference to the aborted transfer.

On August 2, when Charley had been missing for a little more than a month, the first real clue to the mystery was uncovered. Ironically, it came from the New York Police Department. An old sea captain, Gil Mosher, went to the police with his story. He claimed his brother Bill had approached him the previous May with a scheme to kidnap one of Commodore Vanderbilt's grandchildren. He had turned down his brother, feeling the operation was too risky. The scheme was exactly the same as the plan actually implemented to kidnap Charley Ross. Gil figured it was too much of a coincidence. He was sure that his brother and a friend, Joseph Douglas, were the kidnappers. Gil's motive for coming forward was the reward money and a personal vendetta against his brother. He also stated that he could recognize his brother's distinctive handwriting, no matter what pains he had taken to disguise it.

When informed of this new development, Philadelphia Police Chief Kennard H. Jones, accompanied by Christian Ross's brother Joseph, rushed to New York. They heard Gil Mosher's story and had him describe his brother's handwriting before showing him the letter. Gil not only described the writing, but also pointed out his brother's habit of folding the letters in a distinctive fashion. Other minute details convinced the police that Bill Mosher had written the ransom letters.

The word went out to pick up Bill Mosher and Joseph Douglas. Both men were small-time thieves who had been in and out of jail for a number of years. Apprehending them was no easy task, for the police had made the decision to keep their search undercover. They feared for Charley's life if the kidnappers found out that their identity was known.

Abruptly the case took an unexpected turn. Judge Van Brunt owned a large modern summer home in Bay Ridge, Long Island. His brother, Holmes Van Brunt, lived in a large, gracious old Victorian home directly across the judge's lawn. When the judge returned to the city for the winter, he set up an alarm system that would go off in his brother's permanent home if anything was disturbed during his absence.

On the night of December 14, this alarm went off, waking up Holmes Van Brunt. Holmes, his son Albert, together with gardener William Scott and hired hand Herman Frank armed themselves and cautiously headed for the judge's house. They hid in the bushes waiting for the robbers to come out.

Finally the cellar door opened. Van Brunt shouted, "Halt, stop!" Two shots whistled past his head. The four concealed men opened fire. One of the intruders fell, shouting, "I give up," but the other man made it to a lane, where he ran into Albert, who swung his shotgun at the robber, breaking his arm. As the burglar raised his pistol, Albert got two shots away with his revolver, sending bullets into the robber's head and chest. The man fell but was still breathing. The shooting abruptly ceased.

Someone gave the dying man a drink of whiskey. Van Brunt bent over the critically wounded man: "Young man, your time is pretty short now. If you have anything to say, you had better be about it at once. Who are you? What is your name and where did you come from?"

The answer was barely audible: "Men, I won't lie to you. My name is Joseph Douglas. That man lying over there is William Mosher. Mosher and I stole Charley Ross from Germantown."

With a certain degree of desperation, someone asked, "Who has charge of the child now?"

The fallen man replied, "Mosher knows all about the child. Ask him."

The men, now joined by their wives and a few neighbours, huddled over Douglas.

"Mosher is dead," they exclaimed. "Can you tell us where the child is?"

"I don't know where he is. Mosher knows." Then Douglas added, "The child will be returned home safe and sound in a few days." Joseph Douglas closed his eyes and breathed his last.

The search for little Charley Ross continued. He was spotted in several U.S. cities, in Montreal, Toronto and Vancouver, as well as several Mexican and European cities. Over the years many adults have claimed to be Charley Ross, but all such claims have been disproved. Members of Charley's family continued to search for him for the remainder of their lives. When his parents died, his six sisters and brothers continued the search.

On July 1, 1924, the fiftieth anniversary of the kidnapping, Walter, who had become an extremely successful businessman, made a public statement concerning his brother's abduction. He stated that all the claimants to Charley's identity were cranks, but he still held out hope that the mystery might one day be solved.

To this day, no one knows what became of Charley Ross.

# MICHAEL SAMS

## HE PUT HIS VICTIM IN A COFFIN

THIS time would be different, thought Michael Sams as he meticulously planned the perfect crime. His previous attempt had been amateurish in its execution.

On July 9, 1991, he had plucked part-time prostitute Julie Dart off the streets of Leeds, England, and had killed her. A blow to the back of the head with a ball-peen hammer had rendered the girl unconscious. He had finished her off by strangling her with a ligature. Two days after Julie's disappearance, Michael had written a letter to police demanding £140,000 for her safe return. Police responded, but Michael pulled out of the complicated drop-off procedure before it was completed. A few days later, Julie's body was found in a field.

Michael now felt that the time had come to implement the perfect crime. He planned well. The victim was chosen, the plot perfected. Michael would kidnap a female and keep her hostage until the ransom was paid.

On Wednesday, January 22, 1992, Michael had an appointment to meet Stephanie Slater, a 25-year-old real estate agent employed by Shipways, a large real estate organization. Using the name Bob Southwall, he had phoned for an appointment to view a home at 153 Turnberry Road in Birmingham. He was waiting outside the door when Stephanie drove up in her company-owned Ford Escort.

Stephanie showed the house to her client. Without warning, in an upstairs bathroom, Michael pulled out a knife and a chisel. Stephanie couldn't believe this was happening to her. She lunged at him and the pair struggled. Stephanie felt the pain in her hand as the blade sunk into her flesh. Her attacker pushed her backward into the bathtub, helpless. The fight was over. She shouted, "Don't kill me, please don't kill me!" The man's voice rose, "Shut up, shut up. Be quiet. Don't look at me, don't look at me."

Michael knew exactly what he was doing. He tied, gagged and blindfolded his victim. Stephanie decided then and there to do everything this man asked of her. Her life depended on her wits.

Michael led Stephanie downstairs and into a vehicle. Twenty minutes later, they came to a stop. Michael assured Stephanie that she was not going to die unless she caused trouble. He informed her that she was being held for ransom. Michael had Stephanie make a tape recording for her employers. She repeated her captor's words, outlining her precarious position and advising them that they would be contacted again. Michael placed the tape in an envelope, which he had Stephanie lick shut. He told her if he licked the envelope, police would be able to obtain his DNA prints. Stephanie knew she was at the mercy of no ordinary criminal. This guy had thought of everything.

After driving for well over an hour, the pair arrived at their destination. Michael was alternately cruel and kind to Stephanie. He shared a pot of hot tea with her, but interspersed their chat with the threat that if she screamed while the gag was out of her mouth or if her blindfold slipped from her eyes, he would kill her.

Michael placed Stephanie in a coffinlike wooden box which she entered feet first. He undid her handcuffs in order to place her hands over a bar above her head before refastening the cuffs. Stephanie's hips scraped against both sides of the wooden box. It was pitch-black and bitterly cold inside Stephanie's coffin. She heard the sound of her captor's car disappearing in the distance. Stephanie Slater was so very alone.

Michael Sams drove the 15 miles from his workshop in Newark, Nottinghamshire, to his home in Sutton-on-Trent. His plan was now in motion. It would not only make him rich, but would illustrate his brilliance as a master criminal. He had come a long way since that day 15 years earlier when he had been imprisoned for car theft. While in prison, he'd contracted cancer. His leg was amputated and replaced with an artificial limb. All that was behind him now. He crawled into bed with his third wife, Teena.

Next morning, Michael drove to his workshop. Stephanie was in terrible shape. The blood had drained from her hands and arms. Her hips were scraped from rubbing against the side of the box. When her gag was removed, she had difficulty speaking. She had almost frozen during the bitterly cold night. Michael explained that he was demanding £175,000 from her employers, Shipways, which was owned by a large organization, Royal Life Estates. Once the money was turned over to him, he would set her free.

Letters received by Shipways were turned over to the police. From the misspellings, police connected Julie Dart's murder with Stephanie Slater's abduction. They realized they had a bona fide madman on their hands, and a clever one at that.

Four days passed. Stephanie was now following a regimen. Michael had improved the coffin so that her hips no longer scraped its sides and had provided her with blankets. When she awoke, she was allowed out of her capsule for breakfast and exercise. She was permitted to relieve herself, after which she was returned to her coffin. She talked to her captor, all the while being cooperative and complimentary to him. He in turn seemed to enjoy her company and appeared to be growing fond of her. At no time did he sexually interfere with Stephanie in any way.

Finally, the night of the ransom money transfer arrived. Michael gave Stephanie's superior, Kevin Watts, explicit instructions over the telephone as to how to proceed with the £175,000. Watts was to act as courier with the warning that police were not to be present. Police taped this conversation. Michael told Stephanie she would soon be home with her parents.

Kevin Watts started on his journey. He received written instructions at several phone booths, eventually finding himself on a lonesome road with instructions to place the money in a tray on the rail of a stone trestle. Watts did as he was instructed. Down below in the pitch blackness was Michael Sams. Attached to the tray was a length of thin cord. As soon as the sound from Kevin's vehicle faded into the distance, Michael pulled on the cord, causing the ransom money to tumble down at his feet.

Michael returned to Stephanie in his Newark workshop. She was elated. She realized that if he had failed to return, she would have starved to death in her cage.

Originally, Michael had planned to drop Stephanie off in an isolated area and let her walk to a phone. Now he felt some sympathy. He would drive her home. He knew very well her house would be guarded by police, but a block or two away would be safe enough. Michael pulled up near Hembs Crescent and let Stephanie out. His last words were, "Get back to your normal life as soon as possible. You may need some counselling. I'm sorry it had to be you." Stephanie stepped out of the car and removed her blindfold. The streetlights blinded her. She staggered as she walked.

Les Barnaby was up late that night watching a movie on the TV when he heard Michael's car pull up. He glanced out his window and saw an orange Metro speed away. An apparently intoxicated girl staggered down the street. Stephanie made her way to her home, knocked on the door and surprised her overjoyed parents. She had been held prisoner for eight days.

Police now had a description of the man who called himself Bob Southwall, as well as a tape of his voice. Les Barnaby came forward with a description of the suspect's vehicle. The case was featured on the BBC's widely viewed

"Crime Watch" program. Police received more than 1,000 calls claiming to know the identity of the wanted man. One proved to be correct. Michael's first wife, Susan Oake, had no doubt about the kidnapper's identity. She immediately informed police.

Michael was arrested without incident and eventually the ransom money was recovered. He admitted to kidnapping Stephanie, but claimed to have no knowledge of Julie Dart's murder. However, an English jury found him guilty of murder, kidnapping and unlawful imprisonment. Michael Sams received three life sentences. Later, in prison, he confessed to the murder of Julie Dart.

# ED SCHRODER

## HE DRILLED THE DENTIST

ALL the fellows at the London and San Francisco Bank couldn't understand the sudden change that had come over Ed Schroder. For years Ed had been a steady employee. Good family man, too. Salt of the earth. That was before June 12, 1880.

After that date, he hardly talked to anyone, was often absent from work and abruptly stopped playing poker with the boys. Ed just wasn't the same old Ed anymore.

The man his colleagues knew so well had been a career banker for eight years. He had been married for the same length of time to Mary Stebbins, the daughter of Reverend Horatio Stebbins. The reverend, who would later become regent of the University of California and trustee of Stanford University, was no small potatoes. He was furious when his daughter eloped with Ed, but, like many a father before him, resigned himself to the fact that foolish young girls marry boys they love rather than those their fathers choose.

The marriage was a happy one. Ed and Mary lived in a pleasant home at 1164 Alice Street. Two little Schroders blessed the union.

One fine day in 1878, Mary had a toothache. She paid a visit to Dr. Alfred LeFevre, a successful dentist who was well married to a sickly wife and was the father of four children. Mary didn't have a simple cavity. I know that for a fact because she continued to visit the 45-year-old dentist for the next two years. In case there is any doubt, we are talking hanky-panky here.

On the night of June 11, 1880, Ed was supposed to work late, but packed it in around 9 p.m. He returned quite unexpectedly to his home on Alice Street. As he entered the front door, he heard someone rush out the back. His wife was upstairs in bed. Ed asked Mary who had been visiting. She told him that it was Sarah Gallagher, the family maid. When questioned further, Mary changed her story. She told her husband she wasn't a hundred percent sure it was Sarah, it might have been Sarah's boyfriend.

Mary had made the mistake of altering lies in mid falsehood. Ed was suspicious. He begged Mary to tell him the truth. Finally, she blurted out that the visitor had been Dr. LeFevre. She went on to say that the dentist had not only filled her teeth, he had also satisfied one of her more basic needs.

Ed was devastated. Next morning he advised Reverend Stebbins that his daughter was an adulteress. The reverend questioned Mary, who denied all. Folks, Mary lied through her teeth.

To prove his daughter had been visiting the dentist on legitimate dental business for the previous two years, the reverend, accompanied by Ed, paid a visit to Dr. LeFevre. They wanted a detailed accounting of her many visits. Regrettably, the doctor's accountant kept the books and he was not present. Ed said something about blowing the dentist's brains out, which was unfortunate. Such threats have a way of becoming evidence at murder trials.

The pair left the office without the bill for Mary's dental work. Later, Dr. LeFevre gave them a receipted bill in the amount of $83, which was kind of revealing, as it was later proven that Mary had never paid the dentist one penny.

Well, folks, it had been quite a 24 hours for our Ed. His wife had admitted to being unfaithful for two years and it appeared to him that her lover was paying him off with a receipted bill for dental work.

Ed took to the demon rum with a vengeance. It was as if he were attempting to drink the world dry. He became a close- mouthed, brooding man and often stayed away from the bank. His colleagues and friends had no idea what was causing his mental anguish until July 26. That was the day Ed drilled dentist Alfred LeFevre.

It was all very dramatic. The doctor had several patients with teeth just waiting to be drilled, cleaned or pulled. Seated on chairs, leafing through those months-old magazines favoured by dentists, were a Mrs. Spotts and a Miss Agnew. They would only be scared out of their wits. Seated in the dentist's chair at the time was a Mrs. Keeney. She would think the world had come to an end.

The doctor left Mrs. Keeney's side to fetch one of his hideous instruments. At that precise moment, Ed dashed into the office brandishing a pistol. He fired point-blank at the dentist, who staggered across the office to Mrs. Keeney's side before falling to the floor. Displaying a distinct lack of confidence in his aim, Ed fired a second shot at the fallen man. Dr. LeFevre was able to mumble that Ed had shot him in cold blood and without provocation. He died on the office floor. Mrs. Keeney had the dubious distinction of being the doctor's last patient.

A police officer summoned from the street was greeted by Ed with the great line, "Officer, do your duty. I have shot a man. No man can seduce my wife and live."

Ed was taken into custody and charged with the murder of Dr. LeFevre. His trial, which began on November 29, 1880, was the social event of the winter season in the Bay area. Little else was discussed. This one had everything: a backstairs romance between a banker's wife and a married dentist; the shooting beside that torturous chair; Mrs. Keeney's frightening experience. The Schroder murder trial was definitely not to be missed.

On the surface, it appeared as if Ed's goose was cooked. The victim had said he did it, even Ed said he did it. In addition, a gunsmith told the court Ed had purchased the murder weapon on the day of the fatal shooting.

As we all know, however, murder cases are not that simple. The jury was faced with a difficult decision. If they believed that Ed had planned the murder with intent to kill while in a clear state of mind, then he was guilty of murder in the first degree. If convicted, he would be sentenced to death. On the other hand, if Ed had been driven insane by the thought of his wife having sexual intercourse with Dr. LeFevre over a prolonged period, he could be acquitted.

Three days later, the jury returned a verdict of not guilty. Ed burst into tears and embraced the foreman of the jury.

Ed and Mary left the courtroom arm in arm to the cheers of the standing-room-only crowd. They remained in San Francisco only a few months. The notoriety of the murder case forced them to leave the city and they soon disappeared from public view.

It is not known whether his wife Mary required any further dental work.

# CHICKEN STEPHENS

## SENATOR'S DEMISE

JOHN Walter "Chicken" Stephens was a sleaze. He was also a U.S. senator. Occasionally, the two go hand in hand.

Chicken was a good ol' southern boy who couldn't stay out of minor scrapes with the law. In 1849, while still a lad, he apprenticed as a harness maker, an honest profession if not one with a great future. When he stole a quantity of leather from his employer, his family made restitution to keep their boy out of the Leaksville, North Carolina, jail. Despite the occasional misdemeanour, Chicken became an official of the Methodist church in town and sold bibles on the side to augment his meagre income.

Let's take time out to relate how Chicken got his colourful nickname. This doesn't have much to do with the story, but it's so much fun that I can't pass it up.

A neighbour, Tom Ratliff, caught our boy red-handed with two headless chickens he had just stolen from Ratliff's coop. Ratliff was furious and had him charged with theft. When Stephens learned of the charge, he went after Ratliff with a pistol and a club. Two strangers separated the men and received superficial bullet wounds for their trouble. In the end, Stephens paid fines totalling $2,000 for the theft and the assault. The chicken story spread throughout the state, and forever after Stephens was known simply as Chicken. Years later, a local boy commented, "Mr. Stephens stole a chicken and was sent to the state Senate and if he'd steal a gobbler he'd be sent to Congress."

Undaunted by his unfortunate legal encounters, Chicken married a local girl, Nancy Waters, and after the prescribed nine months became the father of a healthy daughter. Seeking greener pastures, he and his family moved to Yanceyville, North Carolina. Once ensconced in his new surroundings, Chicken made the mistake of attempting to cook a crooked deal with Dr. Allan Gunn, a local man who was running for sheriff. He promised to deliver enough votes to assure Gunn's victory for the paltry sum of $4,000. Gunn was outraged and reported the offer to the Methodist Church. As a result, Chicken was excommunicated.

Once again, Chicken overcame a scandal. He ran for the position of state senator and won. Chicken saw the job as a licence to feather his nest. He immediately sought and obtained several minor posts, which enabled him to charge for favours. An unscrupulous judge issued Chicken a licence to practise law. That privilege cost him $20.

Now in high gear, Chicken, as a justice of the peace, reaped a percentage of every fine he levied. He also made a fortune selling political favours. By 1870, Chicken was a wealthy man with a fine family living in a large rambling home. There was one fly in the sarsaparilla: over the years Chicken had made many enemies. To protect himself, he carried several knives and a pistol.

Around this time, the Ku Klux Klan was a formidable force in North Carolina. When the members of that organization thought the legal community was lax, they were not above taking the law into their own hands. The Klan felt that Chicken had had his own way long enough. They would get rid of him in their own unique fashion.

On May 21, 1870, the Democratic Party was holding a convention in the Caswell County Courthouse in Yanceyville. The building was crowded with 300 delegates. Outside, in the town square, citizens came and went. It was a busy, exciting day in the town.

Chicken Stephens attended the convention. He listened to the speeches for some time before leaving with Frank Wiley, a huge man who had formerly been sheriff of the town. The two men were seen in the main lobby of the courthouse at a few minutes after 4 p.m. Wiley left the building alone. No one could remember seeing Chicken after that.

Back at the Stephens' residence, Nancy waited for her husband. He had told her he would be home by five for supper. When Chicken didn't arrive by 6 p.m., she contacted his two brothers, who went around town looking for the missing man. As night fell, they could only trace Chicken's movements to the courthouse lobby. They contacted county officials, who felt that it would be best to search every nook and cranny of the old building in the light of day. Several men were posted to guard the courthouse that night.

Bright and early Sunday morning, in a room used primarily to store firewood, the searchers came across the body of Senator Chicken Stephens. A rope was deeply embedded in his neck and his throat had been slit from ear to ear. He had also been stabbed in the chest with a pearl-handled pocket knife which lay on the floor beside the body. Chicken's gold watch and his money were intact, eliminating robbery as the motive for the crime.

An inquest into the death was conducted immediately. The jury concluded that Chicken had been murdered by persons unknown. That was the official stand, but many believed that the Klan was responsible. Everyone in Yanceyville knew that the leader of the Klan in that area was John Lea, a 27-year-old Confederate veteran. He had been in the courthouse on the day of the murder, as had several members of his organization.

Two months after the murder, Lea, former sheriff Wiley and two other Klan members, J.T. Mitchell and Felix Roan, were taken into custody. Although their guilt was strongly suspected, there was nothing more against them than vague insinuations. They were released from custody, to the elation of the townsfolk. In fact, a celebration parade was held in their honour.

The murder remained unsolved. As the years passed, John Lea was often asked if he had been involved in Chicken's murder. In 1912, he presented a typewritten sealed document to the North Carolina Historical Commission with instructions that it be opened upon his death.

Captain John Lea lived until 1935, when he passed away in South Boston, Virginia, at age 92. The sealed letter was opened. In it, Lea confessed that he had been the leader of the Klan and had organized and planned the murder of Senator Chicken Stephens. The three men arrested with him at the time of the murder were all involved, as were others. Lea named them: James Denny, Joe Fowler, Tom Oliver, Pink Morgan and Dr. S.T. Richmond. Lea had outlived everyone connected with the crime.

In his letter, he described every aspect of the murder in detail. Wiley had lured Chicken to the wood-storage room. The men had made their way singly to the room. When Chicken entered, he found himself staring into the barrel of a Colt revolver. He realized what was about to happen and pleaded for his life. As he pleaded, Mitchell placed a rope around his neck and drew it tight, forcing Chicken to the floor, gasping for air. Tom Oliver stabbed him in the chest and slit his throat. The men stepped back. Chicken Stephens was dead.

The conspirators left the room one by one and met that same night at the outskirts of Yanceyville. At Lea's suggestion they took an oath not to reveal what had happened in the courthouse wood-storage room. None of the men in on the execution-style murder of the senator ever came in conflict with the law during their lifetime. Many led outwardly exemplary lives and several held high public office.

# ANTONIO STROLLO

## BEST FRIEND WAS A KILLER

---

AROUND the turn of the century, times were hard in Italy. For many, the United States was the land of opportunity. Construction was booming along the Eastern seaboard. Docks, railroads and huge buildings were being erected. Labour was in demand, and Italy provided much of the manpower to keep the construction industry going. From Italian stock would emerge names such as La Guardia, Di Maggio, Caruso and hundreds of others from all walks of life who would make their contribution to the development of the United States.

But all were not success stories. In the tiny town of Culiano, in the province of Salano, lived an elderly lady with her two sons. Her husband, after a lifetime of back-breaking work in the stubborn fields, had long since died. Now the widow Torsielli lived only for her two sons, Vito and Toni. For years she prepared their meals and washed their clothing while each day they worked the fields from sunup to sundown.

The years passed. Soon the old woman was confined to bed. She couldn't be left alone. The boys took the bulk of their meagre earnings and hired a woman to look after their mother. The situation looked hopeless. There was no way out. They would all live and die in Culiano without ever enjoying a moment's pleasure.

Other boys from the town were going to America. Some came back wearing bright socks and neckties. They gathered up their parents and took them back with them. Vito and Toni had a meeting. It was decided that they would live on practically nothing until they saved the fare for Vito to go to America. Then he would send money back to Culiano to take care of his mother. Who knows, maybe he would save enough for them all to end up in America.

Toni couldn't help being envious of his older brother but the scheme seemed the only way out of their predicament. Vito left for the New World. Toni and his mother waited for a letter, but no letter came. A month passed, two months, a year; still no letter came. God forbid, Vito might be dead, thought Toni. He and his sick mother might be waiting for nothing.

In the meantime, Toni was in love with Nicoletta Lupero, and had been since he was a child. Their situation seemed hopeless. Toni hardly made enough money to support himself and his mother, without taking on the added burden of a wife. Toni reached his thirtieth birthday. Nicoletta was 25. Some of their friends had been married for 10 years. From time to time, a former resident of the village would return from America. Some said that Vito was now rich, though no one said they had actually seen him. All tried to convince Toni that he was crazy if he didn't go to America.

Finally, he and Nicoletta decided that they would dismiss the woman who was looking after his ill mother. Nicoletta would move in with the aged Mrs. Torsielli and Toni would go to America, save enough money and bring them both to the New World. The day Toni left Culiano, the parish priest had to physically pull him out of his mother's arms.

Once in America, Toni met several other men his age from his home province. Through his acquaintances, he obtained pick-and-shovel work in Lambertville, New Jersey, 70 miles from New York City. Toni didn't mind the hard manual labour. It was no worse than what he had done back home. The big difference was that now he was getting paid good wages. Sometimes he made as much as $40 a month. Toni sent money home every pay day. Even after deducting his living expenses and the money he sent home, he still had some left over to put in the bank.

The months flew by. Toni made friends in Lambertville. Antonio Strollo was his best friend. It was Strollo who actually wrote Toni's letters to his mother and Nicoletta. He read the replies as well, for Toni could neither read nor write.

For three years, Toni worked and saved, always keeping an eye open for news of his brother, Vito. It was Strollo who got the bright idea that they should advertise for the missing man. Strollo was a true friend. Toni wouldn't listen when other men said Strollo was lazy and couldn't hold a job. Moreover, they said, he drank far too much Chianti. Strollo wrote and inserted the advertisement for the missing Vito in the *Il Progresso,* New York's Italian newspaper.

A letter came from Vito. He had seen the ad. He begged Toni to forgive him for not writing to their mother. Now that the ice was broken, he wanted desperately to see his brother. He told Toni he was prosperous, married and had children. He lived in Yonkers.

Toni was overjoyed. Vito was rich. Everything would still work out. Toni dictated a reply, which Strollo wrote and mailed to Vito. Several letters were exchanged by the brothers. It was decided that at the end of the month, pay day, Toni would leave his job, withdraw his savings of $300 and visit Vito. Toni would then continue to Italy, settle his family's affairs before returning to

America with Nicoletta and his mother. Strollo would accompany Toni to Yonkers. As the great day approached, Toni's landlord, Sabbatto Gizzi, wrote down his name on a piece of paper and gave it to Toni. He wanted Toni to be sure to write.

On August 16, 1903, Toni and his friend Strollo boarded the train for New York. They transferred to a trolley. At the end of the line they continued on foot. Soon the pair found themselves in the country. Toni was hungry. He spotted a man digging in a field of mushrooms. He strolled over and asked where the closest restaurant was located. The man told him that there was a good Italian restaurant—The Promised Land—in Yonkers. Toni chatted for a while. Later the man was to state that the last he saw of Toni and Strollo, they were taking a short cut through some woods that adjoined his field.

Once in the woods, Strollo pulled a knife on Toni and stabbed him more than 30 times. Then he cleaned Toni's clothing of everything that could identify the dead man and took the $300. He had never seen so much money in his life. In the ferociousness of his attack, he almost hadn't noticed his cut hand and knee. They didn't hurt. That night Strollo took a room at the Mills Hotel on Bleecker Street in New York City. He felt good, even though the cuts on his hand and knee got blood all over his bedsheets.

Next morning, Strollo ate a hearty breakfast, bought a cigar and a new suit. He bought a book, *Sua Maesta a Sua Moneta (His Majesty and His Money),* to read on the trip back to Lambertville. Strollo was supremely confident that the body, if ever found, would never be identified. Back in Lambertville he would tell Toni's friends that he had left Toni with his brother in Yonkers. He didn't have to account for Toni's absence.

Toni's body was found the very next day by the mushroom digger. He immediately recognized the body as that of the man who had inquired about a restaurant the previous day. Police searched the body and found only one tiny piece of paper, which had obviously been overlooked by the killer. On it was written: Sabbatto Gizzi, P.O. Box 239, Lambertville, New Jersey. Detectives questioned Gizzi in Lambertville, and within 36 hours of the murder, they were face-to-face with Antonio Strollo.

The story of the lost brother was revealed to the police. Strollo told the whole story, but denied killing Toni. Soon the authorities located the store where Strollo had purchased the new suit. When they questioned the hotel clerk at the Mills Hotel, he told them of the bloodstained bedding. The mushroom digger identified Strollo as the man who was with Toni shortly before the victim was killed.

Strollo was taken into custody. Informers were placed in his jail cell, and soon the whole story came out. Vito had never been found. All the time it was Strollo who had written the letters to Toni, duping him into believing they were from his long lost brother. It was all an elaborate scheme to get Toni to withdraw his savings of $300, lure him to some isolated spot, kill him and steal his money.

On March 11, 1908, Antonio Strollo was put to death in the electric chair for the murder of Toni Torsielli.

Vito Torsielli was never found.

# LARRY SWARTZ

## STABBING FRENZY

ROBERT and Kate Swartz met when both were students at the University of Maryland. Bob became a highly qualified electronic engineer, while Kate pursued a teaching career. They married and eventually settled in Annapolis, Maryland, where they purchased a suburban home at 1242 Mount Pleasant Drive.

The Swartzes had all the creature comforts, as well as the security that comes with two substantial salaries. There was one flaw in their apparently happy marriage. Kate couldn't have children. They decided to adopt a family.

Larry, the first child to be adopted, was a handsome six-year-old with a crop of jet-black curly hair. He had been shunted from foster home to foster home since birth, but seemed to be an appreciative, loving youngster who fit in well with Bob and Kate.

Michael, the second boy to be adopted by the Swartzes, was an angular eight-year-old. He too had been brought up in a series of foster homes. Unlike Larry, he didn't hit it off well with his adoptive parents right from the beginning. Although he had a relatively high IQ, his school work wasn't up to par. The Swartzes placed a high value on education and it rankled that their oldest son wasn't doing well in school. Michael was confrontational and seemed to be always at loggerheads with his mother and father. At times Bob would lose his temper with the boy and give him a sound thrashing. Larry didn't do that well in school either but he had a more placid, easy-going personality than his older brother. The two boys got along famously.

The Swartzes adopted a third child, four-year-old Annie, who had been abandoned by her South Korean parents. Annie soon became the star of the entire family. The two boys loved to teach her English and both Bob and Kate doted on her. As the years passed, there was still animosity between Michael and his parents.

One day, when Michael was 14 years old, he had promised his parents that he would stay at home. He disobeyed them and sneaked out a window. Meanwhile, Kate and Bob returned. It was a case of the straw that broke the camel's back.They locked the boy out and called his social worker. Bob and Kate made their views crystal clear. They simply didn't want Michael anymore. In their view, they had tried everything. Their lanky son, who had sprouted to six feet six inches, was more than they could handle. Michael moved out and for the next few years was transferred from one mental institution to another.

With Michael's departure, it seemed to Larry that all his parents' wrath descended upon him. True, his school work was deplorable, but nothing he did seemed to satisfy them. That's not entirely true. When he decided to become a priest and entered a high-school seminary in Pennsylvania, Bob and Kate were extremely proud. It didn't last. Larry dropped out of the seminary and returned home. The bickering continued, mainly over Larry's poor school work. When he turned 17, he told friends that he couldn't wait until his eighteenth birthday so that he could legally move out of his parents' home.

On the night of January 17, 1984, police were called to the comfortable home on Mount Pleasant Drive. A neighbour had summoned them. They were greeted by Larry Swartz and his nine-year-old sister, Annie. The boy was calm, considering the sight he had seen. In the study, police came across Bob Swartz's body. He had been stabbed many times. Furniture was overturned and there was blood on the floor and walls. Just outside the house in the snow, another officer found Kate Swartz's nude body. She too had received several stab wounds. The snow in the area of the body was soaked with blood.

Larry was able to answer the officers' questions. The bodies were those of his parents, 51-year-old Bob Swartz and 43-year-old Kate. Larry told police that a noise had awakened him about 11 p.m. Annie was already awake and told him that their parents weren't in their bed. Larry looked out the kitchen window and saw his mother's body lying in the snow. He went on to tell detectives who were now at the scene that his brother, Michael, no longer lived at home. He was undergoing tests at the Crownsville Hospital Center, a psychiatric institution located only a few blocks from the Swartz residence. Larry explained that Michael was no longer welcome in their house because of the bad feeling between him and his parents. In fact, Kate had often mentioned to Larry that Michael was a mental case and that she was afraid of him.

An autopsy indicated that Bob had been stabbed 17 times from his neck to the pit of his stomach. He also had a number of defensive stab wounds to his hands and arms. Kate had been subjected to seven stab wounds, but had been killed by a blow to the back of her head that had caved in the top of her skull.

Michael Swartz immediately became the prime suspect in his parents' murder. Officials at the Crownsville Hospital informed detectives that the psychiatric dormitory where Michael was housed was totally secure. At the time of the murder he had been behind locked doors. Despite the hospital authorities' word that Michael had been confined, detectives tested the premises by having themselves locked in the dormitory. They found that other than the locked door, there was only one way out and that was through a heavily barred window, which proved to be impenetrable. It would have been impossible for Michael Swartz to have killed his parents. Police looked for another suspect, someone who hated the victims enough to stab them time and again after they were dead.

Three days after the Swartzes' funeral, Larry confided to his lawyer that he had murdered his parents. According to his statement, he and his father had argued that evening over one of Bob's computer programs which Larry had messed up. Larry went upstairs to his room and proceeded to finish off what was left of a bottle of rum he had hidden there. When he came downstairs, his mother started bugging him about exams he was then in the process of writing. Larry picked up an axe and struck Kate from behind. He then grabbed a steak knife and proceeded to stab her over and over again.

Bob must have heard the noise and suddenly appeared before Larry. Without a word, Larry spun around and plunged the knife into his father's chest. Bob staggered backward, but Larry was upon him like a wild animal, stabbing in a crazed frenzy until his victim lay still.

Larry dragged his mother's body outside into the snow and undressed her. He tossed the knife and axe into a swamp backing onto their property. Re-entering the house, he went upstairs and told Annie that everything was all right. She had just been awakened by a bad dream.

With Larry's assistance, the murder weapons were retrieved. His lawyers were able to plea-bargain the first-degree murder charges to two counts of second-degree murder in return for a guilty plea. Larry was sentenced to two concurrent 20-year prison terms with the rather lenient stipulation that eight years of each sentence be suspended. The sentence also stipulated that he receive psychiatric therapy.

Larry Swartz served his time at Maryland's Patuxent Correctional Institute, where he succeeded in earning his high-school equivalency diploma before being paroled.

# KATHY TELEMACHOS

## BAD BLOOD

GEORGE Telemachos wanted the best for his only daughter. He tried his hardest, but it just didn't work out.

George and his wife moved from New Zealand to the United States because of their chronically ill baby son. The family settled on the southeast coast of Florida in Broward County, where Kathy, their second child, was born. Unfortunately, she suffered from the same serious liver ailment as her brother. Four years after Kathy's birth, her brother died.

George went into the restaurant business and prospered. No matter how hard he worked to make a living, he devoted much of his time to his sickly daughter. In hindsight, there are those who say she was his obsession. George flew Kathy around the country to consult with specialists. He opened more restaurants to defray Kathy's substantial medical bills. In the end, his devotion to his daughter affected his marriage. George's wife filed for divorce in 1977. It took two years before the decree was granted and another eight years for the courts to award shared custody of Kathy to her parents.

All the while, Kathy's health was failing. In 1981, at the age of 10, she underwent a liver transplant at Pittsburgh's famed Children's Hospital. A year later it was necessary to replace her rejected liver with another transplant. The second operation was a success. It was the first successful transplant of its kind to take place in the United States.

During Kathy's ordeal, George was constantly at her bedside. When she was well enough to travel, he brought her home to Florida. With the help of her father and mother, Kathy regained her strength. As the years passed, she was able to take part in normal everyday activities. During her last year in high school, she experienced a stunning setback when her kidneys failed. At age 18, Kathy received a kidney transplant with her mother as donor.

Upon Kathy's release from hospital, George gave her a car as a present. When she mentioned she didn't like the vehicle, her father bought her another. Whatever Kathy wanted, she got. George well realized he was spoiling his daughter, but he loved her so. After all, she had been seriously ill since birth.

Kathy was now a beautiful young woman. George wanted her to attend college against her wishes. Perhaps this was the turning point in their relationship. Kathy began to hang around with the wrong crowd. When George sold his restaurants and purchased the Baker Street Tobacconist Shop in the Hollywood Fashion Mall, he employed his daughter. George believed it would occupy her mind and keep her off the streets. The ploy backfired.

One day, Erik J. Delvalle, a high-school dropout, strolled into the shop to purchase a pack of cigarettes. Within weeks, he and Kathy were engaged to be married. To say that George was displeased with the match would be an understatement. He was devastated. In simple terms, he didn't believe Erik was good enough for his Kathy. He felt that Erik was a bum, which wasn't that far off the mark. By now George was well aware that Kathy had been introduced to marijuana. One day he noticed a .38-calibre revolver sticking out of her purse. When George discovered that money had been taken from his shop's cash register, he fired Kathy and ordered her out of the house. Kathy and Erik took an apartment of their own.

On July 23, 1990, after George hadn't been seen for almost two days, neighbours entered his home. They found George dead in his bed. He had been shot in the centre of the forehead with a weapon held only inches from his head. The entire house was in a shambles. Drawers had been pulled out and the contents of closets scattered about the floor. Detectives on the scene didn't feel that robbery had been the motive. It appeared to them that the murder had been a cold-blooded execution-style assassination made to look like the work of burglars.

It wasn't long before detectives learned of the bad blood that had existed between the victim, his daughter and her boyfriend. In addition, it was discovered that on the night of July 21, a police officer had questioned Kathy, Erik and a friend, Vince Magona, near George's home. The three were left to go on their way, but the officer had taken their names. Now that encounter took on a greater significance.

Kathy, Erik and Vince were picked up and questioned. Vince immediately spilled his guts. He told police that Kathy had led him and Erik on a dry run of the house a few days before the murder so that they would be acquainted with the layout. On the night of the murder, all three entered George's home. Vince and Erik made their way to George's bedroom, where Erik shot the hapless man as he lay asleep in bed. Vince told police he had been promised $300 by Kathy, but that she had only given him $100 from money she had taken out of her dead father's wallet. Kathy was definitely not a loving daughter.

When Erik heard that Vince had talked, he too decided to tell all. He added that he had tossed the .38-calibre revolver into a canal as they fled the murder scene in Kathy's car. Initially, Erik admitted that he had pulled the trigger, but upon learning of Florida's death penalty, he changed his story, stating that Kathy had fired the fatal shot. For her part, Kathy refused to discuss her father's murder.

Through questioning the young people's friends, detectives learned that the threesome had bragged about the murder before George's body was found. Kathy and Erik believed George to be worth close to $5 million. They had often mentioned that upon his death Kathy would be one rich girl. In reality, George had spent great amounts of money on Kathy's health problems. Although comfortable, he was worth considerably less than one million dollars. Ironically, it was revealed after the murder that George was suffering from heart and lung ailments and had only a few months to live.

Vince Magona was permitted to plead guilty to second-degree murder and conspiracy to commit first-degree murder in exchange for his testimony against Erik and Kathy. In this way he avoided the possibility of a date with Florida's electric chair. Hoping to be sentenced as a juvenile, Vince took the witness stand and told his story. He got off lightly. The presiding judge sentenced him as a youthful offender, imposing a prison term of three years, to be followed by two years' probation.

Erik pleaded guilty to second-degree murder. He was sentenced to life imprisonment with no possibility of parole for 25 years. During Erik's sentencing process, the direct motive for the murder surfaced. While it was true that the killers knew that Kathy would inherit her father's money upon his death, they had a more urgent matter with which to contend. They had stolen blank cheques from George and had forged his signature. In all, they had cashed $8,600 worth of cheques to purchase furniture for their apartment. George had to be killed before he discovered the theft.

Kathy refused to plea bargain. Vince and Erik both testified for the state at her trial. It wasn't pretty. Vince said that Kathy had insisted on being in the bedroom so that she could watch her father die. After deliberating for two days, the Florida jury found Kathy guilty of conspiracy to kill and first-degree murder. They recommended by an eight to four count that she be put to death. Despite this recommendation, the presiding judge overruled the jury's wishes and sentenced Kathy Telemachos to life plus 30 years' imprisonment.

# BILL THACKER

## MOB LYNCHED THACKER

OUR neighbours to the south take their politics seriously. Not only have they developed the distressing habit of assassinating their presidents, they are also not above killing each other over minor political differences.

Back in 1900, Bill Thacker lived, loved and drank locally brewed bourbon in his home town of Noah, Kentucky. Bill owned the general store and was one of the town's leading citizens. Yes, it's true, he slugged back that bourbon like it was going out of style. But say what you will about Bill, he was a good family man. He and Mrs. Thacker had five strapping children.

Bill hated Democrats. It is unclear why or how he acquired this abnormal distaste, but it was a well-known fact around Noah that when Bill was in his cups it was a good idea for anyone belonging to the Democratic Party to give him a wide berth.

On Monday, July 30, 1900, Bill was downing rotgut with a vengeance. He rounded up his 16-year-old son Robert and told him they were going hunting. Robert wasn't averse to spending a day in the woods with his dad. Who knows, if they were lucky they would bag one of those mean black bears. Bill explained that that wasn't the type of hunting he had in mind. He figured that they would round up a few Democrats and have some good old-fashioned fun with them.

Father and son mounted their horses and trotted off toward the nearby town of Foxport. On the way, Bill took long swigs from his bottle of bourbon. He didn't seem to mind telling everyone he met about his mission. He even told grocery-store owner Elijah Boling that he planned to hunt down a few Democrats. To emphasize his point, Bill flashed a pistol he was carrying in his coat pocket.

Out on the street, Bill met John Gordon, a strapping 21-year-old local farm boy. He asked John two questions—if he was a Democrat, which was answered in the affirmative, and if he wanted a fight, which was answered in the negative.

Bill strolled into Million's General Store. Inside were Homer Million, the son of the owner, and Miles Earls, another local boy. The two were discussing guns, as good old boys down Kentucky way are prone to do. John Gordon strolled in. So did Robert Thacker. Bill wanted to get things percolating. He suggested that his son Robert could beat the pants off John. John replied that he didn't know Robert and had no intention of fighting him.

Bill had tried, but there was no way to entice any Democrats into a friendly little scrap. In disgust, he and Robert mounted their horses and headed for nearby Mount Carmel. No sooner had they started off than they came upon Bert Wykoff and his two sons, Cleveland and Grosey. Bert and his boys were putting up a picket fence. Bill shouted, "Hurray for McKinley!" referring to President William McKinley. Bert replied, "We are going to beat McKinley this time."

Before you could say pork barrel, Bill and the Wykoffs were hurling insults at each other. As the men argued, John Gordon showed up to enjoy the fun. Robert Thacker shouted to his father, "Let's get away from these sons of bitches Democrats." John took exception to the remark and replied, "Who are you calling sons of bitches?" Robert answered clearly enough, "You." With that, John suggested they square off.

Robert pulled out a knife. John reached for a pole, but before he had it in his hands, Bill Thacker shot him directly above the left eyebrow. John slumped to the ground, critically wounded. Bill mumbled to no one in particular, "I hated to do that, but I had to."

Many of the good citizens of Foxport were attracted to the commotion. They stood around watching Bill Thacker, who was now acting like a madman, waving his pistol from side to side. Several men in the crowd attempted to reason with Bill, but he made it clear that he would only surrender to the justice of the peace, Squire Gaebke. Meanwhile, someone had fetched Dr. Emmet Pope, who examined the seriously wounded man and suggested that he be lifted out of the sun into the shade of some nearby trees. Soon after being moved, John Gordon died. Finally, Squire Gaebke showed up and took Bill into custody. He was lodged in the Maysburg jail to await trial.

In January 1901, Bill Thacker stood trial for the murder of John Gordon. Since several reputable citizens had heard all Bill's threats and had seen the cold-blooded killing, you would think that the results would be a foregone conclusion. Such was not the case. Bill claimed that John had picked up a large pole and would have killed his son if he hadn't shot him. In fact, Bill said that he had jumped between his son and John. It was only after John shouted, "I will kill you both" that he drew his weapon and fired. The bogus yarn did him no good. The jury quickly brought in a verdict of guilty.

Bill appealed on a technicality and won a new trial. All the same evidence was paraded before another jury. In addition, Robert Thacker was called on to verify his father's story. Robert made a major mistake by admitting he was carrying a knife when his father shot John. This pretty well destroyed Bill's story of shooting to save his son's life. Once again, Bill was found guilty and sentenced to life imprisonment. Once again, he appealed. The appeal was successful and Bill was returned from penitentiary to be lodged in the Flemingsburg jail to await his third trial.

That summer of 1903, rumours spread throughout the area. Bill Thacker would appeal forever and eventually would be freed. Was there no justice? John Gordon had been a gentle, well-liked boy who had never harmed anyone. He was dead. His killer showed no remorse. Stories about the murder were exaggerated. One such rumour purported that after Bill shot the boy, he sat on his victim's chest and smoked his pipe. Didn't such a man deserve to be punished?

On the night of July 15, 1903, the good folks of Fleming County gathered in secret by lantern light. Their purpose was clear. They fully intended to take the law into their own hands.

The mob met only minimum resistance at the jail. The keys to Bill's cell were handed over without too much discussion. Bill was dragged screaming and struggling from his cell. To quiet him, someone hit him over the head with a rock. The terrified man was taken to an orchard near Mount Carmel and unceremoniously hanged from a fruit tree.

Next day the town was quiet. It seemed no one had actually attended the lynching. A coroner's inquest concluded that Bill Thacker had met his death at the hands of persons unknown.

# ALBERT TIRRELL

## SLEEPWALKING DEFENCE

EVERY so often the public is treated to a murder trial where somnambulism, or sleepwalking, is put forward as the principal defence. Somnambulistic behaviour was first used as a defence in North America by an attorney in 1845. Let's take a peek at the circumstances surrounding this most unusual murder case.

The Tirrell family of Weymouth, Massachusetts, was a proud, wealthy clan, big in the shoe business. They owned the largest factory in the area.

The patriarch of the family shuffled off his mortal coil in 1843, leaving control of his business and personal fortune to his 25-year-old son Albert. Al was a fine cut of a man, standing approximately six feet tall. He was well married to a gracious young woman who, wouldn't you just know it, answered to the name of Prudence. Al and Prudence had brought two little Tirrells into the world.

Al took to the shoe racket like a half sole takes to a brogue. For a year the entire Tirrell clan was ecstatic with the patriarch's choice. The shoe company prospered.

Then Al took a business trip to New Bedford. Old records indicate he was on the lookout for a good deal concerning the purchase of leather. He didn't find leather, but he did find a willing young brunette named Maria Pickford. Maria was a buxom, good-looking New England lass who was definitely tired of the rough whaling crowd she was accustomed to cavorting with around New Bedford. Al was more in keeping with what a girl had in mind when she thought of a good catch.

As for the conscientious shoe manufacturer, he fell about as hard as an ill-fitting, ankle-high reinforced work boot. Al simply forgot about Prudence, the shoe business and the two little Tirrells, pretty well in that order. He couldn't get enough of his Maria. To correct this situation, he installed his new love in a cosy little apartment in Boston. About the only time Al showed up at the factory in Weymouth was to collect his pay.

The entire family got on Al's tail. No Tirrell in the history of the Tirrells had ever strayed from the straight and narrow. In no uncertain terms, they told Al to smarten up. As for Prudence, well, Prudence cried a lot.

Brother-in-law Nathaniel Bayley was delegated by the family to have a serious chat with Al. Nat did the best he could. He pointed out that a man of Al's stature had a responsibility to the family business, not to mention his wife and children. Al agreed. But then the allure of that well-chiselled face and voluptuous figure drew him to Maria like a bee to honey.

One mustn't get the mistaken impression that all was roses with Al and Maria. *Mais non.* They fought like cats and dogs, but always ended up on the proverbial couch where, as we all know, much can be forgiven.

In September 1845, the lovers partied a tad too strenuously at the conservative Hanover House in Boston. They were unceremoniously asked to leave the establishment and seek accommodation in surroundings which catered to a more rowdy clientele.

The Tirrell family was astounded at Al's behaviour. More to teach him a lesson than anything else, they had him arrested and charged with adultery. Naturally enough, they soon relented and helped defend their wayward member. In the end, the court forced Al to post a bond promising to keep the peace for six months and not to associate with Maria.

Al pouted about the harshness of his sentence for an entire day before dashing over to Maria's new digs on Cedar Lane in Beacon Hill. The couple hit the sack with a vengeance. Al and Maria didn't surface for the better part of a week. Actually, Maria didn't surface at all.

On October 27, 1845, a fire broke out in Maria's room. When firemen arrived, they quickly extinguished the small blaze in the mattress. On the bed lay the body of Maria Pickford. Her throat had been viciously cut with a straight razor, which was found on a table a few feet from the body. Al had left several items of clothing in Maria's room when he had hastily departed.

Police traced the wanted man. Hours earlier he had woken up Timothy Fullam, the proprietor of a livery stable. Fullam knew Al and had often rented him rigs. Now his customer appeared to be in a stupor. Al mumbled, "Someone tried to murder me. I'm in a scrape." Fullam thought Al was a bit tipsy.

Al drove to Weymouth, where he met with his brother-in-law Nat Bayley. He insinuated that he had spent the night with Maria, violating the conditions of his bail. Nat had no idea that Al was wanted for murder. He gave his brother-in-law some money and advised him to get out of town. Later, Nat would tell investigators that Al had appeared disoriented and confused.

Al made good his escape. He managed to obtain a berth on the freighter *Sultana* and remained at large for four months. Detectives traced the wanted man and took him into custody when the ship docked in New York.

On March 24, 1846, the apparently open-and-shut case came to trial in Boston. It appeared that Al didn't stand a chance. He admitted spending the night in question with Maria. He also admitted that he had sought help from his brother-in-law. Surely Al would end his days on the gallows. But such was not to be the case.

Al's wily lawyer, Rufus Choate, became intrigued with his client's confused state immediately after Maria's death. He dug deeper and learned that when Al was three years old, he had climbed out of bed and, while sleepwalking, had scrambled out a window to the edge of the roof. His father had pulled him to safety. Al had had no recollection of the incident the following morning.

Al's reputation as a sleepwalker grew as he reached puberty. To control his nocturnal wanderings, his parents locked him in his room at night. The boy chafed at this restriction until his parents relented. At age 16, Al left the house, clad only in his nightshirt, harnessed a horse and drove to an uncle's home some distance away. His amazed uncle discovered Al unhitching the horse in the bitter cold while completely asleep. Once awakened, Al had no idea how he had arrived at his uncle's home.

Prudence Tirrell took the witness stand in her husband's defence and related that she had awakened one night to find Al clutching her throat. She screamed and Al woke with a start. He apologized profusely, although he couldn't remember attempting to strangle her.

Lawyer Choate shouted at the court, "If Albert Tirrell murdered Maria Pickford, he was not responsible for what he did because he was asleep at the time and unaware of what he was doing." Choate went on to explain that on the morning of October 27, when his client reached the livery stable, "He was just awakening from somnambulistic sleep. He did not know where he had been or what he had been doing."

The Massachusetts jury deliberated for only two hours before returning a verdict of not guilty. Albert Tirrell left the courtroom a free man with the loyal and ever-loving Prudence at his side.

# WILLIAM UDDERZOOK

## WHERE THERE'S SMOKE...

I have often pondered why it is considered irresponsible to bet the coin of the realm on one particular horse on the assumption that the chosen steed will dash around an oval faster than its friends. Yet, if a person bets $50 that he, or she, will most certainly depart this world before the first snow falls, that's considered to be sensible, frugal and responsible.

This latter bet, or insurance, if you will, has given rise to a host of criminal activity, all designed to relieve those big bad insurance companies of their reported vast amounts of other people's money.

Everybody is fascinated by a spectacular, honest-to-goodness fire. In the more rural areas of North America, a respectable blaze is, in many instances, the only relief the agricultural set have from the excruciating boredom of just plain living. On many occasions, I have heard the good farmers mention one to the other, "No harm's been done. There was no one inside, and anyway, the insurance company will pay for everything."

Unfortunately, on February 2, 1872, there was someone inside. Four miles outside of Baltimore, on the York Road, a cottage owned by a Mr. Lowndes blazed merrily away. As the flames licked high into the crisp winter air, Lowndes twisted his handkerchief in anguish as one of his choice properties burned to the ground.

While thus engaged, he conversed for almost an hour with another spectator who had the unlikely name William E. Udderzook. You can imagine Lowndes's surprise when, after watching the fire for such a long time, his fellow flame watcher mentioned that he thought his brother-in-law, Winfred Goss, was still in the house.

Lowndes was, of course, familiar with his tenant, Mr. Goss. Now that he thought about it, he never did feel that Goss was the most stable character in the world. He particularly didn't like the idea that his tenant followed the rather precarious occupation of inventor. Goss had the habit of carrying around a ratchet screwdriver, his latest gadget. At the present time, he was working on inventing a substitute for rubber. It seemed right strange to Lowndes that an hour before, when the fire was just getting hot, Udderzook had not mentioned that there was someone in the house. At that time it might have been possible to attempt a rescue. Now it was too late.

As the fire cooled, the remains of what had once been a human being were removed from the blackened ruins. Later it was discovered that Goss had fortunately prepared himself for just such a tragic eventuality. During the previous four years, he had taken out four life insurance policies with a total payoff of $25,000. As recently as a week before the fire, he had the foresight to sign up for the last $5,000. The beneficiary of all four policies was his wife, Eliza Waters Goss, who it is my pleasant duty to report, was not in the house when it burned.

Now, this was all fine, but the police had one sticky question in search of an answer. How did healthy, 37-year-old Winfred manage to get himself trapped in the not-so-towering inferno. His brother, Campbell, could shed no light on the mystery, having only heard of the tragedy the day following the fire.

Our old friend Udderzook volunteered that he and the deceased man had been drinking whiskey on the afternoon of the blaze. Mrs. Goss was not at home. As suppertime approached, Udderzook left the cottage to eat with a neighbouring family, the Engels.

Later, when Udderzook and young Gottlieb Engels started off to rejoin Goss, they saw that the cottage was on fire. They assumed that a kerosene lamp, which had been giving Goss trouble, had exploded. The coroner was inclined to go along with Udderzook's story, but the insurance companies were another thing. They felt that where there was smoke, there was fire of quite another kind.

Those insurance companies had sneaky little investigators turning up all kinds of interesting bits of information. For example, despite Campbell Goss's solemn declaration that he had only heard of the fire the day after it occurred, the insurance men discovered that the very night of the untimely blaze, he had rented a horse and buggy from a livery stable where the chief subject of conversation was the spectacular fire. Not only that, he had galloped away into the country.

Those evil-minded insurance types were convinced that he picked up his brother and drove him to a nearby railway station. They believed Winfred was alive. Try as they might, the insurance operatives just couldn't get it through their heads that a man whose total income was $1,200 annually would legitimately fork over $500 for insurance premiums. Then there was the strange coincidence. You see, Winfred Goss had closed out his bank account the day before the fire.

All of this was reason enough for the insurance companies to hold up payment. Mrs. Goss was the soul of patience. She waited a full year before she brought suit against the companies. The insurance companies gained permission to exhume Goss or whomever, in order to examine his teeth. In this way they would identify the victim once and for all.

Mrs. Goss assured the investigators that her husband had had all his teeth. An autopsy revealed that the man found in the fire had only nine teeth. Based on this rather sound evidence, the insurance companies felt that Goss had not met his death in the fire. They decided to defend themselves against Mrs. Goss's suit.

Despite the evidence, Mrs. Goss was awarded the full amount of the policies, plus interest. It is difficult to reconcile the jury's verdict with the evidence, but suffice it to say, when it came to widows or insurance companies, juries always ruled in favour of widows. At least in 1873 they did.

Not at all discouraged, the insurance companies appealed the verdict. This time it was rumoured far and wide that they would investigate until they turned up the missing W. Goss, assuming, of course, he was alive. These rumours came to the attention of our dear friend with the strange name, William Udderzook.

On June 30, a few weeks after the favourable verdict had been passed down, Udderzook took a little trip to Jennerville, Pennsylvania. He checked into a hotel with a middle-aged stout stranger, who never did give his name. Next evening, Udderzook rented a horse and carriage from a livery stable. He and the stranger drove away. At midnight, Udderzook returned the carriage and the following morning checked out of the hotel. He was alone.

The livery people were not that happy with the condition of the carriage. There were several large bloodstains on the interior walls, a floorboard was broken and two blankets were missing. Partial damages were recovered on the spot when the proprietor of the stable found a man's large ring under a seat.

A week later, a traveller was attracted by a group of buzzards making a racket just off the main road. Upon investigating, he found the head and trunk of what had once been a middle-aged, heavy-set man. Twenty-five yards away, partially buried, were a matching pair of arms and legs.

A coroner's jury identified the body as Udderzook's companion. On July 25, Udderzook was arrested and charged with murder. The insurance companies claimed that the body was that of Winfred Goss. If you have been keeping track, we now have two bodies thought to be W. Goss.

By the time Udderzook came to trial, the plot was clear. Some unfortunate soul, who was never identified, was murdered and placed in the Goss house before it was set ablaze. The real Winfred Goss went into hiding with Udderzook's help, who in turn was in cahoots with the widow and Winfred's brother Campbell.

When the insurance companies didn't come across with the $25,000 and threatened to find Winfred, the three conspirators decided to kill him for real. No one could prove that Mrs. Goss and Campbell were involved with Udderzook. If those blasted buzzards hadn't circled Winfred's assorted parts, Udderzook might have gotten away with it.

Alas, such was not to be the case. The prosecution was able to trace Winfred's activities from the time of the fire to the time he was murdered. Remember that ring found under the seat of the carriage? It was the property of Winfred Goss.

The jury must have studied the case at great length. They deliberated more than two days before finding Udderzook guilty of murder.

On November 12, 1874, in Westchester, Pennsylvania, Udderzook was led to the gallows. To the very end he insisted that all his troubles were caused by those vindictive big bad insurance companies.

# HELEN ULVINEN

## THE PERFECT COUPLE

CAROL and Dave Hoffman were the perfect couple. They owned a lovely home in Corcoran, Minnesota, and were the proud parents of two healthy children, Heidi, 3, and baby Bridgette. It wasn't unusual to see Carol and Dave lugging their small boat down to nearby Weaver Lake early in the morning to fish or scuba-dive.

The Hoffmans had been married for nine years when they realized that although Dave did quite well at his machine operator's job, they were regularly a bit short of funds. It was decided that Carol would re-enter the workforce at a factory in Golden Valley, a few miles from their home.

It was a great idea, but it didn't work out. Carol had to organize babysitters, rush home from work to prepare meals and take care of her two little girls. She was perpetually tired. The couple's social life suffered.

Dave had a solution. He invited his 65-year-old mother to live with them. Helen Ulvinen loved her grandchildren, and the thought of living with them held great appeal. She also felt she could be of help to her son and daughter-in-law. Helen closed her home in Minneapolis early in the summer of 1980 and moved to Corcoran.

There is something awkward about having the mother-in-law move in, isn't there? Sure, it works occasionally, but when things don't go well they tend to get out of hand. Carol couldn't stand having Helen underfoot all the time. It only took a few weeks before the situation became intolerable. Carol spoke to Dave. Naturally enough, he couldn't see anything wrong with his own mother. The subject became a bone of contention in the Hoffman residence.

On Monday morning, August 11, 1980, Dave reported his wife missing to police. According to Dave, he and Carol had a heated argument the night before. Carol had became furious and stormed out of the house. Because she was so upset, Dave wouldn't give her the keys to the family car. She left on foot. Dave waited for his wife to return, but she never did.

The police listened to his story, but thought that Carol Hoffman would return home on her own. Their attitude changed a few hours later when

Carol's purse was found beside the highway just north of town. The contents of the purse, including a wallet containing money and credit cards, were intact.

A full-scale search for Carol was conducted by police and volunteers. There was grave suspicion that Carol had been abducted while walking alone along the road. Dave was inconsolable. He led search parties and appeared on radio and television, begging Carol's abductor to return the mother of his two children. Dave often broke down and cried.

Detectives questioned Carol's acquaintances in an attempt to find out more about the missing woman that could lead them to solving what they feared was now a murder case. In this way, authorities learned that she had often spoken to her friends about the deplorable situation in her home. Although Dave had advised them of the tension in the house, it appeared to be a much more serious problem than police had first realized. Evidently Carol had threatened divorce if her mother-in-law didn't move out.

Colleagues at Dave's place of employment were interrogated. Police learned that Dave was worried sick that Carol would take the two children if she divorced him. One employee told detectives that Dave had once insinuated that he would kill Carol by turning off her air supply when they were scuba-diving. Dave's colleague thought he was joking and dismissed the incident from his mind.

Police were now having second thoughts about Dave Hoffman. They decided to interrogate Dave as a suspect rather than as the grieving husband. He was asked if there was anything he was holding back, anything he wanted to get off his chest. Dave didn't hesitate. He told the stunned detectives that Carol had refused to have sex with him for weeks. He had come to think of her as an evil person and had decided to kill her for the sake of the children.

Once Dave was rolling, he couldn't stop. He told police that he had originally planned on killing Carol while they were scuba-diving at the lake, but on that occasion she was having so much fun he didn't have the heart to do it. On the Sunday that Carol supposedly disappeared, she didn't disappear at all. He simply strangled her as she lay in bed. Dave claimed that God had assisted him in removing an evil presence from his house.

Dave recounted that he had carried Carol into the bathroom, after which he had awakened his mother, who was pleased at what he had done. She agreed to guard the bathroom door against his young daughters disturbing him at his delicate work. Dave went on to describe how he had dissected his wife's body and had attempted to get rid of small portions by putting them down his garburetor, but the unit had seized, forcing him to abandon that method.

Dave had found an old duffel bag and gunny sack in the basement. All of Carol's body parts were placed in the two bags, together with some rocks from her garden. Mother was relieved of her guard duty, while Dave busied himself cleaning up for the next several hours. He went to bed, awoke at six-thirty Monday morning, had a bite to eat and placed the two bags containing his wife's parts into the boat, which he took to the lake. He rowed out to the centre of the lake and threw the two bags overboard. The rocks weighed them down nicely. For appearance's sake, cunning Dave did a little fishing.

Within hours, the Hoffman house was searched. Forensic evidence was found in the bathroom, garburetor and vacuum cleaner, corroborating Dave's fantastic story. His mother, Helen, was arrested. The two children were placed with county authorities and Dave was retained in custody.

On August 20, divers recovered the gunny sack and duffel bag containing Carol's dismembered body. Dave, in his intense way, attempted to explain to detectives that he had really been successful in exorcising an evil presence from his home. He couldn't fathom why they didn't understand.

Detective Bob Salitros of the Hennepin County sheriff's department remembers the 13-year-old case vividly. It ranks as one of the strangest in his long career. During the initial investigation, he and his partner had a nagging feeling that Dave Hoffman was not the grieving husband he seemed to be. Salitros talked to Hoffman every day for 10 days before Hoffman revealed all the startling details of the murder.

Helen Ulvinen was found guilty in the murder of her daughter-in-law. On December 22, 1980, she was sentenced to life imprisonment. However, 11 months later, the Supreme Court of Minnesota overthrew the jury's verdict, claiming there wasn't sufficient evidence to warrant a guilty verdict. Helen was discharged from prison on December 22, 1981.

Her son Dave wasn't nearly as fortunate. On February 11, 1981, he was found guilty of murder and sentenced to life imprisonment. He is presently serving that sentence.

# CHARLES WALTON

## CROSS SLASHED INTO VICTIM'S CHEST

COME along with me now to Lower Quinton, about nine miles down the road from Stratford, England. As everyone knows, this is Shakespeare country. What is far less known is that the area is steeped in superstition and witchcraft. Here you will be told stories of headless horsemen, of figures that are half man and half beast and of a black dog with luminous eyes who roams the countryside seeking victims. According to legend, he who gazes upon the black dog is doomed. To this day, it is believed that the close-mouthed inhabitants of the area practise witchcraft.

It was on Valentine's Day, 1945, that it happened. Seventy-four-year-old Charles Walton lived with his niece Edith in Lower Quinton. The old gent was a loner who did odd jobs around the tiny rural community. Because he was known never to part with a pence, Walton was reputed to be moderately well off.

At the time our story unfolds, Walton worked off and on trimming hedges for a local farmer, Albert Potter. On this particular day, he bade his niece goodbye at 9 a.m., and told her he would return for tea at four o'clock, as usual. Walton was a creature of habit. He always returned home at four and made himself a cup of tea when he worked for Potter.

Edith was employed in a nearby factory that manufactured war materials. Uncle and niece parted. Walton made his way to Meon Hill with the aid of his walking stick. He also carried a hay fork and sickle-shaped slash hood.

That evening, Edith returned home from her job at 6 p.m. fully expecting to find her uncle. Alarmed at not being able to locate the elderly gentleman, she called on a neighbour, Harry Beasley. Together they walked to Albert Potter's house. Potter said that he was pretty sure he had seen Walton from a distance up on Meon Hill shortly after noon. He had assumed it was Walton, but could not positively say it was him.

Darkness fell. With the aid of a flashlight, Potter joined the other two in the trek up Meon Hill. From time to time they called out Walton's name, as they felt that Walton's rheumatic legs may have given out.

Suddenly, Potter stopped short. "Stay there!" he shouted. "Don't come any nearer. You mustn't look at this."

The sight that greeted Potter was not a pleasant one, Walton's throat had been cut with a sickle. More hideous still, his body was held firmly to the ground by the prongs of the hayfork that had been plunged through his neck and into the earth. Walton's killer had slashed a cross into his chest.

Famed detective Robert Fabian of Scotland Yard was called in to lead the investigation. Torontonians may remember Fabian. He was brought to Canada in the summer of 1954 to investigate the riddle of the Marion McDowell abduction. Unfortunately, Fabian was unable to solve the McDowell case, which remains a mystery to this day.

On the morning of February 15, 1945, the colourful Fabian was at the scene of the crime in Lower Quinton. It didn't take the detective long to find out that he wasn't dealing with an ordinary murder, if any murder can ever be called ordinary.

Local police filled him in on the deep superstitions of the inhabitants. They even provided him with books on the subject. One such book described the case of an elderly lady, Ann Turner, who had been murdered in 1875 by a young lad. The motive for the murder had been the killer's belief that Ann had an "evil eye" that caused animals to die and crops to fail.

Fabian attempted to solicit the help of the locals in the area, but was met with a wall of silence. There were fewer than 500 inhabitants in Lower Quinton, nearby Upper Quinton and Admington. No one had seen or heard anything unusual, nor had anyone seen a stranger. In fact, no one even wanted to talk of the murder.

The tales of witches and evil spells was initially scoffed at by Fabian. He had investigated and solved scores of murder cases. Witchcraft was a phenomenon of years past. Then he heard that a few days earlier, a calf had been found dead in a ditch. Folks said it was an evil omen and the direct result of someone with an evil eye. They talked of little else.

Strange events hounded Fabian. While examining the murder scene, a large black dog ran down Meon Hill past the startled detective. When he told local police officers of the black dog he himself had witnessed, they recounted other tales of terror concerning the black dog. Eerily, within hours of Fabian relating his tale, a police car ran into and killed a black dog in Lower Quinton.

When the locals heard that Fabian had seen the phantom black dog, they ostracized the policeman. Pubs would empty when he entered. Citizens crossed the road when he appeared. Within days, another dead calf was found in the ditch. A dead black dog was found slung over a shrub near where Charles Walton's body had been found. In order to better understand what he was up against, Fabian pored over all available literature pertaining to the superstitions of the area. Despite the best efforts of Scotland Yard's most famous detective, Charles Walton's murderer was never apprehended.

As he investigated the background of the area, Fabian grew to respect some of the folklore of the region. He no longer scoffed at the strange tales and firmly believed that covens were meeting in Lower Quinton while the investigation was going on.

In all, Fabian and his assistants took over 4,000 statements, followed every possible clue, but did not make an arrest.

The detective did find out some strange and unusual facts. One such fact was that, in ancient times, in the month of February, bloodletting festivals took place. Blood was allowed to soak into the ground, supposedly to make the earth fertile. A few of the locals who did speak to Fabian claimed that Charles Walton's killing had been a fertility rite.

Fabian was told that the infamous black dog had once appeared 60 years earlier, in 1885, which was within living memory of some of the natives. The dog had been seen on nine consecutive nights by a 14-year-old ploughboy as he headed home at night. On the ninth night, the boy witnessed a headless woman, which everyone agreed was a sign of death. The very next day, the ploughboy's sister died. She had been in the best of health.

After hearing this story, Fabian pored over a book entitled *Folklore, Old Customs and Superstitions in Shakespeare Land*. He came across the story of the ploughboy in more detail and was startled to read the lad's name—Charles Walton.

Detective Superintendent Robert Fabian died of natural causes in 1978.

# NOLA JEAN WEAVER

## NOLA JEAN'S STORY

LONG Grove, Illinois, is one of those tiny towns that makes city dwellers wonder what they are doing living in their crowded, traffic-choked metropolises. Now practically a Chicago suburb, the town has managed to retain a quaint tranquillity despite the large homes built at the edge of the community by wealthy Chicagoans who have found refuge from the city's high crime rate.

Nola Jean and Larry Weaver bought a home in a rather luxurious subdivision on the outskirts of Long Grove. They had been childhood sweethearts back in Camden, Arkansas. In 1962, the attractive, well-educated young couple tied the knot. Both pursued teaching careers. In 1976, after several transfers, they wound up in idyllic Long Grove, where Larry was appointed assistant superintendent of a large school district. Slim, athletic Nola Jean continued as a physical-education teacher. Their daughter, Tiffany, was eight years old when the family moved to Long Grove.

The Weavers had it made in the shade: a beautiful home, a lovely daughter and secure promising careers. On the night of December 4, 1977, their world crumbled. Two days earlier, Earl Goodfellow observed a pickup truck patrolling the neighbourhood. When the two occupants of the truck saw Earl looking at them, they sped away. Earl was suspicious enough of the strangers to mention the incident to his immediate neighbours, the Weavers.

On the night of the fourth, the Weavers followed their usual routine. Tiffany was put to bed. Larry and Nola Jean watched television before they too retired for the night. A little after 1 a.m., the stillness of the crisp winter night was disrupted by Nola Jean's screams. The Goodfellows were awakened by loud knocks on their front door. There stood Nola Jean, clutching Tiffany in her arms. Clad only in a nightgown, Nola Jean blurted out, "Call the police and fire department! There's been some shooting and a fire."

Earl Goodfellow responded to his neighbour's frantic request. In a matter of minutes the local fire department and the police were at the scene. The quiet winter night had been transformed into a beehive of activity centred on 99 Lincoln Avenue.

Initially, police were reluctant to enter the house as Nola Jean had told them that two men had accosted her and her husband. Slowly, armed officers advanced and entered. The house was empty except for the horribly burned body of Larry Weaver, which lay still smouldering on the bed. Firemen extinguished the last vestiges of the localized fire. A coroner would later confirm that over 90 percent of Larry's body had been badly burned.

Detectives questioned Nola Jean at the Goodfellows' residence. She told them that she and Larry were awakened a little after 1 a.m. by sounds in their home. Larry went downstairs to investigate. He returned in a matter of minutes, bent over her in bed and told her in a low voice to grab the .22 rifle they had in the house and get out of there. Nola Jean managed to gather up the rifle and make her way outdoors before being intercepted by one of the intruders. He disarmed her and called for Larry to surrender. Larry appeared with his hands over his head. The two men, now in full control, demanded money, big money. The amount of $750,000 was mentioned, which led Nola Jean to believe that the men had mistaken them for multimillionaires.

Larry pleaded with his captors, telling them that he didn't have that kind of money, but that he could obtain a smaller amount. The men agreed and one of them drove off with Larry in Nola Jean's car. Fifteen minutes later, they returned. Larry's captor growled, "He's lying." He then led Larry into his bedroom. Nola Jean heard one shot. Both men then ran from the house. Nola Jean rushed to Tiffany's room and frantically ran to the Goodfellows'. That in a nutshell was Nola Jean's story.

Detectives examined the interior of the house. Some things didn't jell with Nola Jean's story. There was no forced entry. All windows and doors, other than the patio door, which had been used by everyone, were securely locked from the inside. There was no physical evidence indicating how the men had gained entrance to the house. An examination of Larry's bed revealed that an accelerant had been spread over the bed. It was also ascertained that Larry had been under a sheet and blanket when he had been set on fire. Surely if he had been forced to lie on the bed, he wouldn't have gone under the covers. He had been shot in the head by a .22-calibre rifle. The Weavers' rifle was nowhere to be found.

Nola Jean was able to give such detailed descriptions of the two intruders that a police artist was able to compile composite drawings of the two men. Meanwhile, she was subjected to a lie detector test, ostensibly to remove her as a suspect. The test was inconclusive. When asked to take a second test, Nola Jean refused on the advice of her lawyer. That's when authorities decided the ideal life that the Weavers seemed to have led had to contain some secrets.

They were right. Close friends were questioned. It was learned that energetic Nola Jean was carrying on extramarital affairs with two men. One was her superior at the high school and the other was her brother-in-law. A student came forward with the startling information that he had witnessed his phys-ed teacher doing what comes naturally with her boss on a wrestling mat in the gym. Evidently Nola Jean had fallen out of love with her husband and was playing the field.

Homicide investigators kept digging and continued to come up with incriminating evidence. Although the Weavers' .22-calibre weapon was never found, it was proven that Nola Jean had purchased ammunition for the rifle on a recent visit to Arkansas. The two cars owned by the couple were checked when detectives first heard Nola Jean's story on the night of the murder. The engine of her car was warm and the seat was in the extreme forward position. Was it natural for Larry, a six- footer, to choose his wife's vehicle and not adjust the seat, when his own car was available? Police believed that Nola Jean had driven her own car that night in order to dispose of the murder weapon.

In addition, letters found in the house revealed that Larry had known of his wife's sexual activities. Nola Jean had responded to her husband's notes, describing her sex life with other men in minute detail. To add frosting to the layers of circumstantial evidence, Larry was heavily insured, both personally and through his employer. Nola Jean was the sole beneficiary of all the policies.

Nola Jean was arrested and charged with her husband's murder. All the evidence was presented in sensational detail. Nola Jean's married lovers were forced to take the witness stand and tell their lurid tales of illicit sex. After deliberating a full day, the Illinois jury found her guilty of murdering her husband. She was sentenced to 40 to 60 years' imprisonment.

While incarcerated, Nola Jean was a model prisoner. She taught several classes, all the while fighting for a new trial. On November 6, 1980, after Nola Jean had spent three years in prison, the Illinois Appellant Court overturned the murder conviction on a technicality and granted a new trial. She managed to stay out of jail awaiting the date of her second trial, which was scheduled to take place on June 27, 1983. She stunned the court by pleading guilty in return for a plea-bargain deal. Nola Jean was sentenced to 14 years' imprisonment with credit for time already served. After spending almost five years in prison, she was parolled at age 44.

Since that time, the former Nola Jean Weaver has changed her name, inherited a farm in Missouri left to her by a girlfriend and, in 1989, remarried.

# JOE WILLIAMS

## TRUTH REVEALED AFTER DEATH

---

ANY criminal lawyer will tell you that you can never predict a jury's decision. We must assume that in the vast majority of cases their decisions are correct, but there are those occasions where we have proof that juries have made terrible mistakes.

On May 21, 1939, Walter Dinivan awoke as he did each morning of his retirement. Life was sweet. Walter had made his money in the garage business and had purchased a sizeable villa in Bournemouth, England. He loved to stroll through his extensive gardens.

The villa was large and Walter had divided it into two flats. Two elderly ladies occupied the top floor, while Walter, a widower, shared the first floor with his granddaughter.

On the day in question, Walter's grandson, who was a member of the Royal Navy, visited his grandfather. Walter was delighted and insisted the lad sleep over on the night of the twenty-first. That day, the elderly gentleman enjoyed an outing to Lullworth Cove with his two grandchildren. Upon their return, they had tea. The two young people left the villa at 7:15 p.m. to attend a dance.

Walter Dinivan retired to his drawing room, sat in his favourite chair in front of the fireplace and settled down to a quiet evening at home. At 11:45 p.m., his two grandchildren returned home from the dance. They were surprised to find all the doors of the villa locked. Their grandfather had assured them that he would leave a door open for them.

Finally, unable to get a response to his knocking, Walter's grandson smashed the window of the front door and gained entrance to the villa. He found his grandfather lying in a pool of blood in front of the fireplace. He had been struck viciously about the head with a blunt instrument. Walter was alive, but he died the next day.

An autopsy indicated that ten blows had been inflicted to the elderly gentleman's head. There was also evidence that he had been strangled.

Scotland Yard was asked to assist in the case. The murder scene was straight out of a novel. The position and condition of the body indicated that Walter had not struggled, but had been surprised by his attacker. It was felt that, as there was no forced entry to the villa, Walter may have been acquainted with his killer and had invited him to enter the drawing room.

Walter may have entertained the murderer. On a table in the den was a bottle of beer, two large glasses and a small green glass containing whiskey. One of the beer glasses was overturned, causing a beer stain on the tablecloth. The other large glass contained beer. The whiskey had been Walter's. His grandchildren stated that he never drank beer; he preferred whiskey, which he always drank out of the distinctive small green glass found on the table.

Detectives were able to lift a thumbprint off the beer glass that had been tipped over. There were also several cigarette butts in the ashtray. Since Walter didn't smoke, it was believed the cigarettes had been smoked by his killer.

Remember, this was 1939. Testing of saliva to identify blood type was not in common use, nor was it accepted as evidence in court. Despite this, Scotland Yard sent the cigarette butts for testing. In this way they learned that whoever had smoked the cigarettes had a rare blood type found in only three percent of the population.

On the drawing-room floor, detectives found a woman's hair curler, which did not belong to Walter's granddaughter. They also found a crumpled paper bag, which may have held the murder weapon, quite possibly a hammer. The motive for the murder appeared to be robbery. Walter was known to carry several pounds on his person. This was missing, as were his watch and rings. A safe located in the drawing room had been opened with a key always carried by Walter. The contents of the safe, believed to be several pounds, was missing.

Detectives took the fingerprints of everyone involved. None matched the fingerprint on the beer glass. Laundries were canvassed in an attempt to locate anyone who had brought in bloodstained clothing to be cleaned. Nothing pertaining to the murder was uncovered.

The massive investigation in Bournemouth was the chief topic of conversation in the community. Everyone was discussing the case. It was in this way that detectives learned of one man who was known to be broke the day before the murder and flush with money immediately after the killing.

Joe Williams was a crusty old retired soldier who had spent most of his soldiering years in India. The 69-year-old lived in abject poverty in an ancient dilapidated house that was heavily mortgaged. He had the appearance of Ichabod Crane and often acted in an irrational manner, particularly when provoked.

Joe was interviewed by Scotland Yard's finest and was totally uncooperative. He refused to allow his fingerprints to be taken and defiantly swore that the last time he had seen Walter was on May 17, four days before the murder took place. On that occasion, Walter had invited him inside the villa for a drink. Joe admitted that he had asked Walter for a loan, but Walter would only advance him five pounds, which he had taken from his safe.

Scotland Yard detectives were certain that Joe Williams was their man. They located Joe's favourite pub and dropped in to have a few drinks with their suspect. Surreptitiously, they gathered up Joe's cigarette butts and sent them for testing. Sure enough, Joe's blood type was the same rare type as that of the man who had smoked the cigarettes in Walter's drawing room.

Detectives searched Joe's filthy home. They found paper bags of the same type as the one left at the murder scene. These bags were traced to the manufacturer who had no trouble authenticating that their company had manufactured them. In fact, because the machine used on the paper was now obsolete, they were able to pinpoint the exact machine. Further, they were able to prove without a doubt that the bag left at the murder scene and the one found in Joe's house had come off this particular machine in consecutive order. The serrated edges at the top of both bags underwent scientific testing that proved this was the case.

The hair curler found in Walter's villa was thought to be a remote clue, but proved to be invaluable. The curler was old and was no longer being manufactured. Scotland Yard learned that Joe had been married years before. His wife had left him, but police were successful in tracing her. She had no difficulty identifying the curler as having once belonged to her. She still used the same curlers and willingly showed them to police. Detectives believed Joe had planted the old curler and the extra glass of beer to lead police to think that a woman had also been involved in the murder.

Four months after the tragedy, investigators felt they had an abundance of circumstantial evidence pointing to Joe's guilt. He lamely accounted for the large amount of money he had after the murder by telling his interrogators that he had been extremely lucky at the horse races. Joe's thumbprint matched the one on the beer glass, but Joe dismissed this as having been left there on May 17, when Walter had invited him in for a drink. No one believed him. Joe Williams was taken into custody and tried for the murder of Walter Dinivan.

In October 1939, Joe Williams was inexplicably found not guilty by an English jury. He smiled and joked with his guards as he left the courtroom a free man.

Joe Williams lived on for 12 years until March 1951, when he died peacefully in his sleep. The next day, crime reporter Norman Rae revealed in the *News of the World* what he had known for 12 years. Joe Williams had been guilty of the murder of Walter Dinivan. On the night of his acquittal, Joe had had a few drinks with the crime reporter to celebrate. He told Rae, "I did it. The jury was wrong. It was me." Joe even toasted the hangman, saying, "To the hangman who has been cheated of his victim."

Joe went through his every movement in the villa, revealing details only the killer could have known. Nothing could be done about the confession. Libel laws prevented Rae from writing his story. Joe had been tried and acquitted. There were no technical reasons for a new trial and, having once been acquitted, Joe Williams could not be tried again on the same charge.

# JAMES WILSON

## DID SHEEP FARMER KILL THEM BOTH?

---

WHEN James Wilson left England in 1947 to seek his fortune in New Zealand, he had already formed very definite ideas as to how he would fulfil his ambition. His plans didn't include manual labour.

Within a year, James owned a prosperous sheep farm about 35 miles outside Auckland. He lived in a huge home and led the life of a country squire. And how did he acquire so much wealth in such a short time? Simple. Her name was Norah Harwood and her daddy was one of the most prominent landowners in the area. The day James married Norah, he was elevated from farm labourer to king of the castle.

In January 1964, after 17 years of married life, Norah died under mysterious circumstances. The attending physician refused to issue a death certificate. Norah was in good health one day and very dead the next. A post-mortem revealed that she had died as the result of strychnine poisoning.

When James was questioned, he confessed that he kept strychnine around the farm as a pesticide. Quite possibly, he and Norah had been careless. They stored the strychnine in a lemonade bottle in the kitchen. No doubt Norah had mistakenly mixed up the bottle with similar lemonade bottles she drank from each afternoon while watching her favourite TV program. Unfortunately, James had been in Wellington at the time of the terrible mishap.

Testing of the half-empty bottle of lemonade revealed large quantities of strychnine. Everything checked out, except for one thing. In the course of their investigation into Norah's death, police found out that James had been carrying on a prolonged affair with a younger woman, Freda Smart. Detectives were certain that James had murdered his wife. He had, in fact, committed the perfect murder. With Norah's death, James became the sole owner of the profitable sheep farm. Six months after Norah's untimely demise, James married Freda Smart.

Friends of the Wilsons were of the same opinion as the police. As a result, they shunned Freda. The new Mrs. Wilson had only one friend, Jessica Lacey, who owned a small grocery store and restaurant near the Wilson farm. The two women visited each other often.

Fifteen years later, Freda, now 53 years old, complained of pains in her stomach. She visited her family physician, Dr. Herbert Roventry, in Auckland. He prescribed painkillers, but nothing seemed to help. As the weeks turned into months and the pain increased, the doctor carried out a series of tests. Still, he was unable to diagnose the cause of Freda's discomfort. James was deeply concerned and spent much time with his stricken wife. So did Jessica Lacey. It was Jessica who called Dr. Roventry, imploring him to come to the Wilson farm. Her friend Freda was in excruciating pain and appeared to be near death. Dr. Roventry rushed to his patient's side, but he was too late. Freda Wilson was dead.

Dr. Roventry had no idea what had caused Freda's death. He called police and ordered a post-mortem. The post- mortem revealed that Freda's body was laced with arsenic. Arsenic in her hair indicated that she had been poisoned over a lengthy period of time. It was all too much. Two wives, both poison victims.

Auckland detectives were certain they would nail their man this time around. If James Wilson ran true to form, he would have a mistress stashed away somewhere. It didn't take them long to find beautiful 26-year-old Ivy Thomas. The pair had been seeing each other for about a year before Freda's death.

Investigators confronted James with their suspicions. He admitted to his affair with Ivy, but vehemently denied killing Freda. He claimed he had had no reason to harm his wife. He already owned the farm and was getting all the sex any man could want from Ivy. He simply had no motive to kill Freda. When questioned, Ivy told police that James had never broached the subject of marriage. She added that James wouldn't have been stupid enough to poison Freda, knowing full well he would be suspected of her murder. Police had to agree that her reasoning made some sense. To further complicate matters, James swore he had never kept arsenic around his home, nor had he ever purchased it.

James was interrogated extensively, until finally he confessed, but not in the manner police expected. He told them that when he had fallen in love with Freda, he had risked all to be with her, knowing full well that if Norah found out, she would divorce him. As the farm was in her name, he would lose everything and be reduced to a common labourer. Freda had wanted him to seek a divorce, but he wouldn't hear of it. Gradually the idea of poisoning Norah formed in his mind. Freda was privy to his thoughts. She implored him not to do it, not because it was wrong, but because she was afraid he would be caught. James went through with the scheme and it had worked out just as he had planned. As for Freda, James claimed he was as puzzled as the police. He definitely had had nothing whatever to do with her death.

Despite having confessed to poisoning Norah, James was brought to trial for Freda's murder. The prosecution theorized that Freda had found out about her husband's affair with Ivy. She may have asked for a divorce. James wouldn't hear of it. After all, Freda knew the details of Norah's murder. She had to be killed to silence her. Although James claimed throughout that he was innocent of Freda's murder, he was found guilty and sentenced to life imprisonment.

When sentence was pronounced, James suffered a heart attack. He was rushed to hospital, where he recovered. After being transferred to prison, he suffered a second, fatal heart attack. Between his first and second attack, James insisted that he had been convicted of a murder he had not committed. He continued to tell doctors that he was innocent of Freda's murder right up until he breathed his last.

As soon as James's death was announced, police received a visit from Jessica Lacey. Freda Wilson had confided in her that she had once followed James and had discovered his affair with Ivy Thomas. Freda was devastated. She was well aware that years earlier James had killed his first wife in order to marry her. The two women talked. Jessica suggested that there were two avenues open to her friend. She could let the affair run its course or she could obtain a divorce. Freda rejected both ideas. She revealed to Jessica that James had killed Norah. Maybe he would kill her. Jessica told Freda that James wasn't that stupid. He wouldn't kill her because no one can simply go around killing wives and get away with it. Freda looked at her friend in a strange way and abruptly terminated the conversation.

In the weeks that followed, Freda fed herself arsenic. Jessica had taken a vow not to reveal her friend's secret. She watched as Freda suffered excruciating pain. Unbelievably, Freda Wilson had poisoned herself so that her husband would be convicted of her murder. The scheme had worked perfectly.

# MARIE WITTE

## BOILED BODY PARTS

EVEN as a pre-teenager, Marie simply adored nudist camps. There was something about the fresh air, the freedom of movement and the volleyball. There were also members of the opposite sex. Marie enjoyed the latter most of all.

At age 14, Marie met a young serviceman at a nudist camp. His rank has always been something of a mystery, probably because he hardly ever donned a uniform. Despite her tender years, Marie married her lover. The wedding was a gala affair, covered by many of those magazines that feature nudist camps. That was the only thing covered; Marie took her solemn vows clad only in a wedding veil. The marriage ended in divorce a few months later.

Undaunted by this unfortunate union, Marie continued to frequent nudist camps. It was while sashaying around in the Florida sunshine that Marie met the vacationing Paul Witte. By now, Marie was a mature 16 and had been kissed many times. Paul was 26 and wanted more.

After vacationing in Florida, he returned to his mother, Elaine, in the tiny hamlet of Trail Creek, Indiana. But darn it all, Paul couldn't get his mind off that cute little Marie. He phoned in a proposal. Marie caught the next bus to Trail Creek.

Mummy Elaine didn't exactly take Marie to her ample bosom. After all, the girl was only 16, but who was she to stand in the way of her son's happiness? Within weeks, Marie and Paul tied the knot.

Surprise of surprises, the Witte marriage appeared to be a happy one. Two sons, Eric and John, blessed the union. Years passed. The boys grew up to be strapping teenagers. Everything appeared normal in the Witte household until September 1, 1981. That was the day of the tragic accident. Eric, 17, was fooling around with his father's gun when it discharged. The bullet plowed into the back of his father's head, killing him instantly. Sometime later, when Marie's house burned down, Elaine invited her daughter-in-law and her two grandsons to move in with her.

That was a mistake. The two boys turned out to be undisciplined hellions. Their grandmother couldn't stand them and they couldn't stand her. The tension was relieved somewhat in 1983 when Eric joined the navy and was stationed in San Diego, California. A few months later, Marie told anyone who inquired that her mother-in-law had gone away on vacation to visit relatives. She was a little vague as to when Elaine would return. At the same time, she and John took a trip to San Diego to visit Eric.

Nine months passed. No one had seen hide nor hair of Elaine, Marie or John. When a relative from out of town came to Trail Creek and found Elaine's house devoid of furniture and to all intents and purposes deserted, she went to the police. An inquiry at Elaine's bank revealed that her social security cheques were no longer being deposited there, but were being sent to General Delivery, San Diego. A further inquiry disclosed that the cheques had all been signed by Elaine Witte and endorsed by Marie Witte. A handwriting expert was brought in to examine Elaine's signature. He felt that someone had traced her name from an authentic signature.

The FBI located Marie and Eric, who had cashed some of the cheques. They were taken into custody in San Diego and charged with forgery and conspiracy. But where was Elaine Witte? Marie said she had no idea and could care less.

Back in Trail Creek, a relative of the Wittes went to authorities and, for the first time, police heard that Elaine had been murdered. The relative told a wild tale of murder and intrigue. Detectives were amazed at the horrific nature of the story they were being told. They approached the two Witte boys with the relative's incriminating statement.

John decided to talk. He told detectives that he and his grandmother had argued constantly. Marie had been using Elaine's bank card to withdraw funds from her bank account. When Elaine suspected she was being systematically robbed, she informed Marie that the very next day she was going to her bank to check on her affairs. Marie told John that Elaine would throw them all out of the house. Something had to be done post-haste.

Marie awakened John in the middle of the night and ordered him to kill his grandmother. John took his brother's crossbow and shot Elaine in the chest as she slept. Marie instructed him to clean up, before leaving the house for a few hours. John shoved his grandmother's body into a garbage can. When Marie returned, she called Eric in San Diego, asking his advice. Eric told her to put the body into the family freezer located in the basement. She and John spent three days hacking and chopping Elaine's body so the parts would fit in the freezer. The job became somewhat easier when Marie purchased a chainsaw.

Eric flew home on a 24-hour pass. He assessed the situation and suggested Marie install a garbage-disposal unit and a trash compactor to get rid of the body. The appliances didn't do the job. The garbage disposal unit clogged and burned out the motor, while the trash compactor wasn't capable of accommodating large bones. It too broke down.

Marie spent a full week boiling the body parts so that she could put them into freezer bags and store them easily in the freezer until Eric returned from San Diego and told her how to get rid of her mother-in-law.

Once police informed Eric of John's statement, he decided to confess as well, confirming everything John had already related. In addition, he dropped the bombshell that his father's death had not been an accident. His mother had commanded him to shoot his father. According to Eric, his father had abused him, his brother and his mother for years. After the shooting, Marie had rehearsed her sons on what to say to the police. Everyone had believed Paul Witte's death had been a tragic accident.

When Marie had wanted to stage another accident to get rid of Elaine, Eric had argued with his mother not to do it. He figured police would never fall for two tragic accidents in the same family. That was the reason they so desperately wanted to dispose of Elaine's body.

Eric had finally done the job. He threw the boiled body parts out of a car across three states on his way from Indiana to California. If anyone came across the boiled meat, it would be doubtful they would recognize it as human.

And what happened to the members of this joyous family? Let's see. John was not charged with any complicity in his father's murder. He testified against his mother in exchange for the right to plead guilty to involuntary manslaughter in the case of his grandmother. He was sentenced to 20 years' imprisonment.

Eric was given immunity from prosecution in the case of his grandmother in exchange for his testimony concerning his father's murder. He pleaded guilty to murdering his father and was sentenced to 20 years in prison.

On November 4, 1985, Marie Witte stood trial in Michigan City, Indiana, for the murder of her mother-in-law. All the gory details came out. With her two sons testifying against her, the outcome was a foregone conclusion. Marie was found guilty of murder and conspiracy. She was sentenced to the maximum allowed by law—60 years and 50 years to run consecutively. She was also charged with the murder of her husband. Once again, her sons testified for the state.

During her trial, it was revealed that Marie had attempted but failed to poison her husband with rat poison before eliciting the assistance of her son. She was found guilty of murder and attempted murder. On top of her previous 110-year sentence, she received a further sentence of life imprisonment. Marie Witte will most probably never be set free.

# WILLIAM YOUNGMAN

## SON FROM HELL

WE have in this volume presented for your enjoyment and revulsion some of the most hideous ladies and gentlemen ever to take human lives.

Now allow me to showcase William Godfrey Youngman, definitely a contender for the number-one villain of all time. William's father was a tailor in London, England, over a hundred years ago. The Youngman family, consisting of William Sr., his wife and three sons, lived in the top two floors of a three-storey home.

It was a foregone conclusion that William would take up his father's profession, but after a short while as an apprentice to the senior Youngman, he let it be known that the cut-and-sew game was not for him. William became a footman for a well-known physician, but soon managed to get into trouble. Evidently some of the doctor's belongings found their way into our William's possession. He wasn't prosecuted for this indiscretion, but he was fired.

William returned to his parents' home, where he displayed an aversion to any sort of exertion. He moped around the house all day thinking of ways to make money without indulging in the disagreeable act of manual labour. He mulled over the obvious, such as armed robbery and mugging, but dismissed these activities as far too dangerous. You see, William was not only a stupid oaf, he was also a coward. In his own dull way, he came up with a scheme never duplicated for its many cruel and heartless aspects.

Sly William made the acquaintance of Mary Streeter, the daughter of a farmer who worked his fields just outside the city. Mary, who wasn't exactly rushed off her feet by eligible swains, liked William mainly because no other boy had ever paid her so much attention. When he invited her to London to spend some time as a house guest of his parents, she quickly accepted.

On a beautiful summer day, Mary arrived in London. William met her at the station. Together they started off for the Youngman residence, but because of the heat the young couple stopped off for a bit of liquid refreshment at a pub near London Bridge. While in the pub, an incident took place that would later assume some importance.

The owner of the pub, a man named Spicer, waited on William and Mary. When William let Mary pay for the drinks, Spicer sidled up to her and whispered, "That boy is an idler, a ne'er-do-well, and means you no good." Spicer had disliked William at first sight. When William turned his back, he again spoke to Mary. "I'd rather see a daughter of mine dead in her grave than married to a man as he."

Mary Streeter was in love. Who was this man who spoke so harshly against her William and what right did he have to say such things? She decided to ignore the man's warnings. That same day, William suggested that Mary take out insurance on her life in the amount of £100, a not inconsiderable sum in those days. William didn't let up. He pestered Mary so much that the next day, accompanied by William, she purchased the insurance policy, falsely listing her husband, William, as beneficiary. Mary shelled out the money for the first premium.

A week later, the stage was set for murder most foul. The young couple spent a day in the country, with Mary footing all bills for the day's activities. At 9 p.m. they returned home and ate a hearty meal prepared by William's mother.

One can only picture the Youngmans' satisfaction. Their not-too-ambitious son had met a lovely girl. It was obvious to everyone that it was only a matter of time before he and Mary would wed. The evening meal had been consumed with enthusiastic good cheer. William's two younger brothers, Thomas, 11, and Charles, 6, teased William about his girlfriend. All in all, it was a pleasant evening.

Mr. Youngman was the first to go to bed. He was accustomed to early hours, as he had to rise at 5 a.m. to travel to his place of employment some distance from his home. Mary and Mrs. Youngman shared a room, while William slept with his brothers.

Next morning, bright and early, Mr. Youngman got up and went to work, leaving his family asleep in bed, as was his custom. About 20 minutes later, the occupants of the first floor heard noises loud enough to cause concern. One of them put on his trousers and went upstairs. Halfway up he was met by William in his nightclothes. William was covered with blood. He screamed, "For God's sake, come up. There are several dead and dying. My mother got up in the middle of the night, just now, in fact, and attacked us all. I am afraid I have killed her in self-defence."

Upstairs, on the landing, just in the doorway of her bedroom, lay the bodies of Mrs. Youngman and Mary Streeter. Both had been stabbed to death. The two young boys were both dead in their bed. They too had been stabbed repeatedly.

Police were called and were at the scene in a matter of minutes. William gave them this fantastic statement, "My mother went suddenly mad and did it all. She attacked me with the knife after she had killed the others, and I wrested it from her and stabbed her to protect myself. I was entitled to do so. That's the law."

The officers looked at each other and shook their heads. Why had it been necessary for this strong 25-year-old man to kill his mother after he had "wrested" the knife from her? They pointed out this discrepancy to William, who doggedly stuck to his story.

Poor Mr. Youngman. That morning he had left his family sleeping peacefully. Now he was summoned home to find that they had all been murdered, with the exception of William. When questioned by police, he informed them that his wife had never been erratic in any way and for his son to insinuate that she was mad was in itself ludicrous. The authorities agreed with Mr. Youngman. William was arrested that very day. A search of his room uncovered the insurance policy. In Mary's trunk police found letters that Mary had received from William before her ill-fated visit to London. In these letters, William repeatedly asked Mary to insure her life.

William's trial lasted only one day. Despite the unbelievable nature of his story, he stuck to it throughout. No one believed it for a minute. The jury was convinced that they were staring at a bona fide monster, a man who could plan and carry out the murder of his unsuspecting girlfriend, his two younger brothers and his mother, all for monetary gain. One can despise William for the four murders, but in addition, his plan included another despicable element—he attempted to place the blame on his mother.

William Youngman was found guilty of murder and sentenced to hang. While in jail, he steadfastly held to his original statement and initiated a letter-writing campaign pleading with anyone who might help his cause, including the Queen of England.

All his efforts brought no results and William Youngman was hanged for his horrible crimes. While being led to the scaffold, he was heard to mumble over and over, "My mother done it all." Who knows, by then he might very well have believed his ridiculous story himself.

# PART 3

## MURDER MOST FOUL

# RENE ACKERMAN

## (SWITZERLAND)

WHEN 47-year-old Rene Ackerman was questioned by Swiss police, he told them a straightforward story. According to Rene, on Wednesday, May 12, 1982, he had dinner with his wife, Erika, after she completed her workday at a Lucerne department store. They had dined at a fashionable restaurant and had lingered until shortly after 11 p.m. Erika had driven away in her Austin Mini, supposedly to their apartment in the town of Kriens, about a mile south of Lucerne. Rene had visited with a friend. You might ask why police were so interested in Rene's activities on that particular evening. Well, I'll tell you. His wife never made it home. Folks in the tiny Swiss village of Seelisberg were startled when wild sounds attracted them to the edge of the village, where they saw a screaming woman engulfed by flames flailing about in the middle of the road. Down the road, a vehicle exploded. All in all, it was an exciting night in Seelisberg.

Villagers rushed to the burning woman's aid, using clothing and blankets to extinguish the flames. The unconscious, horribly burned woman was rushed by ambulance to Lucerne, where she died seven days later. During the week, while the woman lay in a coma, police launched an extensive investigation into the incident. The Austin Mini that had exploded was traced through its licence to Erika Ackerman, hence the questioning of her husband, Rene.

Rene proved to be quite a lad. He had divorced his first wife four years earlier and had only been married to Erika for three months. Detectives were interested in the friend Rene had visited on the night of his wife's terrible ordeal. The friend turned out to be beautiful 34-year-old blonde Cornelia Riffel. When interrogated, she swore that Rene had been with her from a little after 11 p.m. until 4 a.m., which encompassed the time that Erika and her Austin Mini went up in flames.

Folks, even the slickest rascal does not generally spend the night with a blonde after only three months of marriage. Rene had a ready explanation. He told authorities that Cornelia was his mistress and had held that position since 1976. They had been doing what comes naturally before he married Erika and simply continued their boudoir gymnastics after he was legally wed. What can I tell you? Rene was just that kind of guy.

Cornelia was married when she met Rene, who was also married at the time. Their chance meeting broke up both marriages when the pair became lovers. What's more, they had the loot to openly enjoy themselves. Cornelia's papa had passed away, leaving her a wad of cash to squander. She and Rene did an excellent job spending it. They dined at the most expensive restaurants and owned three homes with accompanying sports cars. They even owned a racehorse, which didn't run fast, but had an enormous appetite.

Detectives were stymied. They were certain that in some way Rene was responsible for his wife's death, but given Cornelia's statement that he had been with her when the incident occurred, they couldn't get a handle on the case. True enough, Rene had a slight burn on the back of his right hand, but he came up with a convenient explanation for that. He claimed he had burned his hand putting a dish in the oven.

Meanwhile, an autopsy revealed that Erika had been doused with gasoline. Moreover, an examination of the Austin Mini indicated that someone had set the vehicle and Erika on fire. Judging from the position of the Austin, police believed the car had been pushed off the road before being torched.

It was a difficult one to figure out. Why would a man who was living high off the hog, complete with a beautiful mistress, decide to kill his wife of only three months? Why had he married Erika in the first place? There had to be a reason, and there was a good one.

It was left to forensic accountants to come up with the motive. Cornelia and Rene had been living so extravagantly they had slowly exhausted their funds. They had mortgaged the houses and other assets to keep a supply of cash flowing in. Faced with the demise of their luxurious lifestyle, they had come up with a diabolical scheme. Rene would marry someone and insure her life. Erika was picked because she was not wealthy. If he married a rich woman, Rene reasoned, he would be suspected of killing her for her money. Accountants found that Erika had two life insurance policies, one for a value of £30,000 pounds and one for £60,000. Rene was the beneficiary of both policies.

It was a tough case, but Swiss detectives kept digging away. They questioned employees at the restaurant where Erika and Rene had dined on the night in question. They learned that Erika had complained of a headache and Rene had given her some pills. A search of Rene's BMW uncovered an empty five-gallon gas can and a pair of men's gloves. The right glove had a hole burned in the back, which matched perfectly the burn on Rene's right hand.

Rene was arrested and charged with his wife's murder. Cornelia, who stuck to her story that Rene had been with her all night, was charged with being an accomplice to homicide.

In 1985, Rene stood trial. The prosecution contended that Rene had plied his wife with wine and sleeping pills at the restaurant. He then drove her to Seelisberg, where he doused both Erika and the Austin Mini with gasoline; Cornelia had followed the pair in the BMW and picked up Rene. The lovers drove back home, where they spent the remainder of the night.

Rene never confessed. Cornelia finally admitted she had picked up Rene outside Seelisburg, but claimed she had had no knowledge of the murder. The Swiss jury didn't believe either of the accused. Rene Ackerman was found guilty of murdering his wife and was sentenced to life imprisonment, while Cornelia was found guilty of being an accomplice to murder. She received a sentence of 17 years in prison.

# JIM ALLISON

(CANADA)

EVERYONE has heard one of those ribald stories about the farmer's daughter. Too few of us, however, have been fortunate enough to know one in the flesh, so to speak. But a real honest-to-goodness "farmer's daughter" did exist in southern Ontario.

Her name was Emma Borland, and she lived about five miles south of Galt, just before the turn of the 20th century. Mr. and Mrs. Borland knew they had a handful when Emma romanced her way through her teens. She was good-looking, had a figure to match anda yen for action. All those virile young males of Waterloo County provided the action, and Emma provided everything else.

Emma was only 21 when she married John Arnott, a wealthy merchant from Innerkip, who was quite a bit older than she was. Emma turned over a new leaf and was a good and faithful wife to John for two years, and then he passed on to his great reward. There were those around Galt who said she'd been too much for the poor soul in the bedroom. Be that as it may, at 23 Emma found herself completely free and wealthy to boot. So Emma took up where she left off when she married John. She had a barrel of fun for three full years before she turned respectable again.

This time she married Tony Orr, a successful farmer. The entire Orr family was well known socially throughout Waterloo County. Despite Emma's past reputation, she fit, or was pushed gracefully, into the social whirl of rural life. Again Emma settled down, and really was a good wife until she was about 35. Then she simply ran away with the hired hand, just like they do in the stories. A real handsome character named Tim Mulholland had been making love to Emma while Tony was busy tending the fields or whatever. Tony traced the couple to a hotel in Niagara Falls.

Tony really loved his wife. He took her back and this time hired an unattractive, pimply-faced youngster named Jim Allison as his hired hand. Once bitten, twice shy, as they say. Anyway, they all lived happily for three more years, until all of a sudden Emma disappeared.

Tony and young Jim hitched the horses and drove into Galt to Sheriff Maynard Gould's office to report Emma missing. Alex Allison, Jim's father, was a municipal official who worked in the same building as the sheriff. The youngster took the opportunity to go down the hall to see his father. In the meantime, Tony informed the sheriff that both he and Jim had hunted for Emma all morning. He said a neighbour had heard a gunshot earlier, so Tony had looked for his own shotgun, and found that it was missing. The sheriff sympathized with Tony, but suspected that Emma was up to her old tricks again. Sheriff Gould agreed to go out to the farm with Tony. Young Jim was through visiting his father, and joined Tony and Sheriff Gould in the hall. While Tony attended to the horses, the sheriff asked Jim a pointed question: Did Emma have a boyfriend that Tony didn't know anything about? Jim informed him that there were at least two that he knew of, Weldon Trevelyan and Harry Blair.

Telling Tony he would join him at the farm later, the sheriff went looking for Trevelyan and Blair. Trevelyan readily admitted meeting with Emma. In fact, he thought it was a damn shame she was missing. He claimed he would miss her, too. Some stories just ring true; the sheriff believed Trevelyan. Then the sheriff questioned Blair. Upon being interrogated, Blair admitted making love to Emma, but denied any knowledge of her disappearance. The sheriff shook his head. He believed Blair, too.

Gould proceeded to Tony's farm. By the time he arrived, Tony and Jim had already found the missing shotgun. It smelled of cordite, and had obviously been fired recently. At this point the sheriff realized he had a possible murder on his hands. He wired John Murray, head detective of the Ontario police. Word came back that Detective Murray would arrive by train at nine the next morning. The sheriff accepted the invitation to spend the night on the farm. When he awoke at daybreak the next morning and looked out his window, he thought he saw a light go out in a grove of trees on the other side of a cornfield. Being half-asleep, he dismissed it from his mind, deciding he'd probably seen a firefly.

Tony, Jim and the sheriff drove to Galt and met Detective Murray at the train. After being briefed, the detective questioned the two main suspects, Trevelyan and Blair. However, he wasn't as convinced of their innocence as the sheriff was. In fact, Murray thought that possibly Tony had had enough of Emma and had decided to do away with her.

Once at the farm, Detective Murray quickly discovered a patch of grass that was discoloured. The discoloration, which was obviously caused by blood, led down to the cornfield. Detective Murray followed the bent foliage across the meadow to a grove of trees. There he and the sheriff found a shallow half-dug grave with no body in it. Close by, under some leaves, lay the body of poor Emma. She had been killed by a shotgun blast. Detective Murray figured that the murderer had come back after dark to dig the grave. The job wasn't finished. Then Gould remembered the light he had seen when he woke up. It must have been the murderer finishing his work for the night.

Would the killer complete the grave the following night?

In true Hitchcock fashion, the sheriff and the detective hid in the bushes that night and waited for the murderer to show up. At around midnight a lantern came bobbing through the cornfield and up to the grove of trees. The officers grabbed the man with the lantern. To their utter amazement, it was Alex Allison, Jim's father.

Alex told a tragic story. His son Jim had killed Emma, but did not have the courage to conceal the body. Jim had confessed to his father when he and Tony had come to the municipal building to report the woman's disappearance to the sheriff. Alex had dug all the previous night, but had had to stop at daybreak.

They put handcuffs on Alex, and once his son saw him, he broke down and admitted killing Emma. Jim said that he knew about the other men Emma was playing around with and thought he would try his luck with her. Emma laughed at him, and called him ugly. She said she would tell Tony to fire him. In a rage, Jim took the shotgun and killed her.

No charges were ever laid against Alex Allison, but his son Jim was hanged on February 4, 1898, in what was then called Berlin, now known as Kitchener.

# BEVERLEY ALLITT

## (ENGLAND)

---

I am often asked why England has spawned such strange and unusual murders. There is no answer to this question, but it is a fact that the tidy little isle has given rise, pound for pound, to the weirdest group of killers in the world.

Let's take a look at Nurse Beverly Allitt, who was born in the quaint Lincolnshire village of Corby Glen. At school, Beverly was bright and attentive. But when she enrolled at nearby Grantham College with an eye toward a nursing career, her scholastic endeavours took a turn for the worse. Her personality seemed to change as well. She became a shy, introverted, somewhat overweight young woman. Beverly was also plagued by a tendency toward illness, which was to continue throughout her life. She missed classes regularly due to colds, fatigue and a variety of ailments that always seemed to cure themselves. In time, she had to drop out of college, but shortly there-after she enrolled in a two-year course at the South Lincolnshire School of Nursing.

During her stay at nursing school, Beverly suffered from a series of sicknesses, but she managed to complete the course and obtain employment on a trial basis at Grantham Hospital. It had not been easy for Beverly. At various times she had blurred vision, headaches, back problems and swollen breasts. She also had been afflicted with injuries to her feet, arms, legs and fingers. In addition, she suffered from gallbladder pains, ulcers and various infections.

No one even mildly suspected that Beverly suffered from Munchausen's syndrome, a condition in which the patient strives for attention by inflicting wounds or inventing symptoms. It is rare for such individuals to exhibit signs of both Munchausen's syndrome and Munchausen's syndrome by proxy. This latter condition involves inflicting others with injuries or inducing diseases in others so that they themselves will receive reflected attention.

Beverly Allitt had both conditions, but no one knew it. What her superiors and colleagues saw in 1991 was a neat, hardworking, 24-year-old nurse taking care of the children on Ward 4 of Grantham General Hospital.

On February 21, a young woman rushed into Grantham General with her 7-week-old son in her arms. X-rays indicated little Liam Taylor had pneumonia.

Liam's dad soon joined his wife and son. The parents were comforted by the spick-and-span caring nurse who kept them informed of their son's condition. She assured them that Liam was doing fine and told them to go home and get some rest.

Two hours later, at 6 p.m., the Taylors returned to the hospital. Beverly greeted them with the distressing news that Liam's condition had worsened. She explained that she had looked in on him and found he was barely breathing. The baby was rushed to a treatment room, where doctors managed to revive him.

That night, the Taylors slept in the hospital. They were relieved the next day when their son opened his eyes and seemed to be much better. Still anxious, though, they decided to sleep at the hospital that night as well. In the wee hours, Beverly called a colleague to look at Liam. The baby was chalk-white.

Beverly called for the crash team. Within minutes doctors were working frantically to save the baby's life. At 6 a.m. they concluded that Liam had suffered massive brain damage due to lack of oxygen.

While the action was taking place in Ward 4, Beverly Allitt took a back seat as more highly trained nurses and doctors took over. She smiled, washed up and went home. When she came back on duty later that day, she learned that Liam Taylor had died. Death was attributed to a muscle around the baby's heart ceasing to function. Beverly was never suspected of wrongdoing. In fact, she was never even questioned about the death. She had enjoyed the entire episode immensely.

Two weeks later, on March 5, Timothy Hardwick, a helpless 11-year-old cerebral palsy patient, who also suffered from epilepsy, was admitted to Ward 4. Timothy could not walk, talk or see, and had just had a severe epileptic seizure. In due course, he settled down and was resting comfortably.

Beverly was alone with the boy for only a few minutes before she appeared on the floor, shouting, "Quick, cardiac arrest!" A doctor rushed to the area. He was too late. A postmortem failed to ascertain a definite cause of death. Ultimately, it was attributed to epilepsy and cerebral palsy. No one suspected foul play.

March was a bad month at Grantham General. In quick succession, three babies with minor ailments had cardiac arrests. All recovered, but the frequency of these serious incidents caused authorities some concern, particularly when the three youngsters were found to have extraordinarily high levels of insulin in their blood. The only thing the cases had in common was their nurse—Beverly Allitt.

The Phillipses were overjoyed with their identical twin girls, Becky and Katie. Although very tiny, the babies were sent home 33 days after their birth. On April 1, Becky, suffering from what doctors suspected was gastroenteritis, was admitted to Ward 4 at Grantham General. Beverly Allitt spent a lot of time with the little girl. Two days later, Beverly told another nurse that Becky seemed to be in distress. Her colleague disagreed. She felt Becky was doing fine.

Next day, after Beverly fed Becky, the baby was taken home. Her parents were so pleased at her recovery they had her sleep in their bed. At 3 a.m. they awoke to look at Becky. She was dead. A postmortem failed to reveal the cause of death. It was attributed to crib death. Later, blood taken from Becky's heart would show high levels of insulin.

Doctors were concerned about Becky's twin, Katie. They decided to hospitalize her as a precaution. She was placed under the care of Beverly Allitt. That night, Beverly ran down the hall carrying Katie and shouting, "Cardiac arrest, cardiac arrest!" Doctors succeeded in saving Katie's life. Someone remarked that the automatic alarm had failed to go off when Katie stopped breathing. It must have malfunctioned. Katie Phillips was left severely brain-damaged, her right side paralyzed, her hearing impaired and partially blind.

Katie's mother, however, was most appreciative of Nurse Allitt and told staff members the conscientious nurse had saved her daughter's life. She asked Beverly to be Katie's godmother. Humbly, Beverly accepted, saying she was honoured.

Over the next eleven days, four more children unexpectedly suffered cardiac arrests. All four were saved, but some were severely brain-damaged. All of them had the same nurse—Beverly Allitt.

The fourth youngster to die at Beverly's hands was 15-month-old Claire Peck, an asthma patient. Claire was to be outfitted with an intravenous drip and receive nebulizing treatment to help her breathe. For a few minutes, the nurse and doctor attending Claire left her room. Beverly was alone with the child. In less than two minutes Beverly was shouting, "Cardiac arrest!" The doctor and nurse were at the child's side almost instantaneously, administering oxygen. Claire responded immediately. Once again, the nurse and doctor momentarily left the room. As if programmed, the words echoed through the halls once more, "Cardiac arrest, cardiac arrest!" This time the child couldn't be saved. Claire was dead.

It was all too much. Hospital authorities believed a mysterious virus might have swept through the ward. When a postmortem failed to establish the cause of Claire's death, police were called. A poisons expert, conducting tests on materials taken from Claire's body, found traces of lignocaine, a powerful anaesthetic used on patients who have suffered cardiac arrest. Since Claire was asthmatic, there was no reason she would have been given this drug. To police, this was a clear sign that the child had been poisoned.

Investigators reviewed 25 incidents involving 13 children. One nurse, Beverly Allitt, had been present at each of the 25 incidents. Three weeks after the investigation began, Beverly was arrested. She was charged with four murders, three attempted murders and six counts of causing bodily harm.

At her trial, Beverly's history revealed her years of self-maiming to bring attention to herself. Her attacks on the children in her care came about when she graduated from the condition known as Munchausen's syndrome to Munchausen's syndrome by proxy. At the end of her trial, Beverly was sentenced to 13 terms of life imprisonment, the harshest sentence given a woman by a British court in the modern era.

Since her imprisonment, Beverly Allitt has confessed that she killed three children and injured six others.

# DORIS ANDRIST AND ANDRE BODMER

(SWITZERLAND)

OVER the years, I have delved into some strange and unusual murder plots. You might remember Donald Hume, who dropped his victim's body parts from an airplane as his co-pilot, a dog, looked on; or Bob James, who inserted his wife's foot in a box containing a poisonous rattlesnake. Well, folks, Andre Bodmer and Doris Andrist rank right up there with originators of the weirdest murder plots in the vile and checkered history of homicide.

When Andre was only 15 years old, he was madly in love with his 14-year-old girlfriend, Isabella. No puppy love here; this was mature sexual love in every sense of the word. Both sets of parents, strict, affluent and religious Swiss, were aghast at the obvious sexual attraction between their children. When the parents objected too strongly, the teenagers ran away from the Swiss town of Schwyz and lived off the land in the Buednerland Forest.

In due course, they were brought back to town, but the reunion with their parents was less than jovial. Isabella was pregnant. To the delight of the young couple, their parents insisted they marry. After the nuptials, however, they left the newlyweds to fend for themselves.

Andre and Isabella made their way to Gasel, where Andre apprenticed as a butcher and Isabella attended school, her tummy showing the effects of her woodsy escapade.

After Isabella had her baby, times were rough. The Bodmers lived from hand to mouth. Sometimes they went hungry. This desperate state of affairs couldn't continue indefinitely. A solution to their dilemma was agreed upon: the attractive Isabella would become a prostitute.

And that's how it began. Soon Isabella was entertaining men in their apartment while Andre walked the baby. Their lucrative business was interrupted for a short while when Isabella found herself once again pregnant. The Bodmers' second child came into this troubled world, but as soon as Isabella regained her figure, she was back turning tricks.

The lifestyle Isabella had adopted was rather hectic, with two children and business obligations constantly overlapping. She had a tête-à-tête with hubby

Andre, who agreed it was time for him to seek gainful employment. He was accepted as a journeyman butcher with the Denner Wholesale Meat Products Co. in Zurich.

The Bodmers moved to the town of Dielsdorf, about three kilometres outside Zurich. For the first time since they were little more than children, Andre, now 29, and Isabella, 28, were leading normal, productive lives. It would be most pleasant to relate that the Bodmers and their two offspring settled down to a happy, peaceful existence, but such was not to be the case.

At this point, Doris Andrist, a salesgirl in the sausage department at Denner's, enters our story. It began innocently enough. Andre gave the luscious brunette a lift home one day. A few days later, they checked into a hotel room and we can only assume they felt no great compulsion to sleep.

Doris was a knockout in the looks department and a real manipulator in the gray-matter department. Being a single girl, she longed to marry Andre, but that was impossible, as Andre was already well married to Isabella. To Doris, the solution was crystal clear. Isabella had to go.

Doris initially thought divorce might be a solution, but Andre pointed out that he was expecting to inherit his parents' restaurant; the mere mention of divorce would cut him off from this potential windfall.

Doris scratched her pretty cranium and took the giant leap to premeditated murder. She suggested they kill the woman who stood in the way of their happiness. Andre agreed this latter step would certainly achieve the desired result.

Shooting was discussed, but dismissed as being too technical. Neither knew how to fire a gun. After mulling over the problem, they agreed strangulation would suit their purposes perfectly.

Doris suggested that Andre lure Isabella into the woods, where she would strangle her. Andre disagreed. He and Isabella had not been getting along, and it was doubtful that she would be receptive to the idea of a romantic walk in the woods. Besides, he would be an immediate suspect, as is so often the case when wives bite the dust. In addition, inquisitive police might discover the relationship between him and Doris. No, there simply had to be a better plan than that.

It took a few weeks for the diabolical duo to come up with their unbelievable plot, which would divert suspicion from Andre. He would lure Isabella into the forest on the pretense that they were entering a reality contest called Game of Courage. If they won, they would be the recipients of a large sum of money. The game involved entering the woods, where Andre would blindfold Isabella and tie her to a tree. She would be released by an official of the game. There was no risk involved and they stood to win a tidy sum.

It boggles the imagination to believe that anyone would be taken in by such a scheme, but we must remember that although the spark between Isabella and Andre had diminished, he was still the father of her two children and her constant companion for most of her life. Besides, she had no knowledge of Doris's existence.

Meanwhile, Doris was a busy girl. She knew Andre's blood type was AB. If Andre had intercourse with Isabella and they attempted to simulate a rape at the time of her murder, semen left at the scene would be matched to Andre's. It was Doris's intention to leave semen from a different blood type at the site of the murder.

Doris had thought up a way to accomplish this rather difficult task. Posing as a prostitute, she had no difficulty getting picked up in vehicles by cruising males. Eventually, Doris found a gentleman with type O blood. She paid him a fee and collected his semen in a condom, which she carefully stored in her refrigerator.

On September 14, 1985, the unsuspecting Isabella was blindfolded, gagged and tied to a tree in the forest, where the two conspirators took turns throttling her until she was dead. Doris then tore off Isabella's slacks and underwear. She scratched Isabella's face and even broke some of her fingernails. Doris then spread the contents of the condom over Isabella's thighs and legs.

Next day, Andre reported to police that his wife was missing. He told them she had wanted to attend a dance, but because he hadn't wanted to go, they'd argued. Isabella had stormed out of the house and had not returned home. Later that same afternoon, a couple strolling through the woods came across her body.

The physician who performed the autopsy felt that certain aspects of the case were suspicious. There was something unnatural about the crime scene and the condition of the body. Rapists do not usually tie their victims to a tree while raping them. In addition, Isabella had not actually been raped, as her attacker had obviously ejaculated prematurely. From the semen, it was ascertained that the attempted rape had been initiated by someone with type O blood, which eliminated Andre as a suspect.

The pair of killers would have been home free had it not been for one unforeseen circumstance. They both suffered pangs of remorse and fell into a deep depression. Some five weeks after Isabella's murder, they were found unconscious in Buednerland Forest and rushed to hospital, where their stomachs were pumped. Both survived. They had taken massive doses of barbiturates.

Detectives investigating the unsolved murder of Isabella Bodmer questioned Andre. Eventually, he and Doris admitted to the murder, but would disclose no details. It was almost a year later, after Doris's photograph appeared in Swiss newspapers, that the sperm donor came forward with his strange story. Only then did Andre and Doris reveal their diabolical plot.

Andre Bodmer and Doris Andrist stood trial for murder and were found guilty. On January 8, 1988, each received a sentence of 20 years' imprisonment.

# HERB AND DOROTHY ARCHER

(CANADA)

YOU don't hear much about the tiny town of Oak Lake, Manitoba, these days, but back in the winter of 1978, it was the most talked-about community in Canada. Dr. Markus Scherz, 64, was the only medic in town. The beloved doctor and his wife, Stephanie, knew all 350 souls who called Oak Lake home.

A loud knock on the door of the Scherz home in the middle of a cold January night awoke the occupants from a deep sleep. For the first time, Dr. Scherz laid eyes on Herbert Bruce Archer and his wife, Dorothy. They were accompanied by farmer Dave Penny from nearby Routledge.

That Sunday, January 22, 1978, had been quite a night for the three visitors to the Scherz home. The saga that was to follow had started earlier when a man and woman registered as Mr. and Mrs. Maurice Crystal at the Countryside Inn Motel in Virden. Their van was parked beside the motel and had come to the attention of the RCMP. A man named Archer had rented the vehicle weeks earlier in Vancouver. The rental vehicle was supposed to be returned in two days. After several weeks passed, the van was considered to have been stolen.

Four RCMP officers, Corporal Russell Hornseth, and Constables John O'Ray, Dennis Onofrey and Candace Smith, arrived at the motel in two police cruisers to check out the van. They knocked on the door of room 20 and identified themselves as police officers.

The motel room door opened slowly. Apprehensive, Constable Onofrey drew his gun. As soon as Archer saw the weapon, he opened fire. Onofrey was shot dead. Constable Smith, who had just finished her basic training six weeks earlier, ran for cover and drew her weapon. She fired twice and missed. Archer was more accurate. Constable Smith was hit twice, in the hip and stomach.

Archer kept firing. Corporal Hornseth was shot in the head. O'Ray ran for cover, lost his glasses and fell to the ground. He saw the desperate pair make a run toward one of the police cruisers. Archer, realizing the van was low on fuel, decided to take off with his wife in the police car. O'Ray fired several shots. One struck Dorothy Archer, wounding her severely. Speeding away in the police cruiser, Archer realized two things: he needed weapons and ammunition; and it was imperative that his wife receive medical attention.

Archer chose a farmhouse at random. Dave Penny answered the door. He was soon made aware of the situation. The Archers wanted weapons and medical help for Dorothy. Dave told Archer he didn't have any guns, but could accompany his wife to Oak Lake, which had a doctor. Archer and Dorothy proceeded to tie up Mrs. Penny and her daughter. Dorothy was directed to stand guard while her husband took off to procure weapons.

Dave drove while Archer kept him covered. They pulled into Lloyd Hatch's farm. Lloyd and Wilma Hatch were apprised of the circumstances and turned over guns to Herb Archer. With Dave driving, the pair returned to Penny's farm. Dave's family was as he had left them, with badly wounded Dorothy Archer standing guard.

Once again, Dave found himself driving the police cruiser. This time he was heading for Oak Lake and the medical attention Dorothy Archer required.

Dr. Scherz had been practising in the town for a quarter of a century. He had been awakened in the night many times. The doctor calmly examined the patient and advised Archer that she needed surgery, which he was ill-equipped to perform. He suggested they go to Brandon, about an hour's drive away. Archer wouldn't hear of it. Instead, he had the doctor call an ambulance, which soon arrived and whisked Dorothy to hospital.

Herbert Archer had three hostages: Dr. Scherz, his wife, Stephanie, and Dave Penny. Once Dorothy was taken care of, he relaxed. It was now daylight, Monday, January 23. Archer loved to talk, and told his captives his life story. He portrayed himself as not a bad fellow, but one who had done some wrong things in his life. He admitted killing a Mountie and told his prisoners he had nothing to lose. He explained that he must not fall asleep and demanded something from Dr. Scherz to keep him awake. The doctor gave him amphetamines.

The phone rang. The RCMP was making contact with Archer. They assured him that his wife was out of danger. The desperate man demanded $100,000 cash and safe passage by air out of Canada. He also wanted a guarantee that once he was out of the country, the authorities would make no effort to bring him back. Archer advised the Mounties that his three hostages were alive and well.

Although the Archers would never be brought to trial for the murder of Maurice Crystal, the Calgary businessman was found strangled to death in his office that Sunday night. It was Crystal's credit card that Archer had used to register at the motel in Virden, where the shootout with the RCMP had occurred.

When he and Dorothy fled in the police cruiser, they left the credit card behind in room 20.

Another day and night passed. Archer nodded off occasionally, but the slightest noise made him clutch his weapon and wake up. He had no idea that investigators had connected the Calgary murder with the assault on the RCMP.

The RCMP had evacuated the homes close to Dr. Scherz's house. Stores closed. School was suspended. Life in the tiny hamlet had abruptly changed. Only reporters and police were allowed in the general area of the Scherz home.

The individuals in the house had been held captive for more than eighty hours. Constable Dennis Onofrey was buried in Virden. The wait continued. The situation was tense. Archer often said during the course of the siege that he would go down fighting and save the last bullet for himself.

Despite his bravado, Archer's determination to fight it out commenced to wane. On Thursday night, he discussed his options with his captives. They told him he had a better chance if he gave himself up rather than attempt to make a deal. Police don't deal with someone who has killed one of their own. Archer listened and reluctantly agreed. He would only ask for fair treatment.

When the RCMP phoned again, Archer asked that fraud charges against him in Ontario and British Columbia be dropped, that he be provided with competent counsel and have one hour with his wife. The Mounties consented to his terms. Archer then replied, "Come and get me." After five days, the ordeal was over.

In his wake, Archer had left one officer dead and two seriously hurt. Although she recovered from her wounds, Constable Candace Smith is unable to have children. Corporal Russell Hornseth lost the sight of one eye. And an entire community was traumatized.

On November 15, 1978, Herbert and Dorothy Archer stood trial for the murder of Constable Dennis Onofrey. After 20 days of listening to the testimony of witnesses and the summations of lawyers, the jury found the defendants guilty of murder in the first degree.

Herbert and Dorothy Archer were sentenced to life imprisonment with no possibility of parole for 25 years. Herbert Archer died of a heart attack in 1990 while still in prison. Dorothy Archer was released in 1993, after serving 15 years.

# DICK BAKONYI

(CANADA)

IT has been said that the perfect murder is one where murder is not even suspected. The tragic accident that takes place so logically and unavoidably, the missing person who walks away from family and friends, never to be seen or heard of again—all these could very well be homicides. We cannot discuss these cases, for they have never been recognized as anything other than what they appeared to be on the surface.

But the near misses are intriguing.

Raymond Slemko was an electrician employed with the Baldwin Electric Co. in Toronto. On a cool September afternoon, in 1960, Slemko had to check some wiring in a trench beside an artificial rink in Dufferin Grove Park. Raymond thought he detected a slight odour, and asked Moses Spurrel, an employee of the A.J. Martin Excavation Co., to give him a hand. Both men started to dig. Raymond would later tell the Supreme Court how he discovered the body of Eva Blumberger. "The electrical cord binding the blanket broke when I put my shovel under it, and I saw a foot."

Later that very day, cement was to be poured into the trench and the body of Eva Blumberger would never have been discovered. She had been reported missing several days earlier by her family, and most probably would have been missing forever had it not been for the curiosity of Raymond Slemko.

The cause of death was a fractured skull, inflicted by vicious blows to the head. Eva had not been sexually molested in any way. The day after the body was uncovered, two private investigators who had been employed by the dead girl's family to find her turned over their file on the case to the police. The main information in the file contained the results of an interview with one Deszo (Dick) Bakonyi. The police picked up Bakonyi for questioning. After hours of interrogation, he was charged with murder.

Due to marriages between members of Eva's and Dick's families, their relationship to each other was rather complicated. Eva's father had died some years earlier, and her father's brother, who was Bakonyi's father, married her mother. Eva, therefore, was Dick's stepsister, as well as his cousin.

According to Bakonyi, on September 12, Eva asked him if he would let her into his room for a meeting with her boyfriend. When Dick and Eva entered the room, Bakonyi claimed, someone placed a chloroform rag over his mouth from behind. Upon regaining consciousness he realized that Eva was gone and there was blood on his bed. Dick said he had not seen Eva since the time of this attack.

The police came up with a somewhat different set of circumstances and events. Bakonyi's landlady, Mrs. Eugenia Rudski, identified the blanket that was wrapped around the body as her own. It had been used on Bakonyi's bed. She described the evening of September 12, when she thought she heard a dull thud emanate from Dick's room. She yelled through the door, inquiring what was going on, but didn't receive any reply. Next morning she washed some dark stains off Bakonyi's bedroom floor. Other bloodstains were found on the dresser, and on Bakonyi's trousers and shoes. All the bloodstains were the same type as Eva Blumberger's. The electric wire was the same type that Bakonyi used on his hi-fi equipment. Dick was a classical music fan, who owned extensive hi-fi equipment and over $1,000 worth of classical records.

Mrs. Ilene Fraser of St. Clarence Avenue happened to be in Dufferin Grove Park the day before the body was uncovered, and swore she saw Dick Bakonyi in the trench where Eva's body was later discovered. Mrs. Fraser thought nothing of it at the time, but the next day, when the body was found, she came forward with her information. Later she identified Dick from a lineup at police headquarters as the man in the trench.

On December 3, 1960, Bakonyi stood trial for the murder of his stepsister. The evidence against him was all circumstantial, but it spun a tight web of guilt. During the trial it was brought out that Eva thought she was pregnant. She feared exposure, and possibly tried to induce an abortion. An autopsy indicated that she was not pregnant. The day Eva vanished, she left a note in Bakonyi's room, which read: *Dear Dan,* (she sometimes called Bakonyi that) *I was here … you were not here. Get the medicine or there will be troubles. I will call. Eva.*

The prosecution proposed that the motive for the killing could have been that Eva had accused Dick of being responsible for her imagined pregnancy. Even Bakonyi's story of being chloroformed was ridiculed. It was proved that Dick had been with members of his family later on the night of September 12, and hadn't even mentioned the alleged incident to anyone. If you are forcefully chloroformed and your stepsister has been abducted, it would seem quite natural that you would, at the very least, tell your family, if not report the incident to the police.

In Bakonyi's defence, his sister gave evidence that he was in her home at approximately the time Mrs. Rudski heard the dull thud from Dick's room.

After two hours of deliberation, the jury found Bakonyi guilty of murder. When asked if he had anything to say before sentence was passed, the accused said, "I think I have, My Lord. Eva Blumberger was my cousin. Before her death she was in trouble. I wanted to help her. That is the only reason I came to be entangled in this case. Probably because of this, I am going to lose my life. I am not afraid to die."

Bakonyi was sentenced to be hanged on May 23, 1961. On May 19, just four days before the execution was to be carried out, his sentence was commuted by the federal cabinet to life imprisonment in Kingston Penitentiary. Dick Bakonyi has since been released. His present whereabouts are unknown.

# TYRONE BORGLUND AND ERIC PEEVER

(CANADA)

THE murders were atrocious, cold-blooded acts committed by boys not old enough to vote.

In January 1988, seven individuals were living in a three-bedroom bungalow on Fourteenth Avenue in Mission, British Columbia. The inhabitants had experienced diverse upheavals en route to the small town located about sixty-five kilometres east of Vancouver.

Karsten Madsen met Leny van Rikoort in 1977 in Vancouver. Karsten, at 27, had been married, divorced and deeply involved with another woman before meeting Leny. Karsten's marriage to Sharon Peever had brought two children into the world, Eric and Michael, who remained with their mother after the divorce. By the time he met Leny, Karsten was also the father of Jason, a bouncing 8-month-old baby, the result of his last involvement.

Leny and Karsten married in 1978. Their daughter, Michelle, was born that same year. Little Jason was also a part of their family. The Madsens relocated often in the following seven years, eventually settling in Mission. Like many Canadian families with young children, they required two incomes to keep a roof over their heads. Karsten made a precarious living as a drywall installer. Despite the ever-present need for more money, the Madsens appeared to be happy. They were outgoing and well-liked. The family consisted of four individuals living in the bungalow on Fourteenth Avenue. They would all become victims.

In 1985 the Madsens applied to become foster parents. Their motives came under close scrutiny. Certainly the $500 a month they would receive from the B.C. Ministry of Social Services was a factor. There is some evidence that the money enabled them to purchase a new car. Whatever the motivation, 14-year-old Tyrone Borglund moved into the Madsen home. The addition of Tyrone brought the number of residents in the bungalow on Fourteenth Avenue to five.

Initially things went well, but it wasn't long before Tyrone became a disruptive force around the house. From time to time, Leny reported his behaviour to the ministry. On more than one occasion, Tyrone was removed and placed in another home, but was taken back by the Madsens when he promised to mend his ways.

Eric and Michael, who were living with their mother, Sharon Peever, grew to be teenagers. Caught stealing from the house, Eric, the older of the two boys, was thrown out of his home by his mother's common-law husband. He contacted Karsten, his biological father, and moved in with the Madsens in Mission.

Eric and Tyrone seemed to get along well. They were approximately the same age and soon became close friends. The sixth player in the tragedy that was to follow was now onstage. One more player was required to complete the cast. Eric's younger brother, Michael, contacted Karsten and moved into the bungalow in Mission. The full cast of seven individuals was now gathered.

Karsten and Leny knew they had problems. Michelle and Jason behaved like normal youngsters, but the three older boys were a handful. On more than one occasion, the police contacted Leny. The boys had become petty thieves. They even stole from their own home. Karsten had to keep a careful eye on his liquor. Small items often went missing. Leny gave the boys severe tongue-lashings, which seemed to sink in for a while but had little lasting effect.

Tyrone and Michael shared sleeping quarters in the basement and it was there that the three boys planned the murder of the other four members of the family. They'd decided: Karsten, Leny, Michelle and Jason would all be murdered. The boys would take money from the master bedroom, steal Leny's Toyota and take off for Fort St. John.

On the night of January 17, 1988, the stage was set. Tyrone suggested the axes. They were weapons of opportunity, just lying there in the house. The boys practised swinging the axes down in the basement. Upstairs, the house was quiet. Everyone was asleep. Eric sneaked upstairs and returned with some wine and pear brandy. The boys took long swigs from the bottles. Tyrone and Eric, equipped with the axes, slowly climbed the stairs. Michael carried a maul. He would later testify that when the reality of what they were about to do came to him; he couldn't go through with the plan. He left his co-conspirators and returned to the basement.

Tyrone and Eric continued to the master bedroom. Karsten and Leny were sleeping soundly. The moves had been well planned. Tyrone would kill Karsten while Eric took care of Leny. Tyrone lifted the large axe above his head and brought it down with all his might on the sleeping man's skull. The force of the blow split open Karsten's head. Leny awoke with a start. She screamed, her hands instinctively shielding her head, but there was no escape. Eric brought the axe down. Her arms may have deflected the initial blow so that the first swing didn't render her unconscious. We will never know how many times Eric swung that axe, but at some time in the midst of the blood and the passion, he dropped the weapon and ran to the refuge of the basement. Tyrone finished the gruesome task in the bedroom.

Eleven-year-old Jason was awakened by the noise. Rubbing sleep from his eyes, he strolled into the master bedroom. Only half-awake, he likely couldn't quite absorb the scene he was witnessing. He said, "What are you doing to my mum?" Three vicious swings from Tyrone's axe and the little boy lay dead on the bedroom floor.

The next to wake up was 9-year-old Michelle. She too was drawn to the source of the noise. Tyrone intercepted her at the doorway. She met the same fate as Jason. There was no more noise from upstairs in the house on Fourteenth Avenue in Mission, British Columbia.

Down in the basement, there was plenty of excitement. They had actually done it. True, Tyrone was the ringleader, but they had all been involved in one way or another. Now that it was over, Eric felt he owed Tyrone an explanation. After all, he had retreated during the height of the attack. Tyrone assured him there were no hard feelings. In the end they had accomplished what they had set out to do.

The three boys entered the room of carnage. Their plan was working. In minutes they removed all the bills from Karsten's wallet and Leny's purse. The keys to the Toyota were there in Leny's purse, just as they had expected. It didn't take long for them to get out of the house, leaving behind four bodies hacked to death in the bedroom. The teenagers wheeled the Toyota out of the driveway and headed toward Fort St. John, 790 kilometres to the northeast. Good times lay ahead. Only then did Tyrone and Eric notice that their clothing was spattered with blood.

Once in Fort St. John, the boys purchased booze, called friends and partied. Two days after the killing spree, Tyrone was picked up for drunk driving. The Toyota was soon traced to Mission, the bodies discovered and the bloody multiple murders exposed.

What had triggered the vicious attack that had taken four lives? According to Tyrone, they were angry at Leny because she had given them another one of her patented tongue-lashings and had forbidden them to watch television.

All charges against 15-year-old Michael Peever were dropped in exchange for his testimony. After the murder trial, in which he appeared as the Crown's star witness, he was placed, anonymously, in a group home somewhere in British Columbia.

Tyrone and Eric stood trial for murder in adult court. The jury did not believe their claim that they had taken the axes into the Madsens' bedroom solely to frighten the Madsens. It took only three hours' deliberation to find both boys guilty of murder.

Tyrone Borglund, 16, and Eric Peever, 17, were sentenced to life imprisonment with no possibility of parole for 25 years. They are presently serving their sentences.

# IAN BRADY AND MYRA HINDLEY

(ENGLAND)

FOR sheer horror, the Murders on the Moors rank right up there with the worst. If the retelling of this true tale alerts just one parent to the dangers of allowing a child to accompany not only strange men, but strange women, then this effort will have been worthwhile.

Ian Brady was not your average child. While still in his preteens, he threw cats off buildings to prove that they didn't have nine lives. Once he crucified a frog and relished the sheer agony he caused the helpless creature. Between the ages of 12 and 15, he was caught breaking into several shops and houses. Each time he was apprehended, he was put on probation so that he could continue his schooling.

When Ian was 15, he left school and was promptly charged with nine counts of housebreaking. He was given one more chance by another lenient magistrate and left Glasgow to live in Manchester. Ian drank, couldn't keep a job and continued to break into houses. Apprehended again in the act, he finally met a magistrate who sentenced him to two years in Borstal. On June 9, 1958, Ian, at age 20, was released from prison.

In February 1959, Ian obtained a clerical position at Millwards Merchandise Ltd., a chemical supply company in West Gorton, Manchester. At night he read about Adolf Hitler and the Marquis de Sade.

Myra Hindley was born in 1942 in the slums of Manchester. When she was four, her mother gave birth to a second daughter, Maureen. As a result of the overcrowding at Eaton Street, Myra moved in with her grandmother a block down the street.

Although her IQ was slightly above average, Myra was not a good student. She left school while in her teens and drifted from job to job before securing a position as a shorthand typist with Millwards in West Gorton. Much of her typing was for a lean, pale, rather eccentric young man who fascinated Myra. His name was Ian Brady.

Ian introduced Myra to his library of witchcraft, sadism and genocide. She was a quick learner. What Ian said was law; Myra never argued. The pair became inseparable. Myra purchased a minivan and, since Ian didn't drive, it was she who chauffeured them to and from work.

Through the years, Myra had remained friendly with her younger sister, Maureen, who joined Millwards in 1963. Myra confided to Maureen that she was having an affair with Ian Brady. When Myra and her grandmother moved to Wardle Brook Avenue in Hattesley, Ian moved in with them. The elderly grandmother kept to herself and never interfered with the machinations of Myra and her live-in boyfriend. Their evenings were spent experimenting with sexual perversions, drinking cheap wine and wandering the countryside in the minivan. On their days off, Ian would indulge in his hobby of photography. Myra was a willing model, posing in the nude in every conceivable position or stance that Ian suggested.

Mrs. Sheila Kilbride gave her 12-year-old son, John, a peck on the cheek before he scampered off with a friend to go to the movies. After the two lads left the movie theatre at 5 p.m., John's friend caught a bus home. He last saw John talking to a friendly blonde lady. The lady was Myra Hindley. Little John Kilbride never returned home. Police were notified of the boy's disappearance, and a comprehensive search followed, but no trace of the boy was found.

Ten-year-old Lesley Downey was excited on Boxing Day of 1964. Her mother had given her permission to attend a fair being held only two hundred yards from her residence. By 5 p.m., Mrs. Jean Downey became apprehensive when Lesley failed to return home.

A minivan circled the fairgrounds before coming to an abrupt stop. A blonde woman approached Lesley and volunteered to pay for another ride on the merry-go-round. What 10-year-old could resist such good fortune? The little girl jumped on the wooden pony. When the woman offered her a lift home, Lesley knew everything would be all right. Her mother had told her never to accept a ride with a strange man, but she hadn't said anything about taking a ride with a friendly, kind lady. Even though her house was nearby, Lesley climbed into the van beside Myra Hindley. Crouched in the shadows behind the unsuspecting child lurked Ian Brady. Lesley Downey was never seen again.

When Myra's sister, Maureen, married David Smith, it was natural for the two couples to become close friends, especially since the Smiths lived within walking distance of Myra and Ian. David Smith had been in several scrapes with the law and had been convicted of assault. He welcomed Ian's hospitality. The two men were accustomed to staying up half the night drinking cheap wine.

The strange double life of Ian Brady and Myra Hindley came to light on the night of October 6, 1965. On that night, Myra's 77-year-old grandmother took a sleeping pill at 8:30 p.m. and went to bed. Myra and Ian cruised the streets of Manchester in her minivan. Myra parked the vehicle while Ian took a stroll. He returned with 17-year-old Edward Evans, a homosexual who had eagerly accepted an invitation to return to Ian's home for a drink.

Once back at Wardle Brook Avenue, Ian and Edward engaged in conversation while Myra called on her brother-in-law, David Smith. She convinced David to accompany her back home on the pretext that Ian had some miniature bottles he wanted to give away. As David admired the miniature bottles in the kitchen, a blood-chilling scream echoed through the house. Myra shouted, "Dave, Dave, come and help Ian." Smith ran from the kitchen to the living room and into hell.

In the eerie glow of the television set, David saw Edward Evans, whom he didn't know, lying half on the floor and half on a couch. Blood was cascading from Edward's head onto the floor. Ian stood over the fallen youngster with a bloody hatchet in his hand. As David watched in terror, Ian brought the hatchet down on Edward's head over and over again. Edward tried in vain to crawl away from his attacker.

Ian interrupted his murderous frenzy to say, "This one's taking a while to go." Then he wrapped an electric cord around Evans's neck and pulled until his victim was dead. Ian was soaked in blood. Myra's clothing had been spattered with blood as well. David Smith had been an audience to a murder that had been orchestrated just for him. Ian commented, "It's the messiest one yet. Normally one blow is enough."

Myra cleaned up the room while Ian changed clothes. Upstairs, Myra's grandmother slept through it all. Ian solicited David's help in carrying the body upstairs to a bedroom. Myra put on a pot of tea. At about 3 a.m., David suggested that he should head home. He was surprised when his companions said good night and let him leave. David felt as if he had lived through a nightmare. He ran all the way home. He was so terrified of Ian and Myra that he waited three hours before daring to sneak out of the house to call police.

When detectives arrived at 16 Wardle Brook Avenue, they were let in by Myra. A search of the back bedroom revealed the horribly mutilated body of Edward Evans trussed up in a plastic bag. Three bloodstained carpets and the murder weapon were taken from the house by police. A postmortem revealed that Evans had received 14 blows to the skull.

At the police station, Ian confessed to murder and attempted to implicate David Smith. As detectives interrogated Ian and Myra, it appeared that the murderous pair had timed the killing of Edward Evans to coincide with David Smith's arrival so that he would be a witness to murder.

The house on Wardle Brook Avenue was practically dismantled in a search for clues. The investigating officers found Ian Brady's diary. On one page they came across the name of John Kilbride, the little boy who had been missing for almost two years. They also discovered that Ian had checked two suitcases at Manchester's Central Station. The suitcases contained pornographic pictures of Myra, as well as weird photographs of the lonesome moors outside Manchester, showing Myra staring straight down, as if standing over a grave. Police located the sites depicted in the photographs and dug up the bodies of John Kilbride and Lesley Downey.

Myra Hindley and Ian Brady stood trial at historic Chester Castle on April 19, 1966. The pornographic pictures, the photos of the gravesites of the two children and Brady's diary left little doubt as to the guilt of the accused pair.

One piece of evidence was so horrifying that hardened homicide detectives left the courtroom when it was presented. Myra and Ian had recorded Lesley Downey's last moments on tape as they sexually abused and tortured her to death. The 16-minute, 21-second tape had been discovered intact by police.

The jury took only 2 hours and 22 minutes to find Ian Brady guilty of three separate counts of murder. He received three life sentences, while Myra received two life sentences for the murders of Lesley Downey and Edward Evans. She was sentenced to a further seven years for harbouring Brady in the case of John Kilbride. Ironically, Ian Brady and Myra Hindley escaped the hangman's noose. A few months prior to their trial, capital punishment had been abolished in England.

As recently as 1987, Myra Hindley resurfaced when she assisted police in recovering the body of 16-year-old Pauline Reade, another victim of the infamous pair.

Myra Hindley remains incarcerated, while Ian Brady is presently confined in a mental institution.

# BETTY BRODERICK

(UNITED STATES)

---

THIS is a tale about two attractive, wealthy people who, unfortunately, were unable to settle their marital difficulties without the aid of a nickel-plated .38-calibre revolver.

Dan Broderick met Betty Bisceglia while both were university students. Dan had just been accepted at Cornell Medical School in Ithaca, New York. Betty attended the Catholic College of Mount St. Vincent in the same city. The two young people dated, fell in love, and married in April 1969, after Betty graduated and obtained a teaching job.

Following a Caribbean honeymoon, the newlyweds settled into a dormitory room at Cornell. Both realized there would be some rough times in the years ahead. Dan's immediate future would be devoted mainly to study. Betty would teach to assist her husband financially in gaining his medical degree. With student loans they would make out just fine.

They didn't.

A month after the wedding, Betty learned she was pregnant. Nine months later, she gave birth to their first child, a daughter, Kim. After the baby was born, she and Dan obtained part-time jobs to make ends meet. It was rough sledding, but the years passed and eventually Dan obtained his medical degree.

Dan had ambitions that would not be denied. He noted that huge settlements were being dispensed in malpractice suits. What a coup it would be to be a lawyer with a medical degree. Certainly, he would have a leg up on lawyers who would have to depend on medical knowledge and expertise from an outside source. Dan decided to become a lawyer. He applied to, and was accepted by, Harvard Law School.

This time around, however, Betty objected. If Dan had to pursue a legal career, she told him, he could attend night school. Betty let Dan know that another loan on top of his medical school loan would take years to repay. Dan insisted on Harvard. The Brodericks picked up their sparse belongings and moved to Boston. It was a struggle, but once again the years passed and Dr. Dan Broderick graduated as a lawyer.

Dan and Betty moved to San Diego, California. This was it—the good times, the big money. It only took a few years. The student loans were paid off. A large home was purchased in 1976 in posh La Jolla. Little Danny junior was a welcome addition to the family.

It should have been perfect, but it wasn't. Dan threw himself into his work. He became one of the city's leading attorneys. Soon his income exceeded a million dollars a year. Dan was something of a human dynamo. Maybe it was the many years of doing without while he studied that drove him to acquire more and more wealth.

Meanwhile, two more children blessed the Broderick household. Betty hated being neglected. True, she belonged to all the right clubs, socialized with all the right people and wore designer clothing, but at the same time she was sharing her life with a man who was in love with his career and the recognition it brought him. The Brodericks argued constantly.

In 1983, two things occurred in Betty Broderick's life. Dan made it very clear that he was not happy with their marriage. Around the time that Dan revealed his disenchantment, Betty learned that he was having an affair with his tall, attractive receptionist, Linda Kolkena. Betty accused Dan of involvement with Linda, but he vehemently asserted that his relationship with the woman was purely professional. Now Dan did more than neglect his wife. He ignored her. Betty seethed. Her world was crumbling. She complained to friends and attempted to turn her children against their father. Everyone knew the Brodericks were carrying on their own private war.

In February 1985, Dan moved out and filed for divorce. He cited myriad irrational acts committed by Betty, such as destroying household effects, throwing small appliances and breaking windows. Betty defended herself legally as best she could, but Dan held all the cards. Being a lawyer, it was not difficult for him to inundate his wife with legal documents on an almost weekly basis. Betty, on the other hand, had to hire lawyers, at great expense, to ward off her husband's many legal ploys. All the while, friends kept her well informed of Dan and Linda's romance. Throughout the messy, well-publicized divorce, Dan provided Betty with a liberal allowance of $16,000 per month. Betty constantly pressed the courts for an increase.

The Brodericks were finally divorced. Now the battle advanced to the question of custody of their four children and the available funds to support them. The legal skirmishes continued unabated. During this rather hectic period, Dan married Linda Kolkena. Betty went crazy with rage. She phoned

Linda, cursing and threatening like a madwoman. She often stalked their home. Dan obtained a restraining order keeping his ex-wife from coming within 100 yards of their residence.

Was Betty driven to the brink by a callous husband who thought only of himself? Many think so. Others believe that with her liberal allowance, Betty could have built a new life for herself without resorting to revenge.

On November 5, 1989, Betty Broderick went over the edge. At approximately 5 a.m., she drove up to her ex-husband's home in Marston Hills. Inside, Dan lay asleep in bed beside his wife of seven months. We will never know exactly what went through Betty's mind as she silently made her way through the well-appointed home while her 44-year-old ex-husband slept with his 28-year-old wife.

Betty climbed the stairs to the master bedroom. She was carrying her .38-calibre revolver. There in bed reposed the two individuals who had ruined her life. Later, Betty would say she remembered her finger closing on the trigger and the weapon firing once. Her account is inaccurate. She shot five times.

Linda never knew what hit her. One slug tore into her chest, while another entered her head. From the position of Dan's body, it was evident that he made some attempt to reach the telephone on the night table. A bullet entered his lung. He died within a couple of minutes. Betty crossed the room and replaced the phone. She ran from the house and sped away, stopping at a pay phone to call and tell a friend what she had done. The friend phoned acquaintances who, in turn, gained entrance to the house and discovered the bodies. That same day, Betty surrendered to police. In her purse was her .38-calibre revolver.

Betty Broderick's trial caused a sensation in California and, indeed, throughout the United States and the world. Three books and two screenplays have been written about her case. Was Betty a woman scorned or a cold-blooded killer? The California jury couldn't decide. After deliberating for four days, they reported that they were hopelessly deadlocked. The presiding judge was forced to order a mistrial.

Betty's second trial was more conclusive. She was found guilty of two counts of second-degree murder. In February 1992, she was sentenced to 15 years' to life imprisonment for each murder, and two years for possession of a gun, the sentences to run consecutively. Betty Broderick will be eligible for parole in the year 2010.

# SUSAN CHRISTIE

(IRELAND)

WHEN Lieutenant Duncan McAllister first laid eyes on Penny Squire, he thought she was the most beautiful girl he had ever seen. Sure enough, Penny was a knockout and looked far older than her 16 years. Age didn't matter that much to 21-year-old Duncan. He dated Penny and discovered that they both enjoyed the same outdoor sports.

Penny's dad was an English teacher employed in Lippstadt, Germany, where Duncan was posted with the British army. It was here that the young couple met. Soon they were inseparable, and for a full year spent every spare moment together.

When Duncan was posted back to England in 1983, he and Penny discussed marriage. It was a touchy subject, mainly because of Penny's tender age. The 17-year-old Penny talked it over with her parents. They had planned on a university education for their daughter, but consented to the marriage when they realized that her mind was made up.

Duncan and Penny married. For six years their union was an ideal one. Duncan, a career army man, earned an engineering degree and was promoted to captain. Everything was coming up roses for the happy couple until June 1989. That's when Duncan was posted to Northern Ireland. To British army personnel, a posting to Northern Ireland was akin to a stint in purgatory.

Despite his disappointment with the unpopular assignment, Duncan, a product of the stiff-upper-lip school, decided to make the best of a less-than-pleasant situation. Always athletic, he formed a scuba diving club, enlisting divers from members of the armed forces. One member was a cute young thing, Private Susan Christie. Right from their first dive together, it was obvious to Duncan that Susan was infatuated with him. As her instructor, he could either resist her advances or encourage them. Duncan chose to encourage them.

And now, folks, as so often occurs in affairs of the heart, there are two versions of what transpired between Duncan and Susan. Let's review Duncan's version first. He claims that although he was flattered by Susan's advances, he was fair and square with her. He told her to turn off the charm unless she intended to go all the way. Susan responded favourably, suggesting that she would be most amenable to a romp in the hay.

Stout fellow that he was, Duncan pointed out the inherent pitfalls in having the aforementioned romp with a married man who would under no circumstances leave his wife. According to Duncan, after mulling over his negative lecture for a few days, Susan was not deterred in the least. She agreed not only to a one-night romp, but to an on-going affair. As an added incentive, she revealed that she was a virgin. Duncan succumbed and the pair made love in the great outdoors beside one of those romantic lakes.

So much for Duncan's gallant tale.

Susan admitted that she was a virgin at the time of their tryst, but, according to her, that was the only truthful statement in Duncan's version of their liaison. She claimed that she desired to retain her virginity but that Duncan implored, coaxed and pressured her until one day he lured her to his home and seduced her on his own bed. We can only assume that Penny was not at home.

One thing we do know is that Duncan and Susan were doing it all the time. On a scuba-diving expedition in the South Atlantic, Susan told Duncan that she wanted to have sex in a novel manner, something that he and Penny had never done. They decided that making love underwater would be different. The pair made love twenty metres under the chilly waters off Ascension Island.

Despite the obvious thrills the extramarital sex afforded Duncan, he began to tire of his lover. When he suggested they terminate their affair, Susan went into a rage. How dare he cast her aside after he had taken her virginity! She loved him and had no intention of giving him up. Duncan attempted to explain that it had all been great fun, but he loved his wife. He even made the mistake of telling Susan that she wasn't as attractive as Penny.

Susan was furious. As so often happens in the triangle business, she blamed the blameless Penny for all her problems. On March 27, 1990, Susan, who was acquainted with Penny, arranged to take a stroll through Drumkeeragh Forest with the unsuspecting wife of her lover. When Duncan heard of the chummy walk, he was definitely less than pleased. There is a real danger in having one's mistress meet one's wife. A wrong word here or a slip of the tongue there and all hell could break loose.

As it turned out, Duncan had good reason to be concerned. On the afternoon of the infamous walk, Duncan was enjoying a Scotch and soda in the officers' mess when his commanding officer informed him that a terrible tragedy had taken place. A man had attacked Susan and Penny with a knife. Susan was in hospital with several cuts and bruises. Unfortunately, Penny hadn't survived the attack. Her throat had been slashed.

Within minutes, the full resources of the British army were employed scouring Drumkeeragh Forest. Despite their best efforts, however, no suspect was found. Detectives questioned Susan, who could offer only the vaguest description of her attacker. Evidently, one slash had taken Penny's life. The whole thing had happened so quickly that Susan had hardly been able to look at the man.

Duncan was also questioned, but he could shed no light on why anyone would want to harm his wife. As time passed, Duncan realized that the one piece of information that would put an entirely different perspective on the murder was his affair with Susan. He decided to inform police not only of the affair, but of his attempt to terminate it and Susan's reaction to his suggestion.

Now armed with the information that Penny had taken her last walk with her husband's mistress, detectives immediately uncovered clues pointing to Susan's guilt. Police discovered that Susan had been to the location of the attack a week earlier. She also had access to butcher knives, one of which could have inflicted the stab wound to Penny's throat. During her interrogation, Susan described gloves worn by her attacker; similar gloves were found in her possession. Moreover, Susan had received combat training and knew exactly how to slit an adversary's throat from behind. She also had the guts and ability to inflict superficial cuts and bruises to her arms without seriously injuring herself.

In time, Susan confessed to her affair with Duncan and her hatred of his wife. She insisted that although she wanted Penny dead, she had no recollection of the actual act of taking her life.

Susan Christie stood trial for murder. She was found guilty of manslaughter and sentenced to five years' imprisonment. The Crown appealed the light term and was successful in having the sentence increased to nine years.

# REV. D.L.CLARK

## (UNITED STATES)

THE good folks of Greencastle, Pennsylvania, were concerned when Rev. Donald Lewis Clark's wife, Phyllis, took ill. It was in the fall of 1981 that 54-year-old Phyllis complained of stomach trouble. Nothing really serious at first, just recurring stomach cramps. But the discomfort didn't go away.

Rev. Clark and most of the parishioners at the Macedonia United Brethren Church were shocked when Phyllis, obviously in considerable pain, fell down the cellar stairs of the church parsonage. Rushed to Chambersburg Hospital, approximately 15 kilometres from Greencastle, Phyllis didn't respond to treatment. On October 23, she was transferred to the Hershey Medical Centre, where she died the next day.

When asked if he wanted an autopsy performed on his dear wife, Clark suggested it wasn't necessary. He felt his wife of 29 blissful years should be laid to rest intact. Those involved tended to agree. The funeral was a solemn affair, attended by most of the minister's flock.

Clark appeared to be beside himself with grief. No doubt, as he watched the casket being lowered into its final resting place, he thought how different all this was from the breakup of his first marriage. Marriage number one had taken place long ago when he was still a young man. When he and his first wife divorced, it took him only a year to meet and wed Phyllis Miller. The two daughters who blessed their union were a gift from God.

Members of the church shook their collective heads. The reverend wasn't taking his loss well. Of course, they had no way of knowing the Lord had provided Clark with the foresight to insure Phyllis's life for a cool $50,000 just two months before she departed this cruel world.

To ease his great pain, the reverend purchased a couple of new cars, which more than replaced the rickety old rattletrap he had been forced to drive before the tragic loss of his wife. Clark just loved to roar down the country roads in his new Camaro. He changed in other ways, too. When Phyllis was hale and hearty, he attended to his church duties punctually and with great diligence. Now he neglected the church and his devoted flock.

The elders of the church, while sympathetic toward their minister, felt that enough was enough. About a year after Phyllis's departure, they advised Clark that his services were no longer required. They gave him a month's notice, requesting he move out of the church's property by March 31, 1983. Then the date was extended to April 27. A lot happened in that one month.

Let's start off with Ronaele "Candy" Rotz. On April 7, Candy's nude body was found in the bathtub of her home in Chambersburg. An electric space heater was in the tub with the attractive 40-year-old divorcee. She also had a severe gash on the back of her head. It could have been one of those weird accidents that happen from time to time. Candy could have stumbled, hit her head, and knocked the heater into the tub as she fell in. Then again, she could have been murdered.

And how did the unfortunate death of Candy Rotz involve the good and holy Rev. Clark? Well, I'll tell you. Investigators learned that Candy had been an extremely religious woman, who had belonged to every religious organization in the area. Somewhere along the way, she had met Clark, while he was mourning the departure of dear Phyllis. On January 20, 1983, the reverend and Candy had married secretly, but did not live together. No one else knew about their wedding.

After detectives learned the details of the reverend's third marriage, they uncovered other sensitive information. Clark had never told Candy he was a minister. He posed as a police officer to his bride and to the officiating minister. He claimed to be an undercover narcotics agent, explaining to Candy that until his current assignment was concluded, they would have to live separately for her safety.

Clark was in hot water. And speaking of hot water, an autopsy was performed on Candy's body. It was discovered that she had been struck on the head with a sharp instrument and placed in the tub with the space heater in a crude attempt to make her death appear accidental.

Detectives looking into the reverend's activities were now hot to trot. They delved deeper into the devious life of the preacher man. Eight days after his marriage to Candy, he had insured her life for $50,000. Not satisfied with this amount of protection, he waited only a week longer before increasing his bride's insurance to $200,000 should she expire due to an accident.

On April 13, authorities paid a visit to Rev. Donald Lewis Clark. When they received no response to their knocking on his door, they forced their way into his home. There was the minister's body lying nude on the bathroom floor.

An autopsy and toxicology tests indicated that he had taken small amounts of arsenic for several days as the circle of evidence drew him into the police investigation. Two days before his body was found, he gave himself a massive dose, which killed him. The reverend left suicide notes that have never been made public.

Police backtracked. They looked into the untimely demise of wife number two. After conducting an extensive investigation, they concluded that Phyllis had been systematically poisoned with arsenic. Weak and racked with stomach cramps, she had either fallen or been pushed down the stairs and had died within a few days.

Despite Clark's elaborate plans, Candy's murder was botched. The blow to her head had killed her. She was already dead when she was placed in the tub with the heater.

The motive for the murders was the insurance money, but there was another reason for the reverend's strange behaviour. Investigators discovered he had had a teenage lover all the while he was burying and marrying his wives. No doubt Phyllis was murdered so he could gain his freedom, as well as a tidy sum, to carry on with his mistress. He gave himself a false occupation and lived separately from his third wife to avoid her finding out about his lover. Many believe the minister killed Candy for the insurance money to finance a $90,000 home he had purchased in Shippensburg, where he planned to install his teenage paramour.

It matters little. A private funeral service was held for Rev. Donald Lewis Clark, after which he was buried in nearby Burns Hill Cemetery.

The Macedonia United Brethren Church hired a new minister.

# ERIC COOKE

## (AUSTRALIA)

THE city of Perth, Australia, was in a state of crisis. A serial killer was at large and the police appeared powerless to apprehend the murderer.

The first killing took place on February 2, 1959, a sultry summer night down under. Pnena Berkman, a beautiful 33-year-old divorcee, had just returned from an upscale party. Her escort kissed her goodnight at the door of her luxurious apartment. Pnena undressed and retired for the night. Next morning, a neighbour and close friend, who had a key to the apartment, received no response to her ring. She entered and made her way to the bedroom. There lay Pnena amidst blood-soaked bedclothes. She had been stabbed many times all over her body. The neighbour rushed back to her apartment and called police.

It took only a few minutes for homicide detectives to arrive. Their preliminary investigation indicated there was no forced entry, which didn't mean much in Perth. Many residents left doors unlocked due to the low incidence of crime in the city. Pnena's date was questioned and exonerated of any complicity in the crime. Robbery was dismissed as a motive since Pnena's open purse was in plain sight and no money had been removed. There was no indication of a sexual attack of any kind. This was verified by autopsy results.

Because there was no sign of a struggle, police theorized that Pnena might have known her killer and might have welcomed him into her bedroom. Acquaintances of the dead woman came under investigation, but all were able to prove their innocence. The murder, considered an isolated incident, went unsolved.

Ten months later, on December 19, Jillian McPherson Brewster, a 22-year-old heiress, was dropped off at her apartment around midnight by her fiancé. The happy couple had a golfing date for the following morning. At 9 a.m. Jillian's fiancé let himself into the apartment with his key. He found Jillian dead on her bed. She had been stabbed many times.

Detectives noted the similarities between the two murders, one of which was that both women had been stabbed to death while sleeping in their own apartments. Like Pnena's date, Jillian's fiancé was immediately cleared of any guilty knowledge of the crime.

Murder took a sabbatical until January 27, 1963. In the middle of that night, the Walmsley family was awakened by the persistent ringing of their doorbell. George Walmsley, a retired grocer, woke up, threw on his bathrobe and answered the door. He was immediately shot in the head by an intruder who ran away. George's daughter was the first family member to reach the grievously wounded man. No amount of assistance helped. George died moments after arriving at Royal Perth Hospital.

A few blocks away from the Walmsley residence, a 19-year-old student, John Sturkey, was taking advantage of the warm weather. He was fast asleep on his front veranda when someone approached him and shot him in the head. His landlady found him unconscious and bleeding profusely. John was rushed to Royal Perth Hospital, where he died only a few hours after George Walmsley.

Both Walmsley and Sturkey had been murdered with a .22-calibre weapon and both had been shot in the head. Police were reluctant to couple the murders with the earlier Berkman and Brewster killings because the weapons were different. Yet there were similarities. All four murders had taken place between midnight and dawn. There was some evidence the killer had spied on all four victims before killing them.

Six months passed. On August 10, 1963, a cold, windy day, Shirley McLeod, a 19-year-old babysitter, was taking care of a baby on Walell Road. At 2 a.m. the baby's parents returned home. Shirley didn't respond to their greeting. When they heard their infant daughter crying, they knew something was wrong. Shirley would never let the baby cry unattended. In the living room they found Shirley sitting grotesquely in a chair. She had been shot in the head.

Police ascertained that she had been killed by a .22-calibre bullet. Detectives discovered that the killer could have entered the premises through an unlocked garage that had a door leading to the living quarters. Nothing had been taken from the residence. Neighbours had not heard or seen anything unusual.

Another unsolved murder gave the good citizens of Perth something to think about. It seemed that no one was safe. The string of victims came from all walks of life. None were engaged in criminal activity, nor were they connected in any way with each other.

The first real break in the case came August 17, 1963, when an elderly man gathering wildflowers came across a .22-calibre rifle under some brush. Because of the wide publicity given the murders, the man didn't touch the weapon, but went directly to police. Ballistics experts proved that the striations on test bullets fired from the weapon matched those on the bullet taken from Shirley McLeod's head.

Detectives wondered why a killer would toss a murder weapon under brush rather than throw it in the nearby Canning River. They concluded that the murderer was hiding the rifle to retrieve it later rather than attempting to get rid of it. Investigators substituted a similar weapon and placed it under the brush exactly where the killer had hidden it. The area was staked out in the hope that the murderer would show up to collect the rifle.

It took two weeks. On September 1, a car stopped near the planted weapon. A short, slim man walked directly to the rifle and was picking it up when two burly officers took him into custody.

The suspect was Eric Edgar Cooke, a five-foot four-inch, 32-year-old truck driver. Eric was married and the father of seven children. He led detectives to the Swan River, where divers retrieved another .22-calibre rifle. This weapon proved to be the one which had taken the lives of John Sturkey and George Walmsley.

On November 25, 1963, Eric stood trial for three murders. At his trial, his rather difficult childhood was reviewed by defence counsel. Evidently, Eric, who had a harelip and cleft palate, had been cruelly taunted by school chums. He had been abused by his parents and had later suffered several industrial accidents, incurring trauma to his head.

The prosecution hammered away at the cold-blooded acts that had taken three lives. In the case of John Sturkey, Cooke said, "He was on his back sleeping and I walked up to about four feet from him. I pointed the rifle at him and I shot him. I do not know why. I did not have the slightest reason for harming him. He was a complete stranger to me." Eric went on to say that he had tremendous urges to kill. All his victims were strangers. "The power was so great that I could not stop myself. It was not until afterward, when I read the details in the papers, that I fully realized the dreadful things I had done."

Although Eric was strongly suspected in the Berkman and Brewster murders, he never confessed to them and was never charged with these crimes.

Eric Edgar Cooke was found guilty of murder and sentenced to death. On October 24, 1964, he was hanged.

# MARGARET CRUMP

(ENGLAND)

MARGARET Crump felt life was passing her by. There she was, decidedly plump, with ever so tiny crow's feet making their unattractive appearance beside her eyes, which in recent months had developed an involuntary squint.

Margaret, who had seen four decades come and go, looked across the breakfast table at her husband of 14 years. Wasn't he a prize? she thought. David spent most of his time collecting money for worthy causes in and around Folkestone, England. When he wasn't complaining about the state of the Commonwealth, he was moaning about his ulcerated leg. Among David's more disagreeable traits, Margaret felt his bouts of depression ranked right up there as the most annoying. Sometimes David was so low he threatened to commit suicide. No one, least of all Margaret, took his threats seriously. The Crumps' marriage had produced no children.

Year after dreary year, David collected funds for charity, while Margaret pursued her hobby of citizens' band radio. Each evening, after David had taken his sleeping pills and she could hear him snoring, she would plug in her equipment. Her CB handle was Maggie Boo. Her hobby was her one escape from her boring, loveless marriage.

One fog-enshrouded night in 1986, Maggie Boo received a response from Hawaiian Cruiser. It was like no other response she had ever received. Hawaiian Cruiser had a melodious, sexy voice. He flattered Maggie Boo. What's more, he was suggestive. Maggie Boo said nothing to discourage the naughty boy. Each day she would wait to hear David snoring so she could exchange sweet sly insinuations with her Hawaiian Cruiser.

It was agreed. The pair had to meet. Margaret hid those crow's feet as best she could and plucked out the few invading gray hairs. She and Hawaiian Cruiser met in a restaurant. The sexy voice belonged to 20-year-old David Belsham, a skinny young man with a severe case of acne. If you can imagine a young Ichabod Crane, you pretty well have the picture.

Despite the physical deficiencies and the discrepancy in their ages, Maggie Boo and Hawaiian Cruiser got along famously. They met often and soon became lovers. Juices dormant those many years once again flowed freely within Margaret Crump. Life was worth living after all. Belsham was attentive, polite and, above all, terrific in bed.

In time, Margaret introduced Belsham to her husband. David never suspected for a moment that this young lad was anything more than a fellow citizens' band enthusiast. Eventually Margaret met two of Belsham's friends, Stephen Farthing and teenager Paul Thompson. When Belsham requested that the two men, who had recently been asked to leave their rooming house, move in with the Crumps, Margaret agreed it would be a good idea. Even David liked the arrangement. Their boarders could do odd jobs around the place, allowing him more time for his charity work.

For a while, all went well. Farthing and Thompson had a roof over their heads, David had two live-in handymen, Belsham had done a favour for two friends and, of course, we all know what Margaret was receiving in quantities she had once only fantasized about.

In the deception business, one must realize that things can't go on forever. In 1987, David's ulcerated leg bothered him so much that he had to be hospitalized. By this time, the relationship between Margaret and Belsham was such that he moved into the Crump house to keep Margaret company.

Playing house appealed to Belsham. There is good evidence he had fallen in love with Margaret and dreaded the fast-approaching day when her husband would be released from hospital. He and Margaret discussed their predicament. They would do the honourable thing. They would tell David of their love for each other. No doubt, he would be civilized and drop out of the picture. After the divorce, they would marry and live happily ever after.

Well, folks, David did come home from the hospital. Margaret and Belsham told him of their intentions. Rather than take the news calmly, David said he would rather die than grant his wife a divorce. In addition, loud and clear, he ordered Belsham and his two buddies out of the house.

No one left the Crump residence. In the next few days, you could cut the tension with a knife. Each evening, David went to his room, took his sleeping pills and went to sleep alone. Downstairs, Belsham, Margaret, Farthing and Thompson plotted his death. They would make the murder appear to be a suicide. After all, David had suffered from depression for years and had often mentioned suicide to anyone who would listen.

On July 16, 1987, David went to his room. He extracted several sleeping pills from a bottle on his night table and took them with a glass of water, as was his custom. Margaret, realizing that he would take his usual large quantity of sleeping pills as he read his Bible in bed, brought him up a cup of coffee. She had solicitously dissolved several sleeping pills in the coffee before taking it upstairs. David grumbled a thanks and drank his coffee.

Next morning, Stephen Farthing found David dead in bed. He called an ambulance. The ambulance attendants noted the empty medicine bottle, observed the room was otherwise neat and tidy and concluded that David had committed suicide by means of an overdose.

Nothing would have been done about the open-and-shut case had a relative of David's not called the Folkestone Police Station the day following his death with the information that David had written her two weeks before, informing her that he believed the four conspirators living in his house planned to kill him. He also told her of his wife's ongoing affair with Belsham. Evidently, David had sneaked downstairs one night and had overheard the entire plot. Although he was alarmed, he couldn't bring himself to believe that his wife and her friends would actually kill him. David was wrong.

An autopsy was performed. The results indicated that David had taken a large quantity of barbiturates, about 12 pills, several of which had not been absorbed into the bloodstream by the time death occurred. The attending pathologist also discovered cotton fibres in David's nose, mouth and lungs, indicating that the victim could have been suffocated with a pillow.

The investigation might have bogged down at this point had David Belsham kept his mouth shut. However, like so many killers before him, he had an irresistible urge to tell someone that he had committed the perfect murder. Belsham chose a buddy in a pub. He related in detail how Margaret had laced the coffee with sleeping pills. They had waited awhile before climbing the stairs and finishing the job with a pillow. Belsham's drinking buddy scampered down to the Folkestone Police Station and told what he had heard.

All four conspirators were arrested, tried and found guilty of David Crump's murder. Because of his youth, Paul Thompson received an indefinite prison term, while Stephen Farthing, Maggie Boo and Hawaiian Cruiser were sentenced to life imprisonment.

# JOHN DAVID

(ENGLAND)

---

DISPOSING of embarrassing bodies has always been the bane of those ladies and gentlemen who choose to kill. Over the years we have heard about many varied and novel methods of disposal—from a killer who dropped body parts from an airplane over the English Channel, to a demented man who kept his wife's frozen body in a freezer for several months.

This grisly tale breaks new ground!

Beautiful, 25-year-old Miriam Jones lived in the English town of Reading. She ran with the motorcycle crowd and loved life in the fast lane. She loved bikers too. Despite her mother's warnings that no good would come of her association with such unsavoury companions, Miriam ended up marrying one of her biker boyfriends. As her mother had predicted, the marriage wasn't a happy one. For one thing, her hubby was a wild and crazy guy who just wouldn't settle down.

Miriam, who wasn't a saint herself, also had difficulty lavishing her affection on only one man. The newlyweds argued incessantly, but finally came up with a solution to their problems. A baby was exactly what the marriage required. Nine months after that decision was made, Miriam became a mother. The addition to the family didn't help one iota. In due course the couple separated, which left Miriam with a new set of problems, not the least of which was making a living for herself and her baby.

Miriam obtained a position as barmaid at the Cider House Pub in the village of Winkfield. The pub was not exactly a high-class establishment. Not by a long shot. The fact is, the Cider House was a hangout frequented by members of the Hell's Angels. Miriam hung around with the bikers.

One day, charming John David walked into the pub for a refreshing Guiness Stout. John was a handsome 25-year-old hunk who had a way with words. Miriam took one look and thought to herself, "That's for me." It wasn't long before the young people became lovers. Once again, Miriam's mother wasn't thrilled with her daughter's choice of men. Still, the woman thought, it was nice that she had a man to care for her and her child. It wasn't easy for Miriam to keep up her tiny apartment on her income from the Cider House.

John's job wasn't what you would call a top-flight position. He worked part-time as a labourer taking care of hogs at a nearby large hog farm. Be that as it may, during the winter of 1987, John and Miriam were seeing each other on a steady basis. He often stayed all night at her apartment. Many thought they would marry.

Just when events were proceeding smoothly, who should return to the scene but Miriam's estranged husband. He, too, often downed a few at the Cider House. Isn't love grand? Miriam discovered that those feelings she once felt for hubby were now revived. There was one iceberg in the tranquil sea of love and his name was John David. Miriam could see no way out. She would simply have to tell the hog tender that he was out and hubby was in. That's exactly what she did. John David was devastated. He beseeched Miriam to reconsider, but nothing he did or said had any effect. Miriam was adamant that she would return to her husband's bed and board and that was that.

John David didn't take rejection well. He had been abandoned by his mother shortly after his birth. Eventually he was adopted, but always resented that his biological mother had set him adrift. Because of his good looks and charming demeanor, John had no difficulty attracting girlfriends. However, they all broke off with him when he grew serious.

In 1984, 22-year-old Jacqueline Cheer had gone steady with John for some time. At one point, she decided that John was not for her. On December 23, 1984, in nearby Maidenhead, Jacqueline was found dead on her bed. An autopsy indicated that she had engaged in sexual intercourse immediately before her death and that she had been manually strangled. Although John was suspected, he was never charged, due to lack of evidence.

Now, in 1987, it was happening all over again. John was being rejected, but no one knew of his previous brush with the law. On April 9, John called on Miriam's mother with the upsetting news that she was missing. He had been babysitting for her the night before, but she had not returned to the apartment. Miriam's mother reported her daughter missing to the police.

A preliminary investigation revealed that Miriam and her husband were about to be reunited. In fact, Miriam, her husband and baby were scheduled to leave for a vacation in Spain the day after she went missing. Police conducted a massive search of the area. Her husband and John David searched side-by-side for the missing woman. She wasn't found.

John David was routinely questioned. He swore that he had no idea of Miriam's destination on the night she disappeared, nor did he know whom she was meeting. During the course of the interrogation, a detective noticed a small cut on John's cheek. John claimed he had received the cut while shaving, although it was obviously above his beard line. John was asked to remove his shirt. There for all the world to see were a number of scratches on his chest and back. He explained that he had scratched himself while working with wire down at the hog farm. No one was buying his story.

John was lodged in a cell overnight. Apparently the long dark night had its effect. Next morning at dawn, he requested to see his interrogators. He told them that he had been rejected all his life and that Miriam had cooled toward him. On the night of April 8, he decided to make one last attempt to win her affection. In no uncertain terms, Miriam told him thanks, but no thanks. Their affair was over. She was returning to her husband.

John attempted to make love to his former girlfriend, but Miriam pushed him aside. The rejection was complete. He clasped Miriam's throat in his strong labourer's hands until she was dead. At this point, John paused in telling his story, then ceased talking altogether. Detectives urged him on. "What did you do with her body?" they wanted to know. It was as if John wanted to get the actual killing off his chest, but was reluctant to go further.

Finally, he confessed that he had wrapped the body in a bedsheet and carried it down to a car he had borrowed for the evening. He drove to the farm where he worked looking after a hundred fully grown hogs. John managed to lift Miriam's body over a fence and into the hog enclosure. John David wept hysterically as he concluded his terrible recitation.

Police descended on the hog farm. Their disgusting task was to recover what might be left of Miriam's body. At the conclusion of their three-day hunt, they had recovered a small piece of her dress and four bone fragments.

While John awaited trial, additional evidence was provided against him regarding the 1984 murder of Jacqueline Cheer, but it was decided that nothing was to be gained by trying this case.

On December 6, 1988, John David was found guilty of the murder of Miriam Jones. He was sentenced to life imprisonment.

# JOHN DU PONT

(UNITED STATES)

DAVID Schultz didn't pursue his dream of another gold medal at the Atlanta Olympics. A madman shot him dead.

It is difficult to pinpoint just when John Eleuthere Du Pont went around the bend. He was always a bit strange, which is referred to as eccentric if you happen to be very rich. Financially speaking, John was loaded. We are talking here about a family tree dating back to 18th century France. One of John's ancestors had a monopoly on gunpowder. Du Pont's business conglomerates have given us nylon, rayon, lucite, lycra, mylar and teflon. The empire had, and still has, its tentacles in so many enterprises that it would be difficult for you or me to go through a single day without using a Du Pont product.

John was born a multimillionaire. He lived with his divorced mother at Foxcatcher Farm, an 800-acre spread in Newtown Square, Pennsylvania. Naturally enough, as a young man he attended private schools. After graduating from high school in 1957, he enrolled at the University of Pennsylvania, but higher education was not for Du Pont. John knew that with his vast wealth he could do or have anything he wanted. With this in mind, he embarked on various projects that interested him. When he tired of his most recent fad, he moved on to another.

In the early sixties, John devoted himself to birds and seashells, spending most of his time collecting in the South Pacific. After gathering hundreds of thousands of specimens, he quit to take up competitive swimming. His aim was to win a gold medal in the 1964 Olympics, to be held in Tokyo. John enrolled in Villanova University and later switched to the University of Miami, where he earned a place on the varsity swim team in 1962 and 1963. With a singleness of purpose, he joined the Santa Clara Swim Club, then the most prominent club in the United States. Competing with the top swimmers in the world, John was to learn that while he was an excellent swimmer, he would never be world-class.

Undeterred, John switched interests, as he would do all his life. He decided to win a gold medal in the pentathlon, a five-discipline event consisting of swimming, pistol shooting, horseback riding, running and fencing. Unfortunately he sprained his ankle at the Olympic trials and had to withdraw.

John did manage to compete in his specialty all over the world, becoming good enough in 1965 to win the Australian championship. He was enthused about his win, so much so that he invited the National Pentathlon Association to hold its 1967 championship competition at Foxcatcher Farm. The association was thrilled to accept. After all, what organization wouldn't desire to have a wealthy competitor and possible patron interested in its sport? John didn't disappoint. He built an Olympic-size pool and an indoor shooting range on the estate. Other amenities were added, until Foxcatcher Farm was a state-of-the-art facility where John practised and where the championship competition could be held.

In August 1967, John finished fourteenth in the competition. At age 29, in a subsequent competition, he finished twenty-third and dead last. In 1976, he made it to the Montreal Olympics as manager of the U.S. pentathlon team.

For a while, John tried to form an unbeatable swim team. He hired the best coaches, but after sinking a cool half-million dollars into the project he abruptly closed the club. He married an occupational therapist, Gail Wenk, in September 1983. The union lasted until March 1984, exactly six months. The divorce made headlines. Financial arrangements were settled out of court for megabucks.

John needed a diversion. He found it in amateur wrestling. It was John's idea to gather the best coaches, provide the ultimate facilities and attract the most outstanding amateur wrestlers in the country to Foxcatcher Farm. His aim was to have the United States dominate amateur wrestling, in particular to win world championships and gold medals at the Olympics for years to come.

As one of Villanova's prime benefactors, John had no trouble associating himself with the university after promising to finance its entire wrestling program. Of course, John Du Pont took the title of head coach. He gathered the top wrestling coaches in the country. Amateur wrestlers who in the past had to take jobs to finance their low-profile sport were now offered deluxe facilities, a regular salary and a home for themselves, their wives and children, all on the Foxcatcher estate. Many were suspicious, thinking this was too good to be true. But John kept his word. The eccentric Du Pont built the facilities, hired the coaching staff and started a wrestling program. It mattered little to the wrestlers that their sponsor liked to drive around the estate in an armored personnel carrier when he wasn't hopping about in his helicopter.

By 1986, Team Foxcatcher was a major force in U.S. amateur wrestling. World-class athletes were attracted to the club. Everything was provided. David

Schultz, a 1984 Olympic gold-medal winner, was the shining star of the Du Pont stable of athletes. He lived on the estate with his wife and children.

David had devoted most of his life to his sport. He had won athletic scholarships to universities and had reached the pinnacle of his career when he won an Olympic gold medal to go with his world championship victory at Kiev, Russia, in 1983. Amateur wrestling is not a financially rewarding sport. While baseball, football, basketball and hockey pay huge salaries, there is no such reward at the end of the rainbow for amateur wrestlers. David considered himself fortunate to have a rent-free home, a regular salary and, above all, another chance at Olympic gold.

The first few years at Foxcatcher went well for David, although it was difficult for him not to notice that John Du Pont's behaviour was becoming more and more erratic. John drank heavily and suffered from severe mood changes. David seemed to be the one person at Foxcatcher who could calm him down. It wasn't easy to stay friends with a sponsor who, from time to time, referred to himself as the Dalai Lama. No question about it, John was operating a couple of bricks short of a full load. David assured his wrestling buddies that John was harmless. He was wrong.

On January 26, 1996, John placed a .38-calibre pistol in his belt, jumped into his Lincoln Town Car and drove to Dave Schultz's house. For reasons known only to himself, John believed David was his enemy. He aimed the .38 at David, who was sitting in his Toyota Tercel. The rear window shattered. David screamed as he got out of the Toyota and walked toward the Lincoln. John took careful aim. From a sitting position in his car, he extended his arm and fired. David fell onto the snow-covered ground.

Inside the house, David's wife, Nancy, and their two children, Alexander, 9, and Danielle, 6, heard the shots. Nancy opened the front door and gasped in horror. There lay David, face down in the snow. As she stared at the unbelievable scene, John aimed his pistol at her. Nancy retreated into the house. John again focused on the still form in the snow as if transfixed. He aimed twice more at David and fired. The shots went into the fallen man's back. Nancy again opened the door and again was forced back inside when John pointed his pistol at her. Finally, John stepped on the gas and drove to his 18-room mansion on the estate.

Nancy dialed 911 and observed John leaving the scene. She ran to her husband's side and cradled his head in her lap as a red puddle of blood spread around his body. David was still breathing but died as Nancy comforted him.

Police rushed to the estate. It was evident from the outset that John had no intention of surrendering. Police decided against forced entry. They would wait outside the eccentric millionaire's home, all the while attempting to communicate with him. The house was surrounded by police and lit with floodlights. Expert hostage negotiators managed to speak to John by phone. He pleaded with them to turn off the lights so he could sleep. The police complied.

Saturday came and went with no new developments in the standoff. Authorities turned off the heat in the house. By Sunday John complained of the cold. When told that they would turn the heat back on, John, as the experts had anticipated, became angry. Who did these people think they were, telling a Du Pont that they would turn on his heat? He knew how to do it and would turn on the heat himself. The ploy worked. John left the house and started to walk towards a boiler room that supplied heat to the mansion. A swat team converged on him and took him into custody. The siege was over.

John Eleuthere Du Pont, one of the richest men ever charged with murder in the United States, was found guilty of murder in the third degree. He was sentenced to 13 to 30 years' imprisonment.

# CHRISTOPHER ENDERLY

(NEW ZEALAND)

---

WHEN her husband was lost at sea in 1977, Sarah Enderly, at the mature age of 45, made up her mind that she was far too young to take her place on the proverbial shelf. Sarah not only scorned the shelf, she made a concerted effort to sample every available male in Christchurch, New Zealand. It was an open secret that Sarah was a woman of, how shall we put it, loose moral standards.

Sarah lived with her 19-year-old son, Christopher, at 7 Oakdene Road, just outside the city in a rather pleasant, rambling old villa. She worked part-time at a university restaurant. Usually there was a man waiting for her to get off duty at eleven each night.

I would be leading you astray if I have given the impression that our Sarah was a raving beauty. Nothing could be further from the truth. She was decidedly overweight, had pronounced bags under her eyes and wore far too much makeup. To compensate for her unattractive appearance, Sarah often trolled for male companions. She wasn't above picking up sex partners in the various parks around Christchurch. It was these gents who would come a calling at the restaurant at closing time.

For six years, Sarah had one of the busiest sex lives in all of Christchurch. I mean four or five times a week, usually with different partners.

On January 25, 1983, her son showed up at police headquarters and reported his mother missing. She had not returned home after work the previous evening. Christopher provided the police with a photograph of his 51-year-old mother. Two days later, when Sarah still hadn't shown up, police commenced to interview neighbours and acquaintances. It was then that they learned of Sarah's overactive sex life. This knowledge opened up a myriad of suspects. Had one of her lovers done her in for any number of reasons that lovers do away with partners?

Detectives also learned that Chris was as straight as an arrow and had no idea that his mother was so sexually active. It appeared that as far as he was concerned, she worked in the house all day, went to work in the restaurant each evening and returned home.

Colleagues at the university restaurant stated that, uncharacteristically, no boyfriend had shown up for Sarah on January 24, the night she went missing. Since Sarah always travelled by bus, police interviewed bus driver Ralph Daniels, who knew Sarah well. He told investigators that on the night in question, Sarah had been the last person to get off his bus.

What in the world had happened to Sarah? Police speculated that the missing woman might have run off with one of her male friends. However, they felt she would not have left a son she loved, nor would she have left without taking any of her belongings. It just didn't make sense.

Police concentrated their efforts on the area between the bus stop and 7 Oakdene Road. Residents of the neighbourhood were again questioned. All knew Sarah by reputation, but none knew her well. Some expressed sympathy for Chris, whom they felt was not aware of his mother's nocturnal dalliances.

In a weed-infested yard behind a vacant house, police found the body of Sarah Enderly. She had been struck on the head seven times. Four of the blows had been delivered elsewhere and the last three had been inflicted after she lay dead in the field. Sarah might have been attacked as she walked from the bus stop to her home, authorities speculated, after which she had been dragged into the vacant lot, where the killer had struck the last three blows to make sure she was dead.

No money or jewellery had been stripped from the dead woman, nor had Sarah been sexually interfered with in any way. That left investigators with the idea that the culprit was a jealous or vengeful lover. Police undertook the tedious task of seeking out the scores of men in Sarah's life. This process had barely begun when Roger Ackworth walked into police headquarters with a most unusual story.

Straitlaced, artistocratic Ackworth explained that his 23-year-old daughter, Melanie had been engaged to Christopher Enderly. He and his wife had met Chris over the Christmas holidays and found him to be a charming young man. They totally approved of their daughter's choice of a husband. However, since the Ackworths were bluebloods, it was most natural for them to delve into their future son-in-law's family. Their investigation revealed that Chris's mother was nothing more than a tramp. To the Ackworths' way of thinking, although Chris was not responsible for his mother's behaviour, he was not a suitable husband for their daughter.

On January 18, Melanie returned Chris's engagement ring. She told her parents that he was extremely bitter when she advised him of the reason for the termination of their engagement.

Police interviewed Chris. He explained that for the past two years he had been aware of his mother's sex life. He had found out by accident. One night, he was studying late for an exam and left his room to fetch a glass of water. He was walking by his mother's room at the other side of the house when he heard loud moans. Thinking that his mother might be ill, he opened her door. Sarah was too busy to notice her son. She was engaged in frenzied activity in her bed with a member of the opposite sex.

Chris was devastated. Since that incident, a service club had refused him admittance, citing his mother's reputation as their reason. On another occasion he was asked to leave a private club because of Sarah's well-known activities. He grew to hate his mother. For two years, the thought of killing her never left his mind. The broken engagement had been the last straw.

Chris had concealed himself near the bus stop each night, waiting for his mother to come home alone. When she got off the bus on the night of the twenty-fourth, he sneaked up behind her and struck her over the head with a hammer. He then dragged his mother's body into the vacant lot and proceeded to strike her three more times to ensure she was dead.

Christopher Enderly was tried and found guilty of murdering his mother. He was sentenced to life imprisonment.

# GEORGE FARMAKOPOULIS

(ENGLAND)

GEORGE Farmakopoulis met his girlfriend Maureen in a rather unique way. He was serving time in an English prison for a minor con job, and his cellmate was none other than Maureen's husband. When George was released from the slammer, he visited Maureen, whose husband was still in prison.

George was a tall, handsome rascal who could charm the birds out of the willows. His guile worked on Maureen. Before you could say "why not," she and George were living and loving under the same roof. Soon their union was blessed with a baby.

What more can I tell you about George? He was one of those fellows who insisted on living well without an adequate income. When pressed for cash, he delved into crime. Just as many Canadian criminals seem to enjoy preying on convenience stores, British rounders thrive on sub-post offices, where many English people deposit their savings. George picked out a likely target in the village of Thriplow, Cambridgeshire.

On an overcast day in the fall of 1984, George and Maureen dropped off their baby and Maureen's other child by her still-incarcerated husband with friends who would babysit the children for the day. After a pleasant lunch, they proceeded to Thriplow. George had been talking about robbing a sub-post office for weeks. It was his way of getting out of debt in one fell swoop. Initially, Maureen was against the idea, but gradually George wore her down. Now it was too late.

George and Maureen walked into the shop of 53-year-old Doreen Smith. Doreen had lost her husband years earlier. She was alone in the sub-post office. Maureen was shocked when George produced a gun and pointed it at the postmistress. She would later state that she had no idea a weapon was to be used in the robbery. George handed Mrs. Smith a bag with the terse order to fill it with money. As Maureen stepped around a partition, she heard the terrified Mrs. Smith shout, "No, don't!" George responded, "Get in here." Then Maureen heard the sound of a door closing.

As Mrs. Smith cowered in the cupboard where George had placed her, she recoiled in horror as George pointed his gun at her head and fired four times.

Three slugs entered Doreen's head. The fourth bullet missed its mark. George and Maureen left the sub-post office, jumped into their van and drove away. George bragged about the shooting to Maureen. They drove to Grantchester, where they had a spot of tea before picking up the kiddies and making their way to the home of Maureen's mother. Once there, they counted their loot. It came to £415.

Back in Thriplow, Doreen Smith, although horribly wounded, was still alive with three slugs in her head. She crawled out of the cupboard, across the floor of the post office and out into the street. Neighbours immediately rushed her to Addenbrooke's Hospital in Cambridge. Throughout her ordeal, Doreen remained conscious and was able to relate her terrifying experience to police. Unfortunately, this courageous woman died from her wounds after lingering in hospital for 18 days.

The day after the robbery, George and Maureen travelled to Amsterdam. A few weeks later, they read about Doreen Smith's death in the newspaper. Maureen was devastated. What had started out as a grab-and-run theft had turned into the brutal murder of an innocent woman. She implored George to go back to England and face the music. He wouldn't hear of it. George confiscated Maureen's passport, making flight impossible. To complicate matters, Maureen informed George that she was pregnant.

Undeterred, George talked Maureen into moving to Athens. Once in Greece, he kept a tight rein on her, occasionally locking her in their home. As luck would have it, Maureen found her passport. Without hesitation, she flew to England and gave herself up to police. That June, she gave birth to a daughter in prison.

In order to apprehend George, authorities approached Maureen with a deal. She went along with the arrangement. George had no idea she was in custody. In fact, he had often called Maureen's mother's home to speak to her. Maureen was delivered by police to her mother's house to receive his calls from Athens, which were always prearranged. George coaxed Maureen to meet him on the continent. Police urged her to arrange to meet him in Amsterdam.

George travelled to Amsterdam and rang Maureen's hotel before showing up. The hotel staff had been briefed. They told him she was breast-feeding her baby and would call him back shortly. Maureen returned his call. Little did George know that she was still in England. However, he was a cautious man and, at the last moment, changed the site of the reunion to Antwerp, Belgium. He was arrested as he stepped off the aircraft in Belgium.

George was returned to England to stand trial. He swore that he was innocent, insisting that he had been shopping in Cambridge at the time of the crime. His protestations were in vain. Maureen's evidence relating every detail of the cold-blooded crime sealed George's fate. He was found guilty of murder and sentenced to life imprisonment with no possibility of parole for 20 years. When the sentence was read in court, George attacked the officers guarding him. It took a half-dozen police to subdue him.

The same jury found Maureen not guilty of murder, as it was felt she was an unwilling dupe in the hands of her manipulative lover. She was complimented on the assistance she had given authorities in apprehending George Farmakopoulos as well as in giving evidence against him. However, Maureen didn't get off scot-free. She was found guilty of robbery and sentenced to five years' imprisonment.

# KEN FROMANT AND ELIZABETH THOMPSON

(ENGLAND)

OCCASIONALLY murder cases reveal titillating sexual details that dwarf the crime itself. One such murder occurred on November 5, 1971, along a lovers' lane known as Purbrook Heath Road outside Portsmouth, England. A police officer discovered the body of 35-year-old Peter Stanswood in his car, which was parked on the road. He had been stabbed to death with a Japanese paper knife, which was protruding from his chest. The handle was covered with blood.

It was ascertained that Pete and his partner, Ken Thompson, were owners of a boating business on the Isle of Wight. Pete lived in Portsmouth with his wife, Heather, and their two children, Tina and Charles.

An officer had the disagreeable task of informing Mrs. Stanswood of her husband's murder. To say that he was shocked at her reaction would be an understatement. Heather told the investigator that her husband had several mistresses. She provided him with a list of 25 ladies whom she knew had been intimate with her Pete. She added that two of the women had presented Pete with illegitimate children and a third was currently pregnant. Heather thought that her husband had spent the previous evening, the night of the murder, with Wendy Charlton, who was heavy-laden with Pete's child. Detectives scrambled over to Wendy's digs. She confirmed that she had spent the previous evening with Pete. During the course of the evening he had phoned Linda Reading, one of the two women who had borne his offspring. It was Wendy's opinion that he had intended to visit Linda after leaving her flat.

Police scratched their noggins. This guy Pete Stanswood had been one busy boy. It was apparent that he had been carrying on adulterous affairs with more Portsmouth ladies than a porcupine had quills. And there was more. It was learned that Heather Stanswood had none of those attributes that would make her a candidate for sainthood. Heather confessed that she too played the field and had had scores of affairs, some of which were known to her husband. Her current beau was Ken Fromant, a native of Berkshire, who was also married with two children. When questioned, Ken swore that he had been in Berkshire on the evening of the murder. Furthermore, he had broken up with Heather two months before the murder. He had no reason to kill Pete Stanswood, a man he had never met.

Meanwhile, minor mysteries cropped up. Blood found on the handle of the murder weapon and the steering wheel of the car did not match the murder victim's blood type. There were no fingerprints on the Japanese paper knife and it was never traced. Above all, it appeared that all those involved in the case were promiscuous and took their adulterous affairs very lightly.

Nine months passed. While detectives were turning up more dirt than a landfill site, they were having great difficulty coming up with a clue to the killer's identity. Their luck changed while interviewing one Portsmouth woman who mentioned that she had been visited by her lover, Ian Dance, the night Pete was killed. Since police had already interviewed Dance, who had sworn he hadn't been in Portsmouth on the evening in question, they now had someone who had given them a conflicting statement.

Dance was questioned again. When told of his girlfriend's faux pas, he admitted that he had been in Portsmouth with an acquaintance, Ken Fromant. Well, son of a gun, Ken was the lover of Heather Stanswood, the murdered man's wife. Dance was able to prove that Ken had dropped him off late in the afternoon and that he had had absolutely nothing to do with Pete Stanswood's murder.

Matters became complicated. Upon being reinterviewed, Ken Fromant was confronted with Dance's statement. He now admitted he had lied when first questioned. His reason for being in Portsmouth was simple enough. He had spent the night in bed with Elizabeth Thompson, the wife of Pete Stanswood's partner. When Elizabeth was interrogated, she broke down and admitted she had spent the night with Fromant. She too swore that neither she nor Fromant had had anything to do with Pete's murder. They were guilty of adultery and lying, but nothing more.

Police weren't so sure. They located the vehicle that Ian Dance and Ken Fromant had driven to Portsmouth on the night of the murder. By sheer good fortune, it had broken down the day after the murder and been left undriven in a garage parking lot ever since. Samples of earth were taken from the vehicle's tires. This earth proved to be identical to earth taken from the site of the murder. In addition, Fromant's blood type matched the blood found on the murder weapon and on the steering wheel of Pete's car.

Although their case was far from airtight, the police took Ken Fromant and Heather Stanswood into custody and charged them with Pete's murder. After being charged, Heather informed police that Elizabeth Thompson had told her that she and Fromant had murdered Pete. She revealed all the details of the crime. According to Heather, her husband had received a telephone call from Elizabeth to meet her at the Purbrook Heath Road car park with sexual intercourse in mind.

When Pete drove up, he found Elizabeth and Fromant waiting in Elizabeth's car. The two joined Pete in his vehicle. The men argued. Fromant took out his Japanese paper knife, but momentarily Pete got the upper hand and managed to cut Fromant's arm, accounting for the presence of his blood on the knife and the steering wheel. When Ken gained control, he stabbed Pete seven times, causing his death. Elizabeth and Fromant drove to her house, where they changed clothing and patched up Ken's arm.

Heather's startling revelations were extensively investigated. As a result, the charges against her were dropped. In her place, Elizabeth Thompson was charged with Pete's murder.

On October 21, 1975, the 17-day murder trial commenced. It caused a sensation throughout England, mainly because of the sexual dalliances of the participants. It was proven that Elizabeth was in the midst of an affair with Pete Stanswood. Although both were married, she felt that if she couldn't have him exclusively, no one could. Fromant, who was infatuated with Elizabeth, murdered a man he had never met. Both defendants admitted that they had been at the scene of the crime at the time of the murder. Each accused the other of committing the actual stabbing. It mattered little.

Ken Fromant and Elizabeth Thompson were found guilty of murder. Both were sentenced to life imprisonment.

# DENNIS GOLDING

(CANADA)

---

IN the fall of 1974 everyone was wondering what had happened to Lisa Golding. Her husband, Dennis, told friends that he had driven her from their Clonsilla Avenue apartment in Peterborough, Ontario, to Highway 401 so that she could hitchhike to Georgia. According to Dennis, he and Lisa had had a bit of a squabble and Lisa had wanted a little time to herself. He would join her to begin a new life in a couple of weeks when she phoned him to let him know her location.

Acquaintances couldn't quite swallow Dennis's story. Dennis, 24, had a real estate business in Peterborough. It didn't seem likely that he would give up his career to resettle in Georgia without any prospects in that American state.

One of the missing woman's friends called Lisa's mother and stepfather in Halifax and was told that they, too, were concerned. They had not heard from Lisa in several weeks, which was very unusual. The friend's phone call so upset Lisa's parents that they informed Halifax police of their daughter's strange disappearance.

Halifax police listened in when Lisa's stepfather called Dennis in Peterborough. Dennis now told a somewhat different story. He said he had no idea where Lisa had gone. He had driven her to the highway 19 days earlier. At that time she told him that their marriage was finished and that she was never coming back. Dennis claimed he was embarrassed to relate the tale to friends, but felt that Lisa's parents deserved to hear the truth.

Lisa's family conferred with police. They felt that she might very well have walked out on her husband, but they could not believe that she would not have contacted them in almost three weeks.

Within days of these suspicious developments, a male friend of Lisa's visited Peterborough police. Upon hearing that Dennis had officially reported his wife missing, he revealed the saga of his involvement with the missing woman. As a result, police delved into the life and loves of Lisa Golding.

Lisa had met 19-year-old Dennis Golding in Halifax when she was 17 and he was serving in the Canadian navy. He was her brother's closest friend. Dennis spent all his shore leave with Lisa. Soon the young people were deeply in love. Everything was coming up roses. Lisa and Dennis were married in All Saints Cathedral and set up housekeeping in Dartmouth, Nova Scotia. As is the case of thousands of newlyweds, the future appeared bright and full of promise. But with the glamour of the uniform removed and the practical problems of earning a living closing in on the Goldings, their relationship deteriorated.

Dennis received his discharge from the navy and decided that Ontario held far more promise than Nova Scotia for a young fellow who wanted to get ahead. He accepted his stepfather's offer of a place to live in Peterborough until he got on his feet. In the meantime, he would take a real estate course with the idea of joining his stepfather's real estate firm.

Lisa was furious. This wasn't in her plans at all. A gift of a motorcycle pacified her enough to facilitate the move, but Lisa was an unhappy camper. She demanded to hit the open road in an attempt to get a proper perspective on the direction her life was taking. Despite the built-in risks in her plan, Dennis reluctantly acquiesced to his wife taking off with a few friends on their motorcycles headed for Halifax. They would check in with Lisa's parents upon their arrival in the Nova Scotia capital. All seems to have gone well with the Halifax visit. Three weeks later, Lisa arrived back in Peterborough.

Shortly after Lisa's return, Dennis had had enough. He ordered his wife out of the apartment, suggesting she go find the life she sought with her biker friends. Lisa took up the challenge and conferred with a particular friend in Sudbury. Together the couple headed for western Canada. Within a month they reversed their direction and crossed the country to Halifax. When Lisa ran out of money, she called Dennis for airfare back to Toronto. She had a buddy in nearby Ajax and would stay there for a while.

Dennis came through as he always did. He figured his wife was finished with her wild lifestyle and was susceptible to returning to him. He was wrong. Lisa once again flew to Halifax, but was immediately disillusioned.

Dennis was beside himself with his wife's machinations. She was charming one minute, but the next minute treated him like dirt. It was lonesome living alone in the Peterborough apartment, so he took in a border, David Sing-Woon Chan, who occupied the spare bedroom.

For the umpteenth time, Lisa made another move. She returned to Peterborough. The troubled couple seemed to be on the verge of a shaky reconciliation. On October 20, 1974, Dennis took his wife out for dinner. That night they made love, not a frequent activity in the Golding residence. They agreed to start over. Dennis's real estate career was taking off. In the years that lay ahead, they would carve out an idyllic life together. Arm in arm, they arranged a $15,000 loan to see them through the next year. At last their hectic relationship was on an even keel.

That's when Lisa Golding disappeared.

The Ontario Provincial Police (OPP) questioned Dennis. He told them that he had left his wife hitchhiking on the highway. Next day, Dennis's stepfather called police. Dennis hadn't shown up for work and couldn't be reached by phone. For three days authorities had the disconcerting task of attempting to find out what had happened to both Dennis and Lisa.

The mystery of Dennis's absence was soon solved. He had been found unconscious in a hotel room in Toledo, Ohio. Apparently he had taken an overdose of barbiturates and was recovering in hospital. OPP detectives were dispatched to Toledo to accompany Dennis back to Ontario. Initially he stuck to his story of dropping off his wife at the edge of the highway, but changed his tune on his lawyer's advice.

Dennis told detectives that after obtaining the $15,000 loan, he and Lisa had argued over the disposition of the money. He thought a large portion of the loan should go toward a down payment on a house, while Lisa believed that she should receive more than the $500 Dennis had given her. The argument continued in the bedroom. Even after they were in bed, Lisa wouldn't stop. Finally, she blurted out that Dennis wasn't adequate in the lovemaking department. To add insult to injury, she told her husband that her biker friend was a far better sex partner than Dennis would ever be. She went on to tell him that even when he was in the navy she had seen other men and used to joke about how stupid he was not to catch on.

Dennis broke. He bent over his beautiful wife, clasped his hands around her neck and strangled her. He told police that he dressed himself and Lisa, all the while making sure he didn't wake up his roomer, David Sing-Woon Chan, who'd slept through the entire incident. He then had the difficult task of carrying the body out of the apartment and down six flights of stairs. Dennis placed his wife's body in his car and drove around for three hours before deciding to bury Lisa near Chandos Lake.

Throughout his gruesome dissertation, Dennis swore that he had loved his wife and had made every allowance for her erratic behaviour, until he finally had seen red and couldn't control himself. Police located Lisa's body, which was buried in soft earth exactly where Dennis had indicated.

Dennis was charged with murdering his wife. Later the Crown accepted his plea of guilty of the lesser charge of manslaughter. On February 17, 1975, he was sentenced to 10 years' imprisonment, the initial portion of his sentence to be served at the Penetanguishene Hospital for the Criminally Insane. When deemed fit to be released from the hospital, he was to be transferred to prison.

Dennis Golding has long since been paroled.

# STEVE GRAY

## (UNITED STATES)

STEVE Gray knew Dolores's family didn't like him. He attributed their obvious displeasure to the fact that he was black and Dolores was of Hispanic stock. That's not the way Dolores's family saw it at all. They couldn't put a finger on the reason they disliked Steve. It was just one of those things. They simply couldn't stand Steve Gray.

It didn't matter who disapproved of the match. The young couple, in their mid-twenties, appeared to be madly in love. They dated for only a few months before marrying on August 29, 1987. Dolores knew she was marrying a navy man. She realized right from the beginning that she could never get accustomed to being separated from her husband.

A month after their marriage, Steve was assigned to sea duty on the *USS Enterprise*. After a couple of weeks ashore, he was again at sea on the *Enterprise* for more than a month. Dolores, who worked for the U.S. government in Fresno, California, was elated when Steve informed her that he had been granted a 17-day leave. At last they would have a real honeymoon. They would take off in Dolores's 1982 Camaro and drive away with no destination in mind, no schedule, just each other and the good times to cherish and enjoy.

On Saturday December 5, they decided to visit Yosemite National Park at Curry Village. The young couple purchased food and a bottle of champagne. They ate the food before driving up to Discovery View to take in the outstanding view of the valley and consume the champagne. Dolores didn't care for any champagne, so Steve drank it as they listened to the car radio in the parking lot. He became drowsy. As he dozed off, Dolores said she was going to take a walk and enjoy the scenery. It was around 5 p.m., just about the time the setting sun cast brilliant red and orange shadows against the geological outcroppings that dominate the surrounding hills.

Steve remembered Dolores leaving the Camaro. He fell asleep. When he awoke, it was pitch-black and Dolores was nowhere to be seen. The next thing anyone was to hear of the fate of Dolores Gray was when Steve dialled 911 from the Curry Village ice-skating rink and told the dispatcher his wife was missing.

He had searched for her, but simply couldn't locate her in the dark. The dispatcher told Steve not to worry, many people get lost in that area. A U.S. park ranger would be sent to meet him at the rink immediately.

The ranger met with Steve, who repeated the details of his wife's disappearance. Together, they drove to the Discovery View parking lot. The ranger turned on his loudspeaker, broadcasting Dolores's description and requesting a response from her in case she was injured or immobilized for any reason. When he received no response, he phoned his command post for additional assistance. He couldn't help but wonder why Steve had not used either of the two pay phones he had passed between Discovery View and the Curry Village rink.

When reinforcements arrived, one of the Rangers asked Steve if he and Dolores were happily married. Steve assured him that his three-month marriage was extremely happy. About the only negative he could think of was his wife's family's racial attitudes. As Steve was being questioned, several rangers noted he referred to Dolores in the past tense.

As the night wore on, Steve indicated that he had promised to return to Fresno that evening to stand guard for a buddy. It seemed strange that a man whose wife was missing would want to leave the scene to do a favour for a friend. The rangers had to coerce Steve into staying the night at a nearby motel.

Next morning, the search for Dolores in the treacherous terrain intensified. Around noon, a mountain climber came across her battered body at the base of a cliff. She had apparently stumbled over the cliff in the dark. An autopsy indicated the death was accidental. Because of Steve's rather weird behaviour, the rangers decided to discuss the case with the FBI, who agreed a full-scale investigation was warranted.

Friends of the newlyweds were questioned. It was learned that on his wedding night Steve had gone out, found a willing female companion and hadn't returned to his bride's side until 4 a.m. You wouldn't call that getting off on the right foot. They also found out the he'd had several one-night stands with a variety of women since his marriage.

Steve had inquired about insurance on Dolores's life 10 days before she plunged to her death. He said it was the normal inquiry of a man who was newly married. When asked to take a polygraph test, Steve agreed. The test indicated he was giving deceptive answers concerning the events leading up to calling 911. Faced with the lie detector results, Steve weakened and changed his story. He now told detectives that after arriving at the Discovery View parking lot, he and Dolores stood beside the Camaro listening to the car radio and drinking champagne. Dolores left to look for a washroom along one of the trails.

Steve said he heard a blood-curdling scream moments later. He panicked, took a quick, unsuccessful look for Dolores in the dark before jumping in the car and driving to the Curry Village rink. Steve said he had lied for two reasons: he hadn't acted very heroically, and he knew Dolores's family would never accept his story. The investigating officers didn't believe his story either, but they realized they didn't have enough evidence to convict the man they were now convinced had killed his wife.

Although Steve denied having any life insurance outside his normal naval protection, detectives discovered he had three policies on Dolores's life that would pay him more than half a million dollars in case of his wife's accidental death. Despite the undeniable proof that the policies existed, Steve insisted that he had no knowledge of them. Detectives were able to dig into the insurance company's files and find Steve's fingerprints on an application he had signed to take out one of the policies.

A short time after Dolores's death, Steve set himself up with another woman. He didn't treat his live-in girlfriend much better than Dolores. One night, police were called to his apartment. Steve had beaten the girl and had threatened to throw her out a second-storey window. For this adventure, he was charged with assault, found guilty and sentenced to 60 days in jail. He was charged with Dolores' murder while still serving this sentence.

In June 1989, Steve stood trial for his wife's murder. The prosecution proved beyond a reasonable doubt that Steve had lied to Dolores about himself from their very first date. He had falsely glamorized his rank in the navy, had constantly seen other women and had contrived to insure Dolores' life for sums far exceeding his ability to pay for such insurance. There was little doubt he had contrived to kill Dolores, collect the insurance money, leave the navy and live a life of leisure. Had he not passed those pay phones or had he shown more concern for his missing wife before she was found, he might very well have gotten away with murder.

It took the California jury only five hours to find Steve Gray guilty of murder in the first degree. He was sentenced to life imprisonment with no possibility of parole.

# GEORGE GREEN

## (CANADA)

MURDER at any time is a repugnant act. When committed by an adult, we look for deep-rooted motives. What drove the murderer doing the deed? Was it greed? Was it anger or passion? But when murder is committed by a child, we look elsewhere. What emotion or drive could compel a child to take another's life?

In 1849, in the township of Emily, near Peterborough, Ontario, a murder took place that shocked the community and the nation. Eliza and Thomas Rowan were God-fearing, honest folk, who laboured long and hard on their farm. When they heard that the widow O'Connor was having a difficult time making ends meet since the recent loss of her husband, Eliza and Thomas agreed to take in tiny, five-year-old Margaret O'Connor.

Soon the little girl was an integral member of the Rowan family. She loved to play with and feed the animals on the farm, and seemed to be always laughing and smiling. The Rowans loved the little girl as if she were their own. Previous to Margaret's joining the family, the Rowans had adopted another youngster. For two years, young George Green had been living with the family.

As an infant, George had been placed with Rev. Mr. Dick, a Presbyterian minister. Then in 1847, the Rowans had taken George to their farm. When the boy reached the age of nine, the Rowans realized he needed some formal education, but the district school was too far away for him to attend regularly. Every so often they would sit George down at the kitchen table and go over some reading and sums.

The boy seemed to take to his farm chores with vigour and good humour. He fed the chickens, milked the cows, and was a pretty helpful hand around the farm. When Margaret joined the Rowans, George and the little girl often performed chores together.

In the autumn of 1849, George was 11, Margaret was 5. Events were about to unfold that would affect both their lives forever.

Samuel Hannah lived about a mile down the road from the Rowans. One fine day Thomas hitched up his team. He was going to a ploughing bee at Samuel's place. Eliza was planning on spending some time with a neighbour while Thomas was ploughing. Her husband would drop her off on his way to the bee.

Before the Rowans left their farm for the day, Thomas instructed George to "raise ten or twelve rows of potatoes." This sort of casual instruction was over and above the normal chores the young lad was expected to do around the farm. Thomas shouted to George as the team galloped out of the yard, "When Margaret goes out to you, you may have her help you to pick the potatoes, and place them in the wheelbarrow."

George nodded and waved to the Rowans as they drove out of sight. The next time Thomas Rowan was to see George, the boy was running toward him on Samuel Hannah's farm shouting, "Margaret has been eaten by a bear!"

For some reason that he had difficulty explaining later, Thomas Rowan instinctively felt George was lying. He angrily turned upon the young lad, "You have killed the little girl. You have murdered Margaret." The words came fast and furious. They were unnatural words, directed against a protesting, sobbing 11-year-old child. The youngster swore he was telling the truth.

All the men rushed to the Rowan farm to hunt for some trace of the missing girl. George pointed out where the bear had come upon little Margaret. He illustrated how the unsuspecting child had held out her hand to the bear, an act she had performed many times when she gave young calves their milk bottles. The boy pointed to the place in the fence where the bear had jumped, carrying Margaret with him.

The men searched until darkness made it impossible to continue. They could find no evidence that a bear had dragged a child in the soft earth. They found no bear tracks or torn clothing. In fact, they could find no evidence that a bear had been anywhere near the Rowan farm.

With the search at a standstill, the men turned their attention back to George Green. They grilled him until finally he fell asleep, still insisting that a bear had carried away the unfortunate Margaret.

All the farmers in the area, as well as young George, were up bright and early the next morning to continue the search. Around noon they found the pathetic body of tiny Margaret O'Connor. She had been bludgeoned to death with a hoe, which lay beside her body. Her attacker had struck her repeatedly in the head and all over her body until she was dead. Adhered to the blade of the hoe that George had been using to "raise the potatoes" were blood and strands of the dead girl's hair.

The men fixed their stares upon 11-year-old George Green. The savageness of the attack upon the helpless child was beyond comprehension. Adamantly proclaiming his innocence, George was taken into custody and lodged in the Peterborough jail. On May 3, 1850, to my knowledge the youngest defendant ever to stand trial for murder in Canada, faced his accusers.

The scene was strange. Solemn, educated men were to argue the merits of his case. A black-robed, learned judge was to direct the proceedings and, in the end, a jury was to pass judgement on George's innocence or guilt. The object of all this attention was a small, trembling child.

Thomas Rowan explained the circumstances leading up to the discovery of Margaret's body. Eliza Rowan then took up the story. She told the court that George confessed to the murder after he had been placed in jail. Margaret had come out to the field where George was digging the potatoes. George had never thought of killing Margaret before. It was only when she was with him in the field that he had "taken the notion of killing her." All of a sudden he struck her with the hoe again and again until she lay still.

The crowd in the courtroom looked down at the young lad in the prisoner's box. They stared in disbelief. The defence called no witnesses.

George was found guilty of murder and sentenced to hang on June 26, 1850. On June 4, his sentence was commuted to life imprisonment in Kingston Penitentiary.

After a few weeks of confinement, George became pale and weak. Several months later, two prisoners were relieved of their usual work detail. They slowly carried a tiny pine box, which they placed in an unmarked grave. The little boy who had hacked Margaret O'Connor to death had arrived at his final resting place.

# SIMON GUN-A-NOOT

## (CANADA)

IF Simon Gun-a-noot had lived, loved and roamed the wilds of the United States, his saga would be as well-known to us as that of Sitting Bull, Geronimo or Cochise. But Canadians appear to be inherently reluctant to glamorize their heroes or, for that matter, their villains. I'll leave it up to you into which category you wish to place Simon Gun-a-noot.

Come along with me now to a different time and place, where men worked hard and played hard. It is June 18, 1906, and the place is Two Mile Creek, British Columbia. The closest real town is Hazelton, home to some 200 hardy souls.

Simon Gun-a-noot was a Kispiox native who trapped and hunted year round in the wilderness between the Skeena and Stikine Rivers. He often sold the products of his labours in far-off Vancouver, purchasing supplies that he lugged back north to sell in the small shop he owned near Kispiox village. Simon, a handsome, well-built man, lived in harmony with his wife, Sarah, and one child on a small ranch where, in addition to his other activities, he raised cows and horses.

On the fateful night in question, Simon dropped into James Cameron's licensed watering hole for a few drinks. Among the patrons was one Alex McIntosh, a heavy-drinking prospector who would rather fight than eat. That's exactly what happened. No one could remember how the fight started, but before you could say mink pelt, Alex and Simon were going at it hammer and tongs. After each had taken severe punishment, the combatants were parted. Simon said that, given the chance, he would fix McIntosh good. McIntosh had his own problems. During the fight he had badly injured a finger, which required medical attention. He took off on horseback for the hospital in Hazelton. Alex didn't make it. Next morning his body was found face up on the trail about a mile outside town.

The coroner stated that Alex had been shot. The bullet had travelled diagonally upward, exiting through the man's collarbone. Its trajectory was compatible with someone firing from a horizontal position on the ground.

While police were surveying the scene of the crime, they were informed that another body, that of Max Leclair, had been found on the trail leading to Kispiox village on the other side of Hazelton. Like McIntosh, he had been shot while travelling on horseback.

Provincial Constable James Kirby, in charge of the investigation, soon learned of the bad blood between Simon and Alex. Although Leclair had not attended the drinking bout the night before, it was felt that Simon might very well have met him on his way home.

An inquest into the deaths of Alex McIntosh and Max Leclair was speedily conducted. The jurors concluded that Simon had murdered McIntosh. They also strongly suspected that Simon and his brother-in-law, Peter Hi-ma-dan, were responsible for Leclair's death. Evidently Peter had been seen travelling with Simon after the scuffle at Cameron's drinking establishment.

Kirby, with five other constables, travelled to Kispiox village to pick up the wanted men, and so began the Gun-a-noot saga. Simon was not at home, and his wife had no idea where he might be hiding. Later it was learned that he had correctly surmised that the law would widen the search, so he stayed close to home. When the heat died down somewhat, Simon gathered up his wife and child, together with Peter and his wife, and headed north into the wilderness he knew so well. His father, Nah-gun, joined the well-equipped and experienced band of travellers.

All that summer the hunt for the wanted men continued. North West Mounted Police lent their assistance. A $1,000 reward, a small fortune in 1906, was posted for the capture of the two men. Despite the mammoth effort, authorities had difficulty penetrating the rugged mountainous terrain. Summer gave way to one of the coldest winters on record. On occasion, the hunted band was sighted, but not once did they come close to being apprehended. When the weather became intolerable, the hunt was intermittently suspended.

With the coming of summer, the search for Gun-a-noot once again intensified. Expert guides and prospectors were hired to help police, but all were unable to locate or keep up with the fugitives. It was learned that Gun-a-noot and his band occasionally joined other groups of natives for short periods of time, but they were always able to anticipate the authorities and move on.

Years passed. Gun-a-noot was unlike many other wanted natives in several ways. He had no urge to return to his village to visit his wife and child for the simple reason that he had taken them with him. Most important of all, he was intimately acquainted with the uninhabited territory he traversed. He often found himself in remote areas into which no white man had ever ventured. Natives, who usually resented anyone trespassing on their hunting and fishing grounds, became Gun-a-noot's allies and assisted him in any way they could.

Natives and whites alike came to admire Gun-a-noot's endurance and courage. To those who crossed his path in the first decade of his freedom, he swore he had murdered no one but was certain he would not be believed. Years later, Gun-a-noot was at least partially vindicated when his sister-in-law, Peter Hi-ma-dan's wife, confessed on her deathbed that she had killed Max Leclair after he had made sexual advances toward her. According to her story, Gun-a-noot came along the trail moments after the incident and then and there decided to take the blame for Leclair's murder.

By 1919, the now-legendary Gun-a-noot had been at large for 13 years. During his sojourn in the wilderness, he had lost three children to natural causes and longed for a better life for his two remaining offspring. Both his parents had died and his wife was in the midst of a prolonged illness. In essence, Gun-a-noot was tired of running. Word spread throughout the territory that the most notorious fugitive of the era was negotiating a surrender. Friends put him in contact with Stewart Henderson, a graduate of the University of Toronto who had originally headed west to seek gold in the Yukon. In 1919, he was a successful criminal lawyer practising in Victoria.

Henderson met Gun-a-noot in the forest outside Hazelton. To Henderson's surprise, Gun-a-noot had saved up the proceeds of years of trapping while a fugitive. He could easily afford to pay Henderson for his services.

On June 24, 1919, Gun-a-noot, accompanied by his lawyer, gave himself up to authorities at the Hazelton jail. In October of that same year, he stood trial for the murder of Alex McIntosh. After 13 years, Crown witnesses were vague in their recollections. Stewart Henderson tore their testimony to shreds. He relentlessly pointed out that there was no concrete evidence linking his client to the murder, other than a fistfight, which was more the norm than the exception when rugged, tired men have one too many. It took the B.C. jury only fifteen minutes to bring in a verdict of not guilty.

A few months later, no doubt influenced by Gun-a-noot's success, his brother-in-law, Hi-ma-dan, turned himself in. With lawyer Henderson at his side, he was freed following a preliminary hearing.

Gun-a-noot lived on until October 1933, when he collapsed and died while tending his traplines.

# DEBRA HARTMANN

(UNITED STATES)

---

TO say Werner Hartmann was not a devoted family man would be to understate the case. He lived under the same roof with both his current wife and his ex-wife. Folks, that takes guts.

Werner made his bundle in the car-stereo game. It was a prosperous business, but simply didn't pull in enough loot to keep him in the lifestyle to which he had become accustomed. Let's see now, Werner and the ladies lived in Northbrook, a classy suburb of Chicago. They had three vehicles, a Mercedes, a Rolls-Royce and a Lincoln Continental at their disposal. You get the idea. Business was good, but not that good.

On June 8, 1982, Werner was alone in his palatial home. It was a pleasant, warm evening. With nothing else to do, he decided to take a shower. Upon leaving the shower, he wrapped a towel around his body and placed one foot outside the shower stall. Someone poured several shots directly into Werner's chest. The seriously wounded man turned as if to stagger out through the bathroom door. His assailant fired more bullets into his back. Werner Hartmann, 38, lay lifeless on the bathroom floor with a total of 12 bullet holes in his upper torso.

In the wee hours of the morning, Werner's current wife, Debra, returned home after a tour of nightclubs with her 14-year-old stepdaughter. When she went upstairs and found her husband's body in the bathroom, she and her stepdaughter ran out of the house and drove to the nearest police station.

Detectives accompanied Debra to her home. They immediately ruled out robbery as a motive for the murder. Absolutely nothing was missing from the house, and besides, robbers don't usually overkill to such an extent. To the veteran police officers it appeared that someone hated Werner enough to shoot him 12 times. When it was established that a .38-calibre pistol had been the murder weapon, police knew that the killer, in the midst of his murderous spree, would have had to reload in order to keep on shooting.

As the investigation proceeded, detectives learned of Werner's rather weird domestic setup. About a month before the murder, he had contacted his first wife, who lived in Florida with their two daughters. Werner had been married to the woman for 13 years, having tied the knot when he was 20 and the blushing bride a mere 15 years of age. In 1977, they divorced, but before that, wife number one had been bookkeeper for the family business. Now, a month before his demise, Werner had asked his ex-wife to return to Chicago to help him in the business. Debra, his current wife of four years, also worked in the family business. The two women got along so well that Debra invited her husband's former wife and children to move into the large home in Northbrook. All were out of the house on the night of the murder.

An additional complication came to light when a police pathologist informed investigators that several of the fatal bullets had been fired hours before the balance of the bullets had been discharged. All the slugs had been fired from the same .38-calibre weapon.

During the course of the investigation, detectives learned that Debra was having an affair with a tennis pro, one John Korabik. When Debra was faced with the investigators' knowledge, she readily admitted her involvement. In fact, since her husband's death, she had moved in with Korabik. Demure Debra stood to gain approximately a million dollars in insurance from her husband's estate. Surely she had a double-barrelled motive for murder most foul.

Still, there was no proof that Debra had committed the murder. Shortly after the body was found, paraffin tests were conducted on her hands in an effort to trace gunpowder. None was found. Inexplicably, small traces of gunpowder were detected on the hands of Debra's 14-year-old stepdaughter. Months drifted into years. Wife number one returned to Florida with her children.

In 1987, some five years after the murder, out of the blue, convict Ken Kaenel told prison officials that back in 1982 he had been approached by tennis pro John Korabik to murder Werner Hartmann for a fee of $50,000. Korabik had given Ken a .38-calibre pistol to do the job with, but when Ken fired off some rounds in his basement, he found that the pistol misfired. He lost faith in the scheme and returned the weapon. Ken was now coming forward in an attempt to get his own sentence reduced. Such admissions are viewed with a degree of suspicion by police. In order to verify his story, detectives went to Ken's former home and dug the old slugs out of the basement wall. The slugs were compared to those removed from Werner's body. Wouldn't you just know it, they matched perfectly.

Ken agreed to work with police to get the goods on Korabik. Debra and the tennis pro had long since parted company. About a year after Werner's demise, Korabik had been shot in the leg, ostensibly by a prowler. Shortly after the incident, the firm of Debra and Korabik was dissolved.

Detectives outfitted Ken with a wire. He visited with Debra. During the course of their conversation, he told her that he had almost become the killer of her husband, but had turned down Korabik's offer. Debra rose to the bait. She volunteered that she had promised Korabik $200,000 to kill her husband. After the murder, they were planning to go into business together, but her ex-boyfriend had become too greedy and had wanted everything for himself. Their relationship understandably had deteriorated after she shot him in the leg.

In January 1989, Debra Hartmann, John Korabik and Ken Kaenel were arrested and charged with conspiracy to commit murder. Although it was never proved, it is believed that when Debra and her 14-year-old stepdaughter returned home on the morning of the murder, they were met by Korabik, who had killed Werner hours earlier. Realizing that Debra's stepdaughter knew too much, the two schemers had her fire several shots into her father's already-dead body. She was told she was equally guilty of the foul deed and was frightened into silence.

The charges of conspiracy to commit murder were never pursued. Instead, the state felt it could more easily obtain convictions on lesser charges, which carried equally harsh sentences. All three had at various times used the mails to implement their murderous schemes. They were each found guilty of mail fraud. Eight years after the murder, Debra Hartmann was sentenced to 22 years' imprisonment; John Korabik received 20 years; and Ken Kaenel, who was looking to have his sentence reduced, was instead sentenced to 20 years' imprisonment.

Debra Hartmann's stepdaughter who, at the time of the sentencing was 22 years old, was not charged with any crime.

# WALTER HERBERT

(CANADA)

A few miles north of London, Ontario, lies the tiny, peaceful hamlet of Arva. Paved roads have replaced the old dusty thoroughfares, but once you venture off the main road, the area is much the same as it was a hundred years ago when intrigue and bloody murder paid a visit to the Ontario countryside.

Joe Sifton had gone through two wives and was 55 years old if he was a day. You had to hand it to Joe, he looked ten years younger.

Joe lived on his son Gerald's farm, but the two men never got along. It didn't matter what the topic—if Joe said black, Gerald said white. In order to keep peace in the family, Joe moved away to his own farm nearby. Truth is, Joe owned several choice acres in the area. The Sifton clan was never considered poor.

Mary MacFarlane was a fresh, 20-year-old dairy maid who worked for Gerald on his farm. The decaying trial transcript of the case reveals the facts, but only the imagination can do justice to Mary. One can picture the rosy-cheeked lass working away at the butter churn or scurrying around the farm doing her chores. Mary was engaged to Martin Morden, a fine broth of a lad who had formerly worked on Gerald's farm. The young people were to marry the following spring.

Who knows how it started. Maybe it was those rosy cheeks. Maybe Joe was one of those men who require a woman's company. Whatever the reason, 55-year-old Joe took a shine to 20-year-old Mary. Actually, he took more than a shine. He took Mary.

Now don't go blaming Joe. It takes two to tango and the evidence indicates that Mary simply loved to dance. Well, folks, Joe and Mary danced to such an extent that lo and behold, Mary noted the distinct absence of the regular monthly biological occurrence that had never deserted her in the past. Yes, of course, she was pregnant.

Mary approached Joe on Thursday, June 27, 1900, with the disconcerting news. Joe took it well. They would get married. Indeed, there were certain complications. There was the little matter of Mary's engagement to Martin Morden. Mary assured Joe that it was nothing more than a childish infatuation to be ignored. Number two wasn't as easy to dismiss. Gerald would be furious. He stood to inherit his father's substantial estate. The marriage would change all that. Joe assured Mary that Gerald would just have to grin and bear it.

The die was cast. Joe would make arrangements with the Rev. Cooper. The date and time were set. The wedding would take place at 5 p.m. on the following Sunday.

Weddings were never meant to be secret. Mary revealed her marriage plans and delicate condition to Gerald. He reacted as expected and flew into a rage.

That very evening, Joe called on Mary. He was discreet enough not to knock on the farmhouse door, but parked his buggy in the yard. Mary ran out and the pair drove away. That night they told Mary's mother of the impending nuptials. Mrs. MacFarlane was none too happy with the match, but in the end reluctantly gave her blessing.

At 11 p.m., Joe parked his buggy in his son's yard. Before Mary could depart, farmer Edgar Morden suddenly appeared on the scene. Edgar had startling news. In a whisper, he told Joe, "You better get away—out of the country, your life is in danger." Edgar, good friend that he was, insisted that Mary and Joe stay over at his house for their own safety.

The couple took Edgar's advice. They were served supper by Edgar's wife, after which they sat around the stove before going to bed.

On Sunday, Mary awoke brimming with joyful anticipation. This was to be her wedding day. Joe told her the plans. They would drive over to his place, where he would change into his best clothing. From there they would make their way to the church. Despite Edgar's warning, Joe couldn't believe he was in any real danger. After all, Gerald was his own flesh and blood.

Joe had just put on his Sunday best when Gerald showed up with hired hand Walter Herbert, ostensibly to return some equipment. They would place it in the barn. Joe said he would give them a hand when he finished dressing. Mary implored Joe not to go, but he insisted.

Shortly thereafter, Walter Herbert ran to the house and excitedly blurted out, "Oh, Mary, Mr. Sifton has fallen out of the barn and killed himself!" He then called across the road to neighbour John Sinker, "Mr. Sifton fell out of the barn and killed himself!"

Sinker asked, "How did he fall out of the barn?"

"He was knocking boards out of the haymow and fell out of the barn."

Sinker ran to assist his fallen neighbour. He noted an axe and some bricks not far from Joe's head. The badly injured man was carried indoors.

Gerald and Walter rushed the short distance to Dr. David McNeil's home. Gerald told the doctor, "Father is terribly hurt. He fell out of the barn and may not be alive when you get there." Rev. Cooper, a neighbour of Dr. McNeil's, overheard the conversation and he too showed up at Joe's side a few minutes after the doctor. That afternoon, Joe Sifton died.

Initially, Joe's death was considered an accident. Then rumours began to spread throughout the area. Rev. Cooper remembered seeing two pools of blood beside Joe's fallen form, rather unusual for a fall. There were also the axe and bricks close to Joe's head. Dr. McNeil, who was the coroner, also became suspicious.

Twenty-five days after the tragedy, Joe's body was exhumed. There were two distinct and terrible wounds to the man's scalp. Police were called in. They learned that Gerald had offered Martin Morden and his brother, James, $1,000 each if they would help him kill his father. Gerald had suggested a fake suicide. Both men, who had been approached separately, refused the offer. Later, when the investigation into Joe's death intensified, Gerald offered the brothers $1,000 not to tell the authorities about his proposition.

The police, led by famed Detective Inspector John Wilson Murray, picked up Gerald Sifton and Walter Herbert. Both men were charged with murder.

A short time after being taken into custody, Walter confessed. He told authorities that the night before the tragedy, Gerald had offered him $1,000 to be a witness "in case anything should occur to make people suspicious about the job." Walter said that he would go with his boss but would have nothing to do with putting old Joe out of the way.

After breakfast on the day of the murder, they left Gerald's house in a horse-drawn cart. When they arrived at Joe's, Gerald fetched an axe and entered the barn. He then took a large hammer and proceeded to knock boards off the top of the barn up in the haymow. Gerald told Walter, "If my father comes up in the mow, hit him in the head with the axe."

A short while later, Joe came into the barn and climbed up the ladder into the haymow. Walter crouched low. "When his father came up, I struck him with the axe. Gerald came over and struck him three or four blows on the top of the head with the hammer. His father's legs seemed to cave in and he fell through the trapdoor. His legs went through the rungs of the ladder and he hung there. Gerald told me to get down and shove him up. I did so and Gerald pulled him out of the hole and hit him two or three more blows.

"Then we picked him up into the mow and placed him on his back. Gerald picked up the axe and hit him again a couple of times. Gerald took hold of his shoulders and I took his feet and we carried him over and threw him out the end of the barn."

Gerald then told Walter to fetch some bricks and put blood on them. Gerald threw the axe out of the barn and instructed Walter to run to the house and tell Mary of the horrible accident.

A year later, Gerald Sifton was brought to trial. Rarely has a more graphic tale of murder been related in a Canadian court. Defence counsel produced doctors who felt that had Joe received the terrible punishment outlined by Walter Herbert, his injuries would have been more severe. After deliberating for six hours, the jury reported that they could not reach a verdict.

Another long year went by before the entire process was repeated. Once more the crowded courtroom was transfixed by Walter Herbert's account of the murder. After almost five hours of deliberation, the jury returned a verdict most startlingly at odds with the evidence—not guilty. Gerald Sifton was a free man.

Walter Herbert, who had confessed to murder, which the court had ruled was not murder at all, was allowed to change his plea from guilty to not guilty. He, too, was set free.

The notoriety of the murders and the two trials forced the two main participants in the drama to leave the area forever.

# WANDA HOLLOWAY

## (UNITED STATES)

---

WHEN the story broke in 1991, it was beyond comprehension. A woman down Texas way had planned a murder so that her teenage daughter would be assured a place on a seventh-grade cheerleading team. Impossible? Yet it did happen.

Channelview, Texas, is located a few miles outside Houston. It's an industrial blue-collar town, distinct from its sprawling neighbour. Religion is big in Channelview. Most of the hard-working inhabitants belong to one fundamentalist group or another.

Ranking right behind religion for the people of Channelview is football. It is not unusual for 25,000 fans to show up for a high school football game on a Saturday afternoon. Parents groom their sons to excel at the game, knowing full well that only a minuscule few will go on to play college or pro ball. In many cases the athlete's high school football career is the highlight of his entire life.

Just as boys aspire to make their high school football team, ambitious girls attempt to become high school cheerleaders. Positions on the squad are few, and require good looks, athletic skill and a certain charisma. Usually the entire student body votes for candidates to the team. In Texas they take their cheerleading seriously.

Verna Heath and Wanda Ann Holloway were good friends. Both were attractive women in their late thirties. Verna had three children: Sean, age 10, and Aaron and Amber, 14-year old twins. Her husband, Jack, was the manager of a grocery store. Verna was active in church affairs and saw to it that she and her family regularly attended the Truth Tabernacle Pentecostal Church.

Verna had been steeped in the art and lore of cheerleading from childhood. Her mother ran a school solely to train potential cheerleaders. Verna taught at her mother's school. It was only natural that Verna's daughter, Amber, displayed the ability and determination to make her mark in the cheerleading game. At age 14, Amber was one of the finalists trying out for a spot on the Grade 7 cheerleading team.

Wanda Holloway had been married three times. Each time she sashayed down the aisle, she bettered her social and financial position. She had one daughter, Shanna, 14, the product of her ill-fated first marriage to a local man, Tony Harper, whom she had married directly out of high school. But all that was behind her now.

Wanda's third husband, 20 years her senior, was prosperous businessman C.D. Holloway. Wanda had all the creature comforts—fine home, expensive jewellery (some pieces were valued in excess of $100,000) and a Jeep Grand Wagoneer in which to cruise around the countryside. Wanda wanted for very little, but she had a burr under her saddle. There was one thing that eluded her. She longed for her daughter to be a high school cheerleader.

Amber Heath and Shanna Holloway were also good friends. When the two youngsters were in Grade 5, they were deeply involved in training to become future cheerleaders. Their parents encouraged them. Wanda in particular pressed her daughter to excel. She went so far as to build a stage in her garage, complete with lights and mirrors so that Shanna could observe herself going through her routines.

When Shanna finished the fifth grade, Wanda had her transferred to Cobb Elementary Public School. There was a method to her madness. Grade 6 youngsters at Cobb were able to try out to be cheerleaders at Alice Johnson Junior High the following year. Only two girls from the entire student body at Cobb would be chosen.

In the spring of 1989, Shanna tried out for one of the two spots available at the junior high. Wanda kept her daughter on a strict regimen of practice and more practice. She felt Shanna couldn't miss. After all, one of the best cheerleading aspirants, Amber Heath, had chosen to stay at her old school, Channelview Christian, for the sixth grade and so would not be eligible to compete.

Unknown to Wanda, halfway through the school year, Verna Heath went to the junior high school and asked officials to let Amber try out for the school cheerleading team since she was planning to attend the following year. Officials saw no harm in the request and advised Verna that her daughter could try out with the Cobb Elementary applicants.

Here's what happened. Another girl, Summer Rutledge, won the competition. Amber came second. Both girls made the team. Shanna came in third and lost out. Wanda raised Cain with school officials. In her mind, the rules had been changed to include Amber in the competition and eliminate her daughter. Wanda's blind ambition for Shanna became an obsession. She grew to hate Verna and Amber. Next year would be different. Her Shanna would win.

In 1990, Shanna was again a finalist for the team, as was current team member Amber Holloway. Strange as it may seem to us, these youngsters conducted campaigns to garner votes from the student body. The committee governing such events prohibited the use of giveaway gifts by the competing girls. Wanda gave out rulers inscribed with her daughter's name during the campaign. Officials deemed this to be in direct defiance of the rules and disqualified Shanna from competition.

Wanda was fit to be tied. She didn't blame the officials. She blamed Verna Heath and Amber, telling everyone in town in no uncertain terms that Shanna had been cheated out of her rightful place in the sun. When the football season started, Wanda couldn't stand the sight of Amber Heath out there strutting her stuff.

During the 1990 football season, Wanda decided that something drastic had to be done to put those Heaths in their place. She looked up her first husband's brother, Terry Harper. Now, Terry was not what you would call a sterling individual. Over the years he had been arrested for drunk driving, causing a disturbance, and on several drug charges. In recent months, he had been going through one of his crime-free intervals. Terry was also quite the marrying man; he was currently living with his seventh wife.

Wanda approached Terry and didn't mince words, "I hate this girl. I want to get rid of her. I hate her mother. I want to get rid of her." Despite his checkered past, Terry listened in surprise as Wanda asked him if he knew anyone who would do away with Verna Heath and her daughter. Terry related the incident to his brother Tony, who insisted that he contact police. Terry took his brother's advice.

Detectives listened to the unbelievable tale. It was difficult to fathom that this churchgoing wife of a pillar of the community was soliciting the murder of a woman and her teenage daughter all because of a position on a high school cheerleading team.

Police asked Terry if he would wear a wire for his meetings with Wanda. He agreed. A series of encounters took place. The substance of these meetings constituted a verbal contract. Terry would acquire a hit man to kill Verna for $5,000, and Amber for an additional $2,500. Wanda agreed to hand over $2,500 in jewellery as a down payment for Verna's murder, with the balance to be paid in one month. On January 28, 1991, a tape recorder on Terry's body recorded the entire transaction. Wanda handed over the jewellery in a plastic bag. Two days later, she was taken into custody and charged with "solicitation of capital murder," an offence that carries a sentence of five years' to life imprisonment.

Wanda, christened "Pom Pom Mom" by the press, was found guilty. She received a 15-year prison sentence and a $10,000 fine. Two days later, she walked out of court free on $10,000 bail pending appeal. Since 1991, the strange case of Wanda Holloway has not disappeared from public view. In 1994, her defence team was successful in having a new trial ordered on a technicality.

In a civil action, the Heath family sued Wanda and was successful in obtaining a settlement of $150,000 from Wanda's insurance company. Lawyers' fees ate up $50,000 of the settlement.

Meanwhile, life goes on in Channelview. The Holloway family and the Heath family still live only a few blocks from each other. Occasionally, Wanda and Verna bump into each other, but do not exchange pleasantries.

# JULIET HULME AND PAULINE PARKER

(NEW ZEALAND)

IN 1953, at the age of 16, Pauline Parker was an overweight, awkward teenager. She walked with a slight limp, the result of contracting osteomyelitis as a child. Because of her limp, she didn't take part in sports at Christchurch High School in her native New Zealand, but she did own a pony and was an avid member of the Horse and Pony Club.

Pauline's father, Herbert Rieper, was an inoffensive little man who owned a relatively successful wholesale fish business. Herb never did get around to officially marrying Honoura Parker, but their common-law marriage had survived 23 not-always-tranquil years. The Rieper-Parker union produced four children. The eldest, Wendy, 18, was a normal, affectionate daughter who had never caused her parents one moment's anxiety. A younger brother was born mentally ill and was confined to an institution, while a fourth child died at birth.

Dark, brooding Pauline, as we shall soon see, marched to her own drummer. We will never know how Pauline would have turned out had not the fates decreed that her life become entwined with that of 15-year-old Juliet Hulme.

Juliet's father, Dr. Henry Rainesford Hulme, was tall, stooped and cultured. During the Second World War, at age 46, he was one of England's leading mathematical scientists. He was considered a fine acquisition when he became rector of Canterbury University College in Christchurch. With the position came membership in the senate of New Zealand University.

No question about it, Hulme was a heavyweight. But it was not academic recognition that enticed him to leave England for New Zealand. It was his daughter, Juliet. Doctors told him that her tubercular condition would improve in the fresh, clean air of New Zealand. In 1948, Hulme, his aristocratic wife, Hilda, daughter Juliet and his youngest son, Jonathan, arrived in Christchurch.

As part of his compensation, Dr. Hulme was given the use of a 16-room mansion in which to live and entertain. Certainly the brilliant doctor, who held one of the most prestigious positions in Christchurch, could look forward to a bright and promising future.

Things didn't work out as Dr. Hulme planned. After a few years of apparent tranquillity, 15-year-old Juliet met Pauline Parker. Adolescent girls often develop close attachments, but this was different. The two girls were inseparable. The bond between them bothered both families. To Pauline's parents, it appeared the Hulme girl was the cause of all their daughter's problems. Conversely, the Hulmes felt Pauline was an extremely bad influence on Juliet.

But the gods in the heavens decided they had more in store for the two families. Walter Andrew Bowman Perry arrived in Christchurch from England on a prolonged business trip. He became acquainted with the Hulmes, who invited him to be their houseguest in a self-contained flat that was part of their large home. Walt was delighted to partake of Henry's hospitality. Unfortunately, he partook of Henry's wife as well.

One fine afternoon, when everyone was supposed to be out, Juliet strolled into her mother's bedroom. Who should she find there in bed with Mummy but Walter Andrew Bowman Perry? Things were never quite the same between Mummy and Juliet after that.

Dr. Hulme picked this inopportune time to resign his position at the university. He told his family he had decided to return to England with son Jonathan. Dr. Hulme suspected his wife of adultery and his daughter of having a lesbian affair with Pauline Parker. He discussed the situation with Pauline's father, but nothing seemed to do any good. Dr. Hulme decided he would take Juliet as far as South Africa. He would continue on his way to England and she would return to Christchurch.

When Juliet heard of this scheme, she was furious. She wouldn't budge a step unless Pauline went with her. The girls asked Pauline's mother for permission to have Pauline go on the trip. They were bluntly refused.

The human mind is a complicated mechanism. The more the two girls thought about it, the more it seemed to them that Honoura Parker was the one who stood in the way of their happiness. They decided to kill her.

On June 22, 1954, an overcast winter's day in Christchurch, Honoura, Pauline and Juliet walked together along a path. The murder scenario was already in motion. That morning, Juliet had brought half a brick to her friend's house. Now that very brick was in Pauline's pocket inside the foot of an old stocking. Pauline pointed to some pretty pink stones on the path. As her mother stooped to examine the pebbles, Pauline extracted her homemade murder weapon and set it crashing over and over again on her mother's head. She passed the bloody stocking to Juliet, who proceeded to hit Honoura repeatedly. Together, the two girls beat Honoura Parker to death.

Pauline ran to a nearby kiosk, shouting, "It's Mummy. I think she's dead. We tried to carry her. She was too heavy."

Hysterically, Juliet added, "Yes, it's her mother. She's covered with blood."

Pauline interrupted, "We were coming back along the track. Mummy tripped on a plank and hit her head when she landed. She kept falling and her head kept banging and bumping as she fell." The girls washed their hands. Later, witnesses said the pair could be heard laughing uncontrollably as they washed away the blood.

Police examined the 45 wounds that had been inflicted to Honoura Parker's head and detained the girls for questioning. Three weeks later, they were charged with murder. Both girls confessed, making the salient point of New Zealand's most infamous crime not who committed the murder but whether the perpetrators were sane or insane.

The star of the proceedings was not a witness, but Pauline's diary. It remains one of the most diabolical pieces of evidence ever read in a courtroom. Here are a few excerpts:

> February 13, 1954. *Why could not Mother die? Dozens, thousands of people are dying. Why not Mother?*
>
> April 28, 1954. *Anger against Mother boiling inside me as she is the main obstacle in my path. Suddenly, means of ridding myself of the obstacle occur to me. If only she were to die.*
>
> June 21, 1954. *We have decided to use a brick in a stocking rather than a sandbag. Mother has fallen in with our plan beautifully.*
>
> June 22, 1954. *I felt very excited last night and sort of night-before-Christmas.*
>
> On the top of the page dated June 22, Pauline printed: THE DAY OF THE HAPPY EVENT.

As the trial progressed, it was revealed that the two girls spent much of their time writing stories, which they believed were potential best-sellers if they could ever make their way to America and have them published. Honoura Parker had crystallized in their minds as the main obstacle standing between them and their goal. As a result, she had to die. The thought of being apprehended and punished had never entered their minds.

After retiring for 2 hours and 13 minutes, the New Zealand jury found both girls guilty of murder. They were sentenced to prison "during Her Majesty's pleasure," which is usually around 25 years. Pauline Parker and Juliet Hulme spent only four years in prison before they were released.

Author's Note: The movie *Heavenly Creatures* is based on this old New Zealand murder. New Zealand journalists have traced Juliet Hulme to a small village in Scotland, where she now lives. The literary world was shocked to learn that Juliet Hulme is internationally renowned mystery writer Anne Perry, who has written more than twenty murder mystery novels.

# DAILRENE INGRAM AND MATTHEW PEIRIS

(SRI LANKA)

---

FROM time to time the faith-healing business has had the misfortune to fall into disrepute. Remember Mr. Swaggart who, between leading assorted heathens to the light, took great joy in bedding down with prostitutes. Then there was Jim Bakker, who was more concerned with renting the rooms of his luxury hotel than with saving souls.

Now let me introduce you to Father Matthew Peiris, who was somewhat of a heavyweight in his chosen field of healing the afflicted. The good father, a native of Sri Lanka, received his religious education at Lincoln Theological College in England. He held down several ecclesiastical positions there before returning to his native land.

While in England, Father Matthew had met and married Eunice Lois, herself the daughter of a preacher man who claimed to have a direct line to the Archangel Michael. At the time our story unfolds, the couple had three adult children: a son, Munilal; and two daughters, Mihiri and Mairani. Obviously, Father Matthew was partial to the letter M.

For years Father Matthew went about praying, healing and curing with a degree of success. At age 60, something happened to the man of the cloth that cannot be laid at the feet of his profession. It seems that Father Matthew had earthly concerns known to lure less religious men off the straight and narrow. Shall we get right to it?

In 1976, Eunice returned to England for a visit. During her absence, Father Matthew acquired a secretary. He was writing a book and planning to take a future book tour with his wife. The secretary could take care of the vicarage while they were gone.

Dailrene Ingram was a beautiful, ripe 27-year-old when she applied for the position. She had been married for eight years, had three young children and an unemployed husband named Russel. Never mind, Father Matthew would take care of all the problems. To alleviate Mrs. Ingram's pressing financial situation, he moved her entire family into the vicarage. He was successful in finding a job for Russel as an advertising salesman for a local newspaper. Everyone was happy as a bed of clams. Especially Father Matthew. Before you could say Casanova, he was bedding down with Dailrene right there in the vicarage. For shame.

Well, now, Mrs. Peiris returned from her trip abroad, which was most inconvenient for the lovers. Still, they made do with lovemaking on the sly, so to speak. Dailrene in particular was in a tight pickle. With three children and a husband underfoot, it was difficult to find the time and the energy to make love to Father Matthew. It was most annoying on Sundays to have to drag hubby and the kids to church in order to hear her lover's sermon, complete with occasional healing sessions.

Something had to give. Russel was the first to take ill. One fine morning, this healthy athletic specimen could hardly get out of bed. In fact, he remained in bed for five weeks. Rather than call in curious doctors, Father Matthew attempted to cure Russel by his own devices. When incanting a few choice phrases over Russel's stomach failed to bring the desired results, Russel was rushed to hospital. He was hooked up to a saline and dextrose drip, which improved his condition markedly. A few weeks later, he was sufficiently well to be sent home to the vicarage and into the care of Father Matthew and his own ever-loving wife, Dailrene.

When Dailrene was asked why Father Matthew was giving her husband so many pills, she became indignant. "Father knows what he is doing," she replied. The good Father's eldest son, Munilal, also inquired why his father was purchasing so many tablets. He never received a satisfactory explanation. Father Matthew had been buying as many as a hundred tablets of the drug Euglucon at a time.

Father Matthew tried to think of everything. He felt he should have independent witnesses in the vicarage and decided to invite another preacher, Russell Jackson, and his wife, Bridget, ostensibly to observe Russel Ingram's agony. Four days after the patient returned from the hospital, he died. Later, Jackson testified that the sleeping arrangements at the vicarage were somewhat unorthodox. Father Matthew was sleeping with Dailrene, while poor Russel was locked in a room all by his lonesome. Bridget had a most unusual and incriminating story to tell. She revealed that she had overheard a conversation between Father Matthew and Dailrene after Russel's death. He said, "Don't worry, Dailrene, soon I will be in the same condition as you, bereft of a partner."

Russel's death was attributed to hypoglycemia, which had caused irreversible brain damage. Hypoglycemia is due to an extremely low level of sugar in the blood. Diabetes, which is caused by too much sugar in the blood, is sometimes treated with Euglucon. Small amounts of Euglucon, such as a single 2.5 mg tablet, are prescribed to bring down blood sugar. Father Matthew had given Russel, who had suffered from no illness whatsoever, as many as seven tablets at one time, telling Russel that a doctor had prescribed the tablets. He had lied.

A few months after Russel's untimely demise, it was Eunice's turn. She lapsed into unconsciousness and was diagnosed with hypoglycemia. As he had done during Russel's illness, Father Matthew led doctors astray with false information.

He did everything in his power to make an accurate diagnosis an impossibility. Eunice remained unconscious for 47 days before dying. Doctors were extremely suspicious of the death. It could have been suicide or homicide. Several put their feelings on record.

In May, 1979, Father Matthew and Dailrene were taken into custody and charged with the murders of Russel Ingram and Eunice Peiris. The case, built solely on circumstantial and medical evidence, was a complicated one. It took four years for the unholy duo to be placed on trial. The trial lasted 163 days.

Defence lawyers contended that death had been due to natural causes, which accounted for the low levels of sugar in the blood of the victims. Similar to the more recent O.J. Simpson defence, the pair's lawyers claimed that samples of blood had been contaminated during the testing process.

The prosecution came up with a witness who had overheard Father Matthew tell his wife that that Christmas would be her last on earth. Other witnesses revealed the strange sleeping arrangements they had observed on visits to the vicarage.

In the end, Father Matthew and Dailrene were done in by the medical evidence, which proved that Russel and Eunice had died from hypoglycemia. The condition was induced by medication, namely the drug Euglucon, which had been purchased by none other than Father Matthew. Witnesses testified that Dailrene knew what was going on all the time. In Dailrene's closet, police found a book on the topic of sugar in the blood. She had been reading up on the subject.

Father Matthew Peiris and Dailrene Ingram were found guilty of conspiracy to commit murder and murder in both cases. They were sentenced to death, but their sentences were later commuted to life imprisonment.

# ZEIN ISA

## (UNITED STATES)

TO their customers at the Alliance Market, the Isa family appeared to be a happy, industrious one, busy carving out a new life for themselves in America. Their small Shaw Boulevard grocery store in St. Louis was light-years removed from the life they had led in Palestine.

Maria and Zein Isa had four daughters. The three eldest girls worked diligently in the store and strictly adhered to their father's stern Muslim code. Although Zein had become a naturalized American citizen, he felt compelled to maintain his Middle Eastern ways, as his father had before him. To Zein, modern American customs and loose moral standards were for heathens, certainly not for his family.

The three older daughters never questioned their father's wishes. Their lives were directed by the head of the family which, to Zein's thinking, was as it should be. Not so to the youngest daughter, Tina. In 1989, 16-year-old Tina was a beautiful youngster, full of the joy of life. She was a popular, straight-A student at Roosevelt High School. A natural athlete, Tina was on the school's soccer, tennis and hockey teams. She was also a member of the school band.

Zein hated the idea of his daughter taking part in any activities outside the home and the store. He berated Tina on a daily basis. Tina's three oldest sisters, who had been brought up so strictly themselves, sided with their father. If his religious values had been good enough for them, surely Tina should follow his wishes. On occasion, when Zein's wife, Maria, took Tina's part, the wrath of the entire family fell on her shoulders. Soon she was pleading with Tina to change her ways.

But Tina believed America was a land where one should be able to express one's free will. She was doing nothing wrong, simply living the life of an American girl. When her father talked in Arabic to his Mideastern friends, Tina couldn't understand why he didn't speak English. On one occasion, American officials had questioned her father about his association with the Palestine Liberation Organization (PLO). Tina didn't want to know about her father's political leanings. She merely wanted to be herself. It wasn't easy.

There were continual embarrassing incidents. Once Zein, accompanied by his eldest daughters, practically broke up the junior prom dance Tina was attending by dragging her off the gymnasium floor. In her senior year, Tina was forbidden to accompany her class on a trip to the nation's capital. That summer, she begged her parents to allow her to attend a six-week summer course at the University of Missouri. They wouldn't consider such an idea.

In 1989, Tina made the acquaintance of Cliff Walker, a tall, good-looking 18-year-old who often shopped at the Alliance Market. When Zein learned that Tina and Cliff were dating, he was furious. Cliff was black and Zein didn't approve. Despite her father's constant tirades on the subject, Tina continued to see Cliff.

Zein fervently objected to his daughter's lifestyle. He believed there was no hope for his youngest child and convinced his wife that Tina could only be saved by having her leave this world for a far better one beyond. He felt the family's honour was at stake. He believed that Tina was a disgrace to herself, her family and her heritage. In time, Maria came around to his way of thinking.

In November 1989, Tina told her family she was taking a nighttime job at a nearby Wendy's. Zein forbade it. His own store had been good enough for her sisters and it should be good enough for Tina, he told her. Over her father's objections, after finishing her school work, Tina went to work at the fast-food outlet for the first time. She proved to be an excellent employee and a joy to have in the establishment. At the conclusion of her shift, Cliff walked her back to her Delor Street apartment.

One evening, Zein and Maria were waiting for Tina when she got home. They were beside themselves with anger. Their daughter had disobeyed them once too often. Furious Maria yelled at Tina as soon as the apartment door opened. Zein appeared from the kitchen, his right hand concealed behind his back. He accused his daughter of being a prostitute and told her she was a disgrace to the family. Mother and father shouted that they would throw Tina out of the apartment and out of their lives. Tears streaming down her cheeks, Tina volunteered to leave. Her father screamed, "You she-devil, don't you know this is your last day? You are going to die tonight."

From behind his back, Zein extracted a vicious-looking, long boning knife. Maria, who weighed 200 pounds, clutched her daughter's hair from behind and threw her to the floor. Zein bent over Tina and thrust the knife into her chest six times. He shouted at the top of his voice, "Die, die, my daughter."

Then Zein picked up the phone and called each of his daughters, informing them of Tina's death. He called police and told them that Tina had attacked him, but with the aid of his wife he was able to thwart the attack. Unfortunately, in the act of self-defence, he had killed his daughter.

Detectives were dispatched to the Isa apartment. They were amazed at Maria and Zein's calm demeanor as they related how their insane daughter had arrived home demanding money from them. When they refused, she had lunged at them with a knife. Zein had managed to direct the knife away from himself, as his wife had attempted to pull Tina away.

It didn't take long for detectives to learn of the animosity between the entire family and the attractive teenager. An autopsy proved Zein's story didn't wash. The six stab wounds were very close together, which is not compatible with a wild struggle. In addition, the angle of the wounds indicated the victim was lying on her back when the knife entered her chest.

Maria and Zein were charged with the murder of their daughter. Before the trial, the FBI contacted St. Louis police. Because of Zein's involvement with the PLO, the Isa apartment had been bugged for over a year. Every argument and threat directed toward Tina had been recorded. The buildup of hate was there for all to hear. Most relevant of all was the recording of the actual murder. Tina was heard to frantically plead, "Mother, please help!" To this plea, her mother responded, "Shut up."

Maria and Zein claimed self-defence, but the Missouri jury found both defendants guilty of murder. Both were sentenced to death. In 1993, the Missouri Supreme Court overturned Maria's death sentence because the jury had been given flawed instructions. However, her conviction was upheld and she is currently serving a life sentence in prison with no possibility of parole. Zein Isa awaits his fate on death row in Missouri State Prison.

In April 1993, the Isa murder case took a strange turn, when the FBI revealed there might have been an additional motive for the murder of Tina Isa. A federal indictment stated that Zein and three other men in St. Louis were associated with the terrorist arm of the PLO known as Abu Nidal. The indictment accused the four defendants of conspiring to kill Tina, allegedly because she might reveal the Abu Nidal's St. Louis connections. The indictment also accuses the four men of terrorism and of planning to blow up the Israeli embassy in Washington.

# JACK KIRSCHKE

(UNITED STATES)

IF ever a married couple had a unique marital arrangement, it was the one that existed between Elaine Terry Kirschke and her husband, Jack. They agreed in writing that for a full year ending on May 1, 1967, they would not have sex with each other, nor with anyone else. They also agreed that after that date they would continue to live together, but would go their separate ways sexually, if you get my so obvious drift.

Now, folks, these were no lightweights, not by a long shot. Until she sold her lucrative business, Elaine Terry was one of California's leading fashion designers. Jack was considered one of the most accomplished criminal prosecutors in the United States. He held down the position of deputy district attorney and appeared to be a shoo-in for a judgeship. At 45 years of age, handsome Jack had the world by the tail. Elaine, 43, was an attractive redhead who looked 10 years younger. The pair had been married for 24 years and had two adult children.

On April 8, 1967, Frank Cornell, who lived in the same apartment building as the Kirschkes at 185 Rivo Alto Canal in Naples, California, thought he heard a loud noise emanating from the Kirschkes' home at 2:30 a.m. Later that morning, when things were abnormally quiet in the Kirschke apartment, he sent a relative, James Miller, downstairs to take a look.

James couldn't get a response to his loud knocking. He peered through a window and saw two blood-spattered bodies in the bedroom. James called police.

The bodies were quickly identified as Elaine Kirschke and Bill Drankhan. Bill was a well-known local businessman. Among his many accomplishments were his ability to fly a plane and his acrobatics in bed with other men's wives.

Under the circumstances, it was most natural that hubby Jack was strongly suspected of drilling his wife and her lover. Jack was detained as he sped through the Mojave Desert towards Los Angeles.

When he was informed that his wife and Bill were dead, Jack suggested that they must have been shot by a robber, which was rather revealing since no one had mentioned where they had been killed or that they had been shot to death.

Jack refused to take a lie detector test and was immediately charged with two counts of murder.

Detectives soon learned of the strange marital arrangement between Jack and Elaine. They also learned that Bill had been bedding down with Elaine for months and that all their acquaintances knew it. No doubt Jack had found out.

Indignant, Jack swore he was innocent of any involvement in the murders. He told his interrogators that he had prosecuted many men, any of whom might have sought revenge. One of them had obviously mistaken Bill for him.

Jack's theory made a lot of sense, particularly when doctors estimated that the time of death was between midnight and 4 a.m. Jack claimed that on the night before the morning of the double murder, he had driven in his daughter's 1963 beat-up Volkswagen to the Los Angeles International Airport to catch a plane to Las Vegas. He had a speaking engagement the following morning at a Rotary Club convention.

However, at the airport, he learned that three consecutive flights at 8:30 p.m., 9:30 p.m. and 11:30 p.m. were totally booked. At 11 p.m. he gave up and decided to drive to Las Vegas. He drove through San Bernardino to Yermo, where he purchased gas between three-thirty and four in the morning.

At around sunup he arrived in Las Vegas and spent a few hours gambling in order to pass the time until he was scheduled to speak to the Rotary Club. Jack gave his speech and was in the Volkswagen on his way back to Los Angeles when he was stopped and informed of his wife's death.

Jack's attempt to get on three successive flights at the airport was confirmed. Two Yermo gas station attendants, Dennis Baily and Gene Ledet, were located. Both swore they had served gas to Kirschke around three-thirty on the morning in question.

Frank Cornell told police that he had heard a noise, which could have been gunshots, around 2:30 a.m. Another neighbour stated that at 4 a.m. he got up to use the bathroom, looked out the window and saw the light go out in the Kirschke bedroom.

There seemed to be no way that Jack Kirschke could be the killer. If the murders had taken place at 2:30 a.m., it would have been impossible for Jack to have driven the 155 miles to Yermo and have been there between 3:30 and 4 a.m. He would have to have averaged 103 miles an hour in the 1963 Volkswagen which, upon testing, wouldn't go over 80 miles per hour. Of course, if the killer had remained in the Kirschke residence until 4 a.m. when the light was turned off, it was out of the question for Jack to have been the guilty party.

Police went to work in an attempt to dismantle Jack's seemingly airtight alibi. They learned that shortly after the crime, a private detective had accompanied Jack to the garage where Baily and Ledet were employed. At that time, Baily didn't recognize Kirschke. Ledet only said that Kirschke looked vaguely familiar. They also vacillated about the exact time that Kirschke might have stopped for gasoline. Detectives felt that these two men had not lied about the time that Kirschke had been in the garage, but were simply confused.

When the gas station attendants faltered in their evidence, the possible scenario changed abruptly. The murder could have taken place at 2:30 a.m. when Cornell heard what he thought could have been shots. Kirschke would have had plenty of time to drive to Las Vegas and give his speech to the Rotarians at 9 a.m.

Homicide detectives still had to cope with the neighbour's evidence that the bedroom light had gone out at 4 a.m. Once more, they examined the murder scene. This time an investigator had the presence of mind to try to switch on the light. It didn't work. Upon examination, it was discovered that the lightbulb had burned out. The neighbour who had seen the light go out hadn't been privy to the killer turning out the light. He had merely seen darkness envelop the room because the bulb burned out.

Bullets removed from the victims' bodies had been fired from a .38-calibre revolver. The slugs were in such good shape that experts were able to ascertain that they had been fired from a rather rare revolver, a Harrington and Richards Defender. Jack admitted that he had once owned such a weapon. It had been given to him as a souvenir of a case he had prosecuted years before, but he hadn't seen the weapon for months.

The hunt was on for Jack's .38-calibre Defender. Fields and ditches near the murder scene were searched without success. The serial number, 22068, was known to authorities. They traced the weapon to the manufacturer. They learned that it had initially been sold to a sporting goods store in Long Beach, which had been burglarized. One of the weapons stolen had been a Harrington and Richards Defender, serial number 22068. Later the criminals were apprehended and the weapon returned to the sporting goods store. It was verified that while these criminals were in possession of the revolver, it had been used to shoot a woman, one Toni White, in the hip.

After an exhaustive search, detectives found the evidence box pertaining to the Toni White shooting. Inside a dusty file cabinet, in a sealed envelope, were bullets taken from Ms. White's rump. A ballistics expert compared the bullets with those taken from the bodies of Elaine Kirschke and Bill Drankhan. They matched. In this way police were able to prove that the gun given to Kirschke as a souvenir had been used to shoot his wife and her lover.

The Kirschke trial took 121 days to complete. A California jury took another six days to reach a verdict. They found Jack guilty of murder in the first degree and the famous prosecutor was sentenced to life imprisonment.

Jack Kirschke spent eleven and a half years in prison before being paroled in February, 1977. He has since remarried and today lives with his wife, Sara, on an island off the coast of Washington State.

# RALPH LEAHY

(CANADA)

"THERE was no direct evidence that murder had been committed, not even a body, yet I knew that Viola had been murdered, and I had a pretty good idea who killed her. The case was bizarre in many ways," said Inspector Bill Perrin of the Ontario Provincial Police. Sitting in his office at police headquarters talking about the apprehension of murderers, I got the distinct impression that once Bill Perrin becomes convinced of something, he doesn't let go until he either proves or disproves his beliefs.

Inspector Perrin now operates out of the Anti-Rackets Branch, but for years was attached to the Criminal Investigation Branch, where he was in charge of many of Ontario's strange murder cases. None was stranger than that of Viola Leahy.

The Leahy farm is situated along Rural Route 4, outside Lakefield, Ontario, and has been in the Leahy family for as long as anyone can remember, certainly four or five generations. Jim Leahy worked hard on the farm, and supplemented his income by operating heavy excavation equipment. Everyone agrees that Jim was one of the best operators in the Peterborough area. Viola, his wife of over 25 years, also had interests that drew her away from the farm. Before her marriage, she received formal training as a registered nursing aide, a vocation she continued to follow after she became Mrs. Leahy. Both Jim and Viola had independent natures, and this independent bent, combined with their physical absence from each other, drove a wedge into an otherwise normal relationship.

Viola in particular craved some sort of social life. She enjoyed taking in the local dances, and sometimes visited a tavern with a woman friend, Emgard Woodzack, although Viola never drank anything stronger than a soft drink.

The long-standing marriage deteriorated until, finally, in 1972, Jim and Viola had an argument that turned into a fight. Viola charged her husband with assault. He was forced to appear in family court in Peterborough, where the charge was dropped. Viola then separated from Jim for a while and took legal action to obtain a half share of the family farm. For some reason known only to herself, she changed her mind and returned to live with Jim. Things were never the same after that. The Leahys settled down to a strange and unusual lifestyle. Viola supported herself. Jim did likewise. They conversed only when necessary. Viola continued to cook Jim's food and wash his clothing. They slept in separate rooms.

Every Friday, Viola would leave the farm and visit with Emgard. She always returned on Monday. And so, month after month, year after year, the strained lives of Viola and Jim Leahy continued.

Jim's brother Emmett worked a farm directly south of the Leahy farm. Actually, Jim had sold the house to Emmett some years before. Besides farming, Emmett had been steadily employed at the Westclox plant in Peterborough for the past 25 years. Emmett was raising four sons; the oldest, Ralph, was nineteen.

Although all was not well with the Leahy marriage, there was really nothing to distinguish them from hundreds of other farmers throughout the country: two brothers with adjoining farms, supplementing their incomes by working away from the soil—hardly the scene for a bizarre and unusual murder.

In 1975, Jim suffered a fractured skull in a farm accident. From that time on, Emmett and his sons gave Jim a helping hand with the chores. Viola, too, was not well. She suffered from arteriosclerosis, hardening of the arteries, which resulted in serious memory losses.

Because of the coolness between husband and wife, Viola came to depend a great deal on her brother and sister-in-law, Jack and Zetta Leeson. She phoned them every day. If she wanted to go anywhere, it was the Leesons who picked her up and brought her back to the farm.

On Friday, September 17, 1976, Viola was picked up by Jack Leeson and taken to Peterborough, where she stayed with her friend Emgard. Two days later, on Sunday, Jim was admitted to Sunnybrook Hospital in Toronto to have bone chips removed from his skull. This confinement was the result of the fracture he had suffered two years previously. Thus Jim was away from the farm from September 19 until his return from Sunnybrook on October 3. He was never to see his wife again.

Meanwhile, Viola's movements are well documented. On Monday, September 20th, she paid a visit to her doctor in Peterborough. Jack and Zetta Leeson picked her up at Emgard's and gave her a lift to Dr. Flak's office. He prescribed pills and rest. The Leesons then drove Viola back to the farm. They helped the 65-year-old woman into the house with her luggage. They left the farm at about 7 p.m. It was the last time they ever saw Viola.

A half-hour later Emgard received a phone call from her friend. The conversation was normal in every way. Viola gave no indication of unusual stress or anxiety. Emgard assumed that everything was fine.

Next day, Zetta Leeson tried to reach Viola on the phone all day, with no success. On Wednesday, Zetta and Jack drove to the farm. They found Viola's luggage exactly where they had placed it the previous Monday. There were several cigarette butts in an ashtray, which bothered the Leesons, because they knew that neither Viola nor Jim smoked.

On Thursday, they notified Emmett Leahy that Viola could not be located. Together with Emmett, they searched the farmhouse but found nothing that could lead them to the missing woman. On Saturday, five days after she made the phone call to Emgard, Viola was reported missing by Jack and Zetta Leeson. The report was turned in to E.D. Martin of the Peterborough detachment of the OPP.

During the preliminary investigation into the missing-person's case, the OPP turned up three pieces of information that would be of the utmost significance. David Ramsay had cleaned the furnace of the Leahy home on September 22. The only person he had come in contact with on the property was young Ralph Leahy. Ramsay stated that the boy seemed to be lurking near an open barn door when he spotted him. Ramsay was interested in getting someone to sign his bill that the work on the furnace had been completed. He thought it odd that when he approached Ramsay with the bill, the boy said, "I'm not supposed to be here." But Ralph signed the bill.

Another bit of information that gave the investigators food for thought was Emmett Leahy's statement that although he was taking care of his missing sister-in-law's mail, it had disappeared from his house. Jack, Zetta and Emmett remembered that when they searched the house on September 23, Ralph had mentioned that he'd seen Viola at about 8 a.m. on September 21. He thought she was heading for the bus.

The investigation continued. Jim Leahy came home on October 3, into the midst of an investigation into his wife's disappearance. All of Viola's personal effects were found in the house. Increasingly, it became apparent that she had met with foul play.

Two weeks went by. The Lakefield postmaster received an unusual piece of mail. It was a change-of-address notice apparently signed by Viola Leahy, directing her mail to the Sudbury post office, general delivery. The card was turned over to the OPP. They quickly established that the signature on the card was a forgery.

In the meantime, Ralph left his father's farm to seek employment in Edmonton, Alberta. The police checked his handwriting against the signature on the change-of-address card and established that the signature had been forged by Ralph.

Detective Inspector A.D.R. Smith and Constable G. Katz thought that Viola Leahy had been murdered. Despite snide insinuations that she had taken off with a man, neither policeman believed it was true. They flew to Edmonton to interrogate Ralph. At first he denied forging the signature. Then he admitted to having done so, stating that a friend of Viola's had given him $50 to do it. Ralph was returned to Peterborough, and charged with uttering a forged document. On June 9, 1977, he received three months' imprisonment, to be followed by a two years' probation.

On June 13, Detective Inspector Bill Perrin was assigned to the case. "I believed that Viola Leahy was dead," the inspector says, "and that the case could only be solved through her nephew, Ralph Leahy." Perrin made the decision to place Constable Bill Campbell, of the Intelligence Branch of the OPP, into jail with the suspect. Within a day, Campbell was playing cards with Ralph in the Quinte Regional Detention Centre in Napanee. Other prisoners were preparing for a transfer to Kingston Penitentiary. Ralph told his new friend that he too would probably be transferred before he finished his current sentence. He bragged that he and a friend had killed someone during the course of a robbery. Campbell didn't press the matter, but made a date to get in touch with Ralph when both men were released.

On August 9, Ralph Leahy was released. Unknown to him, he was under constant surveillance by the OPP. The following night Campbell met with Ralph at the Jolly Roger Lounge of the Holiday Inn in Peterborough. During their conversation, Ralph boasted to the undercover agent that he had killed his aunt the evening after his Uncle Jim had gone to hospital in Toronto. Once Ralph began talking, he wouldn't stop. He confessed to 17 or 18 robberies, and bragged about serving two years in jail. Ralph thought he was impressing Campbell, who had posed as a member of an auto-theft gang working between Montreal and Ontario. Ralph wanted a job with the gang.

Campbell didn't believe any of Ralph's bragging, with one exception. He firmly believed that he had a murderer on the line. They made a date to meet again on August 13. This time Campbell brought along Constable Terry Hall, posing as his brother and fellow member of the auto-theft gang. Ralph was duly impressed, talked incessantly of having killed his aunt. Late into the night the three men talked. In the end, Ralph promised to show them where he had hidden Viola's body.

The following Friday, the two officers and Ralph left the Holiday Inn at 1:30 a.m. for the Leahy farm. In deep bush beside a swamp, the three man dug for a body. Later, the officers were to relate that while Ralph dug, he made derogatory remarks about his aunt. "You old bitch, where are you? You've given me enough trouble."

Throughout the early morning, the men dug by flashlight, but Ralph couldn't find his victim's body. He promised his two friends that if they returned with him at some future date, he would produce the missing woman.

On August 25, at 11:05 p.m., Inspector Perrin decided to pull the plug on the investigation. He arrested Ralph and, at the same time, picked up Ralph's girlfriend, Barbara Hartwick, for questioning. At the time, Ralph remarked, "You'll never find her in a million years." When questioned, Barbara revealed that Ralph had admitted to her, back in November 1976, that he had killed his aunt. He said he had shot her three times.

Perrin interrogated the suspect. Ralph claimed he had nothing to say. Then he informed Perrin, "You made a mistake picking me up today—you should have waited a day and you would have had the body."

In the wee hours of Friday, August 26, Ralph indicated that he wanted to see Perrin. Perrin questioned and informed the suspect of his rights: "Are you prepared to show us where Viola is buried? You know you don't have to show us or do anything that may be used as evidence, Ralph."

At the ungodly hour of 3:30 a.m., Ralph Leahy led the officers to the area beside the swamp where he and the two undercover agents had dug previously. He stated that he had marched his aunt down to the edge of the swamp, and had shot her three times with her husband's .22-calibre rifle. The murder weapon was turned over to Perrin.

Digging began later the same day, but try as they might, they couldn't find the body. Finally Perrin brought in some heavy earth-moving equipment, and on Tuesday, August 30, the shovel uncovered the body of Viola Leahy. She had been shot three times in the area of the chest and abdomen. Ballistics tests confirmed that two of the bullets had been fired from the Leahys' .22 rifle.

Later, Ralph told doctors that he hated his aunt. The killing had not been a spur-of-the-moment sort of thing. He had mulled over the possibility of killing her for several weeks. After murdering his aunt at the edge of the swamp, he left her where she fell, but returned the next day with a shovel and buried her. He told the doctors that his aunt was not worth the time he was going to spend in prison. He had no remorse for what he had done and was only sorry that he would have to go to jail.

The rather smallish five-foot-six-inch farm boy had killed his aunt because he didn't like her. All indications are that she was kind and considerate to her nephew.

Viola Leahy had spent 11 months and 10 days buried on her farm. On February 4, 1977, her nephew, Ralph Leahy, was sentenced to life imprisonment.

# GEORGE LEMAY

(CANADA)

GEORGE Lemay is unique. Strongly suspected of one murder, acquitted of another, he was also the brains behind one of Canada's most dramatic robberies. Toss in recent capers such as assorted burglaries and trafficking in drugs and you begin to get the idea.

George was born into a well-to-do Montreal family. His early years gave no hint of what was to follow. His mother employed George in her successful real estate business.

In 1950, George met beautiful 19-year-old Huguette Daoust, a Montreal bank secretary. Huguette was petite, weighing no more than 105 pounds, with dark hair that accentuated her large, bright eyes. George fell hard. He pursued Huguette with a passion, until the lovely girl from the respected family consented to marry him.

On May 19, 1951, over the objections of her family, Huguette and George were wed. They honeymooned in Florida, familiar territory to George, who had often been on fishing expeditions to the Sunshine State.

When the newlyweds returned to Montreal, it was evident that they were having difficulty adjusting to married life. For one thing, George didn't seem to be very interested in working for a living. For another, he displayed a nasty temper.

Seven months passed, strained months for the good-looking young couple. When George suggested a second honeymoon in Florida, Huguette thought it was a great idea. On December 27, the Lemays drove to Miami in George's red Studebaker convertible. They rented a room and fished every day.

On Friday, January 4, 1952, they went fishing along the Florida Keys, stopping at Tom's Harbor Bridge #4. According to George, they were fishing off the bridge at around 8 p.m. Huguette, clad only in a halter and shorts, complained of the cold. She told George that she was going back to the Studebaker to change into something warmer.

Fifteen minutes passed. When George's fishing line broke, he walked the hundred feet to the car to get a new line. It was only then that he missed his wife. George shouted. He peered into the car. His wife's shorts and halter were on the seat. A sweater and a pair of jeans were missing. No doubt Huguette had wandered off, but as time passed, George became frantic. He raced to a toll gate and, crying hysterically, told attendant Les Baker, "My wife has been kidnapped! Stop all cars! Have them searched!" Baker called the Florida Highway patrol.

Despite an extensive investigation, and despite the suspicion that George may have been involved in his wife's disappearance, no trace of Huguette Lemay has ever been uncovered since that day 47 years ago when she went fishing with her husband.

For the next ten years, George, who maintained a chalet near St. Jerome in the Laurentians, continued to get into minor scrapes with the law. On the Dominion Day weekend of 1961, he graduated to the big time. That's the weekend he directed the novel and daring break-in of the Ste-Catherine St. branch of the Bank of Nova Scotia in Montreal.

Lemay had rented a building across the street from the bank. Using walkie-talkies, he directed his confederates as they worked all weekend digging a tunnel into the bank's safety deposit box vault. Three hundred and seventy-seven safety deposit boxes were looted. The official loss reported was well over $600,000, but it's believed that many victims were reluctant to disclose the amounts removed from their safety deposit boxes. Some feel that George relieved the bank's clients of over $4 million that weekend.

Within two weeks, the gang was rounded up. Andrew Lemieux, age 27, his brother Yvon, 19, their sister, Lise, Jacques Lajoie, 37, and Roland Primeau, 35, were taken into custody. The four men were convicted and given lengthy prison sentences. Lise pleaded guilty to being an accessory and was sentenced to time already served. Later, she would become George Lemay's second wife.

But where was our George? The answer to that question was partially revealed two weeks later, when George's 42-foot cruiser was found docked near Miami. George had piloted the cruiser almost 2,500 miles from Montreal to Florida. The police had the cruiser, but its owner was long gone.

Meanwhile, a raid on George's St. Jerome chalet uncovered a small portion of the loot taken from the bank's safety deposit boxes. Police found a few thousand dollars secreted in a false panel in George's bedroom.

Two years later, the RCMP, the FBI and Scotland Yard cooperated in using an Early Bird satellite for the first time to send pictures of internationally wanted fugitives across the United States. In this manner, Lemay's picture showed up on TV screens in Florida. Sure enough, a boatyard worker in Fort Lauderdale recognized the wanted Lemay as Rene Roy, the owner of the 43-foot sloop

*Tirana*. Within the hour, Roy was fingerprinted. He was indeed the internationally-sought bank robber from Canada, George Lemay.

Lodged in Dade County jail while deportation proceedings were being instituted, George seemed to take a great interest in strengthening his somewhat flabby, squat physique. He also found time to marry Lise Lemieux. Active George was successful in turning on the charm and bribing the guard with a whopping $35,000 to aid him in his escape. It was a daring venture in the Lemay style.

George was allowed to slip out of his first-floor cell and take the elevator to the seventh floor, where he entered a room with an unbarred window. He fastened a rope to a radiator and made his way seven floors down the rope to freedom. Now everyone knew why George had been devoting so much time to building up his strength. He had, as usual, planned every facet of his escape.

The FBI, RCMP and Interpol searched for George throughout the world. It took them almost a year. On August 19, 1966, the FBI received a phone tip. They picked up Robert Palmer in the Golden Nugget Casino in Las Vegas. Fingerprints proved that Palmer was really our George. To change his appearance, George had shaved off the remaining hair from his almost bald head.

It took four months to get George back to Canada to face the music. On November 16, 1966, he was charged with the old Dominion Day break-in of the Bank of Nova Scotia. His confederates described in detail how he had masterminded the entire operation. They related that, when their hard tunnelling had been completed, George had, like a conquering general, insisted on being the first to enter the vault.

In January 1969, after one of the longest criminal trials in Montreal history, George was found guilty and sentenced to eight years' imprisonment.

After serving his sentence, George was out of jail only a short time before being picked up on a drug trafficking charge. While back in jail awaiting trial, George and three confederates are believed to have orchestrated the killing of one Pierre Quintal to prevent him from testifying against them. Despite Quintal's death, they were convicted on the drug charge.

In 1984, George stood trial for Quintal's murder. He was acquitted, but still had to serve the remainder of his drug-related sentence. Once again, George completed his term in prison and was released.

Where is George now? Your guess is as good as mine. Quebec prison officials assure me that George is now "on the streets." They nonchalantly add that they expect him back any time. George is like that.

# DARREN HUENEMANN, DERIK LORD AND DAVID MUIR

(CANADA)

DORIS Leatherbarrow worked hard all her life, and her efforts bore fruit. By 1990, at age 69, she was the sole owner of four prosperous ladies' dress stores in the Vancouver area. Her personal wealth was estimated at between four and five million dollars

Doris had one daughter, Sharon, who had gone through two husbands by the time she met and married Ralph Huenemann in 1976. Eventually Ralph obtained a doctorate and became a respected professor at the University of Victoria. Sharon brought Darren, her four-year-old son by a previous marriage, to the union.

The Huenemanns maintained a rather palatial home in the Saanich area, just north of Victoria on Vancouver Island, while Doris lived alone at Tsawwassen, near Delta, on the mainland. Despite her age, Doris exercised a hands-on policy regarding her chain of stores. She had the reputation of being a hard-nosed businesswoman, but was also known to be generous to her daughter and grandson.

Sharon raised Darren to be obedient, punctual and polite. Friends of the family felt that the lad was almost too perfect. He was immaculately dressed, never took part in athletics and was overly respectful of his superiors. Although many believed Darren was the ideal son, others felt that his behaviour was unnatural for a teenager.

Doris doted on the boy. On his sixteenth birthday, she presented him with a shiny black Honda Accord. She also saw to it that he had a bulging bank account, amounting to several thousands of dollars. Money played a large part in the lives of Doris and Sharon. Both had known hard times and both appreciated the security and power that money brought to the family. Darren couldn't help but be influenced by the constant references to monetary subjects by his mother and grandmother.

In the spring of 1989, mother and daughter made wills. Doris's will was simple enough. Half of her fortune would go to her daughter, and the other half would be left to her grandson. Sharon left the money inherited from her mother to her son, Darren. Both women told Darren the terms of their wills. In so doing, they signed their death certificates. You see, Darren Huenemann, the perfect teenager, who had never received as much as a traffic ticket in his life, had made up his mind to murder his mother and grandmother.

A short time after learning the terms of the wills, Darren began talking openly to school chums about killing his mother and grandmother. They didn't take him seriously. A devotee of the game Dungeons and Dragons, at first he may have been merely voicing fantasies. At some point, however, the fantasies became a diabolical reality.

Darren went about formulating a plan to commit double murder. He picked his co-conspirators carefully. Fellow high school student, 15-year-old David Muir was a straight-A student. The only son of highly educated parents, David had never been in any trouble in his life. Derik Lord, 16, was also the product of a fine family. Like Darren and Dave, he had never been in any difficulty with police. The three boys lived within a half-hour's drive of each other.

Unbelievably, Darren's suggestion that his two friends carry out the killings was not greeted with revulsion by the boys. Darren made it all sound so convincing, so very easy. He offered them money, cars and property when the deed was done. Cold-bloodedly the boys discussed the method by which they would snuff out the lives of the two innocent women. With Darren acting as leader, it was decided they would wait until Doris and Sharon were together. The boys would club them unconscious then slit their throats.

Darren was ecstatic that his plan was taking shape. He took great pride in confiding the plot to his girlfriend, Amanda Cousins. At first, 16-year-old Amanda didn't believe that clean-cut, polite Darren was serious, but as time went by she realized she was privy to dangerous information. When she asked what would happen if she told police of the plot, Darren vacillated between telling her that no one would believe her and threatening to kill her. Amanda didn't mention a word to anyone about the murderous scheme that was taking shape on a daily basis.

All was set. Darren bought two crowbars at the Capitol Iron Store in Victoria, and outfitted David and Derik with them. They would use knives from Doris's kitchen to slit the women's throats.

On September 21, David and Derik took the ferry across the Strait of Georgia to Tsawwassen, but couldn't find Doris's house from the information supplied by Darren. Although Darren was furious at the failure, he wasn't discouraged. They would try again.

On October 5, all was in readiness for a second attempt. Sharon was visiting her mother in Tsawwassen. The two boys, equipped with crowbars in a knapsack, took the ferry across the strait. This time they had no trouble locating the correct address. Doris and Sharon had just started dinner when the doorbell rang. The boys said they were in the area and had stopped by to say hello.

Sharon greeted her son's friends warmly and asked them to stay for dinner. She quickly put two additional plates on the table. When the women's backs were turned, the boys struck. In minutes, Doris and Sharon lay unconscious on the floor. David and Derik picked up two knives from the kitchen, just as Darren had instructed. They slit their victims' throats. The boys then scurried about the house, opening drawers and scattering their contents. Darren had wanted the scene to look like a robbery. They removed a total of $1,580 from the women's purses.

When the killers returned to Saanich, Darren, accompanied by Amanda, was pleased with a job well done. He reviewed their alibis. If they were ever questioned, Amanda was to say she was with the two boys all afternoon and had dinner with them later in the evening. Darren could easily establish an alibi because he was nowhere near the crime scene at the time of the murders.

That night, Dr. Ralph Huenemann was concerned when his wife failed to return home from a visit with her mother. He couldn't reach either woman on the telephone. Finally he called Delta police, who promised to look in at Doris address. It was they who found the bodies.

Detectives felt something was wrong with the crime scene right from the outset. Valuable jewellery and electronic equipment had not been touched, yet the contents of drawers were strewn about the premises. It looked as if someone had amateurishly attempted to simulate a robbery. Two plates on the table were partially filled with food, while two were untouched. It appeared that the victims had invited their killers to dinner.

Doris and Sharon had been clubbed before they were stabbed. Although the knives used to slay the women had been left behind, the instruments used to club the victims were nowhere to be found. The murders had all the aspects of a premeditated assassination.

When Darren was told of the murders, he became hysterical. Relatives and neighbours were sympathetic. After the initial shock wore off, Darren's behaviour abruptly changed. He seemed obsessed with his grandmother's wealth, taking time to inquire how much her car was worth and the value of her jewellery. He told friends jubilantly that he stood to inherit everything.

When police questioned Amanda Cousins, she told a straightforward story of spending the afternoon and evening with Derik and David. The two boys corroborated the details of her story. Darren offered $12,500 reward for the apprehension of the killers. The offer was duplicated by his stepfather.

Darren's other school chums were questioned. They told police that he had often talked about killing his grandmother. Authorities located a taxi driver who had driven the boys to the ferry on the date of the murders. He picked David's and Derik's pictures out of a police photo line-up. So did a youngster who had seen them near Doris's home on the date of the murder.

David was the first to break under questioning. He confessed in detail to the premeditated murders. When offered the opportunity to testify for the Crown instead of standing accused of being an accessory, Amanda Cousins confessed to her involvement as well. All three boys were arrested and charged with murder in adult court.

David Muir and Derik Lord were found guilty and sentenced to life imprisonment with no possibility of parole for 10 years. Darren Huenemann also received a life sentence, but with no possibility of parole for 25 years.

The perfect son who orchestrated the murders of his mother and grandmother didn't collect a cent of his family's money. Doris Leatherbarrow's brothers and sisters inherited the bulk of her estate.

# FRANK AND FRED MACTEMPLE

(CANADA)

---

ST. Thomas, Ontario, is a peaceful community located south of London, just up the road from Lake Erie. But one day in the spring of 1934, guns blazed and bodies fell like something out of a Wild West shootout.

It all started innocently enough. Fred MacTemple, 21, was wanted for stealing a bicycle. Constable Colin McGregor and Sergeant Sam McKeown were dispatched to bring in the local youth for questioning. By chance, Detective Bert McCully of the Michigan police happened to be in the St. Thomas police station. He volunteered to give the officers a lift to 13 Queen Street, where the MacTemples lived. The street was in the rougher part of town, and the MacTemples were known as tough customers.

The officers decided to take the necessary precautions. They asked McCully to cover the back door as they approached the rundown house. They knocked on the front door. A young boy answered. When the officers asked to speak to Fred MacTemple, the lad was so frightened he could only point to the rear of the house.

The two officers entered. A door opened, and there stood Fred MacTemple, brandishing a wicked-looking blue-black U.S.-army-issue .45-calibre automatic. "Stick 'em up!" he shouted.

Neither officer was expecting such a move. They had felt, at worst, that their young suspect might try to run out of the house. Now they stared at a nervous young man waving around a dangerous weapon. McKeown tried talking his way out of a tough jam. "Just a minute," he said, "We've got a warrant against Fred MacTemple for stealing a bicycle. Why all the gunplay?"

The tall young man rasped, "No cops is going to take me!"

McKeown continued, "It's not that serious."

He was interrupted. "Shut that talk!" Fred shouted.

From a door leading off the kitchen, 55-year-old Frank MacTemple emerged, waving a revolver in each hand. One was an ugly-looking German Luger, the other a white .38 Ivor-Johnson. He took command of the situation and shouted orders. "Shut that talk and both of you put your guns on the table! No tricks!"

McKeown couldn't believe he was facing a total of three handguns, all over a stolen bicycle. Once again he attempted to talk his way out of this unlikely predicament. "You're Frank MacTemple, I take it. Your son is wanted for bicycle stealing. It isn't a serious charge."

MacTemple would have none of it. He pushed a gun into McKeown's ribs and commanded, "Shut the talk and put your gun on the table! We're not going to be taken by any damn cop." Fred MacTemple grabbed Constable McGregor's gun. McKeown didn't respond to the elder MacTemple's orders.

McGregor warned, "Be careful, Sam, the hammer of that Luger is up."

For the third time, Frank cursed, "Put your gun on the table or I'll let you have it!" At that precise moment, McKeown jumped Fred MacTemple. Frank started cursing and shooting.

Constable Colin McGregor took a slug directly in the stomach and fell to the floor. McKeown, in a desperate struggle with Fred, was shot in the wrist. He grimaced in pain as his hand went numb. Frank was still shooting. A bullet entered Fred's neck, spinning him to the floor. MacTemple had missed McKeown and shot his own son.

Frank MacTemple, guns blazing, backed out a side door and escaped. Detective McCully raced into the house but was too late to apprehend the crazed man. McKeown managed to get off one shot, which missed.

From upstairs, Mrs. MacTemple and her young son heard the shooting. When it stopped, she ventured downstairs and saw her son, Fred, lying on the kitchen floor with a bullet through his neck.

The two wounded officers and Fred MacTemple were rushed by ambulance to hospital. The day after the shooting, Constable Colin McGregor died of his wounds. Fred MacTemple lingered between life and death for some hours, but gradually recovered. McKeown's hand was bandaged and he was released from hospital.

As soon as Fred was able to talk, police questioned him. They wanted to know what had motivated the shooting. Fred explained that it was a grudge shooting, not particularly against McGregor, but against the police in general. Evidently, the threat of going to reform school for the theft of the bicycle and of the older MacTemple going to jail for other minor thefts had caused father and son to flee the area. Only after they had purchased guns in Erie, Pennsylvania, did they return, swearing that the police would never take them.

Fred explained, "Police had broken up our home, separated our family and made it impossible for Dad and me to come home."

After they procured the weapons, the MacTemples decided to chance returning to St. Thomas.

Now the hunt was on for Frank MacTemple. One of the largest manhunts ever conducted in that section of Ontario was quickly organized. Frank was spotted in several places, but the quarry always managed to elude the hunters.

On May 9, two days after the shooting, a 16-year-old farmhand, Clifford Anderson, was pitching hay from the haymow to the barn floor below. There was a scream and out popped a dirty man in ragged clothing. The old man implored Clifford not to tell his boss, Malcolm McNeil, that he was hiding in the haymow. Clifford, who suspected he was talking to the most wanted man in the province, was frightened out of his wits. He was relieved when MacTemple allowed him to leave the barn to go to his supper. Two hours later, Clifford told the McNeil family about the stranger in the barn. McNeil immediately called police.

MacTemple left the barn and stayed in nearby woods until dark. He then made his way to West Lorne, where he had a friend, Dick Carnegie, 58, who operated an antique store. Police felt the wanted man might seek refuge in his friend's spartan two-room shack. They decided to encircle Carnegie's home, but to remain hidden. Carnegie was told to expect MacTemple. He agreed to cooperate with police and do anything in his power to apprehend the suspected killer.

About 11:30 that same night, MacTemple showed up at Carnegie's door. He claimed he had been hunting squirrels and had accidentally shot himself in the hand. He showed Carnegie his slightly wounded hand, which he had acquired in the melee two days earlier. Carnegie washed and bandaged the wound.

About an hour after he entered the house, MacTemple jumped up. He thought he had heard a noise outside the shack. Before he could respond further, Carnegie exclaimed, "It can't be anything. I'll go out and see, though." With that, he dashed out the door. He was met by police officers, who were in position around the house.

Carnegie confirmed, "I got him inside. What am I going to do with him? If anyone but me goes in that door, he'll shoot. He's got a gun and he's ready to use it." The courageous man continued, "I guess I'll hafta hold him so he can't use his gun while you boys come in."

Carnegie returned indoors and offered his guest a cigarette. After the man accepted the cigarette, Carnegie threw himself upon the startled MacTemple. He yelled for help and, within seconds, it was over. Carnegie was so exhausted and excited, he fell to the floor in a faint.

On March 26, 1935, Frank and Fred MacTemple were tried for the murder of Constable McGregor. Both were found guilty and sentenced to death. There was a great hue and cry to save Fred's life as he hadn't actually fired the murder weapon. However, all appeals failed. On June 27, 1935, father and son were hanged in the St. Thomas jailyard.

# CHRIS MAGEE

## (CANADA)

THERE are monsters among us. Psychiatrists describe them as pathological personalities of the antisocial type. This is the story of one such deranged individual.

On the night of March 1, 1974, Judy Barksey, 19, purchased a pizza and two bottles of pop to take with her. She already had a chocolate bar. Judy was making her way home that night in Strathroy, Ontario, when she was attacked.

Later, her assailant was to describe the incident in his own words: "It was late at night. I was at home watching a hockey game and I decided to go uptown to get some raffle tickets on the game at the News Depot. After getting the tickets, I started for home. I noticed a girl walking on the street in front of me. I started fantasizing sex with her and I was trying to build up nerve to approach her. As we walked along, I finally built up enough courage, or else my sickness was coming to a head, then I grabbed her after we crossed over the tracks. I told her what I wanted. She struggled and refused. I grabbed her by the throat. She goes down, then I panicked, took my jackknife out and stabbed her in the throat. I got scared and I went into her purse and took some money."

Judy Barksey's monster cleaned off his bloody jackknife in a mud puddle and went home to his wife.

The morning after the attack, Dallas Allan, 66, left his home at 11:45 to mail a letter. As he walked by a fertilizer shed, he looked to his left and spotted the body of a young girl lying on the ground. A pizza, two bottles of pop and a chocolate bar were strewn around her. Moments later police were viewing the body of Judy Barksey.

Despite an extensive investigation, detectives were unsuccessful in tracing the killer.

A year and three months later, the man with the uncontrollable desires was absently looking out the window of his home as Rosalie Winters, 18, wandered into Alexandra Park. A short while later, she felt strong hands clamped around her neck. Schoolbooks flew into the air. Rosalie lost consciousness. She was raped and left in the park. She was unable to give a good description of her attacker.

On October 20, 1975, exactly four months after the attack on Rosalie Winters, the unknown assailant struck again. Twenty-four-year-old Denys Jenner arrived home from work and entered his Strathroy home by the back door. His wife, Louise, was lying dead on the kitchen floor. Someone had slashed her throat and tightly tied a black bootlace around her neck.

Realizing his wife was dead, and fearing for his baby's life, Denys walked over his wife's body to his daughter Rachel's room. He found Rachel unharmed in her crib.

Ontario Provincial Police detectives theorized at the time that Louise's killer was known to her. Photographs were found on a chesterfield as if an acquaintance had been scanning them. Possibly, Mrs. Jenner had excused herself to change her baby's diapers upstairs, giving the killer time and opportunity to undo his bootlace. When Mrs. Jenner came back downstairs, the killer struck. Mrs. Jenner had been sexually attacked but then had been given the opportunity to dress before she was killed.

A 74-year-old neighbour of the Jenners reported seeing a late-model cream-coloured or yellow vehicle, possibly an Oldsmobile, enter the Jenner driveway on the day of the murder. She said the occupant of the vehicle, a white male with dark, collar-length hair, had stood at the Jenner door for three or four minutes before entering the house.

Police conducted thousands of interviews in the Jenner investigation. One man, Chris Magee, loosely fitted the description given by the Jenners' neighbour. He knew Mrs. Jenner, as well as Judy Barksey. His father owned a light-colored Oldsmobile.

Magee remained a suspect, but there was nothing of a definite nature to label him a killer. When interviewed he vehemently denied having any knowledge of the murders.

Sylvia Holly Jennings, 19, was hitchhiking to London. She accepted a lift. She was driven well past her destination to an abandoned sideroad near Mount Brydges, Ontario, where she was raped, beaten over the head with a pop bottle, and left for dead. Miraculously, she survived the attack.

James Frayne, 16, of Forest, Ontario, drove a farm tractor and hayrake to a farm his family owned about four and half miles from his home. When he arrived at the abandoned farm site he spotted a leg and knee in the grass.

Initially, James thought someone was sunbathing. He blew the tractor horn and went about changing the hayrake for a mowing machine. James commenced to cut hay, but the sight he had seen upon entering the property bothered him.

He returned to the spot and took a much closer look. What he thought was a sunbather was, in reality, the body of 15-year-old Susan Lynne Scholes. Susan had been raped and stabbed in the throat. The Scholes family resided in London but was spending the summer at their cottage in nearby Hillsboro Beach.

At 1:00 p.m. Susan had left the cottage with her brother, Geoffrey, to go into Forest to buy batteries for her portable radio. Geoffrey dropped Susan off in town. She purchased the batteries and was seen walking out of town towards County Road 12.

McFarlane's Tile Yard is situated on that road. Mrs. McFarlane heard of the murder on the radio and immediately went to the police. She reported seeing the murdered girl walking in front of the tile yard at 1:30 p.m. Susan was wearing a distinctive green sweater with the word "Hillsboro" printed in white letters across the front.

Mrs. McFarlane's son had been using a forklift to transfer tile to the yard when he saw Susan, who he knew through his association with her brother, Geoffrey. As he watched, a truck stopped and gave Susan a lift. He recognized the truck as the one used in the area to pick up and dispose of dead animals.

OPP inquiries soon uncovered that the suspect truck, a 1975 Ford, was owned by Mr. John Grinsven, a Strathroy-based dealer in dead stock. On the day of Susan's murder, the truck was operated by none other than Chris Magee, the suspect in the Barksey and Jenner murders.

Taken to the OPP detachment in Forest, Magee admitted picking up Susan but claimed that he dropped her off and continued on his way. He told investigating officers that he was married and his children were presently living with his father in Strathroy. Magee had no police record but had been dismissed from various jobs because of petty theft.

Authorities found out that Magee's truck was usually outfitted with a filleting knife, used in his work with dead animals. When the truck was searched, the knife was missing. It was later found on Grinsven's property, sharpened and cleaned. It was obvious that all traces of blood had been thoroughly cleaned away by Magee.

On October 21, 1977, Chris Magee was arrested and stood trial for the murder of Susan Scholes. At no time did he confess to the crime. He was found not guilty by reason of insanity and sent to the Mental Health Centre at Penetanguishene.

Magee, always suspected of committing the other crimes in the area, was reinterviewed on May 11, 1979, by OPP Constables P. De Vlugt and B. Linker.

They learned nothing new from their two-hour session with Magee, but a half-hour after they left the institution they received a radio message that Magee wanted to see them again.

When they returned, Magee blurted out a confession to the two officers: "I'm guilty of everything you suspect me of." He went on to give detailed statements concerning the murders of Barksey, Jenner and Scholes, and the rapes of Winters and Jennings.

On January 18, 1980, Chris Magee stood trial for the murders of Barksey and Jenner. Once again he was found not guilty by reason of insanity and once again confined to the Mental Health Centre at Penetanguishene.

# LINDLEY CHARLES MCARTHUR

(CANADA)

---

IN 1972, when Lee Marie Conway graduated as a registered nurse from St. Joseph's Hospital in Toronto, the future looked bright. She was now qualified to pursue a satisfying and honourable profession. Besides, she had met someone she really cared for—Joe Di Palma. Affection turned to love, and on October 20, 1973, Lee and Joe became husband and wife.

Eventually, the couple moved to Angus, Ontario. In April 1979, a son, Anthony, was born. Joe had a good sales position with Rothmans of Pall Mall Ltd. The pieces were falling into place for the Di Palma family. Sure, there were a few rough spots. Joe had the exasperating habit of putting off fixing things around the house. When Anthony hit the terrible twos, he proved to be a hyper youngster. Lee also felt a bit confined in her rural home and often expressed a desire to move closer to Toronto. But these small differences or complaints were superficial. The Di Palmas had a very successful marriage.

All this was to change on Tuesday, September 21, 1982. On that day, quite by chance, Lee was to cross paths with an amoral monster.

On that fateful morning, Joe got up as usual and left at 7:30 a.m. for his job in Toronto. Lee's parents, Kevin and Audrey Conway, who had spent the previous night with the Di Palmas, rose and had breakfast with their daughter. They left the house at 10:30 a.m. to visit their son in Levack, Ontario.

Lee Marie cleaned up the dishes and tidied the house. She then dressed Anthony for the short ride into Barrie in her black-and-silver 1972 Buick. At twelve o'clock, Lee pulled into Don and Ron's Sunoco Service Station in Angus to purchase gas. Anthony was enrolled at a Stay-and-Play program at the Y. Each Tuesday and Thursday, Lee would drop him off at 1:15 and pick him up at 3:15 p.m. Promptly at 1:15 p.m. she dropped little Anthony off at the Barrie YMCA. The hour between 12:15 and 1:15 is unaccounted for. Quite possibly, Lee went window-shopping and had lunch. There is also the possibility that she was being stalked by a madman.

The previous day Lee had made a hairdressing appointment for that Tuesday at 1:30 p.m. at the House of Bellini's, located in the Bayfield Mall. She never kept the appointment. Later that afternoon, at 3:15 p.m., when she failed to arrive at the Y to pick up Anthony, social program director Heather Fraser grew apprehensive. She called the Di Palma residence and the Royal Victoria Hospital, where Lee worked as a part-time nurse. When she could find no trace of Lee Di Palma, she called police.

At 8:44 that evening, Lee's Buick was found parked in the Bayfield Mall opposite the Pit Stop Gas Bar. The car was unlocked, the window open and an interior garbage container was overturned, all conditions that were foreign to Mrs. Di Palma.

At the request of Barrie police, the Ontario Provincial Police were brought into the case. Inspector Norton Rhiness headed the investigative team. Rhiness had precious little to work with. Mrs. Di Palma had disappeared as if swallowed up by the earth.

Lee Marie Di Palma's past was scrupulously investigated. There were no hidden boyfriends, no affairs, no logical reason why this housewife, nurse and mother would meet with foul play. The disappearance was given wide publicity. A dramatization of the mystery appeared on television. Police were deluged with tips from well-meaning citizens. All had to be checked out. One tip was thought to hold real significance. A citizen came forward stating that she and her daughter had been on a bus on October 22, 1982, a month after Mrs. Di Palma's disappearance. She claimed that she chatted with Lee.

The woman, who was travelling to Sudbury, overheard Lee saying that she was going to Calgary. She said a friend had a large dog. She talked about places she had visited in Calgary and people she had met there two years earlier. She complained that her husband was negligent in fixing things around the house. The woman said she had often been to Bayfield Mall in Barrie. She talked about her sister, Nancy, and said she had a small son. The blond woman with the shoulder bag even stated that her husband once drove a van for Rothmans. Unbelievably, each one of these statements was dead on. They all applied to Mrs. Di Palma. However, the woman on the bus was not Lee Marie Di Palma.

Other sightings occurred in Calgary, Blind River and Vancouver. On December 20, about three months after Di Palma's disappearance, an alcoholic confided to a friend that he had murdered a woman near Barrie. He then committed suicide. For a while, he too was considered a prime suspect.

On May 15, 1983, eight months after Lee Marie failed to pick up her son, her body was found. Malcolm Urquhart and his wife, Pauline, were out picking mushrooms on Laurence Henderson's property in nearby Mulmur Township.

Urquhart notice a white object on the ground. At first he thought it was a puff-ball. It turned out to be the skull of Lee Marie Di Palma. Police were soon at the scene. Nearby, they found evidence that before death, Lee had been tied up with shoelaces and the straps from her shoulder bag.

Five months after Lee Di Palma's disappearance and before her body was found, Lindley Charles McArthur first came to the attention of police. McArthur was accused of kidnapping a 13-year-old girl and driving her to a secluded area, approximately three-quarters of a mile from where Mrs. Di Palma's body was eventually found. The youngster was sexually attacked. McArthur was arrested at that time and lodged in the Barrie Jail.

Once in jail, McArthur had an overwhelming urge to talk about the Di Palma murder. He told several inmates details of the murder. Some thought he was lying; others didn't care one way or the other; many grew tired of listening to him.

During the spring of 1983, McArthur was transferred to the Mental Health Centre at Penetanguishene for assessment. That May, Mrs. Di Palma's body was found. McArthur told a psychiatrist that he thought fingerprints would connect him to the Di Palma killing. After the assessment was completed, McArthur was sentenced to two years less a day for the assault on the 13-year-old girl. He was returned to the Barrie Jail to serve his time.

Inspector Rhiness, aware of McArthur's loose tongue, decided to place an undercover agent in McArthur's cell. Fabricating a story that he had been picked up on Highway 400 and was being held until he could be returned to Calgary to face a rape charge, the undercover agent ingratiated himself with his cell mate. Soon McArthur was confiding in his new friend. "Yeah, I expect to be charged with murder in the first degree." When the undercover policeman feigned ignorance, McArthur went on, "So you never heard about Di Palma. The broad was taken from her car and strangled."

Two days later, McArthur was charged with murder. He told the undercover policeman, "I'm charged with murder. As far as I know, they have three things on me. I hung around there. I was in town that day and I know the area where the body was found. Man, after a year, I thought it was over." Then McArthur, cool as a cucumber, took in a movie on television. He really enjoyed the horror movie, *The Changeling*.

During his stay in jail, McArthur revealed details only the killer would know. He told one inmate that he jumped out of his truck, ran to the driver's side of Mrs. Di Palma's car, stuck his head through the open window and caught her by the throat. She said, "Please don't hurt me." He dragged her from her car to his truck.

Who was Lindley Charles McArthur?

McArthur was born in Collingwood, Ontario on September 21, 1962. He successfully completed Grade 12 at Collingwood High School. He was married on February 28, 1982, but at the time of his confinement, he was already separated from his wife. Factors leading to the breakdown of his marriage were his long stretches of unemployment and his desire for nonstop sex. His wife told police that McArthur demanded sex sessions that sometimes lasted for 12 hours. He was also rough and abusive during sex games. On some occasions, he insisted on performing the sex act as many as 15 times a day.

McArthur's wife revealed that the day after the sex attack on the 13-year-old girl, her husband shaved his beard. He did the same thing the day after Lee Di Palma was reported missing. Mrs. McArthur also told police she noticed that her husband had inexplicably lost the laces to his blue Adidas right after the woman's abduction. She had purchased a new pair.

What had triggered the abduction, rape and murder of a defenceless woman? As McArthur told one of his fellow prisoners, "I done it for kicks." The day he murdered Lee Di Palma was his twentieth birthday.

In June 1984, Lindley Charles McArthur was found guilty of first-degree murder. He was sentenced to life imprisonment with no possibility of parole for 25 years.

# HERBERT MCAULIFFE

(CANADA)

NOT many men attempt to get rich by counterfeiting 50-cent Canadian coins. Herbert McAuliffe not only attempted the trick but did a fairly good job. Unfortunately, Herbie's rather comical criminal endeavours ended in tragedy when his bungling efforts turned to murder.

Born in North Bay, Ontario, Herbie was an above-average student during his formative years. He showed a natural mechanical bent and attended a technical school before leaving North Bay for the tobacco belt around Simcoe.

In 1939, along with thousands of other young Canadians, Herbie joined the army. While in the service, he used his mechanical ability to good advantage and quickly rose to the rank of staff sergeant. However, there must have been a little larceny in his heart even then. In 1944, he was dishonourably discharged for stealing money from his comrades.

Herbie gravitated to Windsor, Ontario, taking with him one of the army's .45-calibre Thompson submachine guns and eight automatic pistols. We have no reason to believe that he intended to use the army weapons. No, Herbie had other devious plans. He had decided to counterfeit 50-cent Canadian pieces, something never accomplished in Canada before.

To facilitate his operation, Herbie rented a double garage from Germain Noel on London Sreet, using the alias Frank West. Noel listened as Herbie explained that his work was rather noisy and was a top-secret government project concerning the invention of a revolutionary new weapon.

Now that his cover was established, Herbie wrote away for books and manuals on coin minting. For weeks he pored over the technical articles. There was one immediate problem—the lack of funds. In order to implement his scheme, he required money to purchase machinery. He overcame this minor difficulty with ease: Herbie became extremely adept at holding up service stations and grocery stores.

Coincidental with his successful robberies, a steady stream of rather sophisticated machinery arrived at the garage on London Street. A turret lathe, dies and punch presses worth more than $15,000 were delivered to Herbie's factory. A $10,000 hydraulic press for stamping out the coins was installed in the garage. Herbie didn't do things half way.

It was hard work. Herbie carried out his experiments from scratch. He had no assistants and no technical advisors. His painstaking experiments continued for four years, interrupted and financed by his periodic stick-ups.

At last he'd perfected his technique. He had invented his own alloy and was actually able to stamp out coins from cheap metal and coat them with silver in an electroplating bath. The end result looked perfect. Just for fun, Herbie produced a bucketful.

That same night, Herbie tested his newly minted 50-cent pieces at a gambling joint in Detroit. He knew betting quantities of 50-cent Canadian coins would be unusual and focus attention to him, but he wanted the coins to be examined. If they were accepted in a gambling den, he decided they would be accepted everywhere. Herbie and his phony fifties passed with flying colours. His coins were identical to the real thing.

Next day, back at the garage, Herbie decided to figure out just how much he would net from his operation. He added up his expenses and was dumbfounded to find out that it cost him 48 cents for every 50-cent coin he produced. If he threw in his own labour he was losing money!

There was a solution. If he had the capital to modernize his plant with new equipment, he could lower costs. Herbie decided that the quickest way to raise capital would be to rob a bank.

In his usual methodical manner, he drove throughout the countryside looking for a suitable bank. He found it in the Imperial Bank of Canada at Langton, Ontario. Now, Langton was not a hustling, bustling metropolis. Located about 20 miles from Simcoe, it was not likely that the 250 souls who called Langton home would interfere with Herbie's nefarious scheme.

In preparation for the heist, Herbie stole a car in Windsor. Into it he threw his .45-calibre Thompson sub-machine gun, a Luger and a .45 revolver. He tossed in a brown paper shopping bag to hold his anticipated loot.

Herbie walked up to bank accountant Henry Thompson and announced, "This is a stick-up. Listen, chum, if you don't open up the combination on that vault, I'll be back tonight to drill you dead." Thompson filled Herbie's paper shopping bag with $22,577 in bills and coins. Herbie waved his gun menacingly and herded 11 customers into the bank vault. He then took off for his waiting car, but in his haste our boy neglected to lock the vault door.

Inside the vault, Arthur Lierman, a 31-year-old tobacco-farm owner, pushed the door open. He shouted to William Goddyn, 24, "Come on, Bill, I've got a .22-calibre rifle in my Buick. Let's get him."

Herbie knew he was being followed. A few miles down the road near Frogmore he stopped, took out his sub-machine gun and fired a burst at the pursuing car. Lierman and Goddyn died in a hail of 30 bullets.

Herbie abandoned the shopping bag full of money on the front seat of his stolen car and took off into the bush. Word of the dramatic daylight bank robbery and the murders of two popular citizens of the area spread like wildfire.

The hunt was on. Herbie was headline news across the nation. The largest manhunt in Canadian history up to that time was organized. For three days Herbie hid out in barns, stole food from farmers and swatted mosquitoes, until Graham Haggerty, a 20-year-old farmhand out deer hunting, discovered Herbie in an old shack near Straffordville.

Initially, Herbie was identified as Frank West or George Walker, the two aliases he had used during his years developing fake 50-cent pieces. Eventually his true identity and his counterfeiting career were uncovered and revealed to the public.

Herbie was tried in Simcoe, found guilty of murder and sentenced to death. On December 19, 1950, he was given the last rites of the Catholic Church and walked briskly to his death on the scaffold at the Simcoe Jail.

So ended the career of Herbert McAuliffe, who will go down in Canadian history as the only man to successfully produce counterfeit 50-cent pieces.

# DANA MCINTOSH

(UNITED STATES)

YOU can never be sure what goes on behind the closed doors of someone else's home, can you? Let's take a peek behind the portals of the McIntosh family of Dallas, Texas.

Susan and Dana McIntosh had been high school sweethearts in Tyler, where both were born. On August 8, 1970, the attractive young couple were married. Those who knew them believed they were made for each other.

As the years drifted by, nothing happened to change anyone's mind. They were as much in love as they had been when Dana carried Susan's books home from school back in Tyler. When Susan's dad died seven years after her marriage, he left her a sizable sum, estimated to be several hundred thousand dollars. That didn't hurt a bit.

By 1990, the McIntoshes had two lovely daughters, aged 8 and 12. Dana was the president of his own computer software company. They all lived in a luxurious home on Sunny Land Lane in the Lakewood section of Dallas. Dana and Susan attended church regularly and were extremely active in church affairs, as well as charitable causes. The McIntoshes were truly the perfect married couple.

Monday, March 19, 1990, appeared to be the same as any other day at the McIntosh residence. Dana drove his Mercedes to his office. A couple of hours later, he elicited a co-worker's assistance in driving one of his cars from his home to a service station for repair. He and his colleague drove out together to pick up the vehicle.

Dana opened his garage door and recoiled in horror. Lying on the floor in a pool of blood was the body of his wife. Susan had been horribly slashed across the throat. Dana, believing she was still alive, insisted they place her in his Mercedes and rush her to hospital. At the nearest hospital, doctors counted 25 stab wounds all over Susan's body. When told his wife had been pronounced dead, Dana collapsed.

Detectives were soon made aware of the pertinent facts surrounding the murder. Some of these facts were strange. Susan's hair and underclothing were wet, yet her outer garments were dry. After examining the McIntosh home, police reported no sign of forced entry. When found, Susan had been fully clothed and had not been sexually interfered with. From an examination of the body and the crime scene, police ascertained that Susan had put up a desperate struggle for her life. She had incurred several defensive wounds to her arms and hands.

The initial investigation was dominated by one circumstance that caused detectives to seriously question Dana McIntosh. He had several scratches about his face, which had obviously been recently inflicted. Dana, rather shocked that police would even insinuate he was involved, told them that the family collie had scratched him. Neighbours verified that Dana often played with the collie in the backyard, but none of them could remember his ever having been scratched before.

Scrapings were taken from underneath Susan's fingernails, but results of these tests were unsatisfactory. In fact, lab reports indicated that Susan's fingernails were uncharacteristically clean for someone who might very well have scratched her assailant. A scientific search of the McIntosh home revealed traces of blood in the master bedroom, the bathroom sink and on the shower-stall floor.

Neighbours, friends and employees at Dana's company were interrogated by the police. They were unanimous in their opinion that Dana McIntosh was not the type of man who would murder his wife. In most cases, they had known him for well over 10 years and believed him to be a loving husband and father.

Police were beginning to doubt the avenue their investigation had taken, when a new element entered the case. McIntosh's office was burglarized. Documents were strewn about the office and photographs of Susan were spread across Dana's desk. Detectives noted that nothing of value was removed from the office. Was there someone out there warning Dana he would be the next to go, or was the break-in an attempt to lead police away from suspecting Dana himself?

As so often happens in murder investigations, the backgrounds of the principals held many answers not apparent at first glance. Detectives delved into Dana McIntosh's business activities. They learned his enterprises had been in deep financial difficulties for years. His computer company had been sued by banks and suppliers on several occasions. Each time, Dana had managed to come up with enough cash to avoid bankruptcy. Throughout the financial storms, his and Susan's lifestyle had remained stable.

Looking still further into Dana's affairs, detectives found out that Susan had often come to the company's rescue with her own money. Employees of the McIntosh computer company were questioned confidentially. In this way police learned that Susan had helped out her husband in the past year to the tune of $200,000. Moreover, employees had witnessed Dana and Susan arguing over finances at the office. All was definitely not as copacetic as it appeared to neighbours and social acquaintances.

The trouble started way back in 1981 when Susan had mortgaged several hundred acres of land she had inherited from her father to raise money to finance one of her husband's emergencies. When Dana was unable to keep up the payments, the bank took the land. Susan was furious at losing property that had been in her family for generations. Shortly after this fiasco, the couple had visited a marriage counsellor.

When police discovered that Susan's life was insured for $250,000 and the balance of her estate amounted to another $250,000, all of which would be Dana's upon her death, they charged him with murder.

On April 8, 1991, Dana stood trial for his wife's murder. The state's case was strictly circumstantial. They contended that Dana killed his wife before he left for work and then saw to it that he had a colleague with him when he found her body in the garage. After the vicious attack, which may have occurred in the master bedroom, he removed his wife's outer garments and washed blood from her wounds in the shower stall. He then dressed Susan and placed her body in the garage. One thing he didn't count on was his wife's struggle for her life, during which he suffered telltale scratches to his face.

The prosecution produced one witness, a nurse, who gave the most startling evidence of the entire trial. When Susan was being examined at the hospital in her husband's presence, she noticed he was sucking her fingers. When she asked him to release Susan's fingers, he did so, but moments later she observed him doing the same thing. This time he snapped at the nurse that he was kissing his wife's fingers. The inference was clear. Realizing Susan had scratched him, Dana knew her fingernail scrapings would be retrieved by police. He was attempting to destroy the evidence.

The Texas jury took only 45 minutes to agree with the state's theory of how Susan McIntosh met her death. They found Dana McIntosh guilty of her murder. He was sentenced to 75 years' imprisonment, a sentence he is still serving.

# BILL MCINTYRE

(CANADA)

---

SOMEONE hated Bill McIntyre enough to kill him, but no one knows the identity of the killer.

The obvious suspects, those individuals who found themselves facing criminal charges as a result of Bill McIntyre's relentless determination, have been exonerated of involvement in his murder. You see, Bill McIntyre was an undercover police officer with the Ontario Provincial Police (OPP). He wasn't killed in a shootout. He wasn't murdered while undercover. He was shot to death in his own luxurious apartment at 1300 Marlborough Court in Oakville, Ontario.

When his family moved from Winona to Oakville, Bill was enrolled in school. In 1969, he graduated from White Oaks Secondary School. After graduation he immediately applied for a position with the OPP, but was rejected because he was too young to join the force. In 1972, he reapplied, was accepted and stationed in Goderich.

Over the years, working out of Goderich, Exeter and Mount Forest, Bill McIntyre took part in many undercover operations. He often worked in conjunction with other police forces. His colleagues, as well as his superiors, speak highly of him. In fact, his tireless efforts won him several commendations. By 1981, he was employed in Hamilton under the direction of the Special Services Branch of the OPP. A year later, he sold a home he owned near Exeter and purchased the condominium in Oakville.

During his 11 years on the force, Bill had become a highly qualified officer. He graduated from the Ontario Police College in Aylmer in 1973. A year later, he completed a marine course, followed by a criminal investigation course, and a physical surveillance course. Finally, in the fall of 1983, Bill successfully completed an analysis and intelligence course. In 1983, Bill McIntyre, career police officer, was promoted to the rank of corporal and assigned to be team leader in the physical surveillance section of the OPP. Six months later, he was found dead on the floor of his condominium.

On Thursday, April 19, 1984, Bill and a colleague were working as a surveillance team in Toronto. Later that day, they visited Grant Brown Motors to look at cars. Bill was interested in a Trans Am. They checked in at OPP headquarters on Harbour Street, after which they joined other officers for a beer at a bar in Burlington. The exact times of Bill's activities that Thursday are well documented.

Subsequent investigation revealed that while Bill was in the bar in Burlington, his neighbours in the condo in Oakville heard strange noises emanating from his apartment. Three neighbours, questioned separately, later told police that they heard doors slamming, and thought they heard two males shouting at each other. Unfortunately, they could not hear the actual conversation.

The next day, Friday, Bill McIntyre worked as usual. In hindsight, some officers who came in contact with him thought he was acting strangely. At a meeting in Bowmanville, Bill left his colleagues in an office and made phone calls in private. In the past, he had always called members of his team in front of the other officers.

That evening at 7 p.m., Bill showed up for a dinner date with his long-time friend, Bill Truax. McIntyre and Truax had known each other since both attended Grade 3 in Oakville. A half-hour later, the two men were digging into the prime-rib special at the Executive Tavern in Burlington. After the meal, the friends parted. Bill McIntyre had less than a day to live.

Bill had promised to help Acting Sergeant Nelson Kincaid move some furniture the next day, Saturday. Bill didn't show up, nor did he answer his pager. Kincaid phoned McIntyre around 2 p.m., but received no response.

The day wore on. Two other officers attempted to contact McIntyre, but no one answered their knock on the apartment door. When McIntyre failed to arrive at a scheduled meeting in Bowmanville, Sergeant Kincaid became concerned. McIntyre was not the type of officer who would fail to show up for an appointment without notifying his superiors. Something had to be wrong.

Kincaid phoned Corporal Ken Allen and advised him of the ominous situation. Allen was ordered to pick the lock of the McIntyre apartment. Together with Acting Corporal Dave Crane, he proceeded to 1300 Marlborough Court. McIntyre's two vehicles were in the underground parking lot. The officers listened at the apartment door. They could hear McIntyre's pager beeping inside.

When the officers gained entrance to the unit, they found McIntyre's body on the floor in the hallway leading to the bedroom. An autopsy performed at the Centre of Forensic Sciences in Toronto indicated that Bill McIntyre had been killed as a result of a single wound to the head from a .22-calibre bullet.

Naturally, when an undercover police officer is murdered, it is most logical to look for the culprit among those he had helped apprehend. Investigators checked McIntyre's previous cases. Although they came up with several suspects, all their investigative efforts indicated that none of these individuals was involved in Bill's death.

Investigative probes into Bill's work life indicated that he was an exceptional police officer. Some described him as a workaholic. His personal life was surprisingly private. Officers who had worked with him for months didn't really get to know him. Many never realized how very little Bill McIntyre related to them of his family or his private life.

Who had been in Bill's apartment that Thursday? Evidently, there was more than one individual present. Why were they there? Why did they shout and slam doors? There was no evidence of forced entry.

The door to McIntyre's apartment could only be locked with a key from the outside. Since Bill McIntyre's keys were found intact in the apartment, it is logical to assume that Bill had given a spare key to his killer, who was cool enough to shoot Bill and calmly lock the door behind him as he left the condo.

Police assure me that they found "physical evidence in the apartment that could help identify the killer if and when he is apprehended." However, it is one thing to conjecture about the whys and hows and quite another to trace the killer.

Here matters stood for almost a year, until a woman, whose identity would serve no useful purpose here, came forward with her story. She was visiting her father, who lived in the same condominium complex as Bill, on the day Bill McIntyre was murdered. That morning she was walking the dog at approximately 10:00 a.m. She noticed a man looking up, talking to someone on a fifth-floor balcony. The woman looked up and later was able to identify Bill McIntyre as the man on the balcony. He was wearing jeans and no shirt, the same way he was dressed when his body was found that evening.

As the woman walked by, the man on the street stopped talking. Inside the condo, her father nonchalantly glanced out the window. He too saw the man talking upward toward the balcony.

What were the two men saying to each other? The woman can't be sure, but she thought she heard the man say, "What are you going to do today?" The reply might have been, "I don't know, maybe nothing."

The woman, who may have been the last person, other than his killer, to see Bill McIntyre alive, was alarmed when she learned that the man on the balcony had been murdered. When she discovered he was a police officer, she and her husband thought the killing might be a gangland slaying. What would prevent the killer or killers from coming after her if she came forward? As a result, she remained silent for almost a year before revealing what she had witnessed on the day of the murder.

The woman's memory was less than perfect after such a lengthy period of time. However, under hypnosis, she gave the following description. The man on the sidewalk that day was a white male, wearing a white shirt, blue jeans, white running shoes and beige jacket. He was holding a motorcycle helmet in his hand. The man, who was approximately 5 feet 9 inches tall, was in his twenties or early thirties. He was clean-shaven, had a light complexion and straight blond hair.

It is now over fifteen years since Bill McIntyre was gunned down in his own apartment. Despite the best efforts of investigating officers, many of them McIntyre's own colleagues, his killer has never been apprehended.

# CHARLOTTE MILLER

(AUSTRALIA)

---

FOR more than 15 years, Hilda Miller had a terrific relationship with her common-law husband, 40-year-old Arthur Houdson.

Life hadn't always been good to Hilda. She had taken her lumps along the rocky road of romance before she met Art. Not the least of her problems had been her first husband, Steve Miller, who went out one day for a pack of cigarettes and never returned. He left Hilda and their three-year-old daughter, Charlotte, high and dry.

Hilda attempted to locate Steve, but to no avail. As a result, she was unable to obtain a divorce and marry Art. Still, the present arrangement was not half bad. Art had been a good provider for both mother and daughter. He treated the now 18-year-old Charlotte as if she were his own flesh and blood.

The Houdson menagerie lived in Melbourne, Australia, in apparent harmony until October 15, 1979. That was the day 41-year-old Hilda took ill. She was admitted to hospital with a mild case of kidney stones, but was soon released. From the outset of her illness she was convinced that she had cancer of the liver. Doctors told her she was totally mistaken. Art attempted to talk some sense into the distraught woman, but nothing could convince her that she was in fine health. At home she wallowed in a state of severe depression.

Hilda remained in bed about 90 percent of the time and in her own psychosomatic way suffered from the ravages of cancer. The family physician, Dr. John Fuller, prescribed tranquilizers and barbiturates to ease Hilda's imagined pain. For three months, Hilda lay in bed. By now her health had deteriorated to the point where Art and Charlotte were seriously concerned for her welfare. They had good cause to be worried.

On January 10, 1980, Charlotte frantically called Dr. Fuller. Her mother was lying motionless in bed and couldn't be roused. When Dr. Fuller arrived at his patient's bedside, he immediately realized that Hilda had been dead for several hours. He noticed an empty glass on the bedside table, the dregs of orange juice adhering to its bottom and sides. Alongside the glass were two empty plastic tubes, each of which had contained 25 barbiturate tablets. It was obvious to the doctor that his patient had committed suicide. Dr. Fuller took care of Charlotte, who had become hysterical when she was told that her mother was dead. Then he called the police and the coroner's office.

A postmortem revealed that Hilda died from a dose of 50 barbiturate tablets dissolved in orange juice. The death was officially labelled a suicide. Hilda was laid to rest.

To all intents and purposes, that was that, except for one fact that came to the attention of one police officer, Inspector Thomas Hunt. It was the inspector's job to rubber-stamp Hilda's file officially closed. In due course the evidence of the suicide case would be destroyed. Hunt was puzzled. When he examined the glass, there were no fingerprints on it, nor was there any information in the file that there had ever been fingerprints on the glass. The inspector questioned Dr. Fuller and the first officer at the scene. The doctor swore that he had never touched the glass. The officer told his superior that he had carefully placed the glass in a plastic evidence bag. When Charlotte was questioned, she couldn't recall whether she had touched the glass, nor could she remember whether she had wiped the glass clean.

Inspector Hunt was convinced that all things being equal, Hilda's fingerprints should have been on that glass. Who had wiped it clean and why?

The inspector dug in like a pit bull. A few months after Hilda's death, he decided to have Art followed. Much to his surprise, he learned that Art and Charlotte were still living in the same flat where Hilda had ended her life. The inspector thought it was unusual for an 18-year-old girl to stay in the same residence where her mother had so recently committed suicide.

Perish the thought—was there hanky-panky going on? Neighbours were discreetly questioned. Sure enough, they thought that Art and Charlotte were behaving more like husband and wife than father and daughter. The inspector had to sit back and think this one through. If Hilda had committed suicide, and if Art and Charlotte were lovers, no crime had been committed by the two occupants of the flat. After all, Art was not legally or biologically Charlotte's father. Perhaps nature had simply taken its course. After all, Charlotte was an extremely attractive young woman.

On the other hand, had Art killed Hilda and wiped his fingerprints off the glass so that he could claim her daughter? Inspector Hunt was a bit disappointed to learn that Art had been 50 miles away in Geelong on the day of the murder. However, it would have been possible for him to make the return trip without being noticed.

A couple of things bothered the investigating officer. Art Houdson had been faithful to Hilda for more than 15 years. He had been a kind, caring father to Charlotte for the same period of time. It was only after Hilda's death that neighbours noted the change in his attitude towards Charlotte. The same could be said for Charlotte. She had been a respectful daughter and had never caused her mother one moment's aggravation in her entire life. In addition, Hilda, convinced that she had cancer, had often talked of committing suicide rather than endure the painful death she firmly believed awaited her. She had even mentioned suicide to Dr. Fuller.

Perhaps suicide was the answer after all. Yet, according to the neighbourhood gossips, Art and Charlotte were living as husband and wife. Had Art managed to commit the perfect murder, and in so doing, traded in the 41-year-old mother for her 18-year-old daughter? Maybe.

As the months passed, detectives, keeping Art under surveillance, reported that his appearance had changed since Hilda's death. Where he had once been a rather dapper dresser, he now looked slovenly. He even walked hunched over, as if he had a great deal on his mind.

Surprise of surprises, one day Art walked into a police station of his own volition with a story to tell. He started at the beginning. When Hilda was in hospital, he and Charlotte were thrown together alone in their flat. The furthest thing from Art's mind was romance. After all, he had brought up Charlotte since she was three years old. But Charlotte had naughty thoughts on her mind. One night, she turned off the lights, lit the candles, poured the wine and seduced Art. According to Art, he was weak and simply couldn't resist her charms.

When Hilda returned home from hospital, the surreptitious affair continued. A week before Hilda's death, Charlotte came up with the super idea of murdering her mother. Charlotte explained that Hilda wanted to die anyway. Everyone would be happy all the way around. Art said that he had admonished Charlotte for suggesting such a thing and told her never to bring up the subject again. After Hilda's death, he asked Charlotte point-blank if she had killed her mother. She didn't say yes, but she didn't say no, either. Art was beside himself with guilty knowledge. When he couldn't stand it any longer, he decided to report the entire matter to the police.

Charlotte was taken into custody and questioned. She confessed immediately. Her motive was crystal clear. She wanted Art for herself and her mother stood in the way. It had been easy. She had fed Hilda the barbiturate-laced orange juice. Of course, it was she who had wiped her fingerprints off the glass. Charlotte added that she had no remorse for what she had done.

Charlotte Miller was examined by psychiatrists and judged to be too ill to stand trial. She was confined to a mental institution for an indefinite period.

# WILLIAM MOTHERSHED

(UNITED STATES)

ON the day before Christmas 1980, 30-year-old Officer Dennis Webb was patrolling in his black-and-white along the relatively peaceful streets of San Fernando, California. It was close to 4 a.m. when his radio crackled with information about the robbery of a 7-Eleven convenience store. The robber was described as a small male Caucasian, 90 pounds, five feet five inches, with blond hair.

Within minutes, Webb spotted a young man who fit the description walking down a deserted street. Webb pulled up beside his suspect, got out of the car and shouted, "Freeze!" In response, the young man drew a handgun from his pocket and poured three slugs into the officer. Webb fell to the ground. The gunman stood over the fallen policeman and fired three more shots into his body. He then jumped into Webb's police car and drove away.

Three minutes later, Dennis Webb, a veteran of six years on the San Fernando Police Force, was found dead by a fellow policeman. His own weapon was still in its holster.

Meanwhile, the killer was listening to the details of the shooting on the police radio. When he learned that detectives were looking for Webb's police car, he decided to ditch the vehicle. He drove the car into a field adjacent to a golf course, turned off the ignition and made his way on foot out of the area. It was approaching daylight when Nancy Webb was informed that her husband of two years had been killed in the line of duty.

A massive investigation was immediately organized. It was learned that another 7-Eleven store had been robbed two days before Webb's murder. The clerks in both stores gave detectives roughly the same description of the undersized suspect. It was reasonable to assume that one man was responsible for both hold-ups and Webb's murder.

Precious few clues were garnered by investigating officers. The police car was found with the driver's door still open, but the vehicle yielded nothing that would lead to the killer. Six 9mm automatic pistol cartridge casings were recovered at the scene of the crime. The casings were reloads—ones that had been used before and loaded again by hand, a practice sometimes followed by gun enthusiasts. By mid-January, rewards totalling $34,000 were being offered for information leading to the policeman's killer.

Bob Berndt was a 26-year-old drifter who had been in and out of jails and mental institutions since age 17. His father, a career police officer, had died of cancer. After his father's death, Bob fell apart. He fantasized about being a Vietnam veteran and sometimes claimed to work for the CIA. Bob was fascinated with Webb's murder. He kept clippings of every scrap of information concerning the case.

Bob stood five feet five inches tall and weighed 125 pounds, with a crop of thick blond hair. It was uncanny how closely he fit the description of the killer. He even bragged to his roommate, 35-year-old Robert Hensley, that he had killed the police officer. It made him a big man in Hensley's eyes. Sometimes Bob lent Hensley his Colt .357 Magnum, even though he didn't trust Hensley as far as he could throw him.

In mid-January, the two drifters, Berndt and Hensley, left L.A. by bus and roamed the country, finally landing in Phoenix, Arizona, where Hensley had a friend named Dick. Because they were running out of money, the three decided to rob the Tinhorn Bar. The robbery didn't go well. Hensley acted like a madman, waving Bob's Colt at the lone female employee and a young couple seated at the bar. Once he had the three occupants of the Tinhorn lying face down on the floor, Hensley bent over and deliberately shot each one in the head. His two companions begged him to leave the bar, but Hensley wouldn't go until he had shot all three. The two customers died where they lay, while the barmaid survived the senseless attack.

Back in their motel room, the three robbers counted their loot: $100. When Dick lectured Hensley on the folly of killing people for such a paltry sum, Hensley unceremoniously shot him in the chest. Rushed to hospital, Dick survived the spontaneous shooting. Bob and Hensley were taken into custody. Bob was released, Hensley detained.

Bob Berndt took off. In Clinton, Oklahoma, he was picked up as a suspicious character. When his belongings were searched, police found an unmailed letter written to Bob's priest back in San Fernando. The letter contained the incriminating sentence, "I also killed a police officer, Dennis Webb, in San Fernando Valley."

Oklahoma police contacted San Fernando police. Detectives quickly ascertained that Bob had been in the San Fernando area at Christmas time.

Besides, he owned a .357 Magnum pistol and had purchased hand-loaded ammunition from a friend. Detectives flew to Clinton to question Bob. Under interrogation, he fell apart. He told detectives about the wild shootout at the Tinhorn Bar and confessed to the murder of Officer Dennis Webb, as well as the robberies of the two convenience stores.

Bob was brought back to San Fernando. He was taken to the street where Webb had been gunned down and immediately pointed out the spot where the killing had taken place. He claimed he had sold the murder weapon. Bob led authorities to the area where the police car had been abandoned. He was pleased with his performance and seemed to delight in cooperating with detectives. About the only flaw in the case was that both convenience store operators failed to positively identify him as the man who had robbed them.

On February 17, 1981, Bob Berndt was charged with the murder of Officer Dennis Webb. While in jail, he continually told guards and fellow inmates how sorry he was that he had killed a police officer. Psychiatrists stated that by murdering Webb, Bob was in reality killing his policeman father.

That's where matters stood when the Los Angeles police received a phone call from the FBI in Hobbs, New Mexico. Some students at New Mexico Tech had come forward with information about a fellow student, 18-year-old William Mothershed. Evidently, Mothershed had spent his Christmas vacation at his home in San Fernando. Although he was a top student with no criminal record, his description fit the convenience store robber in every detail.

New Mexico officers interviewed a student who was an avid gun collector and who had sold Mothershed a 9mm Smith & Wesson before the Christmas break. He had also provided Mothershed with 200 rounds of hand-loaded ammunition. Before selling the weapon, the student had fired off 10 rounds to make sure the gun was in perfect order. He still had the shell casings of those 10 rounds. The casings were flown to Los Angeles, where they were microscopically compared to the shell casings found at the scene of Webb's murder. They matched. Mothershed's 9-mm was the murder weapon.

William Mothershed, a studious young man, had never been in trouble in his life. He was picked up and immediately confessed to robbing the two convenience stores and murdering the police officer. He told police that he had taken apart the Smith & Wesson and had disposed of it piece by piece while driving through the desert. He and his friends at New Mexico Tech had often discussed a life of crime. He had decided it was the easiest way to make money. It was Dennis Webb's misfortune to cross his path.

When told of Mothershed's confession and proof of his guilt, Bob Berndt burst out laughing. He admitted he had lied to show how clever he was. It hadn't been that difficult. He had studied the newspapers and pretty well knew the locations of the murder and the abandoned police car.

Bob wasn't that clever. Although the charge of murdering Officer Webb was dropped, he was found guilty of murder in the two killings in the Tinhorn Bar in Phoenix. For these crimes he received a total of 37 years' imprisonment.

Robert Hensley was found guilty of the same double murder and was sentenced to death.

William Mothershed was found guilty of the murder of Officer Dennis Webb. He was sentenced to life imprisonment and is presently serving that sentence.

# RODERICK NEWELL

(ENGLAND)

LET me introduce you to the Newall family. Nicholas met and married Elizabeth in 1963. Both were teachers. Both came from wealthy British families, which afforded them private personal incomes exclusive of their teaching salaries. A son, Roderick, was born in 1965. A second son, Mark, arrived a year later.

Because of their privileged financial situation, Nicholas and Elizabeth resigned from teaching in 1968 and purchased a yacht, the *Chanson du Lecq*. They would do what so many of us dream of doing. They would find their paradise in the West Indies. The couple were experienced sailors.

On the way to their new life, the Newalls stopped in Jersey, one of the Channel Islands. Once there, they became enamoured with the place. It wasn't the West Indies, but it had a rugged beauty and favourable tax laws. Nicholas and Elizabeth decided to seek their Shangri-La no further.

The family settled into island life. Both Nicholas and Elizabeth obtained part-time teaching jobs, and they purchased a home, the Crow's Nest, which had one of the finest views on Jersey. The two boys were sent to boarding schools in England. From the ages of six until their teens, they were separated from their parents for long periods. Those who knew the family felt there was a coldness between sons and parents. Nicholas was strict, one might even say arrogant. Still, the two lads had all the creature comforts.

The Newalls led an active social life. Their best friends were David and Maureen Ellam, whom they saw at least once a week. To add to their comfortable lifestyle, Nicholas and Elizabeth bought a villa in Spain. Their eldest boy, Roderick, chose the army as a career and rose to the rank of lieutenant. Mark became a financial fund manager. Both parents were proud of their two successful, strapping sons.

If there was any flaw in the portrait of domestic tranquillity, it was the lack of love flowing from parents to offspring. Nicholas adored Elizabeth; Elizabeth adored Nicholas. Neither seemed to express the same affection toward their sons.

In 1987, with their boys away pursuing careers, the Newalls sold the Crow's Nest and moved to a smaller dwelling at 9 Close de l'Atlantique. On October 9, the Newall boys flew to Jersey on a visit. They stayed at a home Mark was building. The boys made a date to take their parents to dinner the next evening at the Sea Crest Restaurant. It was their mother's forty-eighth birthday.

Roderick and Mark arrived at their parents' home at 8 p.m. Everyone appeared to be in good spirits. They knocked back two bottles of champagne. Mark, a moderate drinker, volunteered to drive to the Sea Crest. The party arrived after 9 p.m. and stayed until after midnight. During the meal, more champagne and wine were consumed, followed by liqueurs. After dinner, back at 9 Close de l'Atlantique, the Newalls opened a bottle of Scotch. Tongues loosened, voices rose, and an argument ensued. Roderick was thinking of abandoning his army career. His father objected. Other subjects came under scrutiny. Roderick and his father didn't see eye to eye on anything. Finally, Mark, who had often heard such bickering, tired of the discussion and went home.

The dispute between father and son grew more intense. According to a statement given much later by Roderick, his father gave him a push. He fell to the floor. Within arm's reach were a pair of rice flails, which is a weapon used in martial arts. Roderick clubbed his father to death. Initially, Elizabeth tried to separate the two men. Then she ran into the bedroom in fear for her life. Roderick raced after her and clubbed her until she too was dead.

Hours later, Roderick contacted Mark and told him what he had done, adding that he was contemplating suicide. Mark told his brother to do nothing; he would be there in minutes. Mark arrived and calmed his brother down. He claims to have found some tarpaulins and tools in the garage. The boys wrapped their parents in the tarps and carried them outside to Mark's rented van. They drove to a field near the sea, where they used the tools taken from the garage to bury Nicholas and Elizabeth.

The brothers returned to their parents' home and cleaned up evidence of the murder, most particularly the blood that was everywhere. It was quite a job. In order to dry rugs and walls, they turned up the heat and left. Roderick took some of his parents' possessions and the materials used to wash up the blood. He burned these in a nearby field. Next day, Roderick and Mark left Jersey.

Two days passed. The Ellams figured that their friends had left the island to visit relatives. When they received no word from the Newalls, David Ellam went over to investigate. He found five days' of unopened mail and a hole in the roof of the house from a recent storm. Strangely, the heat was intense in the house.

David turned it down. The Ellams contacted Roderick and Mark, who flew to Jersey and inspected the house with their parents' friends. They too appeared to be mystified. Elizabeth and Nicholas Newall had vanished. Police were notified.

Under questioning by police, Roderick and Mark told straightforward stories. They said they had returned to their parents' home the morning after the birthday party. They had breakfast and lunch, before leaving at around 3 p.m. While they were there, Elizabeth's friend, Maureen Ellam, brought over flowers for their mother. Since Elizabeth was asleep at the time, Roderick took the flowers to her. Everything was normal when the boys left. That evening, taking separate flights, the brothers had left Jersey.

Forensic scientists spent four days examining the interior of the house. Bloodstains were found in the lounge and in the bedroom. Both areas revealed signs of having been washed. J-cloth fibres, identical to those stored in the kitchen, were found adhering to a rug. Specks of blood were analyzed. The samples taken from the lounge were the same type as Nicholas's, while the bedroom samples matched Elizabeth's blood. Officials concluded that Nicholas had been attacked in front of the fireplace in the lounge, and Elizabeth had been accosted in the bedroom. The disappearances were now being treated as murders.

Hundreds of volunteers joined police to search for the bodies of the victims. Helicopters, dogs and radar were used, to no avail. Because Roderick and Mark were the last known individuals to have seen their parents alive, they were questioned extensively. They reiterated that they had left their parents alive and well.

The disappearance of the missing pair was the main topic of conversation on the island. The Ellams insisted that the search continue, but as months turned into years the hunt diminished. Roderick resigned from the army and spent much of his time aboard the family yacht in the Mediterranean. The intensive police investigation revealed the cold relationship that had existed between the Newall brothers and their parents. Both were suspected of involvement in the disappearance, but police uncovered nothing concrete to connect them to the crime.

On January 3, 1991, the Newalls were declared officially dead. Their sons inherited their entire estate. Mark became a huge success in the financial world. Roderick continued to roam the world in his yacht. No one knew Roderick's innermost feelings. He was racked by guilt. Each day he relived the blows landing on his parents' skulls, the blood spattering on the floor, the bodies being placed unceremoniously in the shallow grave.

In June 1992, Roderick visited relatives in England. He constantly brought up the subject of his missing parents and seemed to be on the verge of confessing. He planned to visit Stephen Newall, his father's twin brother, in Scotland. When a relative informed Maureen Ellam in Jersey that Roderick seemed near the breaking point, she called police. They in turn notified Scottish authorities, who asked Stephen Newall to wear a wire during conversations with his nephew. Stephen agreed and arranged to have tea with his nephew in a private room at the Dunkeld House Hotel.

During the dramatic meeting, Roderick broke down and described how he had unmercifully beaten his parents to death. He stated that Mark wasn't present during the killings, but had assisted in the burial of the bodies. At the end of the confession, Stephen asked his nephew the obvious question, "Why?" Roderick replied, "You wouldn't understand, because I don't understand."

Because the confession had been procured in an unorthodox manner, police sought legal opinions as to its admissibility. The process took days. In the meantime, Roderick left in his yacht. On August 7, 1992, the yacht was intercepted by a Royal Navy frigate. Roderick was arrested and incarcerated in Gibraltar. Although he fought extradition, he was eventually returned to Jersey. Mark was picked up in Paris.

Once back in Jersey, Roderick gave authorities a map indicating the location of his parents' grave. With the use of the map and Roderick's personal direction at the site, police recovered the Newalls' bodies.

The murder charges against Mark were dropped. Roderick stood trial for the murders of his parents. Because there was proof that he had purchased tools, tarpaulins and plastic sheets before the killings, he was convicted of premeditated murder. Roderick Newall was sentenced to two concurrent life terms in prison. Mark Newall was convicted of assisting his brother after the fact of murder. He was sentenced to two concurrent six-year terms.

# STELLA NICKELL

## (UNITED STATES)

I have always claimed that, as a group, poisoners are the most reprehensible of all murderers. Among these cowardly individuals are a select few who not only kill their intended victim, but care not one iota if they murder others.

Stella Nickell was one such individual.

In 1986, we find Stella well into her second marriage. Ten years earlier she had tied the knot with second husband Bruce Nickell, who was employed as a part-time heavy-equipment operator with the state of Washington. Stella had brought her daughter, Cynthia, to the union. Cynthia was a striking 20-year-old redhead in 1986. Stella, on the other hand, would never see forty again. Years of drinking and carousing were beginning to take their toll. Stella discerned crow's feet and other nasty signs of aging when she gazed into the mirror of her home in the Seattle suburb of Auburn.

It is difficult to pinpoint exactly when Stella decided she didn't want to take a position on the proverbial shelf. Bruce, a recovered alcoholic with a bad back, only worked a few days each week and would never earn more than a bare living. Life was drab, dull, boring. To Stella's way of thinking, cold hard cash would deliver her out of her predicament. Of course, Bruce, a definite encumbrance, would have to go.

Stella formulated a plan. She studied the effects of the foxglove plant and decided its deadly poison was just what the doctor ordered. She cultivated foxglove plants, harvested her crop of deadly seeds and fed some to the unsuspecting Bruce. The diabolical plan didn't work. In fact, Bruce seemed to be extraordinarily chipper after digesting what should have been his last meal. Cynthia, observing her mother's sudden obsession with foxglove, couldn't help but be curious. When Cynthia asked her about it, Stella insinuated that they would both be better off without Bruce.

The arithmetic worked out fine. The state of Washington had insured Bruce's life for $31,000 with an additional $105,000 payoff if he left this mortal coil due to an accident. To sweeten the pie, Stella took out two additional policies on Bruce's life for $20,000 each. Let's see now, our Stella had a potential $176,000 at stake. She decided to try again.

Scheming Stella remembered the horrendous Tylenol murders that had taken place in the Chicago area in 1982. Someone had placed cyanide into Tylenol capsules and had returned the capsules to store shelves. In that instance, seven people had died. No one was ever convicted of the crimes. Stella saw some merit in the diabolical scheme. There was one drawback—Bruce didn't use Tylenol. He preferred Excedrin.

Stella purchased cyanide-laced rat poison and put some in the Excedrin capsules Bruce kept in a bottle in a kitchen cabinet. On June 5, 1986, Bruce took four capsules and muttered, "I think I'm going to pass out." He fell unconscious to the floor. After being helicoptered to Harborview Medical Center in Seattle, he died several hours later without regaining consciousness.

Cynthia immediately thought her mother was responsible for Bruce's death. Before she could utter an accusatory word, Stella said, "I know what you're thinking and the answer is no."

Neither the attending physician at Harborview nor the coroner detected cyanide in Bruce's body. Death was attributed to pulmonary emphysema. Stella was home free. As matters stood, she would collect $71,000, a tidy little sum, but $105,000 short of what the payoff would have been if her husband's death had been declared accidental.

Stella felt cheated. There had to be a way she could get her hands on that money. Her mind raced back to the Tylenol tragedies. If she planted cyanide in more Excedrin bottles and placed them back on a store shelf, another death would surely take place. With a little help, Bruce's death would be coupled with that of the latest victim. No tight-fisted insurance company could then claim that Bruce had died a natural death.

Stella proceeded with her unbelievable plot. She purchased several boxed bottles of extra-strength Excedrin. Despite improvements in drug packaging since the Tylenol incidents, Stella managed to empty some of the capsules and refill them with cyanide. Her work at repairing boxes and bottles was amateurish, but she was successful in placing the lethal packages back on the shelves of three different stores.

Forty-year-old Susan Snow, the mother of one adult daughter and one teenager, had risen to the position of assistant vice-president of the Puget Sound National Bank. Every morning, Susan and her husband, Paul, each took two extra strength Excedrin to start the day. June 11, 1986, was no exception. Paul rose early, took two Excedrin out of a new bottle Susan had recently purchased and, by the luck of the draw, ingested two bona fide painkillers.

Later, Susan took her usual two capsules. Within minutes, her 15-year-old daughter, Hayley, found her unconscious on the bathroom floor. Susan was rushed to the hospital, where she lived for six hours before her husband agreed to disconnect life-support equipment. Medical examination revealed the presence of cyanide in the Excedrin Susan had taken. Naturally, the unusual death and its horrific ramifications received wide publicity.

Displaying a keen sense of public responsibility, Stella Nickell came forward with the suggestion that her husband might also have been a victim of the tainted medication. Tissue tests proved that Stella's suspicions were correct. Bruce Nickell had been poisoned. Now the Seattle poisoning case received nationwide publicity. Health officials, as well as Bristol-Meyers, the manufacturers of Excedrin, instructed stores to remove all painkillers from their shelves. Two bottles of cyanide-laced Excedrin were uncovered in this manner.

Detectives confiscated bottles of Excedrin from Stella's home. Two of the bottles were found to contain cyanide. Soon, almost a hundred investigators, including FBI agents, were employed to track down the demented person who had taken two lives. Laboratory analysis revealed that the cyanide found in the two bodies and the unused recovered capsules had come from a single source.

Susan Snow's husband, Paul, came under mild suspicion as someone who stood to gain financially from his wife's death. He agreed to take a polygraph test, which indicated he knew nothing whatever about the murders.

Stella was questioned for the same reason. In addition to Washington State's policy on Bruce's life, detectives learned that Stella had taken out other life insurance policies totalling $40,000 shortly before her husband's death. Although Stella was a strong suspect, there was no hard evidence pointing to her guilt.

In conjunction with other drug manufacturers, Bristol-Meyers put up a reward of $300,000 for the arrest and conviction of the poisoner. Whether it was the 300,000 big ones that enticed Stella's daughter, Cynthia, to come forward or whether it was, to quote her own words, "the right thing for me to do," we will never know. Cynthia told authorities of her mother's first attempt to kill hubby Bruce with foxglove and of their many conversations regarding poisons.

In 1988, Stella was taken into custody and charged with "causing death by product tampering." She has the distinction of being the first person ever convicted of this charge. Stella Nickell has never collected one penny of her husband's life insurance money. She was sentenced to 90 years' imprisonment and will be eligible for parole in the year 2018, when she will be 74 years old.

# SAM PARSLOW AND CORDELIA POIRIER

(CANADA)

---

THE quaint villages with their large churches and hard-working farm folk that make up rural Quebec are a strange backdrop for murder most foul. Yet, even here, the passions that simmer, boil and erupt into bloody murder have found their way.

Back before the turn of the century, the tiny village of St. Canute was a remote community. The God-fearing French farmers led a hearty, healthy and, for the most part, happy existence. But not Cordelia Poirier.

You see, Cordelia was unhappily married to Isidore Poirier. Now, Isidore wasn't a bad fellow, really. It was just that he was about as exciting as maple sap dripping into a bucket. Isidore worked hard, was a respected member of the community and attended church regularly. But he was oh so very colourless. Isidore made love as though it was a duty rather than a pleasure. Besides, he was well into his forties, while Cordelia had not yet celebrated her thirtieth birthday.

Sam Parslow, the Poiriers' young hired hand, had none of Isidore's finer qualities, but what he lacked in stability, he more than made up for in bed. Many a chilly winter night, when Isidore was away for one reason or another, Sam would dim the lantern in Cordelia's bedroom and partake of the forbidden fruit which lay within. Some nights Sam attempted to harvest the entire orchard, so eager was Cordelia for his substantial charms.

In 1895, as luck would have it, Isidore received an opportunity to work in California for several months. He jumped at the chance. Cordelia practically pushed him out the door. Sam and Cordelia's sack time increased dramatically.

Mon Dieu, could this go on in a quaint French-Canadian village without tongues wagging? Of course not. The lovers sometimes went out together. They held hands and occasionally stole a kiss in public. Mind you, all the while that Cordelia was performing between the sheets with Sam, she was attending Mass regularly. In fact, both she and Sam sang in the choir. Cordelia also played the organ during Mass.

Can't you just hear the whispers? "A disgrace, and poor Issie in California"; "They should be horsewhipped for carrying on so." It couldn't go on.

Finally, Sam's mother, who felt that her son was being led away from the straight and narrow by the wicked Mrs. Poirier, went to the parish priest, Father Pinault, and asked him to save her boy. The good father, obviously a man of few words, sent a note to Isidore in California. "Come back at once, or else take away your wife."

In response, Isidore wrote a scorching letter to Father Pinault, telling him in no uncertain terms that he had the utmost faith in his wife. Isidore, never one to keep a secret, wrote dear Cordelia about the priest's ridiculous accusations. Cordelia replied that he was right—they were ridiculous.

In due course, Isidore returned to his home in St. Canute. We can only assume that Sam moved out of the master bedroom and into the hired hand's quarters. The gossip grew to a crescendo. Cordelia, by far the most dominant personality in our triangle, knew she had to do something. It didn't take her that long to come up with a murder plan that would turn a dishonest dollar at the same time. She would insure her husband's life before she and Sam killed him.

After paying her insurance agent a brief visit, Cordelia wrote the man a letter. The letter is so incriminating we reproduce it here:

> "I told my husband that I had been to see you with regard to our policy. I forgot to ask you for books in French. My husband wants to understand the thing before disbursing too much money. He is well decided to continue, but he wants first to understand whether if he should die by any means—by being killed or by accident, or by poison or by railway accident—your company would pay, because he has spoken to several people and they say you would not. It seems to me you told me I would be paid no matter what death my husband would meet. My husband today is in perfect health. Reply and I will arrange with you."

The agent assured Cordelia that his company would pay off no matter how Issie might meet his death. In due course, Isidore Poirier's life was insured for $2,000.

With financial matters in place, Cordelia proceeded to cajole, urge and otherwise convince Sam that the only proper thing to do was to kill Isidore. They would allow a decent interval to pass before marrying. Sam didn't need much persuading. He thought it was a great idea.

On November 21, 1898, Isidore attended Mass as usual. Cordelia and Sam filled the church with ecclesiastical melodies. After the service, Isidore stopped off at the blacksmith shop, where he and Smitty Bouvrette had a few blasts out of a whisky bottle the blacksmith kept handy for just such occasions.

Cordelia knew that Isidore would take a nap when he arrived home. The opportunity she and Sam had been waiting for was at hand. Sam hid in the house, fingering the new butcher knife he had purchased in Montreal. Isidore went to bed. In minutes, Sam and Cordelia could hear Isidore snoring. Sam sneaked up to the bed. He was scared stiff. He aimed the knife at the sleeping man's throat, thrust forward, but failed to inflict a fatal wound. Isidore woke up. The two men struggled. Cordelia shouted, "Kill him, kill him!" Thus encouraged, Sam stabbed Isidore in the neck and about the face. Finally, Isidore was dead.

The conspirators lifted the body onto the bed and placed the butcher knife in the dead man's hand. They put a half-empty bottle of whisky beside the body. Then Cordelia slipped out of her blood-soaked dress and burned it in the stove. If you didn't look closely, the gory mess might have passed for a suicide.

Cordelia put on her Sunday best and returned to church, where she played the organ as usual. After services she travelled to her father's home in St. Jerome and spent the night. Next morning she returned to St. Canute to play the organ for a wedding at the church. Cool as a cucumber, Cordelia conversed with several villagers, her parents and the parish priest without giving any sign that her husband had lain dead for more than 24 hours, his head almost severed from his neck.

On the way home from church, Cordelia told blacksmith Bouvrette to walk through the house with her. We all know what they found in the bedroom. The parish priest was the first one called. Father Pinault reluctantly announced that it looked like suicide to him. Cordelia smiled.

A nosy farmer noted that the ashes in the stove didn't look like residue left from wood. He scooped out the ashes and discovered a number of hooks and eyes. Of course, we know they were all that remained of the bloody dress Cordelia had been wearing.

Someone thought a more experienced individual should be brought in to ascertain the cause of Isidore's death. Detective K.P. McCaskill was dispatched from Montreal. He took one look at the bloody footprints on the floor and knew he was investigating murder. One of the prints matched Cordelia's shoe, another matched Sam's. The jig was up. Cordelia and Sam were taken into custody.

Cordelia, by far the stronger personality, immediately confessed, claiming that Sam was the instigator of the plot and the actual killer. No one believed her. Both she and Sam were found guilty and were sentenced to hang.

On March 10, 1899, eight hundred screaming ticket holders were allowed into the prison yard at St. Scholastique to witness the execution. It was a gala affair. They sang songs and even took a few shots at the scaffold.

Sam Parslow had to be practically carried to the noose. Cordelia walked with head erect. When she saw Sam's condition she shouted in disgust, "Stand up!" Then she and her lover plunged into eternity.

# ALAN POOLE

## (ENGLAND)

CONSTABLE Alan Baxter, age 33, woke up on the morning of Monday June 5, 1951, firmly believing that things had to get better. Alan wasn't asking for much. A week earlier, his father had suffered a stroke and died. His wife was still in Chatham, at England's All Saints Hospital, where she had given birth to a stillborn baby. Alan's series of misfortunes would continue. This would be the second to last day of his life.

Alan Poole, 20, woke up that day convinced he was one tough guy. Poole read gangster comic books and never missed a gangster movie. For as long as he could remember, he had attempted to emulate the fictional heroics of bad men. His parents, local God-fearing citizens, couldn't handle their son, who was always in trouble. In 1946 he was incarcerated after being found guilty of no fewer than 19 burglaries.

Sentenced to a term in prison, Alan escaped long enough to rob a sports shop. Once again behind bars, he developed a deep hatred for police. Like his comic-book characters, he knew he was smarter than the coppers and could beat the system. In 1949 he escaped a second time and attacked the first police officer he encountered. Back to prison he went.

On a pleasant spring evening, these two men, Alan Baxter and Alan Poole, born in the same area of England to middle-class families, were destined to cross paths. Their lives and the lives of their families would never be the same.

The Chatham police station received a call that someone in the Luton section of the city was threatening citizens with a Sten gun. Constable Alan Baxter, Sergeant William Langford and Constable John Brown responded to the call in a patrol car. With Baxter behind the wheel, they made their way to a large garbage dump surrounded by a number of shacks. They were told that the gunman was in the area.

Unarmed, Langford and Brown proceeded to check each shack. As Langford approached one of the buildings, the gunman appeared and, without hesitation, opened fire. It was Langford's good fortune that the man was a poor shot. Bullets whizzed past his head as he threw himself to the ground.

The assailant walked directly to the patrol car where Constable Baxter was seated. A hail of bullets shattered the windshield. Baxter was able to open the door and get out before a second fusillade ripped into his body. Langford rushed to his fallen comrade's aid. Baxter could only say, "He's got me in the guts, Sarge. I've had it."

Langford managed to place Baxter back in the patrol car and rush him to St. Bartholomew's Hospital.

Within minutes, surgeons were frantically trying to save Baxter's life. He survived the operation and was able to see his wife, who was brought to his side from All Saints Hospital in an ambulance. From a trolley, Mrs. Baxter spoke briefly with her husband. He died 18 hours after being shot.

A massive search was instituted for the gunman. Roadblocks were set up. Army and navy personnel stationed nearby were pressed into the hunt. At the time, authorities had no idea as to the identity of the shooter. They soon found out from witnesses who had seen the man with the Sten gun. It was local bad boy Alan Poole.

Poole's most recent brush with authority was his desertion from the army. He had enlisted, but promptly went Absent Without Leave. Police learned that Poole's parents lived at 114 Symons Avenue, approximately a mile from where Constable Baxter had been murdered. Evidently Poole had never before solicited assistance from his parents. He chose to live by stealing from local shops and hiding out wherever he could find shelter. Now, with the heat on, police felt Poole would somehow make his way to his parents' house. They dispatched a number of armed officers to stake out the Symons Avenue address.

The night passed uneventfully. Early next morning, police were surprised to hear a burst of gunfire from the rear of the home. Poole, behaving like the gangsters he loved to emulate, had fired his Sten gun just for fun. He had obviously made his way to the house before it was surrounded by police.

Inside the house, Poole's parents were terrified by the unfolding events. Poole's 11-year-old sister, Doreen, sobbed as her brother fired off his weapon through an upstairs window. Finally, Poole came downstairs and faced his parents, "Get your hats and coats on and get out. I'm going to shoot it out with the cops." Albert Poole attempted to reason with his son, "Good God, son, where have you been! The police are after you."

There was no reasoning with Alan. "I'm going to shoot it out with them," he repeated. "They'll never take me alive. I've plenty of ammunition and I'm going to kill some more of the bastards." The ex-convict, army deserter and murderer, turned to his little sister, "Good-bye. You won't see me again," he said.

Later, Albert Poole would state that he thought about staying and reasoning with his son, but he could tell that Poole was crazed with the all-consuming idea of shooting it out with the police. Alan Poole had seen the action too often in American movies and had voraciously read gangster comic books where the anti-hero went down in a hail of bullets. He had cast himself in the real-life role of gangster and there was no turning back. Albert saw the look in his son's eyes, shook his head and calmly escorted his family from the house.

Alan went to an upstairs bedroom. He peered out the window and opened fire. Police scurried for cover. Some returned fire with their single-shot .303 rifles. They realized they had surrounded a madman, armed with an automatic weapon, who had no intention of surrendering. The army and navy threw equipment and manpower into the siege. Scores of police evacuated the inhabitants of nearby homes. Eventually, more than 200 personnel surrounded the house on Symons Avenue.

Realizing the standoff could last indefinitely, police were able to obtain tear-gas grenades from a nearby army base. Due to the danger of fire breaking out in the house, the fire department was brought in to direct streams of water through shattered windows. A volunteer officer dashed to the side of the house and lobbed in the tear-gas grenades.

Alan Poole witnessed the scene he had helped orchestrate. Just like in the movies, he was holed up with no chance of escape. He fired sporadically at any movement, while outside, police returned fire as hoses poured water into the house. Gas billowed up to the bedrooms from the first floor.

In the midst of the siege, the gunfire from the house abruptly ceased. All was silent. For two hours police waited. Finally, they decided to enter the house, not knowing whether the demented man was setting a trap or not. There was grave fear that he was cunning enough to hold his fire in anticipation of killing as many officers as he could when they entered.

Officers broke down the front door and rushed inside. Alan Poole lay dead in his own blood. He had not taken his own life, but had been hit by the last return fire.

On June 11 and 12, there were two funerals in Chatham. Two local men had been killed less than a week earlier. Constable Alan Baxter was afforded a hero's funeral by the police department. Hundreds of citizens lined the streets to pay their last respects. Next day, only Alan Poole's immediate family and a clergyman were present when the boy who wanted to be a gangster was laid to rest.

# JERRY ROSENBERG

(UNITED STATES)

TOUGH little Jerry Rosenberg walked toward me with the aid of a cane. He has had a rough life. You see, Jerry has been imprisoned for 34 years. Those three decades are indelibly etched in the lines of his face. The Wende Correctional Facility guard who accompanied him to meet with me in this maximum-security institution didn't take his eyes off us as Jerry shook my hand.

Jerry Rosenberg was a small-time Brooklyn thief who dabbled in cons, scams and armed robbery back in the late fifties and early sixties. By the time he was 24 years old he had been arrested 26 times, but with the aid of a protective father he beat all the raps with the exception of one. He was convicted of armed robbery and spent four years in prison.

It was just another job for Jerry that May 18, 1962, when he and a buddy, Anthony Portelli, 26, planned to rob the Boro Park Tobacco Co., a wholesale/retail candy and tobacco outlet on New York's 48th Street. The decision to commit the robbery would change Jerry's life forever.

Jerry and Portelli charged into the Boro Park premises. Both men were armed and masked. They demanded money, scooping up whatever loose bills they could find. Waving weapons, they herded seven employees to the rear of the store, shouting at David Goldberg, president of the business, that they wanted more money. Goldberg was shoved into an office, where he produced more bills. Still the men weren't satisfied. One said, "If I don't get some more dough, somebody's going to get hurt." Either by accident or to make a point, one of the robbers discharged his weapon into the ceiling.

Outside, Detective Luke Fallon, 56, a police officer for 25 years, and his partner, John Finnegan, 29, the father of three children and a veteran of six years on the force, had just made a purchase in the Boro Park store. Fallon had bought a box of candy for his wife's birthday. As they were leaving the area, they heard a shot emanating from the Boro Park outlet. Fallon re-entered the premises. He didn't have a chance. Portelli got off three shots, one of which entered the officer's chest. He died in the doorway. Finnegan rushed in. He managed to fire six shots, but missed with every one. Portelli fired twice more, killing Finnegan in a matter of minutes.

The bandits, now frantic to get out of the store, paid little attention to their masks, which had fallen from their faces. Outside, the third member of the robbery party, whose job it was to drive the getaway car, panicked and sped off. The two desperate men got away clean, but dropped their hats and weapons as they fled the crime scene.

All three men were quickly identified. David Goldberg, who claimed to have seen the thinner of the two men in the warehouse when his mask slipped from his face, identified him as Jerome Rosenberg from police mug shots.

Three days after the murder, Portelli, a bachelor, was arrested in the Lido Motel in Chicago. When he wasn't robbing stores, he worked hustling gas at his father's station in Auburn, New York. Anthony Dellernia, the alleged driver of the getaway car, was the father of two children. He was employed at the Navy Submarine Base in New London, Connecticut. Dellernia's wife, Jean, talked him into giving himself up to police the day after Portelli was apprehended.

That left Jerry Rosenberg at large. Jerry worked as a novelty salesman for General Sales Associates, his father's firm. Two days after Dellernia gave himself up, Jerry contacted two *New York Daily News* reporters and had them drive him to the newspaper's office at 220 E. 42nd Street, where they handed him over to the police. The day before had been his twenty-fifth birthday.

On January 14, 1963, the three men stood trial for the murder of the two officers. The mood in the courtroom was tense. Publicity concerning the cold-blooded murder of two of New York's finest had the public in an uproar. Presiding over the trial was famed judge Samuel Leibowitz.

In the case of Anthony Dellernia, a mistrial was ordered on a technicality. Three months later he was retried. The jury deliberated for ten hours before returning a not guilty verdict. Dellernia walked out of the courtroom a free man and has led an exemplary life ever since his close brush with the law.

Jerry Rosenberg and Anthony Portelli didn't fare as well. David Goldberg positively identified them as the two bandits who had been in his premises, Portelli being the trigger-man. The jury found both men "guilty with no recommendation for mercy." A month later, Judge Leibowitz, in the preamble before sentencing, said, "The evidence against Rosenberg was so overwhelming it was a moving picture case." Leibowitz followed Jerry's assertion that he didn't get a fair trial with, "I hereby sentence you to be executed in accordance with the law during the week of March 31, 1963." When Jerry shouted back, the judge added, "Get this killer out of my sight."

Jerry and Portelli were lodged in the death house at Sing Sing. Appeals delayed the execution, but it appeared that nothing on this earth could save these two men from the electric chair housed down the hall at the end of death row.

Jerry's entry into the world of the legal profession was initiated by his lack of confidence in his own lawyer. In frustration, he borrowed a law book from a fellow inhabitant of the death house. Painfully, the Grade 8 dropout struggled over the legal terminology with the aid of a law dictionary. Eventually, Jerry enrolled in a correspondence course, seeking more knowledge. After two years of study, he realized that he was understanding the law and how to manipulate it to his advantage.

Ironically, during the incarceration of Jerry and Portelli, the death penalty was abolished in New York State for all inmates except cop killers. Jerry and Portelli could only watch as death house occupants were transferred to other prisons, their sentences commuted to life imprisonment.

Jerry, now something of a legal beagle, obtained a copy of the bill abolishing capital punishment. There, in black and white, was the description of the circumstances that excluded him and his buddy from having their sentence commuted to life imprisonment. The bill referred to "premeditated murder of police officers." He and his friend had been convicted of "felony murder" and felony murder was punishable only by life imprisonment. Their crime had been committed during the course of a robbery. Jerry had discovered a bona fide loophole. He appealed to Governor Nelson Rockefeller's office and made headlines when he received executive clemency from the governor, having his and Portelli's sentences commuted to life imprisonment. He had spent more than three years on death row.

Portelli was sent to Dannemora; Jerry to infamous Attica State Prison, where he chafed under the inhumane conditions that existed in the institution. The rules were strict and stringently adhered to. Food was substandard and scarce. For example, at that time, the total food cost per prisoner per day was 63 cents. Unlike life on death row, Jerry was put to hard work in Attica. Despite this, he managed to study law at night, receiving his LLB degree in December 1967.

Jerry's career as a jailhouse lawyer was now fully launched. He was well known as the man to see if you wanted your legal rights to get to the attention of the proper authorities.

In September 1971, a portion of the prison population revolted against the harsh treatment meted out by prison authorities. Guards were taken as hostages. Prisoners demanded to be heard. Jerry was chosen by the leaders of the uprising to be a member of their negotiating team. When Governor Nelson Rockefeller refused to come to the prison, negotiations broke down. State troopers opened fire on inmates. Ten minutes later, 39 individuals—some hostages, some prisoners—lay dead. Eighty-nine others suffered serious gunshot wounds. It was the largest massacre ever to take place in a U.S. prison.

After the Attica riot, Jerry was shipped back to his old alma mater, Sing Sing, where he was eventually put in charge of the newly installed law library. Soon Jerry was handling complicated appeals, winning most of them. Frivolous cases were not his style, nor did he represent sex offenders. He took only those cases in which he felt a prisoner's rights had been violated. His reputation as the nation's top-rated jailhouse lawyer grew.

During the intervening years, Jerry resided in what amounts to a list of New York State's more infamous correctional facilities—Sing Sing, Dannemora, Greenhaven, Auburn, Sullivan, and finally Wende.

Over the years he has, in addition to his LLB degree, earned a Doctorate of Law, qualifying him to teach in law school. More than three hundred former prisoners owe their freedom to his legal endeavours. Occasionally Jerry receives dispensation to appear in court. Usually heavily guarded and handcuffed, he is released from his restraints outside the courtroom. Judges and opposing counsel all agree he is a formidable foe, well prepared in all aspects of the law.

In October 1985, Jerry was rushed to the Upstate Medical Center in Syracuse with arterial cardiac disease. During the ensuing bypass surgery, Jerry's heart stopped for more than 90 seconds. He was declared dead by the attending physicians. However, they managed to revive him, and in so doing gave Jerry the foundation for one of the most unusual actions ever brought before the courts. He appealed for immediate release, claiming that he had been sentenced to life and that his life had been terminated when he was declared dead. Jerry lost that one.

Although Jerry's forte has been his indefatigable determination to assist his fellow prisoners, he has the distinction of being the only American convict allowed to appear in a federal court in defence of a non-prisoner.

It is now 37 years since that day in 1962 when two police officers were shot down in cold blood. Anthony Portelli, who fired the fatal shots, died in prison in 1975 after suffering a brain hemorrhage. Jerry is the longest-serving prisoner in New York State. The average sentence served in the United States for murder is 15 years. Many serve far less. He has come up for parole seven times in the last 14 years, but despite his best efforts he has been denied parole each time.

Probably Jerry's most memorable case involved the appeal of Mafia don Carmine Galante. It was Jerry Rosenberg, self-educated jailhouse lawyer, who was instrumental in gaining the release of the notorious mobster. Jerry apologizes with a suppressed smile, "It wasn't my fault he was murdered after he got out."

Jerry has achieved a degree of fame while serving his prison term. A book, *Doing Life,* by Stephen Bello, reviewing Rosenberg's remarkable life, was published in 1982. This was followed by a TV movie on the same subject. Still, there are those who disagree with the acclaim Jerry has received. They are quick to point out that Luke Fallon and John Finnegan were deprived of their lives more than three decades ago.

As we parted, I alluded to the two officers' deaths and the devastation their murders caused their families. Jerry nodded his head in agreement and said, "Remember, Max, I didn't kill anyone."

# PIERRE AND BERNADETTE ROUAUX

## (BELGIUM)

PHILIPPE Rouaux had a few reversals in his young life. At age 20, he attempted to take his own life when a girlfriend broke off their relationship. Two years later, the quiet philosophy student was madly in love with 20-year-old Pascale Iserbiet. The attractive couple were engaged to marry when, for reasons of her own, Pascale broke off the engagement.

Philippe didn't take the rejection well. On December 6, 1982, while sitting in his car in his hometown of Assesse, Belgium, he pointed a .22-calibre rifle at his head, pulled the trigger and ended his life.

Detectives investigating the apparent suicide found Philippe's rifle lying in his lap. His right index fingerprint was on the trigger. They also learned that he'd attempted suicide before and that three members of his mother's family had taken their own lives. Case closed. At least for the time being.

On November 5, 1983, an unrelated incident took place in Assesse when Dr. Michel Delescaille was reported missing by his wife, Jacqueline. She stated that her husband, a 33-year-old general practitioner and psychiatrist, had received a phone call the previous evening and had rushed out of their home, shouting over his shoulder that someone had broken their ankle.

When he didn't return home, Jacqueline went looking for Michel throughout the village, but could find no trace of him or his Opel Kadett car.

Next morning, she notified police. Dr. Delescaille's fate wasn't a mystery for long. Within hours, a jogger, Marie Angares, came across the doctor's car. Marie observed that the door of the vehicle was wide open and thought the scene looked suspicious. She walked around the vehicle and saw Michel's body lying in the mud some thirty feet from the car. Marie ran to a nearby town and alerted police. Soon detectives from Namur, the closest large city, took over the investigation.

A physician examining the body found multiple wounds to the head. In the mud near the body, detectives recovered two large bloody hammers with hair adhering to both. They theorized that when the good doctor got out of his car, he had been struck an initial blow from one of his attackers. Two individuals then hit him continually as he crawled in the mud in a futile attempt to get away from his assailants.

There were faint tire tracks beside the Opel which indicated that the murderers had driven away in their own vehicle. No doubt the phone call to the doctor's house had been a ruse to lure him to this lonely spot and to his death.

Who would have committed such a crime? Jacqueline and Michel were happily married. Detectives made discreet inquiries. Jacqueline was totally devoted to her husband and their two children. There were no lovers lurking in the wings. Likewise, Michel was not involved with any women. There was absolutely no flaw in the couple's married life.

When the investigation wound down, police decided to interview each of Dr. Delescaille's psychiatric patients in case one of them had nurtured a real or imagined grudge against the physician.

It turned out that Michel didn't have many seriously ill mental patients. All were interviewed and proved to have airtight alibis for the time of the murder. Only one was not interviewed, for the simple reason that he was dead. As luck would have it, Philippe Rouaux had been one of Michel's patients.

The doctor had diagnosed Philippe as a manic depressive, which was more or less confirmed when the poor boy shot himself after being rejected by his fiancée.

By nature, police are curious. They took another hard look at Philippe's suicide and turned up some startling discrepancies. Philippe had been left-handed. You may recall that the fingerprint on the trigger was from his right index finger. Strangely, the investigative report indicated that although Philippe had killed himself inside a vehicle, no empty shell had been recovered from the weapon's chamber. At the time, the missing empty shell was attributed to mishandling by investigators.

Detectives interviewed one of Philippe's friends, who said Philippe had confided that he hated his father and was going to kill himself so that his father would have a guilty conscience. At the time of the apparent suicide, it was believed that Philippe had taken his life because of the termination of his engagement. All this served to reopen the Philippe Rouaux case.

Three years had passed since Philippe's death. Police were surprised when they received an anonymous note accusing Philippe's ex-fiancée, Pascale Iserbiet, and her current boyfriend, Georges Landry, of murdering Philippe. Pascale was hurt, and at the same time, insulted that anyone would believe she had anything to do with the tragedy.

She had an airtight alibi for the time of Philippe's death. As for Georges, he wasn't even in the area, nor did he know Pascale at the time. Police wrote them off as suspects, but actively attempted to find out who would send such an incriminating letter.

Because the letter was mailed in Assesse, police showed the envelope to post office clerks. Sure enough, one of the clerks recalled having seen the handwriting before, but couldn't remember where.

Police made photocopies of the envelope and gave a copy to each employee. In this way, they could compare the writing to any other similar mail that passed through their hands. Three days later, letters turned up at the post office with handwriting matching that on the photocopied envelope. The letter accusing Pascale and Georges had been written by Pierre Rouaux, Philippe's father.

When Pierre was questioned, he admitted sending the anonymous letter to police stating that Pascale was responsible for his son's death when she broke off their engagement. Police explained that Pascale may have been indirectly responsible, but that was not a criminal offence. Besides, suicide ran in the Rouaux family, and Philippe had attempted suicide before he ever met Pascale.

The elderly Rouaux underwent extensive questioning. Finally, both he and his wife, Bernadette, broke down. They blamed Dr. Delescaille, their son's psychiatrist, for Philippe's death. It was they who had made the phone call about the broken ankle. Michel had agreed to meet them along the road, believing they would lead him to the patient. Both had rained blows to the physician's head with the big hammers as he crawled in the mud.

On March 29, 1988, Bernadette and Pierre Rouaux were found guilty of murder and sentenced to 20 years' imprisonment. The suspicious death of Philippe Rouaux has never been solved. Had Pierre Rouaux not written the anonymous letter to police, he and his wife would never have been suspected of murdering Dr. Michel Delescaille.

# NORMAN "RED" RYAN

(CANADA)

CAN you name two infamous Canadian bank robbers? If you are over fifty, you might remember Edmond Alonzo Boyd and his notorious gang. It's tough to recall another of his ilk. But of course there was one such desperado. Indeed, Norman "Red" Ryan not only robbed banks, he also hoodwinked the judicial system of an entire country.

Red was born in July 1895 on Markham Street in Toronto and managed to stay squeaky clean until he attained the ripe old age of 12. That's when he was caught stealing a bicycle and was charged with theft. A kindly magistrate looked down at the freckle-faced, red-haired youngster and gave him a suspended sentence. When Red was caught stealing chickens a year later, he was hustled off to St. John's Reform School, but good behaviour had him back on the streets in a matter of months.

In 1912, Red wrecked a motorcycle in what is now Mississauga. When a local man refused to help him, Red pulled a revolver and fired several shots over the man's head. Police apprehended the impetuous youth and found stolen property on his person. Even the motorcycle had been stolen. A realistic magistrate figured this young man was about to become an habitual criminal. He sentenced Red to four terms of three and a half years each, to run concurrently. Red Ryan entered Kingston Penitentiary. He was 17 years old.

Even today, Kingston is not the Holiday Inn. In 1912 it was hell. Red hated eating his meals alone in his cell and despised the isolation—hour upon hour of solitude. He managed to keep his nose clean, did his assigned tasks without complaint and gained parole after two years, on condition that he stay under the supervision of his father.

It should be pointed out that the Ryans were a hard-working, God-fearing family. Red's dad operated a tin shop and was forever urging his son to enter the business and give up his criminal ways. Red promised his father that he would be a good boy.

Within months, Red, along with a buddy whom he had met in Kingston Pen, held up the Dominion Express Co. in Parkdale. This operation was soon followed by a daring armed robbery of the Toronto Piano Factory. The pair's good fortune didn't last long. In June 1915, they were spotted in Owen Sound. A shoot-out ensued before Red was taken into custody.

For the Owen Sound caper, he was sentenced to eight years in Kingston. For the two previous robberies, he received 12 years' imprisonment on each charge. The cold grey walls of Kingston Penitentiary closed in on Red Ryan for the second time. He celebrated his twentieth birthday in the pen, but the redhead with the lengthy sentence to serve had a visit from Lady Luck.

In 1918, with the war in Europe depleting this country's manpower, the Canadian government took unusual steps to fill army ranks. Simply put, penitentiary prisoners were offered their freedom in return for overseas duty. Red jumped at the chance. He was shipped to England, where he deserted and stole from army stores. He was apprehended, convicted and sentenced to six weeks in the lockup. Red escaped, joined the merchant navy under an assumed name, and in 1921, managed to make his way back to Toronto. All in all, it had been quite a three-year adventure.

Red Ryan was back in town looking for banks to rob. He even took time off to get married. Times were tough in Toronto, so Red went down the road to Hamilton and knocked off the Union Bank at the corner of Main and Locke Streets. The take was a cool $5,000. Other banks fell to Ryan and his partner, George McVittie. They relieved the Bank of Hamilton of nearly $4,000 before moving to Montreal, where shots were fired when they attempted a withdrawal from the downtown branch of the Bank of Commerce. No one was hurt. The two men were later apprehended, holed up at the YMCA on Drummond Street

On December 9, 1921, Red received a sentence of 40 lashes and seven years' imprisonment in St. Vincent de Paul Penitentiary. Later he was taken from prison to stand trial in Hamilton. He was found guilty of several charges and received sentences totalling 25 years, to be served at his old home, Kingston Penitentiary.

From the moment Red entered the pen, he thought of little else but escape. He gathered ruthless, desperate men around him—Arthur "Curly" Sullivan, an armed robbery specialist serving a 10-year sentence; Thomas "Runty" Bryans, a Sault Ste. Marie native serving time for manslaughter; habitual criminal Edward "Wyoming" McMullen, serving 20 years; and Gordon Simpson, an armed robber.

On September 10, 1923, these men set fire to a large straw stack. Under cover of smoke, the five men made their way over the twenty-foot stone wall. Ryan, the last man up the homemade ladder, was grabbed by guard Matt Walsh.

But Red, the natural leader of the gang, had prepared for this eventuality. A pitchfork lay beside the ladder. Red clubbed the officer to the ground and quickly joined the other members of his gang.

The men were able to steal an old Chevy from a home near the prison. Guards were hard on their heels and opened fire. A wild car chase took place through the streets of Kingston, in which McMullen was shot in the hand. When the gang abandoned the vehicle a few miles outside Kingston, McMullen, weak from loss of blood, couldn't keep up. He was taken into custody, but the other four members of the gang managed to make it to Toronto, where underworld contacts outfitted them with clothing and a few dollars until they could get on their feet, which literally meant until they could rob banks.

Twelve days after the daring escape, while newspapers featured their photos on the front pages, the gang brazenly knocked off the Bank of Nova Scotia, getting away with $3,000 in cash. The stolen Overland they used in the robbery was found abandoned in the parking lot of the Granite Club on Church Street.

The gang decided to split up. Simpson and Bryans went their own ways and both managed to stay at large for some time. Simpson was captured in New York in 1925, while Bryans wasn't picked up until 1927 in Chicago.

Meanwhile, Red and Sullivan travelled to Minneapolis, where acquaintances knew them as the Miller brothers. The boys kept in pin money doing what they did best, robbing banks. Their undoing was Red's penchant for keeping in touch with friends back in Toronto. It became known to police that he picked up his general delivery mail at a certain post office in Minneapolis.

Red and his sidekick Sullivan were the most wanted men in Canada. No less than R.H. Tucker, deputy warden of Kingston Penitentiary, and Walter Duncan, of the Federal Department of Justice, travelled to the U.S. city to be in on the capture with the local police.

On December 15, 1923, while the city was in a festive Christmas mood, police staked out the post office. Sure enough, Red showed up. A Minneapolis police officer named Maxon opened fire just as Red spotted him. Red pulled out his own weapon and both men fired at the same time, but only Maxon's bullet found its mark. Red was wounded in the right shoulder and was taken into custody.

As he was being ushered away by police, he shouted a warning to Sullivan, who was waiting in a nearby car. Sullivan opened fire and wounded an officer and a bystander. The police returned Sullivan's fire, inflicting only a superficial wound to his nose. He got away clean. However, police learned of his friendship with one Irene Adams. They staked out her apartment and next day, when Sullivan came calling, police shot him dead directly through the heart.

Red Ryan was returned to Canada. Huge crowds gathered to catch a glimpse of the country's most desperate criminal. Red was a broken man when, for his accumulated crimes, he was sentenced to life imprisonment along with 30 lashes, 10 to be delivered each month for the first three months of his sentence.

Red was unceremoniously returned to his home away from home—Kingston Penitentiary. This time, extraordinary security measures were taken to prevent his escape. Red spent the first nine months of his sentence in solitary confinement.

The Roman Catholic chaplain of the penitentiary, Father Wilfred T. Kingsley, often visited the prisoner in the hole. He implored Red to leave his past behind him and embrace the straight and narrow. Red seemed to listen and learn. Father Kingsley noted the gradual change and recommended that Red be removed from solitary confinement. He was transferred to an isolation cell, where he remained for another eighteen months. It wasn't much, but it was at least a small step towards joining the regular prison population.

Red Ryan, who had always been more than willing to shoot his way out of tough scrapes, took to the Bible with a vengeance. It appeared that the notorious badman, with the support of Father Kingsley, had found the path to reformation. Warden Ponsford was impressed.

In 1926, Red was transferred to the mailbag department, a section of the institution devoted to the production of mailbags for the federal government. Red distinguished himself by inventing a theft-proof lock for the bags, a device which was adopted by the federal postal authorities.

Two years later, model prisoner Red Ryan was transferred to the prison hospital as a junior male nurse. After six years Red became head orderly nurse, which was about as high as he could go in Kingston Pen.

Red Ryan became a rare phenomenon in prison. He was admired by inmates for his past daring deeds on the outside and thought highly of by prison authorities for his obvious efforts to totally change his life even though incarcerated.

Year after year, Red continued to be a model prisoner. He quit smoking, tended the sick far into the night and, miracle of miracles, became an altar boy. His hobby was moulding images of the Virgin Mary.

As the years passed, writers visited Kingston to do feature articles on the criminal who had apparently reformed. In the early 1930s there was a groundswell movement afoot to have this intelligent man who had so much to contribute to society released from prison.

Miss Agnes MacPhail, MP for Grey-Bruce, brought the plight of Red Ryan before the House of Commons. Other prominent citizens travelled to Kingston to visit the former badman. All came away impressed. Among their number was none other than the Prime Minister of Canada, the Honourable R.B. Bennett. The two men had a long chat, which culminated with Bennett promising Red that he would take up his case with the Minister of Justice.

The wheels were now in motion. A year later, on July 24, 1935, after serving 12 years in prison, Red Ryan was released. Toronto newspapers vied for his life story. Prime Minister Bennett, Chaplain Kingsley and Warden Ponsford were commended for displaying humanitarian judgement towards a reformed man once destined to spend the rest of his life behind bars.

For weeks Red was a welcome guest at religious functions. He settled down into his brother Russell's home and obtained employment as a car salesman. Dignitaries still wanted to be seen with Red. He attended sporting events with politicians and entertainers. Law enforcement officials, as well as religious leaders, often invited Red to be guest speaker at various meetings.

On May 25, 1936, in an incident seemingly unrelated to the life of Red Ryan, a thief named Harry Checkley entered a Sarnia liquor store with another man. Both wore masks and dark goggles. By chance, a passerby, Geoffrey Garvey, noticed the hold-up in progress and called police. In minutes the store was surrounded.

The two trapped bandits decided to shoot it out. Sarnia Constable John Lewis was shot dead. So were the two masked robbers. When the masks and goggles were removed from their faces, one man looked strangely familiar. A driver's licence in his pocket confirmed his identity. The man was Norman "Red" Ryan.

Later it was learned that Red had led a double life since his release from prison. He had secretly and successfully robbed several banks before being killed in Sarnia. Because of his charade, in succeeding years the number of paroles granted to prisoners diminished appreciably. Red was directly responsible for changing the parole system of the entire country.

# ANNA MARIE SAMBATARO

(ITALY)

EVERY time a native of Sicily shoots a fellow citizen, it is most convenient to chalk it up to another hit by the Mafia and go on one's way.

Despite this nonchalant attitude toward the Secret Society, it is a fact that folks not connected with organized crime do, from time to time, dispose of strangers and, in selected cases, dear friends and relatives.

On May 6, 1987, the quiet small town of Aci Castello was disrupted when four bullets tore into the body of Concetto Centurino. A police doctor told investigating officers the bullets that took the life of the 45-year-old truck driver were of the 9mm variety. The medic explained that the killer had been a better-than-average marksman, who had managed to find Concetto's heart with two of the bullets and had scored near-heart misses with the other two. The police figured this was the work of a professional killer, most probably a member of the Mafia. They went about delving into Concetto's past.

Right from the start, authorities were a bit puzzled. After all, it is most unusual for someone of Concetto's humble stature to be singled out by the Mafia. There had to be some underlying reason for someone to want him out of the way. As it turned out, Concetto proved to be a most unusual truck driver. You see, he was not only a truck driver, he was a pimp. Not your ordinary run-of-the-mill pimp with a stable of prostitutes, but a pimp with feelings. For years, Concetto had managed only one girl at any given time. The proceeds from his meal tickets had provided him with a luxury car and clothing worn only by the rich and famous. Concetto took care of his regular expenses from his salary as a truck driver.

There was more to Concetto's makeup than meets the eye. Get this—he routinely got his prostitutes pregnant and was the proud daddy of two adult daughters and a 17-year-old son.

Concetto was well known and well liked in Aci Castello. In fact, all his prostitutes had thought highly of the handsome devil. When residents were interviewed, they told investigators that Concetto didn't have an enemy in the world. Of course, that was a barefaced lie. Someone had disliked him enough to pump four slugs in and around his heart.

The women in Concetto's life were questioned extensively. Let's see now: there was 56-year-old Mathilde Sambataro, who was the mother of at least one of his daughters, also named Mathilde. Both mother and daughter practised the oldest profession. Though Concetto had left Mathilde, she didn't have a bad word to say about the father of her daughter. Mathilde's other daughter, Anna Marie, denied Concetto was her biological father, although many of the townsfolk attributed Anna Marie's paternity to him. Mathilde, active as she was, couldn't be sure.

Concetto's 17-year-old son, Franco, was the offspring of Grazia Contino. To complicate matters, Grazia and Concetto had married a week before his murder. She had been his lover off and on for many years. Grazia spoke of her husband in glowing terms.

Police figured one of these women must have hired a killer to dispose of Concetto for some as-yet-unknown reason. Try as they might, detectives couldn't come up with any derogatory information about the dead man. The pimp with morals had been faithful to each prostitute while he lived with them.

Four slugs had found their mark. Someone was responsible. Officials decided that since switching prostitutes had been Concetto's lifestyle for years, this was not the motive for his murder. The only unusual occurrence in Concetto's life was his recent marriage. Somehow, his murder had to be connected to his marriage to Grazia.

During their investigation, police learned that immediately after his wedding, Concetto had been fearful for his life. Was it possible his old flame and the mother of his two daughters had been resentful of his marriage? She was the only one with an iota of a motive.

Detectives interviewed Concetto's neighbours, all of whom swore they had noticed nothing unusual about his house, with one exception. One of the neighbours noted the postman had had difficulty delivering mail to Concetto before his death. Concetto had refused to accept certain letters each day. Police checked with the local mailman, who informed them the refused mail was being returned to Anna Marie Sambataro. Now, why in the world was Concetto's daughter writing to him every day and why was he refusing to accept the letters?

Police decided to bring in both Sambataros for questioning. Mother and daughter swore they had nothing to do with the murder, just as they had sworn earlier in the investigation. This time around, their flats were searched while they were in custody. Nothing was found in Mathilde's flat, but police discovered the returned letters in Anna Marie's. It was obvious from their contents that Anna Marie didn't believe Concetto was her biological father. What's more, Anna Marie was madly in love with him. Now that Concetto had left her mother and married Grazia, she was furious and insanely jealous.

The letters were shown to Mathilde. She confirmed that her daughter was deeply in love with Concetto. Mathilde simply wasn't positive her former lover was the girl's father, but to keep peace in the loosely knit family, she had offered to give up Concetto to her daughter. He had vehemently objected because he wasn't sure the young girl who wanted him so badly wasn't his daughter.

In recent months, Anna Marie had made life miserable for her mother and Concetto. It had become so bad, Mathilde gave up Concetto who, resilient as a rubber band, married Grazia. Anna Marie went out of her head with rage.

Detectives told Anna Marie they knew of her relationship with the murdered man. She confessed she had done what any self-respecting spurned lover would do: she had hired a hit man to kill the scoundrel. In that part of Sicily, putting out a contract was not difficult. The alleged killer was 33-year-old Nunzio Ruscica, an accomplished assassin who was well known to police, but who was so efficient at his chosen profession he had never been arrested or charged with any crime.

Nunzio was taken into custody and questioned. He denied any knowledge of the murder. Since police only had Anna Marie's word for his involvement, they were unable to charge him with any criminal act. They reluctantly released Nunzio from custody.

On September 8, 1988, Anna Marie stood trial for the murder of Concetto Centurino. She confirmed her earlier confession and threw herself on the mercy of the court. Anna Marie Sambataro was found guilty of inciting to homicide. She was sentenced to eight years in prison.

# YVONNE SLEIGHTHOLME

(ENGLAND)

YOU wouldn't want to meet a nicer young fellow than William Smith. Will finished school and, following family tradition, took over Bloat's Farm in Yorkshire, England. All the while, Will was keeping steady company with Jayne Wilmore. Many thought the pair would eventually marry, but things didn't turn out that way. Jayne left the rural area to train as a registered nurse. She no longer saw Will and was soon dating other young men.

Will busied himself farming and playing rugby. It was at a rugby social club in 1979 that he met Yvonne Sleightholme. Before you could say touchdown, Will and Yvonne were going steady. Unlike Jayne, Yvonne was an aggressive young lady who knew exactly what she wanted. What she wanted was Will Smith.

A little over a year after they met, Yvonne moved into Bloat's Farm. She was soon hinting about more permanent arrangements. Yvonne suggested marriage. Will was aghast. The live-in relationship was just hunky-dory with him. Why spoil it all with an unnecessary tying of the knot? He even mentioned that if Yvonne insisted on such a drastic change in their relationship, it might be better for all concerned for them to separate now, rather than prolong the union. As a result of their disagreement, Yvonne moved out of Bloat's Farm.

A month later Yvonne informed Will that she had leukemia, which she maintained had been brought on by his ill-treatment of her. Will was devastated. He had no idea that an illness as serious as leukemia could be caused by the trauma of rejection. Under the circumstances, he invited Yvonne to move back to his farm. Yvonne, complete with bag and baggage, moved back to her rightful manipulative position at Bloat's Farm.

The change of venue did wonders for Yvonne, if she ever really had leukemia. Thereafter she never even complained of a headache.

Years passed. Yvonne brought up the subject of holy matrimony once again. This time, Will acquiesced. The blushing bride-to-be figured it would take six months to arrange the gala affair. We're talking wedding dress, showers, reception, honeymoon—in short, the works. Yvonne felt it had taken her years to wear Will down, so she planned to have a wedding with all the trimmings. For his part, Will made inquiries about a new suit.

As the fickle finger of fate would have it, Will was visiting the small town of Salton when he happened to meet his old flame, Jayne Wilmore. Jayne was as charming and beautiful as ever. She told Will that if they hadn't run into each other, she had planned to look him up. It wasn't exactly for old time's sake. Jayne explained that kind, trusting Will was in over his head and it was her duty to warn him. In brief, she told him that Yvonne was no good. Yvonne, she said, was a scheming female who had trapped him into marriage. Jayne felt Will deserved a better fate.

Will listened. Jayne made a lot of sense. He asked her what he should do to remedy his precarious situation. Jayne suggested that it wasn't too late to break off his engagement to Yvonne. In addition, there was their own future to consider. Now that they had met again, Jayne let Will know that she was not averse to continuing their long interrupted friendship.

Friendship be damned! Within weeks, Jayne and Will were spending a large portion of their time doing what comes naturally between the sheets. Both suffered from guilty consciences, but not enough to abstain.

Will attempted to broach the subject of delaying the wedding, but it wasn't easy. Yvonne was busy planning the elaborate affair. When she declared she was pregnant, Will backed off. Three weeks before the great date, Yvonne miscarried. Will decided this would be his last chance to tell his betrothed he could not go through with the wedding. He told her that he would not continue to lead a life of deception and that was that. In tears, Yvonne advised guests to ignore the wedding invitations. There would be no marriage. For the second time she moved out of Bloat's Farm.

Quick as a bunny, Jayne moved in. In May 1988, Will and Jayne married. For some time, they were supremely happy. Will farmed. Jayne continued with her nursing career. Then the threatening anonymous phone calls began. These were followed by a mysterious fire on the farm, which consumed a barn. When Will and Jayne received a funeral wreath in the mail, they advised police that they suspected Yvonne, the only one they felt was capable of such an act.

Police located Yvonne, living with her parents on their farm. She was not exactly what they expected. In fact, she was polite, co-operative, and claimed she had no idea who was harrassing the Smiths. The police believed her, particularly after she told them she was moving out of the area to a cottage on the Scottish border. They told the Smiths the results of their inquiries.

That's where matters stood in December 1989, when Yvonne drove from her cottage to the road just outside Bloat's Farm. It was a Tuesday night. Yvonne knew Will would be attending his usual rugby club function that night. She waited until she saw him leave. Then she drove her vehicle to the front door. Lugging her trusty shotgun with her, she knocked. Jayne answered the door, and found herself staring directly down the barrel of a shotgun. Yvonne marched Jayne across the farmyard in the pouring rain and, without a word, shot her in the back of the head. Jayne Smith died on the soft earth of the farmyard.

Resourceful Yvonne went about simulating a rape scene. She ripped Jayne's blouse, tore away her brassiere and scratched her breasts. She removed Jayne's panties and took them away with her.

Those close to this soap-opera murder feel Yvonne might very well have gotten away with murder if it hadn't been for the one act she performed when her emotions got the better of her. There she was in the pouring rain, tearing and pulling away the clothing of the woman who she believed had ruined her life. She had planned well, but in the heat of the moment she ripped off Jayne's wedding ring.

When Will learned of the missing wedding ring, he told police about Yvonne Sleightholme living in that cottage up near the Scottish border. Yvonne was questioned. Police learned she wasn't at home on the night of the murder. Blood matching Jayne's blood type was recovered from Yvonne's car.

Accused of murder, Yvonne mysteriously lost the sight of both eyes. At her murder trial, she claimed Will had been keeping company with her after his marriage. He wanted to divorce Jayne, but she wouldn't hear of it, so he had hired an assassin to kill her. Thoughtful Will had even provided the assassin with Yvonne's father's shotgun. In an attempt to frame Yvonne, he had summoned her to the farm on the night of the murder.

No one believed Yvonne's fanciful tale. In May 1991, she was found guilty of murder and sentenced to life imprisonment. In 1993, she appealed her conviction, but was turned down.

# ERWIN SPENGLER

(GERMANY)

KATHARINA Kornagel lived in the small German town of Wagen im Allgaeu. The 70-year-old, overweight Katharina planned to spend the rest of her life in relative tranquillity. Things didn't work out that way for her, but that's getting ahead of our story.

In 1987, Katharina lived in a flat on the first floor of her building. She had resided there for years, ever since her mother had died and left her a small fortune. Everyone in the building liked good-natured Katharina. Maria and George Weh, who lived a couple of floors up from her, were dear friends. So was Brigitte Scherer, who often spent pleasant afternoons sipping white wine with Katharina.

For the past five years, Katharina had employed 33-year-old Erwin Spengler as her chauffeur. She had decided it was too tough walking everywhere, so she purchased a second-hand Mercedes and hired Erwin at the same time. She explained to her friends that both parties were happy with the arrangement. She now was able to take comfortable trips for a few days at a time, and Erwin, who didn't have a vehicle of his own, could use the Mercedes when he wasn't chauffeuring his boss. Within months, Erwin, who was grossly overweight himself, was not only Katharina's chauffeur, but her best friend as well.

On January 18, 1988, Erwin walked into the police station in Wagen im Allgaeu and reported Katharina Kornagel missing. According to Erwin, he had driven his boss to the train station on December 11 and hadn't heard from her since. She had left for Bremen to visit relatives and friends, but it wasn't like her to stay away so long. Police decided to take a look inside Katharina's flat. What they found added credence to Erwin's concern for his employer. There was a small brown crusty stain in the front hall, which at first glance looked ominously like dried blood. Plants in the flat had shrivelled and died during Katharina's prolonged absence. Her washing machine was full of wet clothing. The general appearance of the flat indicated the occupant had left hurriedly.

The stain in the hall turned out to be blood that had been there for well over a month. Laboratory technicians meticulously checked the flat. They found that someone had cleaned the bathroom with hydrochloric acid. The taps, sink and particularly the bathtub had been scrubbed with the acid. Pipes leading from the bathtub were taken up and examined. They were clean. Police estimated that several gallons of hydrochloric acid were used to eliminate any foreign material that might have been forced down the drain. Whoever had worked with the acid must have worn rubber gloves and a mask. Of course, the horrible thought that someone had murdered Katharina and dissolved her body parts was uppermost in the minds of the police. Was it possible that a 200-pound woman could be disposed of in such a manner? Detectives studying the scene felt it was not only possible, but that Erwin Spengler was the logical suspect.

Erwin was taken into custody and questioned. He admitted that up until that past December he had been extremely short of funds, but was flush with cash from around Christmas on. Erwin told his interrogators he had hit a lucky streak at the casino in Baden-Baden. Unfortunately, no one could recall a big winner of Erwin's conspicuous description at the time he claimed to have won at the roulette wheel.

Friends and relatives of Katharina's in Bremen had never expected a visit from her, nor had she arrived in their city. Erwin had to backtrack. He now said he had dropped Katharina off at the station and had assumed she was going to Bremen. It was always possible she had gone elsewhere.

Under pressure to account for his new and sudden supply of money, Erwin admitted his winning streak at roulette was a fabrication. He came into his money honestly enough. Katharina had given him two signed blank cheques and he had merely filled in the amounts. She had given him the money because he needed to pay off debts. Besides, he and Katharina were very good friends.

Police traced the cheques and had the signatures examined. They were disappointed when the signatures on both cheques proved authentic. Police were stymied. Katharina had signed those cheques all right. If she had been forced to sign them, she could have stopped payment if she so desired. There was also the matter of a motive. Why would Erwin want to kill Katharina? He wasn't mentioned in her will, a fact he knew very well.

While detectives were pondering how they could nail Erwin, an unsettling series of items were received in the mail by Katharina's friends. Maria and George Weh received a postcard from Bremen, apparently signed by Katharina. Brigitte Scherer received one the following week from the Canary Islands. It too appeared to be signed by the missing woman. Other occupants of the building also received cards. Police checked the signatures. They were all different and none were genuine. Who was sending postcards from different places in the world to Katharina's friends? For sure it wasn't Erwin Spengler. He was resting not so comfortably in the town jail. Detectives thought perhaps the writer was someone who had lived in Katharina's building and had moved out or gone on a long vacation, but such was not the case. The senior citizens who occupied the flats were of the staid variety. No one had moved out and no one had taken a vacation.

It was left to one officer to come up with the solution to this minor mystery. He checked out men who had been in jail with Erwin and had been released. Of the six men who fell into this category, four were traced. One lived in Bremen and one had visited the Canary Islands. Both men were taken into custody and both admitted they had sent the postcards. They explained that while they were in jail, Erwin had given them the names and addresses of people who had lived in Katharina's building. He had even provided them with a bit of personal information about Katharina and her neighbours so the cards would have an authentic ring to them.

When Erwin was faced with this evidence, he claimed he was being framed. He said he had overheard the men planning a robbery. They were telling lies about him so he would be executed and silenced forever.

Detectives were positive their man had killed Katharina Kornagel and disposed of her body down the bathtub drain with the aid of hydrochloric acid. Despite their suspicions, they had no body and no motive. To the investigators, it appeared Erwin would be better off with Katharina alive. After all, he was gainfully employed by a generous boss, and the use of the Mercedes was a pleasant perk of the job.

Police theorized that the murder had been a spontaneous one. No doubt an argument had taken place that had culminated in murder. Erwin had had over a month to clean up the evidence before strolling into the police station. Had he concentrated so much on cleaning up the bathroom area with hydrochloric acid that he had overlooked the brown stain in the hall? Murderers have been known to make such mistakes. The unsuccessful attempt to create the impression that Katharina was alive by having his former cell mates send postcards to acquaintances was just plain stupid.

Still and all, the prosecution was going to trial with a weak case—no motive, no murder weapon, no witnesses and no body. Despite the shortcomings in the prosecution's case, the German jury brought in a guilty verdict. Erwin collapsed and had to be carried from the courtroom when he was sentenced to life imprisonment.

# MICHAEL TAYLOR

(ENGLAND)

---

I have never been a big fan of exorcism. Does all that ranting and raving under the guise of prayer really help drive the devil from the possessed? I think not. Let's go back to the seventies and take a peek at the Taylor family who lived in Ossett, a town of twenty thousand souls in Yorkshire, England.

Michael and Christine Taylor had five sons, ranging in age from 6 to 12 years. Michael, 31, was religious to the point where he didn't feel fulfilled by attending only the Church of England. As a result, he assisted in forming a group known as the Christian Fellowship.

On September 24, 1974, the Taylors hosted the first meeting of the group at their council-house home. Everyone had a jolly good time. There was singing and bible discussion. At the height of the fervour, Michael spoke in tongues which, as you may know from observing Jimmy Swaggart, is a soliloquy of ecstatic spiritual emotion that manifests itself by the worshipper uttering strange words that no one understands, not even the speaker.

The Fellowship meetings rotated from home to home. At one of them a member of the flock demonstrated an amateur attempt at exorcism. Everyone was impressed as all get-out, particularly Michael, who was so affected by the service that he commenced to shake all over.

Five days after the meeting, Michael attended St. Thomas Church, where Father Peter Vincent conducted the service. Later the same day, the Fellowship meeting was held at Michael's home. Once again he witnessed a demonstration of exorcism and was totally enthralled.

A couple of days later, unemployed Michael was extremely depressed. He had applied for a job and had been rejected. On a visit to his mother that day he told her he had seen the devil, who had told him he was a useless bloke who should kill himself. His mother advised Michael that although he wasn't a world-beater, he was definitely not useless. She was no doubt referring to his stud-like ability to sire five offspring.

The following day, people witnessed Michael behaving irrationally on the streets of the town, dropping to his knees before total strangers and preaching to them that the world was about to end. Operating in a religious fog of sorts, Michael left his ecclesiastical street pursuits to attend a meeting of the Fellowship at the home of St. Thomas's choirmaster, Ron Smith. Father Vincent must have been slumming. He was there too.

Michael related to the assorted gathering that he had been seduced by the devil. Collective ears perked up. It was decided that Michael should describe his experience in detail. After all, it isn't every day that one is seduced by Satan himself. Michael must have poured his heart and soul into his recital, because those who met him after the meeting said he appeared pale, tired and agitated.

On Friday, October 4, Michael, in a state of frenzy, ordered Christine to remove all the religious books and crucifixes from their home. Christine did as she was told.

Other members of the community, especially members of the Fellowship, who didn't mind a tad of exorcism and the like, noticed that Michael's behaviour was well beyond the norm, as every so often he would let out a piercing scream. Once, on a drive with a friend, John Eggins, he started screaming so loudly and so often that Eggins drove directly to Father Vincent's vicarage. Michael demonstrated his appreciation by throwing the vicarage cat through a window.

Someone suggested that Michael was possessed of the devil and required exorcising in the worst way. The idea seemed like an excellent one at the time. Everyone agreed that they would call in Rev. Raymond Smith, a Methodist minister, and his good wife, Margaret, who were recognized in the area as real-life honest-to-goodness experienced exorcists. John Eggins and a Methodist lay preacher, Donald James, would complete Team Exorcism.

All was in readiness for the night-long ritual. Michael was taken to the adjoining vestry, where he was placed on his back. In turn, those is attendance asked questions and broke into prayer.

Much later, Michael related that when they told him of sins he had committed, he confessed, even if the allegations were false. He said he would have confessed to anything. Michael said that every time he exhaled, Team Exorcism would congratulate themselves on getting rid of another devil. Many weeks later, doctors stated that Michael was probably hyperventilating.

As the sun came up and poured into the vestry, the job, in the opinion of the assorted members of the group, was over. They figured they had removed about 40 demons from the exhausted subject, but that there might be a couple left. In particular, Rev. Smith felt that the one demon remaining in Michael was the murder demon, which could not be ousted. The reverend's wife, Margaret, went one step further by stating, "I have had word from God that if he goes home this morning he will murder his wife and children."

All this talk about murder made the exorcism group extremely nervous. They discussed restraining Michael from returning to his home. Several suggested they bring in a medical welfare officer, but it was Sunday and none was available. Instead, they called police, who advised them to call a doctor. Christine wouldn't hear of it. She feared Michael's wrath. This was a spiritual matter, not a medical problem.

At 9 a.m., Michael and Christine were delivered to their home. An hour later, Michael attacked his wife with his bare hands. He tore out her tongue, her eyes and ripped flesh from her face before choking her to death.

Neighbours heard the attack and called police. When the authorities arrived at the scene, they found Michael in a kneeling position, covered with blood. He was taken into custody and asked if he had killed his wife.

He replied, "No, not her. I love her. I destroyed the evil within her. It had to be done. I am relaxed. What had to be done has been done. The evil in her has been destroyed. Christine was good. The evil had been put into her by them. I had to kill it. It came through religion. They primed me for this last night."

Michael was tried for murder, but was found not guilty by reason of insanity. He was detained indefinitely at Broadmoor Hospital, an institution for the criminally insane.

# WILLIAM TOWNSEND

(CANADA)

IF you drive along picturesque Highway 3 from Simcoe to Dunnville in southern Ontario, you will pass through the tiny hamlet of Nelles Corners. Just a few miles north of Lake Erie's shores, Nelles Corners is off the beaten track. In 1854 a crime took place in this community that gave rise to a series of events that made it one of the strangest murder cases in Canada's history.

John Nelles operated a general store. He and his wife lived together with his brother, Augustus, and his wife's sister, Lucy Humphreys. On the night of October 18, the family had finished supper. The early evening was no different from hundreds that had preceded it. A chill wind whistled outside as one by one the family retired for the night. John, left alone at the kitchen table, took a long last pull on his pipe before knocking the ashes against the grate of the kitchen stove. He was about to go to bed when it happened.

Four men burst through the front door. Their intent was never in doubt. Their faces were blackened with burnt cork. The desperate men demanded money. Nelles rose from the kitchen chair, but made no attempt to comply with the robbers' wishes.

A shot echoed through the once peaceful home, and John Nelles sank to the floor. The badly wounded man moved slightly, eliciting a further shot from the pistol carried by one of the men. Mrs. Nelles and her sister, Lucy, rushed into the room and ran to John's aid. The four bandits tore a watch from the wounded man. Ignoring the women, they continued to search the house for anything of value.

Augustus Nelles woke up with the first shot. Wisely, he remained in bed; not the most heroic action, but one that most certainly saved his life. As quickly as the wanton killing had taken place, the five men opened the door and disappeared into the darkness.

A few miles down the road the killers bumped into two farmers, who were relieved of the few dollars they had in their possession. Within hours the unknown assailants had boarded a train bound for Buffalo. Once in the U.S., the men separated, having left heartache and tragedy in their wake.

Despite the fact that their faces had been blackened, a good description of the wanted men was given by both the two women, and the two farmers who had been robbed. Three of the men, King, Blowes and Bryson, were quickly apprehended. They were placed in prison in Cayuga, Ontario. All three were tried, found guilty and sentenced to death. King and Blowes were hanged, but Bryson's sentence was commuted to life imprisonment. He probably saved his skin by confessing to being one of the men in the house at the time of the murder. All three men claimed that they hadn't fired the fatal shot. They stated that the trigger had actually been pulled by one William Townsend.

Meanwhile, an event took place that had a direct bearing on the shooting at Nelles Corners. Approximately a month after the murder of John Nelles, two men entered a hotel operated by a Mrs. Jordan at Port Robinson, Ontario. While the two men were eating, other men in the hotel swore that one of the strangers looked like William Townsend, the wanted killer of John Nelles. They notified the authorities.

Several police rushed to the hotel to apprehend the wanted man. One of the policemen, Constable Charles Richards, faced the stranger, who immediately pulled a gun and shot him. The constable died a few hours later. The man known as Townsend got away.

Over two years went by, and again Townsend was recognized in the U.S. This time he was taken into custody without incident by the Cleveland, Ohio, authorities. The government of Canada immediately proceeded to have the wanted man extradited to Canada. In May 1857, he was delivered to the Canadian authorities and placed in jail in Cayuga to await trial for the murder of John Nelles.

From the moment he was taken into custody, William Townsend captured the imagination of the country. Townsend remained hostile towards the authorities, but despite this hostility, well-placed powerful men took an interest in his case. Throughout his stay in custody and his ensuing trial, Townsend claimed that he wasn't Townsend at all. He swore he was Robert J. McHenry, a Scotsman who worked as a mariner out of Cleveland. He further swore that he had been in California searching for gold at the time of John Nelles's murder.

Townsend's unusual trial began on September 27, 1857. The Cayuga courthouse had never seen such an array of legal talent. The Crown was represented by Henry Smith, the Solicitor General of Canada. S.B. Freeman, Q.C., one of the finest orators of his time, represented Townsend. The accused pleaded not guilty. From the beginning, the trial boiled down to the question of whether the accused man was Townsend or McHenry.

Lucy Humphreys identified the prisoner as the robber who had fired the shots that killed her brother-in-law. William Bryson was brought from Kingston Penitentiary to testify, and identified the accused as the murderer Townsend. Sometime previous to the murder of Nelles, Townsend had been employed as a cooper in the neighbouring community of Dunnville. A number of former neighbours of the man in the dock took the stand, and all identified him as William Townsend.

Although this should have been enough to convict the prisoner, such was not the case. Freeman paraded close to a hundred witnesses to the stand, all of whom swore that they knew Townsend well, and that the prisoner was not William Townsend. Townsend's brother-in-law, Ezra Smith, said the man in the dock was a stranger to him. Benjamin Diffin, who worked with Townsend one whole winter, said the accused was unknown to him. No expense was spared to place witnesses in the stand who swore the accused was not William Townsend.

After six hours of deliberation, the jury returned and informed the court that they were undecided. They were dismissed. The accused man was about to be returned to his cell when the deputy sheriff of Welland County read a warrant charging the prisoner with the murder of Constable Charles Richards of Port Robinson.

William Townsend, or whoever he was, was taken from Cayuga and lodged in the Welland (then called Merrittsville) jail.

On March 26, 1858, he again stood trial for murder. Again his case rested on his claim that a terrible mistake had been made. He was not the murderer William Townsend. All the same witnesses were heard again. This time the foreman of the jury spoke out loud and clear, "The prisoner is McHenry, and is not guilty." That night the taverns of old Merrittsville rocked with celebrations held by McHenry's friends.

Townsend-McHenry was returned to Cayuga, for he was still in custody for the Nelles murder. Within a few days, however, he heard that the Crown had no intention of trying him again. He was released on bail with the understanding that he would make himself available if the Crown ever decided to place him on trial once more. This never happened. The strange, silent, hostile prisoner walked out of the Cayuga jail a free man.

For some time after, Robert McHenry was in great demand as a speaker at clubs and fairs throughout the country. Later, he dropped from sight and was never heard from again.

To some, he was a killer named Townsend, who got away with murder. To others he was a harassed, innocent man named McHenry. Who was he? This question remains unanswered.

# REV. JOHN SELBY WATSON

(IRELAND)

THERE was no great mystery about it. Rev. John Selby Watson had bludgeoned his wife to death. The dastardly deed was performed with an old pistol that the man of the cloth kept stored in a display box. Hate was involved in the slaying, which took place well over a hundred years ago. Anne Watson had received a total of eight blows to the head, any one of which could have killed her.

The reverend's history gave no hint of the violence that was to erupt on that pleasant fall day of October 8, 1871. You see, Rev. Watson had never committed as much as a teeny-weeny indiscretion in his entire life.

John Watson was born into abject poverty in London, England, at the wrong time. In those long-ago days, a higher education was a privilege enjoyed only by the wealthy. But Watson wasn't to be denied. By the sweat of his brow and dogged determination, he managed, at age 34, to obtain his bachelor of arts from Trinity College in Dublin.

Nothing came easy for Watson. He met a young woman he fancied while still a student, but with no money and few prospects, it took him seven years to ask Anne to marry him. During those seven years, the scholarly Watson joined the Church of England and rose slowly through the ranks, becoming a curate at age 37. Three years later he was appointed headmaster of Stockwell Grammar School in Surrey. Only then did he ask Anne for her hand in marriage. She accepted, and the respectable, staid pair were married at St. Mark's Church in Dublin.

You would never call the Rev. John a lightweight in the academic world. In his spare time he translated the works of Xenophon, the ancient Greek historian, as well as various materials written by Cicero, Lucretius and Justinian. Many of the reverend's translations were published. He also wrote a book on the life of Scottish patriot William Wallace, recently the subject of the Academy Award–winning movie *Braveheart*.

When Rev. John wasn't attending to his religious duties or teaching, he found time to pick up a Master of Arts degree from Oxford University and a Fellowship of the Royal Society of Literature.

Throughout his career, Rev. John was beloved by pupils and parents, but his sterling efforts were not financially rewarding. For twenty-five years he laboured diligently, but even in those days downsizing was the practice when times got tough. In 1867, enrollment fell off dramatically. The governors of his school gave him three months' notice and the boot. There was no early-retirement package or compensation of any kind. The reverend simply gathered up his pens and left the school, a disillusioned man.

From the time of his dismissal, Rev. John operated in a daze. Those who knew him later stated that he was so depressed he appeared to be disoriented. Anne, his dutiful wife of so many years, had a difficult time adjusting to her husband's personality change. Some say she became a cranky, annoying woman who constantly criticized him for allowing himself to be manipulated into such an unenviable position.

On Sunday, October 8, 1871, the Watsons attended morning prayer at St. Andrew's Church. Ironically, the sermon that day concerned the punishment of those in high office who misused their power.

That afternoon, former employees of the Stockwell Grammar School paid a social call on the Watsons. Mr. and Mrs. Tully found the reverend rather tense. At one point Mrs. Watson confided, "I am so frightened. I am afraid of anybody getting into the house by the back over the garden wall." Shortly after hearing this strange statement, the Tullys left.

At 9 p.m., Ellen Mary Payne, the Watsons' only servant, returned from her afternoon off. When she entered the house, Rev. John told her, "Your mistress won't be home for two or three days." He told Ellen that Mrs. Watson had gone out of town. Ellen thought it strange that her mistress had not mentioned the trip to her that morning. Rev. John accompanied Ellen up the stairs, leading the way with a lit candle. He pointed out some discolouration on the floor near the library door. "This stain on the floor; it is port wine which your mistress has spilt. I have told you in case you might wonder what it was."

The following day was uneventful for Ellen. That night, when the reverend returned, he told Ellen, "If you find anything wrong with me in the morning, go for Dr. Rugg." Somewhat startled, Ellen inquired if he was ill. Rev. John would only say, "I may require medicine in the morning."

Next day there was still no sign of Anne Watson. The reverend was up and about with the birds and passed up breakfast. He dashed down to a hardware shop, where he ordered a packing case to be made to the specific measurements he provided. He then returned home and retired to his bedroom.

Around noon, Ellen thought she heard noises emanating from the bedroom. She went up to investigate and found the reverend spread out on his bed, unconscious and nude. There were four letters and a glass on a night table beside his still form. Ellen picked up the letters. One was addressed to her and included a five-pound note. It read, *"For the servant, Ellen Payne, exclusive of her wages. Let no suspicion fall upon the servant, whom I believe to be a good girl."*

Another letter was addressed to Dr. George Rugg. Ellen ran to the doctor's house and gave him the letter, which read,

> *To the surgeon. I have killed my wife in a fit of rage. Often she has provoked me and I have endeavoured to restrain myself, but rage overcame me and I struck her. Her body will be found in the little room off the library. The key is in a letter on the table. I hope she will be buried as becomes a lady of birth and position.*

Dr. Rugg rushed to the Watson residence. Using the key, he opened the small room. There lay Anne Watson. The doctor could see at a glance there was nothing he could do for Anne. He hurried to Rev. John's room. The good man of the cloth was not in bad shape. Dr. Rugg recognized the smell of bitter almonds about his mouth and knew that he had taken prussic acid. He quickly procured an antidote, which he gave to the cleric. Rev. John recovered rather speedily. It occurred to the doctor that he was at the scene of a half-hearted suicide attempt. He felt that Rev. John might have spat out the prussic acid rather than swallowing any great quantity.

Police were summoned. In a display case they found five old pistols, four of which had not been touched for years. The fifth one was damaged. The wooden stock had been split and there was dried blood on it. This pistol proved to be the murder weapon.

Rev. John was charged with his wife's murder. On January 10, 1872, he stood trial at London's Old Bailey. He was able to explain away the ordered shipping case, stating it was to be used to store his literary works. Besides, he had not even bothered to pick it up. His attorney pleaded insanity. There didn't seem to be much of a motive for the murder. Despite admitting to the killing, Rev. John would not reveal why he had murdered his wife.

Rev. John was found guilty and sentenced to death, a sentence later commuted to life imprisonment at Parkhurst Prison on the Isle of Wight. He stayed in prison for 12 years, until he suffered a fall in his cell and died at the age of 80.

That should have been the end of the Rev. John Selby Watson and his infamous crime, but that's not the case. Remember those letters found in his bedroom? The fourth letter was written in Latin. It is believed that it reveals the real motive for the crime.

The mystery letter reads:

*"Felix in omnibus fere rebus praeterquam quod ad sexum attinet foemineum. Saepe olin amanti amare semper nocuit."*

For more than a hundred years, Latin scholars have been attempting to translate the message and solve the motive for Anne Watson's murder. Here a few of their efforts:

"To one who has often loved, it has always been harmful to love."

How about, "Many men have found that it is a mistake to be too true to the object of a boyish passion."

Or: "It is often injurious or fatal to a man who once loved to go on forever loving."

There are other interpretations of the vexing letter, but so far no one has come up with a satisfactory explanation as to why an educated religious teacher who had never committed a violent act in his life took it upon himself to bludgeon his wife to death and hide her body for three days.

# JAMES WHITE AND BETTY WILSON

(UNITED STATES)

DR. Jack Wilson was a beloved ophthalmologist with a flourishing practice in Huntsville, Alabama. His road to the good life in Huntsville had been a rocky one. Jack had to struggle financially to obtain his education, which was followed by a stint in France and Germany with the U.S. army. After his discharge, he married, but the union ended in divorce. Jack and his first wife had three sons—Perry, Scott and Steven.

After the breakup of his 15-year marriage, Jack met and married Betty Woods, an attractive nurse and the mother of three sons from a previous marriage. None of the couple's six children were implicated in the murder that took place on that Friday in May 1992.

Both Jack and Betty had medical problems. Jack suffered from Crohn's disease, which had grown progressively worse since his days in medical school, necessitating an operation known as an ileostomy, in which a portion of his large intestine was removed. From the date of the operation, more Jack wore an ostomy bag. Betty hated that bag. Over the years, she started drinking heavily, until she realized that her social drinking had evolved into a way of life. Betty joined Alcoholics Anonymous, became a devoted follower of the organization and quit drinking.

Meanwhile, slim, short Dr. Jack was one of the leading eye doctors in the area. He had amassed an estate of more than $8 million and had an annual income in 1991 of slightly more than $1 million. He and Betty were recognized as leading members of Huntsville's medical and scientific community. If Betty had ever been in love with Jack, that love had ceased to exist. She confided to many of her affluent friends that she no longer cared for her husband. To confirm her feelings, she entered into several affairs with local men. It was generally agreed among their mutual friends that Jack must have known his wife was playing the field. Maybe he didn't care.

At nine-thirty on the evening of May 22, Betty returned to her home at 2700 Boulder Circle after attending an AA meeting with a girlfriend. She told her friend that the next day she and Jack would be starting their vacation, which they intended to spend in New Mexico. Betty walked into her home, took one look and ran hysterically from the residence. She rang a neighbour's doorbell, screaming that Jack had been attacked by a burglar. The neighbour dialled 911.

Detectives at the scene came across Jack's body at the top of the stairs, just as Betty had minutes before. Jack had been beaten about the head with what they speculated was a metal baseball bat, and had been stabbed twice in the chest and stomach, most probably after death had occurred. Despite Betty's assertion that a burglar must have been responsible, the investigating officers didn't think so. Nothing had been taken from the house, nor was anything disturbed.

A few hours later, the investigation into the murder of the prominent doctor took a strange turn. The day before Jack's murder, a detective in Columbiana, Alabama, received a visit from Janine Russell. Ms. Russell had a strange tale to tell. A friend of hers, James White, an unemployed handyman, had told her, while drinking, that he had been hired to kill a doctor in Huntsville. He had been approached by a respectable schoolteacher, Peggy Lowe, who said she was acting for her twin sister in Huntsville. Janine didn't know the name of Peggy Lowe's sister.

The conversation about the contract killing had taken place over a period of weeks. At one point, White, who was usually broke, had flashed a sizable amount of money. He told Janine that he had received a down payment for the proposed murder and would soon complete the contract. Badly frightened, Janine decided to share her knowledge with the police.

The detective listening to her story called his counterpart in Huntsville and passed along the information. The lawmen figured they could be dealing with a hoax, but agreed to run a check on James White. They learned White had once been arrested on a drug charge and had escaped from a local jail, remaining at large for five years before being apprehended. He was released from prison on May 27, 1982, after having been incarcerated for almost a year. Since that time he had committed no infractions. His record certainly didn't indicate he was a contract killer.

Within 24 hours of Janine Russell's visit to the police, Dr. Jack Wilson was murdered in Huntsville. His wife, Betty, had a twin sister. Her name was Peggy Lowe. Was it possible that a respectable churchgoing schoolteacher had hired a killer to dispose of her twin sister's unwanted husband? Police thought it was more than possible. They believed that was exactly what had happened.

Unaware that he was being sought by authorities, James White was easily located. Under intense interrogation, he admitted he had killed the doctor. "Betty Wilson paid me to do it." With that sentence, White placed himself in jeopardy of ending his life in the state's electric chair. Eventually, he told how he had made the acquaintance of Peggy Lowe. He said they had become intimate, an accusation denied by Peggy. White professed that he had been in love with Peggy. When asked to do a favour for her twin sister, Betty, he had agreed. To sweeten the pie, he was offered a payment of $5,000 to do the job.

White may not have been the cleverest man in the world, but when it came to saving his own skin, he was cunning enough. He realized the state required his testimony in order to convict the twins. His lawyer made a deal. White would testify against Betty and Peggy in return for a guarantee that he wouldn't be put to death.

White met Peggy when he was doing some work at the school where she taught. They became good friends and chatted on the phone a few times each week. The subject of murdering Betty's husband had been broached gradually. Peggy put White in touch with her sister. He received an advance of $2,500 from Betty for the impending murder.

The date of the murder was set for the day before Betty and Jack were to leave on vacation. Two days before the murder, Betty had provided White with a loaded .38-calibre pistol to do the job. The pistol was found in White's room. It was loaded with distinctive bullets, a box of which were later found in Betty's home. White never used the weapon because he simply didn't like guns.

On the day of the murder, Betty picked up White at the Ramada Inn in Huntsville and drove him to her home in her BMW. He lay in wait for Jack to return from his office. White killed the ophthalmologist with the baseball bat and, to make certain he was dead, stabbed him twice in the chest and stomach. As agreed, he waited in the house until Betty came back and drove him to his waiting pickup truck in a parking lot.

White's story was checked and rechecked. Times, places and circumstances were all authenticated. The three conspirators were sent to trial separately. James White was found guilty of murder and sentenced to life imprisonment. He will be eligible for parole in the year 2001. Betty Wilson was found guilty of capital murder. The state agreed to waive the death penalty and sentenced her to life imprisonment without possibility of parole. She has appealed her conviction. She resides in the Julia Tutwiler Women's Prison in Wetumpka, Alabama, where she is employed in the laundry.

After a nine-day trial, Peggy Lowe was inexplicably found not guilty. Because of her notoriety, she refused to resume her teaching position. She is now employed in administration at her old school.

# ROBERT WOOD

(ENGLAND)

ON September 12, 1907, when Bert Shaw boarded the 7:20 a.m. train at Sheffield, England, for his home in Camden Town, London, he had no idea he was taking part in the first act of what was to become one of England's most infamous murder cases.

Upon arrival at his apartment, Bert was greeted by his landlady, Mrs. Stocks, and his mother, who had picked that precise moment to visit. It was 11:30 a.m. and the two women were mildly concerned that Bert's wife, Phyllis, had not left her apartment all morning. Bert went directly to his quarters and found the door locked. Mrs. Stocks provided a duplicate key. Bert walked into his parlour. Drawers had been opened, their contents strewn over the floor. When Bert found the bedroom door locked, he broke it down. Phyllis's nude body lay on the bed. She had been stabbed in the throat.

Phyllis had been an avid collector of postcards, which she kept in the front room. Bert noticed one of her albums in the bedroom. It was open and several postcards were scattered on the floor. A subsequent check of the apartment revealed that a silver cigarette case, a gold watch and a glass charm were missing. A bloody basin bore evidence that the killer had washed up after the murder. In the parlour, a meal for two had obviously been consumed. Quite possibly Phyllis's dinner guest had been her killer.

Murder investigations uncover embarrassing facts about the participants. In the Camden Town murder, almost everyone involved had a secret. Bert's wife wasn't legally his wife at all. Her name was Phyllis Dimmock and, shame to tell, she was a prostitute. She and Bert had known each other for two years. About nine months earlier, Bert had agreed to have Phyllis move in with him on condition that she never ply her trade again. He had told everyone, including his mother, that he and Phyllis had married.

That was subterfuge number one. There was more. Phyllis hadn't given up her old ways one little bit. Most nights she sold her body, seeking out customers in the many watering holes in Camden Town. She had no difficulty bringing her customers to her apartment. Mrs. Stocks was always sound asleep in her own quarters and Bert worked nights in Sheffield.

Bert learned of Phyllis's deception from the police. He was investigated as a suspect and was able to prove without a doubt that he was miles away at the time of the crime and could not have been the killer.

Police checked out the pubs frequented by Phyllis. They discovered that her favourite hangout was the Rising Sun in Camden Town. In this way they came in contact with Robert Roberts, a ship's cook with a wad of money to blow before accepting his next berth. He had spent three consecutive nights, Sunday, Monday and Tuesday, with Phyllis, leaving early each morning. On Wednesday night, the night of the murder, he had wanted to visit Phyllis for the fourth time, but she told him she already had a date for that night.

Although it was an unlikely story, every word Roberts told police proved to be true. He had more to tell. On Wednesday morning, before he left the apartment for the last time, there was a knock on the door. Two pieces of mail were pushed under the door. Roberts picked them up. One was an advertisement. The other was a letter, which Phyllis read before handing it over to Roberts. He remembered the contents. *"Dear Phyllis, Will you meet me at the Eagle, Camden Town, 8:30 tonight, Wednesday?—Bert."*

After Phyllis showed the letter to Roberts, she went to a bureau and pulled out a postcard. It read, *"Phyllis darling, If it pleases you, meet me, 8:15 p.m. at the* [a drawing of the Rising Sun]. *Yours to a cinder, Alice."*

Roberts had noticed that the letter and the postcard were written by the same hand. Phyllis threw the letter into the fire and returned the postcard to the bureau drawer. It appeared to detectives that Phyllis's killer had desperately searched for the incriminating postcard, which they could not find in the apartment.

The investigation was winding down when Bert Shaw called police with the startling news that he had found the missing postcard. It was under some newspaper lining the bureau drawer. Scotland Yard released copies of the postcard to major newspapers, asking anyone who recognized the writing to come forward.

Out of the millions who saw the reproduction of the postcard, two individuals recognized the writing. Ruby Young had every intention of passing along her information to police, but before she could do so, her friend Robert Wood, whom she knew had written the postcard, called on her. Ruby accused Robert of the being the writer. He didn't deny it, but had a ready explanation as to how his card had ended up in a murdered woman's apartment.

Robert told Ruby that he had met a woman named Phyllis in the Rising Sun. They had a few drinks. When Phyllis told him she collected postcards, he produced one. Phyllis was delighted and asked him to write something nice on it. He wrote the note as a sort of an appointment, but when he went to sign it, Phyllis instructed him to sign it "Alice." He told Phyllis he would mail it, and placed it in his pocket. Next day, strictly by coincidence, he met Phyllis on the street. They talked a bit and separated. The day after that, he mailed the postcard. A day later, he dropped into the Rising Sun and bumped into Phyllis once more, but she left without him and he never saw her again. Ruby believed Robert's story and didn't pass her information on to Scotland Yard. After all, she had known Robert off and on for three years. For two of those years, the pair had been intimate.

The other person who recognized the writing on the postcard was a Mr. Tinkham, who worked with Robert Wood at a fancy glassware manufacturing company. Tinkham told Robert of his suspicions and Robert gave him the same basic story he'd given Ruby Young. He too believed Robert and did nothing. It should be pointed out that Robert Wood was a respected artist and executive with his company. He had been employed by the firm for 14 years, had no criminal record and was considered to be a fine upstanding citizen.

During the height of the investigation, Robert met with his old flame Ruby on several occasions and urged her to tell anyone who asked that he had been with her on the night of Phyllis's murder. Sometimes Ruby wavered, but always agreed to lie for Robert. He also looked up a Mr. Lambert, whom he knew had seen him with Phyllis at a pub about a week before the murder. He implored Lambert not to reveal what he knew. Robert explained that he wasn't guilty of any wrongdoing. He just didn't want to get involved in a murder case as it would be an embarrassment to his father. Lambert agreed that there was no reason for him to tell anyone what he knew.

Robert had effectively stifled those people who could connect him to Phyllis's murder, except for one thing—human nature. Ruby Young couldn't resist telling a friend the whole story. The friend told a newspaperman, who in turn informed Scotland Yard. On October 4, 1907, Robert Wood was taken into custody. Two days later he was charged with Phyllis Dimmock's murder.

In December 1907, Robert stood trial for Phyllis's murder. The Crown produced a witness, Mac Cowan. Although Cowan could not identify Robert by sight as the man he had seen leaving Phyllis's apartment on the morning after the murder, he was able to identify him by his distinctive walk.

Robert Wood was represented by the finest English defence lawyer of his time, Sir Edward Marshall Hall. He pointed out that Robert had no motive for killing Phyllis. None of the articles missing from Phyllis's home were ever traced to Robert, nor was the murder weapon found in his home. As for Robert's attempts to have friends and colleagues lie to protect him, Marshall Hall claimed that he went to such trouble because he didn't want his family to find out that he often associated with prostitutes. Marshall Hall further asserted that despite Robert's suspicious behaviour, there was nothing to connect him to the crime other than he had admittedly known the victim. He dismissed Cowan's eyewitness identification as an honest mistake.

The English jury returned a verdict of not guilty, after which the courtroom crowd gave Robert Wood a standing ovation.

# KAREN ANNE WOODCOCK

(CANADA)

---

CRIMINAL investigation Branch File #621100540/73 is dog-eared. The thick file at the Ontario Provincial Police headquarters has been handled repeatedly. Stark black letters identify the documents inside: KAREN ANNE WOODCOCK—HOMICIDE.

Floyd and Karen Woodcock were married in Peterborough, Ontario, on May 15, 1958. By the summer of 1973, the couple lived in their own home in the village of Villiers in Otonabee Township, a few miles from Peterborough. They had seven children, ranging in age from 4 to 15. Floyd was employed as a welder with the Outboard Marine Co. in Peterborough.

Karen had decided to go back to work. In the fall of 1972, she had enrolled in a commercial stenographic course at Sir Sandford Fleming Community College in Peterborough. Karen was a better than average student. She was active in the school paper and was well liked by both teachers and students. The forty weeks flew by; June 29 was to be Karen's graduation. Certainly a happy day by anyone's standards, but particularly for a woman returning to school after raising seven children.

The Woodcocks' story seems to portray a contented, industrious couple forging their way ahead in the world. This may have been so, but their marriage did have one flaw. Both were heavy drinkers, but not on a day-to-day basis. Every four months or so, Karen would go on a binge. Sometimes with her husband, and sometimes alone, she would stay drunk for three or four days.

Karen was well known in the beverage rooms of Peterborough. Regulars took her to their homes, where all-night drinking bouts would only be interrupted when someone passed out. Karen's drinking habits in no way were a reflection on her morals. No one has ever insinuated that she did anything but drink with her male companions. Usually these periodic bouts ended with Karen sleeping if off at her father's home. Floyd often picked her up there to take her home.

Floyd drove into Peterborough on June 29 to attend his wife's graduation. Quite by chance he ran into Daniel Robert Smith, a co-worker at Outboard Marine. Together they went to the McGillis Hotel. After only one beer they moved to the Grand Hotel. Floyd later excused himself to attend his wife's graduation. Still later, both he and Karen joined Smith at the McGillis. The three of them drank away the rest of the afternoon. At around 6:30 p.m. they left the beverage room to continue the party at Smith's residence. In the meantime, Karen Woodcock took a taxi to a liquor store where she picked up three bottles of gin and two bottles of wine. Smith paid for the two bottles of gin, and the Woodcocks paid the balance.

At around 8:30 p.m., Floyd suggested that it was time to call an end to the party. Karen would hear none of it. Floyd had often left his wife at parties before, and this was one of those times. He left and she remained, drinking with Smith until about 10:30 p.m. Then the pair went hotel hopping, visiting the King George Hotel and Queen Hotel in Peterborough. At the Queen, Smith left Karen for a few moments to say hello to some friends. When he returned she was gone.

Karen left the hotel and contacted another friend, Daniel Johnson. She slept overnight at Johnson's residence on Reid Street. The next day, Saturday, June 30, Karen and Johnson drank all day, consuming three bottles of wine. They had nothing to eat.

At 1:30 a.m. on Sunday, July 1, Mrs. Woodcock showed up at the home of her father, Edwin Mitchell, at 617 Ludgate Street in Peterborough. Mr. Mitchell, who was having a few drinks himself, can only remember that his daughter made a phone call and then left.

Percy Johnson was the father of Mrs. Woodcock's drinking buddy, Daniel Johnson. At 3:15 a.m. his phone rang. A female voice asked for his son. He quite naturally replied that his son was sleeping, and he hung up. It is believed that this is the call Karen made from her father's home.

Unable to reach Daniel Johnson, Karen left her father's house. At 3:30 a.m. Ronald Baldwin had just driven his babysitter home. He was returning to his own home when he spotted Karen. She wanted a lift. Ronald Baldwin drove her to the corner of Parkhill Road and Reid Street. He was back in his own home at 4 a.m.

At 4:20 a.m. Harold Morton, an employee of Canadian Pittsburgh Glass, was on his way to install a window at Minacola's Furniture Store. He noticed a woman hitchhiking about twenty feet south of the Parkhill Road intersection. He thought she was drunk. It was Karen. Other than her killer, Harold Morton was the last person to see Karen Woodcock alive.

At 7:20 a.m. Fred Simmond was driving to work. Beside the road, but plainly visible from his car, Fred spotted the nude body of Karen Woodcock. The exact spot was about two miles north of the Woodcock residence at Villiers, just south of Highway 7. Simmond never got out of his car. Instead, he continued to the home of Grant Elmhairst. The two men viewed the body together. They returned to the Elmhairst residence and called the OPP detachment in Peterborough.

Beside the nude body the police found an indentation in the soil where a rock had been dislodged. Karen had obviously been beaten about the head with the rock. An autopsy revealed that her death had been caused by a fractured skull. She had firmly held on to her purse strap with her left hand. The purse was open and the contents, which included $32.02, appeared intact. Karen had not been sexually interfered with. None of her clothing was ever found.

Between the hours of 4:20 a.m. and 7:02 a.m. on the first day of July, someone picked up Karen Woodcock and rained blows to her head with a rock until she was dead. Who and why?

Every movement made by Karen Woodcock from the time she started partying after her graduation has been gone over moment by moment by the Ontario Provincial Police. They think they know the identity of her killer.

Many months before the murder, a drinking companion attempted to sexually attack Mrs. Woodcock while her husband was asleep upstairs in their home. No charges were ever brought against the man. Two days after the murder, the same man came forward voluntarily to the OPP in Peterborough. He had information which tended to support his claim that he was so drunk the early morning hours of July 1 that he didn't know where he was. Upon investigating this man, police believe he went out of his way to establish his movements as far away from the scene of the murder as possible.

The police succeeded in having this suspect submit to a polygraph test. Partway through the test the man changed his mind and refused to continue. From the amount of testing done, an expert in this field feels that this man had knowledge concerning the death of Karen Woodcock.

Despite this incriminating piece of information, there is no direct link between the murdered woman and the suspect. He is at large and refuses to discuss the case with investigating officers.

# PETER WOODCOCK

(CANADA)

IT was another era, another world, really, almost 43 years ago that January 15, 1957, when it happened. Under the byline of a young *Toronto Telegram* reporter named Douglas Creighton, Torontonians first heard of the disappearance of four-year-old Carol Voyce.

Six hours after the youngster disappeared, her body was found, beaten and sexually assaulted, under an archway of the Prince Edward viaduct in Toronto's East End.

On that fateful January day, Mrs. Bernadette Voyce decided to visit her friend Mrs. William Auld, who lived only a few blocks from the Voyce residence. Bernadette gathered up Carol and together they set off for the Auld home at 1066 Danforth Avenue. When they arrived, they met four-year-old Johnny Auld. Carol stayed outside to play with Johnny.

A few minutes later, Peter Woodcock, 18, rode up on his distinctive cream-and-red bicycle and struck up a conversation with the two children. He asked the pair if they wanted to go for a ride on his crossbar. Both said yes. Peter chose Carol. That choice was to preordain that Johnny Auld would live and Carol Voyce would die.

As Johnny watched, the nice older boy pedalled away down the road with Carol. Johnny then ran into the house and told his mother that Carol had taken a ride with a boy on a bicycle. The two women, sensing that something was amiss, ran outside. Carol was nowhere to be found. They met Constable Earl Newman, who reported Carol missing. The search for the little girl was on.

Hours later, her body was discovered near the Prince Edward viaduct. Her blood-smeared snowsuit, along with other clothing, was found nearby. Carol had been attacked and mauled by some sadistic monster. The child's face had been pressed down into mud. An autopsy revealed that the cause of death was asphyxiation.

Several children had been attacked during the previous eighteen months, and scores of teenagers had been questioned in the course of these investigations. Now police had a description of the wanted boy and his bicycle, provided by little Johnny Auld. They also had impressions of bicycle-tire tracks leading from the scene of the murder. The tracks indicated that the killer had left the little girl's body and had proceeded by way of nearby railroad tracks. He had walked along the tracks with his bicycle, then remounted and pedalled until he reached a paved road, where all traces of the killer disappeared.

The *Toronto Telegram* featured a composite sketch of the wanted boy. North York Constable George Douglas couldn't get the description of the boy out of his mind. Months earlier, while investigating another sex crime, he had questioned a youth named Peter Woodcock. Douglas was sure that the drawing matched Woodcock's appearance in every detail. He passed along his hunch to detectives James Crawford and Edward Blakeley.

The two detectives picked up Woodcock at Bloordale College, a private school he had been attending for three years. At his home, they confiscated a cream-and-red bicycle. Impressions of the tire treads of the bicycle matched those found at the murder scene.

Woodcock appeared to be delighted to be taken to police headquarters. He basked in his new-found importance. When questioned by detectives George Sellers and Dick Gibson, Woodcock admitted being near the murder scene at the time the murder must have taken place. Initially, he described a boy he had seen on a CCM bicycle. The description of the boy and the bicycle was quite unlike his own.

Detectives then informed him of the mounting evidence, such as the bicycle tracks, pointing to him as the killer. Faced with these facts, Woodcock confessed in detail to the mad-dog-type murder of Carol Voyce. He related a tale of horror that placed him as one of the most diabolical killers in Canadian history.

Detective James Crawford, who picked up Woodcock so many years ago, remembers well the slightly built teenager with the horn-rimmed glasses. Crawford recalls, "Woodcock was responsible for the deaths of three children and several other attacks. Some of his victims were sexually attacked, strangled and left for dead, but regained consciousness and lived."

A 14-year-old youngster, who has never been identified, had been committed to the Toronto Psychiatric Hospital for the murder of seven-year-old Wayne Mallette. Woodcock proved without a doubt that it was he who had killed the Mallette child. The boy who had been incarcerated for six months was released.

Peter Woodcock stood trial for the murder of Carol Voyce. There was no doubt that he had committed the murder. The tire tracks, teeth marks on the body that matched an impression made of Woodcock's teeth, as well as his confession, left only his sanity in question. Woodcock was found not guilty by reason of insanity and incarcerated at Oak Ridges, the maximum security unit of the Penetanguishene Mental Health Centre.

It has been almost 43 years since this monster disguised as a human was incarcerated. Wars have been fought since that day when Peter Woodcock snuffed out the life of little Carol Voyce. Detective Jim Crawford rose in the police force to head the homicide squad before retiring. Constable George Douglas left the police force, went into private business and still lives in the greater Toronto area. Detective Edward Blakeley suffered a fatal stroke at age 59. Reporter Douglas Creighton went on to co-found the *Toronto Sun*.

But what of the slightly built boy with the horn-rimmed glasses sent away to the Penetanguishene Mental Health Centre? A few years ago, Woodcock had his name legally changed to David Michael Krueger. The man who terrorized Toronto as an 18-year-old youth is now 61 years old. He was successful in obtaining a transfer from the maximum security unit in Penetang to the medium security unit of the Brockville Psychiatric Hospital.

On July 15, 1991, David Michael Krueger, once known as Peter Woodcock, and former Penetang patient Bruce Hamill were charged with the murder of patient Dennis Kerr. Kerr had been beaten to death in what may have been a homosexual love triangle.

Peter Woodcock has again been charged with murder, just as he was 42 years ago. As you read this, he is back in the Penetanguishene Mental Health Centre, which will no doubt be his home for the rest of his life.

# ACKNOWLEDGMENTS

MANY individuals and organizations have contributed greatly to this book. I am particularly indebted to the Ontario Provincial Police, Scotland Yard and the FBI. I am also grateful to the wardens and other officials of several prisons who gave of their time and insight.

My thanks to the following people whose contributions to this effort are incalculable: Susan Dugas, Clarissa Feliprada, Jillian Goddard, Julie Hornby, Bob Johnston, Julie Kirsh, Selena Ladd, Glenna Tapscott, Joyce Wagler, and Kathy Webb Nelson.

This book would not have been possible without the dedication of co-editors Maureen Hudes and Liba Berry.

My gratitude to my daughters, Susan, Maureen and Eleanor, whose years of encouragement have kept me focused. A special thanks to my wife, Marilyn, whose contributions have been immeasurable.